Idaho, Montana & Wyoming

Are we meeting your travel needs?
Send written comments to:
AAA Member Comments
1000 AAA Drive, Box 61
Heathrow, FL 32746-5063

Published by:

AAA Publishing
1000 AAA Drive
Heathrow, FL 32746-5063

Advertising Rate and Circulation Information
Call: (407) 444-8280

Printed in the USA by Quebecor World, Buffalo, NY

Photo Credit: (Cover & Title Page)
Sawtooth National Recreation Area, ID
© Ron Watts / Corbis

Printed on recyclable paper.
Please recycle whenever possible.

Stock #4611

TourBook Navigator

Comprehensive City Index

Idaho

Montana

Wyoming

Featured Information

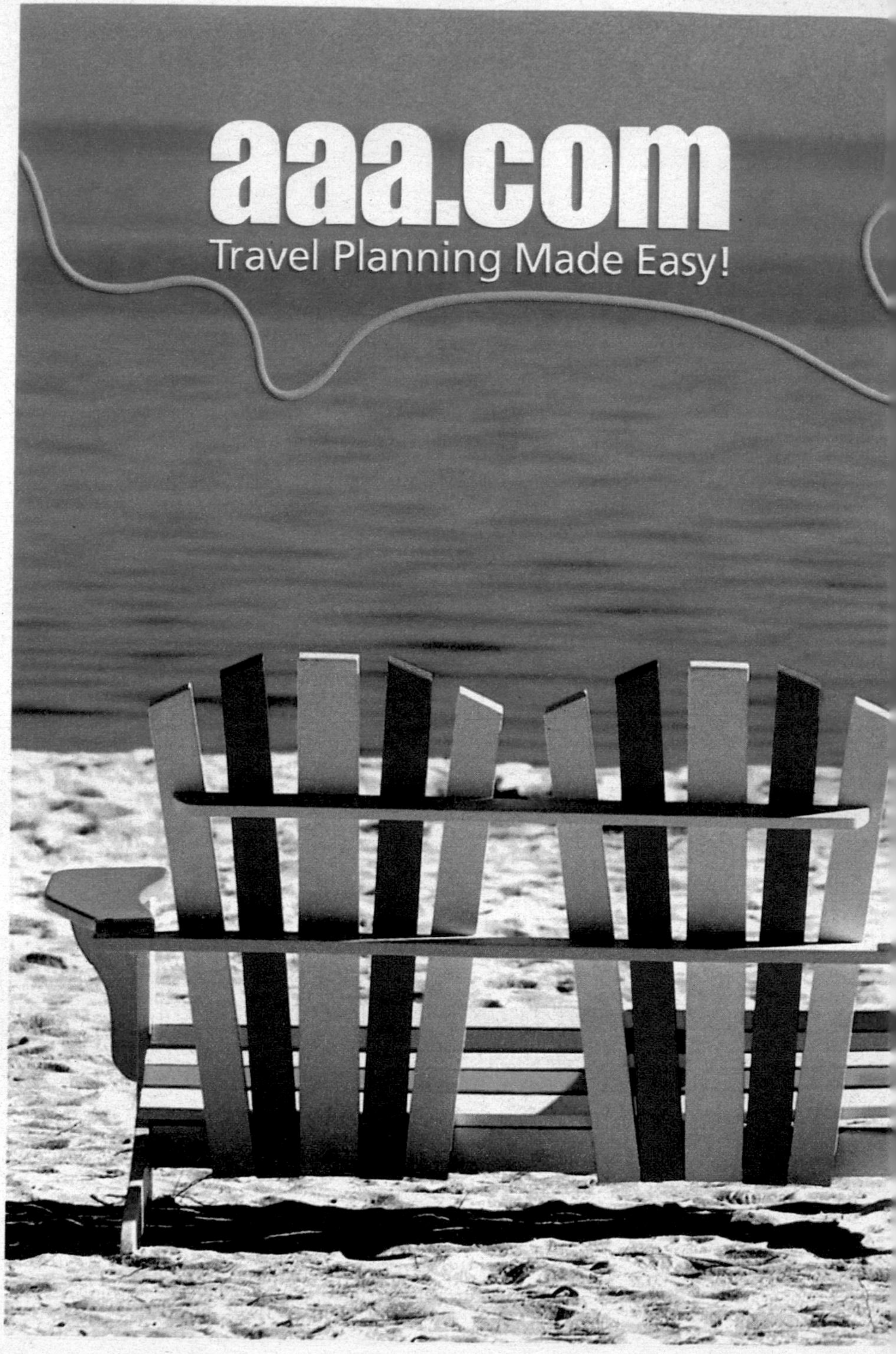
aaa.com
Travel Planning Made Easy!

Look for the Signs of Approval

When you're on the road, look for lodgings that display the AAA Approved sign. It's your sign that the property works hard to win AAA member business. In fact, these properties offer AAA members great room rates*.

When you see AAA Approved signs, you know you've arrived.

* *See TourBook Navigator, page 14, for complete details.*

Trust the AAA TourBook® guide for objective travel information. Follow the pages of the TourBook Navigator to thoroughly understand this unique member benefit.

Making Your Way Through the AAA Listings

Attractions, lodgings and restaurants are listed on the basis of merit alone after careful evaluation, approval and rating by one of our full-time, professionally trained Tourism Editors. Annual evaluations are unannounced to ensure that our Tourism Editors see an establishment just as our members would see it.

Those lodgings and restaurants listed with an [fyi] icon have not gone through the same evaluation process as other rated properties. Individual listings will typically denote the reason why this icon appears. Bulleted recreational activity listings are not inspected but are included for member information.

An establishment's decision to advertise in the TourBook guide has no bearing on its evaluation or rating. Advertising for services or products does not imply AAA endorsement.

How the TourBook is Organized

Geographic listing is used for accuracy and consistency. This means attractions, lodgings and restaurants are listed under the city in which they physically are located—or in some cases under the nearest recognized city. The Comprehensive City Index located in the back of the book contains an A-to-Z list of cities. Most listings are alphabetically organized by state, province, region or island; city; and establishment name. A color is assigned to each state or province so that you can match the color bars at the top of the page to switch from ❶ **Points of Interest** to ❷ **Lodgings and Restaurants.**

3 Dallas

Destination Cities and Destination Areas

The TourBook guide also groups information by destination city and destination area. If a city is grouped in a destination vicinity section, the city name will appear at its alphabetical location in the book, and a handy cross reference will give the exact page on which listings for that city begin. Maps are placed at the beginning of these sections to orient you to the destinations.

❸ **Destination cities,** established based on government models and local expertise, are comprised of metropolitan areas plus nearby vicinity cities.

Destination areas are regions with broad tourist appeal. Several cities will comprise the area.

All information in this TourBook guide was reviewed for accuracy before publication. However, since changes inevitably occur between annual editions, we suggest you contact establishments directly to confirm prices and schedules.

Points of Interest Section

Orientation maps
near the start of each Attractions section show only those places we call points of interest. Coordinates included with the city listings depict the locations of those cities on the map. A GEM symbol (💎) accents towns with "must see" points of interest which offer a *Great Experience for Members®*. And the black ovals with white numerals (**22** for example) locate items listed in the nearby Recreation Areas chart.

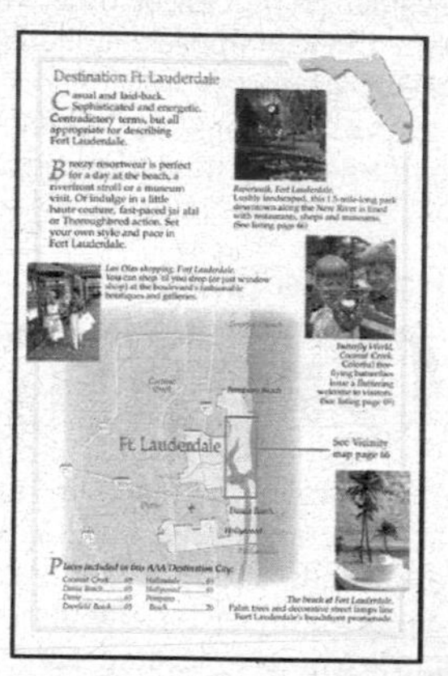

Destination area maps
illustrate key travel areas defined by local travel experts. Communities shown have listings for AAA approved attractions.

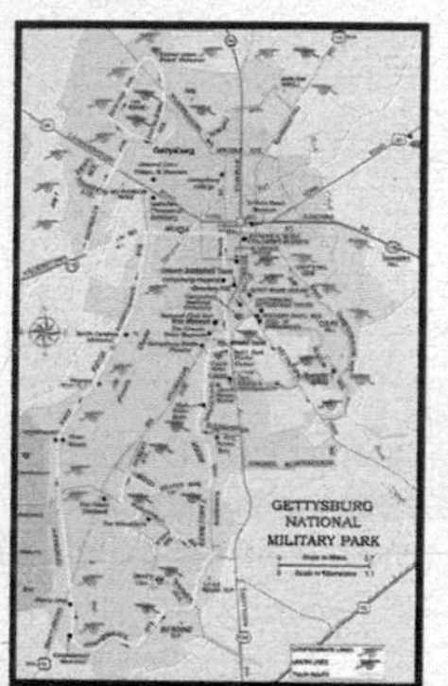

National park maps
represent the area in and around the park. Some campground sites and lodges spotted on the maps do not meet AAA/CAA criteria, but are shown for members who nevertheless wish to stay close to the park area.

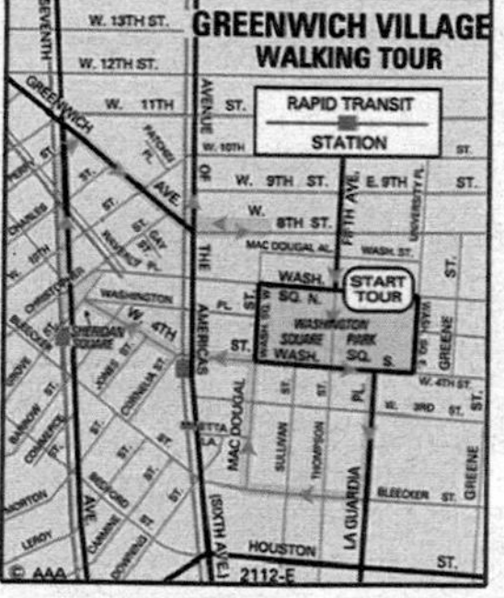

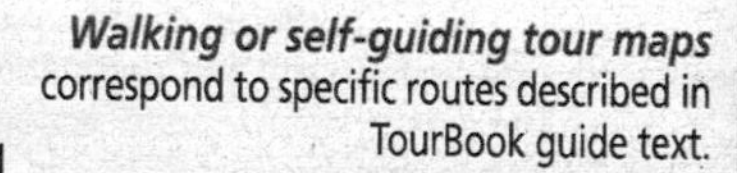

Walking or self-guiding tour maps
correspond to specific routes described in TourBook guide text.

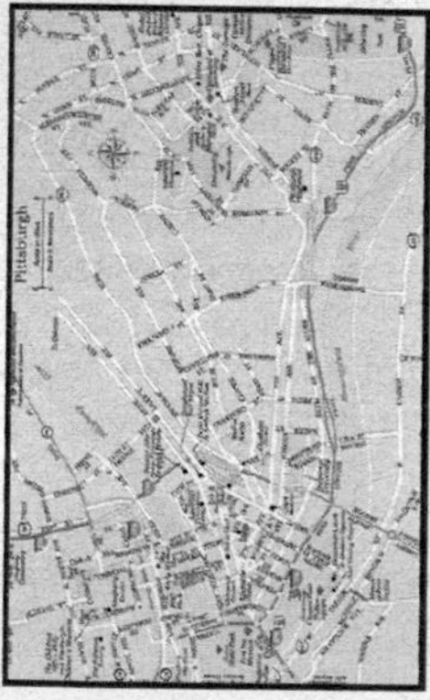

City maps
show areas where numerous points of interest are concentrated and indicate their location in relation to major roads, parks, airports and other landmarks.

Lodgings & Restaurants Section

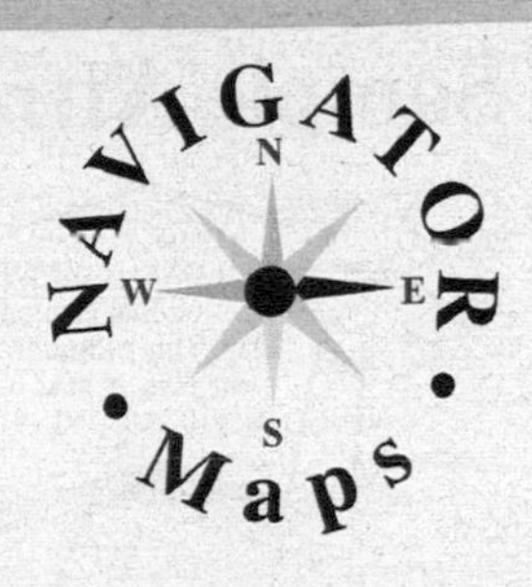

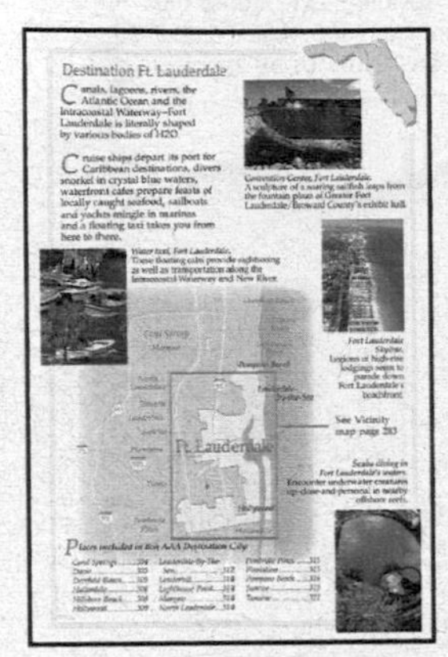

Destination area maps
illustrate key travel areas defined by local travel experts. Communities shown have listings for AAA-RATED® lodgings and/or restaurants.

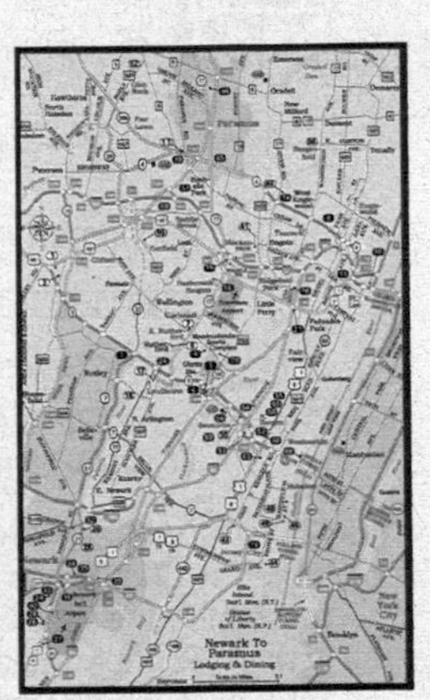

Spotting maps
show the location of lodgings and restaurants. Lodgings are spotted with a black background (22 for example); restaurants are spotted with a white background (23 for example). Spotting map indexes have been placed immediately after each map to provide the user with a convenient method to identify what an area has to offer at a glance. The index references the map page number where the property is spotted, indicates if a property is an Official Appointment and contains an advertising reference if applicable. It also lists the property's diamond rating, high season rate range and listing page number.

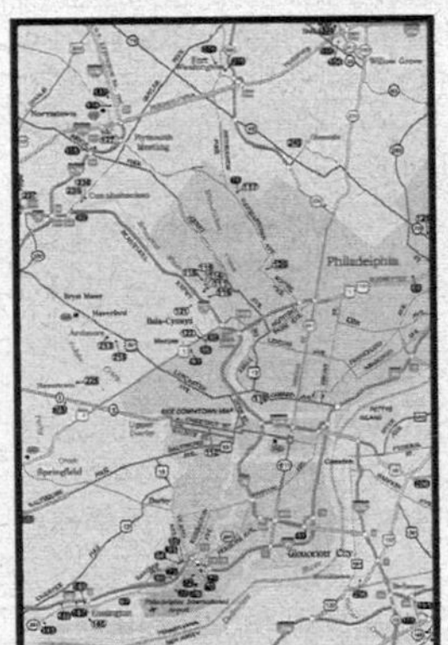

Downtown/city spotting maps
are provided when spotted facilities are very concentrated. GEM points of interest also appear on these maps.

Vicinity spotting maps
spot those properties that are outside the downtown or city area. Major roads, landmarks, airports and GEM points of interest are shown on vicinity spotting maps as well. The names of suburban communities that have AAA-RATED® accommodations are shown in magenta type.

Featured Information Section

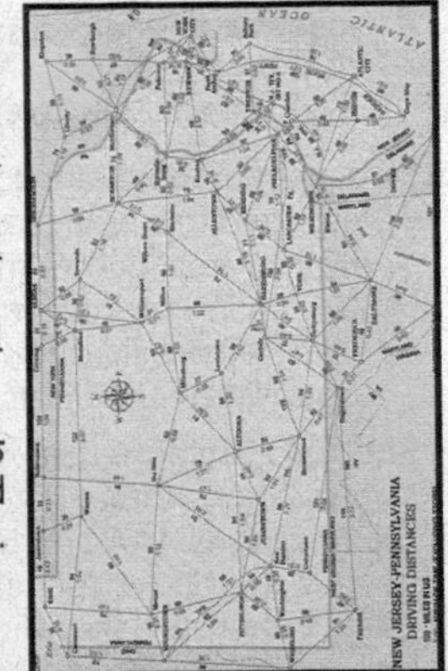

Driving distance maps
are intended to be used only for trip-distance and driving-time planning.

Sample Attraction Listing

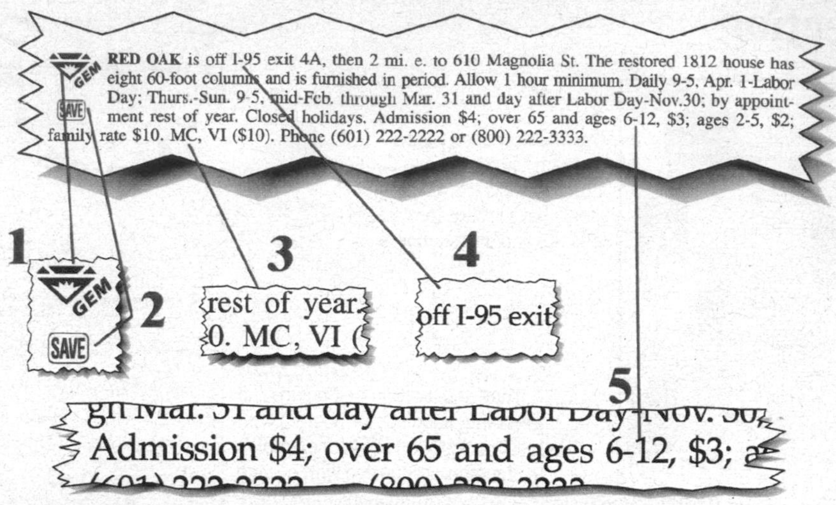

RED OAK is off I-95 exit 4A, then 2 mi. e. to 610 Magnolia St. The restored 1812 house has eight 60-foot columns and is furnished in period. Allow 1 hour minimum. Daily 9-5, Apr. 1-Labor Day; Thurs.-Sun. 9-5, mid-Feb. through Mar. 31 and day after Labor Day-Nov.30; by appointment rest of year. Closed holidays. Admission $4; over 65 and ages 6-12, $3; ages 2-5, $2; family rate $10. MC, VI ($10). Phone (601) 222-2222 or (800) 222-3333.
1
2
SAVE
3
rest of year.
0. MC, VI (
4
off I-95 exit
5
Admission $4; over 65 and ages 6-12, $3;

1 This attraction is of exceptional interest and quality and therefore has been designated a AAA GEM—offering a *Great Experience for Members*®.

2 SAVE Participating attractions offer AAA/CAA, AAA MasterCard or AAA Visa cardholders a discount off the attraction's standard admission; members should inquire in advance concerning the validity of the discount for special rates. Present your card at the admission desk. A list of participating points of interest appears in the Indexes section of the book. The SAVE discount may not be used in conjunction with other discounts. Attractions that already provide a reduced senior or child rate may not honor the SAVE discount for those age groups. All offers are subject to change and may not apply during special events, particular days or seasons or for the entire validity period of the TourBook. Shopping establishments preceded by a SAVE icon also provide discounts and/or gift with purchase to AAA/CAA members; present your card at the mall's customer service center to receive your benefit.

3 AX=American Express
CB=Carte Blanche
DC=Diners Club
DS=Discover
JC=Japan Credit Bureau
MC=MasterCard
VI=VISA

Minimum amounts that may be charged appear in parentheses when applicable.

4 Unless otherwise specified, directions are given from the center of town, using the following highway designations: I (interstate highway), US (federal highway), Hwy. (Canadian or Caribbean highway), SR (state route), CR (county road), FM (farm to market road), FR (forest road), MM (mile marker), Mex. (Mexican highway).

5 Admission prices are quoted without sales tax. Children under the lowest age specified are admitted free when accompanied by an adult. Days, months and age groups written with a hyphen are inclusive. Prices pertaining to points of interest in the United States are quoted in U.S. dollars; prices for Canadian province and territory points of interest are quoted in Canadian dollars; prices for points of interest in Mexico and the Caribbean are quoted as an approximate U.S. dollar equivalent.

Bulleted Listings: Casino gambling establishments are visited by AAA personnel to ensure safety; casinos within hotels are presented for member information regardless of whether the lodging is AAA approved. Recreational activities of a participatory nature (requiring physical exertion or special skills) are not inspected. Wineries are inspected by AAA Tourism Editors to ensure they meet listing requirements and offer tours. All are presented in a bulleted format for informational purposes.

These Show Your Card & Save® partners provide the listed member benefits. Admission tickets that offer greater discounts may be available for purchase at the local AAA/CAA club. A maximum of six tickets is available at the discount price.

Attraction Partners

SeaWorld/Busch Gardens

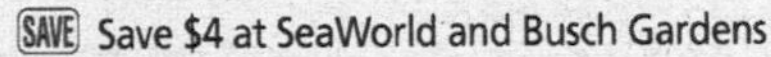

- SAVE Save $4 at SeaWorld and Busch Gardens
- SAVE Save $3 at Sesame Place, Water Country USA and Adventure Island
- SAVE Save 10% on select up-close dining. Reservations are required; visit Guest Relations for details

Six Flags Theme Parks

- SAVE Save $4 on general admission at the gate
- SAVE Save $12 on general admission at the gate each Wednesday
- SAVE Save 10% on selected souvenirs and dining (check at main gate for details)

Universal Orlando (www.aaa.com/Universal)

- SAVE Save $4 on a 2-day/2-park pass or $5 on a 3-day/2-park pass at Universal Orlando's theme parks (savings apply to tickets purchased at the gate)
- SAVE Save 10% on select dining and souvenirs at both Universal Orlando theme parks and at select Universal CityWalk Orlando restaurants (except Emeril's)

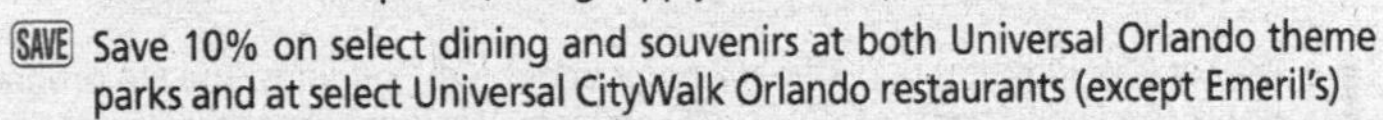

Universal Studios Hollywood

- SAVE Save $3 on a 1-day Universal Hollywood pass (savings applies to tickets purchased at the gate)

- SAVE Save 10% on select dining and souvenirs at Universal Studios Hollywood and Universal CityWalk

Gray Line

- SAVE Save 10% on sightseeing tours of 1 day or less

Restaurant Partners

Landry's Seafood House, The Crab House, Chart House, Muer Seafood Restaurants, Joe's Crab Shack

- SAVE Save 10% on food and non-alcoholic beverages at Landry's Seafood House, The Crab House, Chart House, Muer Seafood Restaurants and Joe's Crab Shack and 10% on merchandise at Joe's Crab Shack. Savings applicable to AAA/CAA members and up to six people

Hard Rock Cafe

- SAVE Save 10% on food, beverage, and merchandise at all U.S., Canada, and select international locations. Members also save 10% at The Hard Rock Vault.

Mexican Partners

- SAVE An alliance between AAA/CAA and AMA (Mexican Automobile Association) provides members visting Mexico savings from Mexicana Airlines, Tony Roma restaurants and Six Flags of Mexico

Visit aaa.com to discover all the great Show Your Card & Save® discounts in your area.

Sample Lodging Listing

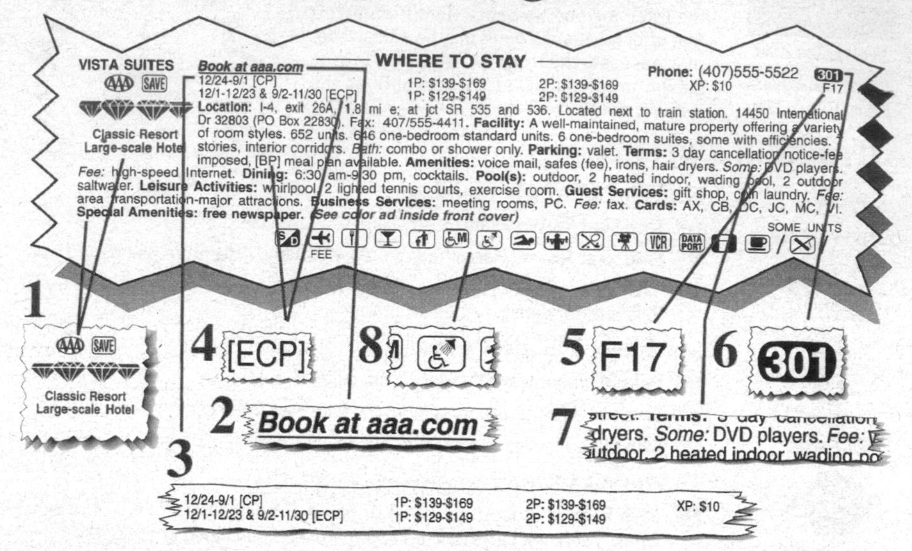

1 AAA or CAA indicates our Official Appointment (OA) lodgings. The OA program permits properties to display and advertise the AAA or CAA emblem. We highlight these properties with red diamonds and classification. Some OA listings include special amenities such as free continental breakfast; expanded continental breakfast or full breakfast; early check-in/late check-out; free room upgrade or preferred room, such as ocean view or poolside (subject to availability); free local phone calls; and free daily newspaper. This does not imply that only these properties offer these amenities. The AAA or CAA sign helps traveling members find accommodations that want member business.

♦♦♦ or ♦♦♦ The number of diamonds—not the color—informs you of the overall level of quality in a lodging's amenities and service. More diamond details appear on page 16.

Classic Resort Large-scale Hotel or Classic Resort Large-scale Hotel: All diamond rated lodgings are classified using three key elements: style of operation, overall concept and service level. See pages 22-23 for details about our Lodging Classifications and Subclassifications.

Member Values

SAVE Official Appointment properties guarantee members a minimum 10% discount off the standard room rates published in TourBook guides or the lowest public rate available at the time of booking for the dates of stay, for standard rooms.

SD Establishments offer a minimum senior discount of 10% off the listed rates. This discount is available to members 60 or older.

A$K Many properties offer discounts to members even though the lodgings do not participate in a formal discount program. The A$K is another reminder to inquire about available discounts when making your reservations or at check-in.

Discounts normally offered at some lodgings may not apply during special events or holiday periods. Special rates and discounts may not apply to all room types. Some Member Values may not apply in Mexico or the Caribbean.

To obtain published rates or discounts, you must identify yourself as a AAA or CAA member, request AAA rates when making reservations and have written confirmation sent to you. The SAVE or senior discount may not be used in conjunction with other discounts. At registration, show your membership card and verify the room rate.

Discounts normally offered at some lodgings may not apply during special events or holiday periods. Special rates and discounts may not apply to all room types. Some Member Values may not apply in Mexico or the Caribbean.

The rates listed for approved properties are provided to AAA by each lodging and represent the regular (rack) rate for a standard room. Printed rates, based on rack rates and last room availability, are rounded to the nearest dollar. Rates do not include taxes and discounts. U.S., Mexican and Caribbean rates are in U.S. dollars; rates for Canadian lodgings are in Canadian dollars.

NAVIGATOR • Lodgings •

2 Book at aaa.com - Internet Reservations

Indicates AAA/CAA members can conveniently check room availability and make reservations in a secure online environment at aaa.com.

3 Rate Lines

Shown from left to right: dates the rates are effective; meal plan provided with rates (see Meal Plan Indicators-if no plan noted, rate includes room only); rates for 1 person or 2 persons; extra person charge (XP); and any applicable family plan indicator.

Rates Guaranteed

AAA/CAA members are guaranteed that they will not be charged more than the maximum regular rate printed in each rate range for a standard room. Rates may vary within the range depending on season and room type. Listed rates are based on last standard room availability. Rates for properties operating as concessionaires for the U.S. National Park Service are not guaranteed due to governing regulations. Rates in the Mexico TourBook are not guaranteed and may fluctuate based on the exchange rate of the peso.

Exceptions

Lodgings may temporarily increase room rates, not recognize discounts or modify pricing policies during special events. Examples of special events range from Mardi Gras and Kentucky Derby (including pre-Derby events) to college football games, holidays, holiday periods and state fairs. Although some special events are listed in AAA/CAA TourBook guides, it is always wise to check, in advance, with AAA travel professionals for specific dates.

Discounts

Member discounts will apply to rates quoted, within the rate range, applicable at the time of booking. Special rates used in advertising, and special short-term, promotional rates lower than the lowest listed rate in the range, are not subject to additional member discounts.

4 Meal Plan Indicators

The following types of meal plans may be available in the listed room rate:

AP = American Plan of three meals daily
BP = Breakfast Plan of full hot breakfast
CP = Continental Plan of pastry, juice and another beverage
ECP = Expanded Continental Plan, which offers a wider variety of breakfast items
MAP = Modified American Plan of two meals daily

See individual listing "Terms" section for additional meal plans that are not included in the room rate.

Check-in times are shown in the listing only if they are after 3 p.m.; check-out times are shown only if they are before 10 a.m.

5 Family Plan Indicators

F = Children stay free
D = Discounts for children
F17 = Children 17 and under stay free (age displayed will reflect property's policy)
D17 = Discount for children 17 and under

6 Lodging Locators

Black ovals with white numbers are used to locate, or "spot," lodgings on maps we provide for larger cities.

7 Unit Types

Unit types, amenities and room features preceded by the word "Some" indicate the item is available on a limited basis, potentially within only one unit.

8 Lodging Icons

A row of icons is included with each lodging listing. These icons represent the member values, member services, and facilities offered by that lodging. See page 19 for an explanation of each icon.

The Lodging Diamond Ratings

AAA Tourism Editors evaluate and rate each lodging based on the overall quality, the range of facilities and the level of services offered by a property. The size, age and overall appeal of an establishment are considered as well as regional architectural style and design.

While guest services are an important part of all diamond ratings, they are particularly critical at the four and five diamond levels. A property must provide a high level of service, on a consistent basis, to obtain and support the four and five diamond rating.

These establishments typically appeal to the budget-minded traveler. They provide essential, no-frills accommodations. They meet the basic requirements pertaining to comfort, cleanliness, and hospitality.

These establishments appeal to the traveler seeking more than the basic accommodations. There are modest enhancements to the overall physical attributes, design elements, and amenities of the facility typically at a modest price.

These establishments appeal to the traveler with comprehensive needs. Properties are multifaceted with a distinguished style, including marked upgrades in the quality of physical attributes, amenities and level of comfort provided.

These establishments are upscale in all areas. Accommodations are progressively more refined and stylish. The physical attributes reflect an obvious enhanced level of quality throughout. The fundamental hallmarks at this level include an extensive array of amenities combined with a high degree of hospitality, service, and attention to detail.

These establishments reflect the characteristics of the ultimate in luxury and sophistication. Accommodations are first-class. The physical attributes are extraordinary in every manner. The fundamental hallmarks at this level are to meticulously serve and exceed all guest expectations while maintaining an impeccable standard of excellence. Many personalized services and amenities enhance an unmatched level of comfort.

The lodging listings with fyi in place of diamonds are included as an "information only" service for members. The icon indicates that a property has not been rated for one or more of the following reasons: too new to rate; under construction; under major renovation; not evaluated; or may not meet all AAA requirements. Those properties not meeting all AAA requirements are included for either their member value or because it may be the only accommodation available in the area. Listing prose will give insight as to why the fyi designation was assigned.

Guest Safety

Room Security

In order to be approved for listing in AAA/CAA TourBook guides for the United States and Canada, all lodgings must comply with AAA's guest room security requirements.

In response to AAA/CAA members' concern about their safety at properties, AAA-RATED® accommodations must have dead-bolt locks on all guest room entry doors and connecting room doors.

If the area outside the guest room door is not visible from inside the room through a window or door panel, viewports must be installed on all guest room entry doors. Bed and breakfast properties and country inns are not required to have viewports. Ground floor and easily accessible sliding doors must be equipped with some other type of secondary security locks.

Tourism Editors view a percentage of rooms at each property since it is not feasible to evaluate every room in every lodging establishment. Therefore, AAA cannot guarantee that there are working locks on all doors and windows in all guest rooms.

Fire Safety

Because of the highly specialized skills needed to conduct professional fire safety inspections, AAA/CAA Tourism Editors cannot assess fire safety.

Properties must meet all federal, state and local fire codes. Each guest unit in all U.S. and Canadian lodging properties must be equipped with an operational, single-station smoke detector. A AAA/CAA Tourism Editor has evaluated a sampling of the rooms to verify this equipment is in place.

For additional fire safety information, read the page posted on the back of your guest room door, or write:

National Fire Protection Association
1 Batterymarch Park
P.O. Box 9101
Quincy, MA 02269-9101

Requirements for some features, such as door locks and smoke detectors/sprinkler systems, differ in Mexico and the Caribbean. If a property met AAA's security requirements at the time of the evaluation, the phrase "Meets AAA guest room security requirements" appears in the listing.

Access for Mature Travelers and Travelers with Disabilities

Qualified properties listed in this guide are shown with symbols indicating they meet the needs of the hearing-impaired or offer some accessible features for mature travelers or travelers with disabilities.

AAA/CAA strongly urges members to call the property directly to fully understand the property's exact accessibility features. Some properties do not fully comply with AAA/CAA's exacting accessibility standards but may offer some design standards that meet the needs of some guests with disabilities.

AAA/CAA does not evaluate recreational facilities, banquet rooms, or convention or meeting facilities for accessibility.

Hearing Impaired

Indicates a property has the following equipment available for hearing-impaired travelers: TDD at front desk or switchboard; visual notification of fire alarm, incoming telephone calls, door knock or bell; closed caption decoder; text telephone or TDD for guest room use; telephone amplification device, with shelf or electric outlet next to guest room telephone.

Accessible Features

Indicates a property has some accessible features meeting the needs of mature travelers and travelers with disabilities. Lodging establishments will provide at least one guest room meeting the designated criteria as well as accessible restrooms and parking facilities. Restaurants provide accessible parking, dining rooms and restrooms.

No fees or deposits, even those normally charged for pets, may be charged for service animals. Service animals fulfill a critical need for their owners—they are *not* pets.

Service Animals

The Americans With Disabilities Act (ADA) prohibits U.S. businesses that serve the public from discriminating against persons with disabilities. Some businesses have mistakenly denied access to persons who use service animals. ADA, a federal mandate, has priority over all state and local laws, as well as a business owner's standard of business, which might bar animals from the premises. Businesses must permit entry to guests and their service animals, as well as allow service animals to accompany guests to all public areas of a property. A property is permitted to ask whether the animal is a service animal or a pet, and whether the guest has a disability. The property may not, however, ask questions about the nature of the disability, the service provided by the animal or require proof of a disability or certification that the animal is a service animal.

Note: These regulations may not apply in Canada, Mexico or the Caribbean.

What The Lodging Icons Mean

NAVIGATOR Lodgings

Member Values

(see p. 14)

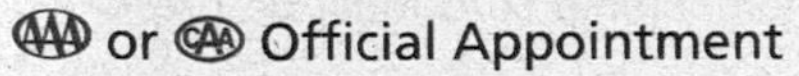

- SAVE Offers minimum 10% discount or lowest public rate *(see p. 14)*
- ASK May offer discount
- Offers senior discount
- fyi Informational listing only

Member Services

- Airport transportation
- Pets allowed
- Restaurant on premises
- Restaurant off premises (walking distance)
- 24-hour room service
- Cocktail lounge
- Child care

Accessibility Feature

(see p. 18)

- Accessible features
- Roll-in showers
- Hearing impaired

Safety Features

(Mexico and Caribbean only)

- S Sprinklers
- D Smoke detectors

Leisure Activities

- Full service casino
- Pool
- Health club on premises
- Health club off premises
- Recreational activities

In-Room Amenities

- Designated non-smoking rooms
- No air conditioning
- No TV
- No cable TV
- VCR
- Movies
- Data port/modem line
- No telephones
- Refrigerator
- Microwave
- Coffee maker

Availability and Additional Fees

If an in-room amenity is available only on a limited basis (in one or more rooms), the term "SOME UNITS" will appear above those icons. Fees may be charged for some of the services represented by the icons listed here. The word "FEE" will appear below each icon when an extra charge applies.

Preferred Lodging Partners

SAVINGS. SELECTION. SATISFACTION. — When contacting one of the partners listed, you will be given AAA's best rates for your dates of stay. Your valid membership card must be presented at check-in.

SATISFACTION GUARANTEE — If you are not satisfied with any part of your stay, you must provide the property the opportunity to correct the situation during your stay. If the matter cannot be resolved, you will be entitled to recompense for a portion of, or your entire, stay. Satisfaction guarantee varies by chain.

Select the chain you want and have your membership card available when making a reservation and checking in.

Special rates and discounts may not apply to all room types. All discounts are off full rates and vary by location and time of year. Special rates and discounts are not available to groups and cannot be combined with other discounts. Restrictions apply to satisfaction guarantees. Valid AAA/CAA membership card must be presented at check-in. Offers good at time of publication; chains and offers may change without notice. Lodging partners offering discounts to AAA/CAA members may vary in Mexico and the Caribbean.

Making Reservations

When making reservations, you must identify yourself as a AAA or CAA member. Give all pertinent information about your planned stay. Ask about the lodging's pet policy, or the availability of any other special feature that is important to your stay. Request written confirmation to guarantee: type of room, rate, dates of stay, and cancellation and refund policies. At registration, show your membership card. Note: Age restrictions may apply.

Confirm Deposit, Refund and Cancellation Policies

Most establishments give full deposit refunds if they have been notified at least 48 hours before the normal check-in time. Listing prose will note if more than 48 hours notice is required for cancellation. However, when making reservations, confirm the property's deposit, cancellation and refund policies. Some properties may charge a cancellation or handling fee.

When this applies, "cancellation fee imposed" will appear in the listing. If you cancel too late, you have little recourse if a refund is denied.

When an establishment requires a full or partial payment in advance, and your trip is cut short, a refund may not be given.

When canceling reservations, phone the lodging immediately. Make a note of the date and time you called, the cancellation number if there is one, and the name of the person who handled the cancellation. If your AAA/CAA club made your reservation, allow them to make the cancellation for you as well so you will have proof of cancellation.

Review Charges for Appropriate Rates

When you are charged more than the maximum rate listed in the TourBook guide for a standard room, question the additional charge. If management refuses to adhere to the published rate, pay for the room and submit your receipt and membership number to AAA/CAA within 30 days. Include all pertinent information: dates of stay, rate paid, itemized paid receipts, number of persons in your party, the room number you occupied, and list any extra room equipment used. A refund of the amount paid in excess of the stated maximum will be made if our investigation indicates that unjustified charging has occurred.

Get the Room You Reserved

When you find your room is not as specified, and you have written confirmation of reservations for a certain type of accommodation, you should be given the option of choosing a different room or finding one elsewhere. Should you choose to go elsewhere and a refund is refused or resisted, submit the matter to AAA/CAA within 30 days along with complete documentation, including your reasons for refusing the room and copies of your written confirmation and any receipts or canceled checks associated with this problem.

How to Get the Best Room Rates

You'll find the best room rate if you book your reservation in advance with the help of a travel professional or agent at your local AAA/CAA office.

If you're not yet ready to make firm vacation plans or if you prefer a more spontaneous trip, take advantage of the partnerships that preferred hotel chains have arranged with AAA. Phone the toll-free number 866-AAA-SAVE that has been set up exclusively for members for the purpose of reserving with these Show Your Card & Save® chain partners.

Even if you were unable to make a reservation, be sure to show your membership card at the desk and ask if you're being offered the lowest rate available for that time. Many lodgings offer reduced rates to members.

Lodging Classifications

To ensure that your lodging needs/preferences are met, we recommend that you consider an establishment's classification when making your travel choices.

While the quality and comfort at properties with the same diamond rating should be consistent (regardless of the classification), there are differences in typical décor/theme elements, range of facilities and service levels. Please see the descriptions below.

Hotel Royal Plaza, Lake Buena Vista, FL

Large-scale Hotel

A multistory establishment with interior room entrances. A variety of guest unit styles is offered. Public areas are spacious and include a variety of facilities such as a restaurant, shops, fitness center, spa, business center, or meeting rooms.

Baymont Inn, Dallas/Ft. Worth-Airport North, TX

Small-scale Hotel

A multistory establishment typically with interior room entrances. A variety of guest unit styles is offered. Public areas are limited in size and/or the variety of facilities available.

Best Western Deltona Inn, Deltona, FL

Motel

A one- to three-story establishment typically with exterior room entrances facilitating convenient access to parking. The standard guest units have one bedroom with a bathroom and are typically similar in décor and design throughout. Public areas are limited in size and/or the variety of facilities available.

Greenville Inn, Greenville, ME

Country Inn

Similar in definition to a bed and breakfast, but usually larger in scale with spacious public areas and offers a dining facility that serves at least breakfast and dinner.

Harbour Town Inn, Boothbay Harbor, ME

Bed & Breakfast

Small-scale properties emphasizing a high degree of personal touches that provide guests an "at home" feeling. Guest units tend to be individually decorated. Rooms may not include some modern amenities such as televisions and telephones, and may have a shared bathroom. Usually owner-operated with a common room or parlor separate from the innkeeper's living quarters, where guests and operators can interact during evening and breakfast hours. Evening office closures are normal. A continental or full, hot breakfast is served and is included in the room rate.

Sands of Kahana, Kahana, Maui, HI

Condominium

Vacation-oriented or extended-stay, apartment-style accommodations that are routinely available for rent through a management company. Units vary in design and décor and often contain one or more bedrooms, living room, full kitchen, and an eating area. Studio-type models combine the sleeping and living areas into one room. Typically, basic cleaning supplies, kitchen utensils and complete bed and bath linens are supplied. The guest registration area may be located off-site.

Desert Rose Inn, Bluff, UT

Cabin/Cottage

Vacation-oriented, small-scale, freestanding houses or cabins. Units vary in design and décor and often contain one or more bedrooms, living room, kitchen, dining area, and bathroom. Studio-type models combine the sleeping and living areas into one room. Typically, basic cleaning supplies, kitchen utensils, and complete bed and bath linens are supplied. The guest registration area may be located off-site.

C Lazy U Ranch, Granby, CO

Ranch

Typically a working ranch with an obvious rustic, Western theme. In general, equestrian-related activities are featured, but ranches may include other animals and activities as well. A variety of guest unit styles is offered in a family-oriented atmosphere.

Vacation Home

Vacation-oriented or extended-stay, large-scale, freestanding houses that are routinely available for rent through a management company. Houses vary in design and décor and often contain two or more bedrooms, living room, full kitchen, dining room, and multiple bathrooms. Typically, basic cleaning supplies, kitchen utensils, and complete bed and bath linens are supplied. The guest registration area may be located off-site.

ResortQuest, Hilton Head Island, SC

Lodging Subclassifications

The following are subclassifications that may appear along with the classifications listed above to provide a more specific description of the lodging.

Casino

Extensive gambling facilities are available such as blackjack, craps, keno, and slot machines. **Note:** This subclassification will not appear beneath its diamond rating in the listing. It will be indicated by a dice icon and will be included in the row of icons immediately below the lodging listing.

Classic

Renowned and landmark properties, older than 50 years, well-known for their unique style and ambience.

Historic

These properties are typically over 75 years of age and exhibit many features of a historic nature with respect to architecture, design, furnishings, public record, or acclaim. Properties must meet one of the following criteria:

- Maintained the integrity of the historical nature
- Listed on the U.S. National Register of Historic Places
- Designated a U.S. National Historic Landmark
- Located in a U.S. National Register Historic District

Separate criteria designate historic properties in Canada, Mexico and the Caribbean.

Resort

Recreation-oriented, geared to vacation travelers seeking a specific destination experience. Travel packages, meal plans, theme entertainment, and social and recreational programs are typically available. Recreational facilities are extensive and may include spa treatments, golf, tennis, skiing, fishing, or water sports, etc. Larger resorts may offer a variety of guest accommodations.

Sample Restaurant Listing

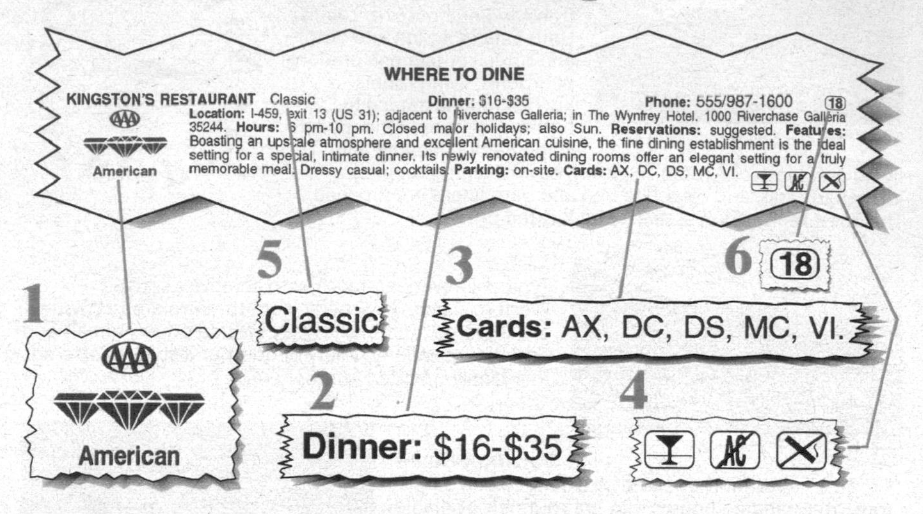

1 AAA or CAA indicates our Official Appointment (OA) restaurants. The OA program permits properties to display and advertise the AAA or CAA emblem. We highlight these properties with red diamonds and cuisine type. The AAA or CAA sign helps traveling members find restaurants that want member business.

[diamonds] or [diamonds] The number of diamonds—not the color—informs you of the overall level of quality for food and presentation, service and ambience. Menus for red Diamond restaurants can be viewed on aaa.com.

A cuisine type is assigned for each restaurant listing. AAA currently recognizes more than 90 different cuisine types.

2 Prices represent the minimum and maximum entree cost per person. Exceptions may include one-of-a-kind or special market priced items.

3

AX=American Express		
CB=Carte Blanche	DS=Discover	MC=MasterCard
DC=Diners Club	JC=Japan Credit Bureau	VI=VISA

4 These three icons are used in restaurant listings. When present, they indicate: the presence of a cocktail lounge, the lack of air conditioning, and/or that the restaurant has a designated non-smoking section or is entirely smoke-free.

5 If applicable, restaurants may be further defined as:

Classic—renowned and landmark restaurant operations in business longer than 25 years, known for unique style and ambience.

Historic—properties must meet one of the following criteria:

- Listed on the U.S. National Register of Historic Places
- Designated a U.S. National Historic Landmark
- Located in a U.S. National Register Historic District

Separate criteria designate historic properties in Canada, Mexico and the Caribbean.

6 These white ovals with black numbers serve as restaurant locators and are used to locate, or "spot," restaurants on maps we provide for larger cities.

The Restaurant Diamond Ratings

AAA Tourism Editors are responsible for determining a restaurant's diamond rating based on established criteria.

These criteria were established with input from AAA trained professionals, members, and restaurant industry experts. They are purposely broad to capture what is typically seen throughout the restaurant industry at each diamond rating level.

These establishments appeal to a diner seeking good, wholesome, no-nonsense eating at an affordable price. They typically provide simple, familiar, and unadorned foods served in a sensible, casual or self-service style. Often quick service and family oriented.

Examples include coffee shops, diners, cafeterias, short order, and modest full service eateries.

These establishments provide for dining needs that are increasingly complex, but still reasonably priced. They typically exhibit noticeable efforts in rising above the ordinary in many aspects of food, service and decor. Service is typically functional yet ambitious, periodically combining informal style with limited self-service elements. Often well-suited to traditional, special occasion, and family dining.

Examples include a varied range of specific concept (theme) and multi-purpose establishments.

These establishments impart an increasingly refined and upscale, adult-oriented experience. This is the entry level into fine dining. Creative and complex menus offer a blend of traditional and trendy foods. The service level is typically semi-formal with knowledgeable and proficient staff. Routinely these restaurants appeal to the diner in search of an experience rather than just a meal.

Examples include high-caliber, chic, boutique, and conventional restaurants.

These establishments impart a luxurious and socially refined experience. This is consistent fine dining. Menus typically reflect a high degree of creativity and complexity, featuring elaborate presentations of market-driven or traditional dishes. A cultured, professional, and highly proficient staff consistently demonstrates a profound desire to meet or exceed guest expectations. Restaurants of this caliber are geared to individuals with an appetite for an elite, fine-dining experience.

Examples include dining rooms associated with luxury lodgings, or exclusive independent restaurants often found in metropolitan areas.

Often renowned, these establishments impart a world-class and opulent, adult-oriented experience. This is "haute cuisine" at its best. Menus are often cutting edge, with an obvious dedication to use of only the finest ingredients available. Even the classic dishes become extraordinary under the masterful direction of highly acclaimed chefs. Presentations are spectacular, reflecting impeccable artistry and awareness. An expert, formalized staff continuously anticipates and exceeds guest expectations. Staff members' unfailing attention to detail appears effortless, well-rehearsed and unobtrusive. Undoubtedly, these restaurants appeal to those in search of the ultimate dining experience.

Examples include renowned dining rooms associated with luxury lodgings, or exclusive independent restaurants often found in metropolitan areas.

The restaurants with fyi in place of diamonds are included as an "information only" service for members. These listings provide additional dining choices but have not yet been evaluated.

Idaho

Ride the Wild Ones

Idaho's rivers are paradise for white-water rafting enthusiasts

Lewis and Clark Revisited

Millions of acres of wilderness await exploration by land, horseback and water

Idaho's Seaport

The Columbia River connects the inland port of Lewiston to the Pacific Ocean

The Renowned Potato

When you think of Idaho, its number one crop comes to mind

World Class Skiing

Sun Valley was America's first resort designed specifically for skiing

Snake River

wild at heart

Snake River, Caribou National Forest / © Tom Algire / SuperStock

Visit Idaho and you'll need an oxygen mask; the scenery is *that* breathtaking. From the serrated granite peaks of the Sawtooth Mountains in the center of the state to the towering Seven Devils near Hells Canyon, Idaho features some of the country's most stunning high-altitude panoramas. And if the views don't steal your breath away, the thin air at these lofty elevations just might.

Fortunately, there's no better place to deeply inhale than within the state's numerous unspoiled wilderness areas. Clean air and peaceful solitude attract pollution- and stress-weary urbanites from around the country to places like the Selway-Bitterroot Wilderness or Craters of the Moon National Monument.

You can expel that fresh air again in a shout of triumph as you conquer exhilarating white water along the Snake, Selway or Salmon rivers. Whoop with excitement as you fly down a powder-covered slope in Sun Valley or on Schweitzer Mountain. Scream with delight at the discovery of a star garnet near Coeur d'Alene, the only place outside of India you can find such treasure and just one reason Idaho's nickname—the Gem State—is appropriate.

Whatever you do, take a deep breath first; you'll want to be ready to enjoy Idaho.

...no,
...on an
...d instead
...un Valley's
...ntains to big,
...way you turn,
...by this state's power
to...

Missio... ...sible

Idaho remains one of the country's most isolated and rugged regions. To early explorers and entrepreneurs, the territory was practically impenetrable. But with a determination undaunted come Hells Canyon or high water, they journeyed west as if on a quest. Follow their lead, and you, too, will be psyched to seize the day.

Meriwether Lewis, William Clark and company were under Thomas Jefferson's orders when they entered what would become Idaho. With help from American Indians whose ancestors' arrival predated theirs by ...nes, the newcomers traced buffalo-...ing trails and hundreds of river miles all ...e way to the Pacific. The journals and maps they created en route enriched a young nation's awareness of the flora, fauna and faces of the West.

Later, trappers, traders and prospectors infiltrated Idaho in pursuit of personal enrichment. While European and East Coast fashions of the early 1800s supported a demand for tall fur hats, trappers made a fine living in Idaho's woodlands. French traders profited from the commerce, and contributed decidedly Gallic names to such Idaho tribes as the Nez Perce and the Coeur d'Alene. The prospectors, meanwhile, found their pot of gold in the state's mountains and streams. Eventually each mother lode went bust, leaving only ghost towns—notably Silver City and DeLamar, both in the Owyhee Mountains—that today entice mostly tourists.

Idaho counts plenty of contemporary dreamers and doers on its dossier. For vacation memories too intriguing to self-destruct, head to their hangouts. In Sun Valley's outskirts, find the memorial that marks one of Ernest Hemingway's favorite fly-fishing spots—it's half-hidden near a shady stream.

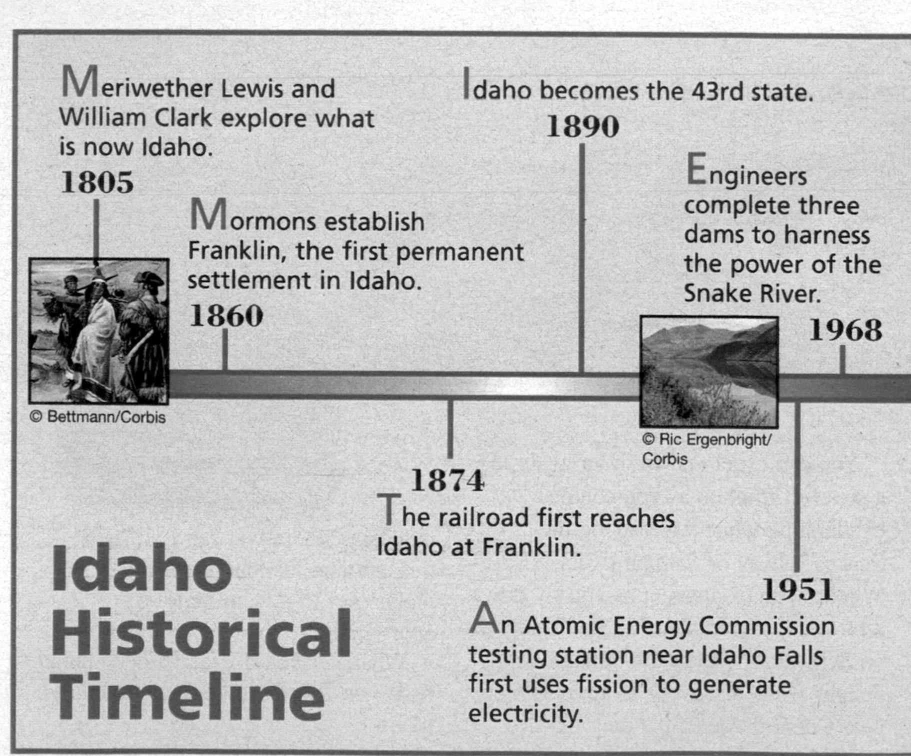

Idaho Historical Timeline
1805
Meriwether Lewis and William Clark explore what is now Idaho.
1860
Mormons establish Franklin, the first permanent settlement in Idaho.
1874
The railroad first reaches Idaho at Franklin.
1890
Idaho becomes the 43rd state.
1951
An Atomic Energy Commission testing station near Idaho Falls first uses fission to generate electricity.
1968
Engineers complete three dams to harness the power of the Snake River.
© Bettmann/Corbis
© Ric Ergenbright/Corbis

Outside Arco, seek clues to Idaho's volcanic past at Craters of the Moon National Monument, the eerie landscape where astronaut Alan Shepard and his crew trained for a lunar landing. And as you shop and stroll in the resort towns of Ketchum and Hailey, keep a covert eye out for famous faces; a who's who of movie stars and Olympic athletes lives here part time.

Idaho's allure sways more than celebrities, though. The state is home to one of the world's largest concentrations of nesting hawks, falcons, owls and other raptors; spy on some of these magnificent birds at Boise's World Center for Birds of Prey.

Not For Your Eyes Only

So, what *is* all the fuss about? Mountains, mostly. Three of Idaho's borders wear crowns topping 9,000 feet. From Bruneau River Canyon's goliathlike stone shoulders to the Precambrian pillars of City of Rocks National Reserve, mountain scenery dominates this state. Gazing upon such grandeur has a way of taking the average human to a slightly higher plane. At least that's what Idaho's famed former senator, Frank Church, seemed to have in mind when he noted, "I never knew a man who felt self-important in the m[illegible] on an [illegible]

Mountains [illegible] its appeal; where [illegible] from the Sawtooths to [illegible] handle, a separate time zone [illegible] gionalism originate. With nearly [illegible] of the state's roads classified as rural[illegible] some unpassable in snow season—it's little wonder locals are so big on self-sufficiency.

Not that less rugged diversions are lacking. State capital Boise offers a fine orchestra and opera. Coeur d'Alene reinforces its resort image with a fun theme park and a golf course featuring one offshore green. And in Sandpoint, the focal point is a city bridge turned popular downtown market.

But it's the outdoors that beckon. Here you can watch the slow, mesmerizing spiral of a golden eagle poised on a canyon-channelled thermal of mountain air, or paddle through a fast, furious white-water spin cycle with a boatful of cohorts. The offerings are as vast as the mountains. Accept the mission and you'll see for yourself: The only thing impossible about Idaho is escaping its captivating spell.

1983
An earthquake registering 7.3 on the Richter scale shakes central Idaho.

1988
Congress establishes Hagerman Fossil Beds National Monument and the City of Rocks National Reserve.

© Don Mason/Corbis

1991
Idaho Attorney General Larry EchoHawk is the first Native American in the country elected to statewide office.

1995
Idaho native Picabo Street wins the World Cup downhill skiing championship.

1999
University of Idaho graduate Jeff Ashby flies aboard the space shuttle *Columbia*.

© NASA

...nd ...g fun ...r, Idaho ... forests are

...isfies your need ...ns as Bogus Basin, 16 ... oise; Silver Mountain, south ... and Sun Valley. Kick up the adrena... notch by taking a helicopter or Snowcat, a treaded vehicle that transports approximately a dozen passengers, to isolated powdery plots in the Brundage, St. Joe or Selkirk mountains.

If you prefer to take in the snowy scenery in more than just fleeting glances, **cross-country skiing** and **snowshoeing** might hold more appeal. Outfitters plan overnight treks through the Boulder, Pioneer, Sawtooth and Teton mountains. Skiers of moderate ability enjoy Fish Creek Meadows and Lolo Pass in Nez Perce National Forest; the scenic trails in Farragut State Park; and the paths winding throughout Sawtooth National Recreation Area. Stick with the difficult 16-mile Banner Ridge Trail, 25 miles northeast of Idaho City near Beaver Creek Summit Pass, and you'll be rewarded with an amazing view.

Running Water

As the snow melts and runs off the mountains, the rivers swell to provide thrills of their own.

Idaho's waterways provide some 3,100 miles of white water, more than enough to tantalize fans of **white-water rafting, kayaking** and **jet boating.** Class III and IV rapids, with names like Split Rock and Whiplash, may explain how the Salmon got its nickname as the "river of no return." Rafting and kayaking also are wild and woolly on the Middle Fork of the Salmon and the Owyhee, Payette and Lochsa rivers, the last of which is a Nez Perce Indian word for "rough water." Jet boats zip along the Snake River through Hells Canyon.

Want to take it slowly? Go **canoeing** between the cliffs rising around the Snake River at Hagerman Fossil Beds National Monument in Hagerman, or watch eagles, ospreys and mink as you enjoy a leisurely float trip down the placid Boise River.

Dories and drift boats take anglers to favorite **fishing** waters on the Clearwater, ...n and Snake rivers, where hardy steel... abound. Healthy populations of rainbow ...d brown trout still swim in one of Ernest Hemingway's favorite **fly-fishing** hideaways—Silver Creek, near Sun Valley. The upper St. Joe River is a haven for cutthroat.

Anglers find the northern lakes no less exciting. Coeur d'Alene, Pend Oreille and Priest lakes teem with chinook and kokanee salmon, Kamloops trout and northern pike.

Back On Dry Land

Climbing expeditions tackle Slick Rock, near McCall; City of Rocks National Reserve, near Almo; and the state's highest peak, Mount Borah. For a less rugged experience, go **hiking** or **backpacking** or make your way up mountains around McCall and Sun Valley on a llama trek. Only pack trains and hikers penetrate the unspoiled terrain of the Frank Church-River of No Return, Sawtooth and Selway-Bitterroot wilderness areas, which blanket more than 2 million acres.

Varied landscapes offer scores of surprises for **mountain bikers.** Ridgelines across such ranges as the Bitterroot, Cougar and Salmon afford outstanding panoramas. A plunging waterfall punctuates the scene at Malad Gorge State Park, near Bliss. For something different, pedal across the lava fields of Craters of the Moon National Monument.

Trail rides around resort areas in the Grand Tetons and near Coeur d'Alene, Sun Valley and Yellowstone entertain **horseback riders.** Sawtooth National Recreation Area and Cascade Reservoir, south of McCall, also are prime for exploration.

The units of the state park system weave history, scenery and recreation to provide memorable **camping** excursions.

Recreational Activities

Throughout the TourBook, you may notice a Recreational Activities heading with bulleted listings of recreation-oriented establishments listed underneath. Similar operations also may be mentioned in Destination City recreation sections. Since normal AAA inspection criteria cannot be applied, these establishments are presented only for information. Age, height and weight restrictions may apply. Reservations often are recommended and sometimes are required. Addresses and/or phone numbers are provided so visitors can contact the attraction for additional information.

Fast Facts

POPULATION: 1,293,953.

AREA: 83,557 square miles; ranks 13th.

CAPITAL: Boise.

HIGHEST POINT: 12,662 ft., Borah Peak.

LOWEST POINT: 710 ft., Snake River at Lewiston.

TIME ZONE(S): Mountain/ Pacific. DST.

MINIMUM AGE FOR DRIVERS: with driver's education training, 15 (restricted to daylight hours until 16); otherwise 17.

MINIMUM AGE FOR GAMBLING: 21.

SEAT BELT/CHILD RESTRAINT LAWS: Seat belts required for driver and front-seat passengers; child restraints required for under 4 and children under 40 pounds.

HELMETS FOR MOTORCYCLISTS: Required for persons under 18.

RADAR DETECTORS: Permitted.

FIREARMS LAWS: Vary by state and/or county. Contact Idaho State Police, 2700 North-South Hwy., Lewiston, ID 83501; phone (208) 743-9546.

HOLIDAYS: Jan. 1; Martin Luther King Jr. Day, Jan. (3rd Mon.); Presidents Day, Feb. (3rd Mon.); Memorial Day, May (last Mon.); July 4; Labor Day, Sept. (1st Mon.); Columbus Day, Oct. (2nd Mon.); Veterans Day, Nov. 11; Thanksgiving; Dec. 25.

TAXES: Idaho's statewide sales tax is 5 percent. There is a 2-percent Travel & Convention Tax on lodgings, with local options to levy up to an additional 5 percent.

STATE INFORMATION CENTERS: Welcome centers that provide details about state attractions, accommodations, historic sites, parks and events as well as road and ski repor[illegible] Milepost 1; 6 miles south of Ma[illegible] along I-90E at Post Falls.

FURTHER INFORMATION F[illegible] VISITORS:

Idaho Division of Tourism Development
Box 83720
Boise, ID 83720-0093
(208) 334-2470
(800) 635-7820

RECREATION INFORMATION:.

Idaho Parks and Recreation Department
P.O. Box 83720
Boise, ID 83720-0065
(208) 334-4199
(800) 635-7820

FISHING AND HUNTING REGULATIONS:

Idaho Fish and Game Department
Box 25
600 S. Walnut St.
Boise, ID 83707
(208) 334-3700
(800) 635-7820

NATIONAL FOREST INFORMATION:

U.S. Forest Service
Northern Region (Northern Idaho)
Federal Building
200 E. Broadway
P.O. Box 7669
Missoula, MT 59807
(406) 329-3511
(877) 444-6777 (reservations)
TTY (877) 833-6777

U.S. Forest Service
Intermountain Region (Southern Idaho)
324 25th St.
Ogden, UT 84401
(801) 625-5306
(877) 444-6777 (reservations)
TTY (877) 833-6777

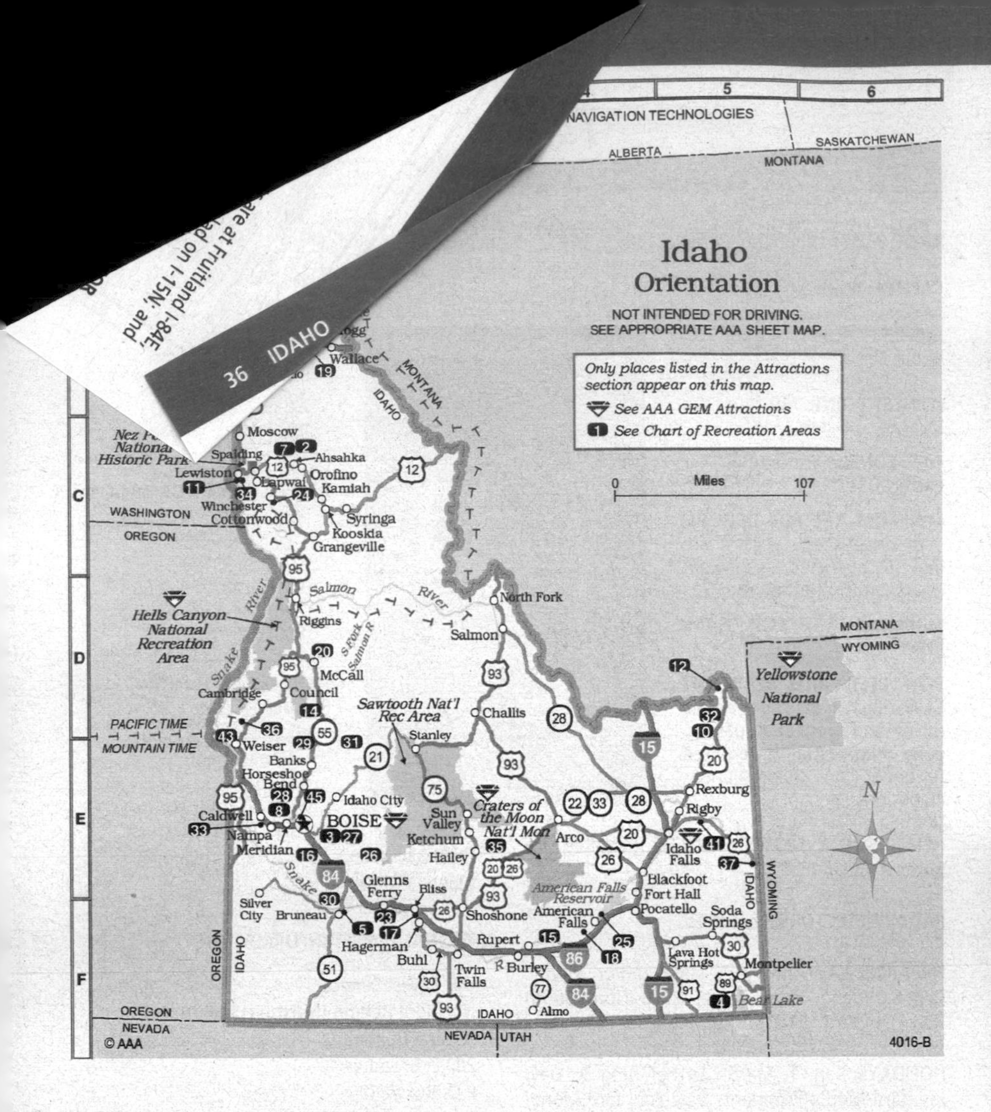

The One For All

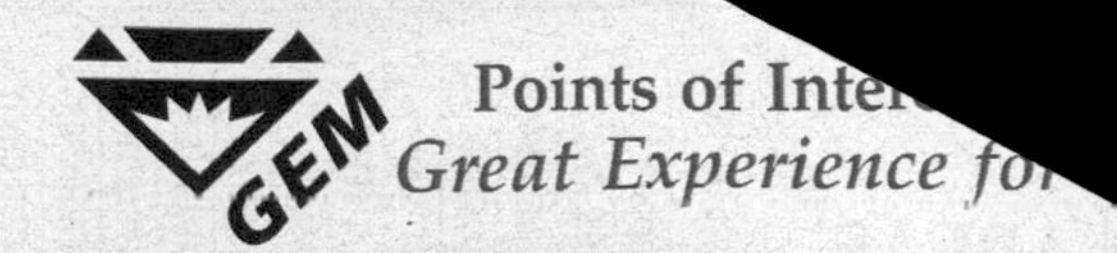

Boise (E-2)

DISCOVERY CENTER OF IDAHO—This family-oriented science museum has hands-on exhibits for all ages. See p. 44.

Craters of the Moon National Monument (E-3)

CRATERS OF THE MOON NATIONAL MONUMENT—The lunar-like volcanic landscape at this national monument can be viewed from a drive along a 7-mile-long loop road. See p. 50.

Hells Canyon National Recreation Area (D-1)

HELLS CANYON NATIONAL RECREATION AREA—North America's deepest gorge is the standout of this ruggedly scenic wilderness region in western Idaho. See p. 52.

Idaho Falls (E-5)

THE MUSEUM OF IDAHO—The state's natural an cultural history—from prehistoric times to the Atomic Age—unfold at this comprehensive museum. See p. 55.

Yellowstone National Park

YELLOWSTONE NATIONAL PARK—The more than 3,400 acres of America's first national park are home to buffaloes, bighorn sheep, elk, moose and pronghorn antelopes as well as thousands of thermal pools and springs. See place listing in Wyoming p. 173.

Idaho Temperature Averages Maximum / Minimum

From the records of the National Weather Service

	JAN	FEB	MAR	APR	MAY	JUN	JUL	AUG	SEP	OCT	NOV	DEC
Boise	36/21	42/26	52/31	62/37	71/45	79/51	90/59	88/57	78/49	65/40	48/30	39/25
Idaho Falls	28/3	33/8	42/18	58/29	68/38	76/44	88/50	86/47	75/38	62/28	43/17	33/9
Lewiston	38/24	44/28	53/33	63/39	71/46	78/52	90/58	88/56	78/49	64/40	48/32	42/28
Pocatello	32/13	37/18	46/26	60/33	69/41	78/48	90/55	87/53	77/44	64/34	45/25	36/19

	MAP	CAMPING	PICNICKING	HIKING TRAILS	BOATING	BOAT RAMP	BOAT RENTAL	FISHING	SWIMMING	PETS ON LEASH	BICYCLE TRAILS	WINTER SPORTS	VISITOR CENTER	LODGE/CABINS	FOOD SERVICE
[illegible]		●	●	●	●	●		●	●	●	●	●	●	●	●
[illegible]		●	●	●				●	●	●		●			
[illegible] Idaho.		●	●	●	●			●	●	●		●	●	●	
[illegible] northern and northwestern Ida[illegible]		●	●	●	●	●	●	●	●	●	●	●		●	
Nez Perce [illegible] North-central Idaho.		●	●	●	●	●		●	●	●	●	●	●	●	
Payette 2,307,89[illegible] [illegible]s. West-central Idaho.		●	●	●	●	●		●	●	●	●	●	●		
Salmon-Challis 4,300,000 acres. East-central Idaho.		●	●	●	●	●		●	●	●		●		●	●
Sawtooth 2,101,422 acres. South-central Idaho. Horse rental.		●	●	●	●	●	●	●	●	●	●	●	●	●	●
Targhee 1,800,000 acres. Southeastern Idaho.		●	●	●	●	●		●	●	●		●		●	●
NATIONAL RECREATION AREAS *(See place listings)*															
Hells Canyon (C-1) 652,977 acres.		●	●	●	●	●		●		●	●	●	●	●	●
Sawtooth (D-3) 756,000 acres.		●	●	●	●	●	●	●	●	●	●	●	●	●	●
ARMY CORPS OF ENGINEERS															
Albeni Cove (B-1) 20 acres 1 mi. e. of Oldtown on a county road. Water skiing.	1	●	●		●	●		●	●	●					
Dworshak Reservoir (C-2) 19,823 acres 7 mi. n. of Orofino. Bird-watching, water skiing.	2	●	●	●	●	●	●	●	●	●			●		
Lucky Peak (E-2) 237 acres 9 mi. s.e. of Boise on SR 21. Water skiing.	3		●	●	●	●	●	●	●	●	●				●
STATE															
Bear Lake (F-5) 966 acres 20 mi. s. of Montpelier off US 89. Snowmobiling, water skiing.	4	●	●		●	●		●	●			●			
Bruneau Dunes (F-2) 4,800 acres 8 mi. n.e. of Bruneau off SR 51. Sand dunes. No motorized boats.	5	●	●	●	●	●		●	●	●		●	●		
Coeur d'Alene Parkway (B-2) 34 acres e. of Coeur d'Alene off I-90 exit 15 on Coeur d'Alene Lake Dr.	6		●	●	●	●		●		●	●				
Dworshak (C-2) 850 acres 26 mi. n.w. of Orofino.	7	●	●	●	●	●		●	●	●				●	
Eagle Island (E-2) 547 acres 8 mi. w. of Boise off SR 44 or US 20/26. Water slide.	8		●					●	●						●
Farragut (B-2) 4,733 acres 4 mi. e. of Athol on SR 54. Historic. Cross-country skiing, snowmobiling.	9	●	●	●	●	●		●	●	●	●	●	●		
Harriman (D-5) 4,330 acres 18 mi. n. of Ashton on US 20. Cross-country skiing; horse rental.	10		●	●				●			●	●	●	●	
Hells Gate (C-1) 960 acres 4 mi. s. of Lewiston on Snake River Ave. Water skiing; horse rental.	11	●	●	●	●	●		●	●	●	●		●		●
Henry's Lake (D-5) 586 acres 15 mi. w. of West Yellowstone off US 20. Bird-watching, water skiing.	12	●	●	●	●	●		●		●					
Heyburn (B-1) 7,825 acres 5 mi. e. of Plummer on SR 5. Cross-country skiing, ice fishing, snowmobiling.	13	●	●	●	●	●		●	●	●	●	●	●	●	●
Lake Cascade (D-2) 4,450 acres n.w. of Cascade.	14	●	●	●	●	●		●	●	●	●	●			
Lake Walcott (F-4) 65 acres 11 mi. n.e. of Rupert off SR 24.	15	●	●	●	●	●		●		●	●				
Lucky Peak (E-2) 240 acres 10 mi. s.e. of Boise off SR 21.	16		●	●	●	●		●	●	●	●				●
Malad Gorge (F-3) 652 acres .2 mi. s. off I-84 exit 147, then .2 mi. w. following signs. *(See Bliss p. 43)*	17		●	●				●			●				
Massacre Rocks (F-4) 990 acres 10 mi. s.w. of American Falls off I-86. Historic.	18	●	●	●	●	●		●		●			●		
Old Mission (B-2) 18 acres 11 mi. w. off I-90 exit 39. Historic. *(See Kellogg p. 48)*	19		●	●	●	●		●		●			●		
Ponderosa (D-2) 1,470 acres 2 mi. n.e. of McCall on E. Lake Dr. Cross-country skiing.	20	●	●	●	●	●		●	●	●	●	●	●		

RECREATION AREAS

	MAP LOCATION	CAMPING	PICNICKING	HIKING TRAILS	BOATING	BOAT RAMP	BOAT RENTAL	FISHING	SWIMMING	PETS ON LEASH	BICYCLE TRAILS	WINTER SPORTS	VISITOR CENTER	LODGE/CABINS	FOOD SERVICE
Priest Lake (A-2) 463 acres 11 mi. n. of Coolin. Cross-country skiing, ice fishing, snowmobiling.	21	•	•	•	•	•		•	•	•		•			
Round Lake (B-2) 142 acres 10 mi. s. of Sandpoint off US 95 on Dufort Rd. Cross-country skiing, ice fishing, ice skating, sledding, snowshoeing. No motorized boats.	22	•	•	•	•	•		•	•	•		•	•		
Three Island Crossing (F-2) 513 acres 1 mi. w. of Glenns Ferry via Commercial St. s. and Madison w. Historic.	23	•	•	•				•		•			•		
Winchester Lake (C-2) 318 acres .25 mi. s. of Winchester on US 95 Bus. Rte. Cross-country skiing, ice fishing, ice skating, sledding. No motorized boats (except with electric motors).	24	•	•	•	•	•		•		•	•	•			
OTHER															
American Falls Reservoir (F-4) 59,893 acres .2 mi. n. of American Falls on I-15. Historic.	25	•	•		•	•		•	•	•			•		
Anderson Ranch Reservoir (E-2) 5,000 acres 30 mi. n.e. of Mountain Home on SR 20 and FR 61.	26	•	•	•	•	•		•	•	•		•		•	•
Arrowrock Reservoir (E-2) 4,000 acres 16 mi. e. of Boise on SR 21 and FR 268.	27	•	•	•	•	•		•	•	•		•		•	
Black Canyon Reservoir (E-2) 2,364 acres 8 mi. n.e. of Emmett on SR 52.	28		•		•	•		•	•	•					
Cascade Reservoir (E-2) 33,788 acres 20 mi. s. of McCall on SR 55. Ice fishing, snowmobiling.	29	•	•		•	•		•	•	•		•			•
C.J. Strike Reservoir (E-2) 7,500 acres. *(See Bruneau p. 47)*	30	•	•		•	•		•	•						
Deadwood Reservoir (D-2) 3,000 acres 34 mi. n.e. of Garden Valley on FR 555.	31	•	•	•	•			•	•	•		•		•	
Island Park Reservoir (D-5) 7,800 acres 27 mi. n. of Ashton off US 20. Snowmobiling.	32	•	•		•	•		•	•	•		•		•	•
Lake Lowell (E-1) 10,587 acres 8 mi. s. of Caldwell via 10th Ave. or SR 55. Water skiing.	33		•		•	•		•	•	•		•	•		
Lake Waha (C-2) 100 acres 18 mi. s.e. of Lewiston on Thain Rd.	34	•	•	•	•	•		•	•	•		•			
Little Wood River Reservoir (E-3) 976 acres 11 mi. n. of Carey on access road.	35	•	•		•	•		•	•	•					
Mann Creek Reservoir (D-2) 4 acres 9 mi. n. of Weiser on US 95. Water skiing.	36	•	•		•	•		•	•	•					
Palisades Reservoir (E-5) 27,845 acres 50 mi. s.e. of Idaho Falls on US 26.	37	•	•		•	•		•	•	•		•			
Pend Oreille Lake (B-2) 94,600 acres. *(See Sandpoint p. 65)*	38	•	•		•	•		•	•	•					
Priest River (A-2) 20 acres .5 mi. e. of Priest River off US 2. Water skiing.	39	•	•	•	•	•		•	•	•					
Riley Creek (A-2) 45 acres 1 mi. s. of Laclede on Riley Creek Rd. Water skiing.	40	•	•		•	•		•	•	•					
Ririe Reservoir (E-5) 6,069 acres 20 mi. n.e. of Idaho Falls on US 26.	41	•	•		•	•		•	•	•			•		
Springy Point (A-2) 13 acres 3.2 mi. w. of Sandpoint on US 95. Water skiing.	42	•	•		•	•		•	•	•					
Steck Park (D-1) 20 mi. n.w. of Weiser via SR 70 on the Snake River.	43	•	•		•			•		•					
Trestle Creek (A-2) 2 acres n.w. of Hope on SR 200. Water skiing.	44		•		•	•		•	•	•					
Veterans Memorial (E-2) 80 acres on SR 44 at 36th St. in Boise. Bird-watching. No motorized boats.	45		•	•	•			•		•	•				

Points of Interest

AHSAHKA (C-2) elev. 1,001′

DWORSHAK DAM VISITOR CENTER is 3 mi. e. on SR 7, following signs, on the North Fork of the Clearwater River. The visitor center overlooks the 717-foot dam, one of the highest straight-axis concrete gravity dams in North America. Behind the dam, Dworshak Reservoir *(see Recreation Chart)* extends 54 miles into wild, rugged timberland.

Free 60- to 90-minute guided tours of the dam are available. Interpretive displays are available and audiovisual presentations are shown in the theater upon request. Visitor center open daily 8:30-4:30, Memorial Day weekend-Labor Day; Mon.-Fri. 8:30-4:30, rest of year. Closed Thanksgiving and Dec. 25. Guided tours are given Mon.-Fri. at 11, 1 and 3, Memorial Day weekend-Labor Day. Free. Phone (208) 476-1255 or (208) 476-1261.

DWORSHAK NATIONAL FISH HATCHERY, s.e. on SR 7 at the confluence of the two forks of the Clearwater River, is one of the world's largest steelhead trout hatcheries. About 3 million steelhead trout and 1 million chinook salmon are raised in environmentally controlled ponds. The best time to see the adult steelhead is March through May; the returning salmon brood stock June through August.

Displays, a viewing balcony above the spawning room, incubators, nursery tanks, 126 outdoor ponds and a self-guiding tour map are available. Allow 30 minutes minimum. Grounds open daily dawn-dusk. Main building open daily 7:30-4; hatchery building closed major holidays. Free. Phone (208) 476-4591.

ALMO (F-4) elev. 5,390′

CITY OF ROCKS NATIONAL RESERVE is 5 mi. s. on HC 61 and 4 mi. w. on an unpaved road. Within the 14,300-acre reserve are massive granite rocks, some 2.5 billion years old, eroded into shapes resembling the ruins of an ancient city. Inscriptions written in axle grease and scratched into the rocks by pioneers traversing the Oregon and California trails afford insights into immigrant trail history.

Rock climbing, sightseeing, hiking through high deserts and primitive camping are possible. Picnicking is permitted. Visitor center open daily 8-4:30, May-Sept.; Mon.-Fri. 8-4:30, rest of year. Day use is free. The overnight fee is $7 for one vehicle, $12 for two vehicles. Only eight persons per site are permitted. MC, VI. Phone (208) 824-5519.

AMERICAN FALLS (F-4)
pop. 4,111, elev. 4,330′

The "Idaho Gem Community" of American Falls, an early campsite on the old Oregon Trail, is the center of irrigation projects that enable the cultivation of thousands of acres of farmland. The American Falls Reservoir *(see Recreation Chart)*, the largest on the Snake River, provides excellent opportunities for boating, sailing, water skiing and rainbow trout fishing. A visitor center is open April through October; phone (208) 226-7214.

American Falls Chamber of Commerce: 239 Idaho St., American Falls, ID 83211; phone (208) 226-7214.

ARCO (E-4) pop. 1,026, elev. 5,320′

EXPERIMENTAL BREEDER REACTOR #1 is 20 mi. e. on US 20 at the Idaho National Engineering Laboratory. On Dec. 20, 1951, the reactor became the first atomic reactor to generate a usable amount of electricity. Exhibits are available to visitors, and free 30- to 60-minute guided tours through the facility are conducted as needed by trained guides. Self-guiding tours are permitted. Pamphlets explaining four nuclear reactors, a reactor control room and detection devices are available upon request.

Allow 1 hour minimum. Daily 9-5, Memorial Day weekend-Labor Day; by appointment rest of year. Last guided tour departs 45 minutes before closing. Free. Phone (208) 526-0050.

ATHOL (B-2) pop. 676, elev. 2,391′

SILVERWOOD, 2 mi. s. on US 95, is a late-1800s mining town theme park with more than 60 rides, live shows, games, attractions and Boulder Beach water park. The Victorian-styled park has three roller coasters, including the wooden coaster Tremors, which goes above and under the ground; a log flume; a steam train; shows and midway games. Music and entertainment, including an ice show, are offered.

Food and camping are available. Allow 3 hours minimum. Silverwood open Sun.-Thurs. 11-9, Fri.-Sat. 11-10, July-Aug.; Sun.-Thurs. 11-7, Fri.-Sat. 11-8, in June; Sat.-Sun. 11-6, May 1-day before Memorial Day weekend and Oct. 1-10; Sat.-Sun. of Memorial Day weekend 11-8, Memorial Day 11-6; Sat.-Sun. of Labor Day weekend 11-10, Labor Day 11-7; Sat.-Sun. 11-7, day after Labor Day-Sept. 30. Boulder Beach open daily 11-7, June 12-Labor Day.

Admission (includes Silverwood and Boulder Beach) $29.99; over 64 and ages 3-7, $18.99. Parking $3. DS, MC, VI. Phone (208) 683-3400.

DID YOU KNOW

The world's largest potato chip resides at the Idaho Potato Expo in Blackfoot.

BANKS (E-2) elev. 2,840′

RECREATIONAL ACTIVITIES

White-water Rafting

- **Bear Valley River Company** meets downstairs from the Banks Store and Cafe for transportation to departure points. Write P.O. Box 38, Banks, ID 83602. Daily 9-4, Memorial Day weekend-Sept. 30. Phone (208) 793-2272 or (800) 235-2327.

BEAVERHEAD-DEERLODGE NATIONAL FOREST—

see Montana p. 82.

BITTERROOT NATIONAL FOREST—

see Montana p. 87.

BLACKFOOT (E-4) pop. 10,419, elev. 4,497′

BINGHAM COUNTY HISTORICAL MUSEUM, 190 N. Shilling Ave., is in a renovated 1905 Southern mansion built of lava rock and lumber. The museum displays period furnishings, clothing, photographs, dolls and other historical items. Allow 30 minutes minimum. Wed.-Fri. 1-4:30, last week in Apr.-last Fri. in Oct. Donations. Phone (208) 785-0397 or (208) 782-0750.

SAVE **IDAHO POTATO EXPO,** 130 N.W. Main St., presents a variety of exhibits related to the potato, including antique machinery and tools, gunny sacks and, at 24 by 14 inches, the "Guinness Book of World Records" world's largest potato chip. Each visitor is offered a free potato product. Videotapes about the potato industry and production processes are shown. Phone for special tour arrangements.

Allow 1 hour minimum. Mon.-Sat. 9:30-5, Apr.-Oct.; 9:30-3, rest of year. Admission $3; over 54, $2.50; ages 6-12, $1. MC, VI. Phone (208) 785-2517.

BLISS (F-3) pop. 275, elev. 3,261′

MALAD GORGE STATE PARK is .2 mi. s. off I-84 exit 147, then .2 mi. w., following signs. Markers indicate points of interest along a 3.5-mile loop road. From a footbridge visitors can see the bottom of a 250-foot-deep gorge where a waterfall plunges into Devil's Washbowl. Hiking trails wind along the gorge's edge and into the park's interior. Wildlife can be seen throughout the park, which also contains prehistoric Indian hunting blinds.

Part of the Oregon Trail, volcanic collapse features and underground springs also can be seen. Picnicking is permitted. Allow 30 minutes minimum. Daily dawn-dusk. Free. Phone (208) 837-4505. *See Recreation Chart.*

BOISE (E-2) pop. 185,787, elev. 2,739′

The woods lining the Boise River were a welcome sight for French-Canadian trappers who were grateful to reach a forest again after trudging across the territory's semiarid plain. As a result, they named the area *Boisé,* meaning "wooded." The city, however, was not founded until 1863, a year after the gold rush reached the Boise Basin.

"The City of Trees," Boise is Idaho's capital and largest metropolitan area. The first sessions of the territorial government were held during 1863 in Lewiston, then moved to this population center the following year. The new territorial capital was the center of commerce and culture for miners and traders from nearby mountain boom towns. Built in 1863, the O'Farrell Cabin on Fort Street is one of the city's oldest buildings.

The quality of life, low cost of living and liberal tax advantages as well as the city's role as state capital and transportation hub, account for Boise's steady economic growth. Many national and multinational firms have their headquarters in Boise, and light industry flourishes. The city also is the home of Boise State University *(see attraction listing)*; the Boise Philharmonic plays in the university's Velma V. Morrison Center for the Performing Arts.

Boise is the southwest terminus of SR 21, the Ponderosa Pine Scenic Route. The route passes through part of Sawtooth National Forest before ending in Stanley; portions of SR 21 are closed in winter.

Protected from unduly harsh winter weather by the Owyhee Mountains, the capital enjoys year-round opportunities for leisure and recreation. Ann Morrison Park, 153 acres between Americana and Capitol boulevards, offers picnicking, playgrounds, ballfields and tennis courts. Skates and bicycles can be rented at Wheels-R-Fun at the south end of 13th Street.

A novel way to reach Ann Morrison Park is by floating down the Boise River on a rental raft or inner tube from Barber Park, which is on the southeast edge of town; at the junction of Warm Springs Avenue and SR 21 turn onto Eckert to reach the park. Rentals are available daily Memorial Day through Labor Day; a return shuttle bus is available.

Kathryn Albertson Park is a 40-acre downtown wildlife sanctuary across Americana Boulevard from Ann Morrison Park. Paved footpaths meander past gazebos, ponds and fountains while offering glimpses of waterfowl and other wildlife. The park also provides access to the Boise Greenbelt, a 25-mile path following the Boise River. A favorite place to walk, jog, skate or ride a bicycle, the greenbelt connects 12 area parks.

Pari-mutuel horse racing takes place at Les Bois Park from early May through August on the Western Idaho Fairgrounds; phone (208) 376-7223.

Note: Policies concerning admittance of children to pari-mutuel betting facilities vary. Phone for information.

Once used as an American Indian lookout, Table Rock rises 1,100 feet above the valley east of Boise. Its flat summit, surmounted by an illuminated cross that can be seen for miles, affords a view of the city and a pioneer route south of the river.

In the 1921 St. Paul Baptist Church building at 508 N. Julia Davis Dr. in Julia Davis Park, the Idaho Black History Museum features biographies and photographs of black inventors as well as examples or re-creations of their inventions; phone (208) 433-0017.

To the southeast, 12 miles south of Kuna, the Snake River Birds of Prey National Conservation Area provides a haven for a number of species of birds and other wildlife. It is home to one of the largest concentrations of birds of prey in the world.

Boise Convention and Visitors Bureau: 312 S. 9th St., Boise, ID 83702; phone (208) 344-7777 or (800) 635-5240. *See color ad p. 43.*

Shopping areas: Boise Factory Outlets, I-84 exit Gowen Road, offers more than 40 factory stores. Boise Towne Square Mall, Milwaukee and Franklin streets, features The Bon Marche, Dillard's, JCPenney, Mervyn's and Sears. Downtown shopping includes 8th Street Marketplace, a former late 1890s warehouse district at 8th and Front streets; Hyde Park on N. 13th Street; and Old Boise Historic District on Main Street between Capitol and 4th streets.

BASQUE MUSEUM AND CULTURAL CENTER, 611 Grove St., in the Basque block, celebrates the legacy of the Basques. Exhibits focus on traditional music, dance, sports, food and houses. Basque history and culture are further depicted through a cultural center, library and genealogy research room. Staff and volunteers are Basques who are knowledgeable about their heritage. Allow 30 minutes minimum. Tues.-Fri. 10-4, Sat. 11-3; closed Jan. 1 and Dec. 24-25. Donations. Phone (208) 343-2671.

BOISE STATE UNIVERSITY, 1910 University Dr. along the Boise River, is an important educational, cultural, theatrical, musical and athletic center. Established in 1932, the university has 16,000 students enrolled in eight schools and colleges.

Highlights of the campus include the Simplot/Micron Technology Center, Christ Chapel, Boise State University Pavilion and the Velma V. Morrison Center for the Performing Arts. Bronco Stadium is noted for its blue artificial turf. Public tours of the university are offered Mon.-Fri. Free. Reservations are required. Phone the New Student Information Center at (800) 824-7017, ext. 4.

SAVE **BOISE TOUR TRAIN,** leaving from the tour train depot across from the rose garden in Julia Davis Park off Capitol Blvd., offers 1-hour narrated tours of the historic and downtown areas of Boise. An enclosed trolley-style bus is used during inclement weather. Other half- and full-day tours also are available.

Tours depart Mon.-Sat. at 10, 11:15, 12:30, 1:45 and 3, Sun. at noon, 1:15, 2:30 and 3:45, Memorial Day-Labor Day; Wed.-Sun. at noon, 1:30 and 3, day after Labor Day-Sept. 30; Sat.-Sun. at 1 and 2:30, Apr.-May and in Oct. Arrive for boarding at least 15 minutes prior to departure. Fare $7; over 62, $6; ages 4-12, $4.50. MC, VI. Phone (208) 342-4796.

GEM SAVE **DISCOVERY CENTER OF IDAHO,** 131 Myrtle St., is a science museum with hands-on displays. More than 130 exhibits invite persons of all ages to touch, explore and discover by doing.

Among the topics investigated are electricity, sound, motion, perception and hearing. Visitors can make a 3-foot bubble, see downtown Boise through a periscope and find out how everyday devices work. Designed to encourage the imagination, Science at Play has nine interactive exhibits designed for pre-schoolers, such as Step and Slide, consisting of foam steps and blocks and a slide for creative play and building.

Allow 1 hour minimum. Tues.-Fri. 9-5, Sat. 10-5, Sun. noon-5, Sept.-May; Mon.-Sat. 10-5, Sun. noon-5, rest of year. Closed Jan. 1, Easter, Thanksgiving and Dec. 25. Admission $6; over 59, $5; ages 3-12, $3.50. AX, MC, VI. Phone (208) 343-9895.

FIRST UNITED METHODIST CHURCH occupies a city block bordered by 11th, 12th, Franklin and Hay sts.; enter through the office at 1110 W. Franklin St. Known as the Cathedral of the Rockies, the church dates from 1872. The present Gothic structure, the third building used by the congregation, contains impressive stained-glass windows. Mon.-Fri. 8:30-5. Free. Phone (208) 343-7511.

IDAHO BOTANICAL GARDEN, 2.5 mi. e. on Main St. and Warm Springs Ave. to 2355 N. Penitentiary Rd., offers 13 themed gardens on 50 acres of the former farm and nursery/hothouse of the Idaho Penitentiary.

Alphabet gardens are found in the Children's Garden, while the Peony Garden has 32 hybrid varieties and fine urns. The Heirloom Rose Garden has pre-1900 roses, and the English Garden contains plants compatible with Idaho's high desert climate. Other features include water, meditation and herb gardens.

Allow 1 hour minimum. Mon.-Fri. 9-5 (also Fri. 5-8, May-Sept.), Sat.-Sun. and holidays 10-6, Apr.-Oct.; Sat.-Sun. and holidays noon-4, rest of year. Closed major holidays. Admission $4; over 65, $3; ages 6-12, $2. AX, MC, VI. Phone (208) 343-8649.

THE IDAHO MILITARY HISTORY MUSEUM is at Gowen Field, with access from Harvard St.; take I-84 exit 52 (Orchard St.) s., following signs to 4748 Lindbergh St., Bldg. #924. Covering a broad spectrum of military history, the museum has uniforms dating to the Spanish American War; an extensive collection of weapons, including firearms, knives and examples of infantrymen's primary rifles from 1795 to the present; field gear from World War I forward; and displays about the Idaho National Guard.

A collection of armored vehicles is outdoors. Allow 1 hour minimum. Fri.-Wed. noon-4; closed major holidays. Donations. Phone (208) 422-4841.

JULIA DAVIS PARK, with entrances on Capitol Blvd. or Myrtle St., contains a lagoon, rose garden, playground and a band shell where concerts are given in the summer. A large portion of the Boise River Greenbelt is accessible from the park. The Discovery Center of Idaho *(see attraction listing)* offers hands-on exhibits for all ages. Boat rentals are available. Picnicking is permitted. Daily dawn-dusk. Free. Phone (208) 384-4240.

SAVE **Boise Art Museum,** 670 S. Julia Davis Dr. at the park entrance, displays the Janss Collection of American Realism and presents more than 15 changing art exhibits annually. Free guided tours are available with a minimum of 2 weeks' notice.

Allow 1 hour minimum. Mon.-Sat. 10-5 (also Thurs. 5-8), Sun. noon-5, June-Aug.; Tues.-Sat. 10-5 (also Thurs. 5-8), Sun. noon-5, rest of year. Closed Jan. 1, Easter, July 4, Thanksgiving and Dec. 25. Admission $8; over 62 and college students $6; grades 1-12, $4; half-price to all first Thurs. of the month. MC, VI. Phone (208) 345-8330.

Idaho Historical Museum, 610 N. Julia Davis Dr., provides an overview of the state's history. Displays include a 19th-century saloon as well as relics of early Idaho. Allow 1 hour minimum. Tues.-Sat. 9-5; closed Jan. 1, Thanksgiving, Dec. 25 and state holidays. Admission $2; ages 6-18, $1. Phone (208) 334-2120.

Zoo Boise, .5 mi. s. off Capitol Blvd., has a variety of animals from around the world, including Amur tigers, zebras, a snow leopard, moose and native bears. Aviaries feature eagles, hawks, owls and vultures. Small Animal Kingdom spotlights animals and plants indigenous to islands, deserts and rainforests. An education center has wildlife exhibits. Food is available. Daily 10-5; closed Jan. 1, Thanksgiving and Dec. 25. Admission $4.80; over 61, $2.55; ages 4-11, $2.30. Family rate (available Thurs.) $2.50; ages 4-11, $1.30. Phone (208) 384-4260.

MORRISON KNUDSEN NATURE CENTER is 2.5 mi. off I-84 exit 54 (Broadway Ave.); cross the Boise River, turn e. onto Park Blvd. then .5 mi. e. to 600 S. Walnut Ave., following signs. This 4.5-acre area features a sampling of the ecosystems present in Idaho. Walking trails pass a mountain stream with logjams and waterfalls, a wetlands pond and a high desert plain with sagebrush and lava rock. Along the way are plants and wildlife indigenous to each area. Windows along the path show how fish are born and how a stream receives oxygen.

The visitor center offers exhibits and occasional lectures. Allow 1 hour minimum. Outdoor area open daily dawn-dusk. Visitor center hours vary; phone ahead. Outdoor area free. Visitor center by donations. Phone (208) 334-2225, or (208) 368-6060 for recorded hours information.

SAVE **OLD IDAHO PENITENTIARY STATE HISTORIC SITE,** 1.5 mi. e. of Broadway and Warm Springs aves. at 2445 Old Penitentiary Rd., was used 1870-1973 as Idaho's prison. Additions to the complex were constructed by prisoners with sandstone they quarried and cut. Exhibits include historic weapons and vehicles, an explanation of the history of tattoos and a video presentation recalling prison history, notorious inmates and conditions of prison life. The grounds and a rose garden are maintained as they were by inmates in the early 1900s.

Picnicking is permitted. Allow 2 hours minimum. Daily 10-5, Memorial Day-Labor Day; noon-5, rest of year. Closed state holidays except Memorial Day, July 4 and Labor Day. Admission $5; over 59, $4; ages 6-12, $3. Phone (208) 368-6080 or (208) 334-2844.

STATE CAPITOL, bordered by Jefferson, W. State, 6th and 8th sts., is Boise's most impressive public building. Built of marble and Idaho sandstone, the Capitol was begun in 1905 and completed in 1920. A 5-foot statue of a golden eagle tops the dome of the classical-style building.

Agricultural, mineral, gemstone and timber products are displayed; a replica of the Winged Victory of Samothrace, a gift from France, and a statue of George Washington, carved from pine and coated in gold, are of interest. Self-guiding tours Mon.-Fri. 8-5, Sat.-Sun 9-5. Guided 1-hour tours are given Mon.-Fri. at 10 and 1:30, early June-late Aug.; by appointment rest of year. Closed holidays. Admission and tours free. Phone (208) 334-5174.

SAVE **WORLD CENTER FOR BIRDS OF PREY** is 7 mi. s. at 5668 W. Flying Hawk Ln. Take I-84 exit 50 to S. Cole Rd., then s. 6 mi. and w. on Flying Hawk Ln. to the top of the hill. This 7,200-square-foot interpretive center features exhibits about birds of prey, biology, ecology and conservation as well as a tropical forest. Live falcons and eagles are available for viewing. Offspring of the birds are released into the wild. Staff is available to answer questions and to lead tours of the visitors center.

Daily 9-5, Mar.-Oct.; 10-4, rest of year. Closed Jan. 1, Thanksgiving and Dec. 25. Admission $4; over 61, $3; ages 4-16, $2. AX, DS, MC, VI. Phone (208) 362-8687.

WORLD SPORTS HUMANITARIAN HALL OF FAME is at 404 S. 8th St., in the 8th St. Marketplace. The hall of fame honors sports greats who also have made significant humanitarian contributions. Interactive displays, sports artifacts and memorabilia are featured. Among the hall's inductees are Arthur Ashe, Bonnie Blair, Roberto Clemente, Rafer Johnson, Tom Landry, Pelé, Mary Lou Retton and Chi Chi Rodriguez.

Guided tours are available. Allow 1 hour minimum. Mon.-Fri. 9-4, Sat.-Sun. by appointment; closed Jan. 1, Thanksgiving and Dec. 25. Admission $3; over 65, $2; ages 5-18, $1. Phone (208) 343-7224.

RECREATIONAL ACTIVITIES

Skiing

- **Bogus Basin Ski Resort**, 16 mi. n. via Bogus Basin Rd. Write 2405 Bogus Basin Rd., Boise, ID 83702. Wed.-Fri. 10-4:30, Sat.-Sun. and holidays 9-4:30, Thanksgiving-early Apr. Phone (208) 332-5100 or (800) 367-4397.

White-water Rafting

- **River Odysseys West (ROW)** offers various departure points. Write P.O. Box 579, Coeur d'Alene, ID 83816. Trips depart mid-May to mid-Sept. Phone (208) 765-0841 or (800) 451-6034.

BOISE NATIONAL FOREST

Elevations in the forest range from 2,860 ft. at Lucky Peak Reservoir to 10,776 ft. at Thomason Peak. Refer to AAA maps for additional elevation information.

In southwestern Idaho, lakes, abandoned mines and ghost towns amid ponderosa pine and Douglas fir dot the 2,648,468 acres of mountainous terrain that make up the Boise National Forest. Large areas of the forest serve as summer range for big game. Black bears, wolves, mountain goats, bighorn sheep, deer and elk inhabit the woods. Upland game birds including chukars, sage grouse, Hungarian partridges and turkeys roam the back country. Salmon, trout and bass thrive in the cold, clear rivers, streams and reservoirs.

Deep canyons, rugged peaks exceeding 9,000 feet and high meadows offer an abundance of recreation opportunities year-round. Cross-country skiing and snowmobiling are popular during the winter. The forest offers more than 900 miles of hiking trails.

Scenic drives wind through the canyons and along the edge of the Sawtooth Wilderness; only trails enter the Frank Church-River of No Return Wilderness in the northeast section. Cascade Reservoir recreation facilities include camping; phone for more information about special facilities and amenities.

Additional information can be obtained from the Public Affairs Office, Boise National Forest, 1249 S. Vinnell Way, Suite 200, Boise, ID 83709; phone (208) 373-4100. *See Recreation Chart and the AAA Northwestern CampBook.*

BONNERS FERRY (A-2)

pop. 2,515, elev. 1,773'

Although trappers David Thompson and Finan McDonald were drawn to the banks of the Kootenai River and established a fur trading post in 1808, it was not until 1864 that a permanent settlement was founded. It was in that year that E.L. Bonner's ferry replaced the canoes of American Indians, who the previous year had carried gold miners rushing to the Canadian Wild Horse lode.

Trapping and river transportation no longer dominate the commerce of Bonners Ferry; today the town, 25 miles south of Canada, maintains a resource-oriented economy of lumbering and farming. Several large hops farms are in the community.

The mountainous terrain of northern Idaho and the gorge cut by the Kootenai River make the Bonners Ferry region popular for its beauty. Katka View Point, 9 miles east on CR 24, provides a view of the Kootenai Valley, the Selkirk Mountains and the proposed Selkirk Crest National Wilderness area. At Smith Creek Falls and View Point, approximately 25 miles north of Bonners Ferry on CR 45 via US 95 and SR 1, a trail leads to an overlook and the falls.

Another scenic trip is provided by traveling US 2 to a point between Mileposts 70 and 71, where an overlook affords a view of the Moyie River canyon, waterfalls and the Big Moyie Canyon Bridge. At 600 feet above the canyon, the span is one of Idaho's highest bridges.

A final route leaves US 2 at Moyie Springs, about 7 miles east of Bonners Ferry, and proceeds through a portion of the Idaho Panhandle National Forests *(see place listing p. 55)* to US 95.

Greater Bonners Ferry Chamber of Commerce: P.O. Box X, Bonners Ferry, ID 83805; phone (208) 267-5922.

KOOTENAI NATIONAL WILDLIFE REFUGE is 5 mi. w. on the dike road along the south shore of the Kootenai River; be alert for logging trucks. Almost 3,000 acres along the river provide feeding, resting and breeding areas for migratory birds. Tundra swans are common in spring; Canada geese and ducks are most numerous in fall. White-tailed and mule deer, moose, black bears and coyotes also use the refuge.

One vehicle route, three observation areas and several foot trails are maintained for visitors. Picnicking is permitted. Refuge open daily dawn-dusk, but entry is limited during the Oct.-Dec. hunting season. Free. Phone (208) 267-3888.

BRUNEAU (F-2) elev. 2,525′

Bruneau, the French name first given the brown-water river that skirts the northern edge of the Great Basin Desert, was founded by 19th-century French-Canadian trappers. The town is the community nearest Bruneau Dunes State Park *(see Recreation Chart and the AAA Northwestern CampBook).* The park's dunes, which rise to 470 feet, are considered the tallest single-structured sand dunes in North America.

BRUNEAU CANYON OVERLOOK is 15 mi. s.e. via a paved and gravel road, then 3 mi. w. on a dirt road, following signs. The Bruneau River courses through a narrow canyon whose vertical walls are 800 feet high in places.

C.J. STRIKE DAM, n.w. via SR 78 on the Snake River, has created a 7,500-acre reservoir. Boating, swimming, fishing, picnicking and camping are permitted. Park open daily 24 hours. Free. Phone (208) 834-2295. *See Recreation Chart.*

BUHL (F-3) pop. 3,985, elev. 3,800′

Buhl (BEWL) is on the Snake River, at the western end of a valley that grew little but sagebrush until 1906, when irrigation transformed the desert into lush farmland. Agriculture and aquaculture are the bases of Buhl's present economy. Tourism and the raising of sheep and beef and dairy cattle are important. The surrounding area produces barley, sugar beets, corn, dry beans, alfalfa, grains, sugar snap peas, seed crops and potatoes.

Buhl is said to be the rainbow trout capital of the United States, since the town is a leader in trout research and production. Trout farms raise and process rainbow trout that are shipped throughout the world; similar farms produce catfish, tilapia and salmon. The products of dirt farms and local craftsmen are available Wednesday 5-7 p.m., mid-June through September, at the farmers' market in the parking lot of the senior citizens' center at 1010 Main St.

An oddity of nature called the Balanced Rock can be seen by taking a short drive south to Castleford, then 6 miles west. The 40-foot-high rock is perched on a base only a few feet in diameter.

Buhl Chamber of Commerce: 716 US 30E, Buhl, ID 83316; phone (208) 543-6682.

THOUSAND SPRINGS, n. on US 30 in Snake River Canyon, appears over a 2-mile area, gushing in beautiful cascades from the sides of the canyon. The springs are believed to be the reappearance of Lost River, which vanishes into the lava fields near Arco, about 90 miles northeast. Three pools are in an area of hot mineral baths.

BURLEY (F-3) pop. 9,316, elev. 4,165′

Hydroplanes, super stock and other powerful racing craft churn up Burley's Snake River waterfront during the month of June, when such national speedboat championships as the Idaho Regatta take place.

Mini-Cassia Chamber of Commerce: 1177 7th St., P.O. Box 640, Heyburn, ID 83336; phone (208) 679-4793.

CASSIA COUNTY HISTORICAL SOCIETY MUSEUM, E. Main St. and Hiland Ave., contains collections of fossils, an early railroad car and caboose, local history items, and tools and wagons of the miners, trappers, loggers and farmers who settled southern Idaho. Audiovisual displays chart the pioneer trails that led immigrants to the Pacific Northwest.

On the museum grounds are furnished replicas of a one-room cabin, general store, schoolhouse, barbershop and a sheepherder's wagon. Allow 1 hour minimum. Tues.-Sat. 10-5, Apr.-Sept.; closed holidays. Donations. Phone (208) 678-7172.

CALDWELL (E-1) pop. 25,967, elev. 2,367′

Situated on the Boise River, Caldwell was established in the late 19th century. The community, which began as a construction camp for the Oregon Short Line Railroad, is now associated with the processing and distribution of farm products. Boone Science Hall, near the corner of 20th and Fillmore streets on the 700-student Albertson College of Idaho campus, houses the Orma J. Smith Museum of Natural History, the Evans Gem and Mineral Collection and the Whittenberger Planetarium; phone (208) 459-5211.

Caldwell Chamber of Commerce: 914 Blaine St., P.O. Box 819, Caldwell, ID 83605; phone (208) 459-7493.

WINERIES

- **Ste. Chapelle Winery**, 8 mi. s.w. on SR 55, then .5 mi. e., following signs. Mon.-Sat. 10-5, Sun. noon-5; closed Easter, Thanksgiving and Dec. 25. Phone (208) 459-7222.

CAMBRIDGE (D-2) pop. 360, elev. 2,739′

CAMBRIDGE MUSEUM, jct. US 95 and SR 71, provides information about area heritage from the arrival of the first settlers in 1869 until the 1930s. Displays focus on geology, farming relics, American Indian life and pioneer days in the community. A blacksmith shop and a replica of a schoolroom with historic items can be seen. A reproduction of a mine entrance has illustrations demonstrating dynamiting techniques. A genealogy section is available.

Allow 30 minutes minimum. Wed.-Sat. 10-4, Sun. 1-4, June-Aug. Schedule may vary; phone ahead. Donations. Phone (208) 257-3485.

RECREATIONAL ACTIVITIES

White-water Rafting

- **Hughes River Expeditions**, location departures vary with trip. Write P.O. Box 217, Cambridge, ID 83610. Expeditions offered May-Sept. Phone (208) 257-3477 or (800) 262-1882.
- **River Odysseys West (ROW)** trips depart from the Frontier Motel. Write P.O. Box 579, Coeur d'Alene, ID 83816-0579. Snake River trips offered May-Sept. Phone (208) 765-0841 or (800) 451-6034.

CARIBOU NATIONAL FOREST

Elevations in the forest range from 4,850 ft. at Mink Creek to 9,957 ft. at Mead Peak. Refer to AAA maps for additional elevation information.

In the southeast extending into Wyoming and Utah, the 972,407-acre Caribou National Forest is noted for rugged scenery marked by towering mountain ranges and beautiful valleys. Drives along the Snake River and through the many canyons provide scenic vistas. A few traces of the ghost towns of Keenan and Caribou City recall the gold rush days. *See Recreation Chart and the AAA Northwestern CampBook.*

CATALDO (B-2) elev. 2,150'

COEUR D'ALENE'S OLD MISSION STATE PARK, off I-90 exit 39, is named for the restored Old Sacred Heart Mission built in the 1850s by Coeur d'Alene Indians under the guidance of Jesuit priest Father Antonio Ravalli. The 18-inch-thick mission walls were built of woven straw and adobe mud without nails. Videotape presentations, mission tours and a visitor center are available. Daily 8-6, June-Aug.; 9-5, rest of year. Admission $3 per private vehicle. Phone (208) 682-3814. *See Recreation Chart.*

CHALLIS (D-3) pop. 909, elev. 5,288'

LAND OF THE YANKEE FORK HISTORIC AREA has its interpretive center on SR 75 just s. of jct. US 93. The center has a slide program about area mine and ghost town history and dioramas and photographs of the mines and miners 1860-1910.

A 91-mile scenic loop, the Custer Motorway Adventure Road (FR 70), begins here on a narrow, gravel and dirt road, and runs past stage stations, ghost towns, abandoned mines and mills, the Yankee Fork Gold Dredge, the Custer Museum and Sunbeam Dam Interpretive Site. The loop's return road is paved SR 75 (the Salmon River Scenic Byway).

Allow 30 minutes for the interpretive center. Allow 3 hours for the loop. The Custer Motorway Adventure Road is not recommended for vehicles with low clearance, trailers or motor homes. Inquire locally for road conditions. Interpretive center open daily 8-6, Apr.-Oct.; Mon.-Fri. 9-5, rest of year. The Custer Motorway Adventure Road is closed by snow late Oct.-June 30. Yankee Fork Gold Dredge open for tours late June-Labor Day. Custer Museum open Memorial Day-Labor Day. Park, interpretive centers and museum free. Gold dredge tour $3, children $1. Phone (208) 879-5244.

CHALLIS NATIONAL FOREST—

see Salmon-Challis National Forest p. 64.

CLARK FORK (B-2) pop. 530, elev. 2,084'

Clark Fork lies at the foot of the Cabinet Mountains, just northeast of Lake Pend Oreille. The town is on the lake's main tributary, the Clark Fork River, just before it flows into the lake. This location experiences unusually warm winters and cool summers.

The town sprang up in the 1880s when the main line of the Northern Pacific Railroad cut through the Bitterroot and Cabinet mountains. The railroad made lumbering profitable, and lumberjacks began arriving on the area's first steam tugboats. Soon nearby trappers were giving up their trade and joining the timber camps. Today the area attracts hikers, anglers and other outdoor enthusiasts.

Hope, Clark Fork & Trestle Creek Chamber of Commerce: P.O. Box 304, Hope, ID 83836.

CABINET GORGE DAM, 8 mi. e. on SR 200, on the Clark Fork River, is a horseshoe-shaped dam in a scenic setting. A lookout point affords an excellent view of the project.

CLEARWATER NATIONAL FOREST

Elevations in the forest range from 1,200 ft. to 8,820 ft. at Ranger Peak. Refer to AAA maps for additional elevation information.

In the northeastern part of the state, large stands of tall trees and many miles of clear, fast-running streams and rivers characterize the rugged, mountainous Clearwater National Forest. Scenic Lewis and Clark Highway (US 12) runs a few miles south of but roughly parallel to the Lolo Trail, the American Indian route across the Bitterroots to buffalo-hunting country.

A portion of the Selway-Bitterroot Wilderness, the second largest wilderness area in the continental United States, makes up part of Clearwater's 1,739,353 acres. US 12 follows the rugged Lochsa Wild and Scenic River, where kayak and raft enthusiasts challenge the stream's white water. Recreation information is available at ranger stations in Kooskia, Orofino, Potlatch and Powell.

Lolo Pass Visitors Center, along US 12 at the crest of the Bitterroots on the Idaho-Montana border, and the restored Lochsa Historical Ranger Station, halfway between Powell and Kooskia on US 12, are open Memorial Day weekend through Labor Day. For further information contact the Supervisor's Office, Clearwater National Forest, 12730 US

12, Orofino, ID 83544; phone (208) 476-4541. *See Recreation Chart and the AAA Northwestern CampBook.*

COEUR D'ALENE (B-1)

pop. 34,514, elev. 2,157'

The largest city in northern Idaho takes its name from the local tribe of American Indians. French trappers dubbed them Coeur d'Alene (CORE-dah-LANE), meaning "heart of the awl," a vernacular phrase describing them as shrewd traders.

Gen. William Tecumseh Sherman established an Army post in 1878 at the point where the Spokane River drains Lake Coeur d'Alene. Fort Sherman, as it was called after the general's death, became the nucleus of a settlement that was named for the lake. The 1880s mining boom in the Silver Valley brought prosperity, as Coeur d'Alene became an important shipping point. For a period it was the busiest steamboat port west of the Mississippi River. By 1900 boats were carrying tourists on excursion cruises.

North Idaho College now occupies the old fort site, and Fort Sherman Chapel survives at the corner of Hubbard Street and Woodland Drive. The community college has an enrollment of 4,100; phone (208) 769-3300.

Idaho's "Lake City" remains a popular resort. In summer the city's beaches, parks and docks throng with outdoor enthusiasts. Boating, houseboating, swimming, water skiing, parasailing and fishing are popular activities. Forested Tubbs Hill Park, beside the lake just south of downtown, offers trails to secluded coves and beaches, and to the summit for panoramic views.

What is said to be the world's longest floating boardwalk runs 3,300 feet from Independence Point in City Park to the foot of Third Street, around the Coeur d'Alene Resort. The North Idaho Centennial Trail, paved for walkers, bicyclists and skaters, extends 24 miles from Higgens Point, east of Coeur d'Alene, west to the Idaho/Washington border, where it connects with Spokane's Centennial Trail.

Coeur d'Alene Chamber of Commerce Visitor & Convention Services: 1621 N. 3rd St., P.O. Box 850, Coeur d'Alene, ID 83816; phone (208) 664-3194 or (877) 782-9232.

Shopping areas: Silver Lake Mall, 3.5 miles north on US 95, offers The Bon-Macy's, JCPenney and Sears. Antiques can be found at Coeur d'Alene Antique Mall's two locations, 3650 Government Way and 408 Haycraft, and at Wiggett's Marketplace, downtown at N. 4th Street and Lakeside.

AERIAL RETARDANT PLANT, 6 mi. n. on US 95, then w. on Wyoming Rd. to the airport, prepares chemical fire retardants for aerial tankers that extinguish fires in the surrounding forests. Visitors can see the planes being loaded in the event of a forest fire. Allow 1 hour minimum. Tours daily 9-4, July-Sept. Free. Phone (208) 772-3283.

LAKE COEUR D'ALENE is s. of town. Once called one of the five most beautiful lakes in the world by *National Geographic,* it is surrounded by mountains and a lush forest. Twenty-five miles long, it averages 2.5 miles in width and has a 135-mile-long shoreline. It has one of the nation's largest populations of osprey, and bald eagles can be seen diving into the lake to catch salmon in winter. Power boating, sailing and fishing are summer sports.

LAKE COEUR D'ALENE CRUISES depart from the Coeur d'Alene city dock at Independence Point. A 90-minute, narrated lake cruise provides glimpses of wildlife and local scenery. Brunch, sunset, full-day and other cruises also are available. Allow 2 hours minimum. Narrated lake cruises daily, late Apr.-late Oct. Fare $15.75; over 55, $14.75; ages 6-12, $9.75. AX, DS, MC, VI. Phone (208) 765-4000.

MUSEUM OF NORTH IDAHO, 115 Northwest Blvd., explores the history of the Coeur d'Alene region. Displays include exploration, transportation and early settler exhibits as well as fire fighting, logging, lumbering and rotating seasonal exhibits. A 20-minute videotape presentation relates the history of the Coeur d'Alene region.

Allow 30 minutes minimum. Tues.-Sat. 11-5, Apr.-Oct.; closed July 4. Admission (includes admission to Fort Sherman Museum) $2; ages 6-16, $1; family rate $5. Phone (208) 664-3448.

Fort Sherman Museum, on the North Idaho College campus, displays artifacts from U.S. military personnel and Coeur d'Alene Indians at Fort Sherman. It also houses an original forest service smoke chasers' cabin. Allow 30 minutes minimum. Tues.-Sat. 1-4:45, May-Sept.; closed holidays. Admission (includes admission to Museum of North Idaho) $2; ages 6-16, $1; family rate $5.

SILVERWOOD—*see Athol p. 42.*

WILD WATERS is off I-90 exit 12, then s. on Lincoln, e. on Ironwood Dr. and n. on Government Way. The park offers a variety of amusements, including waterslides, spas and inner tube river rides. Children's waterslides, an arcade and a playground also are available. Allow 1 hour minimum. Daily 11-6, Memorial Day weekend-Labor Day. All-day pass $16.99, under 48 inches tall $14.99, senior citizens $6.99, under age 3 free. Admission after 3 p.m. $11.99, senior citizens $6.99. MC, VI. Phone (208) 667-6491.

COOLIN (A-2) elev. 2,147'

Coolin is the headquarters for the Priest Lake resort area. Priest Lake, with its 80-mile shoreline, is known for its big Mackinaw trout. The 25-mile-long lake is linked with smaller Upper Priest Lake via a channel called The Thorofare. Of the lake's seven islands, Kalispell, Bartoo, Four Mile and Eight Mile islands are available for camping.

The Roosevelt Grove of Ancient Cedars, a virgin forest, is on the west side of Priest Lake, northwest of Nordman via FS 302 in Washington. Priest Lake State Park, on the east shore of Priest Lake, offers trails through cedar-hemlock forests *(see Recreation Chart and the AAA Northwestern CampBook).*

Priest Lake Chamber of Commerce: P.O. Box 174, Coolin, ID 83821-0174; phone (208) 443-3191 or (888) 774-3785.

COTTONWOOD (C-2) pop. 944, elev. 3,411'

A way station constructed of cottonwood logs was established here in 1862 amid the wheat field of the Camas Prairie. During July 3-5, 1877, the area southeast of Cottonwood was the scene of several skirmishes between the Nez Perce and U.S. Cavalry troops and scouts. State interpretive markers give details of the battles. *See Nez Perce National Historical Park p. 59.*

The Camas Prairie Railroad's 66-mile Second Subdivision passes through Cottonwood. Opened in 1908 to transport the prairie's agricultural bounty, it was known as the "Railroad on Stilts" for its numerous trestles, some of the nation's tallest. Many can be seen from US 95. The line was abandoned in 2000.

The Museum at St. Gertrude's, on the grounds of the Priory of Saint Gertrude, houses collections about local history including mining artifacts, American Indian memorabilia, ceramics and art. The hand-carved wooden high altar was constructed with mortise and glue; not a single nail was used. Near the northern entrance to the town is a large statue of a dog known as the World's Biggest Beagle.

Cottonwood Chamber of Commerce: P.O. Box 15, Cottonwood, ID 83522; phone (208) 962-3231.

WEIS ROCKSHELTER is 7 mi. s. in Grave's Creek Canyon. Archeological excavations of this cliff recess have revealed almost continuous human occupation between 5500 B.C. and A.D. 1400.

COUNCIL (D-2) pop. 816, elev. 2,940'

COUNCIL VALLEY MUSEUM is at 100 S. Galena St. Area history is depicted through early dentist's, doctor's and sheriff's offices; a jail; a dry goods store; and a cowboy's cabin. Also displayed are American Indian artifacts such as tools and weapons as well as items related to local mining and fruit growing boom periods. Allow 30 minutes minimum. Tues.-Sat. 10-4, Sun. 1-4. Donations. Phone (208) 253-6499.

GEM CRATERS OF THE MOON NATIONAL MONUMENT (E-3)

Eighteen miles west of Arco via US 20/26 and US 93, Craters of the Moon National Monument is at the base of the Pioneer Mountains.

This 1,100-square-mile area contains more basaltic volcanic features than any other area of its size in the continental United States. Lava rivers once flooded the surrounding countryside, leaving vast lava fields covered by cinder cones with large central vents that were thought by early observers to resemble the craters on the moon. The volcanic activity dates back about 15,000 years, with the last eruptions occurring about 2,000 years ago.

The area's variety of surface patterns and formations is typical of the world's other basaltic lava sites. Visitors should be cautious of sharp lava formations.

A 7-mile loop drive, open from mid-April to early November, leads past the monument's main points of interest and takes about 25 minutes to complete. The view from the summit of Inferno Cone takes in the cinder cone chain along the Great Rift, a weakened zone of fissures in the Earth's crust. In winter, when the snow is sufficiently deep, the loop road is closed to vehicular traffic and is groomed for cross-country skiing and snowshoeing.

The cones formed when fountains of molten, gas-charged rock shot into the air. The frothy lava then cooled and hardened into cinders that fell around the vent, producing symmetrical cones. Numerous lava bombs, ejected blobs of less frothy lava that range from an inch to several feet in diameter, are scattered over the slopes. Big Cinder, 700 feet high, is one of the world's largest purely basaltic cinder cones.

Nearby is the Big Craters-Spatter Cone Area. These cones formed when clots of pasty lava stuck together as they fell back to Earth. A trail leads from the drive to the Cave Area, a series of lava tubes that range up to 40 feet in diameter and hundreds of feet in length. The largest is 830-foot Indian Tunnel; Boy Scout Cave has a floor of ice, even in summer. Some of the tubes can be explored; wear sturdy shoes and carry a flashlight.

Other trails lead to Devil's Orchard, cinder fields scattered with fragments of a crater wall, and the Tree Mold Area, where lava slowly enveloped a group of living trees.

More than 300 species of plants and many different species of animals live in this seemingly desolate terrain. In early summer, wildflowers burst into bloom on the cinder fields and slopes of the cones.

Near the monument entrance are a visitor center and campground-picnic area *(see the AAA Northwestern CampBook)*. Guided walks and evening programs are provided during summer months; phone for schedule. The entrance fee is $5 per private vehicle, $3 per motorcycle or bicycle.

VISITOR CENTER is at the start of the 7-mi. loop drive. Exhibits explain the geology, plants, animals and history of the monument. Daily 8-6, mid-June through Labor Day; 8-4:30, rest of year. Closed winter holidays. Phone (208) 527-3257.

FORT HALL (E-4) pop. 3,193, elev. 4,754′

One of the first permanent settlements in Idaho, Fort Hall was established as a trading post on the banks of the Snake River in 1834. Later owned by the Hudson Bay Co., the trading post was abandoned in 1856 due to increased hostility with the American Indians and a decline in fur trading.

In 1864 a stage station was constructed a short distance southeast of Fort Hall. Built on the banks of Spring Creek with materials from this original fort, this post also was known as Fort Hall. In 1868 a treaty established the Fort Hall Indian Reservation, and agency offices some 20 miles east of the original post also were identified as Fort Hall. Today the Fort Hall Indian Reservation has its headquarters east of the townsite on US 91.

GLENNS FERRY (E-3)
pop. 1,611, elev. 2,560′

WINERIES

- **Carmela Vineyards**, off I-84 Glenns Ferry exit at 795 W. Madison, next to Three Islands State Park, following signs. Mon.-Sat. 9-9, Sun. 10-8; closed Jan. 1, Thanksgiving and Dec. 25. Phone (208) 366-2313.

GRANGEVILLE (C-2) pop. 3,228, elev. 3,323′

A boom town in gold rush days, Grangeville is a light industry and agricultural center and the largest town on the fertile Camas Prairie, one of the leading wheat-producing areas in the country. The prairie takes its name from *Camissia esculenta,* a tasty onion-like bulb common in the area and favored by the Nez Perce Indians. Today it is a site for an archeological excavation for mammoth bones. *See Nez Perce National Historical Park p. 59.*

A life-size replica of the giant mammoth unearthed in 1995 at Tolo Lake, 6 miles west of town, can be seen in Eimers Park on US 95. Grangeville also is an outfitting point for wilderness and float trips.

South of Grangeville US 95 drops 3,000 feet to the Salmon River Canyon. This 7-mile section of the highway bypasses the dozens of switchbacks and hairpin curves of the original route, which can be seen to the east.

Grangeville Chamber of Commerce: US 95 at Pine, P.O. Box 212, Grangeville, ID 83530; phone (208) 983-0460.

Self-guiding tours: A brochure for a driving tour of White Bird Battlefield is available at the Nez Perce National Historical Park *(see place listing p. 59)* headquarters in Spalding and at the Forest Service office in Grangeville. The battlefield, 16 miles south of Grangeville on US 95, was the site of the first confrontation of the Nez Perce War. The American Indians won the 1877 battle.

HAGERMAN (F-3) pop. 656, elev. 2,959′

1000 SPRINGS TOURS, departing from Sligar's 1000 Springs Resort 7 mi. s. on US 30, offers 2-hour scenic boat trips through the Snake River Canyon and the 1000 Springs area. Waterfalls, wildflowers and waterfowl can be seen as guides relate area history and geography. Lunch, dinner and champagne brunch cruises and airboat rides and tours also are available. Two-hour scenic boat trips depart daily. Departure times vary; phone ahead. Fare $25; under 12, $20. Reservations are required. MC, VI. Phone (208) 837-9006.

HAGERMAN FOSSIL BEDS NATIONAL MONUMENT visitor center is at 221 N. State St., directly across US 30 from the high school. The monument is 4 mi. s. on US 30, then 3 mi. w. on Bell Rapids Rd., following signs. The visitor center has exhibits, fossils, a slide show and maps and is a good place to begin, as some trails and overlooks at the monument may be restricted.

The 3.5-million-year-old fossil beds, one of the continent's best freshwater fish and small-mammal fossil sites, have yielded remains of early forms of horses, including the Hagerman horse.

For preservation reasons, the beds are inaccessible to visitors; maps for a 10.5-mile driving tour are available at the visitor center and at the monument.

Visitor center open daily 8-5, Memorial Day weekend-Labor Day weekend; Thurs.-Sun. 10-4, rest of year. Closed Jan. 1, Thanksgiving and Dec. 25. Monument and visitor center free. Phone (208) 837-4793.

RECREATIONAL ACTIVITIES

White-water Rafting

- SAVE **High Adventure River Tours**, off I-84 exit 147 (Malad Gorge State Park exit) at 1211 E. 2350 S., Hagerman, ID 83332. Other activities are offered. Daily Apr.-Sept. Phone (208) 837-9005 or (800) 286-4123.

HAILEY (E-3) pop. 6,200, elev. 5,330′

Hailey, laid out in the spring of 1881 by John Hailey, was the center of a rich mining district in its early days. An early Northwest pioneer, Hailey had previously taken part in the Boise Basin Gold Rush in 1862 and had established a name for himself as the owner of a stage and freight line. Fortunes in gold, silver and lead were extracted from mines with such names as Black Cinder, Star, Hope, Climax, Democrat and Big Camas until the mining boom played out in the late 1890s.

On May 7, 1883, Hailey residents witnessed the driving of the last spike of the Wood River branch of the Oregon Short Line. In October of that year the Idaho Territory's first telephone exchange went into use at Hailey. Hailey also was the first to have an electric light plant.

Hailey Chamber of Commerce: 13 W. Carbonate, P.O. Box 100, Hailey, ID 83333; phone (208) 788-2700.

BLAINE COUNTY HISTORICAL MUSEUM, N. Main St. (SR 75), displays early pioneer relics and memorabilia of local interest, including a replica of a mine tunnel. The American Political Items collection contains articles from political campaigns since the late 1800s. Allow 30 minutes minimum. Mon. and Wed.-Sat. 11-5, Sun. 1-5, Memorial Day weekend-Oct. 15. Donations. Phone (208) 788-1801.

GEM HELLS CANYON NATIONAL RECREATION AREA (D-1)

Reached via SRs 82 and 86 in northeastern Oregon and US 95 in western Idaho, the 652,977-acre Hells Canyon National Recreation Area straddles the Snake River Canyon and encompasses parts of national forests in both states.

Confined within steep, eroded black basalt walls, the surging Snake River has carved North America's deepest gorge, measuring 7,913 feet from He Devil Mountain to Granite Creek below. Whitewater rapids alternating with deep pools characterize this 71-mile free-flowing portion of the Snake River as it races north to meet the Columbia River.

The varied elevations of Hells Canyon support mixed plant communities sheltering such wildlife as bears, bobcats, bighorn sheep, cougars, elk, mule deer, mountain goats and many smaller birds, mammals and reptiles. Sturgeon, reputedly growing up to 11 feet long, inhabit the Snake River, sharing it with bass, catfish, salmon and steelhead and rainbow trout.

From the desertlike canyon floor to the alpine lakes of the Seven Devils region, the area presents a variety of recreational opportunities, including boating, float trips and backpacking. From Pittsburg Landing the Kirkwood Historic Ranch and Museum, once the home of Idaho governor and U.S. senator Len B. Jordan, is accessible by powerboat, floatboat or pack trail.

The Rapid River originates in the Seven Devils Mountains and eventually joins the lower Salmon River. The forks of the Rapid River provide quality water for raising chinook salmon and therefore house the Rapid River Fish Hatchery.

The 214,000-acre Hells Canyon Wilderness, with its extensive trail system, protects a large portion of the canyon along the Oregon-Idaho border. If you plan to fish the lakes and the Snake River shoreline, you must acquire the appropriate state licenses *(see Fast Facts page)*; both Oregon and Idaho licenses are valid for boat fishing on the river.

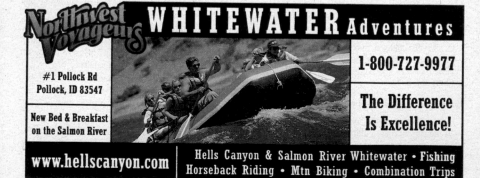

The scenic Hells Canyon All American Road/SR 86 is a series of routes to and through the Hells Canyon National Recreation Area. **On the Oregon side** the best route is a two-lane paved loop which originates in Baker City. From Baker City follow SR 86 to Richland for approximately 41 miles. From Richland continue on SR 86 north for 11 miles to Halfway. From Halfway follow SR 86 for

20 miles to Oxbow and the entrance to Hells Canyon. Nine miles north of Halfway, SR 86 will intersect with FS 39N. Take FS 39N through the heart of the Wallowa Mountains, high mountain country and through the town of Joseph to Enterprise. One mile west of Enterprise on SR 82 is the Wallowa Mountain Visitors Center. Continue along SR 82 west for approximately 64 miles to arrive back to I-84 at La Grande. The entire loop will take approximately 5 hours.

Another possible route from the Oregon side to the recreation area is via SR 82 to Enterprise and Joseph. From Joseph it is possible to go to Hat Point, a 6,982-foot ridge overlooking Hells Canyon, via Imnaha. The route to Hat Point, open summer through early fall, follows FS 4240, a gravel, narrow road with steep grades.

Another route from Imnaha, FS 3955, parallels the Imnaha River as it meanders through rims and benches similar to those along the Snake River. This route connects with the Wallowa Mountain Loop (FS 39), which leads back to Joseph or Halfway. Both FS 3955 and FS 39 are maintained for cars and trailers. FS 39 can be followed east to FS 3965 which leads to the Hells Canyon overlook. With an elevation of 6,000 feet, the overlook provides a spectacular view of the Wallowa Mountains in Idaho and Oregon. These roads are generally closed in winter.

Buckhorn Springs, a scenic area overlooking the Imnaha drainage, can be reached from FS 46 off SR 3, a mostly gravel logging road.

For maps and brochures of different drives contact the Baker County Visitors and Convention Bureau, 490 Campbell St., Baker City, OR 97814; phone (541) 523-3356 or (800) 523-1235.

On the Idaho side the best route to the canyon is SR 71. From Cambridge the road runs 29 miles northwest to Oxbow, Ore., crossing the Snake River near Brownlee Dam. It crosses back into Idaho at Oxbow, then follows the river north to Hells Canyon Dam. The total distance is about 55 miles. Another access point is Pittsburg Landing, 17 miles west of US 95 at White Bird via gravel FR 493.

Note: The Idaho side of the canyon is in the Mountain Time Zone, while the Oregon side observes Pacific Time. It is advisable to check with the Hells Canyon Recreation Area regarding road conditions and construction. Some roads are gravel and caution should be exercised. Phone (541) 426-5546 or (800) 523-1235.

More than 30 outfitters provide float and jet boat trips down the Snake River from Hells Canyon Dam and jet boat trips upstream from the Lewiston/Clarkston area. For a list of local outfitters contact the Supervisor, Hells Canyon National Recreation Area, 2535 Riverside Dr., P.O. Box 699, Clarkston, WA 99403; phone (509) 758-0616 for information or (509) 758-1957 for reservations. *See Recreation Chart and the AAA Northwestern CampBook.*

BEAMERS HELLS CANYON TOURS, departing from the Port of Clarkston dock at 700 Port Dr., offers jet boat excursions through Hells Canyon—North America's deepest river gorge. The 1-day Snake River trip provides opportunities to view three mountain ranges, three states and three rivers. Other excursions also are available. One-day trip daily, May-Sept.; Sat.-Sun., Mar.-Apr. and in Oct. Fare $98; ages 6-12, $49. DS, MC, VI. Phone (509) 758-4800 or (800) 522-6966. *See color ad p. 53.*

HELLS CANYON ADVENTURES is on SR 86 (All-American Rd.) n. of Oxbow, Ore.; tours depart from the landing just n. of Hells Canyon Dam. Guided 2-, 3- and 6-hour jet boat trips as well as white-water rafting trips and fishing and hunting excursions on the Snake River are available.

Tours depart daily May 15-Sept. 15. Two-hour trip departs at 2. Three-hour trip departs at 10. Six-hour and white-water trips depart at 9. Two-hour trip $30; under 12, $10; family rate $90. Three-hour trip $40; under 12, $15. Six-hour trip $105; under 12, $50. Forest service fees are charged. Reservations are recommended. AX, DS, MC, VI. Phone (541) 785-3352 or (541) 785-3480, or (800) 422-3568 out of Ore. *See color ad p. 53.*

HORSESHOE BEND (E-2)

pop. 770, elev. 2,630′

RECREATIONAL ACTIVITIES

White-water Rafting

- **Cascade Raft and Kayak**, 7050 SR 55, Horseshoe Bend, ID 83629. Other activities are offered. Departures daily at 9:30, 1:30 and 5, Mar.-Oct. Phone (208) 793-2221 or (800) 292-7238.

IDAHO CITY (E-2) pop. 458, elev. 4,000′

Soon after gold was discovered in the Boise Basin in 1862, Idaho City became one of the largest cities in the Pacific Northwest. By 1865 it was home to some 7,000 goldseekers; nearly one quarter were Chinese. At its peak the basin was home to 15,000-20,000 miners. The mining district around Idaho City, including nearby Placerville and Centerville, was one of the largest sources of gold ever discovered.

More than 20 pioneer buildings from the 1860s and miles of dredge workings are still visible. The First Masonic Hall, built in 1865 to house Idaho's first Grand Lodge of Masons, displays Masonic items. Idaho City was the site of the territory's first prison, a portion of which has been restored.

Boise National Forest *(see place listing p. 46)* surrounds the town. Idaho City lies on scenic SR 21, also known as the Ponderosa Pine Scenic Route. SR 21 heads northeast through Sawtooth National Forest *(see place listing p. 65)* and ends in Stanley.

BOISE BASIN MUSEUM, Montgomery St. at Wall St., was erected as a post office in 1867 and served as a stage and freight company station before being renovated for its present use. Exhibits, which commemorate the town's origin with memorabilia from its days as a mining boom town, include a working stamp mill model. A video presentation about basin history is shown. Guided 1.5-hour town walking tours are available by appointment.

Museum open Mon.-Sat. 11-4, Sun. 1-4, Memorial Day weekend-Labor Day; Sat. 11-4, Sun. 1-4, May 1-day before Memorial Day weekend and day after Labor Day-Sept. 30; by appointment rest of year. Museum admission $2, over 54 and students with ID $1.50, family rate $5. Town walking tours $3.50, over 54 and students with ID $2, under 6 free with an adult. There is a $30 minimum per group for walking tours. Phone (208) 392-4550.

IDAHO FALLS (E-5) pop. 50,730, elev. 4,742′

Although it lies miles from the silver and gold lodes discovered in the region during the mid-1800s, Idaho Falls owes its formation to these riches. The settlement—originally called Taylor's Crossing—was established about 1860 along one of the few fording points on the upper Snake River. J.M. Taylor's ferry attracted many miners en route to Montana from Salt Lake City.

As the veins of precious metal diminished, transients and disillusioned residents abandoned the area. The few remaining settlers, faced with either adopting a new livelihood or adding the community to the growing list of Western ghost towns, dug channels to irrigate the arid land. Soon the town flourished along with the newly established agriculture. The irrigation system that saved the town now provides water to more than 1 million acres of farmland.

Tautphaus Park has tennis courts, picnic grounds, rides and a zoo. Sandy Downs, 2 miles south of 17th Street on St. Clair Road, is the site of various recreational activities.

Greater Idaho Falls Chamber of Commerce: 630 W. Broadway, P.O. Box 50498, Idaho Falls, ID 83405; phone (208) 523-1010.

IDAHO FALLS is .5 mi. e. off I-15 Broadway exit, then n. on River Pkwy. The low but picturesque and turbulent waterfall in the Snake River is 1,500 feet wide. Next to the scenic falls is a landscaped picnic area and a 2.5-mile greenbelt.

GEM **THE MUSEUM OF IDAHO,** off I-15 Broadway exit at 200 N. Eastern Ave., presents the story of Idaho and the surrounding region from prehistoric times to the Atomic Age. The museum offers permanent displays about early inhabitants and explorers, agriculture, mining and nuclear energy. A hands-on exhibit explores the county's natural history.

Eagle Rock USA is a replica of the 19th-century community that later became Idaho Falls. Guests can visit ten stores and offices that were some of the city's beginning firms. Major temporary exhibits complement these themes. A reference room is available for research.

Allow 1 hour minimum. Tues.-Sat. 10-8, Mon. 6-8 p.m., June-Aug.; Mon.-Sat. 9-8, rest of year. Schedule may vary with some special exhibits; phone ahead. Admission $5; over 61, $4; ages 4-18, $3; family rate (Tues.-Sat.) $18. AX, DC, MC, VI. Phone (208) 522-1400 or (800) 325-7328.

IDAHO PANHANDLE NATIONAL FORESTS

Elevations in the forests range from 2,060 ft. at Pend Oreille Lake to 7,705 ft. at Northwest Peak. Refer to AAA maps for additional elevation information.

In northern Idaho and adjoining parts of Montana and Washington, the many-segmented Idaho Panhandle National Forests have rugged peaks, canyons and valleys. The 2.5-million-acre area includes the former St. Joe, Kaniksu and Coeur d'Alene national forests.

Of particular interest are the stands of old-growth cedars at Hanna Flats and Roosevelt Grove near Priest Lake, the Settlers Grove of Ancient Cedars near Prichard and the Hobo Cedar Grove near Clarkia.

Fishing is available at Priest Lake, Lake Coeur d'Alene and Lake Pend Oreille; nature trails traverse these areas. Float trips are popular on the Coeur d'Alene, St. Joe and Priest rivers. Winter sports areas are off SR 6 between St. Maries and Moscow, at Lookout Pass just off I-90 on the Idaho-Montana border and at 4th of July Pass off I-90.

For a fee, modern-day fortune seekers can collect gem-quality garnets in an area on the east fork of Emerald Creek, 8 miles southwest of SR 3 between Clarkia and Fernwood.

Information is available at the headquarters in Coeur d'Alene and at ranger stations at Avery, Bonners Ferry, Fernan, Priest Lake, St. Maries, Sandpoint and Wallace. For additional information contact the Forest Supervisor's Office, Idaho Panhandle National Forests, 3815 Schreiber Way, Coeur d'Alene, ID 83815-8363; phone (208) 765-7223. *See Recreation Chart and the AAA Northwestern CampBook.*

KAMIAH (C-2) pop. 1,160, elev. 1,196'

Meriwether Lewis and William Clark camped on the north bank of the Clearwater River just north of Kamiah (KAM-ee eye) in the spring of 1806 on their homeward journey. Today a sawmill occupies the site of their month-long encampment.

A pasture about a half mile northwest of Kamiah is supposedly the location of the mission that Asa and Sarah Smith started in 1839. They stayed only 2 years, and their work in this area was not resumed until 30 years later.

The 1871 First Presbyterian Church is said to Idaho's oldest church in continuous use. Scenic US 12 passes through town.

Kamiah Chamber of Commerce: 518 Main St., P.O. Box 1124, Kamiah, ID 83536; phone (208) 935-2290.

EAST KAMIAH, 2 mi. e. on US 12, has a volcanic rock formation, Heart of the Monster, the place of creation in Nez Perce mythology.

Folklore says that in the prehuman years a monster was devouring the animals. Coyote, the chief animal, slew the monster, cut him into pieces and scattered these bits to the winds. Where each bit landed a new Indian tribe arose. The Nez Perce tribe came from blood from the monster's heart. An interpretive center is available. Daily dawn-dusk.

KELLOGG (B-2) pop. 2,395, elev. 2,305'

Kellogg, the Silver Valley's largest town, has made a major transition from mining community to alpine village. The Coeur d'Alene mining district has yielded more than a billion dollars in silver, lead, gold and zinc; the Sunshine Silver Mine is the largest in the United States. The Shoshone County Mining and Smelting Museum, also known as The Staff House Museum *(see attraction listing)*, chronicles the colorful history of Silver Valley.

Historic Silver Valley Chamber of Commerce: 10 Station Ave., Kellogg, ID 83837; phone (208) 784-0821.

SAVE **CRYSTAL GOLD MINE** is at 51931 Silver Valley Rd.; take I-90 exit 51 (Division St.) n. to Cameron Ave. (Silver Valley Rd.), then 1.3 mi. e. The guided tours conducted by experienced miners provide an interesting glimpse into the hand-labor, hard-rock mining of the late 1800s. The temperature inside the cave is 48 degrees Fahrenheit, so dress appropriately.

Picnic and camping facilities are available. Allow 30 minutes minimum. Tours depart every 10 to 20 minutes daily 9-6, May-Oct.; 10-4, rest of year. Closed Jan. 1, Easter, Thanksgiving and Dec. 25. Admission $10; senior citizens $8.50; ages 4-16, $7.50; family rate (five persons) $36. MC, VI. Phone (208) 783-4653.

THE STAFF HOUSE MUSEUM, 820 McKinley Ave., is in a 1906 house built for the Bunker Hill Mine's top executive. The museum has an art gallery, medical and Boy Scout exhibits, a minerals display room, a replica of a primitive mining area, a smelting display, an exhibit about the domestic life of a miner's family and an 1895 Nordberg compressor once used to pump air underground into mines.

Allow 30 minutes minimum. Daily 10-5, Memorial Day weekend-early Oct. Admission $4; over 55, $3; ages 6-18, $1; family rate $6. MC, VI. Phone (208) 786-4141.

RECREATIONAL ACTIVITIES

Skiing

- **Silver Mountain Resort**, off I-90 exit 49 at Kellogg Peak. Write 610 Bunker Ave., Kellogg, ID 83837-2200. Other activities are offered. Daily late Nov.-early Apr. Phone (208) 783-1111 or (800) 204-6428.

KETCHUM (E-3) pop. 3,003, elev. 5,821'

In the late 19th century Ketchum sprang up almost overnight as a shipping and smelting center for the remote mountain mines surrounding the Wood River Valley. Ores and supplies were transported by the giant ore wagons of the Horace Lewis Fast Freight Line. These relics of the area's past are displayed in the Ore Wagon Museum on East Avenue next to City Hall, and once again appear on the streets during the Wagon Days Parade and Celebration Labor Day weekend. The Ketchum Cemetery includes the grave of Ernest Hemingway.

As the gateway to the Sun Valley *(see place listing p. 68)* resort area and the Sawtooth National Recreation Area *(see place listing p. 65)*, the town offers an abundance of activities year-round. Such outdoor recreational activities as swimming, bicycling, hiking, horseback riding, cross-country skiing, snowshoeing and camping are foremost among Ketchum's attractions. For the spectator Ketchum offers some 20 art galleries and the NexStage Theatre where local theater companies perform year-round. For theater information phone (208) 726-3423.

Sun Valley-Ketchum Chamber of Commerce: 411 Main St., P.O. Box 2420, Sun Valley, ID 83353; phone (208) 726-3423 or (800) 634-3347.

Self-guiding tours: The Heritage & Ski Museum, 1st Street and Washington Avenue, has a booklet about the history of Ketchum that includes a walking tour through the downtown area; phone (208) 726-8118.

Shopping areas: Downtown Ketchum offers some 80 shops and restaurants offering everything from antiques and bookstores to children's toys and specialty gifts.

RECREATIONAL ACTIVITIES

Horseback Riding

- **Galena Stage Stop Corrals—Trail Rides**, 24 mi. n. on SR 75. Write HC 64, Box 9999, Stanley, ID 83278. Other activities are offered. Daily 8-5, mid-June through Labor Day. Phone (208) 726-1735.

KOOSKIA (C-2) pop. 675, elev. 1,261'

Kooskia (KOOS-key), founded in 1895 at the confluence of the Middle and South forks of the Clearwater River, takes its name from a Nez Perce phrase meaning "where the waters join." The restored Old Victorian Opera House Theatre, built in 1912, offers live performances; phone (208) 926-0094.

Kooskia Chamber of Commerce: P.O. Box 310, Kooskia, ID 83539; phone (208) 926-4362.

KOOSKIA NATIONAL FISH HATCHERY is 2 mi. s.e. on Clear Creek County Rd. Chinook salmon eggs are collected, incubated and hatched, and the young fish are reared. The best times to visit are in early March before the young chinook are set free or during June and July when the adults return to spawn. Daily 7:30-4; closed major holidays. Free. Phone (208) 926-4272.

KOOTENAI NATIONAL FOREST—

see Montana p. 106.

LAPWAI (C-2) pop. 1,134, elev. 891'

Lapwai is the site of the first military fort in Idaho, built in 1862 to prevent clashes between pioneers and American Indians in the area. The U.S. Army occupied the fort until 1884. Some of the old buildings around the parade ground are still in use. The Old Fort Lapwai Cemetery is located on the ridge just south of the fort.

NORTHERN IDAHO INDIAN AGENCY, 99 Agency Rd. near Fort Lapwai, is the Bureau of Indian Affairs headquarters of Idaho's Nez Perce, Coeur d'Alene and Kootenai Indians. Established in 1862, this is one of the sites that composes Nez Perce National Historical Park *(see place listing p. 59)*. The Nez Perce Tribal Community Building and Bureau of Indian Affairs Office are .25-mile north of Old Fort Lapwai. The agency is open Mon.-Fri. 8-4:30; closed legal holidays. Phone (208) 843-2300.

LAVA HOT SPRINGS (F-5) pop. 521, elev. 5,151'

Lava Hot Springs was named for the mineral springs that boil out of lava rocks at the base of massive cliffs along the Portneuf River. Geologists believe that the pools have remained at the same temperature—110 degrees F—for 50 million years. Lava Hot Springs is a popular health and pleasure resort offering hiking, bicycling, tubing and swimming.

For centuries the Shoshone and Bannock Indians regarded the springs as a neutral site. But the tribes' camp was disrupted during the 19th century when the springs were discovered by Oregon-bound travelers and Utah pioneers who founded a settlement called Dempsey. By 1902 the American Indians had ceded their rights to the springs, granting the land to the U.S. government, which in turn gave the area to the state.

Pioneer Travel Council: P.O. Box 669, Dept. 98A, Lava Hot Springs, ID 83246; phone (888) 201-1063.

IDAHO WORLD FAMOUS HOT POOLS AND OLYMPIC SWIMMING COMPLEX, on US 30E, is a resort that consists of hot mineral pools on the eastern edge of the village and outdoor Olympic-size swimming pools with tube slides on the western edge. The Sunken Gardens bloom on terraces that cling to the walls of an extinct volcano. Snowmobiling and skiing, subject to local weather conditions, are possible on the surrounding mountains.

Mineral baths open daily 8 a.m.-11 p.m., Apr.-Sept.; Sun.-Thurs. 9 a.m.-10 p.m., Fri.-Sat. 9 a.m.-11 p.m., rest of year. Closed Thanksgiving and Dec. 25. Pool open Mon.-Fri. noon-9, Sat.-Sun. and holidays 11-9, May 1 to mid-Aug.; Mon.-Fri. noon-8, Sat.-Sun. 11-8, mid-Aug. to late Aug.

All-day pass allows visitors to exit and re-enter. Mineral baths Fri.-Sun. and holidays $5.50 (all-day pass $7); over 59 and ages 3-11, $5. Mineral baths Mon.-Thurs. $5 (all-day pass $6.50); over 59 and ages 3-11, $4.50 (all-day pass $6). Pool Fri.-Sun. and holidays $5.50; ages 3-11, $5. Pool Mon.-Thurs. $5; ages 3-11, $4.50. Combination pass for baths and pool Mon.-Thurs. $9, Fri.-Sun. and holidays $10. All-day tube slide pass $3; 1-day family pass $12.50 (Mon.-Thurs. only). Family passes are not valid during holidays. MC, VI. Phone (208) 776-5221 or (800) 423-8597.

SOUTH BANNOCK COUNTY HISTORICAL CENTER AND MUSEUM, off US 30 at 110 E. Main St., contains a collection of American Indian and pioneer artifacts and a permanent exhibit showing the effects of transportation on the area and the six communities of south Bannock County. Daily noon-5; closed Thanksgiving and Dec. 25. Donations. Phone (208) 776-5254.

LEWISTON (C-1) pop. 30,904, elev. 738'

At the confluence of the Clearwater and Snake rivers, Lewiston is on a site where Meriwether Lewis and William Clark camped in 1805 and again in 1806. Following the discovery of gold nearby, the settlement became a supply point for mining camps and, subsequently, the state's first territorial capital 1863-65.

Large quantities of grain and other cargo are shipped from Lewiston, known as "Idaho's Seaport," by barge 465 miles down the Snake and Columbia rivers to the Pacific. Boats reach the port by passing through locks at eight dams.

North of the city US 95 climbs 2,000 feet to the top of Lewiston Hill, where a viewpoint overlooks the valley. Lewiston lies on an especially scenic section of US 95 that extends north to Plummer and south to Banks.

Lewiston Chamber of Commerce: 111 Main St., Suite 120, Lewiston, ID 83501; phone (208) 743-3531 or (800) 473-3543. *See ad.*

Shopping areas: Lewiston Center Mall, 1 mile south of US 12 via 18th or 21st streets, features The Bon-Macy's, Gottschalks and JCPenney.

BOAT TRIPS UP HELLS CANYON OF THE SNAKE RIVER are spectacular journeys into the main part of Hells Canyon, the deepest river gorge in North America. Most trips, by aluminum jet boat, return the same day, but others require an overnight stop. All include one or more meals and offer refreshments. Inquire about age restrictions, refund and weather policies. Three- and 5-day float trips depart usually in the early morning. Rates vary; phone ahead. For information phone the chamber of commerce at (208) 743-3531.

LEWIS-CLARK CENTER FOR ARTS & HISTORY is at 415 Main St. The center features the works of local, regional and national artists in various media in a schedule of rotating exhibits. The permanent exhibit, Chinese at the Confluence—Lewiston's Beuk Aie Temple, traces the history of this late 19th-century segment of the community. Mon.-Fri. 11-4, Sat. 10-3; closed national holidays. Free. A fee is charged for special events. Phone (208) 792-2243.

NEZ PERCE COUNTY MUSEUM is at 3rd and C sts. Built in the 1930s, the art deco-style building features displays of American Indian and pioneer artifacts and other relics. Tues.-Sat. 10-4, Mar. 1 to mid-Dec.; closed major holidays. Donations. Phone (208) 743-2535.

CASINOS

- **Clearwater River Casino**, 4 mi. e. on US 12 at 17500 Nez Perce Rd. Daily 24 hours. Phone (208) 746-0723 or (877) 678-7423.

RECREATIONAL ACTIVITIES

White-water Rafting

- **Barker River Trips** on the Clearwater and Salmon rivers meet at 2124 Grelle St., Lewiston, ID 83501. Other activities are offered. Daily June-Sept. Phone (208) 743-7459 or (800) 353-7459.

McCALL (D-2) pop. 2,084, elev. 5,025'

At the southern end of beautiful Payette Lake, McCall is a year-round recreational resort. Fishing, boating, water skiing, horseback riding, white-water rafting, golf, camping and hunting are available. Skiing and snowmobiling are popular winter sports.

Firefighting facilities at the Forest Service's Smokejumper Headquarters feature smokejumping equipment, a fire retardant mixing plant and communications services. Tours are offered; phone (208) 634-0378.

McCall lies on an especially scenic section of SR 55, also called the Payette River Scenic Route. The highway heads north, merges with US 95 and continues toward Coeur d'Alene. The southern terminus of the route is Boise.

McCall Area Chamber of Commerce: 1001 State St., Box 350, McCall, ID 83638; phone (208) 634-7631 or (800) 260-5130.

MERIDIAN (E-2) pop. 34,919, elev. 2,600'

ROARING SPRINGS WATERPARK is off I-84 exit 44 at 400 W. Overland Rd. A variety of waterslides include the mountainous Avalanche, Rattlesnake Rapids, Pipeline Mines and Double Trouble. A wave pool, the Endless River, raft rides, Leisure Lagoon and a children's play area are other options.

Food is available. Allow 4 hours minimum. Daily 11-8, late May-late Aug.; Sat.-Sun. and holidays 11-7, mid-May to late May and late Aug.-early Sept. Admission $21.99; ages 4-12, $17.99; after 3 p.m. $15.99. AX, DS, MC, VI. Phone (208) 884-8842 or (877) 420-7529.

MONTPELIER (F-5) pop. 2,785, elev. 5,934'

Montpelier, one of the state's oldest towns, is at the junction of US 89 and US 30N, the historic Old Oregon Trail. Brigham Young established a Mormon community and named the town for the capital of his home state, Vermont. In 1896 Butch Cassidy relieved the Bank of Montpelier of $7,000. Some of the largest known phosphate deposits are found in this area. Bear Lake resort is about 17 miles south on US 89.

Bear Lake Convention and Visitors Bureau: P.O. Box 26, Fish Haven, ID 83287; phone (208) 945-3333 or (800) 448-2327.

MINNETONKA CAVE is s.w. via US 89 to St. Charles, then 10 mi. w. The cave, 7,700 feet above sea level, contains limestone cave formations and fossils of tropical plants and marine life. The temperature is a constant 40 degrees F. Guided 1.5-hour tours daily on the half-hour 10:30-5, mid-June through Labor Day. Last tour departs at closing. Fee $5; ages 6-15, $4; family rate $20. Phone (208) 847-0375.

SAVE **NATIONAL OREGON/CALIFORNIA TRAIL CENTER** is at jct. US 30 and US 89 at 320 N. 4th St. This living-history center, which sits directly on the site of the historic Clover Creek Encampment on the Oregon Trail, depicts the pioneers' journey across the continent. A wagon master guides visitors through the experience of riding the trail in a covered wagon courtesy of a computer simulation. Displays and artifacts about the history of the Bear Lake valley and the railroad era can be seen in the Rails and Trails Museum.

Allow 30 minutes minimum. Guided tours daily 10-5, May-Sept.; by appointment rest of year. Admission $6; over 59, $5; ages 5-12, $4. MC, VI. Phone (208) 847-3800 or (866) 847-3800.

MOSCOW (C-2) pop. 21,291, elev. 2,574'

Moscow (MOSS-co) is the commercial center of the fertile Palouse country where black volcanic ash soil, ample rainfall and warm autumn temperatures combine to produce lentils, dry peas, wheat and barley. The agricultural yields of the Palouse are processed in Moscow and distributed throughout the country.

The town was once a favorite summer haven for the Nez Perce Indians as well as a base camp in the gold rush of the 1860s. Moscow was a preferred trapping ground of the French Canadians in the early 1800s and is known as the home of the Appaloosa horse. The town lies on an especially scenic section of US 95, which heads north toward Coeur d'Alene and south to Banks.

The University of Idaho was established in 1889, a year before statehood was gained. The 450-acre campus displays a variety of architecture, ranging from Gothic dormitories to the contemporary ASUI-Kibbie Dome Athletic Center.

Exhibits of rocks and minerals in the Life Science and College of Mines buildings at the university are open to visitors, as is the USDA Intermountain Forest and Range Experiment Station, a joint effort of the university and the U.S. Forest Service that conducts research to prevent disease in and insect damage to white pines.

Moscow Chamber of Commerce: 411 S. Main St., P.O. Box 8936, Moscow, ID 83843; phone (208) 882-1800 or (800) 380-1801.

Shopping areas: The Bon-Macy's and Gottschalks are the anchor stores at Palouse Empire Mall, 1.5 miles west on SR 8.

APPALOOSA MUSEUM AND HERITAGE CENTER, w. on SR 8 in the Appaloosa Horse Club building at 2720 W. Pullman Rd., contains Nez Perce regalia and artifacts, cowboy tack, photographs and artwork illustrating Appaloosa history. Live horses can be viewed during summer. Allow 1 hour minimum. Tues.-Fri. 10-5, Sat. 10-4; closed holidays. Donations. Phone (208) 882-5578, ext. 279.

McCONNELL MANSION, 110 S. Adams St., was built in the late 19th century by Gov. William J. McConnell. Now home of the Latah County Historical Society, the mansion displays relics and Victorian-style furniture from the late 1800s. A backyard garden and a research library are available. Allow 1 hour minimum. Mansion open Tues.-Sat. 1-5, May-Sept.; 1-4, rest of year. Research library open Tues.-Fri. 9-5. Closed holidays. Donations. Phone (208) 882-1004.

NAMPA (E-2) pop. 51,867, elev. 2,492'

Col. W.H. Dewey moved his fortune during the 1890s to Nampa, an agricultural hamlet just north of the Great Basin Desert. Dewey brought prosperity to Nampa by attracting several railway branches and constructing the Dewey Palace hotel, which was a town landmark for several decades until it was damaged by fire and torn down. Nampa's name comes from Nampuh, or "Bigfoot," a Shoshone chief who was so large that his feet were supposedly 17 inches long.

Exhibits depicting the region's history can be seen at the Canyon County Historical Museum, which occupies the restored 1906 Union Pacific Railroad depot at 1224 Front St.

Nampa is a central location from which to explore southwestern Idaho's natural wonders and historical sites. Givens' Hot Springs is 17 miles south on SR 45, then 8 miles west on SR 78 on the south side of the Snake River. There are steam baths, an indoor natural hot-water pool and a picnic area.

Silver City and DeLamar, high in the Owyhee Mountains, can be reached by taking SR 45 south to Walter's Ferry, then turning east on SR 78 4.5 miles past Murphy. The towns, at one time thriving mining communities in one of the greatest silver-producing areas in the nation, are on a rough gravel and earth road *(see Silver City p. 66)*. DeLamar has been abandoned.

Nampa Chamber of Commerce: 1305 3rd. St. S., Nampa, ID 83651; phone (208) 466-4641.

DEER FLAT NATIONAL WILDLIFE REFUGE is 4 mi. s.w. The refuge consists of two sections: Lake Lowell, an irrigation reservoir, and 107 islands in the Snake River, from Walter's Ferry downstream to Farewell Bend in Ore. The islands are accessible only by boat.

The refuge harbors waterfowl as well as other birds and mammals. In winter bald eagles move into the area, and in spring and summer marsh and water birds are present.

Shorebirds are plentiful on the mud flats of Lake Lowell in late summer and early fall. In November and December 60,000 mallards can be seen on the lake.

Lake Lowell *(see Recreation Chart)* is one of the Boise-Nampa-Caldwell area's most popular recreation spots. Refuge open daily dawn-dusk. Free. Phone (208) 467-9278.

WARHAWK AIR MUSEUM is at 201 Municipal Dr. at the Nampa Municipal Airport. Centerpieces of the museum, which features restored and flyable aircraft from World War II, include a Curtiss P-40E Kittyhawk, a P-51 Mustang, a Curtiss P-40N Warhawk, a Canadian Hawker Sea Fury and a 1940 Navy N3N biplane trainer. Other items displayed include a restored 1940 DeSoto staff car, period poster art, trench art and uniforms.

Guided tours are available by appointment. Allow 2 hours minimum. Tues.-Sat. 10-5, Sun. 11-5, Apr. 2-Oct. 14; Tues.-Fri. 10-4, Sat. 10-5, rest of year. Admission $5; over 64, $4; ages 4-9, $3. AX, DS, MC, VI. Phone (208) 465-6446.

NEZ PERCE NATIONAL FOREST

Elevations in the forest range from 1,350 ft. in Hells Canyon to 9,393 ft. at Devil's Peak. Refer to AAA maps for additional elevation information.

In the west-central part of the state, Nez Perce National Forest was named for the Nez Perce Indians, whose ancestral lands once included this rugged area of 2,223,594 acres. The forest contains the Gospel-Hump Wilderness and portions of the Selway-Bitterroot Wilderness, Frank Church-River of No Return Wilderness, Hells Canyon Wilderness and Hells Canyon National Recreation Area *(see place listing p. 52)*. Portions of the forest are close to parts of Nez Perce National Historical Park *(see place listing p. 59)*.

More than 150 miles of the Rapid, Salmon and Selway rivers and the Middle Fork of the Clearwater River are classified as wild and scenic rivers. Elk, moose, deer, cougars, mountain goats, bighorn sheep and bears inhabit the forest, while steelhead trout, white sturgeon and small-mouth bass can be found in the rivers and streams.

The historic Magruder Corridor Road (FR 468) is open to forest visitors July through September. The primitive road, rough but passable to two-wheel-drive vehicles, begins at the Red River Ranger Station and ends in Darby, Mont. The wilderness areas adjoining the route together form the largest tract of roadless land in the U.S. outside Alaska.

For road information phone the Red River Ranger District at (208) 842-2255, the West Fork Ranger District at (406) 821-3269, or the supervisor's office in Grangeville. For additional information contact the Forest Supervisor, Nez Perce National Forest, Route 2, Box 475, Grangeville, ID 83530; phone (208) 983-1950. *See Recreation Chart and the AAA Northwestern CampBook.*

NEZ PERCE NATIONAL HISTORICAL PARK (C-1)

Encompassing 28 sites scattered across 12,000 square miles of north-central Idaho as well as 10 sites in Oregon, Washington and Montana, each part of Nez Perce National Historical Park reflects a portion of the history and culture of the Nez Perce Indians and their relationships with white explorers, missionaries, miners, settlers and soldiers.

Some sites are scenic views, some are geologic formations and others contain historic places and buildings. They include the Lolo Trail, American Indian battlefields and former campsites of Meriwether Lewis and William Clark.

For thousands of years the Nez Perce lived in the valleys of the Clearwater and Snake rivers and their tributaries. Their first documented meeting with white settlers in Nez Perce territory took place in September 1805, when the Lewis and Clark expedition encountered them, and the Indians gave supplies and assistance. In 1855 the Nez Perce reluctantly signed a treaty setting aside their ancestral home as a reservation.

A new treaty was negotiated in 1863 with some of the Nez Perce bands after gold was discovered within the reservation; this treaty reduced the reservation to one-tenth of its original size.

The first major battle of the Nez Perce War was on June 17, 1877, near White Bird. The U.S. Army pursued the bands of Nez Perce who had not signed the 1863 treaty across the Nez Perce Trail to Montana. After many battles the Nez Perce surrendered only 40 miles from the Canadian border. They were exiled for 8 years to Oklahoma Territory; the survivors eventually returned to the Pacific Northwest. Today the Nez Perce National Historic Trail parallels much of the original 1877 route.

The Weippe (WEE-eye-p) Prairie, 18 miles east of US 12 on SR 11, is part of Nez Perce National Historical Park. The Idaho section of the Nez Perce Trail and Pass climbs through 150 miles of rough terrain east of Weippe as it ascends the 5,187-foot Lolo Pass through the Bitterroot Mountains.

The park's headquarters and visitor center are in Spalding *(see place listing p. 67)*. A brochure for a self-guiding driving tour of White Bird Battlefield is available here and at the Forest Service office in Grangeville. The battlefield, 16 miles south of Grangeville on US 95, was the site of the first confrontation of the Nez Perce War. The American Indians won the 1877 battle. Also see Cottonwood, Grangeville, Kamiah, Lapwai, Nez Perce National Forest and Orofino.

Park open daily 8-5:30, Memorial Day weekend-Labor Day; 8-4:30, rest of year. Closed Jan. 1, Thanksgiving and Dec. 25. Big Hole Battlefield site $5 per private vehicle, $3 per bicycle. All other sites are free. Phone (208) 843-2261.

NORTH FORK (D-3) elev. 3,620'

RECREATIONAL ACTIVITIES

White-water Rafting

- **North Fork Guides** trips meet at the North Fork Store, Motel and Campground. Write P.O. Box 24, North Fork, ID 83466. Trips run mid-Apr. to mid-Nov. Phone (208) 865-2534 or (800) 259-6866.

OROFINO (C-2) pop. 3,247, elev. 1,027'

In 1805 members of the Lewis and Clark expedition passed near the present site of Orofino on their way west. The first gold miners swarmed into the area 60 years later from California, and soon Idaho's first permanent settlements began to take shape. Orofino is on the Nez Perce Indian Reservation, and the Clearwater River runs through the town's boundaries. The Clearwater National Forest *(see place listing p. 48)* and Nez Perce National Forest *(see place listing p. 59)* are nearby.

Orofino's economy relies on lumbering, farming and government employment. A long growing season, ample precipitation and fertile soil contribute to the prosperity of this agricultural community. Northwest of Orofino, near Ahsahka *(see place listing p. 40)*, is the Dworshak National Fish Hatchery and Dworshak Dam and Reservoir.

Orofino Chamber of Commerce: 217 1st St., P.O. Box 2346, Orofino, ID 83544; phone (208) 476-4335.

LEWIS AND CLARK CANOE CAMP, 5 mi. w. on US 12, is part of the Nez Perce National Historical Park *(see place listing p. 59)*. After crossing the Bitterroot Mountains on horseback, Meriwether Lewis and William Clark camped and built dugout canoes for the remainder of their journey to the Pacific Ocean. Daily dawn-dusk. Free. Phone (208) 843-2261 or (208) 843-7131.

PAYETTE NATIONAL FOREST

Elevations in the forest range from 1,464 ft. in Hells Canyon to 9,545 ft. at Mormon Mountain. Refer to AAA maps for additional elevation information.

Bounded by Boise National Forest, the Snake and Salmon rivers and the Middle Fork of the Salmon River in the west-central part of the state, the Payette National Forest contains 2,307,897 acres that range in elevation from 1,400 to 9,000 feet above sea level. More than 2,000 miles of hiking trails include Lava Ridge National Recreation Trail and Sheep Rock Nature Trail. The forest's many rivers, streams and lakes provide good fishing.

Winter sports include alpine skiing at Payette Lakes Ski Hill as well as cross-country skiing and snowmobiling in many other areas. Major fires in 1994 and 2000 burned several sections of the forest. Phone for trail conditions and availability of picnic areas.

A small portion of the Hells Canyon Wilderness and Hells Canyon National Recreation Area *(see place listing p. 52)* and a large portion of the Frank Church-River of No Return Wilderness lie within the forest. These mountainous areas overlap several national forests and contain extensive trail networks. For more information write Payette National Forest, P.O. Box 1026, 800 W. Lakeside Ave., McCall, ID 83638; phone (208) 634-0700. *See Recreation Chart and the AAA Northwestern CampBook.*

RECREATIONAL ACTIVITIES

Skiing

- **Brundage Mountain Ski Area**, 10 mi. n. of McCall on US 95. Write P.O. Box 1062, McCall, ID 83638. Daily 9:30-4:30, mid-Nov. to mid-Apr. Phone (208) 634-7462, (208) 634-7669 or (888) 255-7669.

POCATELLO (F-4) pop. 51,466, elev. 4,365′

Originally part of the Fort Hall Indian Reservation, Pocatello is named for a 19th-century Bannock chief who granted the Utah & Northern a right-of-way for a Salt Lake City-to-Butte railroad line. The subsequent arrival in 1882 of the Union Pacific Railway, which linked the Midwest and Pacific Northwest, spawned a makeshift community—a congregation of tents at the meeting of the two lines—that was first called Pocatello Junction.

Pocatello maintains its position as one of the region's leading industrial, distribution and transportation centers. Education also is a principal concern; Idaho State University, with 12,000 students, is one of the state's leading 4-year institutions. The town is the northern terminus of an especially scenic section of I-15, which heads south into Utah.

Just off Main Street visitors can see the Union Pacific Depot, a three-story passenger station designed in the late 1800s. Train passengers of the era stayed overnight across the street at the historic Yellowstone Hotel.

Ross Park offers a swimming pool with a waterslide, shady picnic areas, an amphitheater, horseshoe and volleyball areas and a skate park. The park also is home to Bannock County Historical Museum, Fort Hall Replica and Pocatello Zoo *(see attraction listings)*.

Greater Pocatello Information and Visitors Center: 2695 S. 5th Ave., Pocatello, ID 83204; phone (208) 234-4636.

BANNOCK COUNTY HISTORICAL MUSEUM is off I-15 exit 67, then 1 mi. n. on US 30/91 in Upper Ross Park. The museum contains American Indian and railroad displays, a restored stagecoach, a 1915 La France firetruck and a mural history/donor wall. Other displays include a 1900s parlor, a country kitchen, a dental office and a 1947 Linotype press.

Allow 1 hour minimum. Daily 10-6, Memorial Day weekend-Labor Day; Tues.-Sat. 10-2, rest of year. Closed holidays. Admission $1; ages 6-12, 50c. Phone (208) 233-0434.

FORT HALL REPLICA, off I-15 exit 67, then 1 mi. n. on US 30/91 in Upper Ross Park, re-creates the fur-trading post that operated nearby 1834-60. Original Hudson Bay Co. plans were used to create the full-scale replica. Buffaloes, elk, deer and pronghorn antelopes are kept in a field next to the fort.

Allow 1 hour minimum. Daily 10-6, day after Memorial Day-Labor Day; daily 10-2, day after Labor Day-Sept. 30; Tues.-Sat. 10-2, mid-Apr. through Memorial Day. Admission $1.50; over 59 and ages 6-11, $1.25; ages 3-5, 50c. Phone (208) 234-1795 or (208) 234-6237.

IDAHO MUSEUM OF NATURAL HISTORY is on the main floor of the museum building at the corner of 5th and Dillon sts. on the Idaho State University campus. Collections include dinosaur bones, other fossils and mounted animals native to Idaho as well as Shoshone-Bannock basketry. The Discovery Room allows children hands-on encounters with fossils and computers.

Allow 30 minutes minimum. Tues.-Fri. 10-5, Sat. noon-5, Mon. 4-8, June-Aug.; Tues.-Fri. 10-4 (also Mon. 4-8, Apr.-May), Sat. noon-4, rest of year. Closed holidays. Admission $5; over 55, $4; students with ID $3; ages 4-11, $2. Phone (208) 236-3317.

POCATELLO ZOO, 2900 S. 2nd Ave. in the lower level of Ross Park, features native North American wildlife including elk, bison, grizzly and black bears, mountain sheep, pronghorn antelopes, mountain lions and waterfowl in 18 acres of natural habitats.

Allow 1 hour minimum. Zoo daily 9-5, Apr. 1-June 15; daily 10-6, June 16-Labor Day; Sat.-Sun. 10-4, day after Labor Day-Oct.31. Park admission free. Zoo admission $2.25; over 59, $1.75; ages 6-11, $1.50; ages 3-5, 50c. Phone (208) 234-6196.

POST FALLS (B-1) pop. 17,247, elev. 2,169′

On the Spokane River at the Washington-Idaho state line, Post Falls was founded in the late 1800s by Frederick Post when he harnessed the falls to generate power for his sawmill.

State Line Stadium Speedway features stock car racing; phone (208) 773-5019.

Coeur d'Alene-Post Falls Tourism: 4199 W. River Bend Ave., P.O. Box 908, Post Falls, ID 83877; phone (208) 773-4080 or (800) 292-2553. *See color ad.*

Shopping areas: The Factory Outlets Mall, off I-90 exit 2, contains some 60 outlet stores offering discounted name-brand merchandise.

FALLS PARK, off I-90 Spokane St. exit, 2 blks. s. on Spokane St., then 1.5 blks. w. to 305 W. 4th St., offers visitors a view of Post Falls and the gorge as well as trails leading to nearby Treaty Rock *(see attraction listing)* which marks the site of Post Falls' founding. Picnicking is permitted. Daily dawn-dusk (weather permitting). Free. Phone (208) 773-0539 or (208) 773-8147.

Q'EMILN TRAIL SYSTEM, I-90 exit 5, .9 mi. s. on Spokane St., then .2 mi. w. on Park Ave., includes 12 connected trails winding along the south bank of the Spokane River. Trails lead to historic sites, abandoned homesteads, mining camps, logging areas and scenic spots above and below Post Falls Dam. Picnicking is permitted. Allow 1 hour minimum. Daily dawn-dusk. Trails free. Parking $3.50, Memorial Day weekend-Labor Day. Phone (208) 773-0539.

TREATY ROCK HISTORIC SITE, jct. 7th and Compton sts., commemorates the spot where Coeur d'Alene Indian Chief Andrew Seltice transferred land to Frederick Post, the founder of Post Falls. A marked trail features American Indian petroglyphs and paintings. Picnicking is permitted. Allow 30 minutes minimum. Daily dawn-dusk. Free. Phone (208) 773-0539 or (208) 773-8147.

PRIEST LAKE—*see Coolin p. 50.*

PRIEST RIVER (A-1) pop. 1,754, elev. 2,082′

Priest River, at the junction of the Pend Oreille and Priest rivers and 30 miles south of Priest Lake via SR 57, is the gateway to the Idaho Panhandle National Forests *(see place listing p. 55)*. The 1895 Keyser House contains the chamber of commerce and historical displays.

Priest River Chamber of Commerce: 301 Montgomery St., P.O. Box 929, Priest River, ID 83856; phone (208) 448-2721.

ALBENI FALLS DAM, 3.5 mi. w. on US 2 on the Pend Oreille River, offers a scenic viewpoint, visitor center and picnic grounds. Thirty-minute guided tours to the powerhouse overlook, offered in the summer, provide information about the dam and powerhouse; tours do not enter the powerhouse. The films "The Power and Play of the Pend Oreille" and "The Bonneville Power System" are shown in the visitor center, which also has exhibits.

Tours are available daily at 10 and 2, Memorial Day weekend-Labor Day. Visitor center daily 7:30-6, June-Aug.; Tues.-Sun. 7:30-5, Mar.-May and Sept.-Oct.; Tues.-Sun. 7:30-4, rest of year. Free. Phone (208) 437-3133.

REXBURG (E-5) pop. 17,257, elev. 4,861′

In the late 1870s many miners heading into Montana in search of gold stopped along the west side of the Snake River and claimed land under the Homestead Act of 1862. Many of these first homesteaders were Mormons. In 1883 another influx of settlers drove their sleighs to the banks of the Snake River and established the present townsite of Rexburg.

In June 1976 the nearby Teton Dam collapsed, sending 8 billion gallons of flood water into the valley below. To see the site, travel 20 miles northeast on SR 33. Rexburg plays host to the Idaho International Folk Dance Festival in August. The Centennial Carousel, which took 5 years to restore, is in Porter Park.

Rexburg Chamber of Commerce: 420 W. 4th St. S., Rexburg, ID 83440; phone (208) 356-5700.

TETON FLOOD MUSEUM, 51 N. Center, offers shows and picture displays about the 1976 break in the Teton Dam and the subsequent flooding. A film about the flood is shown. Other displays include a variety of quilts and a military exhibit. Mon.-Sat. 9-4, May-Sept.; Mon.-Fri. 10-3, rest of year. Closed holidays. Admission $2; ages 12-18, $1; under 12, 50c. Phone (208) 359-3063.

SAVE **YELLOWSTONE BEAR WORLD,** 7 mi. s. on US 20, re-creates the experience of seeing black and grizzly bears up close from your automobile. Also on the 120-acre grounds are elk, deer and timber wolves.

Guided curator tours are available. Food is available. Allow 1 hour minimum. Daily 9-6, Memorial Day weekend-Labor Day; 9-5, May 15-day before Memorial Day weekend and day after Labor Day-Oct. 15. Admission $10.95; over 64, $9.95; ages 3-10, $6.95; $40 maximum per private vehicle (maximum nine people per vehicle). Curator tour $5. AX, DS, MC, VI. Phone (208) 359-9688.

RIGBY (E-5) pop. 2,998, elev. 4,850′

JEFFERSON COUNTY HISTORICAL SOCIETY AND FARNSWORTH TV PIONEER MUSEUM is at 118 W. 1st South. In addition to exhibits about the history of Jefferson County, the museum also features displays about the city's role in the birth of television.

Philo Farnsworth, said to be the inventor of television, formulated his ideas about the electronic transmission of visual images while a Rigby resident. Vintage TV sets and barber and beauty shops are featured. Allow 30 minutes minimum. Tues.-Sat. 1-5. Admission $2. Phone (208) 745-8423.

RIGGINS (D-2) pop. 410, elev. 1,800′

Riggins, where the Little Salmon pours into the main Salmon River, is a starting point for a drive north along US 95 through the scenic gorge of the Salmon River. The town is considered the area's white-water capital for float trips; for information phone the chamber of commerce.

East of town lies the wilderness of the Payette National Forest *(see place listing p. 61)*. To the west rise the 9,000-foot Seven Devils Mountains, which form a semicircle above the Snake River's chasm, Hells Canyon; some 30 alpine lakes are clustered around the peaks. To the south is the Rapid River Fish Hatchery, one of the Northwest's most successful chinook salmon-breeding operations.

Salmon River Chamber of Commerce: P.O. Box 289, Riggins, ID 83549; phone (208) 628-3778.

RECREATIONAL ACTIVITIES

White-water Rafting

- SAVE **Epley's Whitewater Adventures**, on US 95 at the n. end of town. Write P.O. Box 987, McCall, ID 83638. Trips depart daily at 9:15, May-Sept. Phone (208) 634-5173 or (800) 233-1813.
- **Northwest Voyageurs**, 9 mi. s. on US 95, offers trips on the Salmon, Owyhee and Snake rivers. Write HC2, Box 501, Pollock, ID 83547. Other activities are offered. Departures daily Mar.-Sept. Phone (208) 628-3021 or (800) 727-9977. *See color ad p. 52.*
- **River Adventures** offers Hells Canyon and Salmon River trips, some departing from 1310 S. Main St. Write P.O. Box 518, Riggins, ID 83549. Other activities are offered. Rafting trips depart daily, Apr.-Sept. Phone (208) 628-3952 or (800) 524-9710.
- **Salmon River Challenge**, on US 95 between Mileposts 195 and 196. Write P.O. Box 1299, Riggins, ID 83549. Other activities are offered. Half-day trips depart daily at 12:30, May 1-late Sept. Full- and 2-day trips depart daily at 9, May

1-late Sept. Three- and 5-day trips depart every 8 days, late June-late Sept. Phone (208) 628-3264 or (800) 732-8574.

RUPERT (F-3) pop. 5,645, elev. 4,158′

Rupert was platted by the Bureau of Reclamation, which accounts for its business district being built around a square that is now a public park. Irrigation from dam projects on the Snake River has transformed the surrounding area from semiarid land to one of Idaho's principal agricultural areas. Potatoes and sugar beets are important crops.

Mini-Cassia Chamber of Commerce: 1177 7th St., P.O. Box 640, Heyburn, ID 83336; phone (208) 679-4793.

MINIDOKA NATIONAL WILDLIFE REFUGE extends 20 mi. up the Snake River from Minidoka Dam; refuge headquarters is 12 mi. n.e. via SR 24 and CR 400N. As many as 100,000 waterfowl stop at the refuge as they migrate along the Pacific flyway. Some 200 species of birds plus mule deer, pronghorn antelopes and various predators inhabit the 20,721-acre refuge.

Fishing, boating and picnicking are permitted on the western end of Lake Walcott, though boating is prohibited October through February. There are no tour routes or developed hiking trails; roads are primitive. Refuge open daily dawn-dusk. Office open Mon.-Fri.; closed holidays. Phone (208) 436-3589.

SALMON (D-3) pop. 3,122, elev. 4,040′

Once the winter campsite of fur trappers, including Jim Bridger and Kit Carson, Salmon is at the fork of the Salmon and Lemhi rivers near the edge of the Salmon Valley, a prosperous livestock and mining area. Permanent settlement of this region began with the discovery of gold in 1866. The town is a favorite starting point for pack trips into the Frank Church-River of No Return Wilderness and for float trips down the Salmon River and its wildest branch, the Middle Fork.

Salmon lies on a scenic section of US 93, which heads north to the Montana border and southwest toward Sawtooth National Forest *(see place listing p. 65)*.

Salmon Valley Chamber of Commerce: 200 Main St., Salmon, ID 83467; phone (208) 756-2100 or (800) 727-2540.

LEMHI COUNTY HISTORICAL MUSEUM, 210 Main St., displays tools, domestic items and American Indian artifacts dating to pioneer times. A collection of antiques from China, Japan and Tibet also is exhibited. Mon.-Sat. 9-5, June-Sept.; 12:30-4:30, Apr.-May and in Oct. Hours may vary; phone ahead. Admission $2, under 12 free. Phone (208) 756-3342.

SACAJAWEA INTERPRETIVE, CULTURAL AND EDUCATION CENTER, 1 mi. e. on US 28 (Main St.), is in the Lemhi Valley, the birthplace of the Lewis and Clark expedition's American Indian guide. A visitor center, amphitheater, monument to Sacajawea, displays, kiosks and a 1-mile interpretive trail commemorate the story of Sacajawea and Lemhi Shoshoni culture. The trail features a tipi encampment, a riverside sweat lodge and wildlife exhibits.

Picnicking is permitted. Allow 1 hour minimum. Daily 9-5, June-Aug.; Tues.-Sat. 9-5 in May and Sept.-Oct. Admission $3, under 6 free, family rate $9. Phone (208) 756-1188.

RECREATIONAL ACTIVITIES

White-water Rafting

- SAVE **Idaho Adventures**, on the Salmon River. Write P.O. Box 834, Salmon, ID 83467. Other activities are offered. Rafting trips offered Apr.-Sept. Phone (208) 756-2986 or (800) 789-9283.
- SAVE **Kookaburra Rafting Trips**, on the Salmon River. Write 706 15th St., Salmon ID 83467. Trips run Fri.-Sun., June-Sept. Phone (208) 756-4386 or (888) 654-4386.
- **Rawhide Outfitters**, 204 Larson St., Salmon, ID 83467. Other activities are offered. Trips depart Sun.-Fri., May-Oct. Phone (208) 756-4276.
- **Salmon River Rafting Co.**, on the main channel of the Salmon River, offers ground transportation options from Idaho Falls and Salmon or air from Boise. Write P.O. Box 2043, Salmon, ID 83467 (Apr.-Sept.) or P.O. Box 1887, Jackson, WY 83001 (rest of year). Departures Apr.-Sept. Phone (877) 734-6099.
- SAVE **Silver Cloud Expeditions** trips depart from the Stagecoach Inn, 201 US 93N. Write P.O. Box 1006, Salmon, ID 83467. Other activities are offered. Trips offered daily Mar.-Oct. Phone (208) 756-6215 or (877) 756-6215.

SALMON-CHALLIS NATIONAL FOREST

Elevations in the forest range from 2,200 ft. in the lower canyon of the Salmon River to 12,662 ft. at Borah Peak. Refer to AAA maps for additional elevation information.

From the headwaters of the Salmon River, down the Lost River, Pahsimeroi and Lemhi Mountain Ranges, to the western slope of the Continental Divide, the Salmon-Challis National Forest covers 4.3 million acres. Over 130,000 acres are in the Frank Church-River of No Return Wilderness *(see Payette National Forest p. 61)*.

The historic Lewis and Clark Trail passes through part of the forest, where several monuments to the explorers have been erected. The Custer Motorway Loop and adjacent Salmon River Road provide glimpses of historic mining towns and native wildlife.

Because of swift currents the Salmon River west of Salmon is known as the "River of No Return." Now, however, it is possible to navigate this river upstream via jet boats. Boat trips down the river can be arranged in Salmon *(see place listing p. 64)*.

More than 2,800 miles of trail stripe the forest floor. Hiking season is generally between April and October; hunting, fishing, camping and wildlife viewing also are excellent.

The section of the river between Corn Creek and Riggins can be traveled by kayaks, jet boats or rubber rafts. Skiing is available nearby on the Idaho-Montana border at Lost Trail Pass. For more information write the Salmon-Challis National Forest Headquarters, R.R. 2, Box 600, Salmon, ID 83467; phone (208) 756-5100. *See Recreation Chart and the AAA Northwestern CampBook.*

SANDPOINT (A-2) pop. 6,835, elev. 2,086'

Sandpoint, at the north end of Pend Oreille Lake, is a year-round resort town and artists' community that offers a wide variety of land- and water-based recreational opportunities.

One of the West's great railroad towns, Sandpoint is known as "The Funnel" for the major rail lines that converge here. More than 40 trains a day draw rail fans to the city. A brochure "A Rail Fan's Guide to Sandpoint, Idaho" is available from the chamber of commerce.

The city is the starting point for single- and multi-day train tours through the Montana Rockies to Glacier, Grand Teton and Yellowstone national parks. Guides aboard Montana Rockies Rail Tours provide historic narration and tales of folklore as the *Montana Daylight* follows the original route of the Northern Pacific Railroad; phone (800) 519-7245 for information.

Greater Sandpoint Chamber of Commerce: 900 N. Fifth Ave., P.O. Box 928, Sandpoint, ID 83864; phone (208) 263-0887 or (800) 800-2106.

Shopping areas: One of downtown Sandpoint's focal points is the Cedar Street Bridge Public Market, home to Coldwater Creek Nature and Clothing Store. Formerly a city bridge over Sand Creek, this renovated two-level structure is patterned after the famed Ponte Vecchio bridge shops in Florence, Italy, and contains two long streets of restaurants and shops.

BONNER COUNTY HISTORICAL MUSEUM, 611 S. Ella Ave., uses pioneer relics and other exhibits to chronicle the history of the county, with emphasis on the Kootenai Indians and the local timber industry. Allow 30 minutes minimum. Tues.-Sat. 10-4; closed holidays. Admission $2, students with ID $1, family rate (two adults and three children) $5. Phone (208) 263-2344.

PEND OREILLE LAKE, s. and e. of town, was formed by glaciers and is encircled by lofty mountain peaks. At 43 miles long, Pend Oreille (pon-duh-RAY) Lake is one of the largest freshwater lakes in the Pacific Northwest. Noted for its scenic coves and 1,150-foot depth, the lake is stocked with Kamloops rainbow trout.

Swimming, boating, picnicking and tennis are popular, as are guided boat tours and houseboating. Allow a full day minimum. *See Recreation Chart.*

RECREATIONAL ACTIVITIES

Horseback Riding

- **Mountain Horse Adventures**, 9 mi. n. on Schweitzer Mountain Rd. Write 206 N. Fourth Ave. #132, Sandpoint, ID 83864. Two- to 3-hour trips depart daily at 9 and 1, late June-Aug. 31. Other activities are offered. Phone (208) 663-8768 or (800) 831-8810.

Skiing

- **Schweitzer Mountain Resort**, 11 mi. n. via US 2/95 and Schweitzer Mountain Rd. Write 10000 Schweitzer Mountain Rd., Sandpoint, ID 83864. Daily 9-4, Thanksgiving to mid-Apr. (also Fri.-Sat. 4-9, late Dec. to mid-Mar.). Phone (208) 263-9555 or (800) 831-8810.

SAWTOOTH NATIONAL FOREST

Elevations in the forest range from 4,514 ft. at Rock Creek Drain to 12,009 ft. at Hyndman Peak. Refer to AAA maps for additional elevation information.

In south-central Idaho, the Sawtooth National Forest embraces approximately 2.1 million acres. Offering a wide range of recreational opportunities and spectacular scenery, the forest consists of a northern division containing the Sawtooth National Recreation Area and a southern division along the Nevada and Utah borders.

Adjacent to Sun Valley *(see place listing p. 68)*, the northern division is bisected by the Sawtooth Scenic Route (SR 75 or Sawtooth National Forest Scenic Byway) and provides hundreds of miles of hiking and horseback-riding trails in the Smoky, Pioneer, Sawtooth, Boulder and White Cloud mountains. The Baumgartner Nature Trail, near Baumgartner Campground in the Fairfield District, is a popular hiking area.

The southern division contains the Rock Creek Canyon, Howell Canyon, Black Pine, Raft River and Sublett areas. Alpine and cross-country skiing as well as snowmobiling are available in areas near Twin Falls *(see place listing p. 69)*, Burley *(see place listing p. 47)*, Fairfield and Sun Valley *(see place listing p. 68)*.

Information about campgrounds and recreational opportunities is available at the forest supervisor's office in Twin Falls and the district ranger stations. For further information write Sawtooth National Forest, 2647 Kimberly Rd. E., Twin Falls, ID 83301; phone (208) 737-3200, or TTY (208) 737-3235. *See Recreation Chart and the AAA Northwestern CampBook.*

SAWTOOTH NATIONAL RECREATION AREA (D-3)

In south-central Idaho, the Sawtooth National Recreation Area comprises 756,000 acres of the northern division of the Sawtooth National Forest. The recreation area features three mountain ranges of peaks exceeding 10,000 feet, deep forests and high mountain lakes. The recreation area includes the Sawtooth Wilderness, the White Cloud-Boulder Mountains, the Salmon River and five major lakes. The backcountry has 750 miles of hiking trails and more than 300 lakes.

Nature trails in the forest include the Fishhook Creek Nature Trail, adjacent to Redfish Lake Visitor Center, and the Wood River Adventure Trail, bordering the Wood River Campground. The visitor center, on the northern shore of Redfish Lake 5 miles south of Stanley on SR 75, is open mid-June through Labor Day; phone (208) 774-3376.

A free audiotape tour explaining the area's history and features can be borrowed at the Sawtooth National Recreation Area headquarters, Stanley Ranger Station or the Ketchum Ranger District. For more information write Sawtooth National Recreation Headquarters, HC 64, Box 8291, Ketchum, ID 83340; phone (208) 727-5013 or (800) 260-5970. *See Recreation Chart and the AAA Northwestern CampBook.*

SHOSHONE (F-3) pop. 1,398, elev. 3,968′

Shoshone, in an irrigated farming belt and sheep-raising area, was settled in 1882. Many buildings, including the Community Methodist Church at Apple and C streets, are made from local dark, porous lava rock.

Shoshone Chamber of Commerce: P.O. Box 575, Shoshone, ID 83352; phone (208) 886-2030.

SHOSHONE INDIAN ICE CAVES, 17 mi. n. on SR 75, are caves of ice that maintain a temperature of 18 to 28 degrees F, while a few feet away on the surface the thermometer might register more than 100. Wear sturdy shoes and a coat. The .7-mile tour includes 100 feet of stairs. A museum features collections of gems, minerals and rocks.

Allow 1 hour minimum. Museum and caves open daily 8-7:15, May-Sept. Guided cave tours are given daily. Schedule varies; phone ahead. Last tour begins at closing. Admission $6; over 62, $5.50; ages 5-14, $3.75. AX, DS, MC, VI. Phone (208) 886-2058.

DID YOU KNOW

There are many caves in Idaho, including a cave of ice near Shoshone.

SILVER CITY (F-2) elev. 6,179′

Silver City, high in the Owyhee Mountains of southwestern Idaho, became an important gold and silver mining center after prospectors struck it rich near the headwaters of Jordan Creek in 1862. A 500-pound solid silver crystal from the nearby Poorman mine on War Eagle Mountain won a prize at the 1866 exposition in Paris.

Mining remained a force until 1912, then continued sporadically through the 1930s. In its heyday Silver City boasted a courthouse, hotels, Idaho's first daily newspaper and a population of 3,000. By 1920 its population had fallen to 100.

A walk down Silver City's unpaved streets is a living-history tour. Some 75 buildings remain of this once boisterous mining town. The 1892 schoolhouse and drugstore are now museums. On the knoll near the school is the 1898 Our Lady of Tears Catholic Church. The 20-bedroom Idaho Hotel, which is also a museum, dominates Main Street and was once the finest in the territory. Several historic cemeteries are in the community.

Note: The 23-mile gravel and dirt road leading to Silver City from SR 78 south of Murphy has many rough, winding sections and is not recommended for trailers or oversize vehicles. The road is not maintained in winter and is normally closed early October to late May. Phone (208) 583-4104 or write P.O. Box 75, Murphy, ID 83650-0075, for weather and road conditions.

The first 8 miles of the 25-mile road leading west from Silver City to Jordan Valley, Ore., are rough, winding and narrow. There are no automobile service facilities in the vicinity.

SODA SPRINGS (F-5) pop. 3,381, elev. 5,777′

Since pioneer days Soda Springs has been known for its 30 mineral salt springs. Early trappers called Hooper Spring, a mile north of town, "Beer Spring" because of its natural soda water, which visitors can sample today.

Nearby Captive Geyser is a carbon dioxide geyser controlled to erupt hourly, winds permitting. Foot-deep wagon ruts from the Old Oregon Trail that date from the mid-1800s provide an unusual hazard on the local golf course. The Pioneer Museum downtown displays mementos reflecting area history.

Soda Springs Chamber of Commerce: 9 W. 2nd S., P.O. Box 697, Soda Springs, ID 83276; phone (208) 547-4964 or (888) 399-0888.

SPALDING (C-2) elev. 840′

Catholic, Protestant and Mormon missionaries occupied much of central Idaho during the early and mid-1800s in an attempt to convert the American Indians. Spalding, now within the boundaries of the Nez Perce National Historical Park *(see place listing p. 59)*, is named for Rev. Henry H. Spalding, who built a mission near the present town of Lapwai *(see place listing p. 56)* in 1836.

Two years later he moved the mission 2 miles north to the Clearwater River, where the headquarters of the Nez Perce National Historical Park is today.

Several geologic formations near Spalding have significance in Nez Perce tradition. Coyote's Fishnet, about 4 miles west, is a formation on the bluffs of the Clearwater River's south shore. A talus slope known as The Bear is high on the north side of the river. Ant and Yellowjacket is a rock arch 1.5 miles west off US 12 just before its junction with US 95.

Idaho's first homestead, the Craig Donation Land Claim, is about 8 miles south along US 95. In 1840 mountain man William Craig settled on 630 acres given to him by the Nez Perce. He is buried in the nearby town of Jacques. St. Joseph's Mission, 4 miles south of Jacques in the village of Slickpoo, was dedicated in 1874 and was the first Catholic church in Nez Perce country.

NEZ PERCE NATIONAL HISTORICAL PARK, on US 95, contains exhibits about Nez Perce culture. Audiovisual programs also highlight Nez Perce culture as well as area history. A park folder is available for a self-guiding driving tour of the 38 sites included in the park. Allow 30 minutes minimum. Daily 8-5:30, Memorial Day weekend-Labor Day; 8-4:30, rest of year. Closed Jan. 1, Thanksgiving and Dec. 25. Donations. Phone (208) 843-2261.

SPALDING SITE, .2 mi. e., is the location of the second mission built by Rev. Henry H. Spalding and his wife in 1838. The Presbyterian mission included the territory's first printing press, sawmill and gristmill; it was later used as Indian Agency headquarters. The Spaldings and many Nez Perce are buried in the Spalding Mission Cemetery. The Spaldings' first homesite, 2 miles south at Thunder Hill, was built in 1836, the year they arrived in the Northwest. Allow 30 minutes minimum.

STANLEY (E-3) pop. 100, elev. 6,260′

On the Salmon River (the "River of No Return"), Stanley is at the center of the Sawtooth National Recreation Area *(see place listing p. 65)*, Sawtooth Valley and the spectacular Sawtooth Basin. Most float trips on the Middle Fork of the Salmon River are outfitted at this site. The town lies on two exceptionally scenic highways, SRs 21 and 75.

The Ponderosa Pine Scenic Byway (SR 21) passes through part of the Sawtooth National Forest *(see place listing p. 65)* and ends in Boise; motorists should check for possible temporary closures due to snow. The northeastern segment of SR 75, the Salmon River Scenic Byway, passes through the Sawtooth National Recreation Area and then merges with US 93. The southeastern segment of SR 75, the Sawtooth Scenic Byway, heads south toward Twin Falls and Sun Valley.

Stanley-Sawtooth Chamber of Commerce: P.O. Box 8, Stanley, ID 83278; phone (208) 774-3411 or (800) 878-7950.

SAWTOOTH FISH HATCHERY, 5 mi. s. on SR 75, is used for trapping and holding spring chinook salmon and steelhead trout. The hatchery produces chinook and collects steelhead eggs for later transport to the Hagerman and Magic Valley hatcheries. An observation deck is on the premises. Visitor center daily 8-5. Guided 45-minute tours are given at 10:30, 1:30 and 3, Memorial Day weekend-Labor Day. Free. Phone (208) 774-3684.

RECREATIONAL ACTIVITIES

Horseback Riding

- **Redfish Lake Corrals—Trail Rides**, Red Fish Lake, Stanley, ID 83278. Departures daily 9-3, Memorial Day to mid-Sept. Phone (208) 774-3311 or (888) 722-5432.
- **Sawtooth Wilderness Pack Trips**, on SR 75 in the Sawtooth National Recreation Area. Write Mystic Saddle Ranch, Stanley, ID 83278. Trips depart daily June 15-Nov. 15. Phone (208) 774-3591 or (888) 722-5432.

White-water Rafting

- **Middle Fork River Expeditions**, on the Middle Fork of the Salmon River. Write P.O. Box 199, Stanley, ID 83278. Other activities are offered. Departures June-Sept. Phone (800) 801-5146.
- **The River Company**, .7 mi. w. on SR 21. Write P.O. Box 2329, Sun Valley, ID 83353. Day trip departures daily mid-May through Aug. 31. Phone (208) 788-5775 or (800) 398-0346.
- **River Odysseys West (ROW)** offers trips on the Middle Fork of the Salmon River. Write P.O. Box 579, Coeur d'Alene, ID 83816. One- to 6-day trips depart mid-May to mid-Sept. Phone (208) 765-0841 or (800) 451-6034.
- **Rocky Mountain River Tours**, on the Middle Fork of the Salmon River. Write P.O. Box 8596, Boise, ID 83707. Four- to 6-day trips depart mid-May through Sept. 30. Phone (208) 345-2400, or (208) 756-4808 in summer.
- **Sawtooth Adventure Co.**, 1 mi. n. on US 75. Write P.O. Box 206, Stanley, ID 83278. Other activities are offered. Full-day trips depart daily at 9:30 and 2:30, May 20-Labor Day. Half-day trips depart daily at 9:30, 2:30 and 6. Phone (866) 774-4644.

SUN VALLEY (E-3) pop. 1,427, elev. 5,926′

Sun Valley got its start in 1935 when Union Pacific Railroad Chairman Averell Harriman hired Austrian Count Felix Shaffgotsch to find the most scenic snow spot in the country for a huge ski resort. Passing up places that would become Aspen, Jackson Hole and Mount Hood, Shaffgotsch chose Sun Valley, and soon stars from all across the country came to ski down Bald Mountain and hobnob in the huge wooden lodge Harriman built. Gary Cooper and Clark Gable were frequent visitors; novelist Ernest Hemingway spent his last years in the area, and a memorial to him stands alongside Trail Creek.

Today nearly a quarter-million persons visit the area which somehow still manages to maintain an uncrowded, non-tourist atmosphere. Sun Valley, along with the neighboring town of Ketchum *(see place listing p. 56)*, offers heated outdoor pools, saunas and indoor and outdoor ice skating rinks. The list of local summer activities includes golf, tennis, swimming, white-water rafting, camping, bicycling, hiking, horseback riding, skeet shooting, trapshooting, fishing, mountaineering and kayaking.

Winter brings sleigh rides, snowmobiling and ice skating as well as downhill, cross-country and helicopter skiing. Saturday nights are reserved for hockey games in winter and professional ice shows in summer. Skiing begins on Thanksgiving.

Sun Valley-Ketchum Chamber of Commerce: 411 N. Main St., P.O. Box 2420, Sun Valley, ID 83353; phone (208) 726-3423 or (800) 634-3347. *See color ad.*

RECREATIONAL ACTIVITIES

Skiing

- **Bald Mountain**, SR 75 to Third Ave. Write P.O. Box 10, Sun Valley Sports Center, Sun Valley, ID 83353. Daily 9-4, Thanksgiving to mid-Apr. Phone (208) 622-2231 or (800) 635-4150.
- **Dollar Mountain**, adjacent to Sun Valley. Write P.O. Box 10, Sun Valley Sports Center, Sun Valley, ID 83353. Daily 9-4, Thanksgiving-early Apr. Phone (208) 622-2231.

SYRINGA (C-2) elev. 1,440′

Syringa is named for Idaho's state flower, a variety of mock orange whose creamy white blooms fill the forest in early summer. The town nestles along the Middle Fork of the Clearwater River, a designated Wild and Scenic River.

Lowell/Syringa Chamber of Commerce: HC 75, Box 61, Kooskia, ID 83539; phone (888) 926-4430.

RECREATIONAL ACTIVITIES

White-water Rafting

- **River Odysseys West (ROW)** trips on the Lochsa, Selway and Middle Fork of the Clearwater rivers depart from the ROW office on US 12. Write P.O. Box 579, Coeur d'Alene, ID 83816. Daily mid-May to early Sept. Phone (208) 765-0841 or (800) 451-6034.

TARGHEE NATIONAL FOREST

Elevations in the forest range from 5,300 ft. at Warm River to 12,197 ft. at Diamond Peak. Refer to AAA maps for additional elevation information.

In the south-central part of the state, Targhee National Forest is in the Teton, Centennial, Palisades and Caribou ranges. The forest, named for Tygee, a Bannock Indian Chief, lies partially in Wyoming, but the majority of its 1.8 million acres is in Idaho; it extends in a semicircle around the headwaters of Henry's Fork of the Snake River. The Continental Divide forms most of the northern boundary; Yellowstone and Grand Teton national parks make up most of the eastern border. Canyons, high peaks and desert add to the picturesque scenery.

Water is abundant throughout the forest. Big Springs, one of the largest springs in the United States, is reached by SR 59 from US 20 at Macks Inn. It issues from the base of a high plateau at a constant 52 degrees F and is the headwaters of Henry's Fork.

A 3- to 5-hour canoe/float trip can be taken along a 5-mile national recreation water trail just below Big Springs. Moose, trumpeter swans, ospreys and bald eagles can often be seen. Further down Henry's Fork, boaters must portage around several sections of dangerous water between Macks Inn and Ashton.

Upper and Lower Mesa falls are east of US 20 and north of Ashton on Mesa Falls Scenic Byway. The Upper Mesa Falls is 114 feet high; the Lower Mesa Falls is 65 to 70 feet high.

Trout fishing is excellent throughout the forest: Palisades Reservoir, Henry's Lake, Island Park Reservoir, Henry's Fork and South Fork of the Snake River are noted spots. Winter sports areas near Ashton, Heise, Island Park and Driggs have snowmobiling and downhill and cross-country skiing. More than 1,100 miles of trails provide back-country experiences.

For more information contact the Forest Supervisor's Office, Targhee National Forest, 499 N. 2400 E., St. Anthony, ID 83445-0208; phone (208) 624-3151. *See Recreation Chart and the AAA Northwestern CampBook.*

TWIN FALLS (F-3) pop. 34,469, elev. 3,745'

Twin Falls is in the center of 500,000 acres of prime farmland irrigated by the waters of the Snake River. Since the turn of the 20th century, the "Magic Valley" area has been known as one of the nation's most prolific crop producing regions. Twin Falls also is on the edge of the Snake River Canyon, which was gouged out some 30,000 years ago by the Great Bonneville Flood.

Five miles northeast the white waters of the Snake River plunge more than 212 feet at Shoshone Falls, known as the "Niagara of the West." The best time to view the falls is late April through early June, since irrigation waters are retained upstream during the summer months. **Note:** During periods of drought, the falls may be dry; phone ahead to confirm the status.

Twin Falls Area Chamber of Commerce: 858 Blue Lakes Blvd. N., Twin Falls, ID 83301; phone (208) 733-3974.

THE HERRETT CENTER FOR ARTS & SCIENCE, at 315 Falls Ave. on the College of Southern Idaho campus, contains pre-Columbian and other artifacts from Indian civilizations of the Western Hemisphere. Arranged in various themes, exhibits interpret Indian life and cultures. An art gallery and planetarium offer changing contemporary exhibits and shows.

Allow 30 minutes minimum. Museum open Tues.-Fri. 9:30-4:30 (also Tues. and Fri. 4:30-9), Sat. 1-9, Sept.-May; Tues.-Sat. 1-9, rest of year. Planetarium shows Tues. and Fri. at 7 p.m., Sat. at 2, 4 and 7. Additional shows are presented June-Aug. Hours may vary; phone ahead. Museum admission free. Planetarium $4; over 59, $3; students with ID $2; family rate $9. Under 4 are not recommended in the planetarium. DS, MC, VI. Phone (208) 732-6655.

PERRINE MEMORIAL BRIDGE, on the northern edge of town, spans the Snake River Gorge 486 feet above the water. The four-lane bridge has pedestrian walkways with views of sheer cliffs, the Blue Lakes, waterfalls, a park and two golf courses. A road descends to these areas. The Buzz Langdon Visitor Center is next to the bridge.

Daredevil Evel Knievel attempted to leap across the Snake River Canyon a mile east of the bridge in 1974; the dirt ramp used to launch his rocket-powered vehicle remains. Bridge open year-round. Visitor center open daily 8-8, mid-May to mid-Oct. Phone (208) 733-9458.

WALLACE (B-2) pop. 960, elev. 2,744'

The center of a great lead- and silver-mining region, Wallace is at the junction of four major canyons, three of which lead to important active mining districts. This region claims several of the world's largest and deepest silver mines; some of the mines founded in the late 1800s have 200 miles of tunnels.

Among the historic buildings still standing in town are the railroad depot with its original Chinese bricks; the Smokehouse Building, which was once the courthouse; and the Rossi Building with its Queen Anne-style turret. The turret is an interesting architectural feature seen on most of the corner buildings throughout the historic district.

At the east end of Wallace, SR 4 leads north from I-90 exit 62 into Burke Canyon, one of the district's historic mining areas. The 7-mile road passes tailings, abandoned mines, derelict buildings and the once bustling towns of Gem and Burke. The latter town, in a narrow canyon, was renowned for the 150-room Tiger Hotel, which was not only built over a creek, but also had a rail line tunneling through its center and a street running under its west end; the hotel was razed in 1964.

Area backroads attract all-terrain vehicle enthusiasts in summer and snowmobilers in winter.

Historic Wallace Chamber of Commerce Visitor Center: 10 River St., P.O. Box 1167, Wallace, ID 83873; phone (208) 753-7151 or (800) 434-4204.

Self-guiding tours: Brochures describing driving and walking tours of the mining and historic districts are available at the Wallace District Mining Museum *(see attraction listing).*

NORTHERN PACIFIC DEPOT RAILROAD MUSEUM, 219 Sixth St., occupies a restored station that was built in 1901 and operated until 1980. Exhibits include a re-creation of an early 1900s railroad depot and photographs and railway relics that focus on the railroading history of the Coeur d'Alene mining district.

Allow 30 minutes minimum. Daily 9-7, June-Aug.; daily 9-5 in May and Sept.; Mon.-Sat. 10-3 in Apr. and Oct. 1-15. Admission $2; over 55, $1.50; ages 6-16, $1; family rate $6. Phone (208) 752-0111.

SAVE **SIXTH STREET MELODRAMA** is at 212 Sixth St. Audience participation is encouraged each summer during a family-style melodrama that reflects the area's mining background. The play, staged in the 1899 Lux Building, is followed by the Kelly's Alley Revue, during which visitors can enjoy old-fashioned music and humor. Other plays and musicals are also produced during the rest of the year; phone for schedule and rates.

Allow 2 hours minimum. Summer performances Tues.-Sat. at 8 p.m., early July-late Aug. Admission $10; over 54, college students with ID and children $8; family rate $30. MC, VI. Phone (208) 752-8871 or (208) 752-3081.

WALLACE DISTRICT MINING MUSEUM, 509 Bank St., displays local mining equipment, photographs and a model of a working mine. A 20-minute videotape depicts the life of early miners and the development of one of the richest silver mining districts in the world.

Allow 1 hour minimum. Daily 8-7, July 1 to mid-Aug.; daily 8-6, early June-June 30 and mid-Aug. through Labor Day; daily 9-5, May 1-early June; Mon.-Fri. 9-4, Sat. 10-3, rest of year. Admission $2; over 54, $1.50; ages 6-15, 50c. DS, MC, VI. Phone (208) 556-1592.

SAVE **Sierra Silver Mine Tour,** .5 blk. from the museum at 420 Fifth St., allows visitors to witness mining in the silver-laden veins of the Coeur d'Alene district. Visitors are guided through a tunnel where they can view exhibits, equipment in operation and techniques used to mine silver ore underground. The 1-hour guided tours leave every 30 minutes aboard a San Francisco-style trolley to the mine entrance.

Allow 1 hour, 30 minutes minimum. Daily 9-6, July-Aug.; 9-4, May-June and Sept.-Oct. Fee $9; over 60, $8; ages 4-16, $7.50; family rate $33. Under 4 are not permitted. MC, VI. Phone (208) 752-5151.

WEISER (E-2) pop. 5,343, elev. 2,114'

Named for Sgt. Peter Weiser (WEE-zer) of the Lewis and Clark expedition, Weiser is on the Idaho-Oregon border at the confluence of the Weiser and Snake rivers.

Scenic views of Hells Canyon are afforded from viewpoints north of Weiser; open only in summer, the viewpoints can be reached via US 95 and SR 71. Closer looks at the canyon are made possible by the float trips and jet boat tours that are available from Hells Canyon Dam. The minimum age for most float trips is 6 years; inquire about refund and weather policies.

Greater Weiser Chamber of Commerce: 309 State St., Weiser, ID 83672; phone (208) 414-0452.

WINCHESTER (C-2) pop. 308, elev. 3,968'

Early settlers allegedly named this former logging town for the famous firearm. A replica of a Winchester rifle hangs above Main Street. Winchester Lake State Park *(see Recreation Chart)*, just south on US 95 Bus. Rte., occupies the site of the 1910 Craig Mountain Lumber Company, whose 103-acre millpond is today the centerpiece of the park. Remains of the mill can be seen on the hill near the city water tower.

THE WOLF EDUCATION AND RESEARCH CENTER is w. on Forest Rd., following signs. The center's 20 acres of timberland are home to a resident pack of gray wolves. Visitors have a chance to observe these animals in their natural habitat, courtesy of a .3-mile trail that comes within 50 yards of the wolves' enclosure, though sightings cannot be guaranteed. A visitor center, built to resemble a Nez Perce tribal long house, has displays about wolves.

Allow 30 minutes minimum. Daily 9-5, Memorial Day weekend-Labor Day; Sat.-Sun. 9-4, May 1-day before Memorial Day weekend and day after Labor Day-Sept. 30; by appointment rest of year. Admission $3, under 12 free. Guided tour $10 (includes admission). MC, VI. Phone (208) 924-6960.

WORLEY (B-2) pop. 223, elev. 2,650'

CASINOS

- **Coeur d'Alene Casino**, on US 95. Daily 24 hours. Phone (800) 523-2464. *See color ad p. 197.*

YELLOWSTONE NATIONAL PARK—*see Wyoming p. 173.*

Big Sky Country

Vast plains of prairie grass merge with endless cerulean skies

Cowboys and Indians

Bucking horses and ceremonial dances are the focus at numerous rodeos and powwows

The Treasure State

Rugged mountains yield a wealth of gold and silver

Going-to-the-Sun Road

Stretching across the Continental Divide in Glacier National Park, this engineering marvel climbs 6,680 feet

Rocky Mountain High

Grassy-floored valleys give way to mountains flourishing with towering evergreens and striking alpine vistas

Kintla Lake
Glacier National Park

picture this

Glacier National Park / © Jeffrey Cable / SuperStock

Take a journey through Montana. And bring a camera, preferably one with a wide lens, and lots of film.

Snapping here, there and everywhere, you'll have a choice of views that extend as far as your eye (or lens) can see. Copper-colored wheat fields dance with the wind, spotlighted by the sun; jagged peaks loom in the distance, bathed in evergreen; mesas serve as steps to heaven amid grassy prairies. And a royal blue sky has its own formations: clouds are stretched, feathered and puffed.

You can get a little closer, too. Zoom in on what remains of ghost towns and abandoned homesteads. Catch a candid shot of a tribe member in native dress, celebrating his heritage at a powwow.

Use high-speed film to capture an actual cattle drive.

Focus on wildlife doing what they do best: living peacefully in an unspoiled habitat. More prevalent than people, grizzly bears, thousands of migrating elk, bighorn sheep, mountain goats, moose and bald eagles call Montana home.

The rolling hills, river valleys, deserts, peaks and plains in this state often sit for portraits. "A River Runs Through It," "The Horse Whisperer," "Far and Away" and "The River Wild" are just a sampling of the movies that have relied upon Montana for a backdrop.

Take home the beauty of Montana. You're sure to be back in a flash.

Under a giant sky varying between shades of azure, turquoise and peacock blue, Montana's landscape—encompassing golden wheat fields, timber-covered mountains, flowing trout streams, rocky bluffs and canyon-carved lakes—is a love affair for the eyes.

The state enjoys the best of both worlds. The Continental Divide in western Montana gave rise to the name *montaña*, Spanish for "mountainous." And although the craggy peaks of the northern Rocky Mountains dominate the west, wide open space is the name of the game in the east: Expansive, dizzying prairie grasslands in this region coined the state's nickname, Big Sky Country.

While there are differences between Montana's agriculture- and ranching-based Great Plains and its lumber-dominated west, residents have one thing in common: appreciation for the beauty of their surroundings. With a harsh climate and sparse population, no one will argue that living in Montana is a piece of cake. But the view from a ranch window seems to make it worthwhile.

Spectacular Settings

Take the snowy peaks, ice-sculpted valleys, bright white glaciers, and twinkling lakes and waterfalls of Glacier National Park. Blackfeet Indians were so awed with the majestic region that they deemed it sacred ground. If the grizzlies, mountain lions or wolves could talk, they would probably agree.

Your heart will skip a beat on Going-to-the-Sun Road, a "holy cow!" and "don't look down" scenic byway snaking around cliffs and climbing almost 3,000 feet to the summit of Logan Pass. Bring a panoramic camera to capture the setting.

But save some film for the curiosities occupying Yellowstone National Park, which Rudyard Kipling described as "a howling wilderness ... full of all imaginable freaks of a fiery nature."

For beasts of a hairy nature, visit the National Bison Range in Moiese, where some 500 buffaloes roam the plains. At the Madison Buffalo Jump, a massive cliff in Three Forks, you can discover how natives hunted these shaggy animals by driving them off steep embankments.

Journal notes from the Lewis and Clark expedition suggest that these explorers were enamored with Montana's scenery as well:

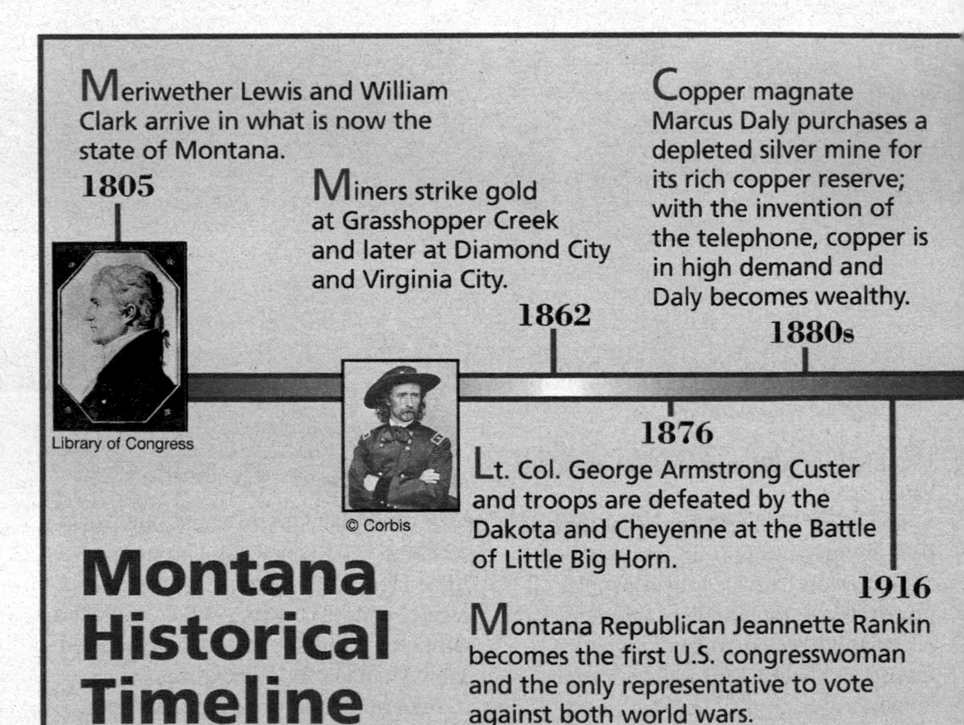

Meriwether Lewis and William Clark arrive in what is now the state of Montana.
1805
Library of Congress
Miners strike gold at Grasshopper Creek and later at Diamond City and Virginia City.
1862
© Corbis
Copper magnate Marcus Daly purchases a depleted silver mine for its rich copper reserve; with the invention of the telephone, copper is in high demand and Daly becomes wealthy.
1880s
1876
Lt. Col. George Armstrong Custer and troops are defeated by the Dakota and Cheyenne at the Battle of Little Big Horn.
1916
Montana Republican Jeannette Rankin becomes the first U.S. congresswoman and the only representative to vote against both world wars.
Montana Historical Timeline

Learn about the journey at Missouri Headwaters State Park, or follow their path along what is now the Upper Missouri National Wild and Scenic River in the eastern plains. Numerous historical sites line the riverbank.

The Treasure State

Vast fortunes were made in Montana, but many would assert they came at the expense of people and land, a notion that doesn't sit well with residents. Many Montanans believe that state resources historically have been exploited in the interests of outsiders.

At Little Bighorn Battlefield National Monument, crooked headstones on a grassy hill attest to the passion that thousands of Lakota, Cheyenne and Arapaho warriors exhibited in an attempt to save their homeland.

And the unearthing of copper ores in Butte began a bitter battle between the "copper kings"—entrepreneurs William A. Clark and Marcus Daly—for control of the area.

Daly eventually won, creating the Anaconda Copper Mining Co., which governed state commerce by controlling mines, smelters, and lumber and railroad operations. Today, mining relics are displayed downtown in old mine shafts, cabins and such stately homes as Clark's lavish Copper King Mansion.

Colorful Virginia City sports reminders of its gold mining past with restored buildings, among them a two-story outhouse. And Helena is home to baroque, Gothic and Italianate mansions recalling the city's golden days.

Residents recently have exhibited an overwhelming drive to protect what they love by fighting to preserve Montana's natural blessings. After the demise of the mining company in the early 1970s, residents amended the state constitution to include strict environmental protection laws, setting a national example.

Laws strive to protect what cowboy artist Charles M. Russell preserves in his paintings: the freedom and romance associated with an undisturbed American West.

Sharing the same sentiment, John Steinbeck wrote, "I am in love with Montana. For other states I have admiration, respect ... even some affection, but with Montana it's love ..."

Become one of many who have experienced the state's beauty. Your memoirs may reflect the same fondness.

1955 The Anaconda Aluminum Co. opens a $65 million plant in northwestern Montana.

1984 Launched in 1967, the Libby Dam hydroelectric project is finally completed.

© G.E. Kidder Smith/Corbis

1987 Originally started in Montana in 1956, the final sections of the nation's first interstate highway system are completed.

© Glenn Oakley/Black Star Publishing/Picture Quest

1988 Numerous forest fires sweep through drought-stricken Montana for nearly 3 months, wiping out trees and wildlife in Yellowstone National Park.

1998 Leaders of the anti-government Montana Freemen are convicted on various charges by federal jurors as a result of their 81-day armed standoff with FBI agents in 1996.

2000 Judy Martz is elected governor and becomes the state's first female chief executive.

Recreation

Bear bells. Quick-dry nylon shorts. Ski poles. Maybe some chest waders. Definitely some dry socks. And, of course, a size 2 Sofa Pillow. Add some sunscreen and a carry-along jacket, and you'll just about have it: the perfect Montana recreation kit.

Dressing the Part

First of all, the quick-dry shorts will come in handy if you plan to immerse yourself in one of this state's top recreation draws—**river rafting.** At Glacier National Park you can drift down placid portions of the wild and scenic Flathead River, savoring arching canyon walls and wildflower-filled meadows. Or strap on some headgear and tackle the bucking, boulder-studded rapids of the Flathead's Middle Fork, where just staying in the boat commands your full attention. Either way, you're likely to slosh in your seat some, so you might as well be dressed for it. Another great rafter's route is Bear Creek, along the park's bottom edge. This run is one of the few where mountain goats are regularly sighted, thanks to Goat Lick, a cliff on the waterway's north side that excretes mineral salts irresistible to goats.

Conditions can vary widely depending on the timing of the spring runoff, so Montana's roughest rivers are best attempted with experienced guides who provide all equipment, helmets included. You'll find outfitters in all of the most-rafted areas. If time allows, try combining a guided river run with an overnight **backpacking** or **horseback-riding** trip; it's a great way to experience several aspects of this magnificent terrain in a single outing.

Cast and Crew

Rafters aren't the only ones who frequent the state's waters, though, and that's where the chest waders come in. As any **fly fisher** worth his tippet knows, Montana is trout territory, and the best ones must be coaxed out of current seams and pocket waters with a deft flick of the wrist and an enticing fly on the end of the line. Such flies can have kind of funny names—hence the Sofa Pillow. Or for something more colorful, tie on a March Brown, Blue Winged Olive or Black Beetle. If in doubt, local fishing shops will gladly recommend what's best for what's biting. For top casting sites, head to Bozeman's outskirts and take your pick of such trout-filled rivers as the Madison, Yellowstone and Gallatin. Folks who don't want to wade will find plenty of rental boats here, complete with guides who will not only do the rowing for you, but also point out the choicest eddies while they're at it.

Fly-fishing may be out if you hit Bozeman mid-winter, but that doesn't mean you're too late to have fun. Excellent **downhill skiing** is just around the corner at Big Sky Resort, which averages 400 inches of powder per year. And locals rave about the bowl and chute skiing available at Bridger Bowl Ski Area, a 1,200-acre city-owned site. Six **cross-country skiing** trails rim the region as well, notably the 10-mile Bozeman Creek to Mystic Lake trail and the 4-mile Hyalite Reservoir Ski Loop. For trail maps, contact the Bozeman Area Chamber of Commerce, (406) 586-5421 or (800) 228-4224.

In addition to Bozeman's offerings you'll find superb ski venues close to many other Montana towns, including Big Mountain near Whitefish, Red Lodge Mountain near Red Lodge and Snowbowl near Missoula. All make great places to put those ski poles you packed to good use.

But don't stop there. Unlikely as it may seem, ski poles can often be just the thing to bring when **hiking** Montana's rugged terrain. Such "walking sticks" are especially useful when the only way to follow your trail is to ford a frigid, knee-high creek. The dry socks are for when you get to the other side.

In fact, Montana has so many great hiking trails, you'd wear out socks and ski poles long before covering a fraction of them. Just try not to miss Cinnamon Mountain Lookout Trail in the Gallatin National Forest, or Stoney Indian Pass in Glacier National Park's Belly River Country. Both reward hikers with sudden, stunning vistas of Montana's treasured mountains. One caveat—while such spectacular scenery can be a pleasant surprise, startling an 800-pound grizzly is just plain hazardous. And *that's* why bear bells are number one on any Montana recreational equipment list.

Recreational Activities

Throughout the TourBook, you may notice a Recreational Activities heading with bulleted listings of recreation-oriented establishments listed underneath. Similar operations also may be mentioned in Destination City recreation sections. Since normal AAA inspection criteria cannot be applied, these establishments are presented only for information. Age, height and weight restrictions may apply. Reservations often are recommended and sometimes are required. Addresses and/or phone numbers are provided so visitors can contact the attraction for additional information.

Fast Facts

POPULATION: 902,195.

AREA: 147,138 square miles; ranks 4th.

CAPITAL: Helena.

HIGHEST POINT: 12,799 ft., Granite Peak.

LOWEST POINT: 1,862 ft., Kootenai River.

TIME ZONE(S): Mountain. DST.

MINIMUM AGE FOR DRIVERS: 15 on completion of driver's education.

SEAT BELT/CHILD RESTRAINT LAWS: Seat belts required for driver and all passengers; child restraints required for under 4 or under 40 pounds.

HELMETS FOR MOTORCYCLISTS: Required for under 18.

RADAR DETECTORS: Permitted.

FIREARMS LAWS: Vary by state and/or county. Contact the Montana Department of Justice, 301 S. Park, Drawer 10081, Helena, MT 59626; phone (406) 444-1263.

HOLIDAYS: Jan. 1; Martin Luther King Jr. Day (3rd Mon. in Jan.); Lincoln's Birthday, Feb. 12; Washington's Birthday, Feb. (3rd Mon.); Memorial Day, May (last Mon.); July 4; Labor Day, Sept. (1st Mon.); Columbus Day, Oct. (2nd Mon.); Veterans Day, Nov. 11; Election Day; Thanksgiving; Dec. 25.

TAXES: Montana does not have a statewide sales tax. Designated resort communities may enact a resort tax of up to 3 percent for goods and services. There is a 7 percent statewide Lodging Tax.

STATE INFORMATION CENTERS: Welcome centers are on US 2 1 mile east of Culbertson; at jct. Main St. and US 2 in Shelby; off I-94 in Wibaux; on I-90 southbound .5 miles east of Hardin; at jct. US 191 and US 20N in West Yellowstone; and off I-15 southbound in Dillon. The Highway Building in Helena shares information about highway conditions and construction; phone (406) 444-6200 or (800) 226-7623.

FURTHER INFORMATION FOR VISITORS:

Travel Montana
1424 Ninth Ave.
Helena, MT 59620
(406) 841-2870
(800) 847-4868 out of Mont.

FISHING AND HUNTING REGULATIONS:

Montana Department of Fish, Wildlife & Parks
1420 E. Sixth Ave.
Helena, MT 59620
(406) 444-2535
(406) 444-1200 (TTY)

NATIONAL FOREST INFORMATION:

U.S. Forest Service
Northern Region
Federal Bldg.
Missoula, MT 59801
(406) 329-3511

Montana Temperature Averages Maximum / Minimum

From the records of the National Weather Service

	JAN	FEB	MAR	APR	MAY	JUN	JUL	AUG	SEP	OCT	NOV	DEC
Billings	33/13	36/15	43/23	57/34	68/43	76/51	89/58	86/55	75/46	63/37	46/26	39/19
Great Falls	32/14	34/15	41/21	55/33	66/42	72/49	84/56	81/54	70/46	59/38	44/26	37/20
Havre	26/6	29/8	40/18	57/32	69/43	75/51	86/57	83/54	72/44	60/35	42/21	33/12
Kalispell	26/9	32/12	40/19	55/30	65/39	72/46	83/49	80/46	69/39	55/31	37/21	29/16
Miles City	27/6	32/9	42/19	59/33	71/44	79/53	90/60	88/58	75/47	62/36	44/22	34/13

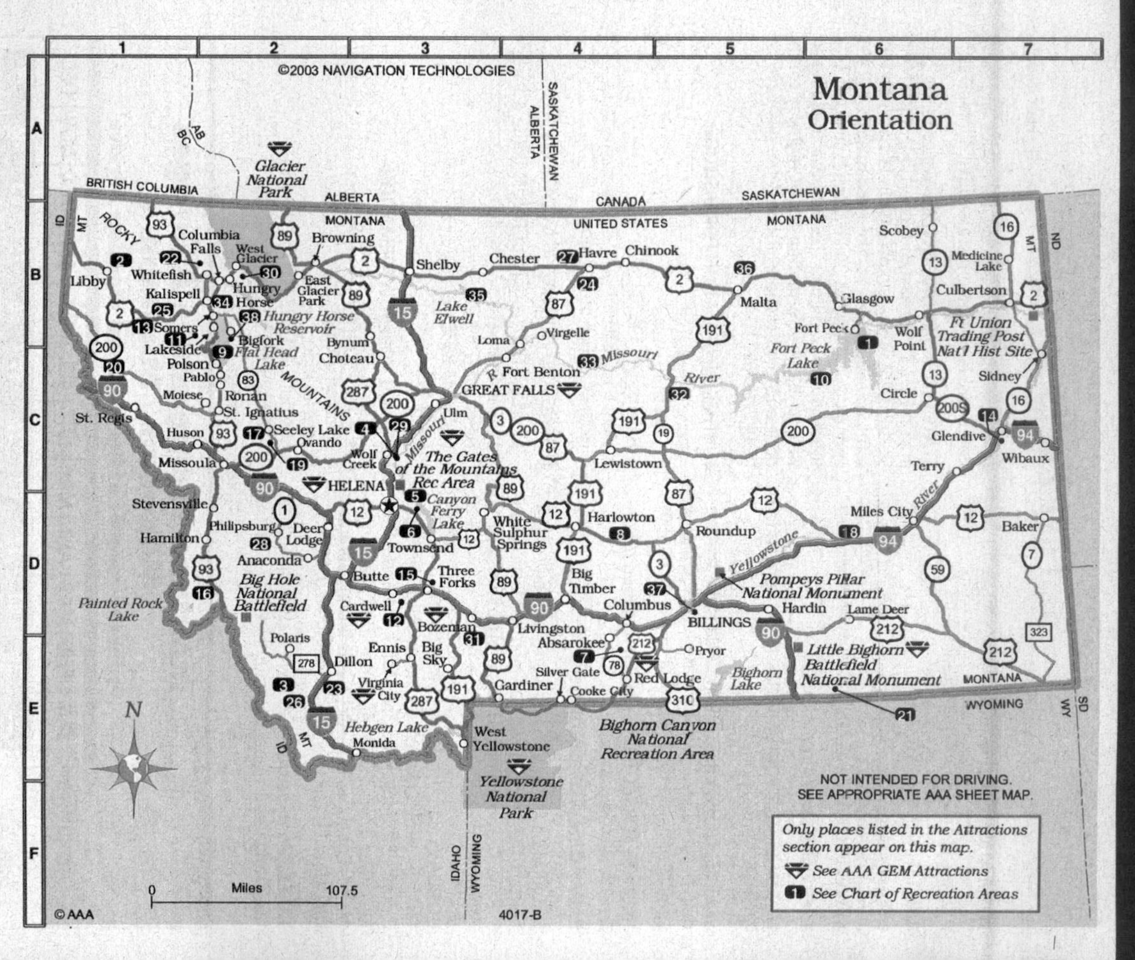
Montana
Orientation
©2003 NAVIGATION TECHNOLOGIES
NOT INTENDED FOR DRIVING.
SEE APPROPRIATE AAA SHEET MAP.
Only places listed in the Attractions section appear on this map.
See AAA GEM Attractions
See Chart of Recreation Areas
CANADA
UNITED STATES
BRITISH COLUMBIA
ALBERTA
SASKATCHEWAN
MONTANA
ND
SD
WY
WYOMING
IDAHO
Glacier National Park
Yellowstone National Park
Bighorn Canyon National Recreation Area
Little Bighorn Battlefield National Monument
Pompeys Pillar National Monument
Big Hole National Battlefield
Ft Union Trading Post Nat'l Hist Site
The Gates of the Mountains Rec Area
ROCKY MOUNTAINS
Fort Peck Lake
Missouri River
Yellowstone River
Flat Head Lake
Hungry Horse Reservoir
Canyon Ferry Lake
Hebgen Lake
Lake Elwell
Bighorn Lake
Painted Rock Lake
HELENA
GREAT FALLS
BILLINGS
Missoula
Kalispell
Whitefish
Columbia Falls
West Glacier
Hungry Horse
Bigfork
Somers
Lakeside
Polson
Pablo
Ronan
St. Ignatius
Moiese
Huson
St. Regis
Libby
Browning
East Glacier Park
Shelby
Chester
Havre
Chinook
Malta
Glasgow
Fort Peck
Wolf Point
Scobey
Medicine Lake
Culbertson
Sidney
Circle
Glendive
Wibaux
Terry
Miles City
Baker
Lewistown
Fort Benton
Loma
Virgelle
Choteau
Bynum
Ulm
Wolf Creek
Seeley Lake
Ovando
Deer Lodge
Anaconda
Philipsburg
Stevensville
Hamilton
Butte
Cardwell
Three Forks
Townsend
White Sulphur Springs
Harlowton
Roundup
Big Timber
Columbus
Livingston
Bozeman
Big Sky
Ennis
Virginia City
Dillon
Polaris
Monida
West Yellowstone
Gardiner
Silver Gate
Cooke City
Absarokee
Red Lodge
Pryor
Hardin
Lame Deer
Miles
0
107.5
4017-B
©AAA

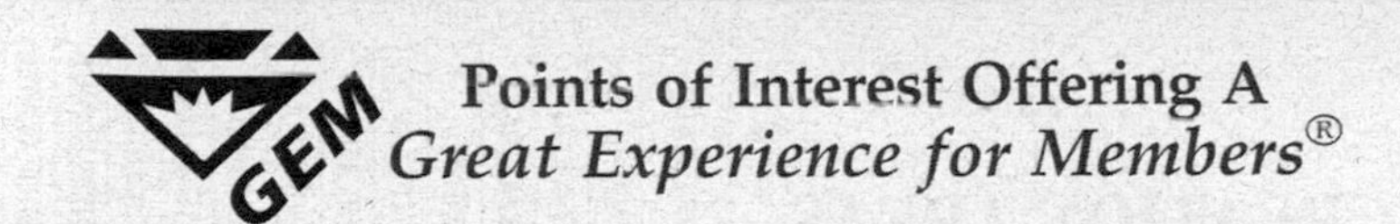

Points of Interest Offering A *Great Experience for Members®*

Bozeman (D-3)

MUSEUM OF THE ROCKIES—Dinosaurs and geology exhibits help explain Montana's past. See p. 88.

Cardwell (D-3)

LEWIS AND CLARK CAVERNS STATE PARK—This 3,005-acre park contains a limestone cavern featuring various rock formations. See p. 90.

Glacier National Park (A-2)

GLACIER NATIONAL PARK—Some 1 million acres of woods, lakes, glaciers and mountains offer refuge to nearly every large mammal found within the country. See p. 96.

GOING-TO-THE-SUN ROAD—Crossing the Continental Divide, this road is one of the most scenic in the country. See p. 100.

Great Falls (C-3)

C.M. RUSSELL MUSEUM—Works of the cowboy artist are displayed here. See p. 101.

LEWIS AND CLARK NATIONAL HISTORIC TRAIL INTERPRETIVE CENTER—The story of an incredible journey is told through displays, costumed interpreters, hands-on exhibits and special programs. See p. 102.

Helena (C-2)

CATHEDRAL OF ST. HELENA—This neo-Gothic church is modeled after the Votive Church in Vienna, Austria. See p. 104.

LAST CHANCE TOUR TRAIN—A 1-hour automotive train tour highlights Helena's past. See p. 104.

MONTANA HISTORICAL SOCIETY MUSEUM, LIBRARY AND ARCHIVES—This museum captures the essence of Montana with exhibits pertaining to area history. See p. 104.

STATE CAPITOL—Charles M. Russell's "Lewis and Clark Meeting Indians at Ross' Hole" is on display in this 1899 building made of Montana granite, copper and sandstone. See p. 104.

Helena National Forest

THE GATES OF THE MOUNTAINS RECREATION AREA—The Missouri River pushes through this area where 1,200-foot granite walls line the canyon. See p. 105.

Little Bighorn Battlefield National Monument (E-6)

LITTLE BIGHORN BATTLEFIELD NATIONAL MONUMENT—This 1.2-square-mile monument commemorates the American Indian wars and features a national cemetery, a visitor center, monuments, memorials and a museum. See p. 107.

Red Lodge (E-4)

BEARTOOTH SCENIC HIGHWAY—A series of scenic overlooks can be found along this 64-mile road that begins in Yellowstone National Park at 5,650 feet and rises to almost 11,000 feet at the Beartooth Plateau. See p. 113.

Virginia City (E-3)

VIRGINIA CITY—This former mining town now features some 20 restored buildings as well as opportunities for fishing, hunting and gold panning. See p. 116.

Yellowstone National Park

YELLOWSTONE NATIONAL PARK—The more than 3,400 acres of America's first national park are home to buffaloes, bighorn sheep, elk, moose and pronghorn antelopes as well as thousands of thermal pools and springs. See p. 173 in Wyoming.

RECREATION AREAS

	MAP LOCATION	CAMPING	PICNICKING	HIKING TRAILS	BOATING	BOAT RAMP	BOAT RENTAL	FISHING	SWIMMING	PETS ON LEASH	BICYCLE TRAILS	WINTER SPORTS	VISITOR CENTER	LODGE/CABINS	FOOD SERVICE
NATIONAL PARKS *(See place listings)*															
Glacier (A-2) 1,000,000 acres. Horse rental.		•	•	•	•	•	•	•	•	•		•	•	•	•
NATIONAL FORESTS *(See place listings)*															
Beaverhead-Deerlodge 3,392,930 acres. Southwestern Montana. Horse rental.		•	•	•	•	•		•	•	•	•	•		•	
Bitterroot 1,577,883 acres. Western Montana.		•	•	•	•	•		•	•	•	•	•	•	•	
Custer/Dakota Prairie Grasslands 1,112,382 acres. Southeastern Montana.		•	•	•				•	•	•	•	•		•	•
Flathead 2,330,029 acres. Northwestern Montana. Horse rental.		•	•	•	•	•		•	•	•	•	•	•	•	
Gallatin 1,735,239 acres. South-central Montana. Horse rental.		•	•	•	•	•	•	•	•	•	•	•	•	•	•
Helena 976,000 acres. West-central Montana.		•	•	•	•	•		•	•	•		•		•	
Kootenai 2,245,000 acres. Northwestern Montana. Horse rental.		•	•	•	•	•	•	•	•	•	•	•	•	•	•
Lewis and Clark 1,843,397 acres. Central Montana.		•	•	•	•	•		•	•	•		•		•	
Lolo 2,100,000 acres. Western Montana. Horse rental.		•	•	•	•	•		•	•		•	•	•	•	•
NATIONAL RECREATION AREAS *(See place listings)*															
Bighorn Canyon (E-5) 120,000 acres.		•	•	•	•	•	•	•	•	•			•		•
ARMY CORPS OF ENGINEERS															
Fort Peck Lake (B-6) off SR 24 in Fort Peck. *(See Fort Peck p. 95)*	1														
Downstream 347 acres 1 mi. e. of Fort Peck off SR 117. Museum, playground.		•	•	•	•	•		•		•					
Dredge Cuts 650 acres .5 mi. n. of Fort Peck off SR 117. Playground.			•		•	•		•	•	•					
Fourchette Bay 80 acres 60 mi. s.e. of Malta off SR 191.		•	•		•	•		•	•	•					
Nelson Creek 468 acres 45 mi. s. of Fort Peck off SR 24.		•	•		•	•		•	•	•					
The Pines 927 acres 4.5 mi. n.w. of Fort Peck on SR 24, 14 mi. s.w. via a gravel road, then 12 mi. s.e. via a gravel road. Playground.		•	•		•	•		•	•	•					
Rock Creek 345 acres 32 mi. s.e. of Fort Peck off SR 24.		•	•		•	•		•	•	•					
Libby Dam (Lake Koocanusa) (B-1) 46,000 acres 17 mi. n.e. of Libby on SR 37. *(See Libby p. 107)*	2	•	•	•	•	•		•	•	•		•	•	•	•
STATE															
Bannack (E-2) 196 acres 21 mi. w. of Dillon on SR 278, then 3 mi. s. Historic. *(See Dillon p. 93)*	3	•	•					•		•		•	•		
Beartooth Wildlife Management Area (C-3) 27,000 acres 10 mi. s.e. of Wolf Creek via a gravel road.	4	•	•		•	•		•	•	•					
Black Sandy (D-3) 55 acres 14 mi. n.e. of Helena via I-15 and CR 415.	5	•	•		•	•		•	•	•				•	
Canyon Ferry Lake (D-3) e. of Helena.	6				•	•	•								
Canyon Ferry 5,000 acres s.e. of Helena off US 287 on Canyon Ferry Lake. Hunting.		•	•		•	•	•	•	•	•					•
Cave Bay 19 mi. e. of Helena via US 287 and CR 284.			•		•	•	•	•	•	•					•
Chinaman 19 mi. e. of Helena via US 287 and CR 284.		•	•		•	•		•	•	•					
Court Sheriff 18 mi. e. of Helena via US 287 and CR 284.		•	•		•			•	•	•					
Hellgate 27 mi. e. of Helena via US 287 and CR 284.		•	•		•	•		•	•	•					
Indian Road 1 mi. n. of Townsend on US 287.		•	•		•	•		•		•					
Ponderosa 18 mi. e. of Helena via US 287 and CR 284.		•	•					•		•					
Riverside 18 mi. e. of Helena via US 287 and CR 284.		•	•		•	•		•		•					
Silos 8 mi. n.w. of Townsend off US 287.		•	•		•	•		•		•					•
White Earth 5 mi. e. of Winston.		•	•		•	•		•		•					
Cooney (E-4) 304 acres 5 mi. w. of Boyd via a gravel road.	7	•	•		•	•		•	•	•					•

RECREATION AREAS

	MAP LOCATION	CAMPING	PICNICKING	HIKING TRAILS	BOATING	BOAT RAMP	BOAT RENTAL	FISHING	SWIMMING	PETS ON LEASH	BICYCLE TRAILS	WINTER SPORTS	VISITOR CENTER	LODGE/CABINS	FOOD SERVICE
Deadman's Basin (D-4) 500 acres 29 mi. e. of Harlowton off US 12.	8	●	●		●	●		●	●	●					
Flathead Lake (C-2) n. of Polson on SR 93. *(See Polson p. 112)*	9				●	●	●	●	●						
Big Arm 55 acres 15 mi. n. of Polson on US 93.		●	●		●	●		●	●	●					
Finley Point 24 acres about 12 mi. n.e. of Polson off SR 35.		●	●		●	●		●	●	●					
Wayfarers 68 acres 1 mi. s. of Bigfork off SR 35.		●	●		●	●		●	●	●					
West Shore 146 acres about 20 mi. s. of Kalispell on US 93.		●	●	●	●	●		●	●	●					
Yellow Bay 10 acres 20 mi. n.e. of Polson off SR 35.		●	●	●	●	●		●	●	●					
Hell Creek (C-6) 172 acres 26 mi. n. of Jordan via a gravel road on Fort Peck Reservoir.	10	●	●		●	●	●	●	●	●				●	●
Lake Mary Ronan (B-1) 76 acres 7 mi. n.w. of Dayton off US 93.	11	●	●		●	●		●	●	●					
Lewis and Clark Caverns (D-3) 3,005 acres 7.3 mi. e. of Cardwell on I-90. *(See Cardwell p. 90)*	12	●	●	●						●			●		●
Logan (B-1) 18 acres 45 mi. w. of Kalispell off US 2.	13	●	●		●	●		●	●	●					
Makoshika (C-7) 11,531 acres 1 mi. s. of Glendive at 1301 Snyder Ave. *(See Glendive p. 101)*	14	●	●	●						●		●	●		
Missouri Headwaters (D-3) 527 acres 3 mi. e. of Three Forks, then 3 mi. n. of US 10. *(See Three Forks p. 116)*	15	●	●	●	●	●		●		●			●		
Painted Rocks (D-1) 263 acres 20 mi. s.w. of Conner off SR 473.	16	●	●		●	●		●		●					
Placid Lake (C-2) 32 acres 6 mi. s.w. of Seeley Lake via CR 83.	17	●	●		●	●		●	●	●					
Rosebud (D-6) 32 acres e. of Forsyth off I-94.	18	●	●		●	●		●		●					
Salmon Lake (C-2) 42 acres 5 mi. s. of Seeley Lake on SR 83.	19	●	●	●	●	●		●	●	●					
Thompson Falls (C-1) 36 acres 3 mi. w. of Thompson Falls off SR 200.	20	●	●	●	●	●		●		●					
Tongue River Reservoir (E-6) 640 acres 6 mi. n. of Decker on CR 314, then 1 mi. e.	21	●	●		●	●		●	●	●					●
Whitefish Lake (B-1) 10 acres 5 mi. w. of Whitefish on US 93.	22	●	●		●	●	●	●	●	●				●	●
OTHER															
Barretts Park (E-2) 38 acres 8 mi. s.w. of Dillon off I-15.	23	●	●		●			●	●	●					
Beaver Creek (B-4) 10,000 acres 11 mi. s. of Havre on CR 234. Birdwatching.	24	●	●	●	●			●	●	●		●			
Bitterroot Lake (B-1) 36 acres 5 mi. n. of US 2 at Marion.	25	●	●		●	●		●	●					●	
Clark Canyon Reservoir (E-2) 4,131 acres 20 mi. s.w. of Dillon on I-15. Hunting.	26	●	●		●	●	●	●	●	●					
Fresno Reservoir (B-4) 25,668 acres n.w. of Havre. Hunting, water skiing.	27		●		●	●		●	●	●					
Georgetown Lake (D-2) 2,850 acres 15 mi. w. of Anaconda on US 10A. Water skiing; playground. *(See Beaverhead-Deerlodge National Forest p. 84)*	28	●	●	●	●	●		●	●	●		●		●	●
Holter Lake (C-3) 22 acres 2 mi. e. of Wolf Creek on Missouri River Rd., then 3 mi. s. via a gravel road. *(See Wolf Creek p. 119)*	29	●	●		●	●		●	●	●				●	●
Hungry Horse Reservoir (B-2) 6,836 acres 10 mi. e. of Columbia Falls on SR 40, then s. 5 mi. via a gravel road. Hunting. *(See Flathead National Forest p. 94)*	30	●	●	●	●	●		●	●		●	●	●		
Hyalite Canyon (E-3) 35,000 acres 14 mi. s. of Bozeman on SR 85.	31	●	●	●	●	●		●	●	●	●	●			
James Kipp (C-5) 465 acres 65 mi. n.e. of Lewistown off US 191.	32	●	●		●	●		●							
Judith Landing (C-4) 44 mi. s.e. of Big Sandy on CR 236.	33	●			●	●		●							
Lake Blaine (B-2) 13 acres 7 mi. e. of Kalispell.	34	●		●	●	●		●	●	●	●			●	●
Lake Elwell (B-3) 6,197 acres 18 mi. s.w. of Chester.	35	●	●		●	●		●	●	●					●
Nelson Reservoir (B-5) 7,702 acres 18 mi. n.e. of Malta off US 2.	36	●	●		●	●		●	●	●					
Riverfront Park (D-5) 1 mi. s. of Billings on CR 416.	37		●	●	●			●			●	●			
Swan Lake (B-2) 10 acres 14 mi. s.e. of Bigfork on SR 83. Water skiing.	38	●	●		●	●		●	●	●					

Points of Interest

ABSAROKEE (E-4) pop. 1,234, elev. 4,039′

RECREATIONAL ACTIVITIES

Horseback Riding

- SAVE **Paintbrush Adventures**, in Stillwater Valley n. of Yellowstone National Park. Write 86 N. Stillwater Rd., Absarokee, MT 59001. Other activities are offered. Trips daily. Phone (406) 328-4158.

White-water Rafting

- **Absaroka River Adventures**, 113 Grove St. Write P.O. Box 328, Absarokee, MT 59001. Other activities are offered. Daily 7 a.m.-10 p.m., May-Aug. Phone (406) 328-7440 or (800) 334-7238.
- SAVE **Beartooth Whitewater** meets passengers off SR 78 at the n. end of town. Write P.O. Box 781, Red Lodge, MT 59068. Other activities are offered. Daily May-Sept. Phone (406) 446-3142 or (800) 799-3142.

ANACONDA (D-2) pop. 9,417, elev. 5,288′

Because it had ample water and was surrounded by one of the world's richest copper deposits, Anaconda was chosen for the site of a copper smelter by the originator of Montana's copper industry, Marcus Daly. Daly, an Irish immigrant who was a manager of a mine in Utah, bought the mine when it was thought worthless after the silver lode ran out. However, Daly saw the mine's potential in its copper reserves—with the invention of the telephone and telegraph, copper wire was in high demand. By the time Daly died in 1900, he was one of the world's richest men.

Daly also founded the nearby town of Hamilton *(see place listing p. 102)*, where he spent summers with his family. Today all that is left of Daly's smelter is the 585-foot smokestack. The Stack Interpretive Center on 4th Street has exhibits about copper production.

A number of buildings from the 1800s remain, including the Montana Hotel, corner of Park and Main streets, which was supposed to house the state legislators; Deer Lodge County Courthouse, 800 S. Main St.; City Hall Center at 401 E. Commercial St.; Hearst Library at Fourth and Main streets; and St. Mark's Episcopal Church, corner of Fifth and Main streets. Anaconda's architecture spans Romanesque to Victorian styles. At 305 Main St. is the art deco, neoclassical 1936 Washoe Theatre.

A popular scenic highway, SR 1, begins in Anaconda and heads west over Flint Creek Pass.

Anaconda Visitor's Center: 306 E. Park St., Anaconda, MT 59711; phone (406) 563-2400.

Self-guiding tours: The visitor center offers a $2 walking-tour map of the historic district.

VINTAGE BUS TOUR departs from the Anaconda Visitor's Center, 306 E. Park St. Highlights of the sightseeing trip in a 1936 touring bus include the historic business district, several churches, the Washoe Theatre, the smokestack interpretive site, a Jack Nicklaus-designed golf course on reclaimed smelter property, the Marcus Daly mansion and one of the state's oldest fish hatcheries. Allow 1 hour minimum. Tours are given Mon.-Sat. at 10 and 2, mid-May to mid-Sept. Fare $5; under 6, $1.50. MC, VI. Phone (406) 563-2400.

BAKER (D-7) pop. 1,695

Named for the superintendent of construction of the Milwaukee Road, Baker is near the middle of vast oil and gas fields. Until 1915 Baker was solely a grazing and farming town. Then a driller in search of water struck a natural-gas pocket, setting fire to his well, which burned as a natural torch for 6 years. Baker is now a center for local petroleum and agricultural interests.

Baker Chamber of Commerce: P.O. Box 849, Baker, MT 59313; phone (406) 778-2266 or (800) 862-2537.

MEDICINE ROCKS STATE PARK is 24 mi. s. on SR 7. The 320-acre park contains huge sandstone formations once used by American Indians for ceremonies. Free.

BEAVERHEAD-DEERLODGE NATIONAL FOREST

Elevations in the forest range from 4,075 ft. in the valleys to 11,361 ft. on Hilgard Peak. Refer to AAA maps for additional elevation information.

Beaverhead-Deerlodge National Forest is part of the huge complex of national forests occupying most of western Montana. In 1996, Deerlodge National Forest's 1,194,124 acres (nearly 100 square miles) were combined with Beaverhead National Forest to form a 3.3-million-acre outdoor recreation area.

Glaciated peaks rise from broad valleys in the area to form some of Montana's most majestic ranges—the Anaconda, Bitterroot, Beaverhead, Flint Creek, Gravelly, Highland, Madison, Tobacco Root and Sapphire. Mountains in these ranges are among the loftiest in the state; more than 40 surpass 10,000 feet. Mount Evans rises to 10,604 feet, and several more, including Hilgard Peak, exceed 11,000 feet.

From the snowpack of these ranges spring the Big Hole, Beaverhead and Ruby rivers, which form

three major tributaries of the Jefferson River. The high country also supplies some of the tributaries of the Madison River. The Clark Fork River flows from its headwaters west of the Continental Divide to Idaho's Lake Pend Oreille.

Through this maze of mountains and river valleys Sacajawea led Meriwether Lewis and William Clark in their search for a passage to the Pacific. This was the land of Sacajawea's people, the Shoshones, who reprovisioned and led the expedition over Lemhi Pass in 1805 and north to a final passage to the West. Despite the inroads of progress—lumbering, mining and ranching—much of the forest's lands have changed little since Lewis and Clark's visit.

Within the forest are portions of the Anaconda-Pintler and Lee Metcalf wilderness areas and a large number of roadless tracts. Typical features of roadless areas are glacial lakes, trout streams and rugged mountain vistas.

The Anaconda-Pintler Wilderness straddles 30 miles of the Anaconda Range and the Continental Divide. The land gradually rises from dense stands of lodgepole pine to open parks dotted with lakes, culminating in jagged peaks in the heart of the range. Anglers prize the clear mountain streams and alpine lakes for their abundance and variety of trout.

Another major area is the Taylor-Hilgard portion of the Lee Metcalf Wilderness. This unit is one of the four portions of wilderness along the spine of the Madison Range, which lies just northwest of Yellowstone National Park. Soaring peaks, knife-edged ridges and alpine lakes are characteristics of this popular area. Birdwatchers will find more than 260 species frequenting a variety of habitats in the forest. The region provides winter range for bighorn sheep and mountain goats and a home to grizzly and black bears, mule deer, mountain lions, elk and moose.

Several endangered species reside in Beaverhead-Deerlodge National Forest. The bald eagle nests in the southeastern Gravelly Range and winters along the Red Rock, Ruby, Jefferson, Madison, Big Hole and Beaverhead rivers. Most migration and wintering activities occur in the large river valleys adjoining the forest. The endangered gray wolf is an occasional visitor to parts of the Continental Divide southwest of Dillon. Threatened grizzly bears occupy portions of the Madison Range within the Lee Metcalf Wilderness and are occasional visitors to the Tobacco Root Mountains and the Gravelly Range.

The forest offers fishing streams, hiking trails, groomed snowmobile trails, developed campgrounds and sites for motorized boating. Visitors can explore many old mines near Deer Lodge, plus the ghost town of Elkhorn, an 1880s mining town with a few corporeal residents. Fourteen miles west of Anaconda on SR 1 is Georgetown Lake *(see Recreation Chart)*, one of the area's busiest recreation sites and an area favored for its excellent fishing. Snowmobiling and cross-country and downhill skiing are available at Discovery Basin, north of Georgetown Lake.

The forest's most unusual feature is Sheepshead Recreation Area, a site designed for the physically impaired. In addition to meadows, forests and a 15-acre lake, the setting offers paved trails, a picnic area and a fishing pier.

Detailed information about campgrounds and recreational opportunities is available at the district ranger stations in Butte, Deer Lodge, Dillon, Ennis, Philipsburg, Sheridan, Whitehall, Wisdom and Wise River. For further information contact the Beaverhead-Deerlodge National Forest Supervisor's Office, USDA Service Center, 420 Barrett St., Dillon, MT 59725; phone (406) 683-3900. *See Recreation Chart and the AAA Northwestern CampBook.*

BIGFORK (B-2) pop. 1,421, elev. 2,968′

On the bay formed by the Swan River on the northeastern shore of Flathead Lake, Bigfork once was a small fishing village and trade center for nearby orchards and farms. Its reputation as an artists' and writers' colony now make it a popular cultural retreat. Among recreational pursuits are snowmobiling and skiing in winter and a host of water sports in summer.

Glacially formed Flathead Lake is the largest natural body of fresh water west of the Mississippi River; at points along its 38-mile length the lake stretches 15 miles wide. Jewel Basin, one of the country's most popular hiking areas with 35 miles of trails, is 11 miles north. A Flathead National Forest *(see place listing p. 94)* ranger station provides information about recreational opportunities in the nearby mountains.

Cultural highlights in Bigfork include the Riverbend Concert Series, which stages Sunday performances throughout the summer. From late June through Labor Day, Bigfork Summer Playhouse presents a regular repertory of Broadway musicals; phone (406) 837-4886 for ticket information.

Bigfork Area Chamber of Commerce: 8155 SR 35, P.O. Box 237, Bigfork, MT 59911; phone (406) 837-5888.

***QUESTA* SAIL BOAT** departs from Bigfork 4. This restored 1929 51-foot racing sloop offers 2-hour tours on Flathead Lake. A sister ship is available in case the *Questa* is filled. Tours depart daily at 1:30 and 7, mid-June to mid-Sept. Day fare $39; over 64 and under 12, $32. Sunset fare $44. Reservations are recommended. MC, VI. Phone (406) 837-5569.

BIG HOLE NATIONAL BATTLEFIELD (D-2)

Big Hole National Battlefield is 10 miles west of Wisdom on SR 43. Covering 655 acres of Nez Perce National Historical Park *(see place listing in Idaho p. 59)*, the site commemorates the battle fought Aug. 9-10, 1877, when U.S. troops aided by civilian volunteers staged a surprise attack against several bands of Nez Perce Indians. The Nez Perce were attempting to escape confinement to a reservation by fleeing to Canada from a conflict begun in Idaho.

Although victorious at Big Hole, the Nez Perce sustained severe losses—approximately 90 men, women and children were killed. These losses forced their surrender 2 months later on Oct. 5, 1877, in the Bear Paw Mountains. Some 150 Nez Perce escaped to Canada.

The battlefield became a military reserve in 1883 and a national battlefield in 1963. The visitor center displays American Indian and military items and presents an audiovisual program about the battle. Interpretive trails traverse the battlefield to the areas where the soldiers retreated and the Nez Perce camped. Guided walks are available.

Allow 30 minutes minimum for the visitor center and 1 hour, 30 minutes for the battlefield. Park open daily 9-5:30, Memorial Day-Sept. 30; 9-5, rest of year. Closed Jan. 1, Martin Luther King Jr. Day, Thanksgiving and Dec. 25. Battlefield road is closed to automobile traffic in winter; skiing and snowshoeing are permitted. Admission $5 per private vehicle or $3 per person arriving by bicycle, bus, motorcycle or on foot, Memorial Day-Sept. 30; free rest of year. Phone (406) 689-3155.

BIGHORN CANYON NATIONAL RECREATION AREA (E-4)

In Montana and northern Wyoming, Bighorn Canyon National Recreation Area centers on a 71-mile-long lake bounded by steep canyon walls. Covering about 120,000 acres, the area features facilities for boat launching, picnicking and camping at Ok-A-Beh Marina, 42 miles southwest of Hardin via SR 313.

Horseshoe Bend in Wyoming, 14 miles north of Lovell, Wyo., via SR 37, and Barry's Landing in Montana, 32 miles south of Yellowtail Dam by boat or north of Lovell, Wyo., via SR 37, have areas for swimming, camping, picnicking and boat launching. Hunting and fishing also are available.

Campfire programs are given at Afterbay and Horseshoe Bend campgrounds on Friday and Saturday from Memorial Day through Labor Day. Guided nature and history walks also are conducted in May and September.

Admission to the recreation area is $5 for a daily pass. Yellowtail Visitor Center in Fort Smith offers an orientation film about the area and exhibits about wildlife, Yellowtail Dam and American Indian culture. The center is open daily 8-5, Memorial Day-Labor Day; schedule varies Apr. 1-day before Memorial Day and day after Labor Day-Sept. 30. Phone (406) 666-3218. The solar-heated Bighorn Canyon Visitor Center, at the junction of US 310 and US 14A in Lovell, Wyo., is open daily 8-6; closed Jan. 1, Thanksgiving and Dec. 25. Phone (307) 548-2251.

For further information, contact Bighorn Canyon National Recreation Area, P.O. Box 7458, Fort Smith, MT 59035; to verify schedule phone (406) 666-2412. *See Recreation Chart and the AAA Northwestern CampBook.*

YELLOWTAIL DAM is near Fort Smith. Yellowtail Dam Visitor Center has historical displays and information about the construction of what is said to be the highest dam in the Missouri River Basin. Allow 1 hour minimum. Daily 9-5, Memorial Day-Labor Day. Free. Phone (406) 666-3218.

BIG SKY (E-3) pop. 1,221

Surrounded by the mountain meadows and forested slopes of Gallatin National Forest *(see place listing p. 96)* and the Spanish Peaks Wilderness, Big Sky is an all-year resort community. Lone Mountain serves as the centerpiece for this village conceived and developed by newsman Chet Huntley.

Skiing and snowmobiling are popular in winter, while summer activity revolves around hiking, horseback riding, white-water rafting and mountain biking.

YELLOWSTONE TOURING COMPANY picks up passengers in the Big Sky and West Yellowstone areas. Narrated van and bus tours of Yellowstone National Park are offered. The Lower Loop Tour includes the Fountain Paintpots, Midway Geyser Basin, Old Faithful, Yellowstone Lake and Mud Volcano. The Upper Loop Tour visits the northern portion of the park and includes Norris Geyser Basin, Mammoth Hot Springs and waterfalls of the Grand Canyon of the Yellowstone.

Tour pickups occur daily 7 a.m.-8 a.m., with returns at 5:30, June-Sept. Lower Loop Tours and Upper Loop Tours are given on alternating days. Fare (depending on pickup point) $49-$60; under 12, $42-$53. Tours require at least five passengers. Inquire about refund policies. AX, DS, MC, VI. Phone (406) 995-4895 or (800) 423-4742.

DID YOU KNOW

Montana is home to
11 American Indian
tribes housed on
11 reservations.

RECREATIONAL ACTIVITIES

Skiing

- **Big Sky Resort**, at Lone Mountain. Write P.O. Box 160001, Big Sky, MT 59716. Other activities are offered. Daily mid-June to mid-Sept. and mid-Nov. to late Apr. Phone (406) 995-5000 or (800) 548-4486.

White-water Rafting

- **Geyser Whitewater Expeditions** is on US 191 1 mi. s. of the entrance to Big Sky Resort at 46651 Gallatin Rd. Write P.O. Box 160729, Big Sky, MT 59716. Daily May 1 to mid-Sept. Phone (406) 995-4989 or (800) 914-9031. *See color ad p. 118.*
- **Yellowstone Raft Co./Mountain Whitewater** is 7 mi. n. on US 191. Write P.O. Box 160262, Big Sky, MT 59716. Daily Memorial Day to mid-Sept. Phone (406) 995-4613 or (800) 348-4376.

BIG TIMBER (D-4) pop. 1,650, elev. 4,075′

BIG TIMBER WATERSLIDE is 9 mi. e. off I-90 exit 377. Seven large waterslides, a Junior Olympic-size pool, wading pools, a train, bumper boats and a moat featuring a lazy river ride are some of the amusements offered. Picnicking is permitted. Food is available. Daily 10-7, early June-Labor Day. Admission $14.95; ages 3-18, $11.95. Pool pass $5.95. Phone (406) 932-6570.

CRAZY MOUNTAIN MUSEUM is off I-90 exit 367, s. to Frontage Rd., then e. to Cemetery Rd. Displays relate the history of the Sweet Grass area. Featured are a one-room schoolhouse, a Norwegian *stabbur* (storehouse), a model of the area as it appeared in 1907, a 1915 Ford, paintings by Jessica Zemsky and Jack Hines, photographs, the Leo Cremer Rodeo exhibit, printed history and memorabilia from the 1900s. Changing exhibits are offered. Tues.-Sun. 1-4:30, Memorial Day-Labor Day. Free. Phone (406) 932-5126.

BILLINGS (D-5) pop. 89,847, elev. 3,124′

In 1823 at Alkali Creek, the site of present-day Billings, 400 Blackfeet attacked American Fur Co. trappers. Some pelts taken by the Blackfeet were traded to Hudson's Bay Co. and later appeared on the London market. An American recognized the stolen pelts, touching off an international incident.

The Northern Pacific Railroad arrived in 1882, literally putting Billings on the map. Refusing to pay the exorbitant prices, the landowners in Coulson were demanding, Northern Pacific Railroad laid out a new city 2 miles upriver and named it in honor of its president, Frederick Billings. In 5 months the town grew from a single building to 250 buildings and 2,000 citizens.

The Rimrocks, Billings' most striking natural feature, rise 400 feet above the Yellowstone Valley, running the length of the city and beyond. Legend has it that Crow warriors once rode over Sacrifice Cliff to appease their gods and to halt the spread of smallpox among their people. At the top of the Rimrocks on Black Otter Trail is Boothill Cemetery. The only vestige of the town of Coulson, the cemetery is the final resting place of two dozen individuals, including peace officers, massacre victims and Muggins Taylor, the scout who brought the world the news of Lt. Col. George Custer's last stand.

Pictograph Cave State Park, 7 miles southeast at the I-90 Lockwood exit, features caverns that have sheltered people of many American Indian cultures. Pictorial records adorn the walls of one cave.

Billings Area Chamber of Commerce and Visitor Center: 815 S. 27th St., P.O. Box 31177, Billings, MT 59107-1177; phone (406) 252-4016 or (800) 735-2635.

Self-guiding tours: A map of historic sites can be obtained at the chamber of commerce.

Shopping areas: Rimrock Mall, at the junction of Central Avenue and 24th Street West, includes Dillard's and JCPenney among its 95 stores.

CHIEF BLACK OTTER TRAIL follows the edge of the Rimrocks north of the city. Chief Black Otter was a Crow war chief who was killed in a battle with the Sioux. His grave and that of Yellowstone Kelly, renowned American Indian scout, trapper and governor of the Philippines, are two points of interest along this scenic drive.

Range Rider of the Yellowstone stands on the Rimrocks off the Chief Black Otter Trail. Cowboy motion picture star William S. Hart posed for the bronze statue of a cowboy and his horse, which commands an impressive view of the city.

FUN ADVENTURES TROLLEY TOURS picks up passengers at area hotels. Among the trolley tours offered are a 1.5-hour downtown tour highlighting historic landmarks and a narrated 3-hour tour tracing Lewis and Clark's route along the Yellowstone River to Pompey's Pillar National Monument. A half-day trip to Little Bighorn Battlefield, combination tours and an architectural walking tour also are available. Allow 1 hour, 30 minutes minimum. Downtown tour departs daily at 9:30 and 11:30. Lewis and Clark tour departs daily at 8:30. Downtown trolley fare $20, under 13 free. Lewis and Clark fare $34; under 10, $24. MC, VI. Phone (406) 254-7180.

MOSS MANSION is at 914 Division St. An Old World-style house designed by architect H.J. Hardenbergh, this massive red sandstone mansion completed in 1903 has ornate ceilings, woodwork, molding and other architectural details. The Moss family occupied the house until 1984 and left the interior intact. Thus the three-story mansion is an unusually complete example of early 20th-century decorative arts.

Guided tours are given on the hour Mon.-Sat. 9-4 (also Wed. 4-7), Sun. 1-3, June 1-Sept. 15; daily 1-3, rest of year. Last tour begins at closing. Closed Jan. 1, third week in Nov., Thanksgiving and Dec. 25. Fee $6; over 62 and students with ID $5; ages 6-12, $3. Phone (406) 256-5100 to confirm schedule.

PETER YEGEN JR. YELLOWSTONE COUNTY MUSEUM is at 1950 Terminal Cir., across from Billings Logan International Airport. Exhibits depict the history of Montana and the northern Plains, including the arrival of Lewis and Clark. The Landmarks Gallery contains works of artists known locally and internationally. Allow 30 minutes minimum. Mon.-Fri. 10:30-5, Sat. 10:30-3; closed major holidays. Donations. Phone (406) 256-6811.

WESTERN HERITAGE CENTER is at 2822 Montana Ave. In the 1901 Parmly Billings Library, the center features changing exhibits about the history and culture of the Yellowstone River region. Audiovisual programs are presented regularly. Allow 1 hour minimum. Tues.-Sat. 10-5, Sun. 1-5; closed holidays. Free. Phone (406) 256-6809.

YELLOWSTONE ART MUSEUM is at 401 N. 27th St. Housed in the original Yellowstone County jail, the museum offers changing exhibitions of historic and contemporary art. A permanent exhibit features contemporary Western art. Historic works by cowboy illustrator Will James also are presented. Guided tours are available by appointment. Allow 30 minutes minimum. Tues.-Sat. 10-5 (also Thurs. 5-8), Sun. noon-5. Admission $7; senior citizens $5; ages 6-18, $3. Phone (406) 256-6804.

ZOOMONTANA is off I-90 exit 443, .9 mi. w. on Zoo Dr., then just s. to 2100 S. Shiloh Rd. A 72-acre home to northern latitude temperate animals, the zoo includes river otters, Sika deer, red pandas, Siberian tigers, gray wolves, bighorn sheep, wolverines, black-footed ferrets and bald eagles. Also featured are a sensory garden, a Native American encampment, an education center with exhibits, an amphitheater and a playground.

Picnicking is permitted. Food is available. Allow 2 hours minimum. Daily 10-5; closed Jan. 1, Thanksgiving and Dec. 25. Last admission 1 hour before closing. Admission $6; over 64, $4; ages 3-15, $3. AX, MC, VI. Phone (406) 652-8100.

BITTERROOT NATIONAL FOREST

Elevations in the forest range from 3,500 ft. at the Kootenai Creek Trail to 10,175 ft. on Trapper Peak. Refer to AAA maps for additional elevation information.

Bitterroot National Forest is in Montana and Idaho. The Montana section curves around the headwaters of the Bitterroot River, reaching into the Sapphire and Bitterroot ranges. This is a region of strong contrasts, with rolling subalpine woodland, open parks and lakes, and jagged, glaciated peaks and canyons.

The national forest takes its name from the bitterroot plant, whose pink flowers carpet the valleys and foothills from late April to July. Meriwether Lewis, on his journey through the region, added the bitterroot flower to his botanical collection and sampled the meal that the American Indians ground from its root. A British botanist later honored Lewis' contribution by using his name as the basis of the flower's Latin name, *Lewisia rediviva.*

As one of the first forest reserves, Bitterroot National Forest also is the site of the first Forest Service ranger station, at Alta. The forest's Idaho portion encompasses the headwaters of the Selway River and a stretch of the Salmon River. Both rivers are components of the National Wild and Scenic River system. Wilderness areas, which occupy about half of the forest's 1.6 million acres, include portions of the Frank Church River of No Return, the Selway-Bitterroot and the Anaconda-Pintler.

For further information contact Bitterroot National Forest, 1801 N. 1st St., Hamilton, MT 59840; phone (406) 363-7161. *See Recreation Chart and the AAA Northwestern CampBook.*

BOZEMAN (D-3) pop. 27,509, elev. 4,755′

Bozeman was named for John Bozeman, who brought the first wagon train of pioneers to settle the Gallatin Valley. The trail he blazed became not only a highway for settlers and miners but also a flashpoint between the American Indians and the settlers. Three years after bringing settlers to the valley, Bozeman was killed by the Sioux, and his trail remained unused for 9 years because of repeated attacks upon wayfarers.

The valley that Bozeman helped settle once was a neutral and sacred hunting ground known to the American Indians as the "Valley of the Flowers." The area has blossomed into one of the state's more agriculturally productive regions.

The city is a gateway to the nearby mountains in the national forests that flank the city and to Yellowstone National Park to the southeast.

One of the city's chief cultural resources is Montana State University, the largest unit of the state university system.

Bozeman Area Chamber of Commerce: 2000 Commerce Way, Bozeman, MT 59715; phone (406) 586-5421 or (800) 228-4224.

Self-guiding tours: Maps and brochures of the South Willson Historic District are available from Museum of the Rockies *(see attraction listing).*

AMERICAN COMPUTER MUSEUM is at 2304 N. Seventh Ave., Suite B, in Bridger Park Mall. Exhibits chronicle the evolution of the computer, from abacus to microchips. Guided tours are available. Allow 30 minutes minimum. Daily 9-5, June-Aug.; Tues.-Wed. and Fri.-Sat. noon-4, Thurs. 4-8, rest of year. Closed holidays. Admission $4; ages 6-12, $2. Phone (406) 582-1288.

GALLATIN COUNTY PIONEER MUSEUM is at 317 W. Main St. Housed in a 1911 county jail, the museum contains old photographs, American Indian artifacts and exhibits about early settlement and

20th-century history. Mon.-Sat. 10-4:30, June-Sept.; Tues.-Fri. 11-4, Sat. 1-4, rest of year. Free. Phone (406) 522-8122.

MUSEUM OF THE ROCKIES is s. of the Montana State University campus at S. Seventh Ave. and W. Kagy Blvd., opposite the football stadium. The museum interprets the history of the northern Rockies through dinosaur exhibits and displays pertaining to American Indians and pioneers. Other exhibits put time into context, explain geological concepts and detail the evolution of humans.

Montana's past is outlined in Paugh History Hall, which includes a furnished 1930s house and gas station. Varied means of transportation, including a stagecoach, sleigh, fire wagon and vintage automobiles, are displayed. Two galleries house changing exhibitions.

A 40-foot domed planetarium uses computer graphics in its changing programs. Laser shows are offered during the school year, and a living-history farm is open during the summer.

Food is available during the summer. Daily 8-8, Memorial Day weekend-Labor Day; Mon.-Sat. 9-5, Sun. 12:30-5, rest of year. Planetarium shows are given daily. Closed Jan. 1, Thanksgiving and Dec. 25. Museum $8; ages 5-18, $4. Laser show $5. Under 5 are not permitted. Planetarium $3, under 5 free. Combination museum and planetarium ticket $9.50; ages 5-18, $6.50. Phone (406) 994-3466 or (406) 994-2251. *See color ad.*

RECREATIONAL ACTIVITIES

White-water Rafting

- **Montana Whitewater** departs from offices 2 mi. n. of Gallatin Gateway. Write P.O. Box 1552, Bozeman, MT 59771. Daily May-Sept. Phone (406) 763-4465 or (800) 799-4465. *See color ad.*

BROWNING (B-2) pop. 1,065, elev. 4,366′

Founded in 1895, Browning is the hub of the Blackfeet Nation and a center for reservation activities. It also is the site of the Blackfeet Tribal Headquarters, which includes a nine-member business council, the governing board of the Blackfeet Tribe. Fifteen miles east on the reservation, a monument marks the northernmost point reached by the Lewis and Clark expedition on July 23, 1806. About 10,000 American Indians live on the Blackfeet Indian Reservation, which covers 1.5 million acres.

MUSEUM OF THE PLAINS INDIAN is at jct. US 2 and US 89W. Murals, dioramas, historical and contemporary American Indian arts and artifacts of the Northern Plains region are displayed. A slide presentation and changing exhibits are offered. Allow 1 hour minimum. Daily 9-4:45, June-Sept.; Mon.-Fri. 10-4:30, rest of year. Closed Jan. 1, Thanksgiving and Dec. 25. Admission June-Sept. $4; ages 6-12, $1. Free rest of year. Phone (406) 338-2230.

BUTTE (D-3) pop. 34,606, elev. 5,716′

Silver Bow Creek's gold and silver first brought the mineral wealth of remote Butte to the attention of the world. But it was copper that made Butte's reputation as "the richest hill on Earth," producing almost 11 billion pounds of the metal. Copper kings fought for control of Butte's wealth. Marcus Daly's Anaconda Co. eventually gained ownership of every mine in Butte and became the dominant power in Montana.

By 1955 the high-grade copper ore was almost played out, and excavation began on Berkeley Open Pit Mine to extract low-grade ore. The mine was one of the larger truck-operated pit mines in the world. The Berkeley Pit Viewing Stand, open daily dawn to dusk, March to mid-November, is free and provides an excellent view of the old open mine. As a transportation hub, the city has become one of the nation's larger inland ports, with containerized cargo from the Orient being cleared and routed to points throughout the Midwest.

The Anselmo Mine Yard, uptown at Caledonia and Excelsior streets, is a fine example of surface support facilities that once served the miners. An interpretive center and tours are offered during the summer. The Granite Mountain Mine Memorial, 1308 N. Main St., is dedicated to the 168 men who died in a 1917 mine disaster.

Butte's historic district contains a large concentration of late 19th- and early 20th-century residential and commercial buildings as well as mining relics such as the steel headframes used to lower miners to a network of more than 2,000 miles of tunnels under "the hill."

Butte is surrounded by Beaverhead-Deerlodge National Forest *(see place listing p. 82)*, which offers varied recreational opportunities. Sheepshead Recreation Area, about 10 miles north via I-15, was designed for the physically impaired. Visitors can experience the beauty of the nearby rugged mountains, verdant forests and meadows by driving either north to Helena or south to Monida on I-15.

Butte-Silver Bow Chamber of Commerce and Visitor Center: 1000 George St., Butte, MT 59701; phone (406) 723-3177 or (800) 735-6814. *See color ad.*

Self-guiding tours: Brochures detailing two walking tours of the historic district are available at the chamber of commerce.

ARTS CHATEAU is at 321 W. Broadway. Built as a home by Charles W. Clark in 1898 and modeled after a French chateau, the building contains the works of Montana artists in exhibits that change periodically. Allow 1 hour minimum. Mon.-Sat. 10-5, Memorial Day-Labor Day; Tues.-Sat. 11-4, rest of year. Admission $3; over 49, $2; under 16, $1; family rate $6. Phone (406) 723-7600.

COPPER KING MANSION is at 219 W. Granite St. The 32-room Victorian house was the residence of W.A. Clark, a U.S. senator and "copper king." Now a national historic landmark and bed and breakfast, the restored 1884-88 mansion is furnished in period and serves as a showcase for numerous collections. Allow 1 hour minimum. Guided tours are given daily 9-4, May-Sept.; Sat.-Sun. 9-4 in Apr. and Oct.; by appointment rest of year. Admission $5; under 15, $3.50. Phone (406) 782-7580.

MINERAL MUSEUM is 1 mi. w. of Montana St. to 1300 W. Park St., in the Museum Building of Montana Tech. The museum exhibits more than 1,500 specimens, including fluorescent minerals, a gold nugget considered to be the largest in Montana and a 400-pound quartz crystal found near Butte. Other features are a geological relief map and an earthquake studies laboratory. Daily 9-6, Memorial Day-Labor Day; Mon.-Fri. 9-4, rest of year. Free. Phone (406) 496-4414.

OLD NO. 1 departs from the chamber of commerce; take I-90 exit 126 to 1000 George St. This replica of an early open streetcar carries passengers on a 90-minute tour of the city. Sights include the historic district, Victorian neighborhoods and Berkeley Pit. Tours depart daily (weather permitting) at 9, 11, 1:30 and 3:30, Memorial Day weekend-Labor Day. Fare $5; ages 4-12, $2.50. Reservations are required. Phone (406) 723-3177 or (800) 735-6814.

SAVE **OUR LADY OF THE ROCKIES** is e. atop the Continental Divide; tours to the site depart from Plaza Mall, 3100 Harrison Ave. The 90-foot-high statue of the Virgin Mary—a nondenominational tribute to motherhood—took 6 years to build and was airlifted into place in 1985. Visitors may step inside the metal structure. The road to the statue is not open to public traffic. A chapel observatory is available. Bus tours lasting 2.5 hours depart Mon.-Sat. at 10 and 2, Sun. at 11 and 2, June-Sept. (weather permitting). Fare $10; over 54 and ages 13-17, $9; ages 5-12, $5. DS, MC, VI. Phone (406) 782-1221 or (800) 800-5239.

WORLD MUSEUM OF MINING & HELL ROARING GULCH is at 155 Museum Way. The museum is on the grounds of the Orphan Girl mine, a silver mine in operation 1875-1956. The mine yard contains the original headframe, hoist house, timber slide and hose house. More than 50 buildings comprise Hell Roaring Gulch, a reconstructed 1890s mining town with mining and regional history exhibits. Allow 2 hours minimum. Daily 9-5:30. Last admission is 1 hour before closing. Admission $7; ages 13-18, $5; under 13, $2. Phone (406) 723-7211.

BYNUM (C-2) elev. 3,972′

TIMESCALE ADVENTURES is at 120 Second Ave. S. Guided 3-hour walking tours of an active dinosaur dig site along the front range of the Rocky Mountains include a discussion about paleontology and an opportunity to search for fossil specimens. Transportation to the field is provided.

Note: The walk may cover up to 2 miles and involve some stooping and bending. Comfortable clothing and shoes are recommended. Phone ahead for additional information about preparations. Tours are given daily at 9 and 1, May-Sept. Departures require a minimum of 2 persons. Fee $35; under 13, $25. Reservations are recommended. AX, DS, MC, VI. Phone (406) 469-2211 or (800) 238-6873.

CARDWELL (D-3) pop. 40, elev. 4,271′

GEM **LEWIS AND CLARK CAVERNS STATE PARK** is 7.3 mi. e. on SR 2. The 3,005-acre park includes a limestone cavern of vaulted chambers, intricate passageways and delicate, varicolored formations that make this one of the most beautiful caverns in the country. Camping facilities are available.

Note: The cavern tour, which involves hiking a three-quarter-mile outdoor path to the entrance and descending more than 600 steps inside, may be cumbersome to the physically challenged and those with heart conditions. Rubber-soled shoes are advised. Because the cavern temperature remains around 50 degrees, a jacket is recommended.

Park open daily 9-9, June 15-Labor Day; 9-7, rest of year. Cavern tours are given 9-6:30, June 15-Labor Day; 9-4:30, May 1-June 14 and day after Labor Day-Sept. 30. Two-hour guided cavern tour $10; ages 6-11, $5. Park entrance fee $5 per private motorized vehicle or $1 per person arriving by bicycle, bus or on foot. MC, VI. Phone (406) 287-3541. *See Recreation Chart and the AAA Northwestern CampBook.*

CHESTER (B-4) pop. 871

LIBERTY COUNTY MUSEUM is at 230 Second St. E. In a former Methodist church, the museum contains artifacts, photographs and other items depicting the homesteading days on the High Plains. Archives and genealogy records are available for research. Allow 30 minutes minimum. Daily 1-5 and 7-9, late May through Labor Day. Free. Phone (406) 759-5256.

CHINOOK (B-4) pop. 1,386, elev. 2,405′

Chinook was named after the American Indian word for the winds that often whip through this area during January and February, causing the temperature to rise as much as 70 degrees in a few hours. Melting the snow and exposing the grass, chinooks have saved many cattle herds from disaster. Charles Russell captured the significance of these winds to the range cattleman in his picture of a starving cow titled "Waiting for a Chinook."

Chinook Chamber of Commerce: P.O. Box 744, Chinook, MT 59523.

BEAR PAW BATTLEFIELD-NEZ PERCE NATIONAL HISTORICAL PARK is 16 mi. s. off US 2 to 100 Indiana St. Chief Joseph, leader of the Nez Perce Indians, surrendered to Col. Nelson A. Miles on this site Oct. 5, 1877. A 1.5-mile walking trail is available. Blaine County Museum *(see attraction listing)*, 16 miles north in Chinook, serves as a visitor center. Picnicking is permitted. Daily 24 hours, May-Sept. Free. Phone (406) 357-3130, or (406) 357-2590 for the museum.

BLAINE COUNTY MUSEUM is 4 blks. s. of US 2 at 501 Indiana St. In addition to fossil exhibits and American Indian and pioneer artifacts, the museum features re-creations of a tar paper homestead, a schoolroom, medical offices and a church. An audiovisual account of the Battle of Bear Paw and information about Bear Paw Battlefield-Nez Perce National Historical Park *(see attraction listing)* also are offered. Allow 1 hour minimum. Mon.-Sat. 8-noon and 1-5, Sun. noon-5, Memorial Day weekend-Labor Day weekend; Mon.-Fri. 8-5, May 1-day before Memorial Day weekend and day after Labor Day-Sept. 30; Mon.-Fri. 1 5, rest of year. Free. Phone (406) 357-2590.

CHOTEAU (C-2) pop. 1,781, elev. 4,000′

Choteau (SHO-toe) was named after French fur trader Pierre Chouteau; the name is spelled with one "u" to distinguish it from the adjoining county, also named after the Frenchman.

Choteau Chamber of Commerce: P.O. Box 897, Choteau, MT 59422; phone (406) 466-5316 or (800) 823-3866.

OLD TRAIL MUSEUM is at 823 N. Main Ave. Set in a Western village, this local history and paleontology museum chronicles the history of the Rocky Mountain Front beginning with the dinosaur era. Hands-on paleontology classes for families and dinosaur enthusiasts are available. Daily 9-6, mid-May to mid-Sept.; Wed.-Sun. 10-3, rest of year. Admission mid-May to mid-Sept. $3; ages 5-17, 50c; family rate $5. Donations rest of year. Reservations are required for classes. Phone (406) 466-5332.

CIRCLE (C-6) pop. 644, elev. 2,424′

Circle takes its name from a cattle ranch that once stood near this site. In the late 19th century the area around Circle was booming cattle country, but the devastation caused by the winter of 1886-87 put many ranchers out of business. Circle remains an agricultural community and the seat of McCone County.

Circle Chamber of Commerce and Agriculture: P.O. Box 321, Circle, MT 59215; phone (406) 485-2741.

McCONE COUNTY MUSEUM is at 801 SR 200S. Featured are a large collection of mounted birds and animals as well as artifacts, farm machinery, tools and guns from the homestead era. Allow 1 hour minimum. Mon.-Fri. 9-noon and 1-5, May-Sept. Admission $2, under 12 free. Phone (406) 485-2414.

COLUMBIA FALLS (B-1) pop. 3,645, elev. 3,098′

The union of the North and Middle forks of the Flathead River has carved out Bad Rock Canyon, at the entrance of which lies Columbia Falls. The abundance of water and timber in the area supports Columbia Falls Aluminum Co. and Plum Creek Timber Co., the town's major industries.

Numerous recreational opportunities are available along scenic CR 486, which follows the North Fork of the Flathead River 20 miles north to the Camas Creek entrance to Glacier National Park. Halfway between Columbia Falls and the park is Wild Eyes Animal Adventures, offering wildlife encounters and photography sessions in natural settings; phone (406) 387-5391 or (888) 330-5391. Hungry Horse Dam *(see Hungry Horse p. 105)* and the Great Bear and Bob Marshall wilderness areas also are nearby.

Flathead Convention & Visitor Bureau: 15 Depot Park, Kalispell, MT 59901; phone (406) 756-9091 or (800) 543-3105.

BIG SKY WATERPARK is 2 blks. w. of jct. US 2 and SR 206. Among the parks amusements are a game arcade, a miniature golf course, a water-wars game and several waterslides. Picnicking is permitted. Allow 2 hours minimum. Daily 10-8, June 19-Aug. 15; 10-6, Memorial Day weekend-June 18 and Aug. 16-Labor Day weekend. Admission $17.95; over 59 and ages 3-10, $13.95. After 4 p.m. $12.95; over 59 and ages 3-10, $10.95. Miniature golf $5.50; over 59 and ages 3-10, $4.50. Phone (406) 892-2139.

COLUMBUS (D-4) pop. 1,748, elev. 3,600′

In 1875 travelers stopped at Countryman stage station on the north bank of the Yellowstone River. The hardy travelers referred to the settlement as Eagle's Nest, or as Sheep Dip, because of its vile whiskey. With the coming of the Northern Pacific Railroad in 1882 the town became a livestock and agricultural center. Initially called Stillwater by the railroad because it lay at the confluence of the Stillwater and Yellowstone rivers, it was renamed Columbus in 1893 to avoid confusion with Stillwater, Minn.

Today the town's economy still rests upon cattle, sheep and small grains but also incorporates Montana's largest platinum mine as well as manufacturers of laminated structural wood, Western-style jewelry and saddle trim.

MUSEUM OF THE BEARTOOTHS is off I-90 exit 408, w. on Fourth Ave., then n. on Fifth St. to the corner of Fifth Ave. Displays illustrate the history of Stillwater County. Items include a caboose, spring wagons and halters, vintage pharmaceuticals and washing machines. The museum also pays tribute to a local Congressional Medal of Honor winner Donald J. Ruhl, in whose name SR 78 was designated a Memorial Highway. An additional building on the grounds displays outdoor machinery. Allow 30 minutes minimum. Tues.-Sun. 1-5, June-Sept. Donations. Phone (406) 322-4588.

COOKE CITY (E-4) pop. 140, elev. 7,675′

Gold miners settled Cooke City in the early 1870s, and by 1880 the town numbered 7,000 fortune-seeking souls. Gold mining continued until the late 1950s, when commercial mining finally ceased. Gold-panning in area streams remains popular.

Cooke City is 4 miles from Yellowstone National Park's northeast gate. Beartooth Scenic Highway *(see Red Lodge p. 113)*, the town's eastern access, usually is open May through September. Cooke City can be reached all year via the road from Gardiner through Yellowstone.

Cooke City Area Chamber of Commerce: P.O. Box 1071, Cooke City, MT 59020; phone (406) 838-2495.

YELLOWSTONE WILDLIFE MUSEUM is on US 212, 3.5 mi. e. of the entrance to Yellowstone National Park. More than 100 mounted animals and birds native to the area are displayed in scenes depicting their natural habitats. Allow 30 minutes minimum. Daily 9-9, mid-May to mid-Oct. Admission $2. Phone (406) 838-2265.

CULBERTSON (B-6) pop. 716, elev. 1,919′

About 20 miles upriver from the site of Fort Union, Culbertson takes its name from the second agent of that fur-trading fort, Maj. Alexander Culbertson. Culbertson's son built a ranch nearby in 1879, and about 10 years later a community was established. Culbertson became a center for the local ranches and farms, a role it continues.

Culbertson Chamber of Commerce: P.O. Box 639, Culbertson, MT 59218; phone (406) 787-5821.

CUSTER NATIONAL FOREST/DAKOTA PRAIRIE GRASSLANDS

Elevations in the forest range from 4,000 ft. near the town of Ashland to 12,799 ft. on Granite Peak. Refer to AAA maps for additional elevation information.

In southeastern Montana, Custer National Forest/ Dakota Prairie Grasslands encompasses nearly 2.5 million acres in two unique districts. The mountainous section, or Beartooth District, includes a portion of the Absaroka-Beartooth Wilderness and Granite Peak, the highest point in Montana. The eastern portions range from the pine-clad hills and rough break country of southeastern Montana to the rolling grassland of northwestern South Dakota and the badlands of western North Dakota.

Beartooth Scenic Highway *(see Red Lodge p. 113)*, usually open May through September, traverses the mountain country. Other good routes provide access to campgrounds and trailheads. Guide and pack services are available in nearby towns.

Trail information, which can be obtained from Forest Service offices, should be checked and updated at Red Lodge Ranger Station before a trip into Absaroka-Beartooth Wilderness is attempted. The ranger station, south of Red Lodge on US 212, is open daily 8-5, June 16-Aug. 31; Mon.-Fri. 8-noon and 1-5, rest of year.

For further information contact the Forest Supervisor, 1310 Main St., P.O. Box 50760, Billings, MT 59105; phone (406) 657-6200. Or write the Grasslands Supervisor, 240 W. Century, Bismarck, ND 58501. *See Recreation Chart and the AAA Northwestern CampBook.*

DEER LODGE (D-2) pop. 3,421, elev. 4,519′

The second oldest city in Montana, Deer Lodge is on the Clark Fork River midway between Yellowstone and Glacier national parks. The city was established in 1862 as the result of a nearby gold discovery. With fresh food and a blacksmith as drawing cards, Deer Lodge was a welcome stop for the many settlers and miners who passed through the area.

Gold West Country: 1155 Main St., Deer Lodge, MT 59722; phone (406) 846-1943. *See color ad.*

Self-guiding tours: Brochures for an automobile tour of the surrounding area are available from Powell County Chamber of Commerce at 1171 Main St.; phone (406) 846-2094.

GRANT-KOHRS RANCH NATIONAL HISTORIC SITE is off exit 184 or 187 on I-90 Bus. Rte. Established in the early 1860s, the ranch had grown to 27,000 acres by the early 1900s, and the owners controlled more than a million acres of public range in four states and Canada. Though much reduced, the 1,500-acre ranch still has livestock and more than 80 buildings, from bunkhouse row to the 23-room ranch house.

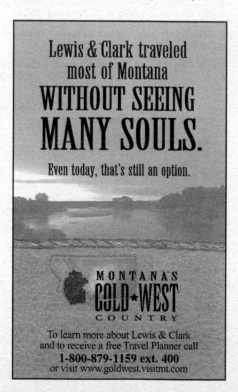

Daily 8-5:30, May 1 to mid-Sept.; 9-4:30, rest of year. Closed Jan. 1, Thanksgiving and Dec. 25. Guided historic house tours are given daily on the

hour 9-4, May 1 to mid-Sept.; 10-3, rest of year. Free. Hours may vary during summer living-history programs; phone ahead. Phone (406) 846 2070, or (406) 846-3388 Sat.-Sun.

SAVE **OLD MONTANA PRISON** is off I-90 exit 184 or 187 at 1106 Main St. Self-guiding tours of the cellhouse, maximum-security areas, hole, tunnel and walled prison grounds together with an exhibit of photographs provide insight into early prison life and area history. The facility served as a prison 1871-1979.

Allow 30 minutes minimum. Daily 8-8, Memorial Day-Labor Day; 8:30-5:30, day after Labor Day-Oct. 31; otherwise varies. Guided tours are available June-Aug. Closed Jan. 1, Thanksgiving and Dec. 25. Admission (includes Frontier Montana Museum, Montana Auto Museum and Yesterday's Playthings Doll & Toy Museum) $9; over 61, $8; ages 10-15, $5. Phone (406) 846-3111 or (406) 846-3114.

Frontier Montana Museum is at 1106 Main St. Two extensive private collections of Western memorabilia from the 1800s are highlights of this museum that also features Civil War items, a gun collection containing 250 weapons, American Indian artifacts, a saloon diorama, a large bourbon-bottle collection and a display of "gambler's essentials." Daily 9:30-5:30, May 15-Oct. 1. Admission included with Old Montana Prison. Phone (406) 846-0026 or (406) 846-3111.

Montana Auto Museum is at 1106 Main St. The museum houses a representative collection of vintage automobiles from 1903 through the early 1970s. Included are a 1903 Model A Ford, a 1928 Pierce Arrow motor home, antique camping vehicles, several 1950s Chevrolets and muscle cars from the late 1960s and early 1970s. Interpretive displays and photographs enhance the collection. Daily 8-8, Memorial Day-Labor Day; 8:30-5:30, day after Labor Day-Oct. 31; otherwise varies. Closed Jan. 1, Thanksgiving and Dec. 25. Admission included with Old Montana Prison. Phone (406) 846-3111.

Montana Law Enforcement Museum is at 1106 Main St. Featured are weapons, uniforms and memorabilia relating to the law enforcement history of Montana. A memorial is dedicated to state law enforcement officers who have died in the line of duty since 1864. Allow 1 hour minimum. Wed.-Sun. 10-6, May 15-Oct. 31. Donations. Phone (406) 846-3777.

Powell County Museum is at 1193 Main St. Permanent and changing exhibits depict the history of Powell County and Deer Lodge Valley. Displays include a weapons collection dating 1776-1970, mining and ranching equipment, and household and school items. A gallery features historic photographs as well as jukebox and slot machine collections. Daily 10-5, June 1-Labor Day. Free. Phone (406) 846-1694 or (406) 846-3111.

Yesterday's Playthings Doll & Toy Museum is at 1106 Main St. The history of children's toys from the 19th century to the present is the focus of this museum. The collection includes dolls from different cultures and dolls made from materials ranging from papier-mâché to china. A working model train also is displayed. Allow 30 minutes minimum. Daily 9:30-5:30, May 15-Sept. 30. Admission included with Old Montana Prison. Phone (406) 846-1480.

DILLON (E-2) pop. 3,752, elev. 5,102′

Named for the president of Union Pacific Railroad, Dillon is a focal point for five rich stock-raising valleys, including Big Hole, Grasshopper and Beaverhead. Beaverhead County is among the top cattle- and hay-producing regions in the state. Dillon was established in 1880 by a group of businessmen who bought out a rancher who refused to give up his land to the railroad.

In 1863 Sidney Edgerton, a lawyer from Ohio, arrived in the area and stayed throughout the winter season. When he visited Washington, D.C., in the spring, he advocated the creation of a new territory; President Abraham Lincoln named Edgerton governor, and Bannack the temporary capital. The following year the territory's seat was moved to the active mining town of Virginia City.

Fishing is a popular recreational pursuit. Some of Montana's higher mountains can be seen from scenic I-15, which follows the Beaverhead and Red Rock rivers to the Idaho border.

Beaverhead Chamber of Commerce: 125 S. Montana St., P.O. Box 425, Dillon, MT 59725; phone (406) 683-5511.

Self-guiding tours: A brochure outlining a walking tour of historic Dillon is available at the visitor center or Beaverhead County Museum *(see attraction listing)*.

BANNACK STATE HISTORIC PARK is at 21 mi. w. on SR 278, then 4 mi. s., following signs. Montana's first territorial capital and one of the original gold-rush towns of this area, the park includes weathered remains of the first capitol, jail, hotel and log cabins. The visitor center offers 19th-century photographs of the region and a videotape about mining. Primitive camping facilities are available.

Picnicking is permitted. Allow 1 hour minimum. Park daily 8 a.m.-9 p.m., Memorial Day-Labor Day; 8-dusk, May 1-day before Memorial Day; 8-5, rest of year. Visitor center daily 10-6, Memorial Day-Labor Day; Sat.-Sun. 11-5, May 1-day before Memorial Day and day after Labor Day-Oct. 31. Closed Dec. 24-25. Admission $3; ages 6-12, $1. Phone (406) 834-3413. *See Recreation Chart and the AAA Northwestern CampBook.*

BEAVERHEAD COUNTY MUSEUM is at 15 S. Montana St., next to the depot. Displays include items pertaining to American Indian and pioneer life in Beaverhead County. An outdoor interpretive area features a 1,300-foot boardwalk and an 1885 homesteader's cabin and sheep wagon. Mon.-Fri. 8:30-5, (also Sat.-Sun. noon-4, Memorial Day-Sept. 30). Donations. Phone (406) 683-5027.

WESTERN MONTANA COLLEGE GALLERY/MUSEUM is at 710 S. Atlantic. Featured are student art, rotating exhibits and a permanent collection centered on Western art. A collection of Asian, African and North American wildlife also is displayed. Mon.-Thurs. 10-3 (also Tues. 7-9 p.m.), Fri. 10-noon; closed mid-Dec. to mid-Jan. and school breaks and holidays. Free. Phone (406) 683-7018 to confirm schedule.

RECREATIONAL ACTIVITIES

Fishing

- SAVE **Watershed Fly Fishing Adventures**, 11 Pierce Dr., Dillon, MT 59725. Mon.-Sat. 8-6, Sun. 8-5, late May-late Oct. Phone (406) 683-6660 or (800) 753-6660.

EAST GLACIER PARK (B-2)

pop. 396, elev. 4,795′

In the Two Medicine Valley, East Glacier Park is the recreational center and eastern gateway to Glacier National Park *(see place listing p. 96)*. The community maintains an Old West appearance.

ENNIS (E-3) pop. 840, elev. 4,939′

Ennis is in the broad, rolling Madison Valley, flanked on both sides by mountain ranges. Built along the Madison River, the town is convenient to the historic gold-mining towns of Virginia City and Nevada City as well as the trout-filled lakes and streams of the Beaverhead-Deerlodge and Gallatin national forests *(see place listings p. 82 and p. 96)*.

Ennis Chamber of Commerce: P.O. Box 291, Ennis, MT 59729; phone (406) 682-4388.

DID YOU KNOW

Montana borders the most Canadian provinces of all the 50 states—British Columbia, Alberta and Saskatchewan.

FLATHEAD LAKE (C-2)

A recreational mecca, Flathead Lake appeals to those who enjoy a wide array of activities ranging from water skiing and fishing to sailing and sightseeing. The 28-mile-long, 15-mile-wide lake boasts several islands; sheep, deer, bears, eagles and ospreys inhabit Wild Horse. Nearby communities include Bigfork, Kalispell, Lakeside, Polson and Somers *(see place listings)*.

FLATHEAD NATIONAL FOREST

Elevations in the forest range from 3,500 ft. at the valley floor to 9,289 ft. on Swan Peak in the Swan Valley. Refer to AAA maps for additional elevation information.

Flathead National Forest stretches along the spine of the Rocky Mountains south from the Canadian border for more than 130 miles. With parts of its eastern and northern boundaries bordering Glacier National Park *(see place listing p. 96)*, the forest shares much of the park's spectacular scenery of high ridges and mountains. Its principal rivers are the Swan, Stillwater and the three forks of the Flathead—the North Fork, Middle Fork and South Fork, all in the National Wild and Scenic River system. This is augmented by 3,400 miles of streams and many small lakes.

Almost half the national forest's 2.3 million acres lies within the Bob Marshall Wilderness complex, which includes the Bob Marshall, Great Bear and Scapegoat wilderness areas. The combined 1.5 million acres attracts those who seek out a challenging recreation experience in a natural setting where mechanized travel and equipment are prohibited.

Popularly known as the "Bob," the Bob Marshall Wilderness straddles the Continental Divide. There are many rugged peaks, alpine lakes, mountain valleys, meandering streams, wildflower-strewn meadows and waterfalls. Sunsets often are highlighted by long streamers of wave-shaped clouds, a phenomenon created partly by strong winds blowing perpendicular to a mountain range.

For those seeking utter solitude, winter use of the "Bob" is almost nil. This vast reserve, appropriately named for the man who helped preserve millions of acres of the wilderness system, shelters one of the country's largest wildlife populations, including elk, bighorn sheep, black bears and several hundred grizzly bears. About 50 outfitting and guiding businesses serve the area.

Other areas of interest in the forest are Mission Mountain Wilderness and Hungry Horse Reservoir *(see Recreation Chart)*, along the shores of which are almost half of the forest's camping and picnic areas. The 15,000-acre Jewel Basin Hiking Area, reached by forest roads from SRs 83 or 35, is a scenic area of rushing waterways, open meadows and subalpine forests; mechanized vehicles and pack animals are not permitted. Hiking, fishing and floating the three forks of the Flathead River are popular activities.

Information about the forest's 34 campgrounds and recreational opportunities is available at the forest headquarters in Kalispell and at district ranger stations. For further information contact the Forest Supervisor, Flathead National Forest, 1935 3rd Ave. E., Kalispell, MT 59901; phone (406) 758-5204. *See Recreation Chart and the AAA Northwestern CampBook.*

FORT BENTON (C-4) pop. 1,594, elev. 2,632'

At the head of navigation on the Missouri River, Fort Benton is one of Montana's oldest communities and was the link between east and west. Thousands of immigrants and miners marked this landing as the beginning of the way west along Mullan Road or north along WhoopUp Trail. Fort Benton also was their chief means of supply, as all goods were brought by steamboat from St. Louis. In 1868, 39 steamboats unloaded 8,000 tons of freight and 10,000 passengers; one steamboat returned to St. Louis with $1.5 million in gold.

The Lewis and Clark Memorial overlooks the Missouri River from the levee not far from the old fort; the memorial stands as a reminder of the explorers' stay in the area and the role they and Fort Benton played in opening the West. A statue of Lt. John Mullan, the first white man to pave the way west from Fort Benton to Walla Walla, WA, and for whom the Mullan Trail is named, also stands on the levee.

Fort Benton is on the western fringe of the Upper Missouri River Breaks National Monument, which corridor traces the Upper Missouri River 149 miles east into the Charles M. Russell National Wildlife Refuge. Recreation information can be obtained from the Upper Missouri National Wild & Scenic River Visitor Center *(see attraction listing).*

Fort Benton Chamber of Commerce: P.O. Box 12, Fort Benton, MT 59442; phone (406) 622-3864.

Self-guiding tours: A brochure outlining a walking and driving tour of Fort Benton is available from the Museum of the Upper Missouri River *(see attraction listing)* and from Fort Benton Visitor Information Center, on Front Street.

MUSEUM OF THE NORTHERN GREAT PLAINS is next to the high school at 1205 20th St. The museum contains the mounted remains of the Hornaday bull, the bovine model for the buffalo nickel, and exhibits relating to agriculture. Allow 1 hour minimum. Daily 10-5, May-Sept.; by appointment rest of year. Admission (includes Museum of the Upper Missouri River) $4; ages 6-12, $1. Phone (406) 622-5316.

MUSEUM OF THE UPPER MISSOURI RIVER is in Old Fort Park at 1900 Front St. Dioramas and exhibits about early trading and river steamers are offered. Daily 10-5, May-Sept.; by appointment rest of year. Admission (includes Museum of the Northern Great Plains) $4; ages 6-12, $1. Phone (406) 622-5316.

UPPER MISSOURI NATIONAL WILD & SCENIC RIVER VISITOR CENTER is at 1718 Front St. Offered is a video presentation about Lewis and Clark's expedition on the 149-mile Upper Missouri River and through the White Cliffs area. The center contains displays about the area's natural and cultural resources and provides assistance in preparing self-guiding river trips. Allow 30 minutes minimum. Daily 8-5, early May to mid-Sept. Free. Phone (406) 622-5185.

RECREATIONAL ACTIVITIES

Canoeing

- **Canoe Montana**, 1312 Front St. Write P.O. Box 591, Fort Benton, MT 59442. Other activities are offered. Trips are available May-Sept. Reservations are required. Phone (406) 622-5882 or (800) 500-4538.

FORT PECK (B-6) pop. 240, elev. 2,100'

The federal government developed Fort Peck in the early 1930s as a support community for the construction of Fort Peck Dam. Built by the U.S. Army Corps of Engineers, the dam harnesses the Missouri River to provide electric power, irrigation and flood control. The town was named after Col. Campbell K. Peck, who established a trading post in the area after the Civil War.

Fort Peck Summer Theatre, west on SR 24, presents contemporary productions from mid-June to early September; phone Fort Peck Fine Arts Council at (406) 526-9943 or (406) 228-2222.

Glasgow Area Chamber of Commerce and Agriculture: 23 US 2E, P.O. Box 832, Glasgow, MT 59230; phone (406) 228-2222.

FORT PECK DAM is on SR 24. The construction of one of the largest hydraulic earth-filled dams in the world created Fort Peck Lake *(see Recreation Chart and the AAA Northwestern CampBook)*, which offers excellent fishing and camping along its 130-mile length. A hard-surfaced highway follows the crest of the dam 250 feet above the tunnel outlets onto the spillway. Illustrated talks and information about the project are available. Phone (406) 526-3411.

Fort Peck Museum is on Lower Yellowstone Rd. at Powerhouse 1. Area geology, paleontology and history are outlined. Nearly 300 specimens of dinosaur bones and other fossils are displayed. Daily 9-5:30. Free.

Powerhouse Tour departs from the museum. The tour describes how the power plants at Fort Peck Dam transform water into electricity. Generators, surge tanks and turbines are displayed. Allow 1 hour minimum. Tours depart daily on the hour 8-4:30, Memorial Day-Labor Day. Free.

FORT UNION TRADING POST NATIONAL HISTORIC SITE (B-7)

Fort Union Trading Post National Historic Site is reached via US 2 and SR 1804, 25 miles southwest of Williston. At its founding by John Jacob Astor for his American Fur Co. in 1828, the trading post was the center for fur trade on the Upper Missouri River. The fort was 1,800 miles by river from St. Louis, the nearest supply point.

Excavators have unearthed the stone foundations of the Bourgeois House, palisades, Indian trade house, icehouse and other structures. The trade house has been rebuilt and furnished as it might have been in the early 1850s. The fort's walls and bastions also have been reconstructed. The Bourgeois House visitor center features exhibits about the fur trade.

Allow 30 minutes minimum. Daily 8-8 CST, Memorial Day weekend-Labor Day; 9-5:30 CST, rest of year. Closed Jan. 1, Thanksgiving and Dec. 25. Donations. Phone (701) 572-9083.

GALLATIN NATIONAL FOREST

Elevations in the forest range from 4,300 ft. at Derby Gulch to 12,799 ft. on Granite Peak. Refer to AAA maps for additional elevation information.

Gallatin National Forest is in south-central Montana. Some of the most rugged mountains in the state can be found in the 1,735,239-acre forest. On the western side are the Madison and Gallatin ranges; to the east, the Absaroka and Beartooth; and to the north, the Bridger Mountains and the isolated block encompassing the Crazy Mountains.

To some, such as the Crow Indians who sought their visions in the Crazies, these mountains inspire a mystical reverence; to others, such as the mountain men who thought the Beartooth Range resembled the teeth of a familiar predator, they inspire a sense of awe. Much of this region remains unchanged, protected in the forest's two wilderness units, the Lee Metcalf and the Absaroka-Beartooth.

Absaroka-Beartooth Wilderness is named for its two very different mountain ranges. Rugged mountains, broad forested valleys and a variety of plant life characterize the Absaroka Range, which receives precipitation that is unusually abundant for this region. In contrast, the Beartooths present a jagged silhouette of monumental walls and spires soaring to heights of more than 12,000 feet. Forming the roof of these massive peaks are broad plateaus of alpine tundra carpeted with summer wildflowers and hundreds of lakes. The ranges are an integral part of the Yellowstone ecosystem, offering shelter to grizzlies, moose, deer, eagles and turkeys.

The Yellowstone, Gallatin, Madison and Boulder, which are the principal rivers, are renowned for excellent fishing. Natural Bridge State Monument, 28 miles south of Big Timber via SR 289, features a 100-foot waterfall at the mouth of Boulder River Canyon. Several short trails lead from the parking area to observation sites of the falls.

Hikers favor Lee Metcalf Wilderness *(see Beaverhead-Deerlodge National Forest p. 82)* and the Hyalite area of the Gallatin Range. Also scenic are the trails in the Bridger Mountains near Bozeman. To experience the region's beauty by car travel Beartooth Scenic Highway *(see Red Lodge p. 113)* or US 191 from West Yellowstone to Gallatin Gateway; or take a self-guiding tour of the Madison River Canyon Earthquake Area.

Information about the forest's 26 campgrounds and recreational opportunities is available at district ranger stations. For further information write Bozeman Ranger District, 3710 Fallon St., Ste. C, Bozeman, MT 59718; phone (406) 522-2520. *See Recreation Chart and the AAA Northwestern CampBook.*

MADISON RIVER CANYON EARTHQUAKE AREA—*see West Yellowstone p. 118.*

GARDINER (E-4) pop. 851, elev. 5,267′

The northern entrance to Yellowstone National Park, Gardiner is the only approach open all year. The Devil's Slide, an unusual rock formation 5 miles northwest on US 89, is visible from the highway. A mile north of town by gravel road is a travertine rock quarry. Theodore Roosevelt dedicated Roosevelt Arch in 1903.

Gardiner Chamber of Commerce: 222 Park St., P.O. Box 81, Gardiner, MT 59030; phone (406) 848-7971.

RECREATIONAL ACTIVITIES

White-water Rafting

- **Montana Whitewater** is at 603 Scott St. Write P.O. Box 1552, Bozeman, MT 59771. Daily Memorial Day weekend-Labor Day. Phone (406) 763-4465 or (800) 799-4465.
- **Yellowstone Raft Co.** is .25 mi. n. of Yellowstone River bridge on US 89. Write P.O. Box 46AA, Gardiner, MT 59030. Daily May 15-Sept. 30. Phone (406) 848-7777 or (800) 858-7781. *See color ad p. 118.*

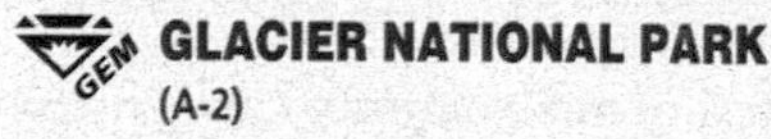

GLACIER NATIONAL PARK (A-2)

See map page 99.

Elevations in the park range from a low of 3,200 ft. in the West Glacier Area to 10,448 ft. on Mt. Cleveland. Refer to AAA maps for additional elevation information.

Glacier National Park is in northwestern Montana. Geologic processes formed and sculpted the peaks, leaving about 50 glaciers and 200 lakes. The mountains to the east are a result of an overthrust of the Earth's crust. Rock layers about a billion years old lie above layers millions of years younger. Some of the finest mountain scenery in America is within this 1-million-acre park.

The U-shaped valleys, as well as most of the lakes, are the legacy of the last ice age. Most glaciers are accessible only by trail; a few can be viewed from the road. Glacier National Park and Waterton Lakes National Park, in Alberta, together form Waterton-Glacier International Peace Park, although each is administered separately. Scenic Going-to-the-Sun Road *(see attraction listing)* connects the east and west sections of Glacier National Park.

Though Glacier is a refuge for nearly every large mammal species native to the United States, most of the animals seek the undisturbed areas, and few are seen along the roads during the travel season. The park also is a haven for 235 species of birds.

The brilliance and diversity of its floral life is one of Glacier's outstanding features; July marks the height of bloom for the 1,000-odd species of flowering plants. In the valleys on the east side are dense stands of Engelmann spruce, subalpine fir and lodgepole pine. The western valleys present a different picture with their many dense stands of western red cedars and other conifers.

General Information and Activities

The park's travel season is roughly from mid-June to mid-October. Visitors can use tour buses for one-way or round-trip travel to various park locations from mid-June to early September. Canoe and motor boat rentals are available at Apgar dock; phone (406) 892-2525.

Note: Vehicles and vehicle combinations longer than 21 feet or wider than 8 feet (including mirrors) are prohibited from traveling Going-to-the-Sun Road between the Avalanche picnic area and Sun Point parking areas, where they may park.

About 700 miles of horseback and foot trails penetrate the park, and many points of interest are within easy walking distance of the hotels and chalets. Mule Shoe Outfitter offers guided horseback rides through the park. Tours depart from Lake McDonald Corral near Lake McDonald Lodge and Many Glacier Corral; phone (406) 888-5121 or (406) 732-4203.

There are more than 60 campsites for backpackers; backcountry camping permits are required ($4 per person per night) and can be obtained at Apgar, St. Mary and Two Medicine visitor centers or the Many Glacier or Poleridge ranger stations. For more information about permits phone (406) 888-7857. Topographic maps can be purchased at the park visitor centers or ordered by mail from Glacier Natural History Association, West Glacier, MT 59936.

Mountain whitefish and cutthroat trout are the most common fish. Lake trout are taken from the larger lakes, principally McDonald, St. Mary and Waterton lakes. Grayling thrive in Elizabeth Lake. No fishing license is required; regulations are available at the visitor centers. When fishing or participating in any activity in or near park water, watch for slippery rocks at the water's edge.

Several concessioners within the park provide tours. Glacier Park Inc. offers trips by bus. Glacier Wilderness Guides arranges guided backpacking trips. Glacier Park Boat Co. operates guided lake cruises on McDonald, St. Mary, Two Medicine, Swiftcurrent and Josephine lakes. Boats and canoes can be rented at Two Medicine, Swiftcurrent and McDonald lakes. Shuttle services is available at Upper Waterton Lake.

CCInc. Auto Tape Tours of the park are available at Glacier Gift Shop in West Glacier or St. Mary's Lodge in St. Mary; phone (201) 236-1666.

Trail rides ranging from 1 hour to all day depart from Lake McDonald Lodge and Many Glacier Hotel. Daily schedules of naturalist-guided hikes, boat trips and campfire programs are printed as a supplement to the *Waterton-Glacier Guide,* the park's newspaper, which is handed out at entrance stations and visitor centers. *See Recreation Chart and the AAA Northwestern CampBook.*

Note: Although the animals in the park might appear tame, they are wild and potentially dangerous. Do not approach, feed, molest or tease them in any manner. Bears and mountain lions especially should be avoided; if one approaches, stay in your closed vehicle. Sightings should be reported to park rangers.

ADMISSION to the park is by a 7-day permit, $10 per private vehicle, $5 per person arriving by bicycle, bus, motorcycle or on foot.

PETS are permitted in the park only if they are leashed, crated or otherwise physically restrained at all times. They are not allowed on park trails or in the water.

ADDRESS inquiries to the Superintendent, Glacier National Park, West Glacier, MT 59936; phone (406) 888-7800.

Points of Interest

AVALANCHE CREEK is on Going-to-the-Sun Rd. A deep, narrow gorge cut through brilliant red mudstone is filled with potholes scoured out by stones swirled in the foaming torrent. From the gorge a 2-mile trail travels to Avalanche Basin and Lake, a semicircular amphitheater with walls more than 2,000 feet high, over which plunge a half-dozen waterfalls. A nature trail with a boardwalk for physically impaired visitors leads to the gorge. Allow 30 minutes minimum.

BELLY RIVER COUNTRY is accessible by trail from Many Glacier through Ptarmigan Tunnel, from

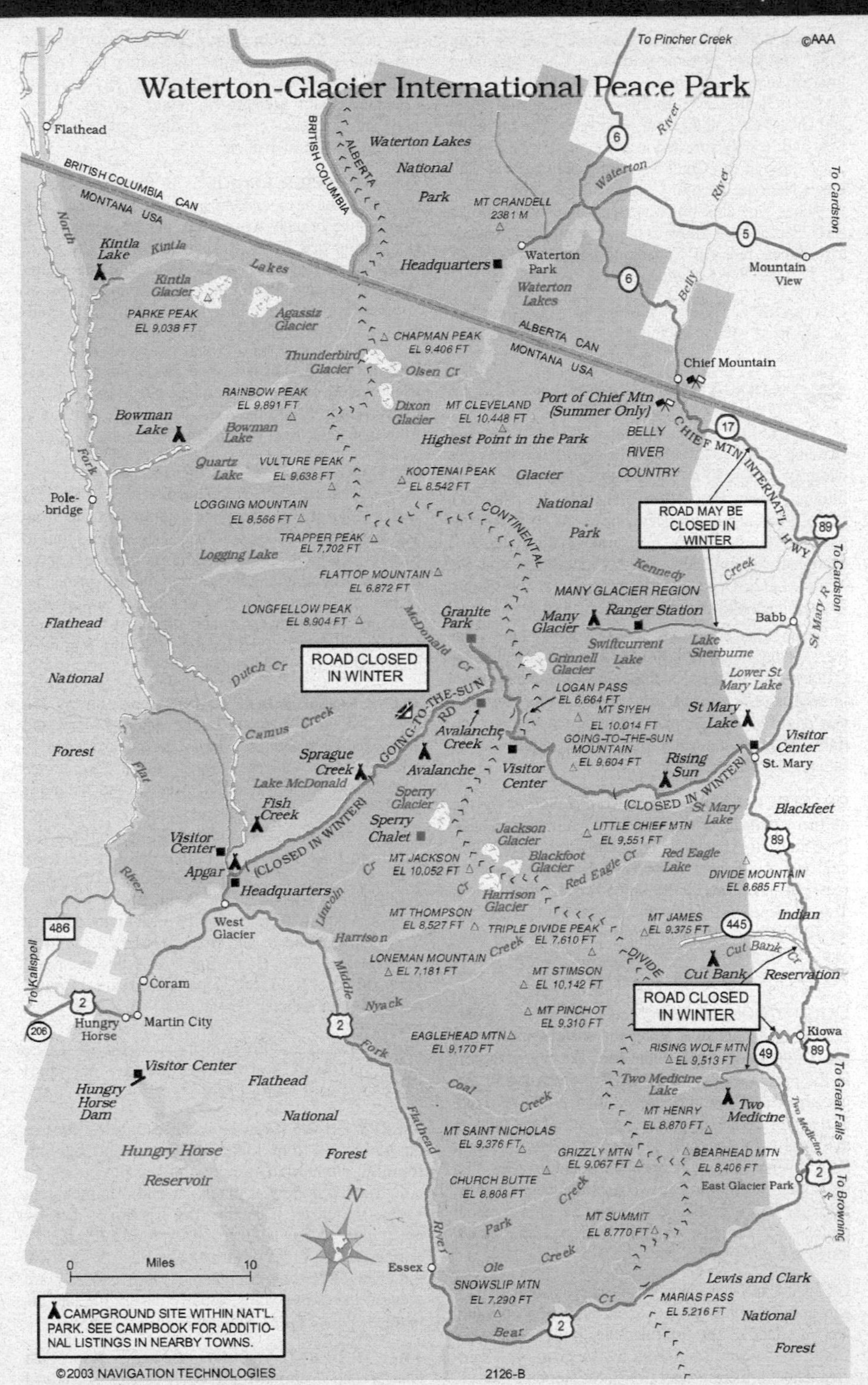
Waterton-Glacier International Peace Park
©AAA
To Pincher Creek
Flathead
BRITISH COLUMBIA CAN
MONTANA USA
ALBERTA CAN
MONTANA USA
Waterton Lakes National Park
MT CRANDELL 2381 M
Waterton Park
Headquarters
Waterton Lakes
Mountain View
To Cardston
Kintla Lake
Kintla Lakes
Kintla Glacier
Agassiz Glacier
PARKE PEAK EL 9,038 FT
CHAPMAN PEAK EL 9,406 FT
Thunderbird Glacier
Olsen Cr
Chief Mountain
Port of Chief Mtn (Summer Only)
RAINBOW PEAK EL 9,891 FT
Dixon Glacier
MT CLEVELAND EL 10,448 FT
Highest Point in the Park
BELLY RIVER COUNTRY
CHIEF MTN INTERNAT'L HWY
Bowman Lake
Quartz Lake
VULTURE PEAK EL 9,638 FT
KOOTENAI PEAK EL 8,542 FT
Glacier National Park
Pole-bridge
LOGGING MOUNTAIN EL 8,566 FT
TRAPPER PEAK EL 7,702 FT
Logging Lake
CONTINENTAL
ROAD MAY BE CLOSED IN WINTER
FLATTOP MOUNTAIN EL 6,872 FT
Kennedy Creek
MANY GLACIER REGION
LONGFELLOW PEAK EL 8,904 FT
Granite Park
Many Glacier
Ranger Station
Babb
Swiftcurrent Lake
Lake Sherburne
Grinnell Glacier
Flathead National Forest
ROAD CLOSED IN WINTER
Dutch Cr
McDonald Cr
LOGAN PASS EL 6,664 FT
MT SIYEH EL 10,014 FT
Lower St Mary Lake
St Mary Lake
GOING-TO-THE-SUN RD
Camus Creek
Avalanche Creek
GOING-TO-THE-SUN MOUNTAIN EL 9,604 FT
Visitor Center
St. Mary
Sprague Creek
Avalanche
Visitor Center
Rising Sun
Lake McDonald
Sperry Glacier
(CLOSED IN WINTER)
St Mary Lake
Blackfeet
Fish Creek
Sperry Chalet
Jackson Glacier
LITTLE CHIEF MTN EL 9,551 FT
Visitor Center
Apgar
(CLOSED IN WINTER)
MT JACKSON EL 10,052 FT
Blackfoot Glacier
Red Eagle Cr
Red Eagle Lake
Headquarters
Harrison Glacier
DIVIDE MOUNTAIN EL 8,685 FT
Flat River
West Glacier
Lincoln Cr
MT THOMPSON EL 8,527 FT
TRIPLE DIVIDE PEAK EL 7,610 FT
MT JAMES EL 9,375 FT
Indian
486
Harrison Creek
LONEMAN MOUNTAIN EL 7,181 FT
DIVIDE
Cut Bank Cr
Cut Bank
Reservation
To Kalispell
Coram
Middle
MT STIMSON EL 10,142 FT
ROAD CLOSED IN WINTER
Hungry Horse
Martin City
Nyack
MT PINCHOT EL 9,310 FT
Kiowa
EAGLEHEAD MTN EL 9,170 FT
RISING WOLF MTN EL 9,513 FT
Fork
To Great Falls
Visitor Center
Hungry Horse Dam
Flathead National Forest
Coal Creek
Two Medicine Lake
Two Medicine
MT HENRY EL 8,870 FT
Flathead
MT SAINT NICHOLAS EL 9,376 FT
Hungry Horse Reservoir
GRIZZLY MTN EL 9,067 FT
BEARHEAD MTN EL 8,406 FT
East Glacier Park
To Browning
CHURCH BUTTE EL 8,808 FT
Park Creek
MT SUMMIT EL 8,770 FT
N
River
Miles
0
10
Essex
Ole Creek
Lewis and Clark National Forest
SNOWSLIP MTN EL 7,290 FT
MARIAS PASS EL 5,216 FT
Bear Cr
CAMPGROUND SITE WITHIN NAT'L. PARK. SEE CAMPBOOK FOR ADDITIONAL LISTINGS IN NEARBY TOWNS.
©2003 NAVIGATION TECHNOLOGIES
2126-B

Waterton Lake over Stoney Indian Pass, or from Chief Mountain customs station on Chief Mountain International Road. Spurs are available to Helen, Cosley, Glenns, Mokowanis and Elizabeth lakes and Gros Ventre and Dawn Mist falls. The region is wild and heavily forested in some places. A 33-mile drive through the Chief Mountain area to Waterton Lakes National Park in Canada offers scenic views. A launch operates on Waterton Lake mid-June to early September. Allow 2 hours minimum. Round-trip launch fare (in Canadian dollars) $14; under 12, $7. One-way $8; under 12, $4.

CUT BANK is a primitive, densely wooded valley. At the head of the valley is 8,011-foot Triple Divide Peak.

GEM **GOING-TO-THE-SUN ROAD** joins US 89 at St. Mary and US 2 at West Glacier. The 52-mile route, acclaimed as one of the outstanding scenic roadways of the world, traverses the width of the park, crossing the Continental Divide through Logan Pass at an elevation of 6,680 feet while affording magnificent views of some of the park's loveliest scenery. From the east, one has exceptionally grand views of the mountains and St. Mary's Lake. Once over Logan Pass a continuous descent begins to the floor of the valley.

Logan Pass closes for the season no later than the Monday morning following the third Sunday in October and reopens in mid-June (weather permitting). *For vehicle restrictions, see General Information and Activities.* A hiker's shuttle stops at several trails along Going-to-the-Sun Road; inquire about fares at the visitor center.

GRANITE PARK is reached from Waterton by the northern portion of the Highline Trail, from Logan Pass along the Highline Trail and from Many Glacier over Swiftcurrent Pass Trail. Exposed is a great mass of lava that once spread over the region. Trails radiate into the surrounding mountains. Granite Park Chalet is open from early July to mid-Sept.; reservations are required. Phone (800) 521-7238.

LAKE McDONALD is reached via Going-to-the-Sun Road, which runs along the eastern shore. Ten miles long and 1 mile wide, the lake is the largest in the park. Its shores are heavily forested, and impressive rocky summits rise 6,000 feet above. Lake McDonald Lodge, near the upper end of the lake, is the focal point for trails to Sperry Chalet, Gunsight Pass, Sperry Glacier, Upper McDonald Valley and the summit of Mount Brown. A cruise boat operates from the lodge mid-June to early September. Boat rentals and naturalist programs are available at the lodge and at Apgar.

LOGAN PASS lies between the headwaters of Logan and Reynolds creeks. At an elevation of 6,680 feet, it straddles the Continental Divide and carries Going-to-the-Sun Road from St. Mary to West Glacier. Though there are no overnight stopping places, easy access by automobile makes it a favorite starting point for several walks, including the trail to Hidden Lake Overlook. Naturalist-led day trips and orientation talks are offered. **Note:** Parking is limited during peak visiting hours, generally mid-morning to late afternoon.

MANY GLACIER REGION is in the n.e. sector of the park. The area encompasses Swiftcurrent Lake, from which branch many deep, glaciated valleys. It can be reached by road 13 miles from US 89 at Babb or by trail from Sun Point, Granite Park, Belly River and Waterton Lake. Launch trips on Swiftcurrent and Josephine lakes depart daily, mid-June to early September.

RED EAGLE LAKE is in Red Eagle Valley. Access to the valley is by trail from the St. Mary park entrance, from Sun Point via Red Eagle Trail and from Cut Bank over Triple Divide Pass.

ST. MARY LAKE lies at the foot of the Lewis Range. Peaks of the front barrier of the Rockies soar a mile above lake waters. Trails radiate from Sun Point; one of the shortest and best is the trail to Baring Falls. Red Eagle Trail along the south shore leads to Red Eagle Lake. Programs are presented nightly in summer at the visitor center and at Rising Sun campground. Launch trips and motorboats are available at the boat landing at Rising Sun from mid-June to early September.

SCENICRUISE BOAT TOURS depart from the docks at Lake McDonald Lodge, Many Glacier and Two Medicine and St. Mary lakes. Narrated trips offer views of wilderness areas, glacial formations, waterfalls and rugged cliffs. Some tours dock for hiking and picnicking.

Allow 1 hour, 30 minutes minimum. Tours depart from Lake McDonald Lodge daily at 10, 1:30, 3:30 and 7 (also at 5:30, July-Aug.), early June-late Sept.; from Many Glacier at 9, 11, 2 and 4 (also at 8:30 and 3, July-Aug.); from Two Medicine Lake at 9, 10:30, 1, 3 and 5; and from St. Mary Lake at 9, 11, 2, 4 and 6:30. Hours may vary; phone ahead. Fare $12; ages 4-12, $6. Departures require a minimum of four adults. Phone (406) 257-2426 year-round, (406) 888-5727 for Lake McDonald boat dock, (406) 226-4467 for Two Medicine Lake, (406) 732-4480 for Many Glacier, or (406) 732-4430 for St. Mary Lake.

SPERRY CHALET can be reached only by foot or on horseback from Lake McDonald and by foot from Sun Point via Gunsight and Lincoln passes. In a high, steep hollow at the upper end of a mountain valley, the chalet is hemmed in on three sides by precipitous peaks. Hiking and exploring the Sperry Glacier and fishing in nearby Lake Ellen Wilson are the chief diversions. Mountain goats frequently are seen on the cirque walls, usually during the late afternoon. Phone (888) 345-2649.

TWO MEDICINE VALLEY is 11 mi. from East Glacier and 7 mi. off SR 49. Features include a lake surrounded by majestic peaks separated by deep, glaciated valleys. Trails for hikers and saddle horse parties radiate to adjacent points of interest; one short trail leads through dense evergreen forest to the foot of Twin Falls. Launch trips across Two Medicine Lake depart daily, mid-June to early September.

GLASGOW (B-6) pop. 3,253, elev. 2,090′

In the midst of the Milk and Missouri River valleys, Glasgow began as a railroad station. It is now an agricultural and commercial trade center for northeastern Montana, and the surrounding area is known as a good fossil-hunting locale.

Glasgow Area Chamber of Commerce and Agriculture: 23 US 2E, P.O. Box 832, Glasgow, MT 59230; phone (406) 228-2222.

VALLEY COUNTY MUSEUM is 5 mi. w. at 816 US 2. Displays include 19th-century American Indian and pioneer artifacts, Lewis and Clark memorabilia, hands-on paleontology specimens, photographs and agricultural tools. Mounted wildlife and a historic barroom exhibit also are shown. Allow 1 hour minimum. Mon.-Sat. 10-8, Sun. 1-5, Memorial Day-Labor Day; by appointment rest of year. Free. Phone (406) 228-8692.

GLENDIVE (C-6) pop. 4,729, elev. 2,070′

Once a center for cattle ranches, Glendive is now a distribution point for diverse agricultural products. The surrounding area is rich in petroleum, natural gas and coal. Another natural resource, the boneless paddlefish, roams the bottom of the Yellowstone River in such numbers that Glendive has assumed the title of "Paddlefish Capital." Paddlefish season is mid-May to late June. Besides anglers, Glendive attracts rockhounds in search of moss agates and fossils, which are plentiful in the area.

Glendive Area Chamber of Commerce and Agriculture: 313 S. Merrill, Glendive, MT 59330; phone (406) 377-5601 or (800) 859-0824.

Self-guiding tours: Brochures of a walking tour of the downtown historic district are available from the chamber of commerce.

FRONTIER GATEWAY MUSEUM is 1 mi. e. off I-94 exit 215 on Belle Prairie Rd. This museum contains dinosaur fossils, American Indian artifacts, farm machinery and other items depicting eastern Montana from prehistoric times to the present. Among buildings on the grounds are a rural schoolhouse, log cabin and smithy. Mon.-Sat. 9-noon and 1-5, Sun. and holidays 1-5, June-Aug.; daily 1-5, mid-May through May 31 and Sept. 1 to mid-Sept. Donations. Phone (406) 377-8168.

MAKOSHIKA STATE PARK is 1 mi. s. at 1301 Snyder Ave. Makoshika comes from the Sioux word meaning "bad earth" or "badlands." The area encompasses 11,531 acres of eroded and vividly colored buttes and gullies, which can be viewed along the Kinney Coulee, Cap Rock and Diane Gabriel nature trails; explanatory brochures are available at trailheads. A visitor center displays fossils and a triceratops skull.

Allow 2 hours minimum. Park open daily 24 hours (weather permitting). Visitor center daily 10-6, May-Aug.; 9-5, rest of year. Admission $5 per private motorized vehicle or $1 per person arriving by bicycle, bus or on foot. Camping fee $12. Phone (406) 377-6256. *See Recreation Chart and the AAA Northwestern CampBook.*

GREAT FALLS (C-3) pop. 56,690, elev. 3,312′

The Great Falls of the Missouri River first was seen by Capt. Meriwether Lewis in 1805. Capt. William Clark mapped the area while the others portaged around a series of five falls. The party returned to this site on its trip from the Pacific coast a year later. In 1882 Paris Gibson visited the site; he returned in the spring of 1883 with a surveyor and an attorney, and a townsite soon was plotted and named Great Falls. Important contributors to the economy are Malmstrom Air Force Base, agriculture and tourism.

River's Edge Trail, which begins north of US 89 on River Drive and stretches along the Missouri River, is popular with pedestrians and bicyclists. The paved trail is about 13 miles long.

A large American flag marks the visitor center on the Broadwater Overlook; follow directional signs on the approach and throughout the city. The center can provide information about guided tours; phone (406) 771-0885. An audio tour tracing 34 miles of the Lewis and Clark National Historic Trail is available from the High Plains Heritage Center, 422 Second St. S.; phone (406) 452-3462.

Great Falls Area Chamber of Commerce: 710 First Ave. N., Great Falls, MT 59401; phone (406) 761-4434.

Shopping areas: Holiday Village Mall, 2.5 miles east of US 15 at 1200 10th Ave. S., houses 95 stores including Herberger's, JCPenney and Sears.

CHILDREN'S MUSEUM OF MONTANA is at 22 Railroad Sq. Hands-on exhibits encourage children to learn about physics, archeology, biology and other topics. Allow 1 hour minimum. Tues.-Fri. 9:30-5; closed Thanksgiving and Dec. 24-25. Admission $2.50, under 2 free. Phone (406) 452-6661.

GEM SAVE **C.M. RUSSELL MUSEUM** is in the n.e. section at 400 13th St. N. Offered are displays of watercolors, sculpture, oil paintings and illustrated cards and letters by the cowboy artist Charles M. Russell. Additional galleries feature historical photographs of the Old West, an exhibit of Browning firearms and the works of other Western artists.

Allow 2 hours minimum. Mon.-Sat. 9-6, Sun. noon-5, May-Sept.; Tues.-Sat. 10-5, Sun. 1-5, rest of year. Closed Jan. 1, Easter, Thanksgiving and

Dec. 25. Admission $6; over 59, $4; students with ID $3; under 5 free. AX, MC, VI. Phone (406) 727-8787. *See color ad p. 266.*

C.M. Russell Home is next to the studio. Russell's permanent residence was built in 1900 and is furnished in period. Mon.-Sat. 9-6, Sun. noon-5, May-Sept.

Log Studio of Charles M. Russell is next to the museum. Built in 1903, the studio contains Russell's pallet and brushes, cowboy memorabilia and American Indian artifacts he used as models. Mon.-Sat. 9-6, Sun. noon-5, May-Sept.; Tues.-Sat. 10-5, Sun. 1-5, rest of year. Closed Jan. 1, Easter, Thanksgiving and Dec. 25.

GIANT SPRINGS FISH, WILDLIFE AND PARKS VISITOR CENTER AND FISH HATCHERY is 2.5 mi. n.e. off US 87 on River Dr. The regional headquarters visitor center has wildlife displays, photographs about park history and film presentations. Across the street is the hatchery for rainbow trout and salmon; a visitor center explains fish raising. The park preserves one of the largest freshwater springs in the world. Scenic overlooks are available from two dams within 2 miles of the site.

Allow 1 hour minimum. Park daily 8 a.m.-10 p.m. Park visitor center Mon.-Fri. 8-5, Sat.-Sun. 1-5, Memorial Day-Labor Day; Mon.-Fri. 8-5, rest of year. Hatchery visitor center daily 8-4:30. Park admission $2. Visitor centers free. Phone (406) 454-5840 for the regional headquarters visitor center, or (406) 452-5734 for the hatchery.

SAVE **GREAT FALLS HISTORIC TROLLEY** departs from High Plains Heritage Center, 422 Second St. S., and picks up passengers at the visitor center and area hotels. Highlights include historic homes, churches, downtown buildings, museums, waterfalls and the Lewis and Clark Trail. Allow 2 hours minimum. Tour departs Mon.-Thurs. at 10 and 4, Fri.-Sun. at 10, 1 and 4, June-Sept.; by appointment rest of year. Fare $20; ages 2-12, $5. Phone (406) 771-1100 or (888) 707-1100.

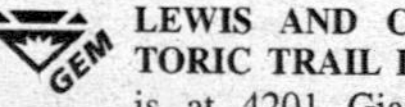

LEWIS AND CLARK NATIONAL HISTORIC TRAIL INTERPRETIVE CENTER is at 4201 Giant Springs Rd. in Giant Springs Heritage State Park. Exhibits detail the 1804-06 Lewis and Clark expedition, particularly the portion that took place in what is now Montana. Highlighted are the Indian tribes of the Plains and Pacific Northwest who aided Lewis and Clark. Costumed interpreters demonstrate skills used on the journey. A 30-minute introductory film by Ken Burns sets the stage for the visitor's own discovery journey.

The center overlooks the Missouri River and features walking trails, scenic overlooks and grounds landscaped with plants described in the explorers' journals. Outdoor living-history programs are presented in the summer.

Allow 2 hours minimum. Daily 9-6, Memorial Day-Sept. 30; Tues.-Sat. 9-5, Sun. noon-5, rest of year. Closed Jan. 1, Thanksgiving and Dec. 25. Admission $5; over 61, $4; ages 6-17, $2. Phone (406) 727-8733.

MALMSTROM AIR FORCE BASE MUSEUM AND AIR PARK is on Malmstrom Air Force Base, just inside the west gate at the east end of Second Ave. N. The museum displays uniforms, equipment and photographs relating to base history. The outdoor air park contains aircraft that date from the mid-20th century. A bus tour is available to selected sites, including the fire department, launch facilities, helicopter area and museum.

Allow 1 hour minimum. Mon.-Fri. 10-4; closed federal holidays. Free. Reservations are recommended for bus tours. Phone (406) 731-2705 for museum information or (406) 731-4050 for reservations.

MEHMKE STEAM MUSEUM is 10 mi. e. on US 87/89. Displays of operable antique steam engines and gas tractors are offered along with exhibits of farming artifacts. Allow 1 hour minimum. Daily dawn-dusk. Donations. Phone (406) 452-6571.

PARIS GIBSON SQUARE MUSEUM OF ARTS is at jct. 14th St. and First Ave. N. in the Norman Architectural Building. The museum contains contemporary art exhibits. Allow 1 hour, 30 minutes minimum. Mon.-Fri. 10-5 (also Tues. 7-9 p.m.), Sat.-Sun. noon-5, Labor Day-Memorial Day; Tues.-Fri. 10-5 (also Tues. 7-9 p.m.), Sat.-Sun. noon-5, rest of year. Closed holidays. Donations. Phone (406) 727-8255.

TOUR DE GREAT FALLS picks up passengers at area hotels. Guided bus tours to museums, parks and natural sites are conducted. Other tours are available. Allow 2 hours, 30 minutes minimum. Daily, June-Sept.; by appointment rest of year. Fare $20; over 64, $18; ages 2-12, $10. Attraction admissions are not included in fare. Reservations are required.. Phone (406) 771-1100 or (888) 707-1100.

RECREATIONAL ACTIVITIES

White-water Rafting

- **River Odysseys West (ROW)**, departs from a local lodging. Write P.O. Box 579, Coeur d'Alene, ID 83816. Trips depart mid-May to mid-Sept. Phone (208) 765-0841 or (800) 451-6034.

HAMILTON (D-1) pop. 3,705, elev. 3,572'

The seat of Ravalli County and headquarters of Bitterroot National Forest, Hamilton was founded by 19th-century copper magnate Marcus Daly.

Bitterroot Valley Chamber of Commerce: 105 E. Main St., Hamilton, MT 59840; phone (406) 363-2400.

SAVE **DALY MANSION** is at 251 Eastside Hwy. (CR 269). The riverside estate of Montana's copper baron, Marcus Daly, contains its original furniture and Italian marble fireplaces. The Georgian Revival house is surrounded by a 22,000-acre stock farm where Daly raised Thoroughbred racehorses. Allow 1 hour minimum. Guided tours are given daily 10-5, Apr. 15-Oct. 15; by appointment rest of year. Fee $6; over 60, $5; students ages 12-17, $4; ages 5-11, $3. Grounds only $1. Phone (406) 363-6004.

RAVALLI COUNTY MUSEUM is at 205 Bedford St. In the original Ravalli County courthouse, the museum contains various exhibits, including an American Indian artifacts collection, a laboratory display about Rocky Mountain tick fever, period rooms, a veterans exhibit and historical photographs and newspapers. A program of cultural or historical significance is presented Sundays at 2. Allow 1 hour minimum. Thurs.-Sat. and Mon. 10-4, Sun. 1-4; closed holidays. Donations. Phone (406) 363-3338.

HARDIN (D-5) pop. 3,384, elev. 2,902′

Hardin borders Crow Indian Reservation and serves as a trading center for its people. The town was named after Samuel Hardin, a rancher from Wyoming who leased land on the reservation. Nearby is the former site of Fort Custer, a military garrison said to have been one of the finest cavalry posts in the world. It was established in 1877, just after Lt. Col. George A. Custer's defeat.

The 4-day Little Big Horn Days celebration takes place the last weekend in June. Festivities include a grand ball with period music, costumes and dances; a re-enactment of Custer's Last Stand; a powwow; arts and crafts shows; and dancing.

Hardin Area Chamber of Commerce: 10 E. Railway St., Hardin, MT 59034; phone (406) 665-1672.

BIG HORN COUNTY HISTORICAL MUSEUM AND STATE VISITOR CENTER is 1 mi. e. off I-90 exit 497. The 22-acre complex features area history exhibits and 20 historic buildings, including a 1911 farmhouse, an American Indian log cabin, a railroad depot, a doctor's building and the Fort Custer stage station. Picnicking is permitted. Museum daily 8-8, June-Aug.; 8-5 in May and Sept.; Mon.-Fri. 9-5, rest of year. Free. Phone (406) 665-1671.

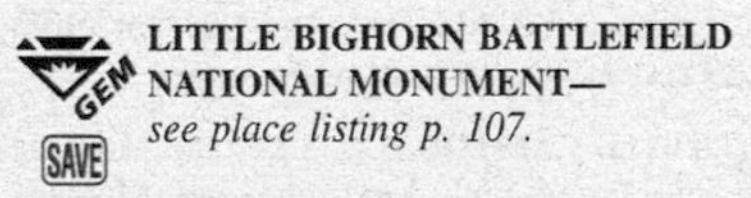

LITTLE BIGHORN BATTLEFIELD NATIONAL MONUMENT—
see place listing p. 107.

HARLOWTON (D-4) pop. 1,062

UPPER MUSSELSHELL MUSEUM is at 11 S. Central Ave. Life in the early 1900s is depicted through replicas of a general store, schoolroom, kitchen and living room. Supplementing these exhibits are displays of period clothing, farm tools and other artifacts. Also displayed is a replica of a dinosaur whose remains were found north of town on Careless Creek. Allow 30 minutes minimum. Tues.-Sat. 10-5, Sun. 1-5, May-Sept.; by appointment rest of year. Admission $2; ages 6-13, $1. Phone (406) 632-5519.

HAVRE (B-4) pop. 9,621, elev. 2,493′

Havre's beginnings as a transportation hub were forged by the railroad, which brought supplies to trappers, miners and the military at nearby Fort Assinniboine. The town was named by railroad officials after the French city Le Havre, but its citizens gave it a different pronunciation: HAV-er.

Area geography can best be described as dichotomous. Here, rolling plains meet the Bear Paw Mountains, providing unlimited summer and winter recreation opportunities. Beaver Creek Park, a 17-mile-long, 1-mile-wide strip park 11 miles south on CR 234, encases Beaver Creek and two lakes and offers a variety of activities including camping, fishing, hiking, cross-country skiing and snowshoeing.

A free guided walking tour of Havre's architecturally diverse historic district departs from the Heritage Center on Third Avenue Saturdays at 7 p.m., May through October (weather permitting). Tours of Fort Assinniboine also are available on selected days June through September; phone (406) 265-6233.

Havre Area Chamber of Commerce: 518 1st St., P.O. Box 308, Havre, MT 59501; phone (406) 265-4383.

Self-guiding tours: Free brochures for self-guiding walking tours of the 36-block historic district are available from the chamber of commerce.

HAVRE BENEATH THE STREETS is at 120 Third Ave. This guided walking tour takes visitors through the city's historical underground. Many of the original buildings built in 1904 are now beneath the city streets. Included are a Chinese laundry, post office, bordello, meat market, bakery, opium den, barber shop and saloon. Allow 1 hour minimum. Daily 9-5, May-Sept.; Mon.-Sat. 10-4, rest of year. Closed holidays. Last tour departs at 3:30. Reservations are recommended. Admission $6; over 55, $5; ages 6-12, $4. Phone (406) 265-8888.

H. EARL CLACK MUSEUM AND GALLERY is at 306 Third Ave. Local history is chronicled through artifacts, dioramas and exhibits about area geological features. A large section of the museum displays items from the 2,000-year-old Wahkpa Chu'gn Buffalo Jump site, one of Montana's largest bison kill sites. Guided tours of Fort Assinniboine, 8 miles southwest off US 87, are offered.

Allow 1 hour minimum. Museum Tues.-Sat. 10-5, Memorial Day-Labor Day; 1-5, rest of year. Hours may vary; phone ahead. Fort tours are given at 5 (weather permitting). Donations. Fort tours $5, students with ID $2. Phone (406) 265-4000.

SAVE **Wahkpa Chu'gn Buffalo Jump** is on US 2 behind the Holiday Village Mall. Pronounced "walk-paw chew-gun," an Assinniboine name for the Milk River, this prehistoric buffalo jump site was occupied by three separate cultures from 600 to 2,000 years ago. A 1-hour guided walking tour features exposed campsites and buffalo bone deposits as deep as 20 feet below the surface. Guided tours daily 10-5 (also Mon.-Sat. at 7 p.m.), June 1-Labor Day; by appointment rest of year. Fee $5; over 62, $4; ages 6-17, $2.50. Phone (406) 265-6417.

ROCKY BOY INDIAN RESERVATION is 15 mi. s. of US 87 in the Bear Paw Mountains. Established in 1916, the Chippewa Cree reservation is named for a Chippewa leader whose Indian name, meaning "Stone Child," later was changed to "Rocky Boy." Tours of historical sites are offered. Fishing is permitted in a number of well-stocked streams and ponds; a tribal license is required. Hiking trails are available. Bear Paw Ski Bowl is on the reservation. Ski area open mid-December to early April. Fishing license $5 for 1 day, $10 for 3 days. Phone (406) 395-4193.

HELENA (C-2) pop. 25,780, elev. 4,047'

Helena succeeded the other gold camps of Bannack and Virginia City as the territorial capital in 1875. It became the state capital in 1889 after a hotly contested fight between W.A. Clark and Marcus Daly. The city owes its existence to "The Georgians," four weary and discouraged Southern prospectors, who in 1864 stumbled down a gulch and grimly dubbed it "Last Chance Gulch," only to find gold where the city's main street now runs.

Later a more suitable name, Helena (He-LAY-na), was put to a vote. But the miners and the bullwhackers did not like the name's feminine ring. Consequently the emphasis was shifted to the first syllable, with the second "e" almost silent, and HEL-e-na became the accepted pronunciation. The gold rush faded quickly, and Helena settled down to become a trade center for the surrounding goldfields.

Marysville, a ghost town, is 25 miles northwest off CR 279. During the 1880s and '90s the town reigned as Montana's leading gold producer. The remnants of its saloons, shops and sidewalks still can be seen.

Helena Area Chamber of Commerce: 225 Cruse Ave., Suite A, Helena, MT 59601; phone (406) 442-4120 or (800) 743-5362.

Shopping areas: Once the quarters of miners, muleskinners and Chinese laborers during the gold rush, the buildings along Reeder's Alley, 100 S. Park Ave., now contain specialty shops.

CATHEDRAL OF ST. HELENA is at jct. Lawrence and Warren sts. This handsome neo-Gothic structure was modeled after the Votive Church of Vienna, Austria. Interior furnishings are of Carrara marble, and the stained-glass windows were made in Munich, Germany. Allow 30 minutes minimum. Mon.-Fri. 8 a.m.-9 p.m., Sat. 8:30 a.m.-9 p.m., Sun. 7:30 a.m.-9 p.m. Guided tours are given Tues.-Thurs. at 1, Memorial Day-Labor Day. Free. Phone (406) 442-5825.

LAST CHANCE TOUR TRAIN departs from Montana Historical Society Museum *(see attraction listing)*. This 1-hour jaunt makes a circuit through the present and past of Helena on "The Last Chancer," an automotive tour train. Tours depart Mon.-Sat. at 10, 11, 1, 2, 3, 4 and 6, July-Aug; at 10, 11, 1, 2 and 3, in June; at 11, 1, and 3, May 15-30 and in Sept. Fare $6; over 59, $5.50; under 12, $5. Phone (406) 442-1023 or (888) 423-1023.

Pioneer Cabin is at 210 S. Park Ave. This 1864 cabin, said to be the oldest in Helena, is furnished with pioneer articles. Allow 30 minutes minimum. Mon.-Fri. 10:30-noon and 1-3, Memorial Day-Labor Day. Guided tours are available by appointment year-round. Admission $1, under 13 free. Phone (406) 443-7641 Memorial Day-Labor Day or (406) 444-1687 rest of year.

MONTANA HISTORICAL SOCIETY MUSEUM, LIBRARY AND ARCHIVES is across from the State Capitol at 225 N. Roberts St. The history of Montana and the Northwest is recounted through an extensive collection of C.M. Russell's paintings and sculpture. The Montana Homeland exhibition uses more than 2,000 artifacts, photographs and documents to trace Montana history from the end of the most recent ice age through World War II.

Mon.-Sat. 9-5 (also Thurs. 5-8), Memorial Day-Sept. 15; Tues-Sat. 9-5 (also Thurs. 5-8), rest of year. Closed holidays. Admission $3; ages 5-18, $1; family rate (two adults and children under 19) $8. Phone (406) 444-2694.

ORIGINAL GOVERNOR'S MANSION is at 304 N. Ewing. Built in 1888, the Victorian mansion was the home of nine Montana governors 1913-59. The house is furnished in period. Allow 30 minutes minimum. Guided tours are given Wed.-Sat. noon-4, Memorial Day-Sept. 15; by appointment rest of year. Closed holidays. Admission $2; ages 5-18, $1; family rate (two adults and children under 19) $6. Phone (406) 442-3115 Apr.-Dec., or (406) 444-4789 rest of year for tour reservations.

STATE CAPITOL is at Sixth and Montana sts. Faced with sandstone and Montana granite, the capitol is topped by a dome of Montana copper. The cornerstone was laid July 4, 1899, and the building was dedicated July 4, 1902. Historical paintings and statues decorate the interior; prominent among these is Charles M. Russell's largest painting, the 12-by-25-foot "Lewis and Clark Meeting Indians at Ross' Hole," in the House of Representatives.

Allow 30 minutes minimum. Mon.-Sat. 9-5, Sun. noon-5; closed holidays. Guided tours are given Mon.-Sat. 10-1, Memorial Day-Sept. 15. Free. Phone (406) 444-4789.

HELENA NATIONAL FOREST

Elevations in the forest range from 3,600 ft. at the gates of the Missouri River to 9,411 ft. on Red Mountain in the Lincoln district. Refer to AAA maps for additional elevation information.

In west-central Montana, Helena National Forest encompasses 976,000 acres. The forest straddles the Continental Divide and embraces the Big Belt and the Elkhorn mountains. The Missouri River passes through the Helena Valley near the center of the forest. Vegetation ranges from sagebrush and bunchgrass to Douglas fir, lodgepole pine and spruce.

There are more than 700 miles of trails and 1,600 miles of forest roads. Continental Divide National Scenic Trail passes through the forest. Ten campgrounds, picnic grounds, good hunting and fishing, historic sites, wilderness areas and several ghost towns are among the forest's attractions. For further information contact the Forest Supervisor, Helena National Forest, 2880 Skyway Dr., Helena, MT 59602; phone (406) 449-5201. *See Recreation Chart and the AAA Northwestern CampBook.*

GEM **THE GATES OF THE MOUNTAINS RECREATION AREA** is 20 mi. n. of Helena via I-15 exit 209 to Gates of the Mountains Landing and is reached by boat or trails. Magnificent 1,200-foot limestone walls line the canyon where the Missouri River pushes through the Big Belt Range. The river is known for good fishing.

Boat trips, with stopovers at Meriwether picnic area, depart Mon.-Fri. at 11 and 2, Sat.-Sun. and holidays at 10, noon, 2 and 4, in June; Mon.-Fri. at 11, 1 and 3, Sat.-Sun. and holidays on the hour 10-4, July-Aug.; daily at 11 and 2, holidays at 11, 1 and 3, Sept. 1-21. Fare $9.50; over 60, $8.50; ages 4-17, $6. MC, VI. Phone (406) 458-5241.

HUNGRY HORSE (B-2) pop. 934, elev. 3,100′

HUNGRY HORSE DAM is 15 mi. s.e. of Glacier National Park. One of the world's largest concrete dams, Hungry Horse's 2,115-foot crest is crossed by a 39-foot-wide roadway. A visitor center 4 miles east of US 2 has interactive displays and a videotape. Guided tours are available. Visitor center open daily 8-3:45, Memorial Day-Labor Day. Free. Phone (406) 387-5241, ext. 361.

HUSON (C-1) elev. 3,015′

THE NINEMILE REMOUNT DEPOT AND RANGER STATION is off I-90 to exit 82, then 4 mi. n. on Remount Rd. A working ranger station on a 5,000-acre ranch features Cape Cod style buildings. A self-guiding tour through the historic site reveals the daily life of the fire-fighting rangers 1930-53. Grand Menard Discovery Trail, 1.5 miles north of the station, features two .7-mile self-guiding tours through a pine forest. Tour and trail brochures are available.

Allow 1 hour minimum. Site open daily dawn-dusk. Ranger station open daily 8-4:30. Visitor center open daily 9-5, Memorial Day-Labor Day. Donations. Phone (406) 626-5201.

KALISPELL (B-1) pop. 14,223, elev. 2,956′

Kalispell (KAL-is-pell) is in the Flathead Valley between Glacier National Park *(see place listing p. 96)* and Flathead Lake, a region noted for the production of sweet cherries. The area was known only to the Salish, who called it "the land between the mountains," until 1891 when the Great Northern

Railroad laid track to this point. The nearby settlements of Demersville and Ashley were moved to create Kalispell.

Kalispell is circled by dense forests, lakes, rivers and mountains. To the east is the Swan Range of the Rocky Mountains, and to the west, the Kootenai Range. Flathead National Forest *(see place listing p. 94)* has its headquarters in the city.

Local parks include Woodland Park, with lagoons, formal gardens and picnicking. Three forks of the Flathead River drain into Flathead Lake, making the area an ideal place for fly fishing, white-water rafting, kayaking and sailing.

Flathead Convention and Visitor Bureau: 15 Depot Park, Kalispell, MT 59901-4008; phone (406) 756-9091 or (800) 543-3105.

Self-guiding tours: Information about walking tours of the historic district is available from Kalispell Chamber of Commerce; phone (406) 758-2800. For information about the greater northwestern Montana area contact Glacier Country at (800) 338-5072.

Shopping areas: The Kalispell Farmer's Market, in the Kalispell Center Mall parking lot, offers more than 100 vendors selling homemade and home-grown products.

SAVE **CONRAD MANSION NATIONAL HISTORIC SITE MUSEUM** is 6 blks. e. of Main St. at Woodland Ave. and Fourth St. E. Built in 1895 for Kalispell's founder, Charles E. Conrad, who traded and freighted on the Missouri River, the 26-room mansion has been restored to its Victorian splendor and contains original furnishings. Visitors can take guided tours of the mansion and self-guiding tours of the gardens on the 3-acre site. Allow 1 hour minimum. Guided tours are given daily 10-5, May 15-Oct. 15. Fee $7; senior citizens $6; under 12, $2. MC, VI. Phone (406) 755-2166.

HOCKADAY MUSEUM OF ART is at 302 Second Ave. E. at Third St. Striking works by local and regional artists and such nationally known artists as Ace Powell are highlighted. Six permanent galleries in a historic Carnegie Library contain etchings, paintings and sculpture that relate Western and American Indian life. The museum also features changing exhibits. Allow 1 hour minimum. Mon.-Sat. 10-6 (also Thurs. 6-8 p.m.), Sun. noon-4, June-Aug.; Tues.-Sat. 10-5, rest of year. Admission $5; over 55, $4; students with ID $2; under 6 free. Phone (406) 755-5268.

SAVE **NORTHWEST MONTANA HISTORICAL SOCIETY CENTRAL SCHOOL MUSEUM** is at 124 Second Ave. E. Exhibits housed in a renovated 1894 school building detail area growth and cover such topics as forest preservation and pioneer life. Noteworthy is an exhibit about cowboy-turned-legislator Frank Bird Linderman, who documented northwest Montana's American Indian culture through sculpture and writings. Allow 1 hour minimum. Mon.-Sat. 10-6, mid-May to mid-Sept.; Tues.-Sat. 11-3, rest of year. Closed Jan. 1, Thanksgiving and Dec. 25. Admission $5; over 62, $4; under 19 free. Phone (406) 756-2048.

RECREATIONAL ACTIVITIES

Hot Air Ballooning

- **Fantasy Flights** departs from various locations in Flathead Valley. Write P.O. Box 7696, Kalispell, MT 59904. Departures daily May-Oct. (weather permitting). Reservations are recommended. Phone (406) 755-4172.

KOOTENAI NATIONAL FOREST

Elevations in the forest range from 1,862 ft. where the Kootenai River crosses into Idaho to 8,736 ft. on Snowshoe Peak. Refer to AAA maps for additional elevation information.

Kootenai National Forest is in the northwest corner of Montana, with a small section extending into Idaho. High, craggy peaks characterize the 2,245,000-acre region; portions of the Cabinet, Whitefish and Purcell mountains are the main ranges, attaining elevations as high as 8,700 feet.

The area's climate is modified Pacific Maritime, and as a result Kootenai has an abundance of plant species more common to the Pacific Coast than to other parts of Montana. Since most of the forest produces commercial timber, there is an extensive network of roads.

The Clark Fork elk herd is well known to hunters. The forest also is home to many nongame species. Throughout the year bald eagles can be seen along the Kootenai River north of Libby; 191 species of birds have been recorded in the forest. Cabinet Mountains Wilderness has 141 lakes; many are scenic, stocked with fish and easily reached by trail. Skiing facilities are available northwest of Libby. The area has 39 campgrounds and 1,500 miles of hiking trails.

Ross Creek Cedars Scenic Area, off SR 56 southwest of Libby, and Ten Lakes Scenic Area, on the Canadian border northeast of Eureka, are reached by local and forest roads. Lake Koocanusa also is a popular recreational spot *(see Libby p. 107)*.

For further information, write the Forest Supervisor, Kootenai National Forest, 1101 US 2W, Libby, MT 59923; phone (406) 293-6211. *See Recreation Chart and the AAA Northwestern CampBook.*

LAKESIDE (C-1) pop. 1,679, elev. 2,900'

On Flathead Lake's west shore, Lakeside offers summer and winter recreation, including boating, fishing, swimming, cross-country and downhill skiing, snowmobiling and ice fishing.

Lakeside-Somers Chamber of Commerce: P.O. Box 177, Lakeside, MT 59922; phone (406) 844-3715.

LAME DEER (D-6) pop. 2,018, elev. 3,380′

Lame Deer is the headquarters for the Northern Cheyenne Indian Reservation. Activities on the reservation include the Sun Dance (dates vary) and a powwow in July. Cheyenne crafts are available at the chamber of commerce, across the street from the police station.

Lame Deer Chamber of Commerce: P.O. Box 328, Lame Deer, MT 59043; phone (406) 477-8844.

LEWIS AND CLARK NATIONAL FOREST

Elevations in the forest range from 4,000 ft. in the valley bottoms to 9,204 ft. on Scapegoat Mountain. Refer to AAA maps for additional elevation information.

Lewis and Clark National Forest is in west-central Montana. Consisting of 1,843,397 acres, the forest has two units. The Rocky Mountain Unit, which embraces about half of the acreage, lies along the eastern slope of the Continental Divide south of Glacier National Park. It includes portions of the Bob Marshall *(see Flathead National Forest p. 94)* and Scapegoat wildernesses.

The Rocky Mountain Unit rises sharply from grasslands to peaks between 7,000 and 8,000 feet in elevation. Access to the area is by a number of gravel roads off US 89 that connect with forest roads and trailheads and serve several campgrounds.

Southeast of Great Falls is the Jefferson Unit, scattered inland mountain ranges dotting the prairie, including the Little Belt, Castle, Highwoods, Big Snowy and Little Snowy mountain ranges and the north end of the Crazy Mountains. The Jefferson Division has short, domelike mountains rather than jagged peaks.

The mountains are forest-covered and have moderate slopes that present less demanding hiking and riding trails than those found in the Rocky Mountain Unit. There are many streams but no large rivers or lakes.

Winter sports are available near Kings Hill Summit, some 40 miles north of White Sulphur Springs *(see place listing p. 119)*, Monarch and Neihart. For further information contact the Forest Supervisor, Lewis and Clark National Forest, 1101 15th St. N., P.O. Box 869, Great Falls, MT 59403; phone (406) 791-7700. *See Recreation Chart and the AAA Northwestern CampBook.*

LEWISTOWN (C-4) pop. 5,813, elev. 3,963′

Lewistown originally was a trading post on the Carroll Trail between Helena and Carroll. First called Reed's Fort, it later was renamed Lewistown after the military officer who established a fort nearby in 1876. Trading, only on a larger scale, continues to support the town, which is a market for the large cattle ranches and wheat farms of central Montana.

Lewistown Area Chamber of Commerce: 408 N.E. Main St., P.O. Box 818, Lewistown, MT 59457; phone (406) 538-5436.

CENTRAL MONTANA MUSEUM is at 408 N.E. Main St. Area history is documented through collections of minerals, guns and American Indian and Western artifacts. Allow 30 minutes minimum. Daily 10-4; closed Jan. 1, July 4, Thanksgiving and Dec. 25. Donations. Phone (406) 538-5436.

LIBBY (B-1) pop. 2,626, elev. 2,086′

Natural resources have been the mainstay of Libby's economy since its settlement in the 1860s. Drawn by stories of gold in the north, prospectors first gathered in this region and named the town after the daughter of one of the men who discovered gold in a nearby creek. Timber and tourism are the town's leading businesses.

Libby's environs contribute to the town's popularity as a recreational center. The nearby Kootenai National Forest *(see place listing p. 106)* provides extensive lands for public use, and anglers enjoy fishing in the Kootenai River and its tributaries. About 17 miles north, Libby Dam *(see Recreation Chart and the AAA Northwestern CampBook)* impounds the Kootenai River, creating 90-mile-long Lake Koocanusa, an excellent area for boating, fishing and swimming.

Libby Area Chamber of Commerce: 905 W. 9th St., P.O. Box 704, Libby, MT 59923; phone (406) 293-4167.

HERITAGE MUSEUM is .5 mi. e. at 1367 US 2S. A 12-sided log building contains exhibits about mining and forestry along with historical information about the Kootenai Indians, local participation in World War II and the work of the Civilian Conservation Corp. Art and wildlife are displayed. Outbuildings include an 1800s log cabin, a miner's cabin and a cookhouse. Archives are available by appointment. Mon.-Sat. 10-5, Sun. 1-5, first Sat. in June-Aug. 31. Donations. Phone (406) 293-7521 or (406) 293-2029.

GEM LITTLE BIGHORN BATTLEFIELD NATIONAL MONUMENT (E-6)

The main entrance to Little Bighorn Battlefield National Monument is 15 miles southeast of Hardin via exit 510 off I-90, then a half-mile east via US 212. In the Valley of the Little Bighorn River in June 1876, Lt. Col. George A. Custer and the 210 men of the 7th Cavalry Regiment under his command made their last stand against several thousand Lakota, Arapaho and Northern Cheyenne, many of whom were fleeing the restrictions of the reservation. Covering 1.2 square miles, the monument commemorates the dramatic climax of the Indian

Wars by preserving the site of this American Indian victory.

The monument embraces a national cemetery established in 1879, various monuments and memorials, and a historical museum with maps, photographs and dioramas depicting the battle. Just inside the entrance is a visitor center where park rangers provide tour information and self-guiding tour brochures.

Auto tour tapes with maps are available at the center and from Big Horn County Historical Museum and State Visitor Center *(see Hardin p. 103)* and other local outlets; phone (406) 638-2465.

Monument 8 a.m.-9 p.m., May 26-Labor Day; 8-6, Apr. 1-May 25 and day after Labor Day-Sept. 30; 8-4:30, rest of year. Visitor center daily 8-7:30. Closed Jan. 1, Thanksgiving and Dec. 25. Admission $10 per private vehicle, $5 per person arriving by bicycle, bus, motorcycle or on foot. Cemetery free. Phone (406) 638-2621.

APSAALOOKE TOURS depart from the Little Bighorn Battlefield National Monument Visitor Center. Narrated van tours of the site of the Battle of the Little Bighorn are given by American Indian guides. Allow 1 hour minimum. Daily 10-3, June-Aug. Fare $8; over 62, $5; under 13, $2. Phone (406) 638-7272 or (406) 638-3223.

LIVINGSTON (D-4) pop. 6,851, elev. 4,489′

The lush grasses of Paradise Valley were ideal for raising cattle, and the valley's warm chinook winds protected the area from bitter Montana winters. When the Northern Pacific Railroad laid tracks in 1882, both the cattle industry and Livingston flourished. Among the town's more memorable residents was Calamity Jane, but after she was jailed following a disturbance, her fondness for Livingston faded and she left town.

Livingston is at the head of Paradise Valley, through which flows the Yellowstone River and around which rise the Crazy Mountains and the Absaroka and Gallatin ranges of the Rockies. The area offers opportunities for wildlife viewing, hunting, fishing, rafting, backpacking, camping, skiing and snowmobiling. A scenic drive, US 89, connects Livingston to Gardiner and the northern entrance to Yellowstone National Park. Livingston was the original entrance to Yellowstone.

Livingston Area Chamber of Commerce: 303 E. Park St., Livingston, MT 59047; phone (406) 222-0850.

Self-guiding tours: A brochure outlining a walking tour of the historic business district is available at Yellowstone Gateway Museum *(see attraction listing)* and the chamber of commerce.

INTERNATIONAL FLY FISHING CENTER is off I-90 exit 333, 1.3 mi. n.e. on US 89, then s.e. on B Street to 215 E. Lewis. Displays include a large collection of fishing art, fly-fishing memorabilia from antique to present-day equipment, hundreds of flies and a hands-on display for fly-tiers. Aquariums with cold- and warm-water fish also are featured. Allow 1 hour, 30 minutes minimum. Mon.-Sat. 10-6, Sun. noon-5, Memorial Day-Sept. 15; Mon.-Fri. 10-5, rest of year. Admission $3; senior citizens, $2; ages 6-13, $1. Phone (406) 222-9369.

LIVINGSTON DEPOT CENTER is at 200 W. Park St. Built in 1902, the restored Northern Pacific Railroad station is in the Italian Renaissance style. It was designed by the same architectural firm that designed New York's Grand Central Station. Featured is the exhibit "Rails Across the Rockies: A Century of People and Places." Events are scheduled throughout the year. Picnicking is permitted. Mon.-Sat. 9-5, Sun. 1-5, late May to late Sept. Admission $3; over 61 and ages 6-12, $2; family rate $8. Phone (406) 222-2300.

SAVE **YELLOWSTONE GATEWAY MUSEUM** is off I-90 exit 333, then 10 blks. n to 118 W. Chinook St. The museum chronicles Northern Pacific Railroad history, native cultures, natural resources and pioneer lifestyles in Montana. Other displays include Yellowstone Park memorabilia, two vintage park stagecoaches and a Northern Pacific caboose. Allow 30 minutes minimum. Daily 10-5, Memorial Day-Labor Day; Tues.-Sat. 11-4, day after Labor Day-Sept. 30; by appointment rest of year. Admission $4; over 65, $3.50; ages 6-12, $2. Phone (406) 222-4184.

LOLO NATIONAL FOREST

Lolo National Forest is in western Montana. With boundaries stretching from the Swan Range in the northeast to the Idaho border, an area 120 miles long and 40 to 80 miles wide, the forest embraces about 2,100,000 acres. Although the Lolo is an important timber producer, many of its south-facing slopes are open and grassy. It also is one of the principal elk areas in western Montana.

Wilderness areas within the park include the 60,000-acre Rattlesnake National Recreation Area and Wilderness as well as Welcome Creek, Great Burn Roadless Area and portions of Scapegoat.

Recreational opportunities abound on 3,500 miles of streams, including Rock Creek, a haven for trout-fishing enthusiasts. Approximately 485 species of fish and wildlife inhabit the forest, which has numerous camping and/or picnic sites and 1,780 miles of hiking trails; winter activities include downhill and cross-country skiing, snowmobiling along 360 miles of designated trails and ice fishing. Some recreation facilities are designed for handicapped access; inquire at a ranger station.

The forest has seven visitor centers: Smokejumpers Visitor Center; Ninemile Remount Depot and Ranger Station *(see Huson p. 105)*; Missoula Area Visitor Information at Fort Missoula; the Northern Region Office in Missoula; and in the outlying districts of Seeley Lake, Superior and Plains/Thompson Falls.

For further information, write Lolo National Forest, Building 24A, Fort Missoula, Missoula, MT 59804; phone (406) 329-3814. *See Recreation Chart and the AAA Northwestern CampBook.*

LOMA (B-3) pop. 92, elev. 2,574′

At the convergence of the Missouri and Marias rivers, Loma was the site of an important decision in June 1805. When the snowmelt swelled both rivers to the point that Lewis and Clark had trouble determining which was the Missouri, they fortunately made the correct call and continued westward.

Lewis named the other river Maria's after his cousin and sweetheart Maria Wood, to whom he later proposed. Eventually the apostrophe was dropped, as was Lewis by his beloved.

MALTA (B-5) pop. 2,120, elev. 2,248′

Named for the island in the Mediterranean, Malta was the center of a cattle empire that reached from Glasgow to Havre and from the Missouri River to Canada during the late 19th century. Wheat and alfalfa have joined cattle as the area's leading products.

A large boulder east at the intersection of US 2 and Sleeping Buffalo Resort looks like a sleeping buffalo. The Assiniboine Indians revered it, and the markings on it had a part in their tribal rituals.

The Little Rocky Mountains, called "island mountains" by early American Indians, are 40 miles southwest on US 191. Gold was discovered in the mountains in 1884, and the historic remains set the scene for the mountain communities of Zortman and Landusky. Legend has it that Butch Cassidy and Kid Curry hid out in this area.

Malta Area Chamber of Commerce: 10½ S. 4th St. E., P.O. Box 1420, Malta, MT 59538; phone (406) 654-1776.

BOWDOIN NATIONAL WILDLIFE REFUGE is 7 mi. e. on CR 2 following signs. This 15,500-acre breeding and feeding area for migratory waterfowl, shorebirds and other wildlife, including deer, is one of the few northwestern nesting areas of the white pelican. The refuge can be seen via a 15-mile, self-guiding automobile tour (weather permitting); ideal viewing times are early fall and late spring. Allow 1 hour minimum. Refuge open daily dawn-dusk. Headquarters open Mon.-Fri. 7:30-4. Free. Phone (406) 654-2863.

PHILLIPS COUNTY MUSEUM is at 431 US 2E. The museum contains exhibits relating to the county's pioneer days, agriculture and mining. Featured are a large collection of American Indian buckskins and beadwork, and an outlaw display centered on Kid Curry. A dinosaur exhibit includes fossils, life-size casts, a complete tyrannosaurus skull, a 33-foot-long brachylophosaurus skeleton and photographs of the dig. Allow 1 hour minimum. Mon.-Sat. 10-5, Sun. 12:30-5, mid-May to mid-Sept. Admission $3, children $1, under 5 free. Phone (406) 654-1037.

MEDICINE LAKE (B-7) pop. 269, elev. 1,951′

MEDICINE LAKE NATIONAL WILDLIFE REFUGE is 24 mi. n. on SR 16. A nesting place for waterfowl and shorebirds, the 31,458-acre refuge houses about 230 species of birds at various times of the year. Fishing and hunting for waterfowl, upland game birds and deer are permitted in season; obtain maps and information at refuge headquarters, 1 mile south and 2 miles east of Medicine Lake. An

18-mile, self-guiding automobile tour route is available. Picnicking is permitted. Refuge open daily dawn-dusk, May-Sept. Headquarters open Mon.-Fri. 7-3:30. Free. Phone (406) 789-2305.

MILES CITY (D-6) pop. 8,487, elev. 2,364′

Miles City developed on the bottomland at the confluence of the Tongue and Yellowstone rivers. Gen. Nelson A. Miles arrived at the mouth of the Tongue River in August 1876 to force the Cheyenne and Sioux to return to the reservations. Miles built Fort Keogh at the site in 1877 and used it as a base for controlling the local tribes.

Main Street in times past was a block of saloons, gambling dens and brothels on the south, and banks, businesses and pawn shops on the north. Miles City has become a growing retail and service hub for eastern Montana and a center for cattle, sheep and crop farms.

Miles City Area Chamber of Commerce: 511 Pleasant St., Miles City, MT 59301; phone (406) 234-2890.

CUSTER COUNTY ART AND HERITAGE CENTER is on Water Plant Rd. Housed in a 1910 former water-treatment plant in a park overlooking the Yellowstone River, the center has two galleries featuring changing exhibits of Western, historical and contemporary art. Tues.-Sun. 1-5, Feb.-Dec.; closed Easter, Thanksgiving and Dec. 25. Free. Phone (406) 232-0635.

SAVE **RANGE RIDERS MUSEUM AND BERT CLARK GUN COLLECTION** is 1 mi. w. on US 10/I-94 Bus. Loop, across the Tongue River Bridge. This 12-building complex features Western antiques and artifacts, archeological and geological specimens, and one of the Fort Keogh officer's quarters. A detailed miniature replica of Fort Keogh is in the coach house. The Bert Clark gun collection comprises more than 400 pieces, including an elephant gun and a set of Belgian dueling pistols. Allow 1 hour minimum. Daily 8-6, Apr.-Oct. Admission $5; over 64, $4; ages 13-22, $1; ages 6-12, 50c. Phone (406) 232-6146.

MISSOULA (C-1) pop. 57,053, elev. 3,223′

Missoula lies astride the Clark Fork River, a tributary of the Columbia River named for William Clark. The town also occupies a valley that was once part of Glacial Lake Missoula, a prehistoric lake.

At the mouth of Hell Gate Canyon, Missoula straddles the route the Salish Indians traveled to reach the Great Plains hunting buffalo. Meriwether Lewis and William Clark later followed the same route through the canyon and camped approximately 9 miles southwest at Travellers Rest, near present-day Lolo. Many American Indians died in the canyon, as the Blackfoot regularly ambushed the Salish, which prompted French-Canadian trappers to christen the site Porte de L'Enfer, "Gate of Hell."

One of the first lumber mills in the region began in Missoula. Lumber remains not only a major industry but also a major concern. The U.S. Forest Service maintains in Missoula its Region No. 1 headquarters, a research station devoted to forest fire research and the smokejumpers' training center. The University of Montana supports these studies with a 22,000-acre experimental forest in addition to conservation and wildlife research stations.

A short drive in any direction will lead into a national forest or a wilderness area. The Rattlesnake National Recreation Area and Wilderness, 6 miles north of downtown, has many small lakes, streams and trails.

A Carousel for Missoula in Caras Park is a hand-carved 1918 merry-go-round created by volunteers. Rides are offered year-round; phone (406) 549-8382.

Missoula Convention & Visitors Bureau: 121 E. Broadway, Suite 103, Missoula, MT 59802; phone (406) 721-4750 or (800) 526-3465.

Self-guiding tours: Brochures outlining a driving tour of the area and a walking tour along the Clark Fork River are available from the convention and visitors bureau.

Shopping areas: Southgate Mall, US 93 and South Avenue, counts Dillard's, Herberger's, JCPenney and Sears among its 105 stores. The restored historic downtown, with a lighted riverfront nearby, also offers distinctive shopping opportunities.

ART MUSEUM OF MISSOULA is at 335 N. Pattee St. Exhibits highlight contemporary artists known nationally and internationally. The museum's collection includes works by Rudy Autio, Dale Chihuly and Miriam Shapiro. Tues.-Fri. 10-6 (also Tues. 6-7 p.m.), Sat. 10-4. Free. Phone (406) 728-0447.

HISTORICAL MUSEUM AT FORT MISSOULA is s. on Reserve St. to South Ave., then 1 mi. w. following signs. The museum is at the center of what was Fort Missoula, established in 1877 at the height of the conflict with the Nez Perce under Chief Joseph. Galleries and exhibits depict the roles of the timber industry, forest management, the fort and early settlement in Missoula County history. Of the 13 structures and original fort buildings that remain, eight have been renovated.

Guided tours are available. Allow 1 hour minimum. Mon.-Sat. 10-5, Sun. noon-5, Memorial Day weekend-Labor Day; Tues.-Sat. noon-5, rest of year. Closed Jan. 1, Easter, Thanksgiving and Dec. 25. Admission $3, senior citizens $2, students with ID $1, family rate $10. Reservations are required for tours. Phone (406) 728-3476.

ROCKY MOUNTAIN ELK FOUNDATION/WILDLIFE VISITOR CENTER is at 2291 W. Broadway. A wildlife art gallery, a collection of world-record elk displays and many life-size mounts, including grizzly bear, mountain goats and bighorn sheep, are highlights. Wildlife films are shown continuously. Mon.-Fri. 8-6, Sat. 9-5, Sun. 9-4, June-Aug.; Mon.-Fri. 8-5, Sat.-Sun. 10-4, Sept.-Dec.; Mon.-Fri. 8-6, Sat. 10-4, rest of year. Hours may vary; phone ahead. Closed Jan. 1, Easter, July 4, Thanksgiving and Dec. 25. Donations. Phone (406) 523-4545.

ST. FRANCIS XAVIER CHURCH is at 420 W. Pine St. Built in 1889, the church is noted for its 144-foot steeple, stained-glass windows and paintings by Brother Joseph Carignano. Visitors may watch a 10-minute videotape explaining the paintings. Allow 30 minutes minimum. Mon.-Sat. 8:30-5. Free. Phone (406) 542-0321.

SMOKEJUMPERS BASE AERIAL FIRE DEPOT is 7 mi. w. on W. Broadway, next to Johnson-Bell Airport. Displays include dioramas, artifacts and photographs relating to the history of U.S. Forest Service firefighting. Service smokejumpers give guided tours of the base and offer firsthand accounts of firefighting and smokejumping. Daily 8:30-5, Memorial Day-Labor Day; by appointment rest of year. Tours are given at 10, 11, 2, 3 and 4. Donations. Phone (406) 329-4934 or (406) 329-4900.

RECREATIONAL ACTIVITIES

Skiing

- **Snowbowl Ski Area** is at I-90 Reserve St. exit. Write P.O. Box 8107, Missoula, MT 59807. Other activities are offered in summer. Wed.-Mon. late Nov. to mid-Apr.; otherwise varies. Phone (406) 549-9777.

White-water Rafting

- **10,000 Waves Raft and Kayak Adventures** is at 1311 E. Broadway. Write P.O. Box 7924, Missoula, MT 59802. Other activities are offered. Trips depart daily at 9, 12:30 and 2:30, Apr.-Oct. Phone (406) 549-6670 or (800) 537-8315.

- **Montana River Guides** departs from Alberton Gorge. Write 210 Red Fox Rd., Lolo, MT 59847. Full- and half-day trips depart daily at 9 and 2, mid-Apr. to mid-Oct. Phone (406) 273-4718 or (800) 381-7238.

- **Pangaea Expeditions** departs from Alberton Gorge. Write 608 Railroad St., Alberton, MT 59820. Daily May 15-Sept. 15. Phone (877) 239-2392.

MOIESE (C-1) elev. 2,600′

NATIONAL BISON RANGE is s.w. via SR 212. Up to 500 bison as well as herds of elk, pronghorn antelope, deer and bighorn sheep live on the 18,540-acre range. From mid-May to mid-October the refuge can be explored via a 19-mile self-guiding driving tour on a one-way gravel road. The tour takes about 2 hours. Only portions of the site are open the rest of the year.

Note: Two-wheeled vehicles are not allowed off the paved roads. Trailers and motor homes are restricted to shorter drives; check at the visitor center. The gravel and dirt roads present some long climbs and steep downgrades. Visitors must keep their vehicles on the tour road, and *must* remain in or near them. Range open daily dawn-dusk. Visitor center open Mon.-Fri. 8-7, Sat.-Sun. 9-7, mid-May to mid-Oct.; Mon.-Fri. 8-4:30, rest of year. Closed holidays mid-Oct. to mid-May. Admission $4 per private vehicle. Phone (406) 644-2211.

MONIDA (E-3)

Monida is a former railroad town at the foot of Monida Pass and the Continental Divide. Scenic highway I-15 passes near town, offering views of the Centennial Mountains to the east and the Italian Peaks to the west. The name Monida is derived from the combination of Montana and Idaho.

RED ROCKS LAKES NATIONAL WILDLIFE REFUGE is off I-15 exit 0, then 28 mi. e. on a gravel road. Established as a refuge for trumpeter swans in 1935, this sanctuary with lakes, marshes, creeks and the isolation of the Centennial Valley has become one of North America's more important nesting areas for the swans. The prime viewing season is June through September. Primitive camping facilities are available. **Note:** No fuel is available after exiting the interstate. Inquire locally about road conditions. Mon.-Fri. 7:30-4. Free. Phone (406) 276-3536.

NEVADA CITY—*see Virginia City p. 116.*

OVANDO (C-2) pop. 71, elev. 4,100′

RECREATIONAL ACTIVITIES

Hunting

- **WTR Outfitters** is n. on SR 200 to 380 Outfitters Ln. Trips are offered Sept. 14-Nov. 30. Other activities are offered June-Aug. Phone (406) 793-5666 or (800) 987-5666.

PABLO (C-1) pop. 1,814, elev. 3,085′

Pablo is home to the 1,244,000-acre Flathead Indian Reservation and the headquarters of the Confederated Salish and Kootenai Indian Tribes. Approximately 3,700 tribal members live on or near the reservation and manage wildlife and natural resources.

THE PEOPLE'S CENTER is 1 mi. n. of the tribal complex at 53253 US 93. Exhibits focus on the history and culture of the Salish, Kootenai and Pend d'Oreille tribes. Art, photographs, oral histories and crafts are included in the collection. "Ed-Ventures," educational tours of nearby Flathead Reservation, are offered for an additional fee. Mon.-Fri. 9-5 (also Sat.-Sun. 10-6, June-Aug.); closed holidays. Admission $3, over 55 and students with ID $2, family rate $6. AX, MC, VI. Phone (406) 675-0160.

PHILIPSBURG (D-2) pop. 914, elev. 5,270′

In the heart of mineral-rich Flint Creek Valley, the town of Philipsburg emerged at the height of a silver mining boom in 1867 and was named for Philip Deidesheimer, a former Comstock engineer who built the area's first ore processing mill. The mill closed in 1869, marking the first of several mining busts and subsequent booms. The demand for manganese in steel production during World War I fueled a final ore producing period that lasted until the Great Depression.

The historic district, centered on Broadway, contains numerous late 19th- and early 20th-century structures. Outlying abandoned mines and ghost towns also attest to Philipsburg's mining legacy, although very few are still accessible. The surrounding Sapphire and Flint Creek mountain ranges attract a new breed of prospector, the rock hound, in search of gems and minerals.

Philipsburg is midway between Drummond and Anaconda on the Pintler Scenic Highway (SR 1). Broad views of Flint Creek Valley are available near mile markers 28 and 42.

Philipsburg Chamber of Commerce: P.O. Box 661, Philipsburg, MT 59858; phone (406) 859-3388.

GRANITE COUNTY MUSEUM & CULTURAL CENTER is at 135 S. Sansome St. An overview of a miner's life includes a mural depicting above-ground activities, an assay office and a reconstructed cabin. Exhibits include a sample of a real vein as well as tools, an ore car and mining memorabilia. Daily 10-4, Apr. 15-Dec. 15. Admission $3, under 12 free. Phone (406) 859-3020.

POLARIS (E-2) elev. 6,355′

Polaris is the beginning point of the Pioneer Scenic Byway, which stretches for 32 miles to the Wise River and affords glimpses of such wildlife as antelope, deer and hawks. The route passes Crystal Park, a natural crystal mountain where visitors can dig for various crystals. Another stop along the drive is Elkhorn Hot Springs, a hot springs pool. This picturesque road is open until the first snowfall.

POLSON (C-1) pop. 4,041, elev. 2,931′

Polson is in a natural amphitheater at the foot of Flathead Lake. During May and June water pours through the 200- to 500-foot perpendicular walls of the Flathead River Gorge at the rate of 500,000 gallons per second. Legend has it that Paul Bunyan dug the channel connecting the river and the lake.

Polson Area Chamber of Commerce: P.O. Box 667, Polson, MT 59860; phone (406) 883-5969.

FLATHEAD LAKE STATE PARK is just n. This is the largest natural freshwater lake west of the Mississippi. Nearby points of interest include Big Arm, Finley Point, Wayfarers, West Shore and Yellow Bay units *(see Recreation Chart and the AAA Northwestern CampBook)*; Somers Fish Hatchery; Montana University Biological Station; Station Creek Fish Hatchery; and Kerr Dam.

Admission $5 per private vehicle or $1 per person arriving by bicycle, bus, motorcycle or on foot. Phone (406) 849-5256 for Big Arm, (406) 887-2715 for Finley Point, or (406) 982-3034 for Yellow Bay.

KWA TAQ NUK PRINCESS is on US 93. Offered are narrated tours of scenic Flathead Lake. A 3-hour tour departs daily at 1:30, June 15-early Sept. Ninety-minute tours depart daily at 10:30 and 7:30. Three-hour tour $19; over 55, $17; ages 6-12, $9; family rate $43. Ninety-minute tour $13; over 55, $11; ages 6-12, $6; family rate $28. Reservations are recommended. MC, VI. Phone (406) 883-2448.

MIRACLE OF AMERICA MUSEUM is 2 mi. s. on US 93. Included in this potpourri of Americana are military collectibles; dolls and toys; logging, pioneer and American Indian artifacts; antique musical instruments and sheet music; and vintage automobiles, motorcycles and bicycles. A pioneer village with 26 walk-in buildings, the Montana Fiddlers Hall of Fame and a 65-foot logging boat also are offered. Picnicking is permitted. Daily 8-8, June 2-Aug. 31; Mon.-Sat. 8-5, Sun. 1:30-5, rest of year.

Closed Easter and Dec. 25. Admission $3; ages 3-12, $1. Phone (406) 883-6804.

POLSON-FLATHEAD HISTORICAL MUSEUM is at 708 Main St. Exhibits preserve the pioneer heritage of the surrounding area. Included are farm machinery, American Indian artifacts, a chuck wagon, a stagecoach and a restored 1881 trading post. Marionettes created by puppeteer Blanche Harding are featured in a Lewis and Clark exhibit. Mon.-Sat. 9-5, Sun. 1-6, Memorial Day-Labor Day. Admission $2.50, senior citizens $2, under 12 free, family rate $6. Phone (406) 883-3049.

RECREATIONAL ACTIVITIES

White-water Rafting

- **Flathead Raft Co.** is on US 93. Write P.O. Box 1596, Polson, MT 59860. Daily early June-early Sept. Phone (406) 883-5838 or (800) 654-4359.

POMPEYS PILLAR NATIONAL MONUMENT (D-5)

Pompeys Pillar National Monument is 1 mi. n. of Pompeys Pillar off I-94 exit 23. Capt. William Clark carved his name on this huge sandstone formation in 1806; it is the only physical evidence of the Lewis and Clark expedition through the area. Clark named the rock after guides Charbonneau and Sacajawea's son, Baptiste, whom he nicknamed Pomp. The pillar also bears American Indian pictographs and the names of early trappers, soldiers and settlers. Interpretive tours are available upon request at the visitor center.

Daily 8-8, Memorial Day-Labor Day; 9-5, day after Labor Day-early Oct. The site is accessible the rest of the year only by a half-mile walk from a parking area. Admission $3 per private vehicle. Phone (406) 875-2233 for the visitor center or (406) 896-5013 for the Bureau of Land Management.

PRYOR (E-5) pop. 628, elev. 4,065′

CHIEF PLENTY COUPS STATE PARK is 1 mi. w. off SR 416 following signs. A museum features relics of Chief Plenty Coups, last traditional chief of the Crow Indians, and interpretive displays about Crow Indian culture. The chief is buried nearby at Medicine Spring. Fishing opportunities are available. Picnicking is permitted. Allow 1 hour minimum. Park open daily 8-8, May-Sept. Visitor center open daily 10-5, May-Sept.; by appointment rest of year. Admission $2. Phone (406) 252-1289.

RED LODGE (E-4) pop. 2,177, elev. 5,548′

At the base of the Beartooth Mountains, Red Lodge is an all-year resort town. Winter sports include downhill and cross-country skiing, while summer pursuits range from trout fishing and boating to water skiing on Cooney Reservoir *(see Recreation Chart)*.

Local legend attributes the town's name to a tribe of Crow Indians called the Red Lodge Clan, who covered their tepees with the local red clay. Coal-mining operations later drew many Europeans to the area.

Red Lodge Area Chamber of Commerce: 601 N. Broadway, P.O. Box 988, Red Lodge, MT 59068; phone (406) 446-1718.

Self-guiding tours: A visitor guide distributed by the chamber of commerce includes information about a walking tour.

BEARTOOTH SCENIC HIGHWAY is US 212 from Red Lodge to the northeastern entrance of Yellowstone National Park via Cooke City. The American Indians called the original Beartooth Pass the "trail above the eagles." This 64-mile road begins at 5,650 feet and rises to the Beartooth Plateau via a series of switchbacks.

After cresting the plateau at an elevation of almost 11,000 feet, where an unobstructed view of more than 75 miles is possible, the road winds past snowfields, small lakes and fields of flowers. Finally it descends into a dense pine forest, passing tumbling waterfalls and streams interspersed with occasional jagged peaks.

Many scenic overlooks have been constructed. Even in mid-summer, cool temperatures can be expected at higher elevations; a jacket or sweater is recommended. Allow 3 hours minimum. The two-lane highway is usually open May through September.

RECREATIONAL ACTIVITIES

Fishing

- **Yellowstone Troutfitters** is at 10 S. Broadway. Write P.O. Box 491, Red Lodge, MT 59068. Daily 10-5, May-Sept.; by appointment rest of year. Phone (406) 446-3819.

Skiing

- **Red Lodge Mountain Resort** is 6 mi. w. to 101 Ski Run Rd. Write P.O. Box 750, Red Lodge, MT 59068. Daily 8-5, Nov.-Apr.; Mon.-Fri. 8-5, rest of year Phone (406) 446-2610.

White-water Rafting

- SAVE **Adventure Whitewater Inc.** meets passengers on SR 78 at the Paintbrush Adventures red barn 1 mi. n. of Absarokee. Write P.O. Box 636, Red Lodge, MT 59068. Other activities are offered. Daily 8-7, Memorial Day weekend-Labor Day. Phone (406) 446-3061 or (800) 897-3061.

RONAN (C-2) pop. 1,812

NINEPIPE AND PABLO NATIONAL WILDLIFE REFUGES are 5 mi. s. off US 93 and 7 mi. n. off US 93, then 3 mi. w. on Reservoir Rd., respectively. Each refuge covers more than 2,000 acres. Primarily of interest to birdwatchers, these areas are inhabited by thousands of ducks, geese and other water birds. A cooperative state, federal and tribal wildlife-viewing area is at Ninepipe National Wildlife Refuge.

Refuges are open daily dawn-dusk. Portions of Ninepipe are closed during hunting season (late Sept.-early Jan.) and nesting season (Mar. 1-July 15). The south and west sides of Pablo are closed to public use; the entire refuge is closed during hunting season. Admission $4 per private vehicle. Phone (406) 644-2211.

ROUNDUP (D-5) pop. 1,931, elev. 3,226′

Renowned for the natural geographical design that made it ideal for herding livestock, Roundup features mountainous scenery and tree-lined streets. Fishing opportunities abound in the Musselshell River and at nearby Fort Peck Reservoir and Deadman's Basin.

MUSSELSHELL VALLEY HISTORICAL MUSEUM is at 524 First St. W. A variety of exhibits detailing Roundup's history include fossils, American Indian artifacts and paintings. Changing exhibits are featured in summer. On the grounds are a smithy, a print shop and the 1884 NF Ranch house. Daily 1-5, late Apr.-late Sept. Donations. Phone (406) 323-1403.

ST. IGNATIUS (C-2) pop. 788, elev. 2,940′

DOUG ALLARD'S FLATHEAD INDIAN MUSEUM is on US 93. Displayed are turn-of-the-20th-century American Indian clothing and regalia. Exhibits also include tools, pottery and artifacts. Allow 30 minutes minimum. Daily 9-7, May-Sept.; 9-5:30, rest of year. Closed Thanksgiving and Dec. 25. Free. AX, DS, MC, VI. Phone (406) 745-2951.

ST. IGNATIUS MISSION is .2 mi. s. on US 93 to sign, then .2 mi. e. Established by Jesuit missionaries in 1854, the mission consists of two original residences, the rectory and a brick church built in 1891. The church is decorated with 58 dry-fresco paintings executed about 1900 by Brother Joseph Carignano, the mission cook. A museum displays American Indian and religious items. Mission open daily 8:30-6, June-Aug.; 9-5, rest of year. Museum schedule varies; phone ahead. Donations. Phone (406) 745-2768.

ST. REGIS (C-1) pop. 315, elev. 2,537′

RECREATIONAL ACTIVITIES

White-water Rafting

- **River Odysseys West (ROW)** departs from SR 135 near the Exxon station. Write P.O. Box 579, Coeur d'Alene, ID 83816. Trips depart daily at 9, July 2-Labor Day. Phone (208) 765-0841 or (800) 451-6034.

SCOBEY (B-6) pop. 1,082, elev. 2,507′

DANIELS COUNTY MUSEUM AND PIONEER TOWN is at 7 County Rd. Some 40 buildings in this restored pioneer town portray early 20th-century homestead life. A collection of period antiques includes vintage vehicles. Guided tours are available. Allow 1 hour, 30 minutes minimum. Daily 12:30-4:30, Memorial Day-Labor Day. Admission $5; ages 6-11, $2.50. Phone (406) 487-5965.

SEELEY LAKE (C-2) pop. 1,436, elev. 4,028′

Seeley Lake is a year-round recreation area tucked between the Mission Mountains and Swan Range on scenic SR 83. In the summer visitors can indulge in fishing, swimming, boating, backpacking and horseback riding. Fewer than 10 miles from town are Placid Lake and Salmon Lake state parks *(see Recreation Chart)*; Seeley Lake itself has three Forest Service campgrounds, and at the north end of the lake is the 3.5-mile-long Clearwater Canoe Trail. Northeast of Seeley Lake is the 2.5-mile-long Morrell Falls National Recreation Trail, rated as "easy." Just east of the Morrell Falls trailhead access road is the Pyramid Pass Trail into Bob Marshall Wilderness Area.

In the winter the average snow on the ground is about 3 feet, and 350 miles of groomed snowmobile trails, primarily in Lolo National Forest, attract enthusiasts. For information about possible logging activities on the trails contact the Seeley Lake Ranger District office at (406) 677-2233. Three miles north of town on SR 83, the ranger station's visitor center provides maps and brochures about the area. Other local wintertime diversions include cross-country skiing, ice fishing and dog sledding.

Seeley Lake Area Chamber of Commerce: P.O. Box 516, Seeley Lake, MT 59868; phone (406) 677-2880.

SHELBY (B-3) pop. 3,216, elev. 3,276′

Shelby was one of the towns that the Great Northern Railroad left in its path as it pushed across the prairie. In its heyday, the town was paradise to cowboys after months on the range. A Saturday night might include carousing, horse racing, or—as once happened—holding up a passing opera troupe and making the train conductor do a clog dance to the rhythm of bullets.

Ranching, farming and the railroad supported the town until the 1922 discovery of oil in the Kevin-Sunburst fields. The area retains a few working oil pumps. Shelby's location on major transportation corridors established its right as an inland port for truck and rail shipping via the Northwest Express Transportation Authority.

Shelby Area Chamber of Commerce: 100 2nd Ave S., P.O. Box 865, Shelby, MT 59474; phone (406) 434-7184.

MARIAS MUSEUM OF HISTORY AND ART is 4 blks. s. of US 2 at 206 12th Ave. N. Exhibits depicting highlights of Toole County history focus on the oil industry, homesteading, the 1923 Dempsey-Gibbons prize fight (which nearly bankrupted the community), barbed wire, and dinosaur and other fossil discoveries. Allow 1 hour minimum. Mon.-Fri. 1-5 and 7-9, Sat. 1-4, Memorial Day-Labor Day; Tues. 1-5, rest of year; other times by appointment. Closed holidays. Free. Phone (406) 434-2551.

SIDNEY (C-7) pop. 4,774, elev. 1,950′

Sidney is a marketing center for sugar beets and wheat and serves an active oil drilling and coal mining region. Tours can be arranged at the Northern Plains Soil and Water Research Center on North Central Avenue. One of the larger auction houses in Montana, the Sidney Livestock Market Center on East Main Street conducts auctions every Wednesday. Local attractions include Fort Union, a late 1800s trapping and trading post, and horseback and wagon train rides.

Sidney Chamber of Commerce: 909 S. Central Ave., Sidney, MT 59270; phone (406) 433-1916.

MONDAK HERITAGE CENTER is at 120 Third Ave. S.E. The complex consists of a 17-unit street scene typical of pioneer Montana. Exhibits include an art gallery, a gun collection, photographs, and dinosaur bones and fossils. Allow 2 hours minimum. Tues.-Sat. 10-6, Sun. 1-5, June 1-Labor Day; Wed.-Fri. 10-4, Sat.-Sun. 1-4, Feb.-May and day after Labor Day-Dec. 31. Closed Easter and Dec. 25. Admission $3; under 12, $1. Phone (406) 433-3500.

SILVER GATE (E-4) pop. 140, elev. 7,389′

Resembling an alpine village, Silver Gate is said to be the only municipality in the nation whose building codes mandate that all structures be made of logs and other materials native to the area.

The town is at the northeast entrance to Yellowstone National Park; nearby Cooke City *(see place listing p. 91)* also has access to the park. Silver Gate is an outfitting center for both cross-country skiing and snowmobiling. Fly fishing is excellent in nearby lakes and streams.

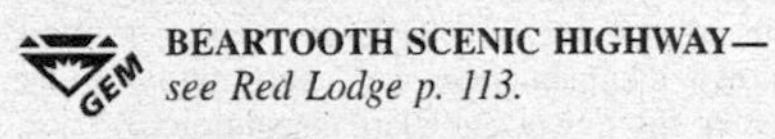

BEARTOOTH SCENIC HIGHWAY—
see Red Lodge p. 113.

SNOWBOWL SKI AREA—
see Missoula p. 111.

SOMERS (B-1) pop. 556, elev. 2,910′

***FAR WEST* CRUISE SHIP** can be boarded 8 mi. s. on US 93 at Somers dock. Offered are 90-minute scenic cruises on Flathead Lake. Brunch and sunset cruises also are available. Cruises depart daily at 1, mid-June to mid-Aug. Sunset cruise departs Sun.-Tues. at 7. Fare $15; under 12, $9. Reservations are required for meal cruises. MC, VI. Phone (406) 857-3203 or (406) 837-5569.

STEVENSVILLE (D-1) pop. 1,553, elev. 3,524′

HISTORIC ST. MARY'S MISSION is at the w. end of Fourth St. The mission was established in 1841 by Father Pierre DeSmet. The present complex includes the 1880s-style restored chapel and a study, dining room and kitchen. Also restored is Father Anthony Ravalli's log house, which contains a pharmacy with a "ride-up" window. Chief Victor's cabin is a small museum that displays original furnishings and American Indian and missionary artifacts.

Picnicking is permitted. Allow 30 minutes minimum. Guided tours are given daily 10-4, Apr. 15-Oct. 15. Admission $3, children $1.50, students with ID $1. Reservations are recommended. Phone (406) 777-5734.

TERRY (C-6) pop. 611, elev. 2,253′

In the heart of agate country, Terry is the home of acclaimed photographer Evelyn Cameron. Many of the pictures she took 1894-1928 to chronicle the lives of Terry's early settlers were compiled in a book more than 50 years later.

Miles City Area Chamber of Commerce: 315 Main St., Miles City, MT 59301; phone (406) 232-2890.

PRAIRIE COUNTY MUSEUM is at Logan and Laundre sts. Housed in the Old State Bank of Terry building, the museum displays local memorabilia. A dentist's office, barber shop, library and butcher shop are among the highlights. Area fossils also are featured. Mon. and Wed.-Fri. 9-3, Sat.-Sun. 1-4, Memorial Day weekend-Labor Day. Donations. Phone (406) 635-4040.

THREE FORKS (D-3) pop. 1,728, elev. 4,061′

Three Forks was a favorite American Indian hunting ground near the headwaters of the Missouri River. In 1805 Meriwether Lewis and William Clark documented their discovery of the beginning of the world's longest river system. Sacajawea, the wife of one of their guides, lived in this area with the Shoshone until she was kidnapped and raised by the Minnetaree. A plaque in Sacajawea Park downtown commemorates her contribution to the success of the Lewis and Clark expedition.

The region supported several trading posts for trappers during the early 1800s; however, due to skirmishes with the Indians, their existence was short-lived. The first permanent non-native settlement was established nearby in 1864. As railroads and highways provided access to the area, settlers arrived, and Three Forks was founded in 1908. Excellent hunting and fishing opportunities attract visitors.

Three Forks Chamber of Commerce: P.O. Box 1103, Three Forks, MT 59752; phone (406) 285-4753.

HEADWATERS HERITAGE MUSEUM is at Cedar and Main sts. Life in an early 1900s village is depicted through replicas of rooms from a settler's house, blacksmith shop, railroad dispatcher's office, schoolhouse and millinery shop. Mon.-Sat. 9-5, Sun. 1-5, Memorial Day-Labor Day; by appointment rest of year. Free. Phone (406) 285-4778 Memorial Day-Labor Day or (406) 285-3644 rest of year.

LEWIS AND CLARK CAVERNS STATE PARK—*see Cardwell p. 90.*

MADISON BUFFALO JUMP STATE HISTORIC SITE is 5 mi. e. on I-90, then 7 mi. s. on Buffalo Jump Rd. As long as 2,000 years ago American Indians hunted by driving buffaloes off a cliff on this 618-acre site. Picnicking is permitted. Allow 30 minutes minimum. Park open daily dawn-dusk. Admission $4 per private motorized vehicle. Trailers are not allowed; the approach road is gravel. Phone (406) 794-4042.

MISSOURI HEADWATERS STATE PARK is 3 mi. e., then 3 mi. n. of US 10 at Trident Junction. Discovered July 27, 1805, by the Lewis and Clark expedition, the headwaters in this 527-acre park are formed by the joining of the Madison, Gallatin and Jefferson rivers. A scenic overlook and a campground are nearby.

Park open daily dawn-dusk. Admission $5 per private vehicle or $1 per person arriving by bicycle, bus, motorcycle or on foot. Camping fee $12. Phone (406) 285-3610. *See Recreation Chart and the AAA Northwestern CampBook.*

TOWNSEND (D-3) pop. 1,867, elev. 3,813′

BROADWATER COUNTY MUSEUM is at 133 N. Walnut St. Featured are pioneer artifacts chronicling local history. Allow 30 minutes minimum. Tues.-Sun. 1-5, mid-May to mid-Sept.; closed July 4. Donations. Phone (406) 266-5252.

ULM (C-3) pop. 750, elev. 3,346′

ULM PISHKUN STATE PARK is off I-15 exit 270, then 3.5 mi. w. on Ulm-Vaughn Rd. The park preserves one of the largest known buffalo jump sites and interprets the buffalo culture. Exhibits depict how American Indians hunted bison by stampeding them over the cliffs. Featured are a large stuffed buffalo, implements fashioned from buffalo remains and a furnished tepee made of buffalo hides. Interpretive trails to the cliffs and grasslands are available.

Allow 1 hour minimum. Daily 9-5, Memorial Day-Sept. 30; Wed.-Sat. 10-4, Sun. noon-4, rest of year. Admission $2; ages 6-12, $1. AX, MC, VI. Phone (406) 866-2217.

VIRGELLE (B-4) elev. 2,560′

RECREATIONAL ACTIVITIES

Kayaking

- **Virgelle Mercantile & Missouri River Canoe Co.** is off US 87, then 7.5 mi. e. on a gravel road. Write 7485 Virgelle Ferry Rd. N., Loma, MT 59460. Other activities are offered. Daily mid-May to mid-Sept. Phone (406) 378-3110.

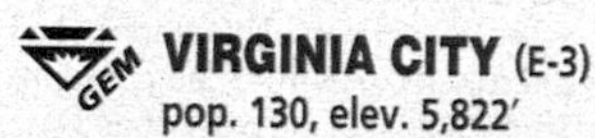

VIRGINIA CITY (E-3) pop. 130, elev. 5,822′

After fruitless panning along the Yellowstone River, six prospectors stumbled onto Alder Creek in May 1863, and their discovery of gold led to the establishment of a town. The settlement attracted thousands of miners and a band of renegades said to have committed more than 190 murders in 6 months. The miners formed a secret group called

---

DID YOU KNOW

More gem sapphires are found in Montana than in any other state.

The Vigilantes, who captured and hanged 21 of the criminals, including the outlaws' leader, the sheriff.

One of the older cities in the state, Virginia City served as territorial capital 1865-76. More than 80 early buildings have been restored; others have been reconstructed and can be visited. Among these are the state's first newspaper office, an equipped pharmacy of the period, the Wells Fargo Express Office, the Bale of Hay Saloon and the general stores, which carry 1860-80 merchandise. Boot Hill Cemetery contains the graves of road agents hanged by vigilantes in 1864.

Gold panning, hunting and fishing opportunities are available. A 1935 gold dredge can be seen at the River of Gold Mining Museum. All facilities are open mid-June through Labor Day.

Virginia City Visitor Information Center: P.O. Box 338, Virginia City, MT 59755; phone (406) 843-5247 or (800) 829-2969.

GILBERT BREWERY is at Hamilton and Cover sts. Featured is "The Brewery Follies," a variety show by the Brewery Players. Performances are given Mon. and Wed.-Sun. at 8:30 p.m. (also Sat. at 4:30 and 9 p.m.), the first Fri. in June-Labor Day. Admission $12.50. Reservations are recommended. Phone (406) 843-5218 or (800) 829-2969.

J. SPENCER WATKINS MEMORIAL MUSEUM is at 219 W. Wallace St. Displays chronicle the history of pioneer miners, ranchers and farmers. Daily 10-5, Memorial Day-Sept. 30. Admission $2; under 12 free; family rate $5. Phone (406) 843-5500.

NEVADA CITY is 1.5 mi. w. on SR 287. The city sprang up with the discovery of gold in 1863. Some of Montana Territory's original buildings have been moved to this site and restored to form the Nevada City Museum. The Music Hall contains a collection of mechanical musical machines. Allow 1 hour minimum. Daily 9-7, mid-May to mid-Sept. Museum $6, under 6 free. Combination ticket for museum and a round-trip ride on the Alder Gulch Shortline Railroad small train $10, under 6 free. Phone (406) 843-5247 or (800) 829-2969.

Alder Gulch Shortline Railroad runs between Virginia City and Nevada City. The small, narrow-gauge train is pulled by a gasoline powered engine dubbed No. 8. A train pulled by a refurbished Baldwin 1910 steam locomotive, No. 12, also operates. Allow 1 hour minimum. No. 8 operates daily 11-6:30, Memorial Day-Labor Day. No. 12 operates Sat.-Sun. 11-6:30, July-Aug. and on Memorial Day, July 4 and Labor Day. Round-trip fare on No. 8 is $6, under 6 free. Combination round-trip fare on No. 8 and Nevada City Museum ticket $10, under 6 free. Round-trip fare for No. 12 is $10, under 6 free.

THOMPSON-HICKMAN MEMORIAL MUSEUM is at 300 E. Wallace St. Offered are state and local memorabilia interpreting the history, geology and culture of 19th-century Virginia City. Allow 30 minutes minimum. Daily 10-5, Memorial Day-Labor Day. Donations. Phone (406) 843-5238.

VIRGINIA CITY OPERA HOUSE is at 340 W. Wallace St. Mysteries, comedies and melodramas are performed in the style of the 19th-century touring companies that regularly stopped in this town. Shows Tues.-Fri. at 8 p.m., Sat. at 4 and 8 p.m., Sun. at 4, mid-June to early Sept. Admission $15; under 12, $8.50. Reservations are required. MC, VI. Phone (406) 843-5314, or (800) 829-2969 for reservations.

WEST GLACIER (B-2) elev. 3,215'

West Glacier is the western rail and highway entrance to Glacier National Park *(see place listing p. 96)*. White-water rafting is the area's most popular recreational activity. Fishing and golf also draw visitors in pursuit of outdoor fun. One golf course has rules that include: "do not throw clubs or balls at tame deer" and "players may move balls without penalty to avoid elk tracks."

RECREATIONAL ACTIVITIES

Backpacking

- **Glacier Wilderness Guides** is 1.5 mi. w. on US 2. Write P.O. Box 330, West Glacier, MT 59936. Other activities are offered. Daily May-Sept. Phone (406) 387-5555 or (800) 521-7238.

White-water Rafting

- SAVE **Glacier Raft Co.** is on Going-to-the-Sun Rd. at the west entrance to Glacier National Park. Write P.O. Box 210, West Glacier, MT 59936. Other activities are offered. Daily May-Sept. Phone (406) 888-5454 or (800) 235-6781. *See color ad p. 97.*

- **Great Northern Whitewater Float Trips** is 1 mi. w. on US 2. Write P.O. Box 278, West Glacier, MT 59936. Other activities are offered.

DID YOU KNOW

Three of Yellowstone National Park's five entrances are in Montana.

Daily May 1 to mid-Sept. Phone (406) 387-5340 or (800) 735-7897. *See color ad p. 98.*

- **Montana Raft Co.** is 1.5 mi. w. on US 2. Write P.O. Box 330, West Glacier, MT 59936. Other activities are offered. Daily May-Sept. Phone (406) 387-5555 or (800) 521-7238.
- **Wild River Adventures** is 1 mi. w. on US 2. Write P.O. Box 272, West Glacier, MT 59936. Other activities are offered. Daily May 15-Sept. 15. Phone (406) 387-9453 or (800) 700-7056. *See color ad p. 98.*

WEST YELLOWSTONE (E-3)

pop. 1,177, elev. 6,667′

As its name suggests, West Yellowstone is at the west entrance to Yellowstone National Park. Due to this strategic location, the town's major industry is tourism. Numerous outfitters and rental operations supply visitors with various sports equipment, particularly snowmobiles and cross-country skis, for use in the park and in bordering national forest areas. Fly-fishing, hiking and horseback riding can be enjoyed during summer.

Two miles north of West Yellowstone on US 287, the Interagency Aerial Fire Control Center provides summer tours that explain firefighting techniques; reservations are required and may be made by phoning (406) 646-7691. For evening entertainment the Playmill Theatre at 29 Madison presents 2-hour musical comedy and melodrama performances; reservations are recommended. For information and schedules contact the theater; phone (406) 646-7757.

West Yellowstone Chamber of Commerce: 30 Yellowstone Ave., P.O. Box 458, W. Yellowstone, MT 59758; phone (406) 646-7701.

GRIZZLY DISCOVERY CENTER is 5 blks. s. of the Yellowstone National Park west entrance at 201 S. Canyon St. in Grizzly Park. Grizzly bears and a gray wolf pack can be viewed in naturalistic habitats. Educational exhibits illustrate the biology, behavior, history and population decline of grizzlies and wolves. The center also offers films and presentations. Allow 1 hour minimum. Daily 8-dusk. Admission (good for 2 consecutive days) $8.50; over 62, $8; ages 5-12, $4. AX, DS, MC, VI. Phone (406) 646-7001 or (800) 257-2570.

MADISON RIVER CANYON EARTHQUAKE AREA is on US 287, 17 mi. n.w. of jct. US 191, in the Hebgen Lake Area. This 37,800-acre tract embraces Hebgen and Earthquake lakes. Traces remain of the 1959 earthquake, which blocked a river, moved huge boulders and tilted a lakebed. An observation room features recorded talks and a videotape telling the story of the quake. The visitor center contains photographs of other devastating earthquakes and exhibits about threatened and endangered wildlife.

Allow 30 minutes minimum. Visitor center open daily 8:30-6, Memorial Day to mid-Sept. Admission $3 per vehicle, $1 per motorcycle or bicycle. Phone (406) 682-7620 or (406) 823-6961.

MUSEUM OF THE YELLOWSTONE is at 104 Yellowstone Ave. Housed in a 1909 Union Pacific Railroad depot, the museum highlights the Yellowstone experience, from early tourism and railroad history to the 1988 fires and the rejuvenation of the park's ecosystems. Exhibits include early park freight wagons, a 1940s snow plane and a variety of films. Old Snaggletooth, a legendary grizzly bear, is prominently displayed among the wildlife specimens.

Allow 1 hour minimum. Daily 9-9, June 11-Aug. 28; 10-6, May 8-June 10 and Aug. 29-Oct. 16. Admission $6; senior citizens and ages 4-18, $4; family rate $15. AX, DS, MC, VI. Phone (406) 646-1100.

YELLOWSTONE IMAX THEATER is at 101 S. Canyon St., adjacent to Yellowstone National Park's west entrance. A 35-minute IMAX film about the history, wildlife, geothermal activity and grandeur of America's first national park is shown on a six-story screen with stereo surround sound. Food is available. Shows daily on the hour 9 a.m.-10 p.m., May 1-Oct. 15; 1-9, rest of year. Hours may vary; phone ahead. Admission $8; ages 3-12, $6. MC, VI. Phone (406) 646-4100 or (888) 854-5862.

WHITEFISH (B-1) pop. 5,032, elev. 3,033′

Whitefish Lake borders Whitefish and extends 7 miles north. The area offers scenic vistas, fishing, swimming, boating and beach activities.

Restored to its 1927 chaletlike appearance, the Great Northern Railway Depot houses railroad artifacts and area memorabilia. On the grounds is the Great Northern Locomotive #181, one of only seven ever built.

Offering spectacular views of the Flathead Valley and Glacier National Park, the Big Mountain Gondola carries passengers to the 7,000-foot summit; phone (406) 862-1900.

Flathead Convention & Visitors Bureau: 15 Depot Park, Kalispell, MT 59911; phone (406) 756-9091 or (800) 543-3105.

Self-guiding tours: Brochures outlining self-guiding tours of the historic area are available from the visitors bureau.

RECREATIONAL ACTIVITIES

Skiing

- **Big Mountain Resort** is 8 mi. n. Write P.O. Box 1400, Whitefish, MT 59937. Other activities are offered. Daily Thanksgiving to mid-Apr. Phone (406) 862-1900 or (800) 858-4157.

WHITE SULPHUR SPRINGS (D-4) pop. 984, elev. 5,100′

Nestled in a valley between the Little Belt Mountains in Lewis and Clark National Forest *(see place listing p. 107)* on the east and the Big Belt Mountains on the west, White Sulphur Springs offers numerous outdoor summer and winter recreational opportunities, including skiing, snowmobiling, hiking and mountain biking. The Smith River and nearby Lake Sutherlin invite fishing and water sports.

Reminders of frontier life during the silver mining era can be found in the surrounding ghost towns of Castle, Copperopolis and Fort Logan.

CASTLE MUSEUM CARRIAGE HOUSE is 4 blks. n.e. off US 12/89 to 310 Second Ave. N.E., entered from the carriage house behind the castle. This restored Victorian house built in 1892 by B.R. Sherman, a cattleman and mine owner, sits on a hilltop overlooking the town. The gray stone chateaulike structure is furnished in period. Allow 30 minutes minimum. Daily 10-5, mid-May to mid-Sept. Admission $3; over 64 and under 13, $2. Phone (406) 547-2324.

WIBAUX (C-7) pop. 567, elev. 2,634′

Wibaux has the distinction of being the first town to greet visitors entering Montana westbound on I-94. A statue of Frenchman Pierre Wibaux (WEE-bo), for whom the town is named, stands on the western edge of town.

Wibaux County Chamber of Commerce: P.O. Box 74, Wibaux, MT 59353.

Self-guiding tours: Brochures of a walking tour are available at the information center in Wibaux Historical Museum.

THE PIERRE WIBAUX MUSEUM COMPLEX is on E. Orgain Ave. It features the restored Pierre Wibaux house, built in 1892, and an adjoining barbershop with antique furnishings. A livery stable and a 1964 Montana Centennial Train railroad car are on the grounds. Displays include dinosaur fossils and homestead artifacts. Daily 9-5, May-Sept. Donations. Phone (406) 796-9969 or (406) 796-2381.

WOLF CREEK (C-3) elev. 3,560′

Wolf Creek is a popular point for sports enthusiasts bound for Holter Lake *(see Recreation Chart and the AAA Northwestern CampBook)*, 6 miles southeast of town. The result of one of a series of dams on the Upper Missouri River, the lake is bordered by the Sleeping Giant Wilderness, Beartooth Wildlife Management Area and Helena National Forest *(see place listing p. 105)*.

Almost all of the lake's recreational facilities are on its eastern shore. A particularly scenic drive begins at the junction of US 287 and SR 200 north of Wolf Creek, proceeds south on US 287 to the junction with I-15, then on to Helena, Butte and the Idaho border, passing some of Montana's most impressive mountains.

WOLF POINT (B-6) pop. 2,663, elev. 2,001'

While sustained mostly by agriculture, Wolf Point's economy also benefits from small manufacturing firms and Honeyland Inc., which maintains more than 4,000 bee colonies and produces about a half-million pounds of honey annually. Wolf Point also is the home of many Sioux and Assiniboine, who perform dances and observe celebrations June through August. The Wild Horse Stampede, said to be the state's oldest rodeo, takes place the second week in July.

Wolf Point Chamber of Commerce & Agriculture: 218 Third Ave. S., Suite B, Wolf Point, MT 59201; phone (406) 653-2012.

WOLF POINT AREA HISTORICAL SOCIETY MUSEUM is in the lower level of the public library at 220 Second Ave. S., 1 blk. w. of the Sherman Motor Inn. The museum exhibits artifacts of the area's American Indians and early settlers, including clothing and arrowheads, as well as Marlin and Winchester rifle collections. A small gallery displays works by local artists. Mon.-Fri. 10-5, June-Aug.; closed holidays. Donations. Phone (406) 653-1912.

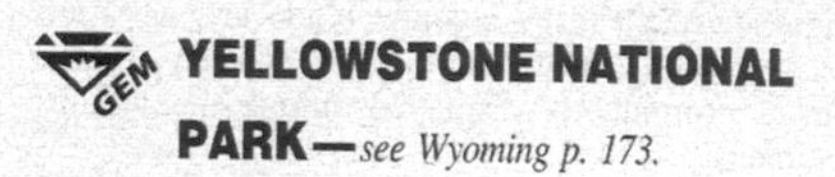

YELLOWSTONE NATIONAL PARK—*see Wyoming p. 173.*

Wyoming

Spectacular Springs
Burgeoning trees, snowmelt swollen streams and verdant valleys

Summer Storms
Leave behind green skies of dazzling clarity

The Land Developers Forgot
Nearly every road is scenic when you're roaming Wyoming

Yellowstone
A "pleasuring ground... [of] natural curiosities... [and] wonders..."

However You See Wyoming
Driving, riding, hiking, biking, rafting or dog sledding, it's forever in your mind's eye

Devil's Tower National Monument / © Henryk T. Kaiser / Camerique Inc., Int'l/Robertstock

her best face forward

Jackson Hole / © Buddy Mays/Words & Pictures / Picture Quest

Deep gorges snaking between high rock walls. Impenetrable stands of ponderosa pines. Intricate systems of limestone caves.

These are but three of the spectacular natural features for which the outdoor wonderland of Wyoming is known.

Some thermal basins in Yellowstone National Park spit bursts of scalding water; others bubble unassumingly. Not far from this heated activity, steam vents utter strange sounds. Bison and bears wander through the back country and along the park's roadways.

Devils Tower National Monument, which resembles a gargantuan stone tree stump, challenges climbers to take on its imposing face.

Shared by Bridger-Teton and Shoshone national forests, 13,804-foot

Gannett Peak is impressive as the state's highest mountain.

Lakes, glaciers, snowfields and forests unite amid the mountains and valleys of Grand Teton National Park. The Jackson Hole valley—a recreational hub—beckons to the adventurous. Hiking, skiing and snowmobiling provide exhilarating thrills; float trips leave you agape at the spectacular scenery along the Snake River.

Wyoming's stunningly diverse landscape is nature's masterpiece.

A land of beauty. A land of serenity. A land of awe.

Mecheweami-ing.

Wyoming is an adaptation of the Delaware Indian word meaning "at the great plains" or "on the great plain."

But the term doesn't fully encompass the geographic diversity for which the region is known. Few would argue that the high plains are anything other than "great," but Wyoming is just as noteworthy for its spectacular mountains, grasslands, canyons, deserts and scores of other natural wonders.

The Continental Divide cuts a diagonal swath across the rectangular state, bisecting it into the Missouri River Basin on the east and the Columbia and Colorado river basins on the west. The divide winds along the curved, jagged spine of the mighty Rockies, from the northwestern Gallatin Range to the southeastern Sierra Madre.

In this mountainous territory are some of the most precious jewels.

Grand Teton National Park makes itself worthy of such gushing adjectives as "breathtaking," "wondrous" and "dramatic." First photographed in 1872, the area continues to inspire snap-happy shutterbugs with its lakes, glaciers, snowfields and lush, green stands of fir, pine and spruce.

Nestled along the park's southern border is the outdoor paradise of Jackson Hole country. This bustling center of activity beckons thrill-seekers with temptations ranging from mountain climbing and windsurfing to skiing and white-water rafting.

Yellowstone National Park is a hot spot for geyser activity, resulting from a volcanic eruption some 600,000 years ago. Although the thermal theatrics of Old Faithful are a sight to behold, many people visit to see the terracelike formations of Mammoth Hot Springs; the colorful hot clay of the vivid paintpots; and the residents of the wildlife sanctuary—grizzlies, black bears, elk, bison and bighorn sheep among them.

Protected Treasures

If the presence of two high-traffic national parks doesn't adequately portend that Americans have long found the Wyoming landscape remarkable, then factor in some of the other acreage the country has protected.

In Bighorn Canyon National Recreation Area sculpted walls rise around a 55-mile stretch of serene Bighorn Lake, a gift the state shares with northern neighbor Montana.

Wyoming Historical Timeline

1807 John Colter discovers "Colter's Hell," an area of waterfalls and geysers.

1834 Fur traders William Sublette and Robert Campbell establish Fort Laramie trading post.

© Lowell Georgia/Corbis

1843 The "Great Migration" along the 2,000-mile Oregon Trail begins.

1849 The United States buys Fort Laramie to use as a base to protect and supply travelers along the Oregon Trail.

© David Hiser/Photographers Aspen/PictureQuest

1868 Wyoming Territory is created from pieces of the territories of Dakota, Utah and Idaho; Wyoming becomes the 44th state in 1890.

1869 Women in Wyoming vote, the first such occurrence in the world.

Bighorn National Forest, too, reveals imposing Shell and Crazy Woman canyons. The Green River carved the kaleidoscopic back drop of Flaming Gorge National Recreation Area.

Sagebrush and grass grow atop Devils Tower National Monument, a massive monolith resembling a stone stump.

The fertile beds of Fossil Butte National Monument teem with extensive deposits of freshwater fish that lived 50 million years ago.

Both Bridger-Teton and Shoshone national forests lay claims to different rugged faces of Gannett Peak, the state's highest at 13,804 feet. The former also boasts live glaciers, an excellent example of a geologic landslide and Two Ocean Creek, which sends streams into both the Atlantic and Pacific.

Rolling Westward

Indeed, the topographic surprises were plentiful for the pioneers who forged their wagon trains westward over the Oregon Trail in the 19th century searching for wealth in the terrain of California and the Pacific Northwest.

The lore of the American West is often commemorated. Sites in Cheyenne, Douglas and Laramie—not to mention Fort Laramie National Historic Site—dig into the details of pioneer history. Cody pays tribute to founder "Buffalo Bill" Cody and remembers visits from Butch Cassidy and his partner the Sundance Kid, who assumed his moniker from the Wyoming town in which he once served time.

While everyone else was trying to get rich during the turbulent period, one group benefited more than any other: women.

Earning its nickname as the Equality State, Wyoming arguably has done more for women's rights than any other state. The government was the first to grant female suffrage in 1869. Months after, Esther Morris became the first female appointed as a justice of the peace. Voters also elected the first female to public office and 30 years later seated the first woman in a governor's chair.

Yes, it is the Equality State. But compared to all others, wonderful Wyoming is in many ways truly unequaled.

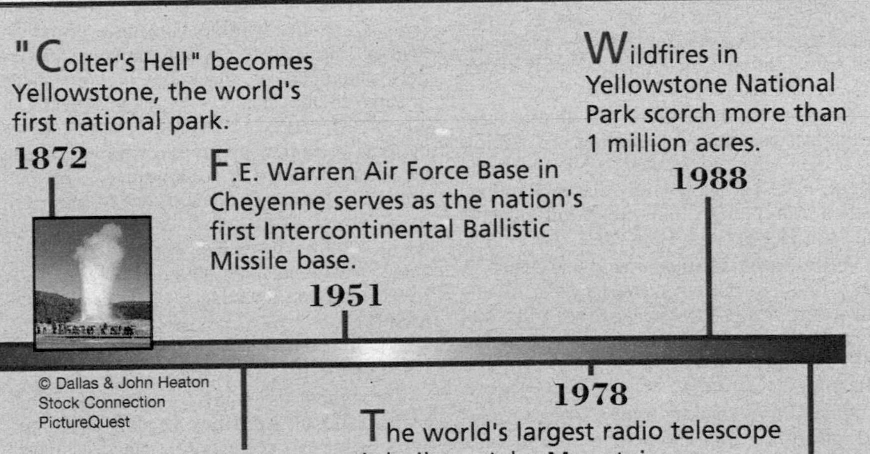

"Colter's Hell" becomes Yellowstone, the world's first national park.
1872
F.E. Warren Air Force Base in Cheyenne serves as the nation's first Intercontinental Ballistic Missile base.
1951
Wildfires in Yellowstone National Park scorch more than 1 million acres.
1988
1925
1978
The world's largest radio telescope is built on Jelm Mountain.
1995

© Dallas & John Heaton Stock Connection PictureQuest

Nellie Tayloe Ross is sworn in as first woman governor in the country; she is appointed first woman director of the United States Mint in 1933.

Fourteen endangered gray wolves are reintroduced into the Yellowstone ecosystem; by 1997 an estimated 163 wolves and their offspring roam the area.

© Tom Brakefield/Bruce Coleman, Inc./PictureQuest

Recreation

The Great Plains meet the Rocky Mountains in Wyoming, offering a varied topography perfect for outdoor recreation. From lush eastern grasslands to towering mountains along the western border, this outdoor wonderland enables visitors to experience the Western way of life. Travelers can venture into the mountains atop a trusty horse, camp in the breathtaking wilderness and end the day relaxing beside an open campfire. Outfitters offer activities ranging from herding cattle to overnight chuck wagon excursions.

Park It

Visitors to any of Wyoming's national areas can explore such recreational pursuits as **hiking, camping** and **wildlife viewing.** Yellowstone, America's first national park, has more than 1,000 miles of hiking trails ranging from easy to strenuous; some venture past the park's bubbling geysers. Yellowstone Lake is popular for **rowboating,** while Shoshone Lake is a favorite for **canoeing.**

A short skip south is Wyoming's other national park, Grand Teton. This area of awe-inspiring mountains is best explored by foot. More than 200 miles of trails allow for short hikes or overnight trips. **Mountain climbing** is a popular summertime activity; climbers should allow 2 days for an ascent of Grand Teton. Rock climbers can head east to the nation's first national monument—Devils Tower looms 1,280 feet above the valley floor.

The snow-clad peaks of the Tetons form the perfect backdrop for **boating** and **fishing** in Jackson and Jenny lakes. While the high-altitude lakes are too chilly for **swimming,** visitors can plunge into the warm mineral waters in Hot Springs State Park.

White-water rafting around Jackson is a great way to check out the spectacular mountain setting. The upper Snake River's flat water is well-suited for the less adventurous, while the lower Snake's white water can take rafters for a wild ride.

Winter in Wyoming brings lots of snow and plenty of outdoor activity. Park trails welcome cross-country skiers and thousands of acres of mountain terrain invite downhill skiers. The packed powder typical of Snow King Mountain in Jackson Hole provides good learning conditions for beginners.

For those who like steep trails and tough terrain, Skillet Glacier on Mount Moran in the Grand Tetons offers a vertical drop of nearly 6,000 feet. Thrill seekers may enjoy hitting the slopes from a helicopter; Jackson Hole is the place to go for extreme **heli-skiing.**

With more than 1,300 miles of groomed trails statewide, **snowmobiling** is as much a form of transportation as it is recreation. Hop aboard a snowmobile to view Yellowstone's steamy geysers. When the snow melts, snowmobile and ski trails beckon hikers and mountain bikers. An autumn **bicycling** excursion beneath the aspen trees in the Sierra Madre Mountains can be invigorating.

A Hunting We Will Go

Whether it is the massive moose or the prevalent pronghorn antelope, **hunting** is quite rewarding. Other game includes black bears, elk, mountain lions and bighorn sheep. Nonresident hunters must be accompanied by a licensed guide for any big game hunts; apply for a license in advance as quantities are limited and demand is high.

Wyoming's cold waters are the ideal place to reel in the big one. **Fly fishing** in mountain creeks as well as within some 200 lakes of the Bighorn National Forest will yield various types of trout, while Fremont Lake is famous for its record-breaking Mackinaw. Most waters are accessible year-round, so **ice fishing** is an option when the lakes freeze over. Don't forget your fishing license.

With nearly 27 million acres of public land, Wyoming is home to some 600 animal species, making wildlife viewing a prime diversion. Head to the plains, home to pronghorn antelopes, or check out bighorn sheep grazing in the shadows of jagged peaks at one of the state's 11 mountain ranges. River bottoms yield the shy moose, while bison can be found wandering Yellowstone. The National Elk Refuge is home to one of the country's largest herds. And birdwatchers will relish spotting trumpeter swans and Canada geese; a walking path along the North Platte River yields an abundance of these feathered friends.

Recreational Activities

Throughout the TourBook, you may notice a Recreational Activities heading with bulleted listings of recreation-oriented establishments listed underneath. Similar operations also may be mentioned in Destination City recreation sections. Since normal AAA inspection criteria cannot be applied, these establishments are presented for information only. Age, height and weight restrictions may apply. Reservations are often recommended and sometimes required. Visitors should phone or write the attraction for additional information, and the address and phone number are provided for this purpose.

Fast Facts

POPULATION: 493,782.

AREA: 97,914 square miles; ranks 9th.

CAPITAL: Cheyenne.

HIGHEST POINT: 13,804 ft., Gannett Peak.

LOWEST POINT: 3,100 ft., Belle Fourche River Valley.

TIME ZONE(S): Mountain. DST.

MINIMUM AGE FOR DRIVERS: 16; under 18 need consent of parent or guardian.

SEAT BELT/CHILD RESTRAINT LAWS: Seat belts required for driver and all passengers; child restraints required for under 5 or under 40 pounds.

HELMETS FOR MOTORCYCLISTS: Required for driver under 18.

RADAR DETECTORS: Permitted.

FIREARMS LAWS: Vary by state and/or county. Contact the Wyoming Highway Patrol, 5300 Bishop Blvd., P.O. Box 1708, Cheyenne, WY 82002-9019; phone (307) 777-4301.

HOLIDAYS: Jan. 1; Presidents Day, Feb. (3rd Mon.); Memorial Day, May (last Mon.); July 4; Labor Day, Sept. (1st Mon.); Columbus Day, Oct. (2nd Mon.); Election Day; Veterans Day, Nov. 11; Thanksgiving; Dec. 25.

TAXES: Wyoming's statewide sales tax is 5 percent, with local options or an additional increment up to 2 percent. Localities may also impose lodgings taxes of up to 4 percent.

STATE INFORMATION CENTERS: Welcome centers are on I-90 at 5th Street interchange east of Sheridan; on I-90 exit 187 at Sundance; on US 26/89/187 on north edge of Jackson; 1 mile south of Cheyenne on I-25 at College Drive interchange; on I-80 on east edge of Evanston; on I-80 exit 401 south of Pine Bluffs; and on I-80, 10 miles east of Laramie at Sherman Hill exit. Daily 8-6, Memorial Day-Labor Day; 8-5, rest of year.

FURTHER INFORMATION FOR VISITORS:

Wyoming Travel and Tourism
Wyoming Business Council
I-25 at College Dr.
Cheyenne, WY 82002
(307) 777-7777 or (800) 225-5996

RECREATION INFORMATION:

Wyoming State Parks and Cultural Resources
Herschler Building/1st floor east
Cheyenne, WY 82002
(307) 777-7519

FISHING AND HUNTING REGULATIONS:

State of Wyoming Game and Fish Commission
5400 Bishop Blvd.
Cheyenne, WY 82002
(307) 777-4600

STATE PARK INFORMATION:

Division of State Parks and Historic Sites
6101 Yellowstone Rd.
Cheyenne, WY 82002
(307) 777-6323
(877) 996-7275 (reservations)

NATIONAL FOREST INFORMATION:

Federal Center
Building 85
Denver, CO 80225
(303) 236-9431

Federal Center
324 25th St.
Ogden, UT 84401
(801) 625-5306
(877) 444-6777 (reservations)

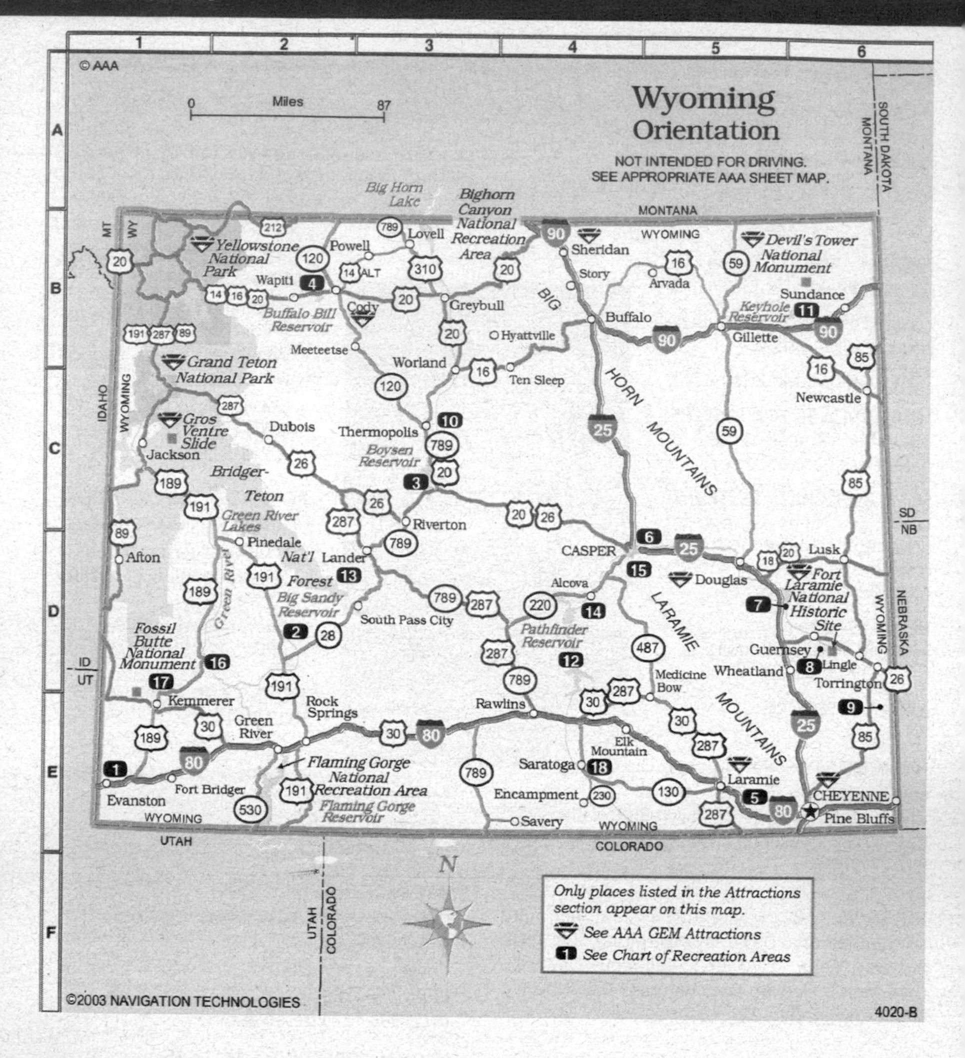

Premium Cruising Defined

Gracious award-winning ships sailing to over 200 of the most fascinating places worldwide. The most extensive menus at sea. Dazzling entertainment and a variety of activities onboard and ashore. Unconditional world-renowned service from the popular international cruise staff.

For more information or reservations, call or visit your local AAA/CAA Travel Office or log on to www.aaa.com.

Travel With Someone You Trust®

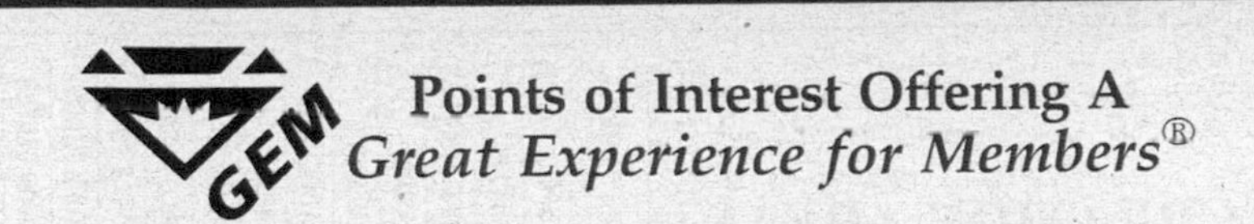

Points of Interest Offering A *Great Experience for Members*®

Bridger-Teton National Forest (B-1)

GROS VENTRE SLIDE—Nature's fury was unleashed here June 23, 1925. See p. 134.

Cheyenne (E-6)

CHEYENNE FRONTIER DAYS OLD WEST MUSEUM—Learn about the rodeo and cowboy life or sit in a bronc-riding saddle. See p. 138.

THE NELSON MUSEUM OF THE WEST—Travel back in time to discover what life was like for the denizens of the Old West. See p. 139.

WYOMING STATE MUSEUM—Explore the history of Wyoming and its residents through historical collections and memorabilia. See p. 141.

Cody (B-3)

BUFFALO BILL HISTORICAL CENTER—Because of the variety of its collections, this museum complex has been called "The Smithsonian of the Old West." See p. 141.

TRAIL TOWN—If raindrops keep fallin' on your head, you might want to duck inside Butch Cassidy and the Sundance Kid's Hole-in-the-Wall cabin. See p. 145.

Devils Tower National Monument (B-5)

DEVILS TOWER NATIONAL MONUMENT—Visitors are permitted to climb the 1,267-foot-high monolith, considered a sacred site of worship by many American Indians. See p. 145.

Douglas (D-5)

WYOMING PIONEER MEMORIAL MUSEUM—The collections here will give you an understanding of the privations the pioneers endured. See p. 146.

Fort Laramie National Historic Site (D-6)

FORT LARAMIE NATIONAL HISTORIC SITE—To travelers along the Oregon and Mormon trails and to Pony Express riders, this command post, staging area, and communications and transportation depot was a welcome site. See p. 148.

Grand Teton National Park (B-1)

GRAND TETON NATIONAL PARK—The recreational possibilities in this magnificent park are endless. See p. 149.

FLOAT TRIPS—Admire mountain scenery and wildlife from the sinuous curves of the Snake River. See p. 153.

Laramie (E-5)

WYOMING TERRITORIAL PARK—Belly-up to the bar, meet Calamity Jane and see the only prison cell ever to hold Butch Cassidy, all in this frontier town. See p. 162.

Sheridan (B-4)

BRADFORD BRINTON MEMORIAL—HISTORIC RANCH AND WESTERN ART COLLECTION—This 20-room ranch house preserves the lifestyle of a prosperous early rancher. See p. 168.

Yellowstone National Park (B-2)

YELLOWSTONE NATIONAL PARK—The more than 3,400 acres of America's first national park are home to buffaloes, bighorn sheep, elk, moose and pronghorn antelopes as well as thousands of thermal pools and springs. See p. 173.

RECREATION AREAS

	MAP LOCATION	CAMPING	PICNICKING	HIKING TRAILS	BOATING	BOAT RAMP	BOAT RENTAL	FISHING	SWIMMING	PETS ON LEASH	BICYCLE TRAILS	NATURE PROGS.	VISITOR CENTER	LODGE/CABINS	FOOD SERVICE
NATIONAL PARKS *(See place listings)*															
Grand Teton (C-1) 485 square miles. Horse rental.		●	●	●	●	●	●	●	●	●	●	●	●	●	●
Yellowstone (B-2) 3,472 square miles. Horse rental. *(See place listing p. 173.)*	●	●	●	●	●	●	●		●		●	●	●	●	
NATIONAL FORESTS *(See place listings)*															
Bighorn 1,115,171 acres in north-central Wyoming. Horse rental.		●	●	●	●	●		●		●		●		●	●
Black Hills 175,000 acres in northeast Wyoming.		●	●	●				●	●			●			
Bridger-Teton 3,439,809 acres in western Wyoming. Horse rental.		●	●	●	●	●		●	●		●	●	●	●	●
Medicine Bow 1,093,618 acres in eastern Wyoming. Horse rental.		●	●	●	●	●		●	●	●	●	●	●	●	
Shoshone 2,466,586 acres in northwestern Wyoming.		●	●	●	●	●		●	●	●	●	●	●	●	●
NATIONAL MONUMENTS *(See place listings)*															
Devils Tower (B-6) 1,347 acres.		●	●	●				●	●	●		●	●		
Fossil Butte (E-1) 8,198 acres.			●	●						●			●		
NATIONAL RECREATION AREAS *(See place listings)*															
Bighorn Canyon (B-3) 120,000 acres. *(See place listing in Montana p. 85.)*	●	●	●	●	●	●	●	●	●			●		●	
Flaming Gorge (E-2) 91 mi. long.		●	●	●	●	●	●	●	●	●	●	●	●	●	●
STATE															
Bear River (E-1) 280 acres on I-80 near Evanston.	1		●	●				●		●	●	●	●		
Big Sandy (D-2) 6,190 acres 6 mi. n. of Farson on US 191.	2	●	●		●	●		●	●	●					
Boysen (C-3) 39,545 acres 14 mi. n.w. of Shoshone off US 20.	3	●	●		●	●		●	●	●		●			●
Buffalo Bill (B-2) 12,000 acres 9 mi. w. of Cody on US 14/16/20.	4	●	●		●	●		●		●		●			
Curt Gowdy (E-5) 1,960 acres 26 mi. w. of Cheyenne off I-80.	5	●	●	●	●	●		●		●		●		●	
Edness Kimball Wilkins (C-5) 315 acres 6 mi. e. of Casper off I-25.	6		●	●				●	●	●	●	●			
Glendo (D-5) 22,430 acres 4 mi. e. of Glendo off US 87.	7	●	●	●	●	●	●	●	●	●		●		●	●
Guernsey (D-6) 8,638 acres 3 mi. w. of Guernsey off US 26.	8	●	●	●	●	●		●	●	●		●	●		
Hawk Springs (E-6) 2,000 acres 39 mi. s. of Torrington off US 85.	9	●	●		●	●		●	●	●		●			
Hot Springs (C-3) 1,034 acres in n.e. Thermopolis on SR 789 and US 20. *(See Thermopolis p. 171)*	10		●	●				●	●	●	●	●	●	●	●
Keyhole (B-6) 15,674 acres 7 mi. n. of I-90 between Moorcroft and Sundance.	11	●	●	●	●	●	●	●	●	●		●		●	●
Seminoe (D-4) 10,381 acres 35 mi. n. of Sinclair off I-80.	12	●	●		●	●		●	●	●		●			●
Sinks Canyon (D-2) 600 acres 7.5 mi. s.w. of Lander on SR 131. *(See Lander p. 161)*	13	●	●	●				●		●		●	●		
OTHER															
Alcova Reservoir (D-4) 3,400 acres 4 mi. s. of Alcova off SR 220. Horse rental.	14	●	●	●	●	●		●	●	●					
Casper Mountain Park (D-4) 3,315 acres 7 mi. s. of Casper on SR 251. Cross-country and downhill skiing, snowmobiling; archery range, braille nature trail, bridle trails, horse rental.	15	●	●	●						●		●			
Fontenelle Reservoir (D-2) 8,000 acres 35 mi. n. of Kemmerer via US 189.	16	●	●		●	●		●		●		●			
Lake Viva Naughton (D-1) 1,375 acres 12 mi. n. of Kemmerer via SR 233.	17	●			●			●							
Saratoga Lake (E-4) 270-acre lake 1.5 mi. n. of Saratoga off SR 130.	18	●	●	●	●	●		●	●	●	●	●			

Wyoming Temperature Averages
Maximum / Minimum
From the records of the National Weather Service

	JAN	FEB	MAR	APR	MAY	JUN	JUL	AUG	SEP	OCT	NOV	DEC
Casper	33/14	37/16	43/21	56/31	66/40	77/49	87/56	85/55	74/45	61/36	44/23	37/18
Cheyenne	38/14	40/15	44/20	55/29	64/39	76/48	84/54	82/53	73/43	62/33	47/22	42/18
Lander	31/8	36/12	45/20	56/31	66/40	76/48	86/55	84/54	73/45	60/34	43/19	35/12
Sheridan	34/9	36/11	43/19	56/31	67/40	75/48	87/56	86/53	74/43	62/33	46/21	39/14
Yellowstone Nat. Park	26/10	30/11	37/17	48/26	57/33	67/41	76/47	74/45	64/37	52/29	38/20	28/12

Points of Interest

AFTON (D-1) pop. 1,818, elev. 6,267′

Mormon emigrants surveyed the already-settled site of Afton in 1896, using a carpenter's square, a rope and an almanac and taking their bearings from the North Star and the sun. An official survey made years later found the plot only about 5 feet off.

In addition to the arch of 3,011 elk antlers that spans Washington Street at the center of town, Afton is noted for Periodic Spring, a natural cold-water geyser. The spring is 5 miles east in Bridger-Teton National Forest *(see place listing p. 134)*.

Afton lies in Star Valley along the scenic portion of US 89, which runs 255 miles between Mammoth Hot Springs in Yellowstone National Park *(see place listing p. 179)* and Geneva on the Idaho border.

Star Valley Chamber of Commerce: P.O. Box 1097, Afton, WY 83110; phone (800) 426-8833.

LINCOLN COUNTY DAUGHTERS OF UTAH PIONEER MUSEUM is .5 blk. e. off US 89 at 46 E. 5th Ave. The museum displays artifacts chronicling Mormon history in southwestern Wyoming. Mon.-Fri. 1-5, June-Aug. Free. Phone (307) 886-5489.

ALCOVA (D-4) elev. 5,364′

Alcova lies in a small valley rimmed by rocky hills. In 1891 a group of Easterners bought a nearby site where hot springs flowed from the walls of a canyon. An analysis of the water showed a high concentration of minerals, but the $250,000 the syndicate planned to spend on improvements never materialized.

The water that finally proved important to the town is that impounded by Alcova Dam, 4 miles south of town off SR 220. The dam stretches 700 feet in length and rises 800 feet from the canyon riverbed. Reservoirs created by Alcova and nearby Pathfinder dams provide popular recreation sites for residents of Casper and other communities. *See Recreation Chart and the AAA Northwestern CampBook.*

One of the more colorful local legends involves Ella "Cattle Kate" Watson, unpopular with townsfolk because of her freewheeling lifestyle and skill at raising cattle. She secretly married rancher Jim Averill so they could double their herd while she retained her homestead in her own name. Other ranchers demanded that both leave town, but before they could make their getaway the two were hanged unceremoniously from a scrub pine. Cattle Kate's 1889 lynching made her the only woman to suffer this fate in Wyoming.

INDEPENDENCE ROCK STATE HISTORIC SITE is 25 mi. w. on SR 220. The site is a well-known landmark on the Sweetwater River. Called "The Great Register of the Desert," it is a 193-foot-high granite boulder with a base that covers more than 27 acres.

Independence Rock was named during a celebration held July 4, 1830, by a party of fur trappers led by William Sublette. Daily dawn-dusk.

ARVADA (B-5) pop. 33, elev. 3,649′

SAVE **POWDER RIVER EXPERIENCE** is 3 mi. s. on CR 273. The attraction offers recreation on a 25,000-acre working ranch. Activities, which vary each month, include horseback riding and lessons. Camping, fishing and wildlife watching also are available. Daily dawn-dusk. Day adventure $120; under 12, $60. Reservations are recommended. Phone (307) 736-2402 or (888) 736-2402.

BIGHORN CANYON NATIONAL RECREATION AREA—

see place listing in Montana p. 85.

BIGHORN NATIONAL FOREST

Elevations in the forest range from 4,600 ft. in the northern section to 13,165 ft. at Cloud Peak. Refer to AAA maps for additional elevation information.

In the Big Horn Mountains of north-central Wyoming, the Bighorn National Forest encompasses 1,115,171 acres. The forest is traversed by US 14 (Big Horn Scenic Byway), which crosses 8,950-foot Granite Pass and winds through scenic Shell Falls and Canyon; US 14A (Medicine Wheel Passage), which passes by Medicine Mountain near the enigmatic medicine wheel; and US 16 (Cloud Peak Skyway), which crosses 9,677-foot Powder River Pass and threads through beautiful Ten Sleep Canyon.

Cloud Peak is the highest peak within the forest. Motorists pulling trailers should use caution on US 14/14A.

Backpacking and saddle and pack trips can be taken into 189,039-acre Cloud Peak Wilderness; horse and foot trails begin at trail heads accessible via gravel roads off US 14 and US 16. This scenic area has miles of streams and more than 200 lakes containing brook, cutthroat, California golden and rainbow trout. Hunters come in search of pronghorns, deer and elk.

Throughout the forest are 47 campgrounds, picnic areas and a good trail network, including the Bucking Mule Falls National Recreation Trail. Downhill skiing is available east of Worland and Greybull (west of Buffalo and west of Sheridan); cross-country skiing can be pursued in all sections of the forest. Mountain climbing and snowmobiling also are popular.

Maps of the forest are available for $6 ($7 laminated) at the District Ranger's office in Sheridan at 2013 Eastside Second St., (307) 674-2600; in Worland at 101 S. 23rd St., (307) 347-5105; in Lovell at 604 E. Main St., (307) 548-6541; or in Buffalo at 1415 Fort St., (307) 684-1100.

Two visitor centers offer nature trails, exhibits, maps and other information about the forest, recreational activities and nearby communities daily 9-5 Memorial Day weekend through Labor Day. Burgess Junction Visitor Center is on US 14 a half-mile east of Burgess Junction; Shell Falls Interpretive Center also is on US 14, but 5 miles west of Burgess Junction.

For additional information contact the Forest Supervisor's Office, 2013 Eastside Second St., Sheridan, WY 82801; phone (307) 674-2600. *See Recreation Chart and the AAA Northwestern CampBook.*

MEDICINE WHEEL is off US 14A on Medicine Mountain, about 27 mi. e. of Lovell. The prehistoric structure, a circular arrangement of stones 245 feet in circumference with 28 spokes extending from a central cairn, is believed to have been used for religious ceremonies or celestial observations.

Note: The road to Medicine Wheel is closed to vehicular traffic. Visitors are required to walk 1.5 miles to the site. Exceptions can be made for elderly or physically impaired visitors.

SHELL CANYON AND FALLS is 30 mi. e. of Greybull on US 14. The site can be seen from the Shell Falls overlook on US 14. An interpretive trail provides views of the imposing limestone cliffs and deep granite gorge cut by Shell Creek.

BLACK HILLS NATIONAL FOREST

The Black Hills National Forest is mostly in South Dakota but includes 175,000 acres of Wyoming's northeast corner. The area typically displays a mixture of Eastern hardwoods with Western coniferous forests. Ponderosa pine, white spruce, burr-oak, birch and quaking aspen provide habitats for a variety of wildlife including turkeys, elk and white-tailed and mule deer. Fire lookout towers at Cement Ridge, Elk Mountain and Warren Peak offer expansive views of the Black Hills and surrounding plains.

Maps and information are available at the District Rangers' offices in Newcastle and Sundance. Maps, which cost $7 each, show roads, streams, recreation areas and public attractions throughout the Black Hills. Most of the forest's developed recreational facilities are in South Dakota, but the Wyoming segment does have four campgrounds with 76 sites.

For additional information contact the Forest Supervisor's Office, 25041 N. US 16, Custer, SD

57730; phone (605) 673-9200. *See Recreation Chart and the AAA Northwestern and North Central CampBooks.*

BRIDGER-TETON NATIONAL FOREST

Elevations in the forest range from 5,660 ft. near Alpine to 13,804 ft. at Gannett Peak. Refer to AAA maps for additional elevation information.

Bordering Grand Teton *(see place listing p. 149)* and Yellowstone *(see place listing p. 173)* national parks, Bridger-Teton National Forest covers 3,439,809 acres in the Gros Ventre, Salt River, Teton, Wind River and Wyoming ranges. Within the forest are several live glaciers, an outstanding example of a geologic landslide and the state's highest mountain, Gannett Peak, shared by Shoshone National Forest *(see place listing p. 169)*. Fishing, hunting, white-water rafting and winter sports attract visitors to the area.

The forest has three wilderness areas, all accessible only on foot or horseback. The Bridger Wilderness, 428,169 acres of scenic mountain country, lies on the west slope of the Continental Divide in the Wind River Range. More than 1,300 lakes, Gannett Peak and many glaciers highlight this rugged landscape, which is traversed by more than 500 miles of hiking trails.

The Green River, beginning at the base of Gannett Peak, races through the Wind River Mountains before turning southward to join the Colorado River. The Teton Wilderness preserves 585,468 acres in the northern section of the forest. Snow sometimes stays on the ground until early July in this barren alpine country of broad meadows, lakes, steep canyons, streams and waterfalls.

At Two Ocean Pass, Two Ocean Creek divides and sends one stream to the Pacific Ocean and another to the Atlantic; this geographic phenomenon supposedly exists nowhere else on the continent. The 287,000-acre Gros Ventre Wilderness, immediately east of Jackson, also is rugged, mountainous country ideally suited to backpacking, fishing and hunting.

Scenic drives include Centennial National Scenic Byway from Dubois to Pinedale, the Green River Road from Pinedale north to the Green River Lakes, and the Skyline Drive from Pinedale northeast to Elkhart Park. Greys River Road leaves US 89 near Alpine and follows the river on its southward run; from its headwaters roads lead to US 89 near Geneva and to US 189 at Big Piney or Fontenelle reservoirs.

Pinedale *(see place listing p. 164)* and the resort town of Jackson *(see place listing p. 157)* are recreational activity centers. Near these two towns are the forest's three ski areas; trails for cross-country skiing also are available. Nearby hot springs include Granite Hot Springs, 35 miles southeast of Jackson on US 189, then 9 miles north. The Jackson Visitor Center, 532 N. Cache St., is open Mon.-Sat. 8:30-4:30.

For additional information contact the Forest Supervisor's Office, P.O. Box 1888, Jackson, WY; phone (307) 739-5500. *See Recreation Chart and the AAA Northwestern CampBook.*

GEM **GROS VENTRE SLIDE** is 5 mi. e. of Kelly on Gros Ventre Rd. When the landslide occurred on the morning of June 23, 1925, this large earth movement dammed up the Gros Ventre (Big Belly) River. In a matter of minutes, trees and land fell from an elevation of 9,000 feet. Two years later part of the slide gave way, and the resulting wall of water, mud and rock destroyed the town of Kelly. A self-guiding tour traverses the area.

PERIODIC SPRING is about 5 mi. e. of Afton on FR 10211 (Swift Creek Rd.). In late summer the spring ceases to flow every 18 minutes, then gradually builds to a thundering, ice-cold torrent. This cycle occurs regularly for 9 months and fluctuates during the period of highest snow melt, from about mid-May to mid-August. A narrow dirt road leads to within half a mile of the spring; the last 200 yards of the hike are very steep. The road, not recommended for trailers, is closed during winter.

BUFFALO (B-4) pop. 3,900, elev. 4,645'

Retaining the atmosphere and hospitality of the Old West, Buffalo is a ranching town on the eastern slope of the Big Horn Mountains. Many American Indian battles took place in this area 1866-77, triggered by the presence of the Bozeman Trail and the forts built to protect it.

After the area was opened to settlement, Buffalo was founded in 1879. Buffalo became known as the "Rustlers' Capital," and by 1892 the tensions between the region's big cattlemen and farmers, or "nesters," had erupted into the Johnson County War. It took the U.S. Army to restore order.

The growth of sheep ranching in the late 1890s brought Basque herders, who were drawn to Buffalo because of the Big Horn Mountains' resemblance to their homeland in the Pyrenees. Basque descendants continue to practice their time-honored traditions.

Guided saddle trips and jeep tours of nearby scenic and historical attractions can be arranged through local operators. Sightseeing is most rewarding along the Cloud Peak Scenic Byway portion of US 16 that runs between Buffalo and Ten Sleep.

Hunters can visit the Hunters Information Station in the chamber of commerce building.

Buffalo Chamber of Commerce: 55 N. Main St., Buffalo, WY 82834; phone (307) 684-5544 or (800) 227-5122. *See color ad p. 135.*

Self-guiding tours: Information about walking and driving tours is available from the chamber of commerce.

CAROUSEL PARK is at 655 E. Hart St. at jct. I-25/US 16 exit 299. The park features a renovated 1925 Spillman carousel with reproductions of bucking horses. Cloud Peak Ferris Wheel, built during the 1930s, faces the Big Horn Mountains and the Cloud Peak Wilderness Area. Visitors also can enjoy miniature golf. Food is available. Allow 1 hour minimum. Daily 8 a.m.-10 p.m., Memorial Day weekend-Labor Day. Carousel and ferris wheel $1.50 each. Phone (307) 684-7033.

JIM GATCHELL MEMORIAL MUSEUM is at 100 Fort St. The museum, which honors a frontier pharmacist known for his friendship with and knowledge of the Plains Indians, houses more than 15,000 artifacts. Included in the displays are a variety of firearms, historical photographs depicting the early days of the West, Indian artifacts and pioneer items. Daily 9-7, day after Memorial Day-Labor Day; Mon.-Sat. 9-5, May 1-Memorial Day and day after Labor Day-Oct. 31; Mon.-Fri. 9-4, Apr. 12-30 and in Nov. Closed July 4 and Thanksgiving. Admission $4; ages 6-16, $2. Phone (307) 684-9331.

OCCIDENTAL HOTEL is at 10 N. Main St. Throughout its history, the 1880 building was the center of community activity and served as town hall, polling place, hospital and headquarters for county government. Mon., Wed. and Fri. 9-4, June 1-Labor Day. Donations. Phone (307) 684-0451.

CARIBOU NATIONAL FOREST—

see place listing in Idaho p. 48.

CASPER (D-5) pop. 49,644, elev. 5,123′

Casper's roots are buried in commerce. The town began as a ferry site on the Oregon Trail in 1847, when a group of Mormon immigrants who were camping realized that there was money to be made by boating travelers across the North Platte River. The idea caught on, and in the early 1850s a toll bridge was built; soon a military post was established to protect the span and its traffic.

The town's real asset, however, was not discovered until 1889, when the first well in the Salt Creek oil field was tapped; by 1915 the town was in an oil boom that matched the frenzy of the California, Colorado and Montana gold rushes.

The boom brought not only prosperity but also a national scandal over the nearby Teapot Dome oil field. In 1927 the U.S. Supreme Court handed down verdicts in the case, which included sentencing Secretary of the Interior Albert Fall to prison for secretly leasing the rich field to Mammoth Crude Oil Co. without taking competitive bids.

Casper is a major service and supply center for mineral, oil, natural gas, uranium and coal industries, as well as a center for many medical and financial services.

Stargazers can view astronomy-related programs at Casper Planetarium, a half-mile north of I-25 exit 188B at 904 N. Poplar, June through August; phone (307) 577-0310.

Pathfinder Dam Museum, southwest on SR 220, features displays relating to the construction of the dam; phone (307) 261-5628. Along SRs 20/26 and 220, markers identify the California, Mormon, Oregon and Pony Express trails.

Casper Area Convention and Visitors Bureau: 330 S. Center St., Suite 420, Casper, WY 82601; phone (800) 852-1889. *See color ad p. 136.*

DAN SPEAS FISH REARING STATION is 10 mi. w. on SR 220, then 4.5 mi. on CR 308 following signs. The station is one of Wyoming's most productive fish hatcheries. Its use of a nearby spring, which promotes rapid fish growth, enables it to produce a 4-inch fish in 120 days. About 1 million fish are stocked annually. Daily 8-5. Free. Phone (307) 473-8890.

FORT CASPAR MUSEUM is .5 mi. n. of SR 220 off Wyoming Blvd. at 4001 Fort Caspar Rd. The site has a reconstruction of Fort Caspar, named in honor of Caspar Collins, a lieutenant killed while trying to reach an army supply train under American Indian attack in 1865. An interpretive center has exhibits of Indian and pioneer artifacts.

Interpretive center open Mon.-Sat. 8-7, Sun. noon-7, mid-May to mid-Sept.; Mon.-Fri. 8-5, Sun. 1-4, rest of year. Fort buildings open Mon.-Sat. 8:30-6:30, Sun. 12:30-6:30, mid-May to mid-Sept. Admission $2; ages 6-17, $1. Phone (307) 235-8462.

HISTORIC TRAILS WEST departs from Fort Caspar. The tour features a wagon train that travels along the actual ruts of the California, Mormon and Oregon trails. Visitors also can take an excursion where they ride horses as American Indian warriors did on the old trails. Historical accounts are given. Other types of expeditions also are available. Daily 10-4, May-Oct. (weather permitting). Fare $25-$95. Reservations are recommended. MC, VI. Phone (307) 266-4868.

INDEPENDENCE ROCK STATE HISTORIC SITE—*see Alcova p. 132.*

NICOLAYSEN ART MUSEUM AND DISCOVERY CENTER is at 400 E. Collins Dr. The center presents changing exhibits by national and regional artists. The Discovery Center offers informal hands-on and supervised programs, including a painting center, an image-rubbing table, a library and an art gallery. Tues.-Fri. 10-7, Sat. 10-5, Sun. noon-4; closed federal holidays. Free. Phone (307) 235-5247.

TATE GEOLOGICAL MUSEUM is on the Casper College campus at 125 College Dr.; take Wolcott St./Casper Mountain Rd. s. Displays include fossils, jade, meteorites and minerals, as well as traveling exhibits. Highlights include bird, dinosaur, fish, mammal and reptile bones and fossils that are more than 50 million years old. Also present is a fossil preparation lab. Allow 1 hour minimum. Mon.-Fri. 9-5, Sat. 10-4. Donations. Phone (307) 268-2447.

WERNER WILDLIFE MUSEUM is s. via Wolcott St. to 405 E. 15th St. The museum houses a pronghorn antelope diorama, a collection of Western birds and mounted specimens of wildlife native to Wyoming and other parts of North America. The Werner Trophy Room exhibits specimens from around the world. Daily 10-5. Free. Phone (307) 235-2108.

CHEYENNE (E-6) pop. 53,011, elev. 6,060'

Cheyenne was named for the tribe of Plains Indians that once roamed southeastern Wyoming. In 1867 Union Pacific Railroad chief engineer Maj. Gen. Grenville M. Dodge built a depot on the site, which was situated at the junction of several roads leading to military camps.

Before the track even reached town, it was overrun by gamblers, cowboys, speculators, shopkeepers and real estate salesmen, thus earning Cheyenne the nickname "Hell on Wheels." The town's reputation was so widespread that in 1868 a resident received a letter from Pennsylvania addressed simply "Cheyenne."

The Lincoln Highway

The horseless carriage rolled onto the American landscape in the 1890s. By 1910 there were more than 450,000 registered automobiles, yet the country still lacked a public road system.

Organized movements for better roads brought issues to the attention of the federal government, which had not participated in major road construction since it funded the National Road project in 1806.

But one particular initiative captured the public's support with a unique idea. In 1913 Carl Fisher—the man who built the Indianapolis Motor Speedway in 1909—and automobile industry leaders chartered the Lincoln Highway Association for the purpose of defining a direct coast-to-coast automobile route.

The LHA's first official act was to delineate a 3,389-mile, 12-state continuous route from New York to California—one that would be passable before the opening of the 1915 Panama-Pacific International Exposition in San Francisco. Although not perfect, the throughway was ready as promised, and a motion picture of America's transcontinental highway was shown at the exposition. Over time, the association improved surfaces by using better materials, shortened the driving distance with realignments and published guidebooks about the Lincoln Highway. Automobile touring had never been so good.

Through example, the LHA educated the public as well as state and federal governments about the value of good roads for almost 15 years. The 1919 moving of a military convoy over the "Lincolnway" foretold the utility of an integrated highway system for national defense and interstate commerce.

By 1869 Cheyenne had outgrown some of its cowtown adolescence to assume the more mature stature of territorial capital, an honor it retained when Wyoming became the 44th state in 1890.

Noted town residents include Nellie Tayloe Ross, the first woman governor in the United States; and Esther Morris, a pioneer for women's suffrage in Wyoming and former justice of the peace of South Pass City *(see place listing p. 169)*. A statue honoring Morris is on Capitol Avenue.

Since it was established in 1867 as a headquarters for the cavalry troops protecting pioneers and railroad construction workers, F.E. Warren Air Force Base has served various branches of the military, including the nation's first intercontinental ballistic missile group. Guided tours of the base museum are available; phone (307) 773-3381.

The renovated, Romanesque-style Union Pacific Railroad Depot downtown now houses a museum. "Big Boy," one of the world's largest steam locomotives, is on permanent display in Holliday Park.

Happy Jack Road (SR 210) is a 38-mile scenic byway to Laramie that runs from rolling grasslands to the rocky foothills of the Pole Mountain Division of Medicine Bow National Forest. Equally interesting is a trip to Snowy Range, a region of fishing streams and mountain lakes.

Cheyenne Frontier Days recaptures the city's Wild West heritage the last full week in July. It features what is claimed to be the world's largest outdoor rodeo, chuck wagon and wild horse races, four parades and nightly entertainment.

Cheyenne Area Convention and Visitors Bureau: 309 W. Lincolnway, Cheyenne, WY 82001; phone (307) 778-3133 or (800) 426-5009. *See color ad p. 140.*

Shopping areas: Frontier Mall, 1400 Dell Range Blvd., has more than 75 stores including Dillard's, JCPenney and Sears.

Self-guiding tours: A pamphlet describing a self-guiding walking tour of Cheyenne's historic downtown area is available at the convention and visitors bureau.

CHEYENNE BOTANIC GARDENS is at 710 S. Lions Park Dr. Located on 8 acres, the gardens include a 6,800-square-foot solar-heated greenhouse conservatory. Tropical foliage, cacti, herbs and roses grown within. A waterfall and a pond also are inside. On the lake side of the grounds is a seven-circuit labyrinth for visitors of all ages to enjoy. Picnicking is permitted. Allow 1 hour minimum. Mon.-Fri. 8-4:30, Sat.-Sun. 11-3:30. Donations. Phone (307) 637-6458.

GEM **CHEYENNE FRONTIER DAYS OLD WEST MUSEUM** is next to Frontier Park on N. Carey Ave. The museum includes among its exhibits a horse-drawn vehicle collection and classic Western art. A bronc-riding saddle lets aspiring cowboys learn the rigors of the rodeo. An interactive electronic program allows visitors to navigate through frontier history. Children can explore hands-on exhibits in the "Hole in the Wall" room.

Mon.-Fri. 9-7, Sat.-Sun. 10-5, with extended hours during Frontier Days; closed holidays. Admission $5, under 12 free with adult. Phone (307) 778-7290. *See color ad p. 140.*

SAVE **CHEYENNE STREET RAILWAY TROLLEY** departs from the intersection of Lincolnway and Capitol. Highlights of the 2-hour sightseeing tours include historic downtown and F.E. Warren Air Force Base. Tickets can be purchased at the convention and visitors bureau. Tours Mon.-Sat. at 10 and 1:30, Sun. at 1:30 (also Fri. at 7 p.m.), mid-May to mid-Sept. (extra tours in July). Fare $8; ages 2-12, $4. Phone (307) 778-3133 or (800) 426-5009. *See color ad p. 140.*

HISTORIC GOVERNORS' MANSION STATE HISTORIC SITE is at 300 E. 21st St. The site was the home of Wyoming's chief executives 1905-76. A videotape provides a historical background of Wyoming's first families and describes the interior design of the 1904 Colonial-style mansion. Allow 1 hour minimum. Tues.-Sat. 9-5, June-Aug.; Tues.-Fri. 9-noon and 1-5, Sat. 9-5, rest of year. Closed Sat. preceding 3-day holidays. Free. Phone (307) 777-7878 or (307) 777-7014. *See color ad p. 140.*

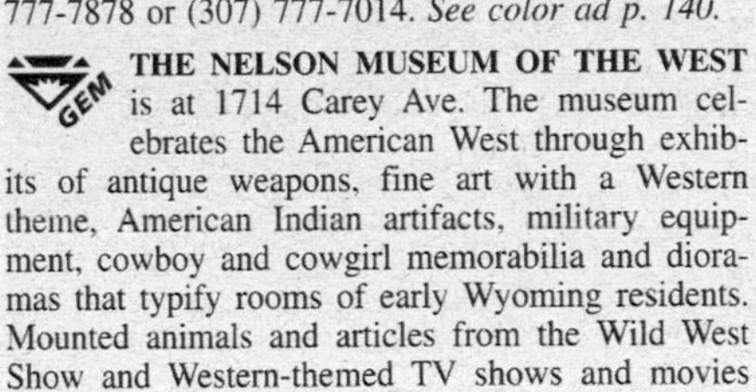

GEM **THE NELSON MUSEUM OF THE WEST** is at 1714 Carey Ave. The museum celebrates the American West through exhibits of antique weapons, fine art with a Western theme, American Indian artifacts, military equipment, cowboy and cowgirl memorabilia and dioramas that typify rooms of early Wyoming residents. Mounted animals and articles from the Wild West Show and Western-themed TV shows and movies also are highlights.

A display focusing on regional lawmen and outlaws is in the basement. A research library is available. Allow 1 hour minimum. Mon.-Sat. 8-5, June-Aug.; Mon.-Fri. 8-noon and 1-5, rest of year. Closed major holidays. Admission $3; over 65, $2; under 12 free. Phone (307) 635-7670. *See color ad p. 140.*

STATE CAPITOL is on Capitol Ave. between 24th and 25th sts. This neoclassic sandstone building, with a golden dome 50 feet in diameter, is architecturally uncommon for the region. Within the building are murals, woodwork, marble floors and displays of native wildlife. Mon.-Fri. 8-4:30; closed holidays. Free. Phone (307) 777-7220.

TERRY BISON RANCH is off I-25 exit 2, then s. on Terry Ranch Rd. to ranch entrance. The historic working bison ranch has more than 3,000 bison. Fishing, horseback rides and wagon tours are offered.

Bison tours daily at 8, 9, 10:30, noon, 1:30, 3, 4:30, 6 p.m. and 7:30 p.m. Bison tours $12; ages 6-12, $9. Horseback rides $21. Under 9 are not permitted on horseback rides, but pony rides are available. DS, MC, VI. Phone (307) 634-4171 or (800) 319-4171. *See color ad p. 140 & p. 141.*

The Lincoln Highway (continued)

With the 1921 Federal Highway Act came the funds for states to construct and maintain connecting arteries. Four years later the United States adopted a highway numbering system, and most of the Lincoln route became US 30, 40 and 50. The association disbanded in 1928, but not before it engaged Boy Scout troops across the country to place some 3,000 concrete Lincoln Highway markers along the route in all 12 states: New York, New Jersey, Pennsylvania, Ohio, Indiana, Illinois, Iowa, Nebraska, Wyoming, Utah, Nevada and California. Many of these markers still exist.

Cheyenne was the first major city encountered by westbound Lincoln Highway travelers entering sparsely populated Wyoming from Nebraska. From there, a 50-mile-long boulevard to **Laramie** climbed to a summit from which Pikes Peak could be seen on a clear day. Today's I-80/US 30 corridor follows the original Lincoln Highway across the state, except where US 30/287 arcs north from Laramie to **Medicine Bow.** The road from **Rawlins** across the Continental Divide was laid along the abandoned Union Pacific Railroad bed. Lincoln Highway guidebooks called the scenery between **Rock Springs** and **Green River** grand and impressive. **Fort Bridger** and **Evanston** were the last stops before entering Utah. **Look for these Wyoming Lincoln Highway landmark towns in this TourBook guide.**

For more information about the old Lincoln Highway contact the new Lincoln Highway Association, P.O. Box 308, Franklin Grove, IL 61031; phone (815) 456-3030.

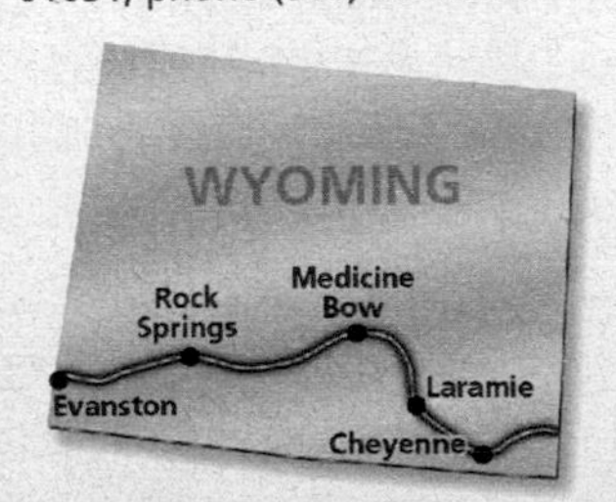

Digital Archives

WILDLIFE VISITOR CENTER is at 5400 Bishop Blvd. (I-25 Central Ave. exit). The center, administered by the Wyoming Game & Fish Department, has photographic displays spotlighting some of the 600-plus species of free-ranging mammals, birds, reptiles and fish that inhabit the state. Also included are several bird and big game mounts. Allow 30 minutes minimum. Mon.-Fri. 8-5, Sat.-Sun. 9-5, Memorial Day weekend-Labor Day; Mon.-Fri. 8-5, rest of year. Free. Phone (307) 777-4538.

GEM **WYOMING STATE MUSEUM** is in the Capitol complex at 2301 Central Ave. The museum showcases items pertaining to Wyoming history. Exhibits include American Indian artifacts, fine art, weapons, military memorabilia, gems and dinosaur bone casts and fossils. Other museum features include a Hands-On History room for children and a wildlife diorama. Allow 2 hours minimum. Tues.-Sat. 9-4:30, May-Oct.; Tues.-Fri. 9-4:30, Sat. 10-2, rest of year. Closed holidays. Free. Phone (307) 777-7022. *See color ad p. 140.*

CODY (B-2) pop. 8,835, elev. 5,095'

Founded by Col. William "Buffalo Bill" F. Cody in 1896, Cody is near the east and northeast entrances to Yellowstone National Park *(see place listing p. 173)*. Some of the state's most scenic areas, including Shoshone National Forest *(see place listing p. 169)*, Sunlight Basin, the Absaroka and Beartooth mountains and the Bighorn Canyon National Recreation Area *(see place listing p. 85)*, are nearby.

US 14/16/20, alternately known as the Buffalo Bill Cody Scenic Byway, was designated the "most scenic 52 miles in America" by President Theodore Roosevelt; of note along the route are the many unusual rock formations. The highway runs 182 miles between Ranchester and Yellowstone National Park. Cody also is the northern terminus of the scenic section of SR 120 that travels 83 miles southeast to Thermopolis *(see place listing p. 171)*. Scenic US 14A heads 107 miles northeast to Burgess Junction.

Outfitters offer fishing, hayrides, horseback riding, hunting and pack trips and river float trips. Scenic flights over the Big Horn Mountains and Grand Teton and Yellowstone national parks can be arranged through Spirit Mountain Aviation; phone (307) 587-6732.

Of interest downtown are historic buildings dating from the beginning of the 20th century. Irma Hotel, 12th Street and Sheridan Avenue, has been a meeting place for local cattlemen, oilmen and shepherds since the early 1900s. Its $100,000 bar was a gift from Queen Victoria to Buffalo Bill in appreciation of his Wild West Show. Pahaska Tepee, Buffalo Bill's first hunting lodge, is at the east entrance to Yellowstone National Park.

Cody Chamber of Commerce: 836 Sheridan Ave., Cody, WY 82414; phone (307) 587-2297. *See color ad starting on p. 142.*

BUFFALO BILL DAM VISITOR CENTER is 7 mi. w. on US 14/16/20. In addition to a dam overlook, the visitor center has a natural history museum, views of Shoshone Canyon, area wildlife displays and dinosaur and fossil exhibits. Allow 30 minutes minimum. Daily 8-8, June 1-Labor Day; 8-6 in May and day after Labor Day-Sept. 30. Free. Phone (307) 527-6076. *See color ad starting on p. 142.*

GEM **BUFFALO BILL HISTORICAL CENTER** is at jct. US 14/16/20 and 720 Sheridan Ave. The five museums that comprise the center have more than 237,000 square feet of exhibit space dedicated to the art, artifacts, crafts, cultures, traditions and history of the American West. In addition, a research library contains book and manuscript collections, historic photographs and an archive of Western songs and ballads.

Food is available. Allow 4 hours minimum. Daily 7 a.m.-8 p.m., June 1 to mid-Sept.; 8-5, mid-Sept. through Oct. 31; 10-5 in Apr.; 8-8 in May; Tues.-Sun. 10-3, rest of year. Admission (valid for 2 consecutive days for all four museums) $15; senior citizens $13; students over 17 with ID, $6; ages 6-17, $4. AX, DS, MC, VI. Phone (307) 587-4771. *See color ad starting on p. 142.*

Buffalo Bill Museum is at jct. US 14/16/20 and 720 Sheridan Ave. at Buffalo Bill Historical Center. The museum displays belongings of the showman,

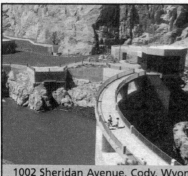

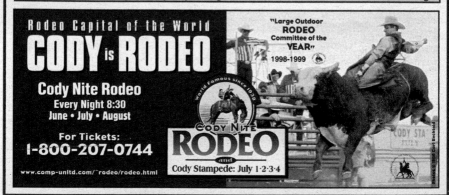

scout and Pony Express rider, along with possessions of Annie Oakley and artifacts of the early West. Exhibits provide insight into the history of the American cowboy, conservation and dude ranching. Daily 7 a.m.-8 p.m., June 1 to mid-Sept.; 8-5, mid-Sept. through Oct. 31; 10-5 in Apr.; 8-8 in May; Tues.-Sun. 10-3, rest of year. Admission included with Buffalo Bill Historical Center.

The Cody Firearms Museum is at jct. US 14/16/20 and 720 Sheridan Ave. at Buffalo Bill Historical Center. The museum is noted for its exhibits of American firearms, including the Winchester collection. The museum, featuring more than 5,000 items, traces the development of firearms from the early 16th century. Examples range from centuries-old projectile arms to flintlocks and Gatling guns to modern sport rifles. Daily 7 a.m.-8 p.m., June 1 to mid-Sept.; 8-5, mid-Sept. through Oct. 31; 10-5 in Apr.; 8-8 in May; Tues.-Sun. 10-3, rest of year. Admission included with Buffalo Bill Historical Center.

The Draper Museum of Natural History is at jct. US 14/16/20 and 720 Sheridan Ave. at Buffalo Bill Historical Center. The museum features exhibits about the region's natural history and human influence from early explorers to ranchers. A highlight is a virtual expedition through mountain forests and valleys. Daily 7 a.m.-8 p.m., June 1 to mid-Sept.;

8-5, mid-Sept. through Oct. 31; 10-5 in Apr.; 8-8 in May; Tues.-Sun. 10-3, rest of year. Admission included with Buffalo Bill Historical Center.

The Plains Indian Museum is at jct. US 14/16/20 and 720 Sheridan Ave. at Buffalo Bill Historical Center. The museum has an extensive collection of art, artifacts, ceremonial items and beadwork as well as dress and weaponry of the Arapaho, Blackfeet, Cheyenne, Crow, Shoshone and Sioux tribes. Exhibits depict the everyday existence of these Plains tribes. Daily 7 a.m.-8 p.m., June 1 to mid-Sept.; 8-5, mid-Sept. through Oct. 31; 10-5 in Apr.; 8-8 in May; Tues.-Sun. 10-3, rest of year. Admission included with Buffalo Bill Historical Center.

Whitney Gallery of Western Art is at jct. US 14/16/20 and 720 Sheridan Ave. at Buffalo Bill Historical Center. The gallery houses a comprehensive collection of paintings, sculpture and prints depicting the West. Artists represented include Albert Bierstadt, George Catlin, Thomas Moran, Frederic Remington, Charles M. Russell and Dallas Sharp. Reconstructed studios enable visitors to view artists' work areas. Daily 7 a.m.-8 p.m., June 1 to mid-Sept.; 8-5, mid-Sept. through Oct. 31; 10-5 in Apr.; 8-8 in May; Tues.-Sun. 10-3, rest of year. Admission included with Buffalo Bill Historical Center.

BUFFALO BILL STATUE is at the w. end of Sheridan Ave. The statue represents young William Cody as a mounted Army scout signaling the discovery of enemy tracks.

CODY CHAPEL MURALS INFORMATION CENTER is in Cody Chapel at Wyoming Ave. and 18th St. The center displays exhibits, artifacts, murals, paintings and sculpture relating to the Mormon colonization of the Big Horn Basin. Film presentations and guided tours are given. Daily 8-8, June 1-Sept. 15; by appointment rest of year. Closed Jan. 1, Thanksgiving and Dec. 25. Free. Phone (307) 587-3290.

CODY NITE RODEO is 2 mi. w. on US 14/16/20. The rodeo features nightly performances. Daily at 8:30 p.m., June-Aug. Special performances are held July 1-4 during Stampede Days. Grandstand seats $12; under 12, $6. Buzzards Roost seats $14; under 12, $8. Phone (307) 587-5155. *See color ad starting on p. 142.*

FOUNDATION FOR NORTH AMERICAN WILD SHEEP is at 720 Allen Ave. The denlike educational area features audio and visual presentations, paintings, prints and mounted exhibits pertaining to North American wild sheep. A variety of bronzed bighorn sheep stand outside. Self-guiding tours are available. Allow 1 hour minimum. Mon.-Fri. 7-5; closed Thanksgiving and Dec. 25. Donations. Phone (307) 527-6261.

TECUMSEH'S OLD WEST MINIATURE VILLAGE AND MUSEUM is 2.5 mi. w. on US 14/16/20. The museum features displays of American Indian and Old West artifacts, guns, other weaponry and wildlife. The history of Wyoming is characterized in miniature in a 66-scene display with moving trains and audio narratives. Allow 1 hour minimum. Daily 8-8, June-Aug.; 9-5 in May and Sept.; by appointment rest of year. Admission $3; ages 6-18, $1. AX, DS, MC, VI. Phone (307) 587-5362.

GEM **TRAIL TOWN** is 3 mi. w. on US 14/16/20. Featured is a group of historic buildings with indoor exhibits reassembled on the first site of the frontier town of Old Cody. Included are the grave of John "Jeremiah" Johnson and a log cabin used as a hideout by Butch Cassidy, the Sundance Kid and other members of the Wild Bunch.

The Museum of the Old West houses guns, carriages, clothing and many prehistoric and historic Plains Indian relics. Daily 8-8 (weather permitting), May 15-Sept. 30. Admission $6; over 59, $5; ages 6-12, $2. Phone (307) 587-5302.

RECREATIONAL ACTIVITIES

White-water Rafting

- **Red Canyon River Trips**, 1374 Sheridan Ave., Cody, WY 82414. Trips depart daily at 9, 1 and 3, May 1 to mid-Sept. Phone (307) 587-6988 or (307) 587-9476.
- **River Runners**, 1491 Sheridan Ave., Cody, WY 82414. Trips run late May to late Aug. Phone (307) 527-7238 or (800) 535-7238.
- **Wyoming River Trips** depart the Holiday Inn/Buffalo Bill Village Complex at jct. SR 120 and US 14/16/20. Write P.O. Box 1541-A, Cody, WY 82414. Trips offered several times daily, May-Sept. Phone (307) 587-6661 or (800) 586-6661.

GEM DEVILS TOWER NATIONAL MONUMENT (B-6)

Devils Tower National Monument is accessible from SR 24, north off I-90 via US 14 or west from Belle Fourche, S.D.; from Alzada, Mont., SR 112 runs southwest off US 212. Occupying 1,347 acres in the area between Sundance and Hulett, the monument contains Devils Tower, the most conspicuous landmark in northeastern Wyoming.

The tower, a huge monolith resembling a colossal stone tree stump, rises 867 feet from its base and 1,267 feet above the Belle Fourche River. The 1.5-acre top has a growth of sagebrush and grass, and the almost perpendicular sides are fluted columns. The tower was formed when numerous sedimentary layers eroded from around a volcanic intrusion that had cooled in a teardrop formation.

About a half-mile from the entrance is a prairie dog colony. Near the monument's campground is an outdoor amphitheater. Ranger-naturalists conduct summer interpretive walks, climbing demonstrations and nightly campfire programs.

The Tower Trail, marked to identify plants and rocks, encircles Devils Tower. Climbing on the tower is permitted, but climbers must sign in before and after expeditions. Fishing, swimming and tubing are permitted on the Belle Fourche River. A visitor center about 3 miles from the park entrance contains geological specimens, artifacts and exhibits. Trailers are prohibited at the monument and must be dropped at the base parking lot. Dogs, which must be leashed, are not permitted on the trails.

Allow 2 hours, 30 minutes minimum. The monument is open daily 24 hours. The visitor center is open daily 8-8, June-Aug.; 8:30-5, Apr.-May and Sept.-Oct. (weather permitting). Admission $8 per private vehicle or $3 per person arriving by bicycle, motorcycle or on foot; under 17 free. Phone (307) 467-5283 Mon.-Fri. 8-4:30. *See Recreation Chart and the AAA Northwestern CampBook.*

DOUGLAS (D-6) pop. 5,288, elev. 4,815′

Known as Tent Town at its founding in 1886, Douglas served as a supply post for cattlemen and a distribution point for railroad consignments. The town's history is typical of the colorful, brawling days when cavalrymen, cowboys and railroad crews were opening the West, but in contrast to many other towns, few killings were recorded.

One of the town's rowdiest characters was George Pike, a cowhand whose rustling habits were so well-known that the cattle companies decided to hire him so he would at least benefit his current employer. One company thought so highly of Pike that at his death it erected an expensive tombstone with the following inscription:

Underneath this stone in eternal rest, Sleeps the wildest one of the wayward west. He was a gambler and sport and cowboy, too, And he led the pace in an outlaw crew. He was sure on the trigger and staid to the end, But was never known to quit on a friend. In the relations of death all mankind's alike, But in life there was only one George Pike.

Douglas also is said to be the original home of the "jackalope," a fanciful creation of Wyoming's taxidermists. Doubters are confronted with dozens of convincing mounted specimens of this animal—best described as a jackrabbit sporting antlers—on display throughout the state. A 10-foot replica of the "hybrid" stands downtown in Centennial Jackalope Square at 3rd and Center streets.

Scenic River Path, running along the bank of the North Platte River in downtown, offers 2.5 miles of trails for walking, bicycling and observing nature.

Douglas Area Chamber of Commerce: 121 Brownfield Rd., Douglas, WY 82633; phone (307) 358-2950.

AYRES NATURAL BRIDGE is in Ayres Park, 12 mi. w. on I-25, then 5 mi. s. on Natural Bridge Rd. La Prele Creek has worn a passageway through thick stone, leaving an arch 30 feet high and 50 feet wide. Camping and picnic facilities are available. Daily 8-8, Apr.-Oct. Free.

FORT FETTERMAN STATE HISTORIC SITE is 7 mi. n.w. via SR 93 off the North Douglas exit of I-25. The site preserves the fort's restored officers' quarters and an ordnance warehouse. Built in 1867, the fort was once a major Army supply post. A museum contains exhibits depicting the history of the military and Fetterman City. Period rooms, weapons, artifacts and clothing are displayed. A living-history program is offered during Fort Fetterman Days the second week of June.

Allow 2 hours minimum. Daily 9-5, Memorial Day weekend-Labor Day. Admission for Wyoming residents $1, nonresidents $2, under 18 free. Phone (307) 358-2864, (307) 777-7014 or (307) 684-7629.

GEM **WYOMING PIONEER MEMORIAL MUSEUM** is on the state fairgrounds off Center St. The museum began as a log structure in 1925 and has since enlarged to accommodate one of the largest displays of historic artifacts in the state. The museum contains an extensive collection of Wyoming pioneer items, military relics, American Indian artifacts, maps, charts, newspapers and photographs from the late 1800s.

The Johnson Gallery houses the museum's American Indian collection that includes such highlights as a 1964 Sioux-style teepee used in the movie "Dances with Wolves," numerous examples of decorative arts and multiple displays of American Indian sculpture. Other museum highlights include clothing worn during Wyoming's territorial period, an art display with changing exhibits, a research library about Wyoming history and an 1885 one-room schoolhouse.

Mon.-Fri. 8-5 (also Sat. 1-5, June-Sept.). Free. Phone (307) 358-9288.

DUBOIS (C-2) pop. 962, elev. 6,917′

Dubois grew from a rendezvous point for French, American and Indian trappers at the head of the Wind River Valley into a headquarters for cattle outfits, tie hack crews and river tie drives. From 1914 to 1946, stacked decks of railroad ties were floated down the Wind River from tie camps west of town to the railhead at Riverton. Dubois now is bordered by extensive cattle and dude ranching operations.

Northwest of Dubois is Union Pass, said to be the only place in the United States from which three rivers flow in different directions: Fish Creek is the source of the Columbia River, Jakeys Fork flows to the Mississippi, and Roaring Fork is part of the Colorado River drainage system.

Pack trips leave Dubois for Gannett Peak, Wyoming's highest peak, and the Fitzpatrick Wilderness, where there are 44 active glaciers.

Snowmobiling, dog sledding and cross-country skiing are popular at Union Pass and Togwotee Pass; both cross the Continental Divide west of Dubois.

Dubois Chamber of Commerce: 616 W. Ramshorn St., P.O. Box 632, Dubois, WY 82513; phone (307) 455-2556.

DUBOIS FISH HATCHERY is 3 mi. e. on US 26/287, then 1.5 mi. s. at 411 Fish Hatchery Rd. Fed by two springs and the Jakeys Fork, the station incubates and ships to other hatcheries nationwide up to 7 million eggs; it also rears nearly a half million fish yearly for stocking. Varieties include cutthroat, rainbow, Snake River and Bear River trout. Daily 8-5. Free. Phone (307) 455-2431.

DUBOIS MUSEUM is at 909 W. Ramshorn St. The museum contains local artifacts depicting the industry, history, cultures and geology of Dubois and the region between the Wind River and the Absaroka Mountains. Daily 9-8, Memorial Day-Sept. 30; Mon-Fri. 9-5, rest of year. Hours may be extended during peak season. Admission $1; under 12, 50c. Phone (307) 455-2284.

NATIONAL BIGHORN SHEEP INTERPRETIVE CENTER is at 907 W. Ramshorn. Through the use of dioramas, mounted animals, hands-on exhibits and videotapes visitors can learn about the history and biology of the bighorn sheep. "Sheep Mountain" replicates the bighorn's natural habitat. It focuses on predator-prey relationships, seasonal changes in habitat conditions, and plant and animal life with which bighorns interact.

Allow 1 hour minimum. Daily 9-8, Memorial Day-Labor Day; 9-5, rest of year. Closed Jan. 1, Thanksgiving and Dec. 25. Guided tours by reservation Nov.-Mar. Admission $2; under 13, 75c; family rate $5. MC, VI. Phone (307) 455-3429 or (888) 209-2795.

ELK MOUNTAIN (E-5) pop. 192, elev. 7,240'

Elk Mountain, originally known as "The Crossing" by pioneers who traversed the Overland Trail, is noted for the wild game that take shelter on the nearby refuge in the shadow of 11,156-foot Elk Mountain. Both Elk Mountain Hotel and Garden Spot Pavilion Dance Hall, next to the hotel, are on the National Register of Historic Places.

ENCAMPMENT (F-4) pop. 443, elev. 7,323'

Encampment takes its name from an Indian camp where tribes gathered to hunt big game between the Medicine Bow and Sierra Madre ranges. It was a copper mining town from 1897 until the vein was exhausted in 1908; a gold strike was reported as late as 1937. Stock raising and lumbering are now the principal industries.

Legend has it that Thomas Edison conceived of the light bulb filament while looking at a frayed line during a fishing trip near Encampment.

GRAND ENCAMPMENT MUSEUM is 3 blks. s. of the post office. The museum houses memorabilia recalling the area's American Indian encampment and copper mining days. The museum complex also encompasses a pioneer village whose 14 buildings include a two-story outhouse and a forest service lookout tower. A park next to the museum has picnic facilities and a playground.

Guided tours are available. Allow 2 hours minimum. Mon.-Sat. 10-5, Sun. 1-5, Memorial Day-Labor Day; by appointment rest of year. Donations. Phone (307) 327-5308.

EVANSTON (E-1) pop. 11,507, elev. 6,743'

Designated the seat of Uinta County in 1870, Evanston lies in the center of the energy-rich Overthrust Belt. It also is a departure point for trips into the Uinta Mountains to the south. Depot Square Park is the center of such summer activities as band concerts and barbecues. Other recreational opportunities include water sports at Woodruff Narrows Reservoir, north via US 89, and cross-country skiing at Bear River State Park. *(see Recreation Chart and the AAA Northwestern CampBook).*

Thoroughbred and quarter horses run during summer weekends at Wyoming Downs, a pari-mutuel track; phone (307) 789-0511.

Note: Policies vary concerning admittance of children to pari-mutuel betting facilities. Phone for information.

Bear River Information Center: 601 Bear River Dr., Evanston, WY 82930; phone (307) 789-6540.

UINTA COUNTY HISTORICAL MUSEUM is 36 10th St. The museum preserves the artifacts and photographs of the area's first pioneers. Displayed are items used on a 19th-century Uinta County ranch, gambling and bootleg whiskey paraphernalia, clothing from the era and objects used by the Indian and Chinese people who emigrated to the region. Mon.-Fri. 9-8, Sat.-Sun. noon-6, Memorial Day-Labor Day; Mon.-Fri. 9-5, rest of year. Closed major holidays. Free. Phone (307) 789-8248.

FLAMING GORGE NATIONAL RECREATION AREA (E-2)

Flaming Gorge National Recreation Area straddles the border between Wyoming and Utah and is reached by SR 530 or US 191 from I-80 in Wyoming or US 191 from Utah. The area includes a 91-mile-long reservoir and the Flaming Gorge and Red canyons, which were carved through the Uinta Mountains by the Green River.

Lake Flaming Gorge is bounded primarily by Red Canyon to the south and by rolling hills and occasional abrupt cliffs and promontories to the north. Of geological interest are the exposed strata in Firehole Canyon and the Sheep Creek Geological Loop.

Once belonging to Mexico, the Wyoming portion of Flaming Gorge region was annexed to the United States after the Mexican War. John Wesley Powell, a one-armed Army major and professor, mapped the area on his way down the Green River in the late 1860s and early 1870s and named Flaming Gorge and many other prominent landmarks.

I-80 is connected to SR 530 and US 191. In Utah, US 191 joins with SRs 43 and 44, which then link with SR 530 again, to form a complete 160-mile loop around the recreation area. Along the route are Flaming Gorge Dam and Visitor Center, Red Canyon Visitor Center, the Sheep Creek Geological Loop and Flaming Gorge.

Known for its bountiful fishing waters, Lake Flaming Gorge also is a popular setting for swimming, boating and water skiing. Large boat ramps are found near campgrounds at convenient access points along the western and eastern sides of the lake.

The western shore, accessible from Buckboard and Lucerne Valley, has campsites and two marinas that provide boat rentals and supplies. Cedar Springs to the southeast is similarly equipped, the latter has a dock and marina. Other campgrounds are scattered throughout the Utah and Wyoming sections.

Red Canyon Visitor Center and Overlook, off SR 44, offers a spectacular view from 1,400 feet above Red Canyon and Flaming Gorge Reservoir. The Red Canyon Visitor Center is open daily 10-5, Memorial Day-Labor Day; phone (435) 889-3713. The Flaming Gorge Dam Visitor Center, off US 191 adjacent to the Bureau of Reclamation offices, is open daily 8-6, Memorial Day-Labor Day; 9-5 in spring and fall; 10-4, rest of year. Phone (435) 885-3135.

The recreation area is open all year, but most facilities are closed during the winter. Seasonal hunting is permitted except near public-use facilities. The reservoir contains a broad sampling of fish, including German brown, lake, rainbow and cutthroat trout; small-mouth bass; and kokanee salmon. Fishing is permitted all year. A license from either Utah or Wyoming is required. Cross-country skiing, snowmobiling and ice fishing are popular winter activities.

A use fee pass is required for all facilities. Passes are $2 (1-day), $5 (16-day) and $20 (annual), beginning from the date of purchase. Golden Age, Golden Eagle and Golden Access pass holders enter free. For further information contact the Flaming Gorge Ranger District, Flaming Gorge National Recreation Area, P.O. Box 279, Manila, UT 84046; phone (435) 784-3445. *See Recreation Chart and the AAA Northwestern CampBook.*

FLAMING GORGE DAM is near Dutch John, Utah. The concrete arch structure rises 502 feet above bedrock. Visitor center open daily 10-4. Guided tours offered daily 11-3. Free. Phone (435) 784-3445.

FORT BRIDGER (F-1) pop. 400

One of Fort Bridger's early residents was the renowned mountain man and scout Jim Bridger. Bridger, who hired himself out as a wilderness guide, was known for telling tall tales. According to popular lore, one of Bridger's most repeated stories was the one in which he tried to jump across a gorge in a petrified forest. The gorge turned out to be wider than he expected, but Bridger managed to escape death by remaining aloft on the gorge's petrified air.

Self-guiding tours: A driving tour atop an original hand-built roadbed of the Union Pacific begins 9 miles west of Fort Bridger at Leroy. The tour continues past the abandoned town of Piedmont, several beehive-shaped charcoal kilns and the Uinta Mountains before entering Evanston *(see place listing p.147)*.

FORT BRIDGER STATE HISTORIC SITE is 3 mi. s. of I-80 exit 34. The fort was established in 1843 by Jim Bridger and Louis Vasquez. Some buildings constructed during Army occupation 1858-90 are in ruins, but many still stand. Recent excavations have revealed the site of the original trading post, which has been reconstructed nearby. A museum offers living-history interpretations throughout the summer.

Picnicking is permitted. Allow 2 hours minimum. Daily 8:30-5, May-Sept.; Sat.-Sun. 9-4:30, mid-Mar. through Apr. 30 and in Oct. Phone ahead to verify hours. Admission for Wyoming residents $1, nonresidents $2. Phone (307) 782-3842.

GEM FORT LARAMIE NATIONAL HISTORIC SITE (E-6)

Fort Laramie National Historic Site is off US 26, 3 miles southwest of the town of Fort Laramie. Near the confluence of the Laramie and North Platte rivers, the site covers 832 acres. From its founding as Fort William in 1834 and until 1849, the fort was an important fur-trading post. Purchased by the U.S. government in 1849 and renamed Fort Laramie, the fort served to aid in the migrations to Oregon and California. By 1890 the fort had outlived its usefulness and was abandoned, its land and buildings sold at public auction.

Eleven structures, including the 1874 cavalry barracks, have been restored and refurnished to recall the flavor of daily life at this post. A visitor center museum displays artifacts relating to civilian, military and Indian history on the northern Plains. From June to mid-August, staff members in period clothing demonstrate aspects of both military and civilian life in the 1870s. A vehicle for the physically impaired is available when the number of staff permits. An 1875 iron Army bridge that spans the North Platte River is 2 miles above the fort.

Grounds open daily 8-dusk. Visitor center open daily 8-7, June 1-Labor Day; 8-4:30, rest of year. Closed Jan. 1, Thanksgiving and Dec. 25. Admission $3, under 17 free; free to all July 4 and Aug. 25. Phone (307) 837-2221.

FOSSIL BUTTE NATIONAL MONUMENT (E-1)

Fourteen miles west of Kemmerer on US 30, Fossil Butte National Monument rises nearly 1,000 feet above the Twin Creek Valley. The buff-to-white beds of the Green River formation contain one of the world's largest deposits of the fossils of freshwater fish that lived 50 million years ago. Fossils of mammals, plants and fish can be seen at the visitor center; a videotape presentation also is available.

A self-guiding hiking trail, 2.5 miles long, leads to the site of a historic fossil quarry, and a 1.5-mile trail takes visitors through an aspen tree grove. Ranger-guided hikes around the monument are offered Sat.-Sun. at 10:30 and 1 by appointment, Memorial Day-Labor Day. Porch programs are offered daily on the hour 11-1.

Allow 2 hours, 30 minutes minimum. Grounds open all year but may be snow covered Oct.-Apr. Visitor center open daily 8-7, June-Aug.; 8-4:30, rest of year. Closed winter holidays. Free. Phone (307) 877-4455. *See Recreation Chart.*

GILLETTE (B-5) pop. 19,646, elev. 4,538′

Gillette lies on a high plateau between the Black Hills and the Big Horn Mountains. The town's livestock industry dates from the early 1800s. Mule deer, pronghorns and buffaloes graze on unspoiled land nearby.

Named for railroad surveyor Edward Gillette, the town was developed as a ranching area and became a hub for transporting livestock to market. Now coal and oil industries fuel Gillette's economy. During summer, free coal mine tours can be arranged through the convention and visitors bureau. The bureau also offers an assistance program for hunters interested in the mule deer, pronghorn antelopes and elk populations in the area.

Campbell County Convention and Visitors Bureau: 1810 S. Douglas Hwy., Suite A, Gillette, WY 82718; phone (307) 686-0040. *See color ad.*

ROCKPILE MUSEUM is 1 mi. from I-90 exit 124 on Second St. (US 14/16E). The museum takes its name from a nearby rock formation. Local history is depicted through extensive displays that include firearms, pioneer and American Indian artifacts, an early horse-drawn hearse and a restored sheep wagon. Next to the museum is a furnished rural schoolhouse that held only 12 students. Mon.-Sat. 9-8, Sun. 12:30-6:30, June-Sept.; Mon.-Sat. 9-5, rest of year. Free. Phone (307) 682-5723.

GRAND TETON NATIONAL PARK (C-1)

See map page 150.

Elevations in the park range from 6,800 ft. at the valley floor to 13,770 ft. at Grand Teton Peak. Refer to AAA maps for additional elevation information.

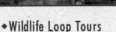

Grand Teton National Park's southern entrance is north of Jackson on US 26/89/191; an eastern entrance is at Moran Junction on US 26/287. From this point US 89/191/287 heads north through the

©2003 NAVIGATION TECHNOLOGIES
© AAA

To Yellowstone National Park
287
191
89
ROAD CLOSED IN WINTER
MOUNT BERRY EL 8,951 FT
WILDCAT PEAK EL 9,693 FT
Bridger-Teton National Forest
Targhee National Forest
Lizard Creek
Arizona Cr.
Pilgrim Creek
Pacific Creek
JOHN D ROCKEFELLER PKWY
Jackson Lake
MOOSE MOUNTAIN EL 10,054 FT
RANGER PEAK EL 11,355 FT
Colter Bay
Colter Bay Visitor Center
Two Ocean Lake
EAGLES REST PEAK EL 11,257 FT
Emma Matilda Lake
BIVOUAC PEAK EL 10,825 FT
Jackson Lodge
Triple Glacier
Signal Mountain
Moran
GREEN MTN EL 9,614 FT
THOR PEAK EL 12,028 FT
MT MORAN EL 12,605 FT
26
287
Buffalo Fork
To Dubois
Hidden Falls And Inspiration Point
Leigh Lake
TR
Jenny Lake
PAINTBRUSH
MOUNT SAINT JOHN EL 11,430 EL
Snake River
ROCKEFELLER PKWY
CASCADE CANYON TRAIL
Jenny Lake Visitor Center
Cunningham Cabin Historic Site
Teton Creek
Teton Glacier
GRAND TETON EL 13,770 FT
Triangle X Ranch Float Trips
MIDDLE TETON EL 12,804 FT
Jenny Lake
SOUTH TETON EL 12,514 FT
NEZ PERCE EL 11,901 FT
AMPHITHEATER LAKE TRAIL
MOUNT LEIDY EL 10,326 FT
MOUNT WISTER EL 11,490 FT
ROAD CLOSED IN WINTER
Chapel Of The Transfiguration
DEATH CANYON TRAIL
BUCK MOUNTAIN EL 11,938 FT
Float Trips
Moose
FOSSIL MTN EL 10,916 FT
Phelps Lake
Menor's Ferry
PROSPECTORS MTN EL 11,241 FT
MOOSE-WILSON RD
Moose Visitor Center
Lower Slide Lake
GROS VENTRE RD
HOUSETOP MTN EL 10,537 FT
MOUNT HUNT EL 10,783 FT
Kelly
Gros Ventre Slide
Gros Ventre
VALLEY TR
Gros Ventre River
Jackson Hole Airport
Teton Village
TETON CREST
390
JACKSON HOLE VALLEY
SHEEP MOUNTAIN EL 11,239 FT
Grand Teton National Park
Teton Pass
JOHN D
MILLERS BUTTE EL 6,775 FT
Miles 0 7.6
To Idaho Falls
22
Wilson
Jackson
JACKSON PEAK EL 10,741 FT
CAMPGROUND SITE WITHIN NAT'L. PARK. SEE CAMPBOOK FOR ADDITIONAL LISTINGS IN NEARBY TOWNS.
26 89 191
To Salt Lake City
2120-B

park into Yellowstone National Park *(see place listing p. 173)*. The park's 485 square miles include the major portion of Wyoming's Teton Range and the valley of Jackson Hole. Together the mountain range and valley frame a majestic landscape of eight large lakes and many smaller ones, glaciers, numerous snowfields and extensive pine, fir and spruce forests.

The Tetons are among the youngest mountains on the continent. The elevations established by the U.S. Geological Survey for the major peaks are Grand Teton, 13,770 feet; Mount Owen, 12,928 feet; Middle Teton, 12,804 feet; Mount Moran, 12,605 feet; South Teton, 12,514 feet; Teewinot Mountain, 12,325 feet; Thor Peak, 12,028 feet; Buck Mountain, 11,938 feet; Nez Perce Peak, 11,901 feet; Mount Wister, 11,490 feet; and Mount St. John, 11,430 feet.

Few mountain ranges have a greater variety of glaciated canyons than the Tetons. The block-faulted mountains of this alpine park are rare in this country. Part of the park area lies above the tree line, which is at about 10,000 feet.

The Tetons were first photographed by William H. Jackson, a member of the Hayden Expedition sent by the government to survey the area in 1872.

General Information

The park is open all year, although most park facilities operate only from mid-May to mid-October. General information is available by; phone (307) 739-3300.

Visitor information is available at Colter Bay, Flagg Ranch, Jenny Lake and Moose visitor centers. Free ranger-led activities in summer include hikes and campfire programs. Entrance stations and visitor centers distribute a schedule of activities, which also is in the park newspaper.

ADMISSION to the park is by private vehicle permit ($20), valid in both Grand Teton and Yellowstone national parks for 7 days; by annual area permit ($40/both parks) or annual permit ($50/entrance to all national parks); by single entry via motorcycle or horseback ($15), or by bicycle or foot ($10). A Golden Age Passport for U.S. citizens over 62 is $10; a Golden Access Passport (for the physically impaired) provides free admission for U.S. citizens.

PETS are permitted in the park only if they are on a leash or otherwise physically restricted at all times. They are not permitted on trails, in the back country or in any public building.

ADDRESS inquiries to the Superintendent, Grand Teton National Park, P.O. Drawer 170, Moose, WY 83012; phone (307) 739-3300.

COLTER BAY VISITOR CENTER is near Jackson Lake. The center exhibits examples of American Indian art and culture, with emphasis on the Plains tribes. Slides and movies are shown regularly. Daily 8-8, Memorial Day-Labor Day; 8-5, early May-day before Memorial Day and day after Labor Day-late Sept. Free. Phone (307) 739-3594.

FLAGG RANCH INFORMATION STATION is at Flagg Ranch, 15 mi. n. of Colter Bay on US 89/191/287. The station provides information about John D. Rockefeller, Jr. Memorial Parkway and the Yellowstone area. Daily 9-6, early June-early Sept. Free.

JENNY LAKE VISITOR CENTER is 8 mi. n. of Moose Junction on Teton Park Rd. The visitor center has exhibits about geology. Daily 8-7, early June-early Sept. Free. Phone (307) 739-3392.

MOOSE VISITOR CENTER is at the park headquarters in Moose. The visitor center has natural history exhibits and provides permits and park information. Daily 8-6, early June-Labor Day; 8-5, rest of year. Closed Dec. 25. Free. Phone (307) 739-3399.

Activities

More than 200 miles of trails afford short walks, strenuous hikes and overnight back country trips. Trail booklets can be found at some trail heads and at the visitor centers. Campsites along back country trails require a camping permit, available at the visitor centers.

Game fish include brook, brown, cutthroat, Mackinaw, and rainbow trout, as well as whitefish. Fish can be taken with artificial flies during most of the summer and autumn, but the Mackinaw trout in Jackson and Jenny lakes are best caught by trolling with heavy tackle.

A Wyoming fishing license is required; a nonresident 1- or 5-day license or season permit is available for a fee. Special fishing regulations apply in the park, and changes are made annually regarding limits and waters open to fishing; check the current regulations.

Mountain climbing is a popular summer pastime. Authorized guide services are available, and because of the difficulty of the Teton peaks, climbers are urged to use them. Prospective climbers should consult rangers for information about routes and appropriate equipment. The Jenny Lake Ranger Station is the park's climbing information center.

The usual alpine equipment is essential: ice axes, ropes and rubber-soled boots or climbing shoes. Two park-approved mountaineering schools offer lessons and guide service.

The climbing season in Grand Teton National Park ordinarily spans mid-June to mid-September, but conditions are best from July to early September. In most cases it is advisable to allow 2 days for an ascent of Grand Teton, Mount Owen or Mount Moran and 1 or 2 days for all the other peaks, depending upon your experience.

Riding on horses trained for mountain trails is another popular way to explore the park. From corrals at Colter Bay Village and Jackson Lake Lodge, the Grand Teton Lodge Co. conducts daily guided

2- and 3-hour rides, half-day trail rides and wagon rides; phone (307) 543-2811.

Morning and evening horse or wagon rides with breakfast or dinner also are available for $38-$45. Guide fees vary according to trail, but all rates are regulated by the park and range from $18 to $42. Restrictions apply to horseback riding.

Boat and canoe rentals, guided fishing trips and scenic boat trips can be arranged at the Colter Bay Marina at Colter Bay Village and at the booking office at Jackson Lake Lodge. Canoe rentals $9; boat rentals $20.

Jackson Lake boat cruises lasting 1 hour, 30 minutes leave the Colter Bay Marina several times daily. Daily trout breakfast cruises to Elk Island as well as Monday, Wednesday and Sunday evening dinner cruises also are offered. Cruise rates range from $15 to $44; under 12, $7 to $26. Contact the Grand Teton Lodge Co. for schedules and exact fares; phone (307) 543-3100.

Jenny Lake Boating Co. offers scenic cruises and shuttle service to the west shore of Jenny Lake. Round-trip shuttle service $7; ages 6-12, $5. One-way shuttle service $5; ages 6-12, $4. The booking office is at the south end of Jenny Lake near the ranger station; phone (307) 734-9227.

Motorboats can be operated on Jackson, Jenny and Phelps lakes, but motors more than 10 horsepower cannot be used on Jenny and Phelps lakes. Hand-propelled craft are permitted on Bearpaw, Bradley, Emma Matilda, Jackson, Jenny, Leigh, Phelps, String, Taggart and Two Ocean lakes and on the Snake River. Water skiing, jet skiing and windsurfing are permitted only on Jackson Lake.

Mandatory boating permits, which are good for the season in both Grand Teton and Yellowstone national parks, cost $5 for nonmotorized craft and $10 for motorized craft. Permits can be purchased at the visitor centers.

Winter activities include snowmobiling, cross-country skiing, snowshoe hikes and ice fishing. All vehicles traveling over snow are subject to special regulations, including a $15 permit.

Concessioner-guided snowmobile trips are available, as are snowcoach tours into Yellowstone National Park from Flagg Ranch daily between mid-Dec. and late March; phone (307) 543-2861. Marked trails for cross-country skiing also are provided.

Five campgrounds, Colter Bay, Gros Ventre, Jenny Lake, Lizard Creek and Signal Mountain, are open on a first-come, first-served basis. Opening dates vary from late April to early June; closing dates are from early September to mid-October. Reservations are not accepted. *See Recreation Chart and the AAA Northwestern CampBook.*

GEM **Float Trips** are conducted by experienced guides who thread rubber rafts down the Snake River through Grand Teton National Park. These trips, which offer spectacular mountain scenery and opportunities to view native wildlife, are carefully supervised by the National Park Service. Reservations are recommended for all trips. **Note:** A minimum weight of 35-40 pounds is required for most float trips.

Barker-Ewing Scenic Float Trips departs from the float trip parking lot at the Moose Visitor Center. Scenic 10-mile trips on the Snake River are offered. Transportation from the meeting place to the launch area is provided. For information write P.O. Box 100-A, Moose, WY 83012. Minimum weight of 40 lbs. is required. Trips depart several times daily, May 15-Sept. 30, water conditions permitting. Fare $40.50; under 13, $27. Under 4 are not permitted.

Reservations are required. AX, DS, MC, VI. Phone (307) 733-1800 or (800) 365-1800. *See color ad p. 150.*

Dornan's Snake River Float Trips provides transportation from Jackson accommodations. The 14-mile scenic float trips provide good opportunities for wildlife and mountain viewing and photography. The trips last 3.5-4 hours. For information write P.O. Box 1176, Jackson Hole, WY 83001. A 14-mile trip departs several times daily, mid-May through late Sept., weather and water conditions permitting. Float trips $38; under 14, $25. Reservations are recommended. MC, VI. Phone (307) 733-2583 or (800) 735-8430. *See color ad p. 153.*

Grand Teton Lodge Co. Float Trips is 5 mi. n.w. of Moran Junction on US 89/191/287. The company offers short float trips; transportation to and from the river is provided. For information write Grand Teton Lodge Co., P.O. Box 240, Moran, WY 83013.

Daily trips from Colter Bay Village run late May-late Sept.; from Jackson Lake Lodge mid-May to late Sept. Luncheon trips, which depart only from Jackson Lake Lodge, are offered late May-late Sept. Dinner trips, departing from Jackson Lake Lodge, also are available. Short float trip $39.50; ages 6-11, $20. Lunch trip $45; ages 6-11, $28. Dinner trip $52; ages 6-11, $35. Under 6 are not permitted. AX, MC, VI. Phone (307) 543-3100.

National Park Float Trips offers free transportation for large parties from Jackson and the float trip parking lot in Moose Village. The operation features 10-mile scenic float rides along the Snake River in Grand Teton National Park. Trips depart several times daily, May-Sept. Fare $38; under 18, $26. MC, VI. Phone (307) 733-5500 or (307) 733-6445 or (888) 860-0005.

Osprey Snake River Float Trips departs near the visitor center at Moose Junction. Trips are 5-mile, 1- to 1.5-hour scenic rides down the Snake River. Trips leave several times daily, early June-late Aug. Fare $26; under 18, $19. Transportation is included. MC, VI. Phone (307) 733-5500 or (307) 733-6445 or (888) 860-0005.

Signal Mountain Lodge Float Trips provides transportation to and from the river. A 10-mile scenic float ride down the Snake River features wildlife viewing opportunities. The trip lasts 3.5 hours. Trips depart daily at 7:30 and 5, mid-May through Sept. 30, weather and water conditions permitting. Float trips $40.50; ages 6-12, $24. AX, DS, MC, VI. Phone (307) 543-2831.

Solitude Float Trips departs the float-trip parking lot near the Moose Visitor Center. Ten-mile scenic trips are available. Trips are offered several times daily, May-Sept., water and weather conditions permitting. Fare $25-$40. Reservations are recommended. MC, VI. Phone (307) 733-2871 or (888) 704-2800. *See color ad p. 151.*

SAVE **Triangle X Ranch Float Trips** begins at the Triangle X Guest Ranch, 11 mi. n. of Moose and 6 mi. s. of Moran Junction on US 26/89. Five- and 10-mile float trips, an evening dinner trip and sunrise and evening wildlife trips are available. For information write Triangle X Float Trips, Grand Teton National Park, Moose, WY 83012. Several trips are offered daily, May-Sept. Fare $26-$48. Reservations are required. MC, VI. Phone (307) 733-5500 or (888) 860-0005. *See color ad p. 151.*

TAPE TOURS are available at gift shops, RV campgrounds, Colter Bay Village, Moose Village Store, Jackson Lake Lodge and Jenny Lake Store. Tours allow drivers to set their own pace while a cassette narrative describes the park's attractions and history. The 90-minute tapes also can be ordered from CCInc., P.O. Box 227, Allendale, NJ 07401. The cost is $12.95, plus $2 postage and handling. Phone (201) 236-1666.

Points of Interest

AMPHITHEATER LAKE TRAIL extends up the eastern slope of Disappointment Peak to two alpine lakes, Surprise and Amphitheater, both at altitudes of more than 9,000 feet. Amphitheater Lake occupies a protected glacial cirque, or steep hollow. An overlook, reached by several trails climbing 3,000 feet above the valley floor, offers a sweeping panorama of Jackson Hole and a view extending eastward 80 miles to the Wind River Mountains. A branch from the trail leads into Garnet Canyon. Trail conditions are available at the visitor centers. Allow 6 hours minimum.

CASCADE CANYON TRAIL explores the deepest recesses of the Tetons, passing through a broad, glacier-carved canyon with walls that rise thousands of feet on either side. Lake Solitude, near the head of the canyon at the tree line, is a pristine example of an alpine lake. Allow 7 hours minimum.

CHAPEL OF THE TRANSFIGURATION is near Moose. Above the altar of the 1925 log chapel is a large window framing a view of the Teton Range. Episcopal services are held during the summer; schedules are posted on a board outside the chapel. Allow 30 minutes minimum.

CUNNINGHAM CABIN HISTORIC SITE is 6 mi. s. of Moran Junction on US 26/89/191. The site was the base of pioneer Pierce Cunningham's Bar Flying U Ranch that once comprised some 560 acres. The site now contains the foundations of the house, barn, shed and outbuildings as well as the remains of a cabin. A leaflet outlining a self-guiding trail through the area also describes the life of the homesteader in Jackson Hole. Allow 30 minutes minimum.

DEATH CANYON TRAIL traverses the length of a canyon of profound depth and grandeur to broad meadows. No canyon better illustrates the contrasts of the Teton area. Allow 6 hours minimum.

GROS VENTRE SLIDE—
see Bridger-Teton National Forest p. 134.

HIDDEN FALLS AND INSPIRATION POINT TRAILS lead from the southern shore of Jenny Lake off Teton Park Rd. A boat ride to the trail head is available in the summer. Ranger-guided tours to Hidden Falls and Inspiration Point depart the trail head daily at 8:30 in season; departure time may vary. Allow 2 hours minimum.

JACKSON HOLE VALLEY, popularly known as Jackson Hole, is a high mountain valley about 50 miles long and 6 to 12 miles wide, completely surrounded by mountains and bisected by the Snake River. The wilderness offers a habitat for many large mammals. The rare trumpeter swan is among the birds inhabiting the area.

Teton Park Road leads to Jenny Lake Lodge, campgrounds, fishing sites and many of the park's trails.

MENOR'S FERRY is near park headquarters in Moose. The ferry is a reconstruction of the craft that was once the only means of crossing the Snake River in central Jackson Hole country. The original home of Bill Menor, one of the area's first settlers, is in the area; it contains historical objects and exhibits. Allow 30 minutes minimum. Daily early July to mid-Sept.

PAINTBRUSH TRAIL starts near the outlet of Leigh Lake, follows the bottom of Paintbrush Canyon, crosses Paintbrush Divide and joins the Cascade Canyon Trail at Lake Solitude. The many wildflowers along this trail give the canyon its name. Wildlife, especially moose, can be seen near lakes and marshes. This trail affords several good views of Jackson and Leigh lakes. Since dangerous snow and ice remain on the divide until late in the year, check conditions at the visitor centers. Horses cannot be taken over the divide to Lake Solitude until late August.

SIGNAL MOUNTAIN is 3 mi. s. of Jackson Lake Junction on Teton Park Rd. The mountain affords a panorama of the valley, Jackson Lake, a portion of southern Yellowstone and the Teton, Gros Ventre and Hoback mountain ranges. A narrow paved road 5 miles long leads to the summit. Trailers are not allowed on this road.

TETON CREST TRAIL traverses the Tetons from Teton Pass to Cascade Canyon. This high alpine country can be explored by foot or horseback.

VALLEY TRAIL runs parallel to the mountains from the e. shore of Leigh Lake s. to Teton Village. The trail is the point of origin of all trails into the Teton range. From this point, trails run westward into Cascade, Death, Granite, Open and Paintbrush canyons; others encircle String Lake, Jenny Lake and Hemitage Point on Jackson Lake. A popular hike follows the south shore of Jenny Lake to Hidden Falls.

The Oregon Trail

Zebulon Pike proclaimed the first westbound trail through the Rockies as "unfit for any but a nomad population." But this warning did not deter the more than 300,000 emigrants who used the trail. The lure of the Oregon country unleashed one of the greatest peacetime migrations in the history of the world.

These early pioneers, with their possessions and dreams for a new beginning, were ill-prepared for the trail's dangers: drought, blizzards, disease, wild animals and hostile Indians. However, as the number of settlements increased, conditions and the nature of the journey improved.

© Jeff Gnass Photography

The gateway to the northwest was actually several major emigrant trails starting at the Missouri River and ending in Oregon City, Ore. In all, the trail extended 2,000 miles and stretched across six states. Traffic along this highway was so relentless, swelled by lengthy wagon trains, that ruts 5-6 feet deep scarred the fragile prairie. Many of the ruts are still visible.

On rock faces of landmark buttes the emigrants chiseled names and dates, poignant testimony to a journey that is now gauged along blacktop highways in hours instead of days.

GREEN RIVER (E-2) pop. 11,808, elev. 6,082′

The northern gateway to the Flaming Gorge National Recreation Area *(see place listing p. 147)*, Green River developed as a stop along the Overland Trail in the mid-1800s. One prominent traveler was Maj. John Wesley Powell, who began his explorations of the Green and Colorado rivers in 1869. The town is a railroad center and the seat of Sweetwater County.

Green River Chamber of Commerce: 541 E. Flaming Gorge Way, Green River, WY 82935; phone (307) 875-5711 or (800) 354-6743.

SWEETWATER COUNTY HISTORICAL MUSEUM is at 3 E. Flaming Gorge Way. The museum contains permanent and temporary exhibits about western American history, including a large collection of historical photographs of southwestern Wyoming. Allow 30 minutes minimum. Mon.-Sat. 10-6, Apr.-Dec.; 9-5, rest of year. Free. Phone (307) 872-6435.

GREYBULL (B-3) pop. 1,815, elev. 3,788′

Greybull derives its name from a local American Indian legend that claimed a great albino buffalo once roamed the area. The American Indians revered the bull, considering it a sign from their Great Spirit. Indian arrowheads, fossils and semiprecious stones can be found around town. The site of widespread oil and mineral activity, Greybull recently has focused its attention on bentonite mining.

Scenic attractions in the vicinity include Shell Canyon Falls *(see Bighorn National Forest p. 132)*, 24 miles east of US 14, and the drive over the Big Horn Mountains via scenic US 14 to Sheridan. Devil's Kitchen, a few miles northeast, and Sheep Mountain to the north are interesting geological formations.

Stone Schoolhouse Gallery & Bookstore, 6 miles east on US 14, is an example of the one-room schoolhouse common to 19th-century America. Area homesteaders quarried sandstone to construct the building in 1903.

Greybull Chamber of Commerce: 521 Greybull Ave., Greybull, WY 82426; phone (877) 765-2100.

GREYBULL MUSEUM is .25 mi. e. on US 14 at 325 Greybull Ave. The museum houses fossils, minerals, Indian artifacts and early Western memorabilia. Of interest are large ammonite fossils, which date from the Mesozoic era when the Greybull area was part of a large inland sea. Daily 10-8, June 1-Labor Day; Mon.-Fri. noon-6, day after Labor Day-Oct. 31; Mon.-Fri. 1-5, Apr.-May; Mon., Wed. and Fri. noon-4, rest of year. Free. Phone (307) 765-2444.

GREYBULL WILDLIFE MUSEUM is at 420 Greybull Ave. The museum features wildlife taxidermy specimens in natural settings. Mon.-Fri. 9-4, May 1-Dec. 15; closed holidays. Free. Phone (307) 765-2002.

GUERNSEY (D-6) pop. 1,147, elev. 4,361′

Just below the mouth of Platte River Canyon, Guernsey is in an area known for its limestone beds and a profusion of such artifacts as agricultural and war implements. Indians driven from their homes east of the Mississippi River and pioneers headed westward followed the river through this area.

During one of his expeditions in 1842, John C. Fremont camped near what is now the Oregon Trail Ruts State Historic Site *(see attraction listing)*. The small prairie next to the river (the present town site) impressed him as a good spot for a military installation because of its cottonwood trees, pines and abundant rock for building.

Prospectors discovered early that the rock formations around Guernsey were good for more than just building. Moss agate stone, unearthed from what is believed to be the first commercially developed deposit of moss agate in the nation, was found in the Guernsey-Hartville region and exported to Germany in the late 1800s. The additional discovery of copper led to the founding of nearby communities Hartville and Sunrise.

Guernsey Visitors Center: 90 S. Wyoming, P.O. Box 667, Guernsey, WY 82214; phone (307) 836-2715.

GUERNSEY STATE PARK MUSEUM is 1.25 mi. w. on US 26, then 2.75 mi. n. on SR 317 in Guernsey State Park *(see Recreation Chart and the AAA*

Northwestern CampBook). Exhibits depict the natural and human history of the region. Allow 30 minutes minimum. Daily 10-6, May-Oct. Park admission $2 per in-state private vehicle, $4 per out-of-state private vehicle. Museum free. Phone (307) 836-2900.

OREGON TRAIL RUTS STATE HISTORIC SITE is 1 mi. s. on S. Wyoming Ave. from jct. US 26. The site presents well-preserved examples of mid-19th-century pioneer trails. Some of the ruts are 5 to 6 feet deep. Next to the ruts are footpaths used by muleteers and others who walked beside the wagons. Self-guiding trails provide an explanation of the site. Allow 30 minutes minimum. No facilities are available.

REGISTER CLIFF STATE HISTORIC SITE is 3 mi. s. on S. Wyoming Ave. from jct. US 26. The site contains a 100-foot cliff with the carved names of thousands of pioneers who journeyed past this point. Many of the inscriptions were made 1840-60. A walkway and an explanatory sign are at the base of the cliff.

HYATTVILLE (B-4) pop. 73, elev. 4,447′

Hyattville, which began as an isolated frontier cow town, is at the confluence of Medicine Lodge and Paintrock creeks in a region that mixes rolling foothills with rugged canyons to create a series of caves, ledges and grassy knolls. The protective nature of this area is what lured its first inhabitants in prehistoric times.

Artifacts of early paleo-Indian family groups were preserved in the layers of sediment beneath a sandstone cliff containing myriad petroglyphs and pictographs. Some of these can be seen at Medicine Lodge State Archeological Site, 6 miles northeast of town off SR 31 on Cold Springs Road (an oiled road); phone (307) 469-2234.

JACKSON (C-1) pop. 8,647, elev. 6,123′

The southern entrance to Grand Teton National Park *(see place listing p. 149)*, Jackson is the supply point and center of activity for ranchers and vacationers in Jackson Hole country. Recreation in the mountain-rimmed valley includes boating, fishing, hiking, horseback riding, mountain climbing, downhill and cross-country skiing, snowmobiling, whitewater rafting and windsurfing on Jackson Lake.

Jackson is on a scenic portion of US 89 that extends south 255 miles from Mammoth Hot Springs to Geneva, Idaho.

Live musical comedies are presented in summer at Jackson Hole Playhouse and Pink Garter Main Stage. The J.H. Rodeo also operates in the summer; phone (307) 733-2805.

Jackson Hole Chamber of Commerce: 532 N. Cache St., P.O. Box 550, Jackson, WY 83001; phone (307) 733-3316.

BAR-T-FIVE COOK OUT AND WILD WEST SHOW is 1 mi. e. on Broadway, then .5 mi. s. on Redmond to 790 Cache Creek Dr. A Western-style dinner show begins with a covered-wagon ride. Mountain men, American Indians and Western musicians offer entertainment. Two shows nightly Mon.-Sat. and holidays at 5:30 and 6:30, mid-May through Sept. 30. Admission $31; ages 6-12, $24. Reservations are recommended. DS, MC, VI. Phone (307) 733-5386 or (800) 772-5386.

JACKSON HOLE—*see Jackson Hole Valley p. 155.*

JACKSON HOLE HISTORICAL SOCIETY is at jct. N. Glenwood St. and Mercill Ave. The historical research facility has changing exhibits featuring artifacts from American Indians and early pioneers. An extensive collection of Old West photographs also is available. Mon.-Fri. 8-5; closed holidays. Free. Phone (307) 733-9605.

JACKSON HOLE IDITAROD SLED DOG TOURS is 20 mi. s. on SR 191/189 at 11 Granite Creek. Sled dog trips in Bridger-Teton National Forest are offered. Warm clothing is recommended. Transportation from lodging is provided. For information write P.O. Box 1940, Jackson, WY 83001. Full- and half-day trips are scheduled mid-Nov. to mid-Apr. Full-day trip $225, half-day trip $135 (meals included). Reservations are required. MC, VI. Phone (307) 733-7388 or (800) 554-7388.

JACKSON HOLE MUSEUM is at jct. N. Glenwood and Deloney sts. The museum features exhibits about archeology, fur-trade and early settler history. Artifacts include firearms, tools and historic photographs. Guided walking tours of Jackson's historic downtown area are available. Mon.-Sat. 9:30-6, Sun. 10-5, Memorial Day weekend-early Oct. Admission $3; over 64, $2; students under 18, $1; family rate $6. Phone (307) 733-2414.

JACKSON NATIONAL FISH HATCHERY is 4 mi. n. on US 26/89/191 at 1500 Fish Hatchery Rd. The hatchery raises predominantly cutthroat trout. Allow 30 minutes minimum. Daily 8-4. Free. Phone (307) 733-2510.

NATIONAL ELK REFUGE is 1 mi. e. on Broadway to Elk Refuge Rd. The refuge is the winter home of approximately 7,500 elk, one of the largest herds in North America. Elk can be seen at the 24,700-acre refuge November through April; during the summer they migrate to various mountain meadows in Grand Teton and Yellowstone national parks and Bridger-Teton National Forest.

The visitor center at 532 N. Cache St. offers exhibits and wildlife videotapes. Refuge open daily 24 hours. Visitor center open daily 8-7, Fri. before Memorial Day-Sept. 30; 9-5, rest of year. Closed Thanksgiving and Dec. 25. Phone (307) 733-9212.

Sleigh Rides is 1 mi. e. on Broadway to Elk Refuge Rd. at the National Elk Refuge. Offered through National Museum of Wildlife Art *(see attraction listing)*, the sleigh rides provide up-close elk viewing. Warm clothing is recommended on the 45-minute trips. Daily 10-4, mid-Dec. through Mar. 31; closed Dec. 25. Fare $12; ages 6-12, $8. Phone (307) 733-9212.

NATIONAL MUSEUM OF WILDLIFE ART is on Rungius Rd. across from the National Elk Refuge. The museum is in a stone building wedged into a Wyoming hillside so that it appears as part of its surroundings. Displays include more than 2,500 paintings and sculptures featuring fine art that depicts wildlife. Artists include Albert Bierstadt, George Catlin, John Clymer, Carl Rungius, C.M. Russell and Conrad Schwiering. Of note are the JKM Collection of big game animals and the American Bison exhibit.

Food is available. Daily 9-5, early Dec.-early Apr. and Memorial Day-Labor Day; Mon.-Sat. 9-5, Sun. 1-5, rest of year. Closed Columbus Day, Thanksgiving and Dec. 25. Admission $8, senior citizens and students with ID $7, under 6 free; family rate $16. Phone (307) 733-5771 or (800) 313-9553.

SAVE **RIPLEY'S BELIEVE IT OR NOT! MUSEUM** is n. of jct. US 26/89/189/191 at 140 N. Cache St. The oddities of this collection include such weird wonders as a shrunken head, a jeweled horse, Annie Oakley's pistol, a huge cigar and art created by using lint from the dryer. Allow 1 hour minimum. Daily 9 a.m.-10 p.m., May-Sept.; 10-8, rest of year. Closed Jan. 1, Thanksgiving and Dec. 25. Admission $8.95; ages 6-12, $5.95. DS, MC, VI. Phone (307) 734-0000.

SAVE **TETON EXPEDITIONS SCENIC FLOATS** depart from 650 W. Broadway. Thirteen- and 21-mile trips allow passengers to view the scenic wildlife, including bald eagles and moose. Food is available. Allow 3 hours minimum. Trips depart daily May-Oct. Thirteen-mile fare $27-$39. Twenty-one-mile fare $53-$69. Phone (800) 700-7238. *See color ad.*

TETON WAGON TRAIN AND HORSE ADVENTURE offers trips along back roads between Grand Teton and Yellowstone national parks. The 4-day, 3-night guided wagon train trips stop at a different camp each night. The excursions also include horseback trips from camp, evening entertainment and canoeing. Under 4 are not permitted. For reservations write Double H Bar Inc., P.O. Box 10307, Jackson, WY 83002.

Departures Mon. at 9, third week in June-third week in Aug. Fare $745; ages 9-14, $695; ages 4-8, $645. Fare includes all transfers, 3 nights' camping and all chuck wagon meals. Sleeping bags and camping gear are provided. Reservations are required. DS, MC, VI. Phone (307) 734-6101 or (888) 734-6101.

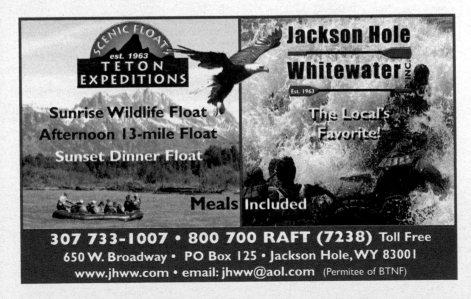

WAGONS WEST picks up passengers at the Antler Inn, 43 W. Pearl Ave. The tour traverses the Mt. Leidi Highlands in Jackson Hole. Two-, 4- and 6-day wagon treks, as well as hourly, daylong and multiday horse pack rides, are available. Marshaled by a wagon master, a covered-wagon train carries passengers along scenic wilderness trails. Gentle riding horses, chuck wagon meals and campfire entertainment are provided. Write Wagons West, P.O. Box 1149, Afton, WY 83110.

Trips depart June-Aug. Two-day trip $357; under 14, $310. Four-day trip $675; under 14, $595. Six-day trip $895; under 14, $795. Horse pack rates $35-$100. Reservations are required. Phone (800) 447-4711.

RECREATIONAL ACTIVITIES

Alpine Slide

- **Snow King Alpine Slide** is 8 blks. s.e. of Jackson Town Square at 400 E. Snow King Ave., Jackson, WY 83001. Daily Memorial Day weekend and early June-Labor Day; Sat.-Sun. day after Labor Day to mid-Sept. Phone (307) 733-7680.

Mountain Biking

- **Teton Mountain Bike Tours** arranges for riders to be picked up at local lodgings. Write P.O. Box 7027, Jackson, WY 83002. Tours daily mid-May to mid-Oct. Phone (307) 733-0712 or (800) 733-0788.

Skiing

- **Jackson Hole Mountain Resort** is 12 mi. w. via SRs 22 and 390. Write P.O. Box 290, Teton Village, WY 83025. Other activities are offered. Daily 9-4, first Sat. in Dec.-first Sun. in Apr. Phone (307) 733-2292 or (800) 443-6931.

- **Snow King Resort**, 400 E. Snow King Ave. Write P.O. Box SKI, Jackson, WY 83001. Other activities are offered. Tues-Sat. 10-8, Sun.-Mon. 10-4, late Nov.-late Mar. (weather permitting). Phone (307) 733-5200 or (800) 522-5464. *See color ad p. 158.*

White-water Rafting

- **Barker-Ewing Whitewater River Trips** begins in Jackson at 945 W. Broadway for both Snake and Salmon rivers. Write P.O. Box 450, Jackson, WY 83001. Daily 8-5, mid-May to late Sept. Other trips are offered. Phone (307) 733-1000 or (800) 448-4202. *See color ad p. 151.*

- **Charles Sands' Wild Water River Trips**, 110 W. Broadway. Write P.O. Box 10489, Jackson, WY 83002. Daily trips available May 15-Sept. 30. Phone (307) 733-4410 or (800) 358-8184. *See color ad p. 157.*

- **Dave Hansen Whitewater River Trips** operates from Wagon Wheel Village at 515 N. Cache St., across from Wyoming Information Center. Write P.O. Box 328-A, Jackson, WY 83001. Five trips depart daily at various times, mid-May 25 to late Sept. Phone (307) 733-6295 or (800) 732-6295.

- **Jackson Hole Whitewater**, 650 W. Broadway. Write P.O. Box 125, Jackson, WY 83001. Five trips depart daily at various times, May 15-Sept. 20. Phone (307) 733-1007, or (800) 700-7238 out of Wyo. *See color ad p. 159.*

- SAVE **Lewis & Clark River Expeditions**, 335 N. Cache Dr. Write P.O. Box 720, Jackson, WY 83001. Trips depart several times daily mid-May to mid-Sept. Phone (307) 733-4022 or (800) 824-5375.

- **Mad River Boat Trips Inc.** has offices at Whitewater Warehouse at 1255 US 89S. Write P.O. Box 10940, Jackson, WY 83002. Snake River trips depart twelve times daily, mid-May to mid-Sept. Phone (307) 733-6203 or (800) 458-7238.

- **Snake River Park Whitewater** is 12 mi. on US 89S. Write 9705 S. US 89, Jackson, WY 83001. Trips depart four to five times daily, May 15-Sept. 5 (weather permitting). Phone (307) 733-7078 or (800) 562-1878.

JACKSON HOLE—

see Jackson p. 157.

KEMMERER (E-1) pop. 2,651, elev. 6,908'

One feature of the boom that followed the discovery of coal near Kemmerer in 1897 was the saloon of "Preaching Lime" Huggins, who maintained that he never sold a drink to a man already under the influence. Over the bar mirror hung such mottos as "Don't buy a drink before seeing that your baby has shoes." One of his patrons liked the establishment because he could do his repenting during his sinning and "get the whole thing over at once."

A nationwide retail chain originated in Kemmerer when J.C. Penney opened his first store, the Golden Rule, in 1902 with an initial investment of $500. The original home of the founder is now a museum at 107 JC Penney Ave.

Native fossils and historical artifacts are displayed at Kemmerer City Visitor Center in Triangle Park.

Kemmerer/Diamondville Area Chamber of Commerce: 800 Pine Ave., Kemmerer, WY 83101; phone (307) 877-9761 or (888) 300-3413.

FOSSIL COUNTRY MUSEUM is at 400 Pine Ave. Permanent exhibits in this museum include a replica of an underground coal mine and a moonshine still, mountain man artifacts, Union Pacific Railroad and World Wars I and II memorabilia, vintage clothing, fossils and a dinosaur footprint from a local coal mine. Allow 30 minutes minimum. Mon.-Sat. 10-4, Labor Day-Memorial Day; Mon.-Fri. 9-5, rest of year. Closed Jan. 1, July 4, Thanksgiving, day after Thanksgiving and Dec. 25. Free. Phone (307) 877-6551.

LANDER (D-2) pop. 6,867, elev. 5,372′

Lander began around 1869 when Camp Augur was built to protect the settlers and Shoshone Indians. In 1884 Lander became the seat of newly created Fremont County, which is as large as some Eastern states. The county covers 5,861,120 acres and is an important wildlife habitat for moose, elk, bighorn sheep, deer and pronghorn antelopes.

North of Lander is the vast Wind River Mountain Range. Part of this range is now the Wind River Indian Reservation. Further northwest near Dubois is an area that was the site of a horse ranch operated by George Parker, alias Butch Cassidy. Cassidy frequently sold his stock in Lander, whose citizens maintained that he always had more to sell than he had raised.

SR 131 follows the middle fork of the Popo Agie River southwest of Lander to Sinks Canyon State Park *(see attraction listing)* and Shoshone National Forest *(see place listing p. 169)*. Lander contains the trailhead for the Continental Divide Snowmobile Trail.

Lander Area Chamber of Commerce: 160 N. 1st St., Lander, WY 82520; phone (307) 332-3892 or (800) 433-0662.

SINKS CANYON STATE PARK is 7.5 mi. s.w. on SR 131. Moose, bighorn sheep and other wild game often can be sighted. The Popo Agie River disappears into the sinks of the Madison Limestone and reappears in a rise one-quarter of a mile down the canyon in a large trout pool.

The Sinks Canyon State Park Visitor Center provides information about natural features and recreational opportunities. Visitor center daily 9-7, Memorial Day-Labor Day. Free. Phone (307) 332-3077. *See Recreation Chart and the AAA Northwestern CampBook.*

WIND RIVER INDIAN RESERVATION is about 15 mi. n.w. on US 287. Of different linguistic stock and cultural background, the Shoshone and Arapaho tribes occupy different sections of the 2.5 million-acre reservation. The graves of Chief Washakie and Sacajawea, as well as the Shoshone Cultural Center, which offers displays and tours, are in Fort Washakie. Arapaho artifacts are in a museum at St. Michael's Mission in Ethete.

Office open Mon.-Fri. 8-4:45. Phone (307) 332-3040 or (307) 332-9106.

LARAMIE (E-5) pop. 27,204, elev. 7,171′

Although American Indians roamed the Laramie Plains as early as 8000 B.C., Laramie's recorded history began in the early 19th century with the arrival of the area's first white man, Jacques LaRamie, a trapper for American Fur Co. In his steps followed mountain men, trappers, emigrants, soldiers and explorers, many tracing the old Cherokee Trail.

Fort Sanders, a short distance south, provided protection for the Overland Stage Line and for the Union Pacific. The railroad brought the bulk of Laramie's citizenry—including a sizable population of lawless riffraff who finally left town at the prompting of self-appointed vigilance committees.

The first women jurors served in Laramie in March 1870. In the fall "Grandma" Eliza A. Swain became the first woman to vote in a general election.

Recreational opportunities abound nearby. Cross-country skiing is available east of Laramie, and downhill skiing and snowmobiling can be found in the Snowy Range of the Medicine Bow Mountains, west of the city on SR 130. Both regions are equally attractive to vacationers during the summer, with many camping and picnic areas.

Of geological interest is Sand Creek, a 6,000-acre natural landmark about 20 miles southwest of Laramie. Some of North America's finest examples of cross-bedded sandstone and "topple blocks" can be seen.

Laramie serves as the eastern end of a scenic portion of I-80, which runs 99 miles northwest to Walcott. Snowy Range Scenic Byway (SR 130), off the I-80 Snowy Range exit, offers a view of mountains, lakes and forests. At the summit, the Libby Flats Observatory and a viewing platform offer a panorama of the area.

Albany County Tourism Board: 210 Custer St., Laramie, WY 82070; phone (307) 745-4195, (307) 755-4073 or (800) 445-5303.

Self-guiding tours: Brochures describing downtown and architectural walking tours are available at the Laramie Chamber of Commerce, 800 S. Third St., Laramie, WY 82070; phone (307) 745-7339 or (866) 876-1012.

ABRAHAM LINCOLN MEMORIAL MONUMENT is 10 mi. s.e. on I-80 exit 323, at the edge of a rest area. The 48.5-foot-tall monument, sculpted by Robert I. Russin, stands at an 8,640-foot summit off I-80 near Sherman Hill. The monument marks the highest point on this transcontinental route. I-80 follows the path of the first transcontinental railroad line.

AMES MONUMENT is 17 mi. s.e. on I-80, then 2 mi. s. on Ames Rd. The 60-foot granite pyramid honors Oliver and Oakes Ames, the two promoters of the transcontinental railroad. Built 1881-82, the monument marks the site of Sherman, a train inspection point before it became a ghost town with the relocation of the Union Pacific tracks. A plaque relates local history.

SAVE **LARAMIE PLAINS MUSEUM** is 1 blk. n. of I-80 and US 30 Business Loop at 603 Ivinson Ave. The museum is the restored 1892 Victorian mansion of Edward Ivinson, one of the city's original settlers. Period furnishings and thousands of artifacts are displayed. The grounds include a carriage house and a one-room log schoolhouse. Guided tours are given Tues.-Sat. 9-5, Sun. 1-4, Sept.-May; Tues.-Sat. 9-5, rest of year. Admission $4.25, students with ID $2.25, under 6 free. Phone (307) 742-4448.

UNIVERSITY OF WYOMING is at 15th and Grand sts.; the visitor center is at 1408 Ivinson St. The university opened its doors in 1887. The 785-acre campus contains buildings of native sandstone. Cultural and fine arts programs and concerts are held year-round. (307) 766-4075.

American Heritage Center is at 22nd St. and Willett Dr. in the Centennial Complex. The center has more than 7,000 historical manuscripts plus photographs, maps and art about Wyoming and Western American history. The center features changing displays from its collections including the art of Henry Farny, Alfred Jacob Miller and Frederic Remington. Mon.-Fri. 8-5, Sat. 11-5, Sept.-May; Mon.-Fri. 7:30-4:30, Sat. 11-5, rest of year. Closed major holidays. Free. Phone (307) 766-2570.

Anthropology Museum is in the Anthropology (Old Law) Building at 14th and Ivinson sts. The museum chronicles Wyoming's cultural history, including information about Northwest Plains Indians and other North American Indians. Collections include archeological and ethnological materials. Mon.-Fri. 8-5, Sept.-May; 7:30-4:30, rest of year. Closed holidays. Free. Phone (307) 766-5136.

Art Museum is at 22nd St. and Willett Dr. in the Centennial Complex. The museum contains more than 7,000 sculptures, prints, paintings and artifacts from many cultures and periods. The permanent collection focuses on American art and art from other countries that has influenced American artists. Works by established artists as well as traveling exhibitions are displayed. Mon.-Sat. 10-5; closed holidays. Free. Phone (307) 766-6622.

Geological Museum is in the e. wing of the S.H. Knight Building. The museum interprets the physical and historical geology of Wyoming through displays of rocks, minerals and fossils. Of interest is a mounted skeleton of a brontosaurus, purported to be one of only five exhibited in the world. Other dinosaur displays include an allosaurus, tyrannosaurus and triceratops. Mon.-Fri. 8-5, Sat.-Sun. 10-3; closed holidays. Free. Phone (307) 766-4218.

VEDAUWOO is 17 mi. s.e. via I-80. The recreation area takes its name from the Arapaho Indian word meaning "earth born spirits." The picnic and camping areas are marked by rock formations developed during the ice age and rounded by weathering. Both expert and novice rock climbers practice their skills on the rocks. Daily 24 hours, May-Oct. (weather permitting). Free. Parking $3. Camping $10. Phone (307) 745-2300. *See the AAA Northwestern CampBook.*

GEM SAVE **WYOMING TERRITORIAL PARK** is at 975 Snowy Range Rd. at jct. I-80. The park features a restored 19th-century prison, a re-created frontier town with living-history characters, special events and a dinner theater.

The Wyoming Territorial Prison, built in 1872, is believed to be the only prison where outlaw Butch Cassidy was incarcerated. Until 1903 it housed some of the most notorious criminals in the West. A highlight is the collection of Western film clips that portrays Hollywood's view of gunfighters. The Horse Barn Dinner Theatre features live Western music and a dinner.

Sites at Frontier Town include a mercantile, saloon, livery stable, smithy, marshal's office and jail; activities include gunfights, stagecoaches, a prison-break posse, puppet theater and ropemaking. A petting corral is featured. Throughout the park visitors will encounter Old West characters like Calamity Jane, saloon hall girls and deputy U.S. marshals.

Guided and self-guiding museum and prison tours are available. Food is available. Allow 4 hours minimum. Daily 9-6, May-Sept. (Frontier Town open only Memorial Day-Labor Day). Theater performances Thurs.-Sat. at 6, June-Aug. Park free. Museum/prison admission $10; under 13 free. Dinner theater $29.95-$33.95. Reservations are required for the theater. AX, DS, MC, VI. Phone (307) 745-6161 or (800) 845-2287.

LINGLE (E-6) pop. 510, elev. 4,171'

WESTERN HISTORY CENTER is 5 mi. w. on US 26. The center has displays about archeological excavations and the physical evidence left behind by the area's earliest citizens. In addition to a working lab, visitors can see fossils, mammoth bones and arrowheads—items found in local digs that enable researchers to understand the lives of early residents of the Western plains. Allow 1 hour minimum. Mon.-Sat. 10-6, Sun. 1-6. Admission $1.50, under 12 free. Phone (307) 837-3052.

LOVELL (B-3) pop. 2,281, elev. 3,837′

Lovell, founded by Mormons in 1900, serves as an outfitting center at the southern entrance to Bighorn Canyon National Recreation Area *(see place listing p. 85)*. A recreation area visitor center offering interpretive displays, movies and campfire programs is at the junction of US 310 and scenic US 14A.

Next to Bighorn Canyon is Pryor Mountain Wild Horse Range, a 32,000-acre area being developed as a refuge for wild horses, elk, bears and bighorn sheep.

Lovell Area Chamber of Commerce: 287 E. Main St., P.O. Box 295, Lovell, WY 82431; phone (307) 548-7552.

LUSK (D-6) pop. 1,447, elev. 5,014′

Named for an early settler, Lusk is a trading center for a ranching and dry-farming district that also is involved in some oil production. To the west are red-colored cliffs from which American Indians obtained material for paint. Through this area ran the Cheyenne and Black Hills Stage Line, whose route is marked by two rows of white posts. Three miles east on US 20, a marker indicates the location of a segment of the Texas Trail. The trail was used to herd cattle from Texas to the open ranges of Wyoming, Montana and the Dakotas.

Niobrara Chamber of Commerce: 119 W. 3rd St., P.O. Box 457, Lusk, WY 82225; phone (307) 334-2950 or (800) 223-5875. *See color ad.*

STAGECOACH MUSEUM is 322 S. Main St. The museum displays many relics of pioneer and Indian days, including an original Concord stagecoach, which was the last running stagecoach. The coach's Cheyenne-Deadwood running mate is in the Smithsonian Institution in Washington, D.C. Mon.-Sat. 10-5. Admission $2, under 10 free. Phone (307) 334-3444. *See color ad.*

MEDICINE BOW (E-5) pop. 274, elev. 6,564′

Faced with no available lodgings when he arrived in Medicine Bow in 1885, American author Owen Wister was forced to spend his first night at the counter of the town's general store. Had he visited 26 years later, he could have slept at the Virginian Hotel, named after his well-known novel "The Virginian." Published in 1902, Wister's book became the inspiration for two stage plays, two silent films, a "talking" film and a television series in the 1960s.

Although Wister first described the modest town of Medicine Bow as a "wretched husk of squalor," he later wrote: "I don't wonder a man never comes back [East] after he has once been here a few years." Medicine Bow's general store and still-operating Virginian Hotel now stand as town landmarks. A landmark of a different sort is the giant wind turbine 5 miles south of town.

MEDICINE BOW MUSEUM is at 405 Lincoln Hwy. The museum is housed in a 1913 railroad depot. Local and traveling historical exhibits depict the history of Medicine Bow and the West. Among the displays are such Western items as cowboys' chaps and branding irons. A picnic area, restored caboose and Owen Wister's cabin are on the grounds. Allow 30 minutes minimum. Mon.-Sat. 10-5, Sun. noon-5, Memorial Day-Labor Day. Donations. Phone (307) 379-2383 or (307) 379-2581.

MEDICINE BOW NATIONAL FOREST

Elevations in the forest range from 5,000 ft. north of the Laramie River to 12,013 ft. at Medicine Bow Peak. Refer to AAA maps for additional elevation information.

In southeastern Wyoming, Medicine Bow-Routt National Forest consists of three separate districts that together cover 1,093,618 acres. Scenic SR 130 (closed in winter) crosses the Laramie and Brush Creek/Hayden districts, which extend northward from Colorado along the Snowy Range.

The Brush Creek/Hayden District spans the Continental Divide in the Sierra Madre Mountains west of Encampment. Douglas District, the northernmost section, is high in the rugged Laramie Mountains south of Douglas. Between Cheyenne and Laramie I-80 crosses the Pole Mountain Unit, noted for its unusual rock formations.

The Thunder Basin National Grassland *(see place listing p. 171)* lies in the energy-rich Powder River Basin north of Douglas. There also are four wilderness areas with 79,135 acres of forested land west of Laramie.

Opportunities for such winter sports as cross-country skiing and snowmobiling abound in the area. Camping, fishing, hiking and hunting also are available. For additional information contact the Forest Supervisor, 2468 Jackson St., Laramie, WY 82070. Phone (307) 745-2300. *See Recreation Chart and the AAA Northwestern CampBook.*

MEETEETSE (B-3) pop. 351, elev. 5,798′

Meeteetse lies along the scenic portion of SR 120, which runs 83 miles between Cody and Thermopolis.

CHARLES J. BELDEN MUSEUM AND MEETEESE MUSEUM is at 1947 State St. Two separate museums are located within the building. The Charles J. Belden Museum features personal effects, sculpture and Western photography that led to Belden's fame. The far end of the building holds The Meeteese Museum and includes artifacts gathered from local ranches and homesteads. Picnicking is permitted. Food is available. Allow 1 hour minimum. Mon.-Sat. 10-4, Sun. 1-5, May-Oct.; Mon.-Tues and Thurs.-Fri. 10-4, rest of year. Donations. Phone (307) 868-2264.

MEETEETSE BANK ARCHIVES is at 1033 Park Ave. It occupies a former 1901 bank building. Artifacts and records document local and regional history. Allow 1 hour minimum. Mon.-Sat. 10-4, May-Oct.; Mon.-Tues and Thurs.-Fri. 10-4, rest of year. Donations. Phone (307) 868-2423.

MEETEETSE HALL MUSEUM is at 942 Mondell. The museum displays local artifacts in an early 1900s Masonic hall. Mon.-Sat. 10-4, Memorial Day-Labor Day. Donations. Phone (307) 868-2423.

NEWCASTLE (C-6) pop. 3,065, elev. 4,321′

Founded in 1889 when coal was discovered in the area, Newcastle was named after its sister community in England, Newcastle-Upon-Tyne. Mining is a continuing industry, along with ranching, lumbering and petroleum exploration. The yield of Newcastle's oil field is processed by its own refinery.

Newcastle Area Chamber of Commerce: 1334 Washington Blvd., WY 82701; phone (307) 746-2739.

Self-guiding tours: Brochures about driving tours are available from the visitor center at the junction of US 85 and US 16.

ACCIDENTAL OIL CO. is at 5297 US 16. The site features a rare hand-dug oil well created in 1966 with a pick and a shovel. Guided tours offer a history of the pump, then take visitors 24 feet below the well where oil-producing rock is displayed under a blacklight. Antique oil pumps and other equipment are on view outside. Daily 9-6, June-Aug. Admission $5, ages 6-18, $3. Phone (307) 746-2042.

ANNA MILLER MUSEUM is 1 mi. e. on US 16 at Delaware St. The museum displays wildlife, antique firefighting apparatus, pioneer articles, fossils, minerals and American Indian artifacts.

Also at the site is the Jenny Stockade, built in 1875 by the expedition sent into the Black Hills area by the U.S. government to investigate reports of gold. The structure is best known as a way station on the Cheyenne-Deadwood stage line, which began in 1876. Mon.-Fri. 9-5; closed holidays. Free. Phone (307) 746-4188.

PINE BLUFFS (F-6) pop. 1,153, elev. 5,047′

Pine Bluffs, named for the stunted pine trees on the bluffs overlooking the area, was once an important watering place along the Texas Cattle Trail. In 1871 more than 600,000 head of cattle were herded through the Pine Bluffs Crossroads, making it the largest cattleshipping point in the world.

Texas Trail Museum preserves historic treasures of the area; phone (307) 245-3713. The University of Wyoming Archaeological Dig presents a look into civilization 10,000 years ago through extracted nomadic American Indian artifacts displayed at the University of Wyoming Archaeological Educational Center, Second and Elm streets. Also of interest is the Our Lady of Peace Shrine. Reputed to be one of the largest Marian statues in the United States, it can be seen from the north side of I-80.

Pine Bluffs Area Chamber of Commerce: P.O. Box 486, Pine Bluffs, WY 82082; phone (307) 245-3695.

PINEDALE (D-2) pop. 1,412, elev. 7,176′

Pinedale serves as an outfitting point for recreation in the Bridger-Teton National Forest *(see place listing p. 134)*. Outdoor activities in the area include trout fishing and various water sports on nearby Fremont Lake, the second largest natural lake in Wyoming. Fishing float trips originate on the Green River, while camping, climbing, backpacking and cross-country and downhill skiing also are available.

Ten miles west of town, Father DeSmet Monument designates the site where the first Catholic Mass in Wyoming was held in 1840.

Upper Green River Rendezvous National Historic Landmark is 6 miles west of Pinedale on US

191. American Indians from throughout the West and such legendary mountain men as Jim Bridger and William Sublette gathered each year during the 1830s to meet the supply caravans from St. Louis and barter, trade for furs and cavort.

Pinedale Area Chamber of Commerce: 32 E. Pine St., P.O. Box 176, Pinedale, WY 82941; phone (307) 367-2242.

Self-guiding tours: Brochures detailing a tour of the historic district as well as day trips in the area are available at the chamber of commerce.

MUSEUM OF THE MOUNTAIN MAN is at Fremont Lake Rd. The museum contains exhibits relating to the rugged individuals who opened the West to settlers. Displays focus on the fur trade, exploration, Plains Indians and early settlement. Allow 30 minutes minimum. Daily 10-5, May-Sept.; by appointment rest of year. Admission $4; over 60, $3; ages 6-11, $2. Phone (307) 367-4101.

POWELL (B-3) pop. 5,373, elev. 4,365′

American Indians from the Blackfoot, Crow, and Shoshone tribes inhabited the area exclusively until explorer John Colter arrived in 1807. Following his arrival came a stream of explorers, trappers and miners. Powell was named after Mayor John Wesley Powell, an early-day explorer.

A memorial and honor-roll marker are 10 miles west on US 14A, where people of Japanese descent were imprisoned during World War II.

A variety of wildlife inhabits the area, and recreational activities are readily available. Historic walking tours of the city also are available.

Powell Valley Chamber of Commerce: 111 S. Day St., P.O. Box 814, Powell, WY 82435; phone (307) 754-3494 or (800) 325-4278.

HOMESTEADER MUSEUM is at 133 S. Clark St. at 1st St. The museum features exhibits about Powell's early settlers as well as displays of old farm machinery and implements. Tues.-Fri. 10-5 (also Thurs. 5-7), Sat. 10-3, May-Sept.; Tues.-Wed. and Fri. 11-3, rest of year. Free. Phone (307) 754-9481.

RAWLINS (E-4) pop. 8,538, elev. 6,758′

In traditionally wool- and hay-producing Carbon County, Rawlins was a departure point for the Union Pacific Railroad and for miners bound for the gold-rich Black Hills. Nearby mines produced the "Rawlins Red" pigment that was used on the Brooklyn Bridge in 1874. The ruins of Fort Fred Steele, built in 1868 to protect early railroads and settlers, are 15 miles east of town off I-80.

During the 1870s Rawlins was a wild town with more than its share of outlaw activity. However, it came to an abrupt halt by the end of the decade when exasperated citizens employed vigilante tactics against one of the region's most notorious outlaws, Butch Cassidy and the Sundance Kid. After the lynching of "Big Nose" George Parrot, warnings were sent out to 24 other known outlaws, who left town the next morning.

On the southern edge of the Sweetwater jade fields and the eastern edge of the gem-riddled Red Desert, Rawlins is noteworthy for its geological features.

Rawlins Carbon County Chamber of Commerce: 519 W. Cedar St., P.O. Box 1331, Rawlins, WY 82301; phone (307) 324-4111 or (800) 935-4821. *See color ad.*

CARBON COUNTY MUSEUM is at 9th and Walnut sts. The museum has displays of Western artifacts, including a sheep wagon, large stained-glass windows and a 1920 hook-and-ladder firetruck. Mon.-Fri. 1-8, Sat. 1-5, June-Aug.; Mon.-Fri. 1-5, Sept.-May; by appointment rest of year. Donations. Phone (307) 328-2740.

SAVE **WYOMING FRONTIER PRISON** is at 500 W. Walnut St. The prison replaced the territorial prison in Laramie in 1901 and operated until 1981. A 1-hour guided tour includes the cell blocks, exercise yard, visiting rooms, gas chambers and death house. The reception area contains a museum with photographs and prison artifacts. Tours daily 8:30-5:30, Memorial Day-Labor Day; by appointment rest of year. Last tour begins 1 hour before closing. Night tours are by appointment only. Admission $5;

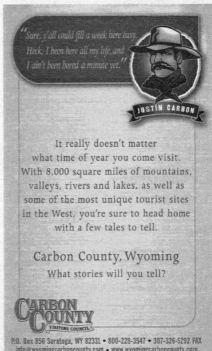

over 55 and ages 6-12, $4.50; family rate $20. Night tours $6. Phone (307) 324-4422.

RIVERTON (D-3) pop. 9,310, elev. 4,956′

Once part of Wind River Indian Reservation *(see Lander p. 161)*, the lower Wind River Basin now supports 130,000 acres of farmland surrounding Riverton. Castle Gardens, a state historical monument 40 miles east, is a formation of knobs, pinnacles and spires rising abruptly 10 to 100 feet above the prairie. Petroglyphs depicting warriors, hunters and animals decorate the soft sandstone formations.

Riverton Area Chamber of Commerce: 213 W. Main St., Suite C, Riverton, WY 82501; phone (307) 856-4801 or (800) 325-2732.

RIVERTON MUSEUM is at 700 E. Park Ave. The museum interprets the story of 20th-century homesteaders who brought the town to life in 1906. Displays include fixtures and merchandise from an early 20th-century general store, drugstore, school, beauty salon, dentist's office, church and post office. An outdoor display features early 20th-century farm machinery. Northern Arapaho and Shoshone Indian artifacts also are exhibited. Allow 1 hour, 30 minutes minimum. Tues.-Sat. 10-6, Memorial Day-Labor Day; 10-4, rest of year. Closed holidays. Schedule may vary; phone ahead. Free. Phone (307) 856-2665.

ROCK SPRINGS (E-2) pop. 18,708, elev. 6,261′

Rock Springs began in 1862 as a way station along the Overland Stage route. The Union Pacific also chose this route because of the area's rich coal deposits that fueled the railroad's locomotives. Mining and refining are still major industries, with resources expanding to include trona and natural gas. Some of the world's largest deposits of trona, used in the manufacture of glass, phosphates, silicates and soaps, lie 30 miles west of the city.

To the north and stretching more than 100 miles between the town of Eden and the Seminoe Mountains is the Red Desert, an area of moving sand dunes second in size only to the Sahara Desert. Of archeological and geological interest, the Sands, as the region is known, has produced evidence of human habitation as far back as 5000 B.C.

Petroglyphs and pictographs adorn the walls of rock outcrops in Cedar, Pine and Killpecker canyons and White Mountain. Visitors also can see evidence of prehistoric Wyoming at Western Wyoming Community College, which maintains a collection of fossils.

Boars Tusk, a volcanic monolith, rises 400 feet above Killpecker Valley at the edge of the Sands. The rock tower, 28 miles north of Rock Springs, is visible from US 191.

The Red Desert is home to one of the nation's largest herds of wild horses. To control the size of the herds, the Bureau of Land Management (BLM) conducts roundups; Mustangs captured by the BLM are kept at Rock Springs' Wild Horse Holding Facility, which conducts an Adopt-a-Horse program; phone (307) 352-0292.

Note: When traveling in desert areas, be sure to start with a full tank of gas and plenty of food and water. Off-road vehicles and cellular phones are recommended for travel in remote areas.

Rock Springs Chamber of Commerce: 1897 Dewar Dr., P.O. Box 398, Rock Springs, WY 82902; phone (307) 362-3771 or (800) 463-8637.

Self-guiding tours: A self-guiding walking tour of downtown Rock Springs covers sites related to the community's coal mining history. Brochures are available at the chamber of commerce.

COMMUNITY FINE ARTS CENTER is at 400 C St. The center contains a collection of more than 490 works by Wyoming and other Western artists as well as nationally and internationally known artists such as Loren McGiver, Grandma Moses and Norman Rockwell. Mon.-Thurs. 10-6, Fri.-Sat. 10-5. Free. Phone (307) 362-6212.

ROCK SPRINGS HISTORIC MUSEUM is at 201 B St. This museum depicts local coal mining history and the diverse nationalities that settled Rock Springs. The building was constructed in 1894 and restored in 1992. Allow 1 hour minimum. Mon.-Sat. 10-5, Memorial Day-Labor Day; Wed.-Sat. 10-5, rest of year. Free. Phone (307) 362-3138.

WESTERN WYOMING COMMUNITY COLLEGE NATURAL HISTORY MUSEUM is off I-80 exit 103, then 1 mi. s. to 2500 College Dr. The museum contains life-size replicas of dinosaurs, prehistoric fossil specimens and artifacts gathered from various formations around southwestern Wyoming. Exhibits, which are scattered throughout the student center, include reproductions of cave art from the Upper Paleolithic era and a 9-ton replica of an Easter Island statue. Maps are available at the entrance. Allow 30 minutes minimum. Daily 9-9. Free. Phone (307) 382-1666 or (307) 382-1600.

SARATOGA (E-4) pop. 1,726, elev. 6,791′

Saratoga, named for Saratoga Springs, N.Y., is a supply center and access point for recreation on the North Platte River and in Medicine Bow National Forest *(see place listing p. 163)*. The 64 miles of the North Platte River between the Colorado border and Saratoga are a nationally designated blue-ribbon trout fishery and include a stretch of white water rated as high as 10 on the U.S. Forest Service scale.

Saratoga Hot Springs offers a natural hot springs pool open free to the public. Fishing areas are available on the Platte and golf facilities are nearby.

Saratoga-Platte Valley Chamber of Commerce: 115 W. Bridge St., P.O. Box 1095, Saratoga, WY 82331; phone (307) 326-8855.

SARATOGA MUSEUM is at 104 Constitution St. The museum, in the 1917 Union Pacific Railroad depot on SR 130, contains historical and archeological artifacts depicting the settlement and growth of the Platte Valley. Geological displays and a sheep wagon also are included. Allow 1 hour minimum. Daily 1-5, Memorial Day weekend-Labor Day; by appointment rest of year. Free. Phone (307) 326-5511.

SARATOGA NATIONAL FISH HATCHERY is 2.5 mi. n. on SR 130, then 1.5 mi. e. on a dirt road, following signs. Constructed in 1915, the hatchery produces lake and brown trout eggs for export. Allow 1 hour minimum. Daily 8-4. Free. Phone (307) 326-5662.

RECREATIONAL ACTIVITIES

Fishing

- **Great Rocky Mountain Outfitters Inc.**, 216 E. Walnut St., Box 1636, Saratoga, WY 82331. Daily 7-7, May-Oct.; Mon.-Sat. 9-5, rest of year. Phone (307) 326-8750.

SAVERY (E-4) elev. 6463'

LITTLE SNAKE RIVER MUSEUM is at 2301 Central Ave. Until 1972, the main building of the museum was used as the Savery School. Items pertaining to the history of Little Snake River Valley and its residents are displayed inside. Also on the grounds is the Strobridge-Groshart-Hays House, built in 1882. The house has been restored to its original state since being donated to the museum site in 1993. Picnicking is permitted. Allow 1 hour, 30 minutes minimum. Daily 11-5, Memorial Day-late Oct. Free. Phone (307) 383-7262.

SHERIDAN (B-4) pop. 15,804, elev. 3,724'

Sheridan is located halfway between the Black Hills and Yellowstone National Park in the valley of the Little and Big Goose. Access through the Bighorn Mountains via US 14 (Bighorn Scenic Byway) or US 14A (Medicine Wheel Passage) offers spectacular sightseeing opportunities. The majestic Bighorn Mountains rise to the west and rolling plains slope to the east.

Sheridan is rich in Western history. In 1866 the area was part of unreserved American Indian territory that was home for the Sioux, Cheyenne and Arapaho. Indian chiefs such as Dull Knife, Red Cloud and Crazy Horse fought battles to keep the white man from their precious hunting grounds.

The Bozeman Trail, a shortcut scouted by John Bozeman through eastern Wyoming, cut across Indian hunting grounds to the rich gold fields of Montana. The trail, which ran south of Sheridan along part of what is now US 87, was the scene of so many battles that it became known as the Bloody Bozeman. The U.S. Cavalry forbade trains of fewer than 100 wagons to take this trail.

The discovery of gold in the Black Hills brought a new influx of fortune seekers and further confrontations, culminating in the Battle of Little Big Horn just north of Sheridan in southern Montana *(see Little Bighorn Battlefield National Monument in Mont. p. 107)*.

Many battle sites are in the area, including those of the Wagon Box Fight and the Fetterman Massacre, near Fort Phil Kearny in Story *(see attraction listing p. 170)*; Dull Knife Battle, south of town; the Sawyer Fight, 20 miles north near Dayton; Rosebud Battle, north in Montana; and the Conner Battlefield in Ranchester, 15 miles north of Sheridan.

After the wars ended, Sheridan was incorporated and built up by the profitable businesses of cattle ranching, farming and coal mining. For today's outdoor enthusiast, recreational activities are nearly unlimited in the nearby Bighorn National Forest *(see place listing p. 132)* and include wildlife viewing, hiking, fishing, hunting, snowmobiling and cross-country and downhill skiing.

The town recaptures the Old West during the Sheridan Wyo Rodeo in mid-July. In addition to several PRCA rodeo performances, highlights include a chuck wagon breakfast, a carnival, concerts, parades and a golf tournament.

City of Sheridan Convention & Visitors Bureau: P.O. Box 7155, Sheridan, WY 82801; phone (307) 673-7120 or (888) 596-6787. *See color ad p. 167.*

Self-guiding tours: A walking tour of the city's historic Main Street District covers many original buildings from the late 1800s and early 1990s. A map is available from the convention and visitors bureau.

GEM **BRADFORD BRINTON MEMORIAL—HISTORIC RANCH AND WESTERN ART COLLECTION** is reached from the s. by the Meade Creek exit off I-90, then US 87N to SR 335; from the n. by I-90 exit 25, then US 87S to Big Horn turnoff. The facility re-creates the atmosphere of Western ranch life. A large collection of Western art includes paintings, sculpture and etchings by Edward Borein, Frank Tenney Johnson, Frederic Remington and Charles M. Russell.

Extensive collections of equipment, Plains Indian crafts, rare books and documents, and items pertaining to the history of the ranch are displayed in a reception gallery, the 20-room main house and other buildings.

Allow 1 hour minimum. Daily 9:30-5, mid-May through Labor Day. Admission $3; over 63 and under 13, $2. Phone (307) 672-3173.

FETTERMAN MONUMENT stands 20 mi. s. on US 87. On this site in 1866 Col. William J. Fetterman disobeyed orders to stay off the Bozeman Trail and took to the trail with only 81 men under his command. Crazy Horse and 2,000 warriors ambushed and killed the entire force. The site is near Fort Phil Kearny.

FORT PHIL KEARNY STATE HISTORIC SITE— *see Story p. 170.*

HISTORIC SHERIDAN INN is at Fifth and Broadway sts. The inn opened June 22, 1893, and was the first building in town to have electricity, steam heat, a telephone and running water. Exhibits highlight the history of the inn, Sheridan and the lives of "Calamity Jane" Canary, "Buffalo Bill" Cody, Ernest Hemingway, Presidents Herbert Hoover, Theodore Roosevelt and William Taft, and Will Rogers.

Food is available. Allow 1 hour minimum. Mon.-Fri. 10-2; otherwise varies. Closed Jan. 1 and Dec. 25. Guided tour $5; over 55 and ages 12-18, $3; family rate $10. Phone (307) 674-5440 to verify schedule.

TRAIL END STATE HISTORIC SITE is at 400 Clarendon Ave. The site is the former home of Sen. John B. Kendrick, the "Cowboy Senator." Set on 3.5 acres, the fully furnished Flemish-style mansion has elaborate woodwork, stained-glass windows, chandeliers and hand-painted walls and ceilings. Guided tours are available by appointment. Allow 1 hour minimum. Daily 9-6, June-Aug.; 1-4, Apr.-May and Sept. 1-Dec. 14. Admission $2, under 18 free. Phone (307) 674-4589.

WYO THEATER is at 42 N. Main St. The theater is an art deco structure built in 1923 and renovated in 1989. It is said to be the oldest operating vaudeville theater in the state. Musical entertainment, ballets and stage presentations are featured year-round.

Box office Tues.-Fri. noon-5. Admission varies depending on event. Phone (307) 672-9084. *See color ad p. 168.*

SHOSHONE NATIONAL FOREST

Elevations in the forest range from 4,600 ft. at Clarks Fork Canyon to 13,804 ft. at Gannett Peak. Refer to AAA maps for additional elevation information.

In northwestern Wyoming, the Shoshone National Forest was established by presidential proclamation in 1891 as the nation's first forest reserve. It occupies nearly 2.5 million acres. Its boundaries extend south from Montana and include parts of the Beartooth, Absaroka and Wind River mountains. The forest includes the state's highest mountain, Gannett Peak.

Forest watersheds and glacial runoff feed several rivers of the Missouri River Basin and serve as a major water source for many communities and ranches within or near the forest.

Scenic drives include Buffalo Bill Cody Scenic Byway (US 14/16/20) through the North Fork of the Shoshone River canyon en route to the east entrance of Yellowstone National Park *(see place listing p. 173)*; the Wyoming Centennial Scenic Byway over Togwotee Pass on US 287/26 between Dubois and Moran Junction; the Beartooth Highway Scenic Byway (US 212) over the Beartooth Plateau; and the Chief Joseph Scenic Highway (SR 296) from its junction with SR 120 to the junction of US 212. SRs 296, 291 and 131 also travel past spectacular mountain scenery.

Back country hiking, trail riding, fishing and primitive camping are available in the Fitzpatrick Wilderness Area, which has two of Wyoming's highest peaks and some of the nation's largest glaciers; the Washakie Wilderness Area, remarkable for its abundance of petrified wood; the Popo Agie Wilderness Area, dotted by more than 200 lakes; the Absaroka-Beartooth Wilderness Area, containing many lakes and granite peaks; and the North Absaroka Wilderness Area, scored by steep canyons. Skiing also is available.

Information and maps (a fee is charged) can be obtained by writing the Forest Supervisor, 808 Meadow Ln., Cody, WY 82414-4516. Phone (307) 527-6241. *See Recreation Chart and the AAA Northwestern CampBook.*

SOUTH PASS CITY (D-3) elev. 7,805′

When early travelers traversed South Pass, the gradual incline often left them unaware that they were crossing the Continental Divide. From 1840 to 1860 an estimated 300,000 settlers traveled through the gap.

Gold was discovered at a site about 12 miles north of the pass in 1842, but takings were not impressive at first. In 1867 the Carissa, a hard-rock lode, was found and a boom began. By 1871 South Pass City boasted 2,000 inhabitants and was the

High-Altitude Health

Temples throbbing, gasping for breath and nauseated, you barely notice the scudding clouds or the spectacular view.

You might be suffering from Acute Mountain Sickness (AMS). Usually striking at around 8,000 feet (2,450 m) in altitude, AMS is your body's way of coping with the reduced oxygen and humidity of high altitudes. Among the symptoms are headaches, shortness of breath, loss of appetite, insomnia and lethargy. Some people complain of temporary weight gain or swelling in the face, hands and feet.

Digital Archives

If your AMS is severe, you should stop ascending; you will recover in a few days. If the AMS is mild, a quick descent will end the suffering immediately. You can reduce the effect of high altitude by being in top condition. If you smoke or suffer from heart or lung ailments, consult your physician. Alcohol and certain drugs will intensify the symptoms.

A gradual ascent with a couple days of acclimatization is best if you have time. On the way up, eat light, nutritious meals and drink plenty of water. A spicy, high-carbohydrate diet may mitigate the effects of low oxygen and encourage you to drink more.

Other high-altitude health problems include sunburn and hypothermia. Dress in layers to protect yourself from the intense sun and wide fluctuations in temperature.

Finally, after you lounge in the sauna or whirlpool bath at your lodging, remember to stand up carefully, for the heat has relaxed your blood vessels and lowered your blood pressure.

seat of Carter County, which encompassed a third of Wyoming.

William H. Bright, a South Pass City saloon keeper and Wyoming senator, introduced a bill granting women the right to vote, hold office and own property. With passage in 1869, Wyoming women became the first in the nation to participate in government, and Wyoming became nicknamed the "Equality State." One town citizen was Esther Hobart Morris, who in 1870 became the city's justice of the peace, the first woman in the country to hold any political office.

Despite its successes, South Pass City was not to escape the usual fate of boom towns: By 1875 the city was nearly deserted. The death of the mines did not, however, mean the end of South Pass City. In the 1950s a new boom came—one that involved not gold but iron ore. While the iron mines are now closed, the gold mines periodically operate, helping the town's economy. Tourism also has enabled the town to capitalize on its rambunctious past.

LIVING HISTORY WAGON TRAILS departs from 5 mi. s. at 231 Three Forks Atlantic City Rd. Covered-wagon excursions and overnight trail rides are offered. The 3-day trip departs Tues. at noon and returns Thurs. at noon, July-Aug. Sat. night trail rides depart Sat. at noon and return Sun. at noon, July-Aug. Other excursions are available. Three-day trip $400; ages 6-12, $300; under 6, $75. Trail rides $125. Rates may vary; phone ahead. Reservations are recommended. Phone (307) 266-4863.

SOUTH PASS CITY STATE HISTORIC SITE encompasses the entire town; turn off SR 28 at Milepost 43 and follow signs. This ghostly reminder of South Pass City's mining era is being restored. Twenty-five log, frame and stone structures remain on 39 acres of land, including Carissa Saloon, South Pass Hotel, a jail, livery stable and butcher shop. A visitor center has interpretive displays and a movie describing the town's past. Living-history programs also are offered. The site has a historic nature trail and picnic facilities.

Allow 2 hours minimum. Buildings open daily 9-6, May 15-Sept. 30. Admission for Wyoming residents $2, nonresidents $5, under 18 free. Phone (307) 332-3684.

STORY (B-4) pop. 887

Story took its name from Charles P. Story, an early mayor of nearby Sheridan who was related to Nelson Story, one of the first to drive Texas cattle over the Bozeman Trail into Montana in 1866. His northbound trip was the only significant use of the trail. Because the costs of maintaining the forts along the trail were immense in terms of both money and lives lost, the U.S. government eventually abandoned them and closed the Bozeman Trail.

Nestled at the base of the Big Horn Mountains in thick stands of Ponderosa pine and aspen, Story offers abundant recreational activities. Camping, hiking, fishing, hunting and horseback riding are readily available.

FORT PHIL KEARNY STATE HISTORIC SITE is reached by following signs from I-90 exit 44. The site preserves the remains of Fort Phil Kearny. Of the three forts built along the Bozeman Trail, Fort Phil Kearny suffered the worst. A visitor center houses displays and photographs. Markers identify the sites of the Fetterman interpretive trail and Wagon Box fights.

A self-guiding tour is available. Allow 2 hours minimum. Visitor center open daily 8-6, May 15-Sept. 30; Wed.-Sun. noon-4, Oct. 1-May 14. Admission $2, under 18 free. Phone (307) 684-7629 or (307) 684-7687.

THE STORY FISH HATCHERY is 2 mi. w. to end of SR 194. The hatchery was built 1907-08 and is the oldest operating fish hatchery in the state. The hatchery raises lake, rainbow and splake trout. Besides incubating and hatching fish eggs, the hatchery serves as a holding facility for fish and eggs destined for other stations throughout Wyoming. It includes an indoor hatchery and outdoor raceways and ponds. Daily 8-5. Free. Phone (307) 683-2234.

SUNDANCE (B-6) pop. 1,161, elev. 4,750′

Sundance lies at the foot of Sundance Mountain, so named because the Sioux Indians held their councils and religious ceremonies at a place called Wi Wacippi Paha, or Temple of the Sioux. It is believed that Harry Longabaugh, better known as "The Sundance Kid," assumed his nickname in Sundance during his 18-month sentence in the Crook County jail for horse stealing.

Sundance is a convenient departure point for trips to nearby Devils Tower National Monument *(see place listing p. 145)* and Black Hills National Forest *(see place listing p. 133)*. An 82-mile circle tour via US 14, SRs 24 and 111 and I-90 circles a portion of the national forest and offers opportunities to see the volcanic core of Devils Tower as well as pronghorns, wild turkeys and white-tailed deer.

Sundance Area Chamber of Commerce: P.O. Box 1004, Sundance, WY 82729; phone (307) 283-1000.

CROOK COUNTY MUSEUM AND ART GALLERY is on the lower level of the courthouse at 309 Cleveland St. The gallery contains more than 20,000 items from the Old West, including a re-creation of the original county courtroom. Photographs and legal papers of the Sundance Kid, who was incarcerated in the county jail for 18 months, also are displayed. Works by local artists are exhibited. Daily 8-5. Free. Phone (307) 283-3666.

TARGHEE NATIONAL FOREST—

see place listing in Idaho p. 68.

TEN SLEEP (C-4) pop. 304, elev. 4,513′

Because American Indians who traversed the Big Horn Basin of Wyoming reckoned time and distance in "sleeps," this midway point across the Big Horn Basin became known as Ten Sleep.

Range wars between cattle and sheep ranchers—quite common in the West during the 1890s and early 1900s—reached a climax with the Ten Sleep-Spring Creek Raid in 1909. This attack on the camp of an ex-cattleman who had brought a large herd of sheep into Big Horn Basin resulted in an investigation that eventually led to a peaceful arbitration.

Nearby Ten Sleep Canyon, on the western side of the Big Horn Mountains, is an outstanding feature of Bighorn National Forest *(see place listing p. 132)*. Near the mouth of the canyon are a trout hatchery and a fish-rearing station; visitors are welcome at both stations. A scenic section of US 16 runs between Ten Sleep and Buffalo *(see place listing p. 141)*.

THERMOPOLIS (C-3) pop. 3,172, elev. 4,326′

A treaty between the Shoshone and Arapaho nations and the United States specified that the waters of the hot mineral springs at Thermopolis would be available to everyone free of charge. The agreement continues to be honored at Hot Springs State Park. Petroglyphs, 21 miles north of Thermopolis on SR 120, are etched on a south-facing cliff at Legend Rock State Petroglyph Site.

Thermopolis is a favorite destination for hunters in search of pronghorn antelopes, game birds, elk and deer. South of Thermopolis on US 20 is Boysen Reservoir, with developed recreational facilities at Boysen State Park *(see Recreation Chart)*.

Thermopolis provides access to two scenic highways—US 20 along Wind River Canyon and SR 120 traveling north to Cody.

Thermopolis-Hot Springs Chamber of Commerce: 119 S. 6th St., P.O. Box 768, Thermopolis, WY 82443; phone (307) 864-3192 or (800) 786-6772. *See color ad p. 144.*

HOT SPRINGS HISTORICAL MUSEUM is at 700 Broadway. The museum complex contains period rooms, a cherrywood bar said to be visited by the Hole in the Wall gang, American Indian artifacts, a restored country school, wildlife and mining exhibits, arts and crafts and geological, agricultural and oil industry displays. Mon.-Sat. 9-7, Sun. 1-5, Memorial Day-Labor Day; Mon.-Sat. 9-5, rest of year. Closed Jan. 1, Thanksgiving and Dec. 25. Admission $4; over 60 and ages 6-12, $2. Phone (307) 864-5183.

HOT SPRINGS STATE PARK is at the n.e. edge of town on US 20 and SR 789. The park contains mineral baths, pools, hot mineral springs, terraces and hot waterfalls, and is home to the state's bison herd. Of particular interest is Bighorn Hot Spring, which releases 3.6 million gallons daily and is one of the largest hot mineral springs in the world. Black Sulphur Springs, White Sulphur Springs, Railroad Springs and Big Springs are other springs within the park. Daily 6 a.m.-10 p.m. Free. Phone (307) 864-2176. *See Recreation Chart.*

WIND RIVER CANYON is 5 mi. s. via US 20. The canyon is a channel carved more than 2,000 feet deep by the rushing waters of the Wind River.

Remarkable rock formations highlight the canyon walls, which are identified in terms of geological era and formation by strategically placed highway signs. One of the canyon's most prominent landmarks is Chimney Rock, about 10 miles south of Thermopolis.

WIND RIVER CANYON WHITEWATER is at 210 US 20S, Suite 5. Scenic float trips as well as whitewater, dinner and fishing trips are offered. Daily 8-5, Memorial Day-Labor Day. Scenic trip fare $30. Fares may vary; phone ahead. Under 6 are not permitted (age may vary depending on river conditions). Reservations and deposit are required for full-canyon, dinner or fishing trips. DS, MC, VI. Phone (307) 864-9343 in season or (307) 486-2253 rest of year. *See color ad p. 144.*

THE WYOMING DINOSAUR CENTER AND DIG SITES is at 110 Carter Ranch Rd. on the e. side of town. The center houses a recent extensive find of well-preserved dinosaur remains from the nearby Morrison Formation. Visitors may tour the preparation lab, where bones are recovered and prepared, and the paleontological site where discoveries are being made.

Daily 8-6, May-Sept.; 10-5, rest of year. Museum admission $6; over 60, veterans and ages 4-12, $3.50. Dig site admission $10; over 60, veterans and ages 4-12, $7. Combination museum and dig site admission $12; over 60, veterans and ages 4-12, $8. Full-day dig $125; family rate $300 (up to three people), $75 for each additional person. DS, MC, VI. Phone (307) 864-2997. *See color ad p. 144.*

THUNDER BASIN NATIONAL GRASSLAND

Thunder Basin National Grassland is in Campbell, Converse, Crook, Niobrara and Weston counties. Covering 1,800,339 acres, the national grassland was once a dust bowl. Settlers from the East, familiar only with the homesteading methods for a humid climate, met with disaster when they tried to establish farms in Wyoming's semiarid plains. Poor soil and recurrent droughts foiled attempts to cultivate the land, which soon deteriorated into dust bowls.

The grassland serves as an example of the regenerative use of land deemed unsuitable for cultivation. Sheep and cattle graze on the grassland's vast acreage, which also supports one of the world's largest herds of pronghorns. The Bozeman and Texas trails traverse a portion of the grassland.

The grassland lies within the Powder River Basin and contains a wealth of natural resources for energy development, including oil, gas and coal. The Black Thunder Mine, 9 miles from SR 59 on east SR 450, is one of the largest coal mines in the country. It operates on the grassland under a special state permit with forest service consent and produces more than 30 million tons of coal per year. For further information phone (307) 939-1300.

TORRINGTON (D-6) pop. 5,776, elev. 4,098′

Traversed by the Oregon, Mormon and California trails and the Overland Stage, Pony Express and overland telegraph lines, Torrington served as a Western gateway for pioneers. Named after settler William Curtis' hometown in Connecticut, Torrington is primarily a livestock exchange center, with cattle raising and agriculture as its main economic contributors.

Goshen County Chamber of Commerce: 350 W. 21st Ave., Torrington, WY 82240; phone (307) 532-3879. *See color ad.*

HOMESTEADERS MUSEUM is s. on US 85 at 495 Main St. The museum is in the former Union Pacific depot and contains artifacts that depict the homestead period, which occurred from 1882-1929. Mon.-Sat. 9:30-4, Sun. noon-4, Memorial Day-Labor Day; Mon.-Fri. 9:30-4, rest of year. Free. Phone (307) 532-5612.

WAPITI (B-2) elev. 5,641′

The Wapiti Valley was popularized by William F. "Buffalo Bill" Cody. He brought guests to the area to enjoy the beauty of the valley and Yellowstone National Park. Wapiti Valley provides a scenic byway into or out of Yellowstone National Park *(see place listing p. 173)*. Among wildlife inhabiting the valley are elk, deer, buffaloes, moose, bighorn sheep, bears, coyotes, bald and golden eagles, and even mountain lions.

Characterized by historic resorts, the valley also offers abundant recreational activities, including hiking, horseback riding, fishing, windsurfing, snowmobiling and skiing.

WHEATLAND (E-6) pop. 3,548, elev. 4,738′

Attracted by the cheap land and irrigation water that were made available by the Carey Act of 1894, settlers streamed into Platte County and transformed its dry landscape into productive farmland, dotted with such aptly named towns as Wheatland.

Wheat continues to be the region's principal crop, sustained in part by the Wheatland Irrigation Project, one of the largest privately owned enterprises of its type in the country. Wheatland also is the home of a white marble quarrying business and Laramie River Power Station, which supplies electric power to Wyoming and six neighboring states.

Recreational opportunities include camping and winter sports in nearby Medicine Bow National Forest *(see place listing p. 163)*. Grayrocks Reservoir, 16 miles northeast, is stocked with game fish and offers boating.

Platte County Chamber of Commerce: 65 16th St., P.O. Box 427, Wheatland, WY 82201; phone (307) 322-2322.

LARAMIE PEAK MUSEUM is 2 mi. n. on 16th St. from exit 78 off I-25. The museum displays items relating to the early settlers of Platte County, the Oregon Trail and the cattle baron era. Some artifacts date from the late 1800s. Allow 30 minutes minimum. Mon.-Tues. and Thurs.-Fri. 10-8, Wed. and Sat. 10-3, June-Aug.; Mon.-Fri. 10-5, Sat. 10-3, late May to mid-Sept.; by appointment rest of year. Closed holidays. Free. Phone (307) 322-2764.

WORLAND (C-3) pop. 5,250, elev. 4,061′

Worland is in a rich farming and stock-feeding area in the center of Wyoming's Big Horn Basin. Sugar beets, beans, malt barley and hay are harvested on irrigated lands; local industries produce aluminum cans, soft drinks, beet sugar and cat litter.

On the grounds of the county courthouse is a 260-year-old Douglas fir that has been carved into a monument honoring American Indians, part of sculptor Peter Toth's "Trail of the Whispering Giants." Among the city's nine parks is Pioneer Square, which has statues honoring the area's early settlers. A nearby drinking fountain offers artesian mineral water from the Big Horn Mountains.

Washakie County Museum and Cultural Center exhibits mammoth bones and archeological finds discovered in Big Horn Basin.

The Big Horn Mountains are popular with campers, hikers, hunters, skiers and snowmobilers. Passing through the city is Big Horn River, offering abundant fishing opportunities.

Vestiges of a far earlier time are the Gooseberry Formations and Painted Desert west on SR 431. In this area of dramatically eroded formations were found the remains of eohippus (dawn horse), the earliest known equine. Wild horses still can be viewed north of town.

Worland Area Chamber of Commerce: 120 N. 10th St., Worland, WY 82401; phone (307) 347-3226.

GEM YELLOWSTONE NATIONAL PARK (B-2)

See map page 174.

Elevations in the park range from 5,314 ft. at the northern entrance in Gardiner, Mont., to 11,358 ft. at Eagle Peak in the southeastern side of the park. Refer to AAA maps for additional elevation information.

Yellowstone National Park has five entrances: Gardiner, Mont. (north); West Yellowstone, Mont. (west); Jackson, via Grand Teton National Park (about 60 miles south); Cody (about 53 miles east); and Cooke City, Mont. (northeast). The area was established in 1872 as the world's first national park. Yellowstone was named from the Minnetaree Indian phrase *mi tsi a-da-zi* (Yellow Rock River).

The approach to Cooke City from Red Lodge, Mont., via the Beartooth Scenic Highway (US 212), negotiates Beartooth Pass at an elevation of almost 11,000 feet. From Cody the approach to Sylvan Pass follows US 14/16/20 through the carved red walls of Wapiti Valley.

The road between Canyon and Tower-Roosevelt is particularly scenic. This drive runs along Mount Washburn and passes Tower Fall, where the spectacles of the gorge, the falls on Tower Creek and the palisades of rock high above the Yellowstone River have few equals.

Although most of the park's 3,472 square miles lie in northwestern Wyoming, they also extend into Montana and Idaho. The central portion of the park is essentially a broad, elevated volcanic plateau that lies between 6,500 and 8,500 feet above sea level. On the south, east, north and northwest are mountain ranges with peaks and ridges rising between 2,000 and 4,000 feet above the enclosed tableland.

The most outstanding of Yellowstone's natural phenomena are the thousands of displays that compose the world's largest thermal basins. Bursts of scalding water spurt high into the air from some of these, while others bubble and spit in murky depths.

Multihued pools born from steaming springs tint the land's surface. Algae and bacteria color the formations in areas of thermal activity, while not far away vigorous steam vents emit uncanny sounds.

Note: Visitors should keep a close watch over children while in the thermal areas of the park, and be sure to stay on established boardwalks.

Yellowstone National Park is one of the most successful wildlife sanctuaries in the world. Grizzly and black bears can be seen occasionally in the back country and sometimes from park roadways. The park also has several thousand elk; many mule deer, pronghorn antelopes and moose; bands of bighorn sheep; and about 2,200 bison. These animals are visible along park roadways and trails in the more remote areas.

General Information

The park roads are open to automobile travel from May through October (weather permitting). The 60 miles of road between Gardiner and Cooke City, Mont., is open all year. During the off-season this road is accessible only from the northern entrance near Gardiner, Mont.; the northeastern entrance via Red Lodge, Mont. is open from about June through September.

Most park facilities are open May 30 to October 15, but food and lodging facilities are limited after October 1. During the off-season gas is available only at Gardiner and Cooke City, Mont. Interior park roads are open to snowmobiles from mid-December through the first week in March. During the summer, rental cars are available at Cody and

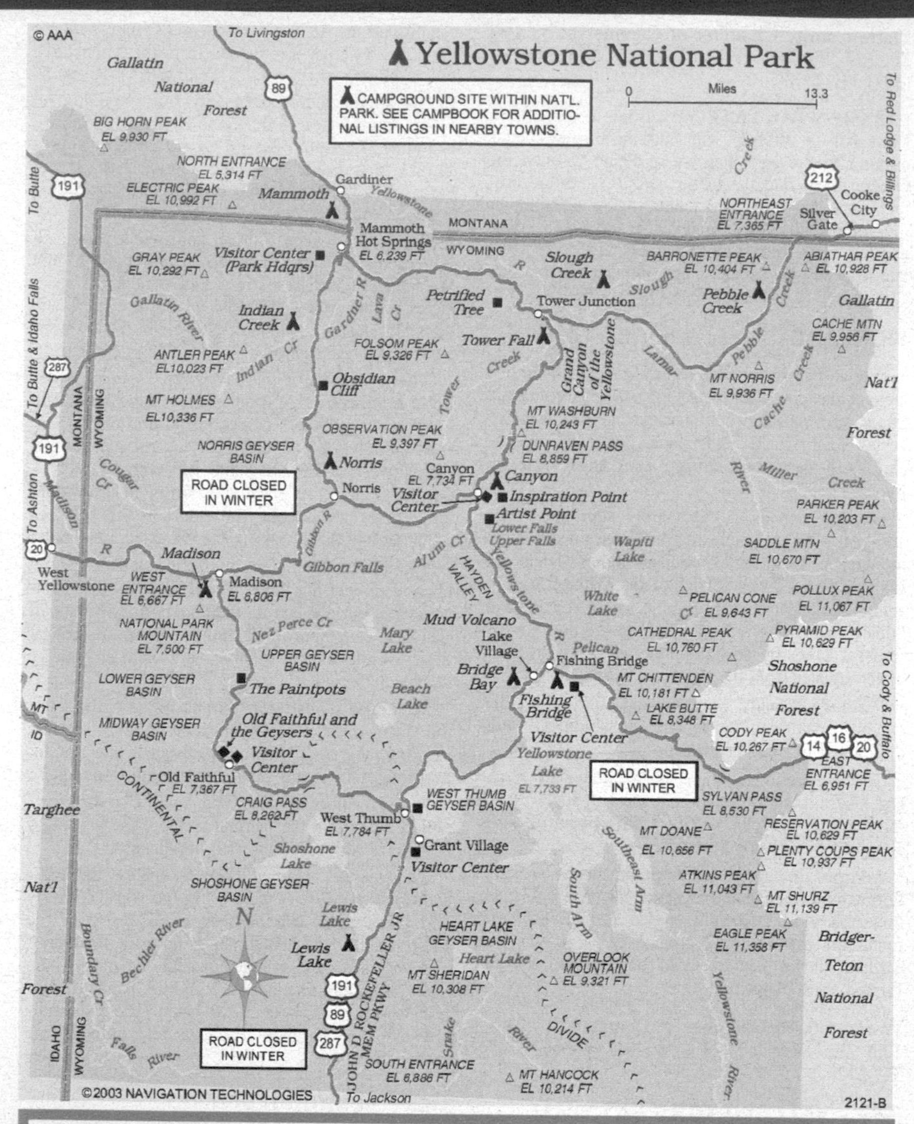
© AAA
Yellowstone National Park
CAMPGROUND SITE WITHIN NAT'L. PARK. SEE CAMPBOOK FOR ADDITIONAL LISTINGS IN NEARBY TOWNS.
Miles
0
13.3
To Livingston
Gallatin National Forest
BIG HORN PEAK EL 9,930 FT
NORTH ENTRANCE EL 5,314 FT
ELECTRIC PEAK EL 10,992 FT
Mammoth
Gardiner
Yellowstone
To Butte
191
89
MONTANA
WYOMING
Mammoth Hot Springs EL 6,239 FT
Visitor Center (Park Hdqrs)
GRAY PEAK EL 10,292 FT
Gallatin River
Indian Creek
Indian Cr
Gardner R
Lava Cr
Petrified Tree
Slough Creek
Tower Junction
Slough
NORTHEAST ENTRANCE EL 7,365 FT
Silver Gate
Cooke City
212
To Red Lodge & Billings
BARRONETTE PEAK EL 10,404 FT
ABIATHAR PEAK EL 10,928 FT
Pebble Creek
Gallatin
CACHE MTN EL 9,956 FT
Nat'l
Forest
Tower Fall
Grand Canyon of the Yellowstone
Lamar
Pebble
Creek
MT NORRIS EL 9,936 FT
Cache
FOLSOM PEAK EL 9,326 FT
ANTLER PEAK EL10,023 FT
To Butte & Idaho Falls
287
Obsidian Cliff
MT HOLMES EL10,336 FT
Tower
MT WASHBURN EL 10,243 FT
OBSERVATION PEAK EL 9,397 FT
DUNRAVEN PASS EL 8,859 FT
NORRIS GEYSER BASIN
Norris
Canyon EL 7,734 FT
Canyon
Inspiration Point
Artist Point
Lower Falls
Upper Falls
Visitor Center
Miller
Creek
River
PARKER PEAK EL 10,203 FT
ROAD CLOSED IN WINTER
Cougar Cr
Madison
To Ashton
20
West Yellowstone
R
Madison
WEST ENTRANCE EL 6,667 FT
Madison EL 6,806 FT
Gibbon R
Gibbon Falls
Alum Cr
HAYDEN VALLEY
Yellowstone
Wapiti Lake
SADDLE MTN EL 10,670 FT
White Lake
PELICAN CONE EL 9,643 FT
POLLUX PEAK EL 11,067 FT
NATIONAL PARK MOUNTAIN EL 7,500 FT
Nez Perce Cr
Mud Volcano
Mary Lake
Lake Village
CATHEDRAL PEAK EL 10,760 FT
PYRAMID PEAK EL 10,629 FT
UPPER GEYSER BASIN
Bridge Bay
Pelican
Fishing Bridge
Shoshone National Forest
LOWER GEYSER BASIN
The Paintpots
Beach Lake
MT CHITTENDEN EL 10,181 FT
Fishing Bridge
LAKE BUTTE EL 8,348 FT
MT
ID
MIDWAY GEYSER BASIN
Old Faithful and the Geysers
Visitor Center
Visitor Center
Yellowstone Lake EL 7,733 FT
CODY PEAK EL 10,267 FT
To Cody & Buffalo
14
16
20
EAST ENTRANCE EL 6,951 FT
Old Faithful EL 7,367 FT
CONTINENTAL
WEST THUMB GEYSER BASIN
SYLVAN PASS EL 8,530 FT
Targhee
CRAIG PASS EL 8,262 FT
West Thumb EL 7,784 FT
Shoshone Lake
Grant Village
Visitor Center
MT DOANE EL 10,656 FT
Southeast Arm
RESERVATION PEAK EL 10,629 FT
PLENTY COUPS PEAK EL 10,937 FT
ATKINS PEAK EL 11,043 FT
Nat'l
SHOSHONE GEYSER BASIN
South Arm
MT SHURZ EL 11,139 FT
N
Lewis Lake
HEART LAKE GEYSER BASIN
EAGLE PEAK EL 11,358 FT
Bridger-Teton National Forest
Bechler River
Lewis Lake
Heart Lake
OVERLOOK MOUNTAIN EL 9,321 FT
MT SHERIDAN EL 10,308 FT
Yellowstone River
Forest
Boundary Cr
191
89
287
JOHN D ROCKEFELLER JR MEM PKWY
Snake
River
DIVIDE
IDAHO
WYOMING
Falls River
SOUTH ENTRANCE EL 6,886 FT
MT HANCOCK EL 10,214 FT
©2003 NAVIGATION TECHNOLOGIES
To Jackson
2121-B

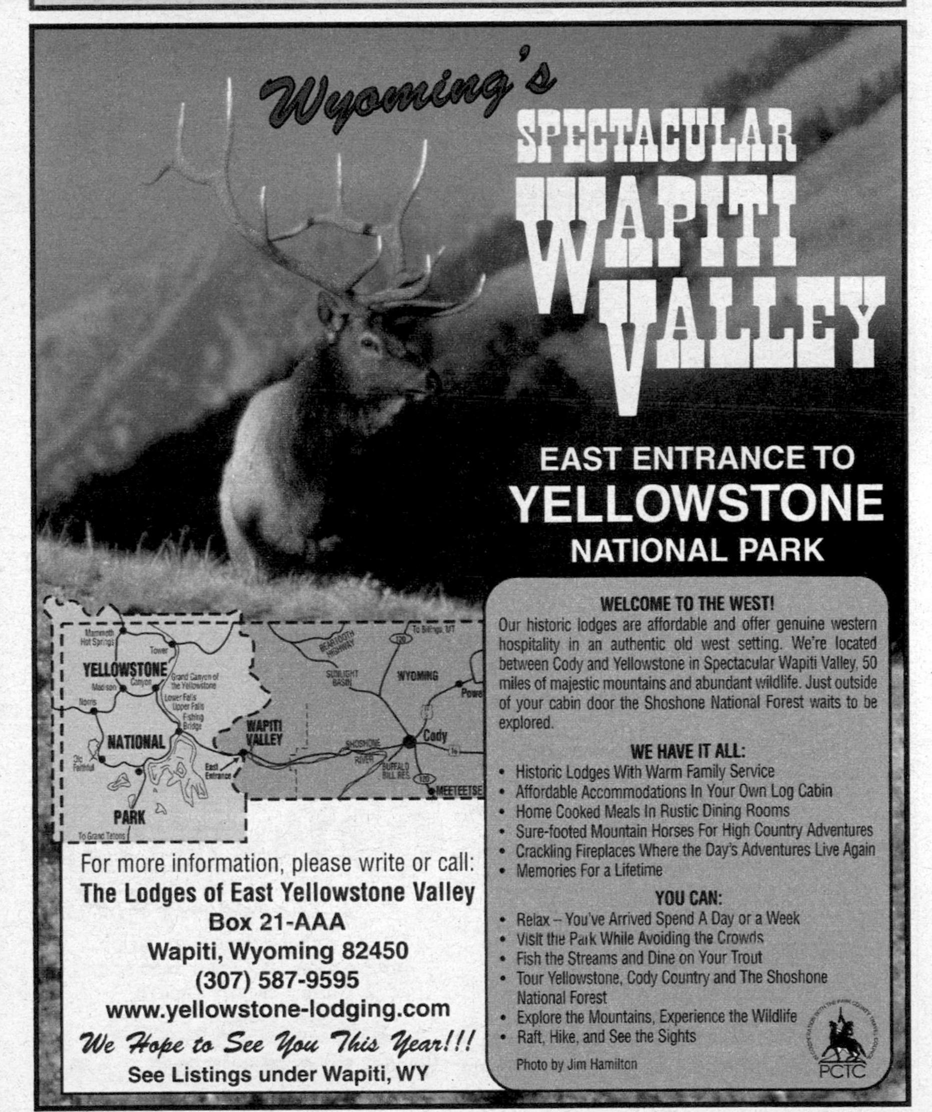

Wyoming's
SPECTACULAR
WAPITI VALLEY
EAST ENTRANCE TO
YELLOWSTONE
NATIONAL PARK
WELCOME TO THE WEST!
Our historic lodges are affordable and offer genuine western hospitality in an authentic old west setting. We're located between Cody and Yellowstone in Spectacular Wapiti Valley, 50 miles of majestic mountains and abundant wildlife. Just outside of your cabin door the Shoshone National Forest waits to be explored.
WE HAVE IT ALL:
• Historic Lodges With Warm Family Service
• Affordable Accommodations In Your Own Log Cabin
• Home Cooked Meals In Rustic Dining Rooms
• Sure-footed Mountain Horses For High Country Adventures
• Crackling Fireplaces Where the Day's Adventures Live Again
• Memories For a Lifetime
YOU CAN:
• Relax – You've Arrived Spend A Day or a Week
• Visit the Park While Avoiding the Crowds
• Fish the Streams and Dine on Your Trout
• Tour Yellowstone, Cody Country and The Shoshone National Forest
• Explore the Mountains, Experience the Wildlife
• Raft, Hike, and See the Sights
Photo by Jim Hamilton
PCTC
YELLOWSTONE
NATIONAL
PARK
WAPITI VALLEY
WYOMING
Cody
MEETEETSE
East Entrance
Tower
Canyon
Madison
Norris
For more information, please write or call:
The Lodges of East Yellowstone Valley
Box 21-AAA
Wapiti, Wyoming 82450
(307) 587-9595
www.yellowstone-lodging.com
We Hope to See You This Year!!!
See Listings under Wapiti, WY

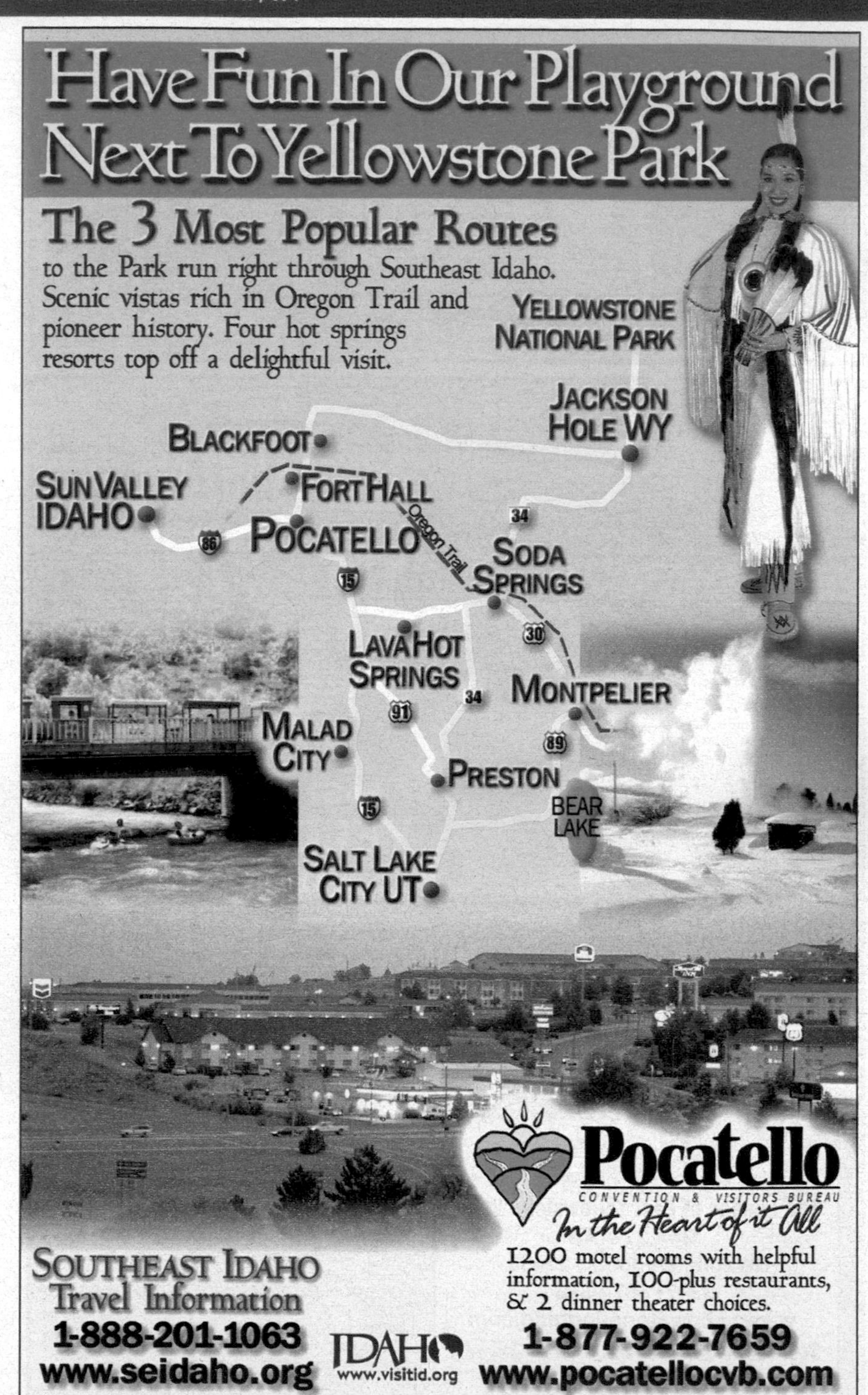
Have Fun In Our Playground
Next To Yellowstone Park
The 3 Most Popular Routes
to the Park run right through Southeast Idaho. Scenic vistas rich in Oregon Trail and pioneer history. Four hot springs resorts top off a delightful visit.
YELLOWSTONE NATIONAL PARK
JACKSON HOLE WY
BLACKFOOT
SUN VALLEY IDAHO
FORT HALL
POCATELLO
Oregon Trail
34
86
15
SODA SPRINGS
30
LAVA HOT SPRINGS
34
91
MONTPELIER
MALAD CITY
89
PRESTON
BEAR LAKE
15
SALT LAKE CITY UT
Pocatello
CONVENTION & VISITORS BUREAU
In the Heart of it All
1200 motel rooms with helpful information, 100-plus restaurants, & 2 dinner theater choices.
SOUTHEAST IDAHO
Travel Information
1-888-201-1063
www.seidaho.org
IDAHO
www.visitid.org
1-877-922-7659
www.pocatellocvb.com

Jackson as well as at Billings, Bozeman and West Yellowstone, Mont.

The roads through the park make many of the most prominent attractions readily accessible. During the summer travel season visitors may encounter slow traffic. Be especially alert for others stopped in the road to watch wildlife; if you must stop, pull well off the highway onto a marked wayside.

Note: According to National Park Service figures, about 80 percent of the park roads are "in a structurally deficient state...including narrow shoulders and rough surfaces." The roads are being gradually repaired under a 20-year program. For up-to-date road information, phone (307) 344-7381.

The park headquarters is at Mammoth Hot Springs, 5 miles from the north entrance. The main post office is at Mammoth; ranger stations are at Old Faithful, Grant Village, Tower-Roosevelt, Mammoth Hot Springs, Lake, Madison, South Entrance and Canyon. The Mammoth and Tower-Roosevelt ranger stations, which are open all year, are accessible by car in winter via the north entrance.

Park information can be received by tuning radios to 1610 AM. Low-powered transmitters broadcast from entrance stations and campgrounds.

From Memorial Day through Labor Day ranger-naturalists conduct geyser walks, natural and living-history talks, photographic workshops and children's programs at Bridge Bay, Canyon, Fishing Bridge Lake, Grant Village, Madison, Mammoth Hot Springs, Norris Geyser Basin, Old Faithful, Tower-Roosevelt and West Thumb Geyser Basin. Free evening programs are given at most park campgrounds during the summer season.

The park's visitor centers offer a variety of interpretive exhibits and information. The Albright Visitor Center at Mammoth Hot Springs concentrates on a general survey of the natural and human history of the park; the Madison Museum, 14 miles east of the west entrance, is the home of the Caldera Art Center, which features literary, visual and performing art. The Old Faithful Visitor Center is devoted largely to geyser activity and its effects.

The Museum of the National Park Ranger, Norris, at Norris Geyser Basin, traces the development of the park ranger profession. The Fishing Bridge Visitor Center/Museum deals primarily with the biological life in the park. The Grant Village Visitor Center houses an exhibit about "Fire and Yellowstone."

The Canyon Visitor Center displays a bison exhibit. A field exhibit near Obsidian Cliff explains the mountain, which was created from a lava flow containing obsidian, a glassy rock.

The TourGuide System consists of a CD player with an accompanying disc available for half- and full-day rental mid-May through October. It features stories about the folklore, history, wildlife, geology and ecology of the park. Visitors can select information about park attractions at their convenience. The unit plugs into the vehicle's cigarette lighter. The TourGuide can be rented at Xanterra Parks and Resorts Activity Desks located in lodging facilities throughout the park. Rates are $24.95 for a full day and $15.95 for a half-day.

ADMISSION to the park is by private vehicle permit ($20), valid in both Yellowstone and Grand Teton national parks for 7 days; by annual area permit ($40/both parks) or annual permit ($50/entrance to all national parks); by single entry via motorcycle or snowmobile ($15 per machine); or by bicycle, foot or horseback ($10 per person). A Golden Age Passport for U.S. citizens over 62 is $10; a Golden Access Passport (for the physically impaired) provides free admission for U.S. citizens.

PETS are permitted in the park only if they are on a leash, crated or otherwise physically restricted at all times. They are not permitted more than 25 feet from the roads, and are not permitted in the back country or on the board walkways or around the hot springs; it is illegal to leave pets unattended.

ADDRESS inquiries to the Superintendent, Yellowstone National Park, P.O. Box 168, Yellowstone National Park, WY 82190; phone (307) 344-7381. For lodging and guest service information write the Travel Director, Xanterra Parks and Resorts, P.O. Box 165, Yellowstone National Park, WY 82190; phone (307) 344-7311.

Activities

Not all of Yellowstone's grandeur can be seen from the boardwalks. More than 1,200 miles of back-country trails lead to many of the park's less accessible attractions. A free back-country use permit, obtainable from any area ranger station, is required for those who wish to camp in the back country. The permit can be obtained in person and no more than 48 hours in advance; for a $15 fee, the permit can be obtained by mail.

There is no better way to explore the park than on horseback over the trails. Private stock can be ridden, or 1- or 2-hour guided rides are available at Mammoth Hot Springs, Tower-Roosevelt and Canyon from Xanterra Parks and Resorts. Horses cannot be rented without a guide.

Motorboats and rowboats can be rented from Xanterra Parks and Resorts at the Bridge Bay Marina. Guided fishing trips also are available. Privately owned boats are permitted on Yellowstone and Lewis lakes, but operators must obtain a $5 permit for nonmotorized craft or a $10 permit for motorized craft. The permits are good for 10 days in Yellowstone National Park; it may be used in Grand Teton National Park after obtaining an upgrade from a park ranger.

Guided snowcoach tours by Xanterra Parks and Resorts to the interior of the park are available mid-December through early March from Mammoth Hot Springs, at the north entrance; West Yellowstone, Mont., at the west entrance; and at Old Faithful and Flagg Ranch, at the south entrance. Snowmobiles can be rented, and guided cross-country ski trips are offered.

Most of the streams and lakes below the timberline contain one or more species of trout. Roadside streams and Yellowstone Lake offer some of the best fishing in the park. Fishing tackle is sold by Hamilton General Stores located throughout the park.

Persons over age 15 are required to purchase a fishing permit. A 10-day permit costs $10. A free fishing permit is required for ages 12-15. For further information write the Chief Rangers Office, P.O. Box 168, Yellowstone National Park, WY 82190. Fishing regulations and permits can be obtained at any ranger station, visitor center or Hamilton General Store. The opening of the season varies from the Saturday of Memorial Day weekend to July 15 for different lakes and streams; it closes the first Sunday in November.

Check at park headquarters or ranger stations for season variations and legal limits. *See Recreation Chart and the AAA Northwestern CampBook.*

Note: It is not only contrary to park regulations but also dangerous to feed, touch or tease any wildlife. Animals in the park are wild and should be viewed only from a safe distance. Because the presence of food in a tent or camp may attract bears and other unwanted guests, it must be kept in locked, hardtopped cars or in locked metal boxes or containers. All leftovers should be disposed of in bear-proof garbage cans provided for that purpose.

Points of Interest

GRAND CANYON OF THE YELLOWSTONE is a section along the Yellowstone River between Canyon and Tower-Roosevelt. The canyon is noted for its spectacular coloring. Vista points offer superb views; among the best are Artist's Point on the south rim and Inspiration Point on the north rim. Lookout Point provides the best view of the Lower Falls.

Allow 1 hour minimum.

MAMMOTH HOT SPRINGS are near the park headquarters at the n. entrance. The springs are characterized by terrace-like formations created by limestone deposits. Well-marked trails allow the safe viewing of the formations at close range; however, visitors must stay on the trails at all times, since in many places the thin crust is dangerous. Allow 1 hour minimum.

OLD FAITHFUL AND THE GEYSERS exhibit character and action. Many, like Old Faithful and Riverside, spout at predictable intervals; others are irregular. Most of the approximately 10,000 thermal features (geysers, fumaroles, hot springs and mud pots) are in the principal geyser basins—Heart Lake, Lower, Midway, Norris, Shoshone, Upper and West Thumb—in the western and south-central sections.

Allow 2 hours minimum.

THE PAINTPOTS are large springs filled with hot clay ranging in color from white to shades of pink and black. Fountain Paintpot, one of the most famous in the park, is in the Lower Geyser Basin.

Allow 30 minutes minimum.

YELLOWSTONE LAKE is e. and s. of the park road between West Thumb and Fishing Bridge. With a shoreline of 110 miles and at 7,733 feet above sea level, the lake is the largest body of water in North America at so high an altitude. The area is a haven for several rare bird species. Allow 1 hour minimum.

RECREATIONAL ACTIVITIES

Hiking

- **Adventure Yellowstone Inc.** picks up at area lodgings. Write P.O. Box 574, Yellowstone National Park, WY 82190. Other activities are offered. Trips depart daily. Phone (406) 585-9041. *See color ad p. 177.*

AMERICA ON THE MOVE

A NEW EXHIBITION ON TRANSPORTATION IN AMERICAN HISTORY

Smithsonian
National Museum of American History
Behring Center

AMERICA
ON THE MOVE

Idaho

Snake River
© Alpen Glow Images
Alamy Images

BLACKFOOT pop. 10,419

WHERE TO STAY

BEST WESTERN BLACKFOOT INN *Book at aaa.com* **Phone:** (208)785-4144

AAA SAVE

Small-scale Hotel

All Year [CP] 1P: $55-$99 2P: $55-$99

Location: I-15, exit 93, just e on Bergener, 0.4 mi n on Parkway. 750 Jensen Grove Dr 83221. Fax: 208/785-4304. **Facility:** 60 one-bedroom standard units. 2 stories (no elevator), interior corridors. **Parking:** on-site, winter plug-ins. **Terms:** 30 day cancellation notice-fee imposed, [CP] meal plan available. **Amenities:** irons, hair dryers. *Some:* high-speed Internet. **Pool(s):** heated indoor. **Leisure Activities:** whirlpool, exercise room. **Business Services:** meeting rooms. **Cards:** AX, CB, DC, DS, MC, VI. **Special Amenities: free continental breakfast and free local telephone calls.**

SOME UNITS

DATA PORT / /

BLISS pop. 275

WHERE TO STAY

AMBER INN MOTEL **Phone:** (208)352-4441

AAA SAVE

Small-scale Hotel

All Year 1P: $33 2P: $39 XP: $4 D18

Location: I-84, exit 141, just s. Located in a rural area. 17286 US Hwy 30 83314. Fax: 208/352-1115. **Facility:** 30 units. 29 one-bedroom standard units. 1 one-bedroom suite ($45-$60). 2 stories (no elevator), interior corridors. **Parking:** on-site. **Terms:** office hours 7 am-11 pm, pets ($4 extra charge). **Cards:** AX, DS, MC, VI. **Special Amenities: free local telephone calls and preferred room (subject to availability with advanced reservations).**

SOME UNITS

FEE / /

BOISE pop. 185,787

Airport Accommodations

OA	BOISE AIR TERMINAL-GOWEN FIELD	Diamond Rating	Rate Range High Season	Listing Page
AAA	**Best Western Airport Inn, adjacent to airport entrance**	3 Diamonds	$69-$81 SAVE	187
AAA	**Best Western Vista Inn, adjacent to airport entrance**	3 Diamonds	$79-$91 SAVE	188
	Boise Super 8 Motel, just n of airport	2 Diamonds	$59-$79	188
AAA	**Comfort Inn Boise, 0.3 mi e of airport**	2 Diamonds	$59-$89 SAVE	188
	Extended Stay America, 1 mi n of airport	2 Diamonds	$55-$70	190
	Fairfield Inn by Marriott, 0.5 mi n of airport	3 Diamonds	$84	190
	Hampton Inn, 0.5 mi n of airport	3 Diamonds	$79-$129	190
	Holiday Inn Boise Airport, 0.5 mi n of airport	3 Diamonds	$85-$92	191
	Holiday Inn Express, 1 mi n of airport	3 Diamonds	$69-$89	191
AAA	**Inn America, adjacent to airport**	3 Diamonds	$55-$71 SAVE	191
AAA	**Sleep Inn, adjacent to airport**	2 Diamonds	$55-$99 SAVE	192

WHERE TO STAY

A JJ SHAW HOUSE BED & BREAKFAST INN — **Phone:** 208/344-8899

Historic Bed & Breakfast

All Year 1P: $79-$119 2P: $79-$119 XP: $20

Location: Between 14th and 15th sts, north edge of downtown. 1411 W Franklin St 83702-5024. Fax: 208/344-6677. **Facility:** This charming home was built in 1907 and is within walking distance of a historic park and the downtown area. Smoke free premises. 5 units. 4 one-bedroom standard units. 1 one-bedroom suite with whirlpool. 3 stories (no elevator), interior corridors. *Bath:* combo, shower or tub only. **Parking:** street. **Terms:** check-in 4 pm, age restrictions may apply, 7 day cancellation notice-fee imposed, weekly rates available, [BP] meal plan available. **Cards:** AX, DS, MC, VI.

SOME UNITS

AMERISUITES (BOISE/TOWNE SQUARE MALL) *Book at aaa.com* — **Phone:** (208)375-1200

AAA SAVE

Small-scale Hotel

All Year 1P: $99-$109 2P: $99-$109 XP: $10 F17

Location: I-84, exit 49 (Franklin St), just w, 0.5 mi n. 925 N Milwaukee St 83704. Fax: 208/375-2900. **Facility:** 128 one-bedroom standard units. 4 stories, interior corridors. *Bath:* combo or shower only. **Parking:** on-site. **Terms:** [ECP] meal plan available, small pets only. **Amenities:** video games (fee), high-speed Internet, voice mail, irons, hair dryers. *Some:* dual phone lines. **Pool(s):** heated indoor. **Leisure Activities:** exercise room. **Guest Services:** valet and coin laundry, area transportation-within 5 mi. **Business Services:** meeting rooms. **Cards:** AX, CB, DC, DS, JC, MC, VI. **Special Amenities: free expanded continental breakfast and free newspaper.**

SOME UNITS

VCR DATA PORT

AMERITEL INN BOISE SPECTRUM *Book at aaa.com* — **Phone:** (208)323-2500

Large-scale Hotel

All Year [ECP] 1P: $95-$130 2P: $95-$130 XP: $10 F18

Location: I-84, exit 50A westbound; exit 50B eastbound. 7499 W Overland Rd 83709. Fax: 208/323-9400. **Facility:** 133 units. 129 one-bedroom standard units, some with efficiencies. 4 two-bedroom suites with efficiencies. 4 stories, interior corridors. *Bath:* combo or shower only. **Parking:** on-site. **Amenities:** video games (fee), high-speed Internet, dual phone lines, voice mail, irons, hair dryers. **Pool(s):** heated indoor. **Leisure Activities:** whirlpool, exercise room. **Guest Services:** valet and coin laundry. **Business Services:** meeting rooms, business center. **Cards:** AX, CB, DC, DS, MC, VI.

SOME UNITS

ASK DATA PORT

AMERITEL INN-BOISE TOWNE SQUARE *Book at aaa.com* — **Phone:** (208)378-7000

Small-scale Hotel

All Year [ECP] 1P: $95-$130 2P: $95-$130 XP: $10 F18

Location: I-84, exit 49 (Franklin St), just w, 0.5 mi n on Milwaukee St to Emerald St, then just e. 7965 W Emerald St 83704. Fax: 208/378-7040. **Facility:** 124 units. 121 one-bedroom standard units, some with efficiencies. 3 one-bedroom suites. 4 stories, interior corridors. *Bath:* combo or shower only. **Parking:** on-site, winter plug-ins. **Amenities:** video games (fee), high-speed Internet, dual phone lines, voice mail, irons, hair dryers. **Pool(s):** small heated indoor. **Leisure Activities:** whirlpool, exercise room. **Guest Services:** valet and coin laundry. **Business Services:** meeting rooms, fax. **Cards:** AX, CB, DC, DS, MC, VI. ***(See color ad p 186)***

SOME UNITS

ASK DATA PORT

BEST WESTERN AIRPORT INN *Book at aaa.com* — **Phone:** (208)384-5000

AAA SAVE

Small-scale Hotel

All Year 1P: $69-$71 2P: $79-$81

Location: I-84, exit 53 (Vista Ave), just s. 2660 Airport Way 83705. Fax: 208/384-5566. **Facility:** 50 one-bedroom standard units. 2 stories (no elevator), exterior corridors. **Parking:** on-site. **Terms:** [CP] meal plan available. **Amenities:** high-speed Internet (fee), voice mail, irons, hair dryers. **Pool(s):** small outdoor. **Guest Services:** valet and coin laundry. **Cards:** AX, CB, DC, DS, MC, VI. **Special Amenities: free continental breakfast and free newspaper.**

SOME UNITS

DATA PORT

BEST WESTERN NORTHWEST LODGE *Book at aaa.com* **Phone:** (208)287-2300

All Year [ECP] 1P: $72 2P: $81 XP: $10 F18

Small-scale Hotel

Location: I-84, exit 57, just e. 6989 Federal Way 83716. Fax: 208/287-2310. **Facility:** 69 one-bedroom standard units, some with whirlpools. 3 stories, interior corridors. *Bath:* combo or shower only. **Parking:** on-site, winter plug-ins. **Amenities:** high-speed Internet (fee), dual phone lines, voice mail, irons, hair dryers. **Pool(s):** small heated indoor. **Leisure Activities:** whirlpool, exercise room. **Guest Services:** valet and coin laundry, area transportation. **Business Services:** meeting rooms, fax (fee). **Cards:** AX, CB, DC, DS, JC, MC, VI. **Special Amenities: free expanded continental breakfast and free newspaper.**

SOME UNITS

BEST WESTERN SAFARI MOTOR INN *Book at aaa.com* **Phone:** (208)344-6556

6/1-2/28 [ECP] 1P: $68-$78 2P: $74-$84 XP: $6 F17
3/1-5/31 [ECP] 1P: $66-$76 2P: $72-$82 XP: $6 F17

Small-scale Hotel

Location: At 11th and Grove sts; center. 1070 Grove St 83702. Fax: 208/344-7240. **Facility:** 103 one-bedroom standard units, some with whirlpools. 3 stories, interior corridors. **Parking:** on-site, winter plug-ins. **Terms:** pets (in smoking units). **Amenities:** voice mail, irons, hair dryers. **Pool(s):** small heated outdoor. **Leisure Activities:** sauna, whirlpool, exercise room. **Guest Services:** valet laundry. **Business Services:** meeting rooms, fax (fee). **Cards:** AX, CB, DC, DS, MC, VI. **Special Amenities: free expanded continental breakfast and free local telephone calls.**

SOME UNITS

BEST WESTERN VISTA INN *Book at aaa.com* **Phone:** (208)336-8100

All Year 1P: $79-$81 2P: $89-$91 XP: $5 F18

Small-scale Hotel

Location: I-84, exit 53 (Vista Ave), just s. 2645 Airport Way 83705. Fax: 208/342-3060. **Facility:** 87 one-bedroom standard units. 2 stories (no elevator), interior/exterior corridors. *Bath:* combo or shower only. **Parking:** on-site. **Terms:** [CP] meal plan available. **Amenities:** voice mail, irons, hair dryers. *Some:* dual phone lines. **Pool(s):** small heated indoor. **Leisure Activities:** whirlpool, exercise room. *Fee:* game room. **Guest Services:** valet and coin laundry. **Business Services:** conference facilities. **Cards:** AX, CB, DC, DS, MC, VI. **Special Amenities: free continental breakfast and free newspaper.**

SOME UNITS

BOISE SUPER 8 MOTEL *Book at aaa.com* **Phone:** (208)344-8871

6/1-9/30 1P: $59-$63 2P: $69-$79 XP: $5 F12
3/1-5/31 & 10/1-11/30 1P: $47-$55 2P: $56-$65 XP: $5 F12
12/1-2/28 1P: $45-$53 2P: $54-$59 XP: $5 F12

Small-scale Hotel

Location: I-84, exit 53 (Vista Ave), just n. 2773 Elder St 83705. Fax: 208/344-8871. **Facility:** 108 one-bedroom standard units. 3 stories, interior corridors. **Parking:** on-site. **Terms:** pets ($25 deposit). **Amenities:** safes (fee). **Pool(s):** small heated indoor. **Guest Services:** coin laundry. **Cards:** AX, DC, DS, MC, VI.

SOME UNITS

ASK

FEE FEE FEE

BUDGET HOST INN **Phone:** (208)322-4404

All Year [ECP] 1P: $45-$55 2P: $60-$70 XP: $5 F14

Motel

Location: I-84, exit 50A westbound, just s, just w, then just n; exit 50B eastbound, just w, then just n. Located behind WalMart. 8002 Overland Rd 83709. Fax: 208/322-7487. **Facility:** 87 one-bedroom standard units. 2 stories (no elevator), exterior corridors. **Parking:** on-site. **Terms:** weekly rates available, pets ($10 fee, dogs only). **Amenities:** high-speed Internet, voice mail. **Pool(s):** heated outdoor. **Leisure Activities:** whirlpool. **Cards:** AX, DC, DS, MC, VI. **Special Amenities: free expanded continental breakfast and free local telephone calls.** ***(See color ad p 189)***

SOME UNITS

FEE

COMFORT INN BOISE *Book at aaa.com* **Phone:** (208)336-0077

All Year 1P: $59-$69 2P: $69-$89 XP: $10 F18

Small-scale Hotel

Location: I-84, exit 53 (Vista Ave), just s. 2526 Airport Way 83705. Fax: 208/342-6592. **Facility:** 62 one-bedroom standard units, some with whirlpools. 2 stories (no elevator), interior/exterior corridors. **Parking:** on-site. **Terms:** [ECP] meal plan available. **Amenities:** dual phone lines, voice mail, irons, hair dryers. **Pool(s):** small heated indoor. **Leisure Activities:** whirlpool. **Cards:** AX, CB, DC, DS.

SOME UNITS

COURTYARD BY MARRIOTT *Book at aaa.com* **Phone:** (208)331-2700

Small-scale Hotel

All Year 1P: $69-$119 2P: $79-$129 XP: $10 F17

Location: I-84, exit 54 (Broadway Ave), 3 mi n. 222 S Broadway Ave 83702. Fax: 208/331-3296. **Facility:** 162 units. 157 one-bedroom standard units. 5 one-bedroom suites ($129-$169). 4 stories, interior corridors. *Bath:* combo or shower only. **Parking:** on-site. **Terms:** [BP] meal plan available. **Amenities:** video games (fee), high-speed Internet, dual phone lines, voice mail, irons, hair dryers. **Dining:** 6:30-10 am, Sat & Sun 7-11 am, cocktails. **Pool(s):** small heated indoor. **Leisure Activities:** whirlpool, exercise room. **Guest Services:** valet and coin laundry. **Business Services:** meeting rooms, fax. **Cards:** AX, DC, DS, MC, VI. **Special Amenities: free newspaper.** ***(See color ad below)***

SOME UNITS

DOUBLETREE CLUB HOTEL *Book at aaa.com* **Phone:** (208)345-2002

Small-scale Hotel

All Year 1P: $59-$164 2P: $69-$174 XP: $10 F18

Location: I-84, exit 54 (Broadway Ave), 2 mi n, 0.3 mi e on Beacon and Parkcenter Blvd. 475 W Parkcenter Blvd 83706. Fax: 208/345-8354. **Facility:** 158 one-bedroom standard units. 6 stories, interior corridors. **Parking:** on-site. **Terms:** cancellation fee imposed, [AP] meal plan available, pets ($10 extra charge). **Amenities:** voice mail, irons, hair dryers. *Fee:* video games, high-speed Internet. **Pool(s):** heated outdoor. **Leisure Activities:** whirlpool, exercise room. **Guest Services:** valet laundry, area transportation. **Business Services:** meeting rooms, business center. **Cards:** AX, CB, DC, DS, JC, MC, VI.

SOME UNITS

FEE

DOUBLETREE HOTEL RIVERSIDE *Book at aaa.com* **Phone:** (208)343-1871

Small-scale Hotel

All Year 1P: $69-$169 2P: $69-$179 XP: $10 F18

Location: I-184, exit Fairview Ave, just n, then just w on Garden. Located adjoining the Boise Greenbelt. 2900 Chinden Blvd 83714. Fax: 208/344-1079. **Facility:** 304 units. 302 one- and 2 two-bedroom standard units, some with whirlpools. 2 stories, interior corridors. *Bath:* combo or shower only. **Parking:** on-site. **Terms:** pets ($25 extra charge). **Amenities:** high-speed Internet (fee), voice mail, irons, hair dryers. **Pool(s):** heated outdoor, wading. **Leisure Activities:** sauna, whirlpools, rental bicycles, jogging, exercise room. **Guest Services:** gift shop, valet and coin laundry. **Business Services:** conference facilities, business center. **Cards:** AX, CB, DC, DS, JC, MC, VI.

SOME UNITS FEE

ECONO LODGE BOISE *Book at aaa.com* **Phone:** (208)344-4030

AAA SAVE

Small-scale Hotel

All Year 1P: $55-$65 2P: $65-$75 XP: $10 F18

Location: I-184, exit Fairview Ave, just n. 4060 Fairview Ave 83706. Fax: 208/342-1635. **Facility:** 52 one-bedroom standard units. 3 stories, interior corridors. **Parking:** on-site. **Terms:** [CP] meal plan available, pets ($10 fee, dogs only). **Amenities:** voice mail, safes (fee). *Some:* irons, hair dryers. **Cards:** AX, DC, DS, MC, VI. **Special Amenities: free continental breakfast and free local telephone calls.**

SOME UNITS FEE

EXTENDED STAY AMERICA *Book at aaa.com* **Phone:** 208/363-9040

Small-scale Hotel

All Year 1P: $55-$59 2P: $64-$70

Location: I-84, exit 53 (Vista Ave), 0.7 mi n. 2500 S Vista Ave 83705. Fax: 208/363-9039. **Facility:** 107 one-bedroom standard units with kitchens. 2 stories, interior corridors. *Bath:* combo or shower only. **Parking:** on-site. **Terms:** office hours 7 am-11 pm, weekly rates available. **Amenities:** voice mail. **Guest Services:** coin laundry. **Cards:** AX, DC, MC, VI.

SOME UNITS

FAIRFIELD INN BY MARRIOTT *Book at aaa.com* **Phone:** (208)331-5656

Small-scale Hotel

6/1-10/31 1P: $84 2P: $84
3/1-5/31 & 11/1-2/28 1P: $79 2P: $79

Location: I-84, exit 53 (Vista Ave), just n, then just w on Elder St. 3300 S Shoshone St 83705. Fax: 208/424-3169. **Facility:** 63 one-bedroom standard units. 3 stories, interior corridors. *Bath:* combo or shower only. **Parking:** on-site. **Terms:** [CP] meal plan available. **Amenities:** voice mail, irons, hair dryers. **Pool(s):** small heated indoor. **Leisure Activities:** whirlpool, exercise room. **Guest Services:** valet laundry. **Cards:** AX, CB, DC, DS, MC, VI.

SOME UNITS

THE GROVE HOTEL-A WESTCOAST GRAND HOTEL *Book at aaa.com* **Phone:** (208)333-8000

AAA SAVE

Large-scale Hotel

All Year 1P: $124-$144 2P: $144-$164 XP: $20 F18

Location: At Capitol Blvd and Front St; center of downtown. 245 S Capitol Blvd 83702. Fax: 208/333-8800. **Facility:** The Grove is a luxury high-rise offering added amenities and refined service. 254 units. 247 one-bedroom standard units, some with whirlpools. 1 one- and 6 two-bedroom suites ($219-$269) with whirlpools, some with kitchens. 17 stories, interior corridors. *Bath:* combo or shower only. **Parking:** on-site (fee) and valet. **Terms:** [AP], [BP] & [ECP] meal plans available. **Amenities:** dual phone lines, voice mail, honor bars, irons, hair dryers. *Fee:* video games, high-speed Internet. *Some:* fax. **Dining:** 2 restaurants, 6 am-11 pm, cocktails, entertainment. **Pool(s):** heated indoor. **Leisure Activities:** sauna, whirlpool, steamroom. **Guest Services:** gift shop, valet laundry, area transportation-city center. **Business Services:** conference facilities, business center. **Cards:** AX, DC, DS, MC, VI. **Special Amenities: free newspaper and free room upgrade (subject to availability with advanced reservations).** ***(See color ad below)***

SOME UNITS FEE

HAMPTON INN **Phone:** (208)331-5600

Small-scale Hotel

5/1-8/31 1P: $79-$119 2P: $84-$129
3/1-4/30 & 9/1-2/28 1P: $69-$109 2P: $74-$114

Location: I-84, exit 53 (Vista Ave), just n to Elder St, then just w. 3270 S Shoshone St 83705. Fax: 208/389-1220. **Facility:** 64 one-bedroom standard units. 3 stories, interior corridors. *Bath:* combo or shower only. **Parking:** on-site. **Terms:** cancellation fee imposed, [CP] meal plan available. **Amenities:** voice mail, irons, hair dryers. **Pool(s):** small heated indoor. **Leisure Activities:** whirlpool. **Guest Services:** valet laundry. **Cards:** AX, CB, DC, DS, JC, MC, VI.

ASK SOME UNITS

HILTON GARDEN INN BOISE SPECTRUM *Book at aaa.com* **Phone:** (208)376-1000

Small-scale Hotel

All Year 1P: $89-$149 2P: $89-$149 XP: $15 F18

Location: I-84, exit 50A westbound; exit 50B eastbound, just s. 7699 W Spectrum St 83709. Fax: 208/321-7916. **Facility:** 137 units. 128 one- and 2 two-bedroom standard units. 6 one- and 1 two-bedroom suites ($125-$269). 4 stories, interior corridors. *Bath:* combo or shower only. **Parking:** on-site, winter plug-ins. **Terms:** [BP] meal plan available. **Amenities:** video games (fee), high-speed Internet, dual phone lines, voice mail, irons, hair dryers. **Pool(s):** heated indoor. **Leisure Activities:** whirlpool, exercise room. **Guest Services:** sundries, valet and coin laundry. **Business Services:** conference facilities, business center. **Cards:** AX, CB, DC, DS, MC, VI.

SOME UNITS

HOLIDAY INN BOISE AIRPORT **Phone:** (208)343-4900

Small-scale Hotel

6/1-8/31 1P: $85-$92 2P: $85-$92 XP: $10 F12

3/1-5/31 & 9/1-2/28 1P: $75-$81 2P: $75-$81 XP: $10 F12

Location: I-84, exit 53 (Vista Ave), just n. 3300 Vista Ave 83705. Fax: 208/343-9635. **Facility:** 265 units. 262 one-bedroom standard units. 3 one-bedroom suites. 2 stories (no elevator), interior corridors. *Bath:* combo or shower only. **Parking:** on-site. **Terms:** small pets only ($25 extra charge, in designated units). **Amenities:** voice mail, irons, hair dryers. **Pool(s):** heated indoor, wading. **Leisure Activities:** whirlpool, exercise room. *Fee:* game room. **Guest Services:** valet and coin laundry. **Business Services:** conference facilities, fax (fee). **Cards:** AX, CB, DC, DS, JC, MC, VI.

(See color ad opposite title page)

SOME UNITS

FEE FEE FEE

HOLIDAY INN EXPRESS *Book at aaa.com* **Phone:** (208)388-0800

Small-scale Hotel

All Year [ECP] 1P: $69-$85 2P: $69-$89 XP: $6 F

Location: I-84, exit 53 (Vista Ave), 0.5 mi n. 2613 S Vista Ave 83705. Fax: 208/388-0846. **Facility:** 63 one-bedroom standard units. 3 stories, interior corridors. *Bath:* combo or shower only. **Parking:** on-site, winter plug-ins. **Amenities:** video library (fee), voice mail, irons, hair dryers. **Pool(s):** small heated indoor. **Leisure Activities:** whirlpool. **Guest Services:** valet laundry. **Cards:** AX, CB, DC, DS, MC, VI.

SOME UNITS

IDAHO HERITAGE INN BED & BREAKFAST **Phone:** 208/342-8066

Historic Bed & Breakfast

All Year 1P: $70-$110 2P: $70-$110 XP: $15

Location: I-84, exit 54 (Broadway Ave), 3 mi n, then just w. Located in the historic district. 109 W Idaho St 83702. Fax: 208/343-2325. **Facility:** Built in 1904, this home served for a time as the governor's mansion. Smoke free premises. 6 one-bedroom standard units. 3 stories (no elevator), interior/exterior corridors. *Bath:* combo or shower only. **Parking:** on-site. **Terms:** age restrictions may apply, [BP] meal plan available. **Amenities:** dual phone lines. **Leisure Activities:** rental bicycles. **Guest Services:** complimentary evening beverages. **Business Services:** fax (fee). **Cards:** AX, MC, VI.

SOME UNITS

INN AMERICA *Book at aaa.com* **Phone:** (203)389-9800

AAA SAVE

Small-scale Hotel

5/2-9/15 1P: $55-$61 2P: $65-$71 XP: $5 F18

4/1-5/1 1P: $45-$51 2P: $55-$61 XP: $5 F18

3/1-3/31 & 9/16-2/28 1P: $41-$47 2P: $51-$57 XP: $5 F18

Location: I-84, exit 53 (Vista Ave), 0.3 mi se. 2275 Airport Way 83705. Fax: 208/338-1303. **Facility:** 73 one-bedroom standard units. 3 stories, interior corridors. *Bath:* combo or shower only. **Parking:** on-site. **Terms:** cancellation fee imposed, [CP] meal plan available. **Amenities:** high-speed Internet (fee), irons, hair dryers. **Pool(s):** small heated outdoor. **Guest Services:** valet and coin laundry. **Cards:** AX, DC, DS, MC, VI. **Special Amenities: free local telephone calls and early check-in/late check-out.**

SOME UNITS

OWYHEE PLAZA HOTEL *Book at aaa.com* **Phone:** (208)343-4611

AAA SAVE

Historic Small-scale Hotel

All Year 1P: $85-$135 2P: $95-$145 XP: $10 F18

Location: At 11th and Main sts; center. 1109 Main St 83702. Fax: 208/336-3860. **Facility:** This restored 1910 hotel is close to shopping and attractions; some poolside rooms are offered. 100 units. 99 one-bedroom standard units, some with whirlpools. 1 one-bedroom suite ($250-$275) with whirlpool. 3 stories, interior/exterior corridors. *Bath:* combo or shower only. **Parking:** on-site. **Terms:** pets ($25 deposit, in designated units). **Amenities:** high-speed Internet (fee), hair dryers. *Some:* honor bars, irons. **Dining:** 2 restaurants, 6 am-5 pm, Sun 7 am-9 pm, cocktails, also, Gamekeeper Restaurant, see separate listing. **Guest Services:** valet laundry. **Business Services:** conference facilities, fax (fee). **Cards:** AX, DC, DS, MC, VI.

SOME UNITS

FEE FEE FEE

THE PLAZA SUITE HOTEL *Book at aaa.com* **Phone:** (208)375-7666

Small-scale Hotel

All Year [ECP] 1P: $99-$125 2P: $99-$125 XP: $9 F5

Location: I-84, exit 50A, 0.5 mi n. 409 S Cole 83709. Fax: 208/376-3608. **Facility:** 38 one-bedroom standard units, some with whirlpools. 4 stories, interior corridors. *Bath:* combo or shower only. **Parking:** on-site. **Terms:** cancellation fee imposed. **Amenities:** high-speed Internet (fee), voice mail, irons, hair dryers. **Pool(s):** heated indoor. **Guest Services:** valet laundry, area transportation. **Business Services:** meeting rooms, fax (fee). **Cards:** AX, CB, DC, DS, JC, MC, VI.

SOME UNITS

FEE

RED LION HOTEL BOISE DOWNTOWNER *Book at aaa.com* **Phone:** (208)344-7691

Large-scale Hotel

All Year 1P: $59-$109 2P: $69-$119 XP: $10 F18

Location: I-184, exit Fairview Ave, 1 mi n. 1800 Fairview Ave 83702. Fax: 208/336-3652. **Facility:** 182 units. 180 one-bedroom standard units. 2 one-bedroom suites with whirlpools. 3-7 stories, interior corridors. *Bath:* combo or shower only. **Parking:** on-site. **Terms:** cancellation fee imposed, small pets only ($15 extra charge). **Amenities:** voice mail, irons, hair dryers. **Pool(s):** small heated outdoor. **Leisure Activities:** whirlpool, exercise room. **Guest Services:** valet laundry. **Business Services:** conference facilities. **Cards:** AX, DC, DS, MC, VI. ***(See ad p 192)***

SOME UNITS

FEE FEE

RED LION PARKCENTER SUITES - BOISE *Book at aaa.com* **Phone:** (208)342-1044

Small-scale Hotel

All Year 1P: $79-$119

Location: I-84, exit 54 (Broadway Ave), 2.3 mi n, just e on Beacon and Parkcenter Blvd. Located in a business park. 424 E Parkcenter Blvd 83706. Fax: 208/342-2763. **Facility:** 237 one-bedroom standard units, some with whirlpools. 3 stories, interior corridors. *Bath:* combo or shower only. **Parking:** on-site. **Terms:** cancellation fee imposed, [ECP] meal plan available. **Amenities:** high-speed Internet (fee), voice mail, irons, hair dryers. **Pool(s):** heated outdoor. **Leisure Activities:** whirlpool, exercise room. **Guest Services:** sundries, valet and coin laundry, area transportation. **Business Services:** meeting rooms, business center. **Cards:** AX, DC, DS, MC, VI. ***(See ad below)***

SOME UNITS

RESIDENCE INN BY MARRIOTT *Book at aaa.com* **Phone:** (208)344-1200

Small-scale Hotel

6/1-10/15 [ECP] 1P: $133-$175
3/1-5/31 [ECP] 1P: $128-$165
10/16-2/28 [ECP] 1P: $125-$165

Location: I-84, exit 53, 2.5 mi n, then just w. Located adjacent to Ann Morrison Park. 1401 Lusk Ave 83706. Fax: 208/384-5354. **Facility:** 104 units. 71 one-bedroom standard units with kitchens. 7 one- and 26 two-bedroom suites with kitchens. 2-3 stories (no elevator), exterior corridors. *Bath:* combo or shower only. **Parking:** on-site. **Terms:** pets ($10 extra charge). **Amenities:** high-speed Internet, dual phone lines, voice mail, irons, hair dryers. **Pool(s):** heated outdoor. **Leisure Activities:** whirlpools, exercise room, sports court. **Guest Services:** coin laundry. **Business Services:** meeting rooms, fax (fee). **Cards:** AX, CB, DC, DS, JC, MC, VI. ***(See color ad below)***

SOME UNITS

FEE

RODEWAY INN OF BOISE *Book at aaa.com* **Phone:** (208)376-2700

Small-scale Hotel

All Year [CP] 1P: $65-$95 2P: $65-$100 XP: $8 F17

Location: I-184, exit 2, just se. 1115 N Curtis Rd 83706. Fax: 208/377-0324. **Facility:** 98 one-bedroom standard units. 2 stories (no elevator), interior/exterior corridors. **Parking:** on-site. **Terms:** weekly rates available, small pets only ($15 deposit). **Amenities:** safes (fee), irons, hair dryers. **Pool(s):** heated indoor/outdoor. **Leisure Activities:** sauna, whirlpool, putting green, shuffleboard. **Guest Services:** valet laundry, area transportation. **Business Services:** meeting rooms. **Cards:** AX, CB, DC, DS, MC, VI.

SOME UNITS

FEE

SLEEP INN *Book at aaa.com* **Phone:** (208)336-7377

AAA SAVE

Small-scale Hotel

All Year [ECP] 1P: $55-$89 2P: $55-$99 XP: $5 F18

Location: I-84, exit 53 (Vista Ave), just s. 2799 Airport Way 83705. Fax: 208/336-2035. **Facility:** 69 one-bedroom standard units. 2 stories (no elevator), interior corridors. *Bath:* combo or shower only. **Parking:** on-site. **Terms:** cancellation fee imposed. **Amenities:** high-speed Internet (fee), voice mail, irons, hair dryers. **Guest Services:** valet laundry. **Cards:** AX, CB, DC, DS, MC, VI. **Special Amenities: free expanded continental breakfast and free local telephone calls.**

SOME UNITS

STATEHOUSE INN *Book at aaa.com* **Phone:** (208)342-4622

Small-scale Hotel

All Year 1P: $94-$109 2P: $104-$119 XP: $10 F

Location: At 10th and Grove sts; center. 981 Grove St 83702. Fax: 208/344-5751. **Facility:** 112 units. 107 one-bedroom standard units, some with whirlpools. 5 one-bedroom suites ($175-$250) with whirlpools. 6 stories, interior corridors. *Bath:* combo or shower only. **Parking:** on-site. **Terms:** [BP] meal plan available. **Amenities:** video library (fee), dual phone lines, voice mail, irons, hair dryers. **Leisure Activities:** sauna, whirlpool, exercise room. **Guest Services:** valet laundry. **Business Services:** meeting rooms, fax (fee). **Cards:** AX, CB, DC, DS, MC, VI.

SOME UNITS

ASK VCR DATA PORT

UNIVERSITY INN *Book at aaa.com* **Phone:** (208)345-7170

SAVE

Motel

6/1-10/31 [ECP] 1P: $59-$72 2P: $65-$78 XP: $6 F18

3/1-5/31 & 11/1-2/28 [ECP] 1P: $55-$68 2P: $61-$74 XP: $6 F18

Location: I-84, exit 53 (Vista Ave), 2.5 mi n. Located next to the university. 2360 University Dr 83706. Fax: 208/345-5118. **Facility:** 84 one-bedroom standard units, some with whirlpools. 1-2 stories (no elevator), exterior corridors. **Parking:** on-site. **Amenities:** *Some:* irons, hair dryers. **Pool(s):** heated outdoor. **Leisure Activities:** whirlpools. **Guest Services:** valet laundry. **Business Services:** meeting rooms, fax (fee). **Cards:** AX, CB, DC, DS, MC, VI.

SOME UNITS

DATA PORT VCR

The following lodging was either not evaluated or did not meet AAA rating requirements but is listed for your information only.

COMFORT SUITES AT AIRPORT **Phone:** 208/472-1222

fyi

Small-scale Hotel

All Year [ECP] 1P: $79-$99 2P: $89-$109 XP: $10 F18

Too new to rate. **Location:** I-84, exit 53 (Vista Ave), just n. 2906 Vista Ave 83705. Fax: 208/472-1210. **Amenities:** 83 units, coffeemakers, microwaves, refrigerators, pool. **Cards:** AX, CB, DC, DS, JC, MC, VI.

WHERE TO DINE

ANGELL'S BAR & GRILL **Lunch:** $9-$10 **Dinner:** $16-$30 **Phone:** 208/342-4900

American

Location: At 9th St; downtown. 999 Main St 83702. **Hours:** 11:30 am-close, Sat-Mon from 5 pm. Closed: 7/4, 12/25. **Reservations:** suggested. **Features:** With snug booths and a decor rich in woodwork and forest green, the cozy restaurant is reminiscent of an old-time gentleman's club. Creative specials share menu space with the customary steaks and chops at this award-winning spot, which was established in 1981. Casual dress; cocktails. **Parking:** on-site. **Cards:** AX, CB, DC, DS, JC, MC, VI.

BARDENAY **Lunch:** $4-$14 **Dinner:** $7-$14 **Phone:** 208/426-0538

International

Location: Downtown. 610 Grove St 83702. **Hours:** 11 am-10 pm, Thurs-Sat to midnight. Closed: 7/4, 11/25, 12/25. **Features:** The first in the country licensed to operate its own distillery, the large, popular restaurant serves a wide variety of dishes. Vodka, rum and gin are produced on the premises. The restaurant is appropriately named: Bardenay is a term sailors use loosely in place of the word "cocktail.". Casual dress; cocktails. **Parking:** street. **Cards:** AX, CB, DC, DS, MC, VI.

BOISE RIVER RAM & BIG HORN BREWING CO **Lunch:** $5-$14 **Dinner:** $5-$14 **Phone:** 208/345-2929

American

Location: I-84, exit 54 (Broadway Ave), 2.8 mi n. 709 E Park Blvd 83712. **Hours:** 11 am-2 am. Closed: 12/25. **Reservations:** accepted. **Features:** Close to Boise State University, this sports-oriented eatery features a variety of burgers, sandwiches, grilled chicken, pizza, fresh salad, steak and seafood. The service is attentive and knowledgeable. Casual dress; cocktails. **Parking:** on-site. **Cards:** AX, CB, DS, MC, VI.

CAZBA **Lunch:** $9-$14 **Dinner:** $12-$20 **Phone:** 208/381-0222

East Mediterranean

Location: Between Idaho and Bannock; downtown. 211 N 8th St 83702. **Hours:** 11 am-9:30 pm, Fri-10 pm, Sat 8 am-10 pm, Sun 8:30 am-9 pm. Closed: 5/31, 11/25, 12/25. **Reservations:** suggested. **Features:** While Greek dishes are prominent, the menu also lists a variety of Eastern Mediterranean offerings. Original sauces and seasoning combinations are subtle, distinctive and enjoyably flavorful. In addition to more traditional items, there are 14 types of wraps. The artistic decor and ambience are light, airy and relaxing. Casual dress; beer & wine only. **Parking:** street. **Cards:** AX, DS, MC, VI.

COTTONWOOD GRILLE **Lunch:** $6-$11 **Dinner:** $14-$21 **Phone:** 208/333-9800

American

Location: I-84, exit 53 (Vista Ave), 2.8 mi n, just w. 913 W River St 83702. **Hours:** 11 am-4 & 5-10 pm. Closed: 7/4, 12/25. **Reservations:** suggested. **Features:** The casually elegant restaurant serves contemporary American cuisine. Dishes are prepared with certified prime-grade beef, aged in house, and the freshest of local ingredients. Dressy casual; cocktails. **Parking:** on-site. **Cards:** AX, MC, VI.

EL CAZADOR MEXICAN GRILL **Lunch:** $4-$7 **Dinner:** $8-$12 **Phone:** 208/323-1801

Mexican

Location: I-184, exit Curtis Rd, just n, then w. 5900 Fairview Ave 83704. **Hours:** 11 am-10 pm, Fri & Sat-11 pm, Sun-9 pm. Closed: 11/25, 12/25. **Reservations:** accepted. **Features:** Travelers and young professionals are attracted to the traditional and distinctive Mexican dishes served in this festive, family-owned restaurant. House specials include chimichangas, tacos and fresh guacamole. The service staff is friendly and efficient. Casual dress; cocktails. **Parking:** on-site. **Cards:** AX, DS, MC, VI.

GAMEKEEPER RESTAURANT **Dinner:** $16-$60 **Phone:** 208/343-4611

Continental

Location: At 11th and Main sts; center; in Owyhee Plaza Hotel. 1109 Main St 83702. **Hours:** 5:30 pm-10 pm. Closed: 1/1, 12/25; also Sun. **Reservations:** suggested. **Features:** The varied menu includes an extensive selection of Continental and American entrees, such as rack of lamb, duck, seafood, steak, pepper steak and scampi. The crowd is lively in the lounge, quiet in the dining room. The service is impeccable. Dressy casual; cocktails. **Parking:** on-site. **Cards:** AX, MC, VI.

GOODWOOD BARBECUE COMPANY **Lunch:** $6-$18 **Dinner:** $6-$18 **Phone:** 208/658-7173

Barbecue

Location: I-84, exit 50A westbound; exit 50B eastbound, just s, then just w. 7849 W Spectrum 83709. **Hours:** 11 am-9:30 pm, Fri & Sat-10:30 pm, Sun-9 pm. Closed: 11/25, 12/25. **Reservations:** accepted. **Features:** The lively, casual, family-friendly restaurant specializes in traditional barbecue fare, as well as new twists on such old favorites as smoked prime rib. The menu lists comfort food at its best. Barbecue lovers shouldn't miss this place. Casual dress; cocktails. **Parking:** on-site. **Cards:** AX, MC, VI.

JJ NORTH'S GRAND BUFFET **Lunch:** $7 **Dinner:** $9 **Phone:** 208/375-7161

American

Location: I-184, exit 2, just n, 0.5 mi w. 6681 Fairview Ave 83704. **Hours:** 7 am-8:30 pm, Sat 8 am-9 pm, Sun 8 am-8 pm. **Features:** The numerous buffet bars run the gamut from entrees to salad to dessert and everything in between. Fresh, nicely presented and tasty food is consistent throughout. The service is prompt and helpful. A breakfast buffet is served on weekends. Casual dress. **Parking:** on-site. **Cards:** DS, MC, VI.

JOHNNY CARINO'S **Lunch:** $5-$9 **Dinner:** $8-$14 **Phone:** 208/373-4968

Italian

Location: I-84, exit 50A westbound; exit 50B eastbound, just s to Spectrum Rd, just w; in Boise Spectrum. 1700 S Entertainment Ave 83709. **Hours:** 11 am-10 pm, Fri & Sat-11 pm. Closed: 11/25, 12/25. **Features:** The restaurant invites guests to comfortable, casual dining in a simulated Italian country-style environment. Casual dress; beer & wine only. **Parking:** on-site. **Cards:** AX, CB, DC, DS, JC, MC, VI.

KOPPER KITCHEN **Lunch:** $5-$9 **Dinner:** $7-$13 **Phone:** 208/344-4271

American

Location: I-84, exit 53 (Vista Ave), just s. 2661 Airport Way 83705. **Hours:** 5 am-midnight. **Features:** In an appealing modern building with a shake roof, this three-meal restaurant appeals to travelers looking for a quick and convenient place to eat. The menu offers a full breakfast, sandwiches and several steak, chicken and pasta dishes. Casual dress; cocktails. **Parking:** on-site. **Cards:** AX, MC, VI.

KULTURE KLATSCH **Lunch:** $4-$8 **Dinner:** $6-$10 **Phone:** 208/345-0452

Vegetarian

Location: Between Myrtle and Front sts; downtown. 409 S 8th St 83702. **Hours:** 7 am-10 pm, Fri-11 pm, Sat 8 am-11 pm, Sun 8 am-3 pm, Mon 7 am-3 pm. Closed: 1/1, 11/25, 12/25. **Features:** The restaurant focuses on vegetarian dishes, a multicultural selection of natural food items and many varieties of beverages from the juice bar. Patrons should call ahead for the entertainment timing and billing so they don't miss the musical talent. Casual dress; beer & wine only; entertainment. **Parking:** street. **Cards:** MC, VI.

MCGRATH'S FISH HOUSE **Lunch:** $6-$13 **Dinner:** $8-$20 **Phone:** 208/375-6300

Seafood

Location: I-84, exit 50A westbound; exit 50B eastbound, just s, then just w. 1749 S Cole Rd 83709. **Hours:** 11 am-10 pm, Fri & Sat-11 pm. Closed: 11/25, 12/25. **Features:** The Pacific Northwest original is a favorite choice for seafood lovers. Widely varied menu selections, including freshly shucked oysters on the half shell and oyster shooters from the oyster bar, can satisfy any taste. Those who prefer seafood cooked can find a generous array of tastes on the platters. Other options are seafood with pasta or in classic combinations with steak or prime rib. Casual dress; cocktails. **Parking:** on-site. **Cards:** AX, CB, DC, DS, JC, MC, VI.

MILFORD'S FISH HOUSE **Dinner:** $18-$26 **Phone:** 208/342-8382

Steak & Seafood

Location: Corner of 8th and Broad sts; center. 825 Broad St 83702. **Hours:** 5 pm-10 pm, Sun & Mon-9 pm. Closed: 12/25. **Reservations:** suggested. **Features:** Northwestern seafood is served in this former railroad freight warehouse decorated with many antiques and interesting historic pieces from the early days of the city. Casual dress; cocktails. **Parking:** street. **Cards:** AX, DS, MC, VI.

MONGOLIAN BBQ **Lunch:** $5-$9 **Dinner:** $6-$10 **Phone:** 208/387-0393

Ethnic

Location: I-84, exit 54 (Broadway Ave), 1.7 mi n. 1808 Broadway Ave 83706. **Hours:** 10:45 am-9 pm, Fri & Sat-10 pm. Closed: 1/1, 11/25, 12/25; also Sun. **Features:** Mongolian stir-fry is featured as are fresh vegetables, noodles, beef, chicken and pork. Buffet selections are attractively displayed and cooked to order. Diners can rely on a helpful, attentive staff to help them with their questions and choices. Casual dress. **Parking:** on-site. **Cards:** DS, MC, VI.

MOON'S KITCHEN CAFE **Lunch:** $3-$8 **Phone:** 208/385-0472

American

Location: Between 8th and 9th sts; center. 815 W Bannock 83702. **Hours:** 7 am-3 pm, Sat 8 am-3:30 pm, Sun 9 am-2 pm. Closed major holidays. **Reservations:** accepted. **Features:** Step back in time to the 1950s when the traditional soda fountain and sandwich shop was the social gathering spot. This old-time eatery specializes in flavorful shakes, malts, sirloin burgers, chicken, sandwiches and big, home-style breakfasts. Casual dress. **Parking:** street. **Cards:** AX, MC, VI.

MORTIMER'S IDAHO CUISINE **Dinner:** $18-$26 **Phone:** 208/338-6550

Regional American

Location: Jct Main and 5th sts; downtown. 110 S 5th St 83702. **Hours:** 5 pm-10 pm. Closed major holidays; also Sun & Mon; 1st week of July. **Reservations:** suggested. **Features:** Menu preparations feature fresh local and regional ingredients, some from the chef's own carefully tended garden. A signature item is Idaho trout roulade: stuffed trout on a crisp potato cake. All dishes are expertly prepared and served in artfully arranged presentations. Also offered is a prix fixe tasting menu that introduces several dishes and flavors of the Northwest. All this takes place in the fine-dining environment of a historic stone building. Dressy casual; beer & wine only. **Parking:** street. **Cards:** AX, DC, MC, VI.

MURPHY'S SEAFOOD & STEAKHOUSE **Lunch:** $7-$14 **Dinner:** $10-$30 **Phone:** 208/344-3691

Steak & Seafood

Location: I-84, exit 54 (Broadway Ave), 2 mi n. 1555 Broadway Ave 83706. **Hours:** 11 am-11 pm, Sun 10 am-10 pm. **Reservations:** suggested. **Features:** Near Boise State University, the restaurant caters both to those looking for a fine-dining experience and those interested in a sports-bar setting. Patrons include an eclectic mix of families, students and travelers. The fine dining is provided in a large, richly appointed, mirror-lined room, while across the way an equally large sports bar thrives. Casual dress; cocktails. **Parking:** on-site. **Cards:** AX, DC, DS, MC, VI.

PIPER PUB & GRILL **Lunch:** $6-$15 **Dinner:** $6-$15 **Phone:** 208/343-2444

American

Location: At 8th and Main sts; center. 150 N 8th St, Suite 200 83702. **Hours:** 11 am-midnight, Sun 9 am-2 pm; closing hours may vary. Closed major holidays. **Features:** This congenial, nicely decorated downtown pub offers a large selection of appetizers, sandwiches and salad, along with two house specials: meatloaf sandwich and blue cheese/cracked pepper burgers. A bustling atmosphere predominates on Friday and Saturday. Casual dress; cocktails. **Parking:** street. **Cards:** AX, DC, DS, MC, VI.

BONNERS FERRY pop. 2,515

— WHERE TO STAY —

BEST WESTERN KOOTENAI RIVER INN & CASINO *Book at aaa.com* **Phone:** (208)267-8511

AAA SAVE

Small-scale Hotel

6/1-9/30	1P: $109-$119	2P: $109-$119	XP: $7	F18
5/1-5/31	1P: $89-$99	2P: $89-$99	XP: $7	F18
3/1-4/30 & 10/1-2/28	1P: $79-$89	2P: $79-$89	XP: $7	F18

Location: On US 95; city center. 7169 Plaza St 83805. Fax: 208/267-3744. **Facility:** 65 units. 64 one-bedroom standard units. 1 one-bedroom suite ($250-$350). 3 stories (no elevator), interior corridors. *Bath:* combo or shower only. **Parking:** on-site. **Amenities:** voice mail, safes, irons, hair dryers. **Dining:** 6 am-9 pm, Fri & Sat-10 pm; Sunday brunch, cocktails. **Pool(s):** small heated indoor. **Leisure Activities:** sauna, whirlpool, exercise room. *Fee:* game room. **Guest Services:** coin laundry. **Business Services:** conference facilities. **Cards:** AX, DS, MC, VI.

SOME UNITS

DATA PORT

BONNERS FERRY LOG INN **Phone:** 208/267-3986

AAA SAVE

Motel

6/1-9/30	1P: $56-$77	2P: $72-$77	XP: $8	F8
3/1-5/31 & 10/1-2/28	1P: $49-$65	2P: $60-$65	XP: $8	F8

Location: 2.5 mi n on US 95. HCR 85, Box 6 83805. Fax: 208/267-8687. **Facility:** 22 one-bedroom standard units. 1 story, exterior corridors. *Bath:* shower only. **Parking:** on-site, winter plug-ins. **Terms:** office hours 7 am-10 pm, [CP] meal plan available. **Leisure Activities:** whirlpool. **Guest Services:** gift shop. **Cards:** AX, DS, MC, VI. **Special Amenities: free continental breakfast and free local telephone calls.**

SOME UNITS

BURLEY pop. 9,316

— WHERE TO STAY —

BEST WESTERN BURLEY INN & CONVENTION CENTER *Book at aaa.com* **Phone:** (208)678-3501

AAA SAVE

Small-scale Hotel

6/1-9/30	1P: $60-$67	2P: $66-$73	XP: $6	F17
3/1-5/31 & 10/1-2/28	1P: $55-$62	2P: $60-$67	XP: $6	F17

Location: I-84, exit 208, just s. 800 N Overland Ave 83318. Fax: 208/678-9532. **Facility:** 126 units. 125 one-bedroom standard units. 1 one-bedroom suite. 2 stories (no elevator), interior/exterior corridors. *Bath:* combo or shower only. **Parking:** on-site. **Terms:** small pets only. **Amenities:** irons, hair dryers. **Dining:** 6 am-midnight, cocktails. **Pool(s):** outdoor, wading. **Leisure Activities:** whirlpool, playground, volleyball. **Guest Services:** valet and coin laundry. **Business Services:** conference facilities. **Cards:** AX, CB, DC, DS, MC, VI. **Special Amenities: free newspaper.**

SOME UNITS

DATA PORT VCR FEE FEE

BUDGET MOTEL **Phone:** (208)678-2200

AAA SAVE

Motel

6/1-9/30	1P: $50-$62	2P: $55-$68	XP: $6	F17
3/1-5/31 & 10/1-2/28	1P: $45-$55	2P: $50-$60	XP: $6	F17

Location: I-84, exit 208, just s. 900 N Overland Ave 83318. Fax: 208/677-2576. **Facility:** 139 one-bedroom standard units. 2 stories (no elevator), exterior corridors. *Bath:* combo or shower only. **Parking:** on-site, winter plug-ins. **Terms:** small pets only. **Pool(s):** small outdoor. **Leisure Activities:** whirlpool. **Guest Services:** valet and coin laundry. **Cards:** AX, CB, DC, DS, MC, VI.

SOME UNITS

DATA PORT

CALDWELL pop. 25,967

— WHERE TO STAY —

BEST WESTERN CALDWELL INN & SUITES *Book at aaa.com* **Phone:** (208)454-7225

AAA SAVE

Motel

All Year [ECP]	1P: $59-$149	2P: $64-$154	XP: $5	F12

Location: I-84, exit 29, just s. 908 Specht Ave 83605. Fax: 208/454-3522. **Facility:** 69 units. 66 one-bedroom standard units, some with whirlpools. 3 one-bedroom suites with whirlpools. 3 stories, interior corridors. *Bath:* combo or shower only. **Parking:** on-site, winter plug-ins. **Terms:** pets ($50 deposit, in smoking units, 3 day maximum). **Amenities:** voice mail, irons, hair dryers. *Some:* dual phone lines. **Pool(s):** heated indoor. **Leisure Activities:** whirlpool, exercise room. **Guest Services:** valet and coin laundry. **Business Services:** meeting rooms, business center. **Cards:** AX, CB, DC, DS, MC, VI.

SOME UNITS

FEE DATA PORT

LA QUINTA INN *Book at aaa.com* **Phone:** (208)454-2222

AAA SAVE

Motel

All Year	1P: $65-$120	2P: $65-$120	XP: $8	F18

Location: I-84, exit 29, just s. 901 Specht Ave 83605. Fax: 208/454-9334. **Facility:** 65 one-bedroom standard units, some with kitchens and/or whirlpools. 3 stories (no elevator), interior corridors. **Parking:** on-site, winter plug-ins. **Amenities:** irons, hair dryers. **Pool(s):** heated indoor, wading. **Leisure Activities:** whirlpool, exercise room. **Guest Services:** gift shop, valet and coin laundry. **Business Services:** meeting rooms, fax. **Cards:** AX, DC, DS, MC, VI. **Special Amenities: free expanded continental breakfast and free local telephone calls.**

SOME UNITS

DATA PORT FEE FEE

CASCADE pop. 997

WHERE TO STAY

The following lodging was either not evaluated or did not meet AAA rating requirements but is listed for your information only.

THE ASHLEY INN **Phone:** 208/382-5621

fyi

Not evaluated. **Location:** On SR 55. 500 N Main St 83611 (PO Box 777). Facilities, services, and decor characterize a mid-range property. *(See color ad below)*

COEUR D'ALENE pop. 34,514

WHERE TO STAY

AMERITEL INN ***Book at aaa.com*** **Phone:** (208)665-9000

Small-scale Hotel

All Year [ECP] 1P: $95-$120 2P: $95-$120 XP: $10 F18

Location: I-90, exit 12, just s. 333 Ironwood 83814. Fax: 208/665-9900. **Facility:** 118 units. 114 one-bedroom standard units, some with efficiencies. 4 one-bedroom suites with efficiencies. 4 stories, interior corridors. *Bath:* combo or shower only. **Parking:** on-site. **Amenities:** high-speed Internet, voice mail, irons, hair dryers. **Pool(s):** small heated indoor. **Leisure Activities:** whirlpool, exercise room. **Guest Services:** valet and coin laundry. **Business Services:** meeting rooms. **Cards:** AX, CB, DC, DS, MC, VI. *(See color ad p 186)*

ASK DATA PORT / SOME UNITS /

BEST WESTERN COEUR D'ALENE INN & CONFERENCE CENTER *Book at aaa.com* **Phone:** (208)765-3200

Small-scale Hotel

	1P	2P	XP	
6/16-9/15	1P: $99-$159	2P: $99-$159	XP: $10	F17
3/1-6/15	1P: $79-$149	2P: $79-$149	XP: $10	F17
9/16-2/28	1P: $79-$139	2P: $79-$139	XP: $10	F17

Location: I-90, exit 12, just nw. W 414 Appleway Ave 83814. Fax: 208/664-1962. **Facility:** 122 units. 121 one bedroom standard units, some with whirlpools. 1 one-bedroom suite. 2 stories (no elevator), interior corridors. *Bath:* combo or shower only. **Parking:** on-site, winter plug-ins. **Terms:** check-in 4 pm, cancellation fee imposed, pets ($10 extra charge). **Amenities:** video games (fee), high-speed Internet, voice mail, irons, hair dryers. *Some:* CD players. **Pool(s):** small heated indoor. **Leisure Activities:** whirlpool, exercise room. **Guest Services:** gift shop, valet laundry. **Business Services:** conference facilities. **Cards:** AX, CB, DC, DS, JC, MC, VI. ***(See color ad p 196)***

ASK FEE FEE DATA PORT / SOME UNITS /

COEUR D' ALENE BED & BREAKFAST **Phone:** 208/667-7527

Bed & Breakfast

	1P	2P	XP
3/1-10/31 [BP]	1P: $80-$100	2P: $80-$100	XP: $35
11/1-2/28 [BP]	1P: $68-$85	2P: $68-$85	XP: $30

Location: I-90, exit 13 via 3rd St, 1 mi to Foster Ave, just e. 906 Foster Ave 83814. **Facility:** This 1906 Colonial-style house features a Japanese-style spa gazebo with sliding windows in a private, enclosed garden offering mountain views. Designated smoking area. 4 one-bedroom standard units. 2 stories (no elevator), interior corridors. **Parking:** on-site, winter plug-ins. **Terms:** check-in 4 pm, cancellation fee imposed. **Leisure Activities:** sauna, whirlpool. **Guest Services:** complimentary evening beverages. **Cards:** MC, VI.

THE COEUR D'ALENE RESORT — Phone: (208)765-4000

Resort
Large-scale Hotel

All Year 1P: $99-$549 2P: $99-$549 XP: $10 F17

Location: I-90, exit 11, 2 mi s. 115 S 2nd St 83814 (PO Box 7200, 83816). Fax: 208/664-7276. **Facility:** This service-oriented lakefront resort's golf course features one offshore green. Designated smoking area. 336 units. 331 one-bedroom standard units, some with whirlpools. 5 one-bedroom suites, some with whirlpools. 3-17 stories, interior/exterior corridors. *Bath:* combo or shower only. **Parking:** on-site (fee) and valet. **Terms:** check-in 4 pm, 7 day cancellation notice-fee imposed, small pets only ($50 fee). **Amenities:** video games (fee), dual phone lines, voice mail, honor bars, irons, hair dryers. *Some:* CD players, high-speed Internet. **Dining:** Beverly's, see separate listing. **Pool(s):** heated outdoor, heated indoor, wading. **Leisure Activities:** sauna, whirlpools, steamroom, rental boats, marina, fishing, recreation programs, rental bicycles, spa. *Fee:* golf-18 holes, 4 lighted tennis courts, racquetball court, game room. **Guest Services:** gift shop, valet laundry, area transportation (fee). **Business Services:** conference facilities, business center. **Cards:** AX, CB, DC, DS, MC, VI.

ASK DATA PORT
FEE FEE

DAYS INN-COEUR D'ALENE *Book at aaa.com* — Phone: (208)667-8668

Small-scale Hotel

3/1-5/1 & 11/1-2/28	1P: $49-$109	2P: $49-$109	XP: $5	F18
5/2-8/31	1P: $97-$107	2P: $97-$107	XP: $5	F18
9/1-10/31	1P: $65-$70	2P: $65-$70	XP: $5	F18

Location: I-90, exit 11, just se. Located in a business park. 2200 Northwest Blvd 83814. Fax: 208/765-0933. **Facility:** 62 units. 60 one-bedroom standard units. 1 one- and 1 two-bedroom suites ($90-$160), some with efficiencies or kitchens. 2 stories (no elevator), interior corridors. *Bath:* combo or shower only. **Parking:** on-site, winter plug-ins. **Terms:** 30 day cancellation notice, weekly rates available, small pets only. **Amenities:** hair dryers. *Fee:* video library, safes. **Leisure Activities:** sauna, whirlpool, exercise room. **Business Services:** meeting rooms. **Cards:** AX, CB, DC, DS, JC, MC, VI.

SOME UNITS
ASK DATA PORT / VCR /
FEE

FAIRFIELD INN *Book at aaa.com* — Phone: (208)664-1649

Small-scale Hotel

5/1-9/30 [ECP]	1P: $89-$99
10/1-12/31 [ECP]	1P: $59-$79
3/1-4/30 & 1/1-2/28 [ECP]	1P: $59-$69

Location: I-90, exit 13, just n. 2303 N 4th 83814. Fax: 208/664-1649. **Facility:** 69 one-bedroom standard units. 3 stories, interior corridors. *Bath:* combo or shower only. **Parking:** on-site. **Amenities:** irons, hair dryers. **Pool(s):** small heated indoor. **Leisure Activities:** whirlpool. **Guest Services:** valet and coin laundry. **Cards:** AX, DC, DS, MC, VI.

SOME UNITS
ASK DATA PORT / /

FLAMINGO MOTEL — Phone: (208)664-2159

SAVE

Motel

6/1-9/20	1P: $69-$89	2P: $69-$99	XP: $5	F12
9/21-10/20	1P: $59-$69	2P: $59-$79	XP: $5	F12
3/1-5/31 & 10/21-2/28	1P: $49-$69	2P: $49-$79	XP: $5	F12

Location: I-90, exit 15 (Sherman Ave), 1.1 mi s. Located adjacent to city park. 718 Sherman Ave 83814. **Facility:** 13 units. 11 one- and 2 two-bedroom standard units, some with efficiencies or kitchens. 1 story, exterior corridors. **Parking:** on-site, winter plug-ins. **Terms:** 7 day cancellation notice-fee imposed. **Guest Services:** airport transportation (fee)-Spokane Airport. **Cards:** AX, DC, DS, MC, VI. **Special Amenities: free local telephone calls.**

SOME UNITS
/ /
FEE

GREGORY'S MCFARLAND HOUSE BED & BREAKFAST — Phone: 208/667-1232

Historic Bed & Breakfast

4/15-1/6 [BP]	1P: $115-$195	2P: $115-$195	XP: $45
3/1-4/14 & 1/7-2/28 [BP]	1P: $90-$150	2P: $90-$150	XP: $45

Location: I-90, exit 13, 1.3 mi s on 3rd St, then just e. Located in a quiet, residential area. 601 Foster Ave 83814. **Facility:** This historic Victorian house is on a shady, tree-lined street; a sun room features floral fabrics and white wicker furniture. Smoke free premises. 5 one-bedroom standard units. 2 stories (no elevator), interior corridors. **Parking:** street. **Terms:** office hours 3 pm-6 pm, 2 night minimum stay - seasonal, age restrictions may apply, 14 day cancellation notice-fee imposed. **Amenities:** video library. **Guest Services:** TV in common area. **Cards:** DS, MC, VI.

LA QUINTA INN *Book at aaa.com* — Phone: (208)765-5500

SAVE

Small-scale Hotel

6/1-8/31 [CP]	1P: $100-$160	2P: $100-$160
3/1-5/31 [CP]	1P: $70-$110	2P: $70-$110
12/1-2/28 [CP]	1P: $43-$83	2P: $43-$83
9/1-11/30 [CP]	1P: $60-$100	2P: $60

Location: I-90, exit 12, just ne. 280 W Appleway Ave 83814. Fax: 208/664-0433. **Facility:** 51 units. 50 one-bedroom standard units, some with efficiencies and/or whirlpools. 1 one-bedroom suite ($90-$160) with kitchen and whirlpool. 3 stories (no elevator), interior corridors. **Parking:** on-site, winter plug-ins. **Terms:** weekly rates available. **Amenities:** irons, hair dryers. **Pool(s):** small heated indoor. **Leisure Activities:** sauna, exercise room. **Guest Services:** gift shop, valet and coin laundry. **Business Services:** meeting rooms. **Cards:** AX, DC, DS, MC, VI. **Special Amenities: free continental breakfast and free local telephone calls.**

SOME UNITS
/ DATA PORT /

LA QUINTA INN & SUITES *Book at aaa.com* — Phone: (208)667-6777

SAVE

Small-scale Hotel

6/15-9/6	1P: $89-$179	2P: $89-$179
5/1-6/14	1P: $59-$99	2P: $59-$99
9/7-2/28	1P: $39-$99	2P: $39-$99
3/1-4/30	1P: $49-$89	2P: $49-$89

Location: I-90, exit 15 (Sherman Ave), just s. 2209 E Sherman Ave 83814. Fax: 208/769-7332. **Facility:** 62 one-bedroom standard units, some with efficiencies and/or whirlpools. 3 stories (no elevator), interior corridors. **Parking:** on-site. **Terms:** small pets only (in smoking units). **Amenities:** video library (fee), voice mail, irons, hair dryers. **Pool(s):** small heated indoor. **Leisure Activities:** sauna, hot soak pool, exercise room. **Guest Services:** valet and coin laundry. **Business Services:** meeting rooms, business center. **Cards:** AX, CB, DC, DS, JC, MC, VI. **Special Amenities: free expanded continental breakfast and free local telephone calls.**

SOME UNITS
DATA PORT / VCR /

RESORT CITY INN — **Phone:** 208/676-1225

AAA SAVE — Motel

3/1-9/14	1P: $69-$79	2P: $79-$89	XP: $10	F12
9/15-2/28	1P: $59	2P: $69	XP: $10	F12

Location: I-90, exit 11, 2.5 mi e via Northwest Blvd and Sherman Ave; downtown. 621 Sherman Ave 83814. Fax: 208/676-8757. **Facility:** 17 one-bedroom standard units. 2 stories (no elevator), exterior corridors. *Bath:* combo or shower only. **Parking:** on-site. **Terms:** office hours 7 am-10 pm, 14 day cancellation notice-fee imposed, weekly rates available, [CP] meal plan available. **Leisure Activities:** sun deck. **Cards:** DS, MC, VI. **Special Amenities: free continental breakfast and free newspaper.**

SOME UNITS / VCR /

RODEWAY INN PINES RESORT *Book at aaa.com* — **Phone:** (208)664-8244

AAA SAVE — Motel

6/14-9/5 [CP]	1P: $62-$90	2P: $71-$99	XP: $7	F16
3/1-6/13 [CP]	1P: $55-$73	2P: $59-$80	XP: $5	F16
9/6-10/31 [CP]	1P: $55-$73	2P: $59-$80	XP: $7	F16
11/1-2/28 [CP]	1P: $44-$52	2P: $50-$62	XP: $5	F16

Location: I-90, exit 11, 0.8 mi s. Located in a quiet area. 1422 Northwest Blvd 83814. Fax: 208/664-5547. **Facility:** 65 units. 58 one- and 7 two-bedroom standard units, some with whirlpools. 1-2 stories (no elevator), exterior corridors. **Parking:** on-site, winter plug-ins. **Terms:** office hours 7 am-11 pm, small pets only. **Pool(s):** small heated outdoor, small heated indoor. **Leisure Activities:** whirlpool. **Guest Services:** valet and coin laundry. **Cards:** AX, CB, DC, DS, JC, MC, VI. **Special Amenities: free continental breakfast and free local telephone calls.**

SOME UNITS / /

THE ROOSEVELT, A BED & BREAKFAST INN — **Phone:** 208/765-5200

AAA SAVE — Historic Bed & Breakfast

4/15-10/15 [BP]	1P: $109-$289	2P: $109-$289	XP: $20
3/1-4/14 & 10/16-2/28 [BP]	1P: $79-$199	2P: $79-$199	XP: $20

Location: I-90, exit 13, 2 mi s, then just w; downtown. 105 Wallace Ave 83814 (PO Box 2379, 83816). Fax: 208/664-4142. **Facility:** Shaded by towering pines, The Roosevelt is a 1905 red-brick schoolhouse complete with a bell tower. Smoke free premises. 12 units. 8 one- and 3 two-bedroom standard units. 1 one-bedroom suite. 3 stories, interior corridors. *Bath:* combo or shower only. **Parking:** on-site. **Terms:** age restrictions may apply, 14 day cancellation notice-fee imposed, pets ($25 extra charge). **Amenities:** CD players. **Leisure Activities:** sauna, whirlpool, limited exercise equipment. *Fee:* massage. **Guest Services:** TV in common area. **Business Services:** PC, fax. **Cards:** DS, MC, VI. **Special Amenities: free full breakfast and free local telephone calls.**

FEE FEE

SILVER LAKE MOTEL *Book at aaa.com* — **Phone:** (208)772-8595

Motel

7/1-9/30 [CP]	1P: $85-$95	2P: $95-$105	XP: $10	F12
5/1-6/30 [CP]	1P: $75-$85	2P: $85-$95	XP: $10	F12
3/1-4/30 & 10/1-2/28 [CP]	1P: $56-$60	2P: $60-$66	XP: $10	F12

Location: I-90, exit 12, 2.2 mi n. 6160 Sunshine St 83815. Fax: 208/772-2368. **Facility:** 49 one-bedroom standard units, some with kitchens and/or whirlpools. 2 stories (no elevator), exterior corridors. *Bath:* combo or shower only. **Parking:** on-site, winter plug-ins. **Terms:** check-in 4 pm, weekly rates available. **Amenities:** video library, voice mail. *Some:* DVD players (fee), hair dryers. **Pool(s):** small heated outdoor. **Leisure Activities:** whirlpool, exercise room. *Fee:* game room. **Guest Services:** valet and coin laundry. **Business Services:** meeting rooms. **Cards:** AX, CB, DC, DS, MC, VI.

SOME UNITS ASK DATA PORT / VCR / FEE

WHERE TO DINE

BEACHOUSE — **Lunch:** $5-$9 — **Dinner:** $11-$24 — **Phone:** 208/664-6464

American

Location: I-90, exit 15 (Sherman Ave), just s, then 1 mi e. 3204 E Coeur d'Alene Lake Dr 83814. **Hours:** 5 pm-10 pm, Fri & Sat 11:30 am-3 & 5-11 pm, Sun 11:30 am-3 & 5-10 pm; Wed & Thurs 5 pm-9 pm, Fri & Sat 5 pm-10 pm 11/1-3/31. Closed: 1/1, 12/24, 12/25. **Reservations:** suggested. **Features:** This eatery offers excellent views of the lake and marina, creating somewhat of a boathouse ambience. Breaded halibut with parmesan, garlic mashed potatoes and a veggie medley is a signature dish, but there's also a full menu of steak and barbecue. Casual dress; cocktails. **Parking:** on-site. **Cards:** AX, CB, DC, DS, MC, VI.

BEVERLY'S — **Lunch:** $8-$14 — **Dinner:** $22-$42 — **Phone:** 208/765-4000

Continental

Location: I-90, exit 11, 2 mi s; in The Coeur d'Alene Resort. 115 S 2nd St 83814. **Hours:** 11 am-2:30 & 5-10 pm. **Reservations:** suggested. **Features:** Located on the seventh floor of The Coeur d'Alene Resort, Beverly's serves tantalizing food in a sleek, casually elegant dining room with panoramic views of pristine Lake Coeur d'Alene. The seasonal menu takes advantage of the freshest Northwest seafood and local produce and complementing the dining experience is one of the finest wine cellars in the world. Casual dress; cocktails; entertainment. **Parking:** on-site. **Cards:** AX, CB, DC, DS, MC, VI.

THE CEDARS FLOATING RESTAURANT — **Lunch:** $9-$17 — **Dinner:** $18-$50 — **Phone:** 208/664-2922

Steak & Seafood

Location: I-90, exit 12, 1.5 mi s on US 95. No. 1 Marina Dr 83814. **Hours:** 11:30 am-3:30 & 5-9:30 pm. Closed: 11/25, 12/24, 12/25. **Reservations:** suggested. **Features:** Floating seafood and steak restaurant on Lake Coeur d' Alene. This restaurant weighs 1.2 million pounds. Large windows to take in the expansive view of the lake and forest. The house specialty is Biergarten steak - a filet mignon basted with beer. Casual dress; cocktails. **Parking:** on-site. **Cards:** AX, DC, DS, MC, VI.

CRICKET'S STEAKHOUSE & OYSTER BAR — **Lunch:** $5-$10 — **Dinner:** $9-$22 — **Phone:** 208/765-1990

Steak & Seafood

Location: Downtown. 424 Sherman Ave 83814. **Hours:** 11 am-9 pm; to 10 pm in summer. Closed: 11/25, 12/25. **Reservations:** suggested, in summer. **Features:** A model train running on an overhead track contributes to the eclectic decor of the fun and lively establishment. Prime rib, slow-roasted for five hours, is the signature dish. The fresh sheet for seafood changes daily. Oysters on the half shell are a specialty. Casual dress; cocktails. **Parking:** street. **Cards:** AX, DS, MC, VI.

LAS PALMITAS Lunch: $5-$7 Dinner: $7-$12 Phone: 208/664-0581

Mexican

Location: I-90, exit 11, 2 mi s, just e on Lakeside. 201 N 3rd 83814. **Hours:** 11 am-10 pm. Closed: 4/11, 11/25, 12/25. **Reservations:** suggested. **Features:** The festive, tropical atmosphere complements a truly creative menu, featuring traditional and some eclectic Mexican dishes. House specials include a variety of fajitas and crab enchiladas. The service is fast, efficient and friendly. Casual dress; cocktails. **Parking:** on-site. **Cards:** AX, DS, MC, VI.

MOON TIME **Lunch:** $6-$10 **Dinner:** $8-$14 **Phone:** 208/667-2331

International

Location: I-90, exit 18 (Sherman Ave), 0.5 mi s. 1602 Sherman Ave, #116 83814. **Hours:** 11 am-10 pm, Fri & Sat-11 pm. Closed: 11/25, 12/25; also Mon. **Features:** The informal restaurant has the feel of a neighborhood pub. With dishes ranging from gumbo and burritos to Caribbean pork sandwiches and vegetarian Anasazi bean burgers, the food is as eclectic as the restaurant itself. Casual dress; beer & wine only. **Parking:** on-site. **Cards:** MC, VI.

STONEGRILL AT JIMMY D'S **Lunch:** $7-$10 **Dinner:** $14-$21 **Phone:** 208/664-9774

American

Location: Downtown. 320 Sherman Ave 83814. **Hours:** 11 am-10 pm. Closed major holidays. **Reservations:** accepted. **Features:** The restaurant, which features sidewalk dining during summer, is a favorite for its chicken, seafood and beef dishes. Casual dress; beer & wine only. **Parking:** on-site (fee). **Cards:** AX, DS, MC, VI.

TOMATO STREET **Lunch:** $7-$8 **Dinner:** $8-$13 **Phone:** 208/667-5000

Italian

Location: I-90, exit 13, just n, then w. W 221 Appleway Ave 83814. **Hours:** 11:30 am-9 pm, Fri & Sat-10 pm; 11:30 am-10 pm, Fri & Sat-10:30 pm in summer. Closed: 11/25, 12/25. **Features:** This family-oriented, Italian market-style restaurant features brick-oven pizza, calzone, salad, sandwiches and traditional items. An attentive and efficient wait staff cheerfully dons outlandish headgear, which sets this eatery apart from the norm. Casual dress; beer & wine only. **Parking:** on-site. **Cards:** AX, DS, MC, VI.

THE WINE CELLAR **Dinner:** $8-$14 **Phone:** 208/664-9463

International

Location: Downtown. 313 Sherman Ave 83814. **Hours:** 4 pm-10 pm, Fri & Sat-midnight. Closed major holidays; also Sun. **Features:** The cozy, inviting basement bistro features unobtrusive live music. Guests can enjoy the varied but predominantly Italian cuisine or just drop in for entertainment and a glass of wine from the extensive list. Casual dress; beer & wine only. **Parking:** on-site. **Cards:** AX, DS, MC, VI.

The following restaurant has not been evaluated by AAA but is listed for your information only.

IRON HORSE **Phone:** 208/667-7314

fyi

Not evaluated. **Location:** 407 Sherman Ave 83815. **Features:** The family restaurant, appointed in a railroad theme, serves prime rib and seafood.

DRIGGS pop. 1,100—*See also GRAND TETON NATIONAL PARK.*

WHERE TO STAY

BEST WESTERN TETON WEST MOTEL *Book at aaa.com* **Phone:** 208/354-2363

AAA SAVE

Small-scale Hotel

5/23-9/29 & 12/24-2/28 [CP]	1P: $60-$100	2P: $70-$110	XP: $8	F12

Location: 0.7 mi n on SR 33. 476 N Main St 83422 (PO Box 780). Fax: 208/354-2962. **Facility:** 40 one-bedroom standard units, some with whirlpools. 2 stories (no elevator), interior corridors. **Parking:** on-site, winter plug-ins. **Terms:** open 5/23-9/29 & 12/24-2/28, small pets only ($25 deposit, in designated units). **Amenities:** irons, hair dryers. **Pool(s):** small heated indoor. **Leisure Activities:** whirlpool. **Guest Services:** coin laundry. **Business Services:** meeting rooms, fax (fee). **Cards:** AX, CB, DC, DS, MC, VI. **Special Amenities: free continental breakfast.**

SOME UNITS

FEE

INTERMOUNTAIN LODGE **Phone:** 208/354-8153

AAA SAVE

Cabin

6/16-9/16 [CP]	1P: $69-$74	2P: $69-$74	XP: $5
3/1-4/15 [CP]	1P: $59-$69	2P: $59-$69	XP: $5
9/17-2/28 [CP]	1P: $49-$69	2P: $49-$69	XP: $5
4/16-6/15 [CP]	1P: $49-$59	2P: $49-$59	XP: $5

Location: 0.8 mi e on Little Ave from SR 33 E. Located in a rustic area. 34 Ski Hill Rd 83422 (PO Box 468). Fax: 208/354-2998. **Facility:** Designated smoking area. 20 cabins. 1 story, exterior corridors. *Bath:* combo or shower only. **Parking:** on-site, winter plug-ins. **Amenities:** video library. **Leisure Activities:** whirlpool, picnic tables, volleyball. **Guest Services:** coin laundry. **Cards:** AX, DS, MC, VI. **Special Amenities: free continental breakfast and free local telephone calls.**

SOME UNITS

VCR

FEE

SUPER 8 TETON WEST **Phone:** 208/354-8888

AAA SAVE

Motel

7/1-8/25	1P: $85-$95	2P: $85-$95	XP: $8	F12
8/26-9/30	1P: $60-$70	2P: $70-$80	XP: $8	F12
10/1-2/28	1P: $46-$75	2P: $46-$75	XP: $8	F12
3/1-6/30	1P: $46-$56	2P: $56-$66	XP: $8	F12

Location: 1.3 mi n. 133 N SR 33 83422 (PO Box 780). Fax: 208/354-8953. **Facility:** 46 one-bedroom standard units, some with efficiencies and/or whirlpools. 2 stories, interior corridors. **Parking:** on-site, winter plug-ins. **Terms:** [CP] meal plan available. **Pool(s):** small heated indoor, wading. **Leisure Activities:** sauna, whirlpool. **Guest Services:** coin laundry. **Cards:** AX, CB, DC, DS, MC, VI. **Special Amenities: free continental breakfast and free local telephone calls.**

SOME UNITS

DATA PORT

EAGLE pop. 11,085

WHERE TO STAY

The following lodging was either not evaluated or did not meet AAA rating requirements but is listed for your information only.

HILTON GARDEN INN-BOISE/EAGLE **Phone:** 208/938-9600

fyi

Small-scale Hotel

All Year 1P: $89-$139 2P: $89-$139 XP: $10 F18

Too new to rate, opening scheduled for October 2003. **Location:** I-84, exit 46 (Eagle Rd), 7 mi n, then e. 145 E Riverside Dr 83616. Fax: 208/938-5200. **Amenities:** 97 units, coffeemakers, microwaves, refrigerators, pool. **Cards:** AX, CB, DC, DS, MC, VI.

GIBBONSVILLE

WHERE TO DINE

THE GARDEN CAFE **Lunch:** $5-$9 **Dinner:** $10-$18 **Phone:** 208/865-2222

American

Location: SR 93, MM 336. 3099 Hwy 93 83463. **Hours:** 7 am-8 pm, Sun 8 am-6 pm. Closed major holidays; also Mon. **Features:** You'll enjoy this all around family restaurant specializing in pasta dishes and homemade potato chips. Your delicious meal will be enhanced by the setting of this cafe, which is located in the foothills of the beautiful Lemhi Mountain Range. So, whether you're steelheading, hunting, or just passing through, once you've drunk in mother nature, come drink and dine in this homey cafe. Casual dress; beer & wine only. **Parking:** on-site.

AC

GLENNS FERRY pop. 1,611

WHERE TO DINE

CARMELA VINEYARDS RESTAURANT **Lunch:** $5-$14 **Dinner:** $11-$30 **Phone:** 208/366-2313

American

Location: I-84, exit 120, 0.5 mi s to Bannock, 0.4 mi e to Commercial, 0.5 mi s to Madison Ave, then 0.7 mi w. 1289 W Madison Ave 83623. **Hours:** 11 am-9 pm, Sun 10 am-8 pm. Closed major holidays. **Reservations:** suggested, weekends. **Features:** This castle-like restaurant sits on a bluff just off the river and is surrounded by picturesque grape arbors. The dining room is comfortable, bright and well appointed, and the food tasty and fresh. Steak, seafood and pasta are dinner menu mainstays. Casual dress; cocktails. **Parking:** on-site. **Cards:** AX, DC, DS, MC, VI.

GRANGEVILLE pop. 3,228

WHERE TO STAY

DOWN TOWNER INN **Phone:** (208)983-1110

AAA SAVE

Motel

All Year 1P: $39-$48 2P: $44-$52 XP: $3 F12

Location: 0.5 mi e on SR 13 from jct at US 95, just n on Hall St, then just e. 113 E North St 83530. **Facility:** 16 one-bedroom standard units. 1 story, exterior corridors. **Parking:** on-site, winter plug-ins. **Terms:** weekly rates available. **Cards:** AX, DS, MC, VI. **Special Amenities: free local telephone calls and early check-in/late check-out.**

SOME UNITS

MONTY'S MOTEL **Phone:** 208/983-2500

AAA SAVE

Motel

6/1-10/31 1P: $45-$50 2P: $50-$55 XP: $4 F5

3/1-5/31 & 11/1-2/28 1P: $42-$47 2P: $46-$51 XP: $4 F5

Location: Jct SR 13 and US 95. W 700 Main 83530. Fax: 208/983-1458. **Facility:** 23 one-bedroom standard units. 2 stories (no elevator), exterior corridors. *Bath:* combo or shower only. **Parking:** on-site. **Terms:** office hours 7 am-10 pm, [ECP] meal plan available, small pets only. **Pool(s):** heated outdoor. **Cards:** AX, DC, DS, MC, VI. **Special Amenities: free continental breakfast and free local telephone calls.**

SOME UNITS

SUPER 8 MOTEL **Phone:** 208/983-1002

Small-scale Hotel

4/1-9/30 1P: $64-$115 2P: $68-$128 XP: $5 F17

10/1-2/28 1P: $60-$112 2P: $67-$125 XP: $5 F17

3/1-3/31 1P: $58-$110 2P: $65-$122 XP: $5 F17

Location: Jct SR 95 and 13. 801 SW 1st St 83530. Fax: 208/983-1995. **Facility:** 39 units. 38 one-bedroom standard units. 1 one-bedroom suite with whirlpool. 3 stories, interior corridors. *Bath:* combo or shower only. **Parking:** on-site, winter plug-ins. **Terms:** pets ($10 extra charge). **Pool(s):** heated indoor. **Leisure Activities:** whirlpool, exercise room. **Guest Services:** coin laundry. **Business Services:** meeting rooms, business center. **Cards:** AX, DC, DS, MC, VI.

SOME UNITS

ASK FEE DATA PORT

HAGERMAN pop. 656

WHERE TO STAY

HAGERMAN VALLEY INN **Phone:** (208)837-6196

Motel

All Year 1P: $48-$52 2P: $48-$52

Location: South end of town on US 30. 661 Frog's Landing 83332 (PO Box 480). **Facility:** 16 one-bedroom standard units. 2 stories (no elevator), interior/exterior corridors. **Parking:** on-site. **Terms:** cancellation fee imposed, weekly rates available, pets ($5 extra charge). **Business Services:** meeting rooms. **Cards:** MC, VI. **Special Amenities: free local telephone calls.**

SOME UNITS

FEE

WHERE TO DINE

SNAKE RIVER GRILL & RESTAURANT **Lunch:** $4-$6 **Dinner:** $5-$15 **Phone:** 208/837-6227

American

Location: South end of town on US 30. 611 Frog's Landing 83332. **Hours:** 7 am-9:30 pm, Fri & Sat-10 pm, Sun-9 pm, Mon-2 pm. Closed: 1/1, 12/25. **Reservations:** accepted. **Features:** This rustic restaurant is located in a small town and very near the Snake River. This three-meal restaurant will appeal to the traveling family. However, with the owner doing the cooking, it will also appeal to the stout hearted as they offer distinct wild game dinners, where you provide the game. Casual dress; beer & wine only. **Parking:** on-site. **Cards:** DS, MC, VI.

HAILEY pop. 6,200

WHERE TO STAY

AIRPORT INN **Phone:** (208)788-2477

Motel

All Year 1P: $78-$105 2P: $78-$110 XP: $8 F12

Location: Just n of SR 75 at 4th Ave; near airport. Located adjacent to Wood River Trail System. 820 4th Ave S 83333 (PO Box 984). Fax: 208/788-3195. **Facility:** 29 units. 28 one-bedroom standard units, some with efficiencies. 1 one-bedroom suite. 1-2 stories (no elevator), exterior corridors. **Parking:** on-site, winter plug-ins. **Terms:** office hours 7 am-10 pm, 7 day cancellation notice, [CP] meal plan available, pets ($5 extra charge, in smoking units). **Amenities:** high-speed Internet (fee), voice mail. **Leisure Activities:** whirlpool. **Guest Services:** coin laundry. **Cards:** AX, DC, DS, MC, VI.

FEE DATA PORT / SOME UNITS VCR / FEE

WOOD RIVER INN **Phone:** (208)578-0600

Small-scale Hotel

All Year [ECP] 1P: $92-$97 2P: $92-$97 XP: $10 F18

Location: Just n of downtown on SR 75. 603 N Main 83333. Fax: 208/578-0700. **Facility:** 56 units. 44 one-bedroom standard units. 12 one-bedroom suites ($119-$149), some with efficiencies and/or whirlpools. 3 stories, interior corridors. *Bath:* combo or shower only. **Parking:** on-site, winter plug-ins. **Terms:** office hours 6 am-11 pm, pets ($25 fee). **Amenities:** hair dryers. **Pool(s):** small heated indoor. **Leisure Activities:** whirlpool. **Guest Services:** coin laundry. **Business Services:** meeting rooms, fax (fee). **Cards:** AX, DC, DS, MC, VI.

ASK FEE DATA PORT SOME UNITS / /

HEYBURN pop. 2,899

WHERE TO STAY

SUPER 8 - BURLEY **Phone:** 208/678-7000

Small-scale Hotel

4/1-6/30	1P: $50-$86	2P: $58-$86	XP: $5	F12
7/1-9/30	1P: $61-$66	2P: $67-$71	XP: $5	F12
3/1-3/31 & 10/1-2/28	1P: $50-$54	2P: $56-$59	XP: $5	F12

Location: I-84, exit 208, just n. 336 S 600 W 83336. Fax: 208/678-8003. **Facility:** 68 one-bedroom standard units. 3 stories, interior corridors. *Bath:* combo or shower only. **Parking:** on-site. **Terms:** pets ($5 extra charge). **Pool(s):** heated outdoor. **Leisure Activities:** whirlpool. **Guest Services:** coin laundry. **Business Services:** meeting rooms. **Cards:** AX, CB, DS, MC, VI.

ASK FEE DATA PORT / SOME UNITS / FEE

IDAHO CITY pop. 458

WHERE TO STAY

A ONE STEP AWAY B&B LODGING **Phone:** 208/392-4938

Historic Bed & Breakfast

All Year [BP] 1P: $45-$65 2P: $50-$90 XP: $20 F10

Location: Just w of SR 21; center. 112 Cottonwood St 83631 (PO Box 55). Fax: 208/392-4938. **Facility:** This 102-year-old building in a small mountain community began as a dredging company's workplace. Smoke free premises. 4 one-bedroom standard units. 1-2 stories (no elevator), exterior corridors. *Bath:* combo or shower only. **Parking:** on-site. **Terms:** age restrictions may apply, 31 day cancellation notice-fee imposed, weekly rates available. **Amenities:** hair dryers. **Leisure Activities:** fishing, cross country skiing, hiking trails, jogging. **Guest Services:** complimentary evening beverages. **Business Services:** fax. **Cards:** AX, DS, MC, VI.

VCR

IDAHO FALLS pop. 50,730

WHERE TO STAY

AMERITEL INN *Book at aaa.com* **Phone:** (208)523-1400

Small-scale Hotel

All Year [ECP] 1P: $89-$119 2P: $99-$129 XP: $10 F18

Location: I-15, exit 118 (Broadway), 0.4 mi e, then just n on Lindsay Blvd; exit 119, 0.4 mi se. 645 Lindsay Blvd 83402. Fax: 208/523-0004. **Facility:** 126 units. 122 one-bedroom standard units, some with whirlpools. 4 one-bedroom suites with efficiencies. 4 stories, interior corridors. *Bath:* combo or shower only. **Parking:** on-site, winter plug-ins. **Terms:** cancellation fee imposed. **Amenities:** video games, high-speed Internet, dual phone lines, voice mail, irons, hair dryers. **Pool(s):** heated indoor. **Leisure Activities:** whirlpool, exercise room. **Guest Services:** valet and coin laundry. **Business Services:** meeting rooms. **Cards:** AX, DC, DS, MC, VI. ***(See color ad p 186)***

ASK DATA PORT / SOME UNITS VCR /

AMERITEL INN-IDAHO FALLS SPECTRUM Book at aaa.com **Phone:** (208)552-2500

Small-scale Hotel

5/16-9/15	1P: $119-$129	2P: $119-$129	XP: $10	F12
3/1-5/15 & 9/16-2/28	1P: $84-$94	2P: $84-$94	XP: $10	F12

Location: I-15, exit 118 (Broadway), 1 mi e, 0.5 mi s on Yellowstone, 3.8 mi e on 17th St to Hitt Rd, then just s. 2501 S 25th St E 83406 (10200 W Emerald St, BOISE, 83704). Fax: 208/524-0025. **Facility:** 84 units. 71 one- and 1 two-bedroom standard units, some with efficiencies. 12 one-bedroom suites, some with whirlpools. 3 stories, interior corridors. *Bath:* combo or shower only. **Parking:** on-site, winter plug-ins. **Terms:** [ECP] meal plan available. **Amenities:** high-speed Internet, voice mail, irons, hair dryers. **Pool(s):** heated indoor. **Leisure Activities:** whirlpool, exercise room. **Guest Services:** valet and coin laundry. **Business Services:** meeting rooms, fax (fee). **Cards:** AX, CB, DC, DS, MC, VI.

ASK DATA PORT

BEST WESTERN COTTONTREE INN Book at aaa.com **Phone:** 208/523-6000

SAVE

Small-scale Hotel

6/1-8/31 [ECP]	1P: $69-$99	2P: $69-$99	XP: $8	F18
3/1-5/31 & 9/1-2/28 [ECP]	1P: $59-$89	2P: $59-$89	XP: $8	F18

Location: I-15, exit 119, just e. 900 Lindsay Blvd 83402. Fax: 208/523-0000. **Facility:** 93 units. 92 one-bedroom standard units, some with efficiencies and/or whirlpools. 1 one-bedroom suite with efficiency. 3 stories, interior corridors. **Parking:** on-site, winter plug-ins. **Terms:** 30 day cancellation notice. **Amenities:** irons, hair dryers. **Pool(s):** heated indoor. **Leisure Activities:** whirlpool, exercise room. **Guest Services:** valet and coin laundry, airport transportation-Fanning Field Airport. **Business Services:** meeting rooms. **Cards:** AX, CB, DC, DS, MC, VI. **Special Amenities: free expanded continental breakfast and free newspaper.**

SOME UNITS

DATA PORT / /

BEST WESTERN DRIFTWOOD INN Book at aaa.com **Phone:** (208)523-2242

SAVE

Small-scale Hotel

5/16-9/30	1P: $79-$119	2P: $79-$119	XP: $8	F18
10/1-2/28	1P: $65-$89	2P: $69-$89		
3/1-5/15	1P: $65-$89	2P: $69-$89	XP: $5	F18

Location: I-15, exit 118 (Broadway), 0.5 mi e, then 0.3 mi n. 575 River Pkwy 83402. Fax: 208/523-0316. **Facility:** 74 units. 59 one-bedroom standard units. 13 one- and 2 two-bedroom suites ($69-$129) with kitchens, some with whirlpools. 2 stories (no elevator), exterior corridors. *Bath:* combo or shower only. **Parking:** on-site, winter plug-ins. **Terms:** [ECP] meal plan available, package plans - seasonal, small pets only ($3-$10 extra charge). **Amenities:** voice mail, irons, hair dryers. **Pool(s):** heated outdoor. **Leisure Activities:** bicycles, exercise room. **Guest Services:** valet and coin laundry, airport transportation-Fanning Field Airport. **Business Services:** conference facilities, PC. **Cards:** AX, CB, DC, DS, JC, MC, VI. **Special Amenities: free expanded continental breakfast and free room upgrade (subject to availability with advanced reservations).** *(See color ad below)*

SOME UNITS

FEE DATA PORT / /

COMFORT INN Book at aaa.com **Phone:** 208/528-2804

Small-scale Hotel

5/1-9/30	1P: $69-$89	2P: $69-$89	XP: $5	F18
3/1-4/30 & 10/1-12/31	1P: $64-$84	2P: $64-$84	XP: $5	F18
1/1-2/28	1P: $59-$79	2P: $59-$79	XP: $5	F18

Location: I-15, exit 118 (Broadway), just w to Colorado Ave, then just s. 195 S Colorado Ave 83402. Fax: 208/522-3083. **Facility:** 56 one-bedroom standard units, some with whirlpools. 2 stories (no elevator), interior corridors. *Bath:* combo or shower only. **Parking:** on-site, winter plug-ins. **Terms:** 14 day cancellation notice, [ECP] meal plan available, pets ($10 fee). **Amenities:** safes, irons, hair dryers. **Pool(s):** small heated indoor. **Leisure Activities:** whirlpool. **Guest Services:** valet and coin laundry. **Business Services:** fax (fee). **Cards:** AX, CB, DC, DS, JC, MC, VI.

SOME UNITS

ASK FEE DATA PORT / /

FAIRFIELD INN & SUITES BY MARRIOTT *Book at aaa.com* **Phone:** (208)552-7378

Small-scale Hotel

All Year 1P: $79 2P: $129

Location: I-15, exit 118 (city center/Broadway); just e. 1293 W Broadway St 83402. Fax: 208/552-7379. **Facility:** 81 one-bedroom standard units, some with whirlpools. 3 stories, interior corridors. *Bath:* combo or shower only. **Parking:** on-site, winter plug-ins. **Amenities:** video games, high-speed Internet, dual phone lines, voice mail, irons, hair dryers. *Some:* CD players. **Pool(s):** heated outdoor. **Leisure Activities:** whirlpool, exercise room. **Guest Services:** valet and coin laundry. **Business Services:** meeting rooms, business center. **Cards:** AX, CB, DC, DS, MC, VI.

SOME UNITS

ASK / DATA PORT / /

HAMPTON INN *Book at aaa.com* **Phone:** (208)529-9800

Small-scale Hotel

5/28-9/7	1P: $74-$84	2P: $84-$94
9/8-2/28	1P: $69-$79	2P: $84-$94
3/1-5/27	1P: $69-$79	2P: $79-$89

Location: I-15, exit 118 (Broadway), 1 mi e, 0.5 mi s on Yellowstone, 2.8 mi e on 17th St, then just s. Located next to a shopping mall. 2500 Channing Way 83404. Fax: 208/529-9455. **Facility:** 63 one-bedroom standard units, some with whirlpools. 3 stories, interior corridors. *Bath:* combo or shower only. **Parking:** on-site, winter plug-ins. **Terms:** [ECP] meal plan available. **Amenities:** high-speed Internet, voice mail, irons, hair dryers. **Pool(s):** small heated indoor. **Leisure Activities:** whirlpool, exercise room. **Guest Services:** valet and coin laundry, area transportation. **Business Services:** meeting rooms, fax (fee). **Cards:** AX, DC, DS, MC, VI.

SOME UNITS

ASK / DATA PORT / /

LE RITZ HOTEL & SUITES *Book at aaa.com* **Phone:** (208)528-0880

Small-scale Hotel

All Year	1P: $69-$99	2P: $69-$99	XP: $5	F18

Location: I-15, exit 118 (Broadway), 0.5 mi e, then just n. 720 Lindsay Blvd 83402. Fax: 208/528-9929. **Facility:** 130 units. 121 one-bedroom standard units, some with whirlpools. 9 one-bedroom suites ($189-$209). 2 stories (no elevator), interior corridors. **Parking:** on-site, winter plug-ins. **Terms:** cancellation fee imposed, small pets only. **Amenities:** high-speed Internet, dual phone lines, voice mail, irons, hair dryers. **Pool(s):** heated indoor. **Leisure Activities:** whirlpool, exercise room. **Guest Services:** complimentary evening beverages, valet and coin laundry. **Business Services:** meeting rooms, business center. **Cards:** AX, DC, DS, MC, VI. **Special Amenities: free expanded continental breakfast and free local telephone calls.**

SOME UNITS

NATIONAL 9 EXECUTIVE INN **Phone:** (208)523-6260

Small-scale Hotel

5/16-9/15 [BP]	1P: $59-$89	2P: $65-$95	XP: $7	F12
9/16-2/28 [BP]	1P: $52-$65	2P: $62-$75	XP: $7	F12
3/1-5/15 [BP]	1P: $49-$59	2P: $55-$65	XP: $7	F12

Location: I-15, exit 119, just e. 850 Lindsay Blvd 83402 (2285 S Main, Suite 9, SALT LAKE CITY, UT, 84115). Fax: 208/522-8840. **Facility:** 125 units. 124 one-bedroom standard units, some with whirlpools. 1 one-bedroom suite with kitchen. 2 stories (no elevator), interior/exterior corridors. **Parking:** on-site, winter plug-ins. **Terms:** weekly rates available, small pets only ($10 extra charge). **Amenities:** video library (fee), hair dryers. *Some:* irons. **Dining:** 6 am-1 pm, cocktails. **Pool(s):** heated outdoor. **Leisure Activities:** whirlpool. **Guest Services:** coin laundry. **Business Services:** meeting rooms, fax (fee). **Cards:** AX, CB, DC, DS, JC, MC, VI. **Special Amenities: free full breakfast and free newspaper.** *(See color ad p 204)*

SOME UNITS

FEE FEE

RED LION HOTEL ON THE FALLS *Book at aaa.com* **Phone:** (208)523-8000

Small-scale Hotel

All Year	1P: $89-$109	2P: $89-$109	XP: $10	F17

Location: I-15, exit 118 (Broadway), 0.5 mi e, then just n. 475 River Pkwy 83402. Fax: 208/529-9610. **Facility:** 138 units. 137 one-bedroom standard units. 1 one-bedroom suite ($300). 2-8 stories, interior/exterior corridors. *Bath:* combo or shower only. **Parking:** on-site, winter plug-ins. **Terms:** [BP] meal plan available, package plans, small pets only. **Amenities:** video games (fee), irons, hair dryers. **Pool(s):** heated outdoor. **Leisure Activities:** sauna, whirlpool, exercise room. **Guest Services:** valet and coin laundry. **Business Services:** conference facilities, fax (fee). **Cards:** AX, DC, DS, MC, VI. *(See color ad p 204)*

SOME UNITS

ASK

TOWNE LODGE **Phone:** (208)523-2960

Motel

6/1-9/10	1P: $50-$65	2P: $55-$70	XP: $5	F12
3/1-5/31 & 9/11-2/28	1P: $40-$48	2P: $48-$58	XP: $5	F12

Location: I-15, exit 118 (Broadway), 0.6 mi e, just n on Memorial, then just e; from US 20 N, exit city center to E St; from US 26 (N Yellowstone) to E St. 255 E St 83402. Fax: 208/523-2960. **Facility:** 40 one-bedroom standard units. 2 stories (no elevator), interior/exterior corridors. *Bath:* combo or shower only. **Parking:** on-site, winter plug-ins. **Business Services:** fax (fee). **Cards:** AX, DC, MC, VI. **Special Amenities: free continental breakfast and free local telephone calls.**

SOME UNITS

WHERE TO DINE

BROWNSTONE RESTAURANT **Lunch:** $8-$18 **Dinner:** $8-$18 **Phone:** 208/535-0310

American

Location: I-15, exit 118 (Broadway), 0.5 mi e to River Pkwy, then just n. 455 River Pkwy 83402. **Hours:** 11:30 am-10 pm. **Features:** A good variety of Western American cuisine is served at this brew pub amid an attractive setting overlooking the falls. Friendly, informal service prevails. Polished steel and copper brewing tanks are all part of the decor. Brewery tours are available. Casual dress; cocktails. **Parking:** on-site. **Cards:** AX, DC, DS, MC, VI.

JJ NORTH'S GRAND BUFFET **Lunch:** $6 **Dinner:** $8 **Phone:** 208/529-0181

American

Location: I-15, exit 118 (Broadway), 0.9 mi e, 0.5 mi s on Yellowstone, then 3 mi e on 17th; northeast corner of Grand Teton Mall parking lot. 2450 E 17th St 83404. **Hours:** 11 am-8:30 pm, Fri-9 pm, Sat 8:30 am-9 pm, Sun 8:30 am-11:30 & noon-8 pm. **Features:** This good value, family-friendly establishment, features a home-style buffet spread providing something to suit everyone's tastes, even children. Saturday and Sunday there is a voluminous breakfast buffet. Casual dress. **Parking:** on-site. **Cards:** AX, DC, DS, MC, VI.

MELINA'S MEXICAN RESTAURANT **Lunch:** $5-$10 **Dinner:** $5-$10 **Phone:** 208/524-5430

Mexican

Location: I-15, exit 118 (Broadway), 0.8 mi e, 0.5 mi n on Yellowstone, then just e. 187 E First St 83401. **Hours:** 11 am-9 pm, Fri & Sat-10 pm. Closed major holidays; also Sun. **Features:** If you're in search of good Mexican food, you've come to the right place. Traditional dishes are served in a festive, family atmosphere. A typical selection includes chips with two salsas, soup, a hearty burrito, plus rice and beans. Service is courteous. Casual dress. **Parking:** on-site. **Cards:** AX, MC, VI.

RUTABAGA'S RESTAURANT **Lunch:** $6-$9 **Dinner:** $14-$22 **Phone:** 208/529-3990

International

Location: I-15, exit 118 (Broadway), 0.5 mi e to River Pkwy, then just n. 415 River Pkwy 83402. **Hours:** 5 pm-9 pm, Fri also 11 am-2 pm, Sun 10 am-2 pm. Closed major holidays; also Mon & first two weeks of Jan. **Reservations:** suggested. **Features:** The chef owns this small, intimate bistro, which benefits from a warm atmosphere, friendly service and colorful preparations of well-presented international cuisine. Daily specials are tantalizing and imaginative. Casual dress; beer & wine only. **Parking:** on-site. **Cards:** AX, DS, MC, VI.

THE SANDPIPER — Dinner: $8-$27 — Phone: 208/524-3344

Steak & Seafood

Location: I-15, exit 119, just e. 750 Lindsay Blvd 83402. **Hours:** 4 pm-11 pm. Closed major holidays. **Reservations:** accepted. **Features:** This small-town, locally popular restaurant, adjacent to the Snake River, serves immense amounts of food. For starters, try the tasty pan-fried oysters, then move on to an entree of hearty barbecued ribs. Seasonal patio dining is also available. Casual dress; cocktails. **Parking:** on-site. **Cards:** AX, DS, MC, VI.

SNAKE BITE RESTAURANT — **Lunch:** $5-$9 — **Dinner:** $5-$16 — **Phone:** 208/525-2522

American

Location: I-15, exit 118 (Broadway), 0.5 mi e to River Pkwy, just n. 425 River Pkwy 83402. **Hours:** 11 am-2 & 5-9 pm. Closed: Sun & Mon. **Features:** The contemporary decor and notable food are nice departures from the endless supply of fast food outlets in the area. There's a large selection of sandwiches and soup, along with some full entrees. Service is friendly. Counter service is available. Casual dress; beer & wine only. **Parking:** on-site. **Cards:** DS, MC, VI.

THAI HOUSE — **Lunch:** $5-$8 — **Dinner:** $7-$12 — **Phone:** 208/529-2754

Thai

Location: I-15, exit 118 (city center/Broadway), 1 mi e, then just n. 366 Shoup Ave 83402. **Hours:** 11 am-9 pm. Closed major holidays; also Sun. **Features:** You'll find authentic cuisine served in hearty portions at this downtown eatery. The food is prepared to your desired level of spiciness and always brought to the table by a friendly waitstaff. Casual dress. **Parking:** street. **Cards:** AX, DC, MC, VI.

ISLAND PARK pop. 215

WHERE TO STAY

SAWTELLE MOUNTAIN RESORT — **Phone:** 208/558-9366

AAA SAVE

5/16-9/9	1P: $53-$74	2P: $58-$74	XP: $5	F12
12/21-2/28	1P: $48-$71	2P: $53-$71	XP: $5	F12
9/10-12/20	1P: $43-$59	2P: $48-$59	XP: $5	F12
3/1-5/15	1P: $39-$57	2P: $44-$57	XP: $5	F12

Small-scale Hotel

Location: On US 20 between MM 394 and 395, corner of US 20 and Sawtelle Park Rd. Located in the Targhee National Forest. 4133 Lodge Pole 83429 (PO Box 338). Fax: 208/558-9769. **Facility:** 38 one-bedroom standard units, some with kitchens (no utensils). 1-3 stories (no elevator), interior/exterior corridors. *Bath:* combo or shower only. **Parking:** on-site, winter plug-ins. **Amenities:** video library (fee). **Pool(s):** small heated indoor. **Leisure Activities:** whirlpool, large deck, picnic pavilion. **Guest Services:** gift shop, coin laundry. **Business Services:** meeting rooms. **Cards:** AX, DS, MC, VI.

/ SOME UNITS / VCR FEE /

JEROME pop. 7,780

WHERE TO STAY

BEST WESTERN SAWTOOTH INN AND SUITES — *Book at aaa.com* — **Phone:** (208)324-9200

AAA SAVE

6/1-9/30 [ECP]	1P: $79-$89	2P: $89-$99	XP: $10	F18
3/1-5/31 & 10/1-2/28 [ECP]	1P: $69-$79	2P: $79-$89	XP: $10	F18

Small-scale Hotel

Location: I-84, exit 168, just n on SR 79. 2653 S Lincoln 83338. Fax: 208/324-9292. **Facility:** 67 units. 63 one-bedroom standard units, some with whirlpools. 3 one- and 1 two-bedroom suites ($79-$200), some with whirlpools. 2 stories (no elevator), interior corridors. *Bath:* combo or shower only. **Parking:** on-site. **Terms:** small pets only ($50 deposit). **Amenities:** irons, hair dryers. *Some:* high-speed Internet. **Pool(s):** heated indoor. **Leisure Activities:** whirlpool, exercise room. **Guest Services:** coin laundry. **Business Services:** conference facilities. **Cards:** AX, CB, DC, DS, JC, MC, VI. **Special Amenities: free expanded continental breakfast and free local telephone calls.**

FEE DATA PORT / SOME UNITS /

KAMIAH pop. 1,160

WHERE TO STAY

HEARTHSTONE ELEGANT LODGE BY THE RIVER — **Phone:** (208)935-1492

All Year [BP]	1P: $125-$250	2P: $125-$250	XP: $20	D5

Bed & Breakfast

Location: West of Kamiah, at MM 64. Hwy 12 at Milepost 64 83536 (PO Box 1492). Fax: 208/935-2422. **Facility:** Comfortable, refined decor, in a rural setting, is a feature of this B&B. You'll also find high quality beds with down comforters and triple sheets. Smoke free premises. 5 one-bedroom standard units with whirlpools. 1-2 stories (no elevator), exterior corridors. **Parking:** on-site. **Terms:** check-in 4 pm, 3 day cancellation notice. **Amenities:** CD players, voice mail, irons, hair dryers. *Some:* high-speed Internet. **Leisure Activities:** fishing, hiking trails. *Fee:* massage. **Guest Services:** coin laundry. **Business Services:** PC, fax (fee). **Cards:** AX, DC, MC, VI.

ASK FEE VCR DATA PORT

LEWIS-CLARK RESORT & MOTEL — **Phone:** (208)935-2556

All Year	1P: $36-$45	2P: $41-$50	XP: $5	F3

Motel

Location: 1.5 mi e on US 12. (Rt 1, Box 17X). Fax: 208/935-0366. **Facility:** 21 one-bedroom standard units. 1-2 stories (no elevator), exterior corridors. *Bath:* combo or shower only. **Parking:** on-site. **Amenities:** video library (fee). **Pool(s):** heated outdoor. **Leisure Activities:** whirlpool, horseshoes. **Guest Services:** gift shop, coin laundry, tanning facility. **Business Services:** meeting rooms. **Cards:** AX, DS, MC, VI.

ASK / SOME UNITS / VCR FEE /

QUILT HOUSE BED & BREAKFAST — Phone: (208)935-7668

Bed & Breakfast

All Year [BP] 1P: $80-$115 2P: $90-$125 XP: $35

Location: US 12 at Kamiah, 12 mi on Woodland Rd, follow signs. HC 11, Box 142 83536. Fax: 208/935-7686. **Facility:** The Quilt House is a spacious, spectacular log home, with breathtaking views of the surrounding countryside from its windows and decks. Smoke free premises. 5 one-bedroom standard units. 3 stories (no elevator), interior corridors. *Bath:* some shared or private. **Parking:** on-site. **Terms:** check-in 4 pm, 14 day cancellation notice-fee imposed, [AP] meal plan available, package plans. **Guest Services:** TV in common area. **Business Services:** meeting rooms. **Cards:** MC, VI.

SOME UNITS

FEE

KELLOGG pop. 2,395

WHERE TO STAY

SILVERHORN MOTOR INN — **Phone:** 208/783-1151

Small-scale Hotel

All Year 1P: $43-$61 2P: $53-$71 XP: $5 F12

Location: I-90, exit 49, just ne. 699 W Cameron Ave 83837. Fax: 208/784-5081. **Facility:** 40 one-bedroom standard units. 2 stories (no elevator), interior corridors. **Parking:** on-site, winter plug-ins. **Terms:** package plans. **Leisure Activities:** whirlpool. **Guest Services:** gift shop, complimentary laundry. **Business Services:** meeting rooms. **Cards:** AX, CB, DC, DS, MC, VI.

SOME UNITS

SUPER 8 MOTEL-KELLOGG — **Phone:** 208/783-1234

AAA SAVE

Small-scale Hotel

Dates	1P	2P	XP	
6/8-9/30 & 12/18-2/28 [CP]	1P: $53-$59	2P: $59-$64	XP: $5	F12
3/1-6/7 & 10/1-12/17 [CP]	1P: $45-$50	2P: $50-$55	XP: $5	F12

Location: I-90, exit 49, 0.5 mi s. 601 Bunker Ave 83837 (PO Box 808). Fax: 208/784-0461. **Facility:** 61 units. 56 one-bedroom standard units. 5 one-bedroom suites ($65-$100). 2 stories (no elevator), interior corridors. **Parking:** on-site, winter plug-ins. **Terms:** package plans - seasonal, pets ($20 deposit). **Pool(s):** small heated indoor. **Leisure Activities:** whirlpool, ski storage room. **Guest Services:** coin laundry. **Cards:** AX, CB, DC, DS, MC, VI. **Special Amenities: free continental breakfast and free local telephone calls.**

SOME UNITS

FEE

KETCHUM pop. 3,003

WHERE TO STAY

BEST WESTERN KENTWOOD LODGE *Book at aaa.com* — **Phone:** (208)726-4114

AAA SAVE

Small-scale Hotel

Dates	1P	2P	XP	
6/4-9/25 & 12/17-2/28	1P: $139-$249	2P: $139-$249	XP: $10	F12
3/1-6/3 & 9/26-12/16	1P: $95-$165	2P: $95-$165	XP: $10	F12

Location: South end of town on SR 75 (Main St). 180 S Main St 83340 (PO Box 2172). Fax: 208/726-2417. **Facility:** Smoke free premises. 57 one-bedroom standard units, some with efficiencies and/or whirlpools. 3 stories, interior corridors. *Bath:* combo or shower only. **Parking:** on-site. **Terms:** 2 night minimum stay - with Saturday stayover 6/1-9/30, 7 day cancellation notice-fee imposed. **Amenities:** irons, hair dryers. **Pool(s):** heated indoor. **Leisure Activities:** whirlpool, exercise room. *Fee:* game room. **Guest Services:** coin laundry. **Business Services:** meeting rooms. **Cards:** AX, CB, DC, DS, MC, VI. **Special Amenities: free local telephone calls and early check-in/late check-out.** *(See ad below)*

SOME UNITS

BEST WESTERN TYROLEAN LODGE *Book at aaa.com* — **Phone:** (208)726-5336

AAA SAVE

Small-scale Hotel

Dates	1P	2P	XP	
6/11-9/25 & 12/17-2/28	1P: $129-$169	2P: $129-$169	XP: $10	F12
3/1-6/10 & 9/26-12/16	1P: $85-$115	2P: $85-$115	XP: $10	F12

Location: South end of town, just w of SR 75 (Main St) on Rivers St, just s on 3rd Ave. 260 Cottonwood 83340 (PO Box 802). Fax: 208/726-2081. **Facility:** 56 one-bedroom standard units, some with whirlpools. 3 stories (no elevator), interior corridors. *Bath:* combo or shower only. **Parking:** on-site, winter plug-ins. **Terms:** 3 day cancellation notice-fee imposed, [ECP] meal plan available, package plans - in winter, small pets only ($10 extra charge). **Amenities:** high-speed Internet, voice mail, irons, hair dryers. **Pool(s):** small heated outdoor. **Leisure Activities:** sauna, whirlpool, exercise room. *Fee:* game room. **Guest Services:** coin laundry. **Business Services:** meeting rooms. **Cards:** AX, CB, DC, DS, MC, VI. **Special Amenities: free continental breakfast and free newspaper.**

SOME UNITS

FEE FEE

CHRISTOPHE CONDO HOTEL Phone: (208)726-5601

Condominium

All Year 1P: $60-$336

Location: South end of town, just w of SR 75 (Main St) on Rivers St, just s. 351 2nd Ave S 83340 (PO Box 21). Fax: 208/726-5617. **Facility:** Both single-room and condo accommodations are offered at the hotel; registration is off site. Smoke free premises. 30 two-bedroom suites with kitchens and whirlpools. 3 stories, exterior corridors. **Parking:** on-site. **Terms:** office hours 9 am-7 pm, check-in 4 pm, 30 day cancellation notice-fee imposed. **Amenities:** voice mail, irons. *Some:* DVD players. **Pool(s):** small heated outdoor. **Leisure Activities:** whirlpool. **Guest Services:** coin laundry. **Cards:** AX, MC, VI.

SOME UNITS

ASK FEE DATA PORT / VCR /

CLARION INN OF SUN VALLEY **Book at aaa.com** Phone: (208)726-5900

Small-scale Hotel

6/1-9/30 & 12/17-2/28	1P: $160-$210	2P: $160-$210	XP: $10	F18
3/1-5/31	1P: $140-$180	2P: $140-$180	XP: $10	F18
10/1-12/16	1P: $100-$150	2P: $100-$150	XP: $10	F18

Location: North end of town on SR 75 (Main St), corner of 6th and Main sts. 600 N Main St 83340 (PO Box 660, SUN VALLEY, 83353). Fax: 208/726-3761. **Facility:** 58 one-bedroom standard units, some with whirlpools. 3 stories, interior/exterior corridors. *Bath:* combo or shower only. **Parking:** on-site. **Terms:** 3 day cancellation notice, pets ($25 fee, $10 extra charge). **Amenities:** voice mail, hair dryers. **Pool(s):** heated outdoor. **Leisure Activities:** whirlpool, exercise room. **Business Services:** meeting rooms. **Cards:** AX, DC, MC, VI.

SOME UNITS

ASK FEE DATA PORT / /

TAMARACK LODGE Phone: (208)726-3344

Motel

All Year	1P: $69-$129	2P: $69-$129	XP: $10	F16

Location: Just ne on Sun Valley Rd from jct SR 75 (Main St); downtown. 291 Walnut Ave N 83340 (PO Box 2000, SUN VALLEY, 83353). Fax: 208/726-3347. **Facility:** 26 units. 22 one-bedroom standard units. 4 one-bedroom suites ($89-$169). 2-3 stories (no elevator), interior/exterior corridors. **Parking:** on-site. **Terms:** office hours 7 am-10 pm, 7 day cancellation notice. **Amenities:** hair dryers. **Pool(s):** small heated indoor. **Leisure Activities:** whirlpool. **Cards:** AX, DC, DS, MC, VI.

SOME UNITS

ASK DATA PORT / /

WHERE TO DINE

DEAN'S RESTAURANT **Dinner:** $17-$26 **Phone:** 208/726-8911

International

Location: Corner of 2nd Ave and 6th St; downtown. 180 W 6th St 83340. **Hours:** 5:30 pm-10 pm. Closed: Mon 4/1-5/31 & 10/1-11/30. **Reservations:** accepted. **Features:** The eatery offers casually elegant dining, a varied menu of international delights and highly personable and friendly service. Outdoor dining is available, weather permitting. Casual dress; beer & wine only. **Parking:** street. **Cards:** AX, MC, VI.

THE KNEADERY **Lunch:** $5-$10 **Phone:** 208/726-9462

American

Location: SR 75 (Main St), e on Sun Valley Rd, just s. 260 Leadville 83340. **Hours:** 7 am-2 pm. Closed: 12/25. **Features:** Tasty, well prepared, wholesome food is served in a rustically eclectic setting. The varied menu features creative breakfast selections, sandwiches, salad and soup. The service staff is friendly and casual. Seasonal deck dining is available. Casual dress; beer & wine only. **Parking:** street. **Cards:** AX, MC, VI.

MICHEL'S CHRISTIANIA RESTAURANT & OLYMPIC BAR **Dinner:** $12-$30 **Phone:** 208/726-3388

French

Location: Just n of SR 75 (Main St) on Sun Valley Rd. 303 Walnut Ave N 83340. **Hours:** Open 3/1-4/30 & 6/1-2/28; 6:30 pm-10 pm; from 6 pm in winter. Closed: 11/25, 12/25; also 5/1-5/31. **Reservations:** suggested. **Features:** This casually elegant restaurant serves a variety of fresh dishes in one of the country's premier ski and summer resort communities. The lounge is a local favorite and draws a lively, conversational crowd. Seasonal patio dining is available. Casual dress; cocktails. **Parking:** street. **Cards:** AX, DS, MC, VI.

SAWTOOTH CLUB **Dinner:** $11-$22 **Phone:** 208/726-5233

American

Location: Corner of 2nd Ave SR 75 (Main St); downtown. 231 N Main St 83340. **Hours:** 6 pm-10 pm; from 5:30 pm in winter. Closed: 4/11, 11/25. **Reservations:** suggested. **Features:** This rustic and at times loud and energetic, but always popular watering hole, appeals to the casual apres-ski crowd as well as the summer tourist. The distinctive flavor of mesquite grilling infuses the large cuts of beef and the house specialty, Idaho rack of lamb. Their signature potato skins appetizers are produced in a near constant flow. Casual dress; cocktails. **Parking:** street. **Cards:** AX, MC, VI.

The following restaurants have not been evaluated by AAA but are listed for your information only.

CHANDLER'S **Phone:** 208/726-1776

fyi Not evaluated. **Location:** 200 S Main St 83340. **Features:** The menu features American cuisine, especially seafood and exotic game.

EVERGREEN BISTRO **Phone:** 208/726-3888

fyi Not evaluated. **Location:** 171 First Ave 83340. **Features:** The bistro serves such specialties as venison, rack of lamb and fresh fish.

KETCHUM GRILL **Phone:** 208/726-4660

fyi Not evaluated. **Location:** Corner of East Ave and 5th St; downtown. 520 East Ave N 83340. **Features:** A casual, rustic eatery located in a converted house close to the downtown area, with patio dining available.

PLACE RESTAURANT **Phone:** 208/727-6678

fyi Not evaluated. **Location:** At the Knob Hill Inn. 960 N Main 83340. **Features:** Located in the Knob Hill Inn, this restaurant is extremely popular with locals and tourists alike.

THE ROOSEVELT GRILLE **Phone:** 208/726-0051

fyi Not evaluated. **Location:** Corner of SR 75 (Main St) and Sun Valley Rd; downtown. 280 Main St 83340. **Features:** Located on the main street of town, this Old West style saloon and restaurant features rooftop dining overlooking the town.

WARM SPRINGS RANCH **Phone:** 208/726-2609

fyi Not evaluated. **Location:** 1801 Warm Springs Rd 83340. **Features:** Outdoor seating affords views of the mountains and spring-fed trout ponds.

KOOSKIA pop. 675

WHERE TO STAY

REFLECTIONS INN (FORMERLY LOOKING GLASS INN) **Phone:** 208/926-0855

5/15-10/15 [BP]	1P: $69-$79	2P: $79-$89	XP: $15
3/1-5/14 & 10/16-2/28 [CP]	1P: $55-$65	2P: $65-$75	XP: $10

Bed & Breakfast

Location: 11 mi e on US 12 (between MM 84 and 85). Located in a quiet, secluded area. HCR 75, Box 32, US Hwy 12 83539-9052. Fax: 208/926-7860. **Facility:** Ten wooded acres lend a retreat-like ambience to this river-view inn; a detached guest house affords even more privacy. Designated smoking area. 7 one-bedroom standard units. 2 stories (no elevator), exterior corridors. **Parking:** on-site. **Terms:** age restrictions may apply, 3 day cancellation notice-fee imposed, weekly rates available, package plans - off season, small pets only ($10 extra charge, in limited units). **Amenities:** video library, hair dryers. **Leisure Activities:** whirlpool, fishing, hiking trails. **Cards:** MC, VI. **Special Amenities: free full breakfast and free local telephone calls.**

SOME UNITS

FEE

LEWISTON pop. 30,904

WHERE TO STAY

COMFORT INN *Book at aaa.com* **Phone:** (208)798-8090

3/1-11/1 [ECP]	1P: $79-$139	XP: $10	F
11/2-2/28 [ECP]	1P: $69-$129	XP: $10	F

Small-scale Hotel

Location: 1.2 mi s on US 12 from jct US 95, just s on 21st St. 2128 8th Ave 83501. Fax: 208/798-8988. **Facility:** 52 one-bedroom standard units, some with whirlpools. 2 stories (no elevator), interior corridors. *Bath:* combo or shower only. **Parking:** on-site. **Terms:** pets ($10 extra charge). **Amenities:** safes (fee), irons, hair dryers. **Pool(s):** small heated indoor. **Leisure Activities:** whirlpool. **Guest Services:** valet and coin laundry. **Cards:** AX, CB, DC, DS, JC, MC, VI.

SOME UNITS

ASK FEE FEE

HOLIDAY INN EXPRESS *Book at aaa.com* **Phone:** (208)750-1600

All Year [ECP]	1P: $89-$94	2P: $89-$94

Small-scale Hotel

Location: 1.2 mi s on US 12 from jct US 95, 1.2 mi s on 21st St, just e. 2425 Nez Perce Dr 83501. Fax: 208/750-1800. **Facility:** 80 one-bedroom standard units, some with efficiencies and/or whirlpools. 3 stories, interior corridors. *Bath:* combo or shower only. **Parking:** on-site, winter plug-ins. **Terms:** small pets only ($20 fee). **Amenities:** dual phone lines, voice mail, irons, hair dryers. **Pool(s):** heated indoor. **Leisure Activities:** whirlpool, exercise room. **Guest Services:** gift shop, coin laundry. **Business Services:** business center. **Cards:** AX, DC, DS, MC, VI.

SOME UNITS

FEE FEE

HOWARD JOHNSON EXPRESS *Book at aaa.com* **Phone:** (208)743-9526

Motel

5/1-9/30 [ECP] 1P: $58-$78 2P: $58-$78 XP: $10 F18
3/1-4/30 & 10/1-2/28 [ECP] 1P: $48-$68 2P: $48-$68 XP: $10 F18

Location: 1.6 mi s on US 12 from jct US 95. 1716 Main St 83501. Fax: 208/746-6212. **Facility:** 66 units. 64 one-bedroom standard units, some with kitchens. 2 one-bedroom suites ($68-$88). 1-2 stories (no elevator), exterior corridors. **Parking:** on-site. **Terms:** package plans, small pets only ($15 fee). **Amenities:** *Fee:* high-speed Internet, safes. *Some:* video games. **Pool(s):** small heated outdoor. **Leisure Activities:** whirlpool. **Guest Services:** complimentary laundry. **Business Services:** meeting rooms. **Cards:** AX, DC, DS, MC, VI.

SOME UNITS
ASK / FEE / DATA PORT / VCR

INN AMERICA *Book at aaa.com* **Phone:** (208)746-4600

SAVE

Motel

All Year 1P: $49-$61 2P: $55-$71 XP: $5 F

Location: 1.2 mi s on US 12 from jct US 95, just s. 702 21st St 83501. Fax: 208/746-7756. **Facility:** 61 one-bedroom standard units. 3 stories, interior corridors. *Bath:* combo or shower only. **Parking:** on-site, winter plug-ins. **Terms:** [CP] meal plan available. **Amenities:** irons, hair dryers. **Pool(s):** small heated outdoor. **Guest Services:** valet and coin laundry. **Cards:** AX, CB, DC, DS, MC, VI. **Special Amenities: free local telephone calls and early check-in/late check-out.**

SOME UNITS
DATA PORT

RED LION HOTEL *Book at aaa.com* **Phone:** (208)799-1000

Small-scale Hotel

5/1-10/31 1P: $79-$89 2P: $79-$89 XP: $10 F18
3/1-4/30 & 11/1-2/28 1P: $69-$79 2P: $69-$79 XP: $10 F18

Location: 1.2 mi s on US 12 from jct US 95, just s. 621 21st St 83501. Fax: 208/748-1050. **Facility:** 183 units. 182 one-bedroom standard units, some with efficiencies and/or whirlpools. 1 one-bedroom suite ($99-$129) with whirlpool. 2-4 stories, interior corridors. *Bath:* combo or shower only. **Parking:** on-site. **Terms:** cancellation fee imposed. **Amenities:** voice mail, irons, hair dryers. *Some:* dual phone lines. **Pool(s):** heated outdoor, heated indoor. **Leisure Activities:** saunas, whirlpools, racquetball courts. **Guest Services:** valet and coin laundry. **Business Services:** conference facilities, business center. **Cards:** AX, DC, DS, MC, VI.

SOME UNITS
ASK / DATA PORT / VCR / FEE

SACAJAWEA MOTOR INNS **Phone:** (208)746-1393

SAVE

Motel

All Year [CP] 1P: $56-$59 2P: $63-$66 XP: $2 F12

Location: 1.5 mi s on US 12 from jct US 95. 1824 Main St 83501. Fax: 208/743-3620. **Facility:** 90 units. 84 one-bedroom standard units, some with whirlpools. 6 one-bedroom suites ($74-$88). 1-2 stories (no elevator), interior/exterior corridors. *Bath:* combo or shower only. **Parking:** on-site. **Terms:** cancellation fee imposed, pets ($2 extra charge, in designated units). **Dining:** 6 am-10 pm, Sun-9 pm, cocktails. **Pool(s):** heated outdoor. **Leisure Activities:** whirlpool, limited exercise equipment. **Guest Services:** complimentary laundry. **Business Services:** meeting rooms. **Cards:** AX, CB, DC, DS, MC, VI. **Special Amenities: free continental breakfast and free local telephone calls.**

SOME UNITS
FEE / DATA PORT / VCR / FEE

SUPER 8 MOTEL *Book at aaa.com* **Phone:** 208/743-8808

Motel

All Year [BP] 1P: $40 2P: $42-$45 XP: $5 F13

Location: Just e on US 12 from jct US 95. Located in a busy, commercial area. 3120 North & South Hwy 83501. Fax: 208/743-8808. **Facility:** 60 one-bedroom standard units. 2 stories (no elevator), interior corridors. **Parking:** on-site, winter plug-ins. **Terms:** pets ($5 fee). **Guest Services:** coin laundry. **Cards:** AX, CB, DC, DS, MC, VI.

SOME UNITS
ASK / FEE

WHERE TO DINE

JONATHAN'S RESTAURANT AND MARTINI GRILL **Lunch:** $4-$10 **Dinner:** $6-$30 **Phone:** 208/746-3438

International

Location: Just e of downtown. 1516 Main St 83501. **Hours:** 11 am-9:30 pm, Sat & Sun from 4 pm. Closed major holidays. **Reservations:** suggested. **Features:** The restaurant specializes in the freshest seafood, never-frozen Angus beef and dishes prepared only with local, seasonal produce. Casual dress; cocktails. **Parking:** on-site. **Cards:** AX, MC, VI.

THE OLIVE PIT **Lunch:** $6-$10 **Dinner:** $7-$15 **Phone:** 208/750-1131

Italian

Location: 1.9 mi s on US 12 from jct US 95. 1303 Main St 83501. **Hours:** 11 am-2 & 5-9 pm. Closed major holidays; also Sun & Mon. **Features:** Enjoy your Italian cuisine in this very popular restaurant which is decorated in such a way as to evoke a combination of city bistro and Tuscan garden. Casual dress; beer & wine only. **Parking:** on-site. **Cards:** AX, CB, DC, DS, JC, MC, VI.

WAFFLES CAFFE' **Lunch:** $5-$7 **Phone:** 208/743-5189

American

Location: 1.3 mi e of Snake River. 1421 Main St 83501. **Hours:** 6:30 am-2:30 pm. Closed: 12/25. **Features:** Servers are energetic and friendly at the favorite breakfast and lunch spot. In addition to excellent waffles, the menu lists varied good-value breakfast items, including the iron man or iron woman for hearty appetites. Lighter fare also is available. Casual dress. **Parking:** on-site. **Cards:** AX, MC, VI.

WAYBACK CAFE **Lunch:** $5-$8 **Dinner:** $6-$11 **Phone:** 208/743-2396

American

Location: 1.2 mi s on US 12 from jct US 95, 0.6 mi s on 21st St, just e. 2138 13th Ave 83501. **Hours:** 6:30 am-11 pm. Closed: 11/25, 12/25. **Reservations:** accepted. **Features:** Guests can return to the Eisenhower era and dine in a classic 1950s-themed diner, complete with jukebox, fuzzy dice and servers in poodle skirts. Casual dress; beer & wine only. **Parking:** on-site. **Cards:** AX, DS, MC, VI.

ZANY'S HOLLYWOOD GRILL **Lunch:** $5-$7 **Dinner:** $5-$14 **Phone:** 208/746-8131

American

Location: 1.2 mi s on US 12 from jct US 95, 1 mi s on 21st St. 2006 19th St 83501. **Hours:** 10:30 am-9:30 pm, Fri & Sat-10 pm, Sun from 11 am. Closed major holidays. **Features:** Burgers, sandwiches, salad and steak are featured at this casual family restaurant accented by a madly eclectic and lively 1950s decor simply chock-full of odd little treasures that are sure to delight the eye. Seasonal patio dining is also available. Casual dress; beer & wine only. **Parking:** on-site. **Cards:** AX, CB, DC, DS, MC, VI.

The following restaurants have not been evaluated by AAA but are listed for your information only.

CHAMBERLAIN'S **Phone:** 208/798-0822

fyi

Not evaluated. **Location:** 1407 Main St 83501. **Features:** The no-nonsense, family-style restaurant offers good old-fashioned home cooking and large portions served with a smile.

MERIWETHERS **Phone:** 208/746-9390

fyi

Not evaluated. **Location:** 1.2 mi s on US 12 from jct US 95, just s; in Red Lion Hotel. 621 21st St 83501. **Features:** Comfortable dining.

LUCILE

WHERE TO STAY

STEELHEAD INN **Phone:** (208)628-3044

Motel

All Year 1P: $55 2P: $55 XP: $5

Location: 5 mi n on US 95 at MM 210. (HC-01, Box 14). Fax: 208/628-3546. **Facility:** 10 one-bedroom standard units, some with efficiencies. 1 story, exterior corridors. **Parking:** on-site. **Leisure Activities:** fishing. **Guest Services:** gift shop. **Cards:** DS, MC, VI.

SOME UNITS

MACKAY pop. 566

WHERE TO STAY

WAGON WHEEL MOTEL **Phone:** 208/588-3331

Motel

All Year 1P: $35-$75 2P: $40-$80 XP: $4 F3

Location: 0.3 mi n on US 93. 809 W Custer 83251 (PO Box 22). Fax: 208/588-3334. **Facility:** 16 one-bedroom standard units, some with kitchens. 1 story, exterior corridors. *Bath:* combo or shower only. **Parking:** on-site, winter plug-ins. **Terms:** cancellation fee imposed, weekly rates available, pets ($5 extra charge). **Leisure Activities:** playground, basketball, volleyball. **Guest Services:** coin laundry. **Cards:** AX, DS, MC, VI.

SOME UNITS

FEE

WHERE TO DINE

KEN'S CLUB **Lunch:** $3-$8 **Dinner:** $8-$20 **Phone:** 208/588-9983

American

Location: Center. 302 S Main 83251. **Hours:** 11 am-2 & 5-10 pm, Fri & Sat-11 pm, Sun 9 am-4 pm. Closed: 11/25, 12/25. **Features:** Serving locals as well as visitors, the casual eatery offers daily specials and home cooked meals. The steaks are mouthwatering. Casual dress; cocktails. **Parking:** street. **Cards:** AX, DS, MC, VI.

MARSING pop. 890

WHERE TO DINE

SANDBAR RIVER HOUSE **Lunch:** $5-$8 **Dinner:** $8-$19 **Phone:** 208/896-4124

Steak & Seafood

Location: SR 55, just w of bridge, then just n. 18 Sandbar Ave 83639. **Hours:** 11 am-9 pm, Fri & Sat-10 pm, Sun noon-8 pm. Closed: 7/4, 11/25, 12/24, 12/25; also Mon. **Reservations:** suggested. **Features:** Dine on a variety of well-prepared menu offerings, including soup, salad and sandwiches, while enjoying the view of the Snake River in southwest Idaho's wine country. Outside deck dining is available. Idaho and Northwestern wines are featured. Casual dress; beer & wine only. **Parking:** on-site. **Cards:** CB, DC, DS, MC, VI.

MCCALL pop. 2,084

WHERE TO STAY

BEST WESTERN MCCALL *Book at aaa.com* **Phone:** (208)634-6300

AAA SAVE

Small-scale Hotel

5/26-9/15 & 12/16-2/28 [CP]	1P: $60-$90	2P: $65-$95
3/1-5/25 & 9/16-12/15 [CP]	1P: $55-$80	2P: $55-$85

Location: SR 55, just s of jct with Lake St. 415 3rd St 83638. Fax: 208/634-2967. **Facility:** 79 one-bedroom standard units. 2 stories (no elevator), interior/exterior corridors. *Bath:* combo or shower only. **Parking:** on-site, winter plug-ins. **Amenities:** voice mail, irons, hair dryers. **Pool(s):** heated indoor. **Leisure Activities:** whirlpool, limited exercise equipment. **Guest Services:** coin laundry. **Business Services:** meeting rooms. **Cards:** AX, DC, DS, MC, VI. **Special Amenities: free continental breakfast and early check-in/late check-out.**

SOME UNITS

HOTEL MCCALL — Phone: (208)634-8105

Historic Country Inn

All Year [ECP] 1P: $55-$350 2P: $55-$350 XP: $10 F10

Location: SR 55 at jct of Lake St; center. 1101 N 3rd St 83638. Fax: 208/634-8755. **Facility:** The hotel has room styles ranging from very modern to smaller yet comfortable accommodations within the original building: a 1904 railroad inn. Smoke free premises. 33 units. 26 one-bedroom standard units, some with whirlpools. 7 one-bedroom suites with whirlpools, some with efficiencies or kitchens. 2-3 stories, interior corridors. *Bath:* some shared or private, combo or shower only. **Parking:** on-site. **Terms:** 3 day cancellation notice-fee imposed. **Amenities:** video library, voice mail. *Some:* DVD players, irons, hair dryers. **Dining:** 5 pm-9:30 pm; closed Mon & Tues, wine/beer only. **Leisure Activities:** bocci. **Guest Services:** complimentary evening beverages, airport transportation-McCall Airport. **Business Services:** meeting rooms. **Cards:** AX, DC, DS, MC, VI. **Special Amenities: free expanded continental breakfast and free local telephone calls.**

SOME UNITS

MCCALL SUPER 8 LODGE *Book at aaa.com* — Phone: (208)634-4637

Motel

6/1-10/18 1P: $79-$94
3/1-5/31 1P: $60-$85
10/19-2/28 1P: $55-$75

Location: South end of town on SR 55. 303 S 3rd St 83638. Fax: 208/634-4637. **Facility:** 61 one-bedroom standard units. 2 stories (no elevator), interior corridors. *Bath:* combo or shower only. **Parking:** on-site, winter plug-ins. **Terms:** pets ($5 extra charge, with prior approval). **Amenities:** *Some:* hair dryers. **Leisure Activities:** whirlpool. **Guest Services:** coin laundry. **Business Services:** meeting rooms. **Cards:** AX, DC, DS, MC, VI. **Special Amenities: free continental breakfast and free local telephone calls.**

SOME UNITS

FEE FEE

The following lodging was either not evaluated or did not meet AAA rating requirements but is listed for your information only.

WHITETAIL CLUB — **Phone:** 208/634-2244

fyi

Not evaluated. **Location:** 1.5 mi w on SR 55. Located on Payette Lake. 501 W Lake St 83638. Facilities, services, and decor characterize an upscale property.

WHERE TO DINE

THE MILL — **Dinner:** $10-$44 — **Phone:** 208/634-7683

Steak & Seafood

Location: Just s on SR 55. 324 N 3rd St 83638. **Hours:** 6 pm-10 pm, Fri & Sat-11 pm. Closed: 11/25, 12/25. **Reservations:** accepted. **Features:** Beef is served in large portions, so bring a healthy appetite when you visit. Your surroundings are casual with antiques and nostalgic memorabilia, with heavy wooden beams and supports, log slab tables in the lounge, and a carnival resort town atmosphere. Casual dress; cocktails; entertainment. **Parking:** on-site. **Cards:** AX, CB, DC, DS, MC, VI.

ROMANO'S RISTORANTE — **Dinner:** $8-$25 — **Phone:** 208/634-4396

Italian

Location: SR 55, just w of jct with 3rd St. 203 E Lake St 83638. **Hours:** 5:30 pm-10 pm; to 9 pm in winter. Closed: 11/25, 12/25; also Sun & Mon in winter. **Features:** Located on the ground floor of the yacht club, Northern Italian cuisine dominates the menu. Specialties include a variety of pasta, veal, beef and seafood entrees. Seasonal patio dining affords gorgeous views of Payette Lake and the surrounding mountains. Casual dress; beer & wine only. **Parking:** street. **Cards:** AX, MC, VI.

MERIDIAN pop. 34,919

WHERE TO STAY

BEST WESTERN RAMA INN *Book at aaa.com* — Phone: (208)887-7888

Small-scale Hotel

All Year [ECP] 1P: $74-$109 2P: $74-$109 XP: $5 F12

Location: I-84, exit 44, just ne. 1019 S Progress Ave 83642. Fax: 208/887-7600. **Facility:** 61 units. 54 one-bedroom standard units, some with whirlpools. 7 one-bedroom suites ($109-$150). 2 stories (no elevator), interior corridors. *Bath:* combo or shower only. **Parking:** on-site. **Amenities:** voice mail, irons, hair dryers. **Pool(s):** heated indoor. **Leisure Activities:** sauna, whirlpool, exercise room. **Guest Services:** valet and coin laundry. **Business Services:** meeting rooms. **Cards:** AX, CB, DC, DS, JC, MC, VI. **Special Amenities: free expanded continental breakfast and free newspaper.** *(See color ad p 213)*

SOME UNITS

HOLIDAY INN EXPRESS HOTEL & SUITES *Book at aaa.com* **Phone:** (208)288-2100

AAA SAVE

Small-scale Hotel

All Year [ECP] 1P: $89-$149 2P: $89-$149 XP: $10 F

Location: I-84, exit 46, northwest corner. 800 Allen St 83642. Fax: 208/898-9436. **Facility:** 67 one-bedroom standard units, some with whirlpools. 3 stories, interior corridors. *Bath:* combo or shower only. **Parking:** on-site. **Amenities:** high-speed Internet, voice mail, irons, hair dryers. **Pool(s):** heated indoor. **Leisure Activities:** whirlpool, exercise room. **Guest Services:** valet and coin laundry. **Business Services:** meeting rooms, business center. **Cards:** AX, CB, DC, DS, JC, MC, VI.

SOME UNITS

MOTEL 6 INN & SUITES *Book at aaa.com* **Phone:** (208)888-1212

AAA SAVE

Small-scale Hotel

All Year [CP] 1P: $49-$79 2P: $59-$79 XP: $5 F12

Location: I-84, exit 44. 1047 S Progress Ave 83642. Fax: 208/887-3737. **Facility:** 68 one-bedroom standard units. 3 stories, interior corridors. *Bath:* combo or shower only. **Parking:** on-site. **Amenities:** voice mail. **Pool(s):** heated indoor. **Leisure Activities:** whirlpool. **Guest Services:** valet and coin laundry. **Cards:** AX, DC, DS, MC, VI. **Special Amenities: free continental breakfast and free local telephone calls.**
(See color ad below)

SOME UNITS

FEE

MR. SANDMAN INN & SUITES *Book at aaa.com* **Phone:** (208)887-2062

Small-scale Hotel

6/1-8/31	1P: $59-$89	2P: $67-$89	XP: $8	F16
3/1-5/31 & 9/1-2/28	1P: $54-$89	2P: $62-$89	XP: $8	F16

Location: I-84, exit 44, southwest corner. 1575 S Meridian Rd 83642. Fax: 208/887-2062. **Facility:** 106 units. 105 one- and 1 two-bedroom standard units. 2 stories (no elevator), interior corridors. *Bath:* combo or shower only. **Parking:** on-site. **Terms:** weekly rates available. **Amenities:** high-speed Internet. *Some:* hair dryers. **Pool(s):** heated outdoor. **Leisure Activities:** whirlpool. **Guest Services:** complimentary laundry. **Cards:** AX, CB, DC, DS, MC, VI.

SOME UNITS

ASK / /

MONTPELIER pop. 2,785

WHERE TO STAY

BEST WESTERN CLOVER CREEK INN *Book at aaa.com* **Phone:** (208)847-1782

AAA SAVE

Small-scale Hotel

4/16-10/15	1P: $69-$89	2P: $79-$99	XP: $10	F13
3/1-4/15 & 10/16-2/28	1P: $57-$79	2P: $67-$89	XP: $10	F13

Location: Just n on US 30 from jct US 89 S. 243 N 4th St 83254. Fax: 208/847-3519. **Facility:** 65 one-bedroom standard units. 2 stories (no elevator), exterior corridors. **Parking:** on-site, winter plug-ins. **Terms:** [ECP] meal plan available, small pets only ($10 fee). **Amenities:** video library (fee), irons, hair dryers. **Leisure Activities:** whirlpool, exercise room. **Guest Services:** coin laundry. **Business Services:** meeting rooms. **Cards:** AX, DC, DS, MC, VI. **Special Amenities: free continental breakfast and free local telephone calls.**

SOME UNITS

FEE / VCR FEE /

THE FISHER INN **Phone:** (208)847-1772

AAA SAVE

Motel

5/26-9/5	1P: $36-$44	2P: $39-$52	XP: $5
3/1-5/25 & 9/6-2/28	1P: $29-$39	2P: $33-$44	XP: $5

Location: 0.8 mi n on US 30 from jct of US 89 S. 601 N 4th St 83254. **Facility:** 10 one-bedroom standard units. 1 story, exterior corridors. **Parking:** on-site, winter plug-ins. **Terms:** cancellation fee imposed, weekly rates available, small pets only ($5 extra charge). **Pool(s):** small heated outdoor. **Leisure Activities:** playground. **Guest Services:** coin laundry. **Cards:** AX, DS, MC, VI.

SOME UNITS

FEE / VCR /

SUPER 8 MOTEL MONTPELIER *Book at aaa.com* **Phone:** (208)847-8888

Small-scale Hotel

6/1-10/15	1P: $45-$60	2P: $45-$80	XP: $5	F12
3/1-5/31 & 10/16-2/28	1P: $43-$61	2P: $43-$75	XP: $5	F12

Location: Just n on US 30 from jct US 89 S. 276 N 4th St 83254. Fax: 208/847-3888. **Facility:** 50 one-bedroom standard units. 2 stories (no elevator), interior corridors. **Parking:** on-site, winter plug-ins. **Leisure Activities:** whirlpool. **Guest Services:** gift shop, coin laundry. **Business Services:** meeting rooms. **Cards:** AX, CB, DC, DS, MC, VI.

SOME UNITS

ASK / /

WHERE TO DINE

BUTCH CASSIDY'S **Lunch:** $4-$9 **Dinner:** $7-$20 **Phone:** 208/847-3501

American

Location: Jct US 89 and 30 N. 230 N 4th St 83254. **Hours:** 6 am-10 pm. Closed: 12/25. **Features:** Homemade bread and dessert are most notable, along with healthy portions of specially cut beef. The atmosphere and accompanying decor are decidedly Western and extols the life and times of Butch Cassidy. This eatery is just 15 minutes from Bear Lake. Casual dress; cocktails. **Parking:** on-site. **Cards:** AX, DC, DS, MC, VI.

THE CABIN SMOKEHOUSE BBQ **Lunch:** $6-$12 **Dinner:** $6-$15 **Phone:** 208/847-1824

American

Location: Just n on US 30 from jct US 89 S. 194 N 4th St 83254. **Hours:** 8 am-10 pm. Closed: 11/25, 12/25. **Features:** The Cabin Smokehouse BBQ is BBQ and a whole lot more. A local dining favorite, this rustic setting is family friendly. Casual dress. **Parking:** on-site. **Cards:** AX, CB, DC, DS, JC, MC, VI.

MOSCOW pop. 21,291

WHERE TO STAY

BEST WESTERN UNIVERSITY INN *Book at aaa.com* **Phone:** (208)882-0550

AAA SAVE

Small-scale Hotel

All Year	1P: $85-$130	2P: $90-$135	XP: $5	F18

Location: Jct US 95, 1 mi w on SR 8. Located next to the university and shopping mall. 1516 Pullman Rd 83843. Fax: 208/883-3056. **Facility:** 173 units. 168 one-bedroom standard units. 5 one-bedroom suites. 2 stories (no elevator), interior corridors. **Parking:** on-site. **Terms:** check-in 4 pm, 3 day cancellation notice, pets ($25 extra charge). **Amenities:** video games (fee), high-speed Internet, voice mail, irons, hair dryers. **Dining:** 2 restaurants, 6 am-10 pm, Fri & Sat-1 am, cocktails. **Pool(s):** small heated indoor, wading. **Leisure Activities:** sauna, whirlpool, exercise room. **Guest Services:** valet laundry, area transportation-university. **Business Services:** conference facilities, business center. **Cards:** AX, DC, DS, MC, VI.

SOME UNITS

FEE / VCR /

HAMPTON INN *Book at aaa.com* **Phone:** 208/882-5365

Small-scale Hotel

All Year [ECP]	1P: $59-$129	2P: $69-$139

Location: 1.6 mi w on SR 8 from jct US 93, just n. 185 Warbonnet Dr 83843. Fax: 208/882-5374. **Facility:** 76 one-bedroom standard units, some with whirlpools. 3 stories, interior corridors. *Bath:* combo or shower only. **Parking:** on-site. **Amenities:** dual phone lines, voice mail, irons, hair dryers. **Pool(s):** small heated indoor. **Leisure Activities:** whirlpool, exercise room. **Guest Services:** coin laundry. **Business Services:** meeting rooms, business center. **Cards:** AX, DC, DS, MC, VI.

SOME UNITS

ASK / /

MARK IV MOTOR INN **Phone:** (208)882-7557

Motel

All Year 1P: $49-$129 2P: $49-$129

Location: Jct SR 8, 0.4 mi n on US 95. 414 N Main St 83843. Fax: 208/883-0684. **Facility:** 86 units. 85 one-bedroom standard units. 1 one-bedroom suite. 2 stories (no elevator), interior/exterior corridors. *Bath:* combo or shower only. **Parking:** on-site, winter plug-ins. **Terms:** 14 day cancellation notice, pets ($10 extra charge, in designated units). **Amenities:** *Some:* hair dryers. **Dining:** 6 am-9 pm, Fri & Sat-10 pm, cocktails. **Pool(s):** small heated indoor. **Leisure Activities:** whirlpool. **Guest Services:** area transportation-university. **Business Services:** meeting rooms. **Cards:** AX, CB, DC, DS, MC, VI. **Special Amenities: free local telephone calls and early check-in/late check-out.**

SOME UNITS

FEE

WHERE TO DINE

BASILIOS **Lunch:** $7-$10 **Dinner:** $9-$14 **Phone:** 208/892-3848

Italian

Location: Downtown. 100 W 4th St 83843. **Hours:** 11 am-9 pm, Fri & Sat-10 pm. Closed: 1/1, 11/25, 12/25. **Features:** This downtown restaurant is quietly elegant and is a great choice for traditional Italian food in comfortable surroundings with a Mediterannean feel. Casual dress; beer & wine only. **Parking:** street. **Cards:** MC, VI.

MOUNTAIN HOME pop. 11,143

WHERE TO STAY

BEST WESTERN FOOTHILLS MOTOR INN *Book at aaa.com* **Phone:** (208)587-8477

Small-scale Hotel

All Year 1P: $62-$79 2P: $67-$84 XP: $5 F12

Location: I-84, exit 95, just n. 1080 Hwy 20 83647. Fax: 208/587-5774. **Facility:** 76 units. 75 one-bedroom standard units. 1 one-bedroom suite. 2 stories (no elevator), exterior corridors. *Bath:* combo or shower only. **Parking:** on-site, winter plug-ins. **Terms:** pets ($5 extra charge). **Amenities:** voice mail, irons, hair dryers. *Some:* dual phone lines. **Pool(s):** heated outdoor. **Leisure Activities:** whirlpool, exercise room. **Guest Services:** coin laundry. **Business Services:** meeting rooms. **Cards:** AX, CB, DC, DS, MC, VI. **Special Amenities: free local telephone calls and free newspaper.**

SOME UNITS

FEE

SLEEP INN *Book at aaa.com* **Phone:** (208)587-9743

Small-scale Hotel

All Year 1P: $59-$71 2P: $65-$77 XP: $5 F17

Location: I-84, exit 95, just n. 1180 Hwy 20 83647. Fax: 208/587-7382. **Facility:** 60 one-bedroom standard units. 2 stories (no elevator), interior corridors. *Bath:* combo or shower only. **Parking:** on-site. **Terms:** [CP] meal plan available, pets ($5 extra charge). **Amenities:** video library (fee), voice mail, irons, hair dryers. **Cards:** AX, CB, DC, DS, MC, VI.

SOME UNITS

FEE

WHERE TO DINE

CARLOS' MEXICAN STYLE FAMILY DINING **Lunch:** $5-$8 **Dinner:** $5-$8 **Phone:** 208/587-2966

Mexican

Location: I-84, exit 95, 1.6 mi sw to N 2nd East St. 210 E 5th N 83647. **Hours:** 11 am-9 pm. Closed major holidays; also Sun. **Features:** If you're looking for a casual, friendly, family-style restaurant with an extensive menu of traditional Mexican fare (with a few surprises) and warm service and hospitality, you've found it. Imaginative cooking sets this one apart from the usual. Casual dress; cocktails. **Parking:** on-site. **Cards:** AX, DS, MC, VI.

NAMPA pop. 51,867

WHERE TO STAY

INN AMERICA **Phone:** (208)442-0800

Small-scale Hotel

All Year [CP] 1P: $39-$49 2P: $49-$59 XP: $5 F18

Location: I-84, exit 35, just s. 130 Shannon Dr 83687. Fax: 208/442-0229. **Facility:** 61 units. 57 one- and 4 two-bedroom standard units. 3 stories, interior corridors. *Bath:* combo or shower only. **Parking:** on-site. **Amenities:** irons, hair dryers. **Pool(s):** small heated outdoor. **Guest Services:** coin laundry. **Cards:** AX, DC, DS, MC, VI.

SOME UNITS

ASK

SLEEP INN-NAMPA *Book at aaa.com* **Phone:** (208)463-6300

Small-scale Hotel

All Year [CP] 1P: $61-$81 2P: $69-$89 XP: $8 F18

Location: I-84, exit 36, just s. 1315 Industrial Rd 83687. Fax: 208/463-6300. **Facility:** 81 one-bedroom standard units. 3 stories, interior corridors. *Bath:* combo or shower only. **Parking:** on-site. **Terms:** small pets only ($10 extra charge). **Amenities:** video library (fee). *Some:* irons, hair dryers. **Pool(s):** heated indoor. **Leisure Activities:** whirlpool. **Guest Services:** valet and coin laundry. **Business Services:** meeting rooms. **Cards:** AX, DC, DS, JC, MC, VI.

SOME UNITS

ASK

FEE FEE FEE

WHERE TO DINE

NOODLES — **Lunch:** $5-$9 — **Dinner:** $7-$13 — **Phone:** 208/466-4400

Italian

Location: I-84, exit 36, just n. 1802 Franklin Blvd 83687. **Hours:** 11 am-9 pm, Fri-10 pm, Sat noon-10 pm, Sun noon-8 pm. Closed: 11/25, 12/25; also Super Bowl Sun. **Reservations:** accepted. **Features:** Hearty portions of traditional homemade Italian cuisine are served in an informal atmosphere. Try the house specialty: smoked salmon and penne pasta with zucchini, peas, mushrooms and red peppers in a light cream sauce. The service is prompt and relaxed. Casual dress; cocktails. **Parking:** on-site. **Cards:** AX, MC, VI.

NEW MEADOWS pop. 533

WHERE TO STAY

HARTLAND INN & MOTEL — **Phone:** (208)347-2114

Motel

All Year — 1P: $59-$150 — 2P: $59-$150 — XP: $10

Location: US 95, just n of jct SR 55. 211 Norris St 83654 (PO Box 636). Fax: 208/347-2535. **Facility:** 19 one-bedroom standard units. 1-3 stories (no elevator), interior/exterior corridors. *Bath:* combo or shower only. **Parking:** on-site. **Terms:** 3 day cancellation notice-fee imposed, pets ($7 extra charge, in limited units). **Amenities:** *Some:* hair dryers. **Leisure Activities:** whirlpool, overnight horse facilities available, limited exercise equipment. **Business Services:** PC, fax (fee). **Cards:** AX, DS, MC, VI. **Special Amenities: free local telephone calls and preferred room (subject to availability with advanced reservations).**

SOME UNITS

FEE

OROFINO pop. 3,247

WHERE TO STAY

KONKOLVILLE MOTEL — **Phone:** (208)476-5584

Motel

All Year — 1P: $50-$55 — 2P: $50-$55 — XP: $4 — F10

Location: 2.7 mi e on Michigan Ave. 2000 Konkolville Rd 83544. Fax: 208/476-3268. **Facility:** 39 one-bedroom standard units. 2 stories (no elevator), exterior corridors. **Parking:** on-site. **Terms:** office hours 7 am-11 pm, cancellation fee imposed, weekly rates available, [CP] meal plan available, pets ($5 extra charge, in designated units). **Amenities:** video library (fee). *Some:* hair dryers. **Pool(s):** heated outdoor. **Leisure Activities:** whirlpool. **Guest Services:** coin laundry. **Business Services:** business center. **Cards:** AX, DS, MC, VI.

SOME UNITS

FEE — VCR — FEE

POCATELLO pop. 51,466

WHERE TO STAY

AMERITEL INN — *Book at aaa.com* — **Phone:** (208)234-7500

Small-scale Hotel

All Year [ECP] — 2P: $80-$140 — XP: $10 — F16

Location: I-15, exit 71, just e. 1440 Bench Rd 83201. Fax: 208/234-0000. **Facility:** 148 units. 142 one-bedroom standard units, some with efficiencies and/or whirlpools. 6 one-bedroom suites ($100-$250) with efficiencies. 3 stories, interior corridors. *Bath:* combo or shower only. **Parking:** on-site. **Amenities:** high-speed Internet, voice mail, irons, hair dryers. **Pool(s):** heated indoor. **Leisure Activities:** whirlpool, exercise room. **Guest Services:** valet and coin laundry. **Business Services:** meeting rooms. **Cards:** AX, DC, DS, MC, VI. *(See color ad p 186)*

SOME UNITS

BEST WESTERN COTTONTREE INN *Book at aaa.com*

Small-scale Hotel

All Year 1P: $64-$69 2P

Location: I-15, exit 71, just e. 1415 Bench Rd 83201. Fax: 208/2 standard units, some with kitchens. 1 one-bedroom suite with ridors. **Parking:** on-site, winter plug-ins. **Terms:** / day cancell deposit). **Amenities:** video games, irons, hair dryers. **Po ties:** whirlpool, sun deck. **Guest Services:** valet and coin lau Airport. **Business Services:** meeting rooms. **Cards:** AX, CB, DC, DS, JC, MC, V **nental breakfast and free room upgrade (subject to availability with advanced**

FEE

COMFORT INN *Book at aaa.com*

Small-scale Hotel

5/1-8/31 1P: $62-$79 2P: $69-$8

3/1-4/30 & 9/1-2/28 1P: $49-$69 2P: $56-$79 F18

Location: I-15, exit 71, just e. 1333 Bench Rd 83201. Fax: 208/237-56 ...one-bedroom standard units. 2 stories (no elevator), interior corridors. **Parking:** on-site, wi... ...ins. **Terms:** [ECP] meal plan available, pets ($10 extra charge). **Amenities:** safes, irons, hair dryers. **Pool(s):** heated indoor. **Leisure Activities:** whirlpool. **Guest Services:** valet laundry. **Business Services:** fax (fee). **Cards:** AX, CB, DC, DS, JC, MC, VI.

ASK FEE / SOME UNITS /

ECONO LODGE-UNIVERSITY *Book at aaa.com* **Phone:** (208)233-0451

Small-scale Hotel

All Year 1P: $40-$60 2P: $50-$70 XP: $5 F17

Location: I-15, exit 67, 1.8 mi n. Located across from Idaho State University. 835 S 5th Ave 83201. Fax: 208/478-1618. **Facility:** 54 one-bedroom standard units. 2 stories (no elevator), interior corridors. **Parking:** on-site, winter plug-ins. **Terms:** cancellation fee imposed, weekly rates available, [ECP] meal plan available, pets ($20 deposit). **Amenities:** *Some:* irons, hair dryers. **Guest Services:** valet and coin laundry. **Business Services:** meeting rooms, fax (fee). **Cards:** AX, DS, MC, VI.

ASK FEE / SOME UNITS /

HOLIDAY INN-POCATELLO *Book at aaa.com* **Phone:** (208)237-1400

Small-scale Hotel

All Year 1P: $59-$76 2P: $59-$76

Location: I-15, exit 71, just e. 1399 Bench Rd 83201. Fax: 208/238-0225. **Facility:** 197 units. 189 one-bedroom standard units. 8 one-bedroom suites. 2 stories (no elevator), interior/exterior corridors. *Bath:* combo or shower only. **Parking:** on-site. **Terms:** small pets only (in selected units). **Amenities:** video games, high-speed Internet, dual phone lines, voice mail, irons, hair dryers. **Pool(s):** heated indoor. **Leisure Activities:** sauna, whirlpool, exercise room. *Fee:* game room. **Guest Services:** valet and coin laundry. **Business Services:** meeting rooms, fax (fee). **Cards:** AX, CB, DC, DS, JC, MC, VI. ***(See color ad opposite title page)***

DATA PORT / SOME UNITS VCR FEE /

POCATELLO SUPER 8 MOTEL *Book at aaa.com* **Phone:** (208)234-0888

Small-scale Hotel

All Year [CP] 1P: $48-$71 2P: $52-$79 XP: $4 F12

Location: I-15, exit 71, just e. 1330 Bench Rd 83201. Fax: 208/232-0347. **Facility:** 80 one-bedroom standard units, some with whirlpools. 3 stories, interior corridors. *Bath:* combo or shower only. **Parking:** on-site. **Terms:** small pets only ($2-$10 extra charge). **Amenities:** video library (fee), voice mail. *Some:* hair dryers. **Guest Services:** coin laundry. **Cards:** AX, CB, DC, DS, MC, VI. **Special Amenities: free continental breakfast and free local telephone calls.**

FEE DATA PORT / SOME UNITS VCR FEE /

218 POCATELLO — POST F...

RAMADA INN & CONVENTION... 6/1-8/31 9/1-2/... Small-scale Hotel units. 2 stories ($20 deposit) exercise ro... MC, VI

...N CENTER **Book at aaa.com** **Phone:** (208)237-0020
1P: $56-$70 2P: $56-$70
...28 1P: $55-$70 2P: $55-$70
...5/31 1P: $52-$65 2P: $52-$65
Location: I-86, exit 61, just n. 133 W Burnside 83202. Fax: 208/237-3216. **Facility:** 116 one-bedroom standard ...o elevator), interior corridors. **Parking:** on-site, winter plug-ins. **Terms:** [AP] & [BP] meal plans available, pets ... **Amenities:** video library (fee), irons, hair dryers. **Pool(s):** heated outdoor. **Leisure Activities:** sauna, whirlpool, ...om. **Guest Services:** valet and coin laundry. **Business Services:** conference facilities, fax (fee). **Cards:** AX, DC, DS,

SOME UNITS
FEE FEE

RED LION HOTEL POCATELLO **Book at aaa.com** **Phone:** (208)233-2200
Small-scale Hotel
All Year 1P: $65-$75 2P: $65-$75 XP: $10 F18
Location: I-15, exit 71, just e. 1555 Pocatello Creek Rd 83201. Fax: 208/234-4524. **Facility:** 150 units. 144 one-bedroom standard units. 6 one-bedroom suites ($101-$135), some with whirlpools. 2 stories (no elevator), interior corridors. **Parking:** on-site, winter plug-ins. **Terms:** [AP] meal plan available, small pets only (in designated units). **Amenities:** video games (fee), irons, hair dryers. **Pool(s):** heated indoor, wading. **Leisure Activities:** sauna, whirlpool, exercise room. **Guest Services:** valet and coin laundry, area transportation. **Business Services:** conference facilities, fax (fee). **Cards:** AX, CB, DC, DS, MC, VI. *(See color ad p 217)*

SOME UNITS

THUNDERBIRD MOTEL **Phone:** (208)232-6330
Motel
All Year 1P: $40-$46 2P: $46-$55 XP: $3
Location: I-15, exit 67, 1.3 mi n; just s of Idaho State University. 1415 S 5th Ave 83201. Fax: 208/232-6330. **Facility:** 45 one-bedroom standard units. 1-2 stories (no elevator), exterior corridors. **Parking:** on-site, winter plug-ins. **Terms:** weekly rates available, pets ($5 extra charge). **Pool(s):** small heated outdoor. **Guest Services:** coin laundry. **Cards:** AX, DC, DS, MC, VI.

SOME UNITS
FEE FEE FEE

WHERE TO DINE

BUDDY'S **Lunch:** $5-$16 **Dinner:** $5-$16 **Phone:** 208/233-1172
Italian
Location: I-15, exit 69 (Clark St), 1 mi w, just s on 6th St. 626 E Lewis 83201. **Hours:** 11 am-midnight; 11 am-11 pm, Thurs-Sat to midnight 9/6-5/30. Closed major holidays; also Sun. **Features:** The locals love the bustling atmosphere and good food at this family-owned restaurant—in business for more than 40 years. Italian fare dominates the menu, right up to the handmade ravioli house specialty and the famous salad dressing. The atmosphere is warm and friendly. Casual dress; beer & wine only. **Parking:** on-site. **Cards:** MC, VI.

CONTINENTAL BISTRO **Lunch:** $5-$7 **Dinner:** $9-$22 **Phone:** 208/233-4433
Continental
Location: Between Lewis and W Center; city center. 140 S Main 83204. **Hours:** 11 am-10 pm. Closed: 1/1, 12/25; also Sun. **Reservations:** suggested. **Features:** American Continental cuisine with northern Italian and French influences is inventive as evidenced by several interesting combinations and a wide array, including fresh fish and game. Seasonal patio dining is offered. Parking lot is available after 5 pm. Casual dress; beer & wine only. **Parking:** street. **Cards:** AX, DC, DS, MC, VI.

THE SANDPIPER **Dinner:** $7-$32 **Phone:** 208/233-1000
Steak House
Location: I-15, exit 71, just e, then just n. 1400 Bench Rd 83201. **Hours:** 4:30 pm-10 pm, Fri & Sat-10:30 pm, Sun-9 pm. Closed major holidays. **Reservations:** suggested, weekends. **Features:** Good choices are the house salad with shrimp & creamy garlic dressing and the prime rib entree at this informal, bustling restaurant that's convenient to several area motels and to the interstate. Deck dining is available in season. Casual dress; cocktails. **Parking:** on-site. **Cards:** AX, DS, MC, VI.

POST FALLS pop. 17,247

WHERE TO STAY

HOLIDAY INN EXPRESS **Book at aaa.com** **Phone:** (208)773-8900
SAVE
Small-scale Hotel
All Year 1P: $69-$109 2P: $69-$109
Location: I-90, exit 7, just sw. 3175 E Seltice Way 83854. Fax: 208/773-0890. **Facility:** 47 one-bedroom standard units. 2 stories (no elevator), interior corridors. **Parking:** on-site, winter plug-ins. **Terms:** cancellation fee imposed, [ECP] meal plan available, pets ($10 fee). **Amenities:** irons, hair dryers. **Leisure Activities:** Fee: game room. **Guest Services:** valet laundry. **Cards:** AX, CB, DC, DS, MC, VI. **Special Amenities: free expanded continental breakfast and free newspaper.** *(See color ad p 197)*

SOME UNITS
FEE

HOWARD JOHNSON EXPRESS **Book at aaa.com** **Phone:** (208)773-4541
SAVE
Small-scale Hotel
6/15-9/15 [ECP] 1P: $79-$129 2P: $84-$139 XP: $5 F17
3/1-6/14 & 9/16-2/28 [ECP] 1P: $59-$89 2P: $64-$94 XP: $5 F17
Location: I-90, exit 2, just ne. 3647 W 5th Ave 83854. Fax: 208/773-0235. **Facility:** 99 units. 97 one-bedroom standard units. 2 one-bedroom suites ($109-$179) with whirlpools. 2-4 stories, interior corridors. *Bath:* combo or shower only. **Parking:** on-site. **Terms:** pets ($5 extra charge). **Amenities:** voice mail, irons, hair dryers. **Pool(s):** small heated indoor. **Leisure Activities:** whirlpool. *Fee:* game room. **Guest Services:** coin laundry. **Cards:** AX, CB, DC, DS, JC, MC, VI. **Special Amenities: free expanded continental breakfast and free newspaper.**

SOME UNITS
FEE FEE FEE

RED LION TEMPLIN'S HOTEL ON THE RIVER - POST FALLS *Book at aaa.com* **Phone:** (208)773-1611

AAA SAVE — Small-scale Hotel

6/16-9/15 [BP]	1P: $99-$129	2P: $109-$139	XP: $10	F18
3/1-6/15 & 9/16-2/28 [BP]	1P: $75-$95	2P: $85-$105	XP: $10	F18

Location: I-90, exit 5 eastbound, just s to First Ave; exit 6 westbound, 0.7 mi w on Seltice Way to Spokane St, 0.5 mi s, then just e. 414 E First Ave 83854. Fax: 208/773-4192. **Facility:** 164 units. 161 one-bedroom standard units, some with whirlpools. 3 one-bedroom suites. 2-3 stories, interior corridors. *Bath:* combo or shower only. **Parking:** on-site, winter plug-ins. **Terms:** cancellation fee imposed, pets ($5 deposit, in designated units). **Amenities:** voice mail, irons, hair dryers. **Dining:** 6 am-10 pm; 6:30 am-9 pm in winter, cocktails. **Pool(s):** small heated indoor. **Leisure Activities:** sauna, whirlpool, rental boats, rental canoes, rental paddleboats, marina, fishing, boat ramp across river, guest moorage, 2 tennis courts, exercise room, horseshoes, volleyball. *Fee:* pontoon boats, river cruises. **Guest Services:** valet and coin laundry. **Business Services:** conference facilities, PC. **Cards:** AX, CB, DC, MC, VI. **Special Amenities: free full breakfast and free newspaper.** ***(See color ad below)***

SOME UNITS

FEE FEE

RIVERBEND INN *Book at aaa.com* **Phone:** (208)773-3583

AAA SAVE — Small-scale Hotel

5/22-9/30	1P: $59-$79	2P: $70-$89	XP: $5	F12
3/1-5/21 & 10/1-2/28	1P: $39-$50	2P: $44-$55	XP: $5	F12

Location: I-90, exit 2, just s. Located adjacent to outlet mall. 4105 W Riverbend Ave 83854. Fax: 208/773-1306. **Facility:** 71 units. 70 one-bedroom standard units, some with efficiencies. 1 one-bedroom suite ($100-$150) with efficiency. 2 stories (no elevator), interior corridors. *Bath:* combo or shower only. **Parking:** on-site, winter plug-ins. **Terms:** cancellation fee imposed, [CP] meal plan available. **Pool(s):** small heated outdoor. **Leisure Activities:** whirlpool. **Guest Services:** valet and coin laundry. **Cards:** AX, CB, DC, DS, MC, VI.

SOME UNITS

SLEEP INN *Book at aaa.com* **Phone:** (208)777-9394

AAA SAVE — Small-scale Hotel

All Year [ECP]	1P: $49-$129	2P: $49-$129	XP: $10	F18

Location: I-90, exit 2, just s. Located adjacent to outlet mall. 157 S Pleasant View Rd 83854. Fax: 208/777-8994. **Facility:** 84 one-bedroom standard units. 2 stories (no elevator), interior corridors. *Bath:* combo or shower only. **Parking:** on-site, winter plug-ins. **Terms:** check-in 4 pm, pets ($15 extra charge). **Amenities:** *Some:* irons, hair dryers. **Pool(s):** small heated indoor. **Leisure Activities:** whirlpool. **Guest Services:** coin laundry. **Business Services:** meeting rooms. **Cards:** AX, CB, DC, DS, JC, MC, VI. **Special Amenities: free expanded continental breakfast and free local telephone calls.**

SOME UNITS

FEE

WHERE TO DINE

THE WHITE HOUSE GRILL **Lunch:** $5-$15 **Dinner:** $5-$15 **Phone:** 208/777-9672

Mediterranean

Location: I-90, exit 5, just n. 620 N Spokane St 83854. **Hours:** 11 am-10 pm. Closed: 7/4; also Sun & 12/28-1/6. **Reservations:** suggested. **Features:** Not for the faint of heart or those who worry about their breath, the restaurant is a virtual shrine to garlic. The intimate and casual setting incorporates outdoor seating when the weather permits. The primarily Mediterranean menu highlights Chilean sea bass, as well as wonderful homemade baklava. Casual dress; beer & wine only. **Parking:** on-site. **Cards:** DS, MC, VI.

PRIEST RIVER pop. 1,754

WHERE TO STAY

EAGLE'S NEST MOTEL **Phone:** 208/448-2000

Motel

5/16-2/28	2P: $50-$85
3/1-5/15	2P: $45-$80

Location: US 2, 0.5 mi w. 1007 Albeni Hwy (US 2) 83856 (PO Box 1028). Fax: 208/448-4864. **Facility:** 30 one-bedroom standard units, some with whirlpools. 1 story, exterior corridors. *Bath:* combo or shower only. **Parking:** on-site. **Terms:** office hours 7 am-10 pm, pets (in designated units). **Business Services:** meeting rooms. **Cards:** AX, DS, MC, VI.

SOME UNITS

ASK / FEE FEE

REXBURG pop. 17,257

WHERE TO STAY

BEST WESTERN COTTONTREE INN *Book at aaa.com* **Phone:** (208)356-4646

SAVE

Small-scale Hotel

6/15-8/31	1P: $82-$102	2P: $87-$107	XP: $5	F18
9/1-2/28	1P: $74-$94	2P: $79-$99	XP: $5	F18
3/1-6/14	1P: $72-$92	2P: $77-$97	XP: $5	F18

Location: US 20, exit S Rexburg, 1 mi e. 450 W 4th St S 83440. Fax: 208/356-7461. **Facility:** 98 one-bedroom standard units, some with whirlpools. 2 stories (no elevator), interior corridors. **Parking:** on-site, winter plug-ins. **Terms:** [ECP] meal plan available, small pets only. **Amenities:** video library (fee), irons, hair dryers. **Dining:** 7 am-10 pm, Fri & Sat-11 pm. **Pool(s):** small heated indoor. **Leisure Activities:** whirlpool, exercise room. **Guest Services:** valet and coin laundry. **Business Services:** meeting rooms, business center. **Cards:** AX, CB, DC, DS, JC, MC, VI. **Special Amenities: early check-in/late check-out and free room upgrade (subject to availability with advanced reservations).**

SOME UNITS

DATA PORT / VCR / FEE

COMFORT INN *Book at aaa.com* **Phone:** (208)359-1311

SAVE

Small-scale Hotel

All Year [CP]	1P: $55-$99	2P: $55-$99

Location: Just e of jct of US 20, exit Salmon/Rexburg and SR 33. 885 W Main St 83440. Fax: 208/359-1387. **Facility:** 52 one-bedroom standard units. 2 stories (no elevator), interior corridors. **Parking:** on-site, winter plug-ins. **Terms:** 30 day cancellation notice-fee imposed. **Amenities:** irons, hair dryers. **Pool(s):** small heated indoor. **Leisure Activities:** whirlpool. **Business Services:** meeting rooms, fax (fee). **Cards:** AX, CB, DC, DS, JC, MC, VI. **Special Amenities: free continental breakfast and free local telephone calls.**

SOME UNITS

DATA PORT / /

DAYS INN *Book at aaa.com* **Phone:** (208)356-9222

SAVE

Motel

6/15-8/31	1P: $55-$75	2P: $60-$80	XP: $5	F18
3/1-6/14 & 9/1-2/28	1P: $50-$70	2P: $55-$75	XP: $5	F18

Location: US 20, exit S Rexburg, 1.8 mi e, just n. Located adjacent to Ricks College. 271 S 2nd W 83440. Fax: 208/356-9242. **Facility:** 42 one-bedroom standard units. 2 stories (no elevator), exterior corridors. **Parking:** on-site, winter plug-ins. **Terms:** [CP] meal plan available, small pets only. **Amenities:** irons, hair dryers. **Pool(s):** small heated outdoor. **Cards:** AX, CB, DC, DS, JC, MC, VI.

SOME UNITS

DATA PORT / /

WHERE TO DINE

FRONTIER PIES RESTAURANT & BAKERY **Lunch:** $6-$8 **Dinner:** $9-$14 **Phone:** 208/356-3600

American

Location: 1 mi se of US 20. 460 W 4th St S 83440. **Hours:** 7 am-10 pm, Fri & Sat-11 pm, Sun 8 am-8 pm. Closed major holidays. **Features:** No matter what you choose from the menu — sandwiches, soup or chicken-fried steak — don't budge before savoring a slice of any one of some 25 varieties of made-from-scratch pie. A recent visit afforded a quite delicious portion of strawberry pie. Casual dress. **Parking:** on-site. **Cards:** AX, DS, MC, VI.

ME 'N STAN'S RESTAURANT **Lunch:** $4-$8 **Dinner:** $7-$16 **Phone:** 208/356-7330

American

Location: Center. 167 W Main St 83440. **Hours:** 6:30 am-9 pm, Fri & Sat-10 pm. Closed: 11/25, 12/25. **Features:** The menu selections are well prepared and promptly served by a cordial, efficient staff in a simple, pleasant decor. It's hard to resist a tasty helping of liver and onions, mashed potatoes, green beans, bread and traditional tapioca pudding. Casual dress. **Parking:** on-site. **Cards:** AX, DS, MC, VI.

RIGBY pop. 2,998

WHERE TO STAY

BLUE HERON INN — Phone: (208)745-9922

Bed & Breakfast

	1P	2P	XP
5/24-9/30 [BP]	1P: $109-$185	2P: $109-$185	XP: $15
3/1-5/23 & 10/1-2/28 [BP]	1P: $99-$170	2P: $99-$170	XP: $15

Location: 18 mi n on US 20 from jct I-15, just e. 4175 E Menan Lorenzo Hwy 83442. Fax: 208/745-9922. **Facility:** Scenic views of the Snake River and the surrounding mountains create a relaxing Old West ambience at this B&B. 7 one-bedroom standard units, some with whirlpools. 2 stories (no elevator), interior/exterior corridors. *Bath:* combo or shower only. **Parking:** on-site. **Terms:** 7 day cancellation notice. **Amenities:** video library (fee), hair dryers. **Leisure Activities:** whirlpool, exercise room. *Fee:* massage. **Guest Services:** complimentary evening beverages. **Business Services:** fax. **Cards:** AX, DC, MC, VI.

SOME UNITS

RIGGINS pop. 410

WHERE TO STAY

BEST WESTERN SALMON RAPIDS LODGE — *Book at aaa.com* — Phone: (208)628-2743

Small-scale Hotel

	1P	2P	XP	
4/29-9/5 [ECP]	1P: $83-$115	2P: $83-$115	XP: $10	F17
3/1-4/28 & 9/6-11/30 [ECP]	1P: $73-$105	2P: $73-$105	XP: $10	F17
12/1-2/28 [ECP]	1P: $68-$95	2P: $73-$105	XP: $10	F17

Location: Just e of US 95; downtown. Located on the Salmon River. 1010 S Main St 83549 (PO Box 408). Fax: 208/628-3834. **Facility:** 55 units. 51 one-bedroom standard units. 4 one-bedroom suites ($114-$179) with whirlpools. 2 stories (no elevator), interior corridors. *Bath:* combo or shower only. **Parking:** on-site, winter plug-ins. **Terms:** package plans - seasonal, pets ($15 extra charge, in designated units). **Amenities:** hair dryers. *Some:* dual phone lines, irons. **Pool(s):** heated indoor. **Leisure Activities:** whirlpool, limited exercise equipment. **Guest Services:** gift shop, coin laundry. **Business Services:** meeting rooms. **Cards:** AX, CB, DC, DS, JC, MC, VI.

SOME UNITS

FEE FEE

PINEHURST RESORT COTTAGES — Phone: 208/628-3323

Cottage

	1P	2P	XP	
3/1-12/1	1P: $40-$60	2P: $45-$65	XP: $5	D12

Location: 13 mi s on US 95. Located in a quiet area. MM 182 on US 95 83654 (5604 Hwy 95, NEW MEADOWS). **Facility:** 6 cottages. 1 story, exterior corridors. *Bath:* shower only. **Parking:** on-site. **Terms:** open 3/1-12/1, 7 day cancellation notice, weekly rates available, pets ($5 extra charge). **Leisure Activities:** fishing, horseshoes. **Cards:** AX, MC, VI.

SOME UNITS

FEE

SAGLE

WHERE TO STAY

BOTTLE BAY RESORT & MARINA — Phone: 208/263-5916

Cabin

	1P	2P	XP
6/15-9/14	1P: $95	2P: $95	XP: $8
3/1-6/14 & 9/15-2/28	1P: $75	2P: $75	XP: $8

Location: 8.3 mi e on Bottle Bay Rd from US 95. 115 Resort Rd 83860. Fax: 208/265-8300. **Facility:** 8 cabins ($100-$150). 2 stories (no elevator), exterior corridors. **Parking:** on-site, winter plug-ins. **Terms:** check-in 4 pm, 2 night minimum stay - weekends, 60 day cancellation notice-fee imposed, package plans, pets ($8 extra charge). **Amenities:** video library (fee). **Leisure Activities:** rental boats, rental canoes, marina, fishing. **Guest Services:** coin laundry. **Cards:** DS, MC, VI.

SOME UNITS

FEE

WHERE TO DINE

SWAN'S LANDING — **Lunch:** $6-$16 — **Dinner:** $12-$28 — **Phone:** 208/265-2000

AAA

Steak & Seafood

Location: Just s of Longbridge, 1 mi from Sandpoint, on US 95. 41 Lakeshore Dr 83860. **Hours:** 11 am-10 pm; Sun from 10 am. Closed: 12/25. **Reservations:** suggested. **Features:** Fine Northwestern fare is spotlighted at this casually elegant mountain lodge surrounded by sweeping waterfront and mountain views from both the dining room and patio (in season). Emphasis is on beef, lamb, pork and seafood. Dressy casual; cocktails. **Parking:** on-site. **Cards:** AX, DS, MC, VI.

ST. ANTHONY pop. 3,342

WHERE TO STAY

BEST WESTERN HENRY'S FORK INN — *Book at aaa.com* — Phone: (208)624-3711

Small-scale Hotel

6/1-8/31	1P: $58-$79	2P: $58-$79
9/1-2/28	1P: $52-$75	2P: $52-$75
3/1-5/31	1P: $50-$75	2P: $50-$75

Location: US 20, exit St. Anthony, just w. 115 S Bridge St 83445. Fax: 208/624-3711. **Facility:** 30 one-bedroom standard units. 2 stories (no elevator), exterior corridors. **Parking:** on-site, winter plug-ins. **Terms:** [AP] & [BP] meal plans available, small pets only ($20 deposit). **Amenities:** hair dryers. **Business Services:** fax (fee). **Cards:** AX, DC, DS, MC, VI.

SOME UNITS

FEE

SALMON pop. 3,122

WHERE TO STAY

GREYHOUSE INN BED & BREAKFAST — **Phone:** 208/756-3968

Bed & Breakfast

5/1-10/31	1P: $70-$90	2P: $70-$90	XP: $20	D3
3/1-4/30 & 11/1-2/28	1P: $65	2P: $65	XP: $20	D3

Location: 12 mi s on US 93 (Milepost 293). 1115 Hwy 93 S 83467. **Facility:** Smoke free premises. 7 one-bedroom standard units. 1-2 stories (no elevator), interior/exterior corridors. *Bath:* some shared or private, combo or shower only. **Parking:** on-site. **Terms:** check-in 4 pm, age restrictions may apply, 30 day cancellation notice-fee imposed, [BP] meal plan available. **Cards:** AX, DS, MC, VI.

SOME UNITS

MOTEL DELUXE — **Phone:** 208/756-2231

Motel

All Year	1P: $37-$42	2P: $40-$45	XP: $5	F12

Location: Just s of Main St; downtown. 112 S Church St 83467 (PO Box 863). **Facility:** 24 units. 20 one- and 4 two-bedroom standard units, some with kitchens (no utensils). 1 story, exterior corridors. *Bath:* combo or shower only. **Parking:** on-site, winter plug-ins. **Terms:** 7 day cancellation notice-fee imposed. **Amenities:** voice mail. **Guest Services:** coin laundry. **Cards:** AX, CB, DC, MC, VI.

ASK DATA PORT SOME UNITS

STAGECOACH INN — **Phone:** 208/756-2919

Motel

All Year	1P: $53-$69	2P: $61-$75	XP: $6	F12

Location: Just n on US 93 from jct SR 28. 201 Hwy 93 N 83467. Fax: 208/756-3456. **Facility:** 100 one-bedroom standard units. 2 stories (no elevator), interior corridors. **Parking:** on-site, winter plug-ins. **Terms:** 7 day cancellation notice, [CP] meal plan available. **Amenities:** voice mail, hair dryers. **Pool(s):** heated outdoor. **Guest Services:** coin laundry. **Business Services:** meeting rooms. **Cards:** AX, CB, DC, MC, VI.

SOME UNITS DATA PORT

TWIN PEAKS RANCH — **Phone:** (208)894-2290

Ranch

6/13-9/19 Wkly [AP]	1P: $1636-$1957

Location: 18 mi s on US 93, 2 mi w. Located in a secluded, rural area. 199 Twin Peaks Ranch Rd 83467 (PO Box 774). Fax: 208/894-2429. **Facility:** Twin Peaks is a true Western ranch. Designated smoking area. 27 units. 26 one-bedroom standard units, some with whirlpools. 1 two-bedroom suite with whirlpool. 1 story, exterior corridors. *Bath:* combo or shower only. **Parking:** on-site. **Terms:** open 6/13-9/19, check-in 4:30 pm, 60 day cancellation notice-fee imposed, daily rates available. **Pool(s):** heated outdoor. **Leisure Activities:** whirlpool, boating, fishing, hiking trails, horseback riding, horseshoes. *Fee:* charter fishing. **Guest Services:** coin laundry. **Business Services:** fax. **Cards:** MC, VI.

ASK

WHERE TO DINE

SHADY NOOK RESTAURANT — **Dinner:** $10-$30 — **Phone:** 208/756-4182

Steak & Seafood

Location: From jct SR 28, 0.8 mi n on US 93. 401 1/2 Hwy 93 N 83467. **Hours:** 5 pm-10 pm; to 9 pm in winter. Closed: 11/25, 12/25; also Sun in winter. **Reservations:** suggested, in summer. **Features:** Experience the relaxed atmosphere and Western ambience of this local landmark restaurant. Enjoy the patio dining and weekday happy hour from 5:30 pm to 6:30 pm but call for hours and days of operation in the winter when schedules may vary. And, while here, treat yourself to a piece of the tart, tangy and tasty Key Lime pie. Casual dress; cocktails. **Parking:** on-site. **Cards:** AX, DC, MC, VI.

SANDPOINT pop. 6,835

WHERE TO STAY

BEST WESTERN EDGEWATER RESORT — *Book at aaa.com* — **Phone:** (208)263-3194

Small-scale Hotel

6/27-9/3 [CP]	1P: $129-$149	2P: $129-$149	XP: $6	F16
9/4-2/28 [CP]	1P: $89-$109	2P: $89-$109	XP: $6	F16
5/16-6/26 [CP]	1P: $89-$99	2P: $89-$99	XP: $6	F16
3/1-5/15 [CP]	1P: $79-$89	2P: $79-$89	XP: $6	F16

Location: Just e of US 95 N; downtown. 56 Bridge St 83864 (PO Box 128). Fax: 208/263-3194. **Facility:** 54 units. 53 one-bedroom standard units, some with whirlpools. 1 one-bedroom suite with whirlpool. 2-3 stories (no elevator), interior corridors. **Parking:** on-site. **Terms:** pets ($5 extra charge). **Amenities:** video library (fee), irons, hair dryers. **Pool(s):** heated indoor. **Leisure Activities:** saunas, whirlpool, boat dock, fishing, exercise room. **Business Services:** meeting rooms. **Cards:** AX, CB, DC, DS, JC, MC, VI.

ASK FEE DATA PORT SOME UNITS VCR FEE FEE

COIT HOUSE BED & BREAKFAST — **Phone:** (208)265-4035

Bed & Breakfast

7/1-9/15 [BP]	1P: $80-$95	2P: $80-$95
3/1-6/30 & 9/16-2/28 [BP]	1P: $65-$90	2P: $65-$90

Location: Just ne of US 95 at Fourth Ave and Alder St. 502 N Fourth Ave 83864. Fax: 208/265-5558. **Facility:** This restored Victorian gingerbread house is within walking distance of the downtown shopping district and the city beach. Smoke free premises. 4 one-bedroom standard units. 2 stories (no elevator), interior corridors. *Bath:* combo or shower only. **Parking:** street. **Terms:** check-in 4 pm, age restrictions may apply, 3 day cancellation notice, weekly rates available, no pets allowed (owner's pet on premises). **Amenities:** hair dryers. **Cards:** AX, MC, VI.

ASK

HIDDEN LAKES GOLF RESORT **Phone:** (208)263-1642

Small-scale Hotel

6/15-8/31	1P: $125-$199	2P: $249	XP: $25	F16
3/1-6/14 & 9/1-2/28	1P: $85-$125	2P: $175	XP: $25	F16

Location: 8.0 mi e on SR 200, 0.5 mi n, just past MM 38. 151 Clubhouse Way 83864. Fax: 208/263-1925. **Facility:** Designated smoking area. 8 one-bedroom suites with whirlpools. 2 stories (no elevator), interior corridors. **Parking:** on-site. **Terms:** office hours 6 am-8 pm, 30 day cancellation notice-fee imposed, weekly rates available, package plans. **Amenities:** hair dryers. **Leisure Activities:** whirlpools, cross country skiing, hiking trails, jogging. *Fee:* golf-18 holes, massage. **Guest Services:** gift shop, complimentary laundry, area transportation (fee). **Business Services:** meeting rooms. **Cards:** AX, MC, VI.

ASK FEE

THE K2 INN **Phone:** (208)263-3441

Motel

All Year [CP]	1P: $28-$39	2P: $28-$64	XP: $10	F10

Location: US 95, just e. 501 N Fourth Ave 83864. Fax: 208/263-5718. **Facility:** 18 units. 13 one- and 4 two-bedroom standard units, some with efficiencies or kitchens. 1 two-bedroom suite ($84) with kitchen. 1 story, exterior corridors. *Bath:* combo or shower only. **Parking:** on-site. **Terms:** office hours 7 am-11 pm, cancellation fee imposed, weekly rates available. **Amenities:** *Some:* irons. **Leisure Activities:** whirlpool. **Cards:** AX, MC, VI.

SOME UNITS

DATA PORT / /

LA QUINTA INN *Book at aaa.com* **Phone:** (208)263-9581

Small-scale Hotel

7/1-8/31 [ECP]	1P: $109-$129	2P: $119-$139	XP: $10	F17
3/1-6/30 & 9/1-2/28 [ECP]	1P: $79-$89	2P: $89-$99	XP: $10	F17

Location: Jct US 95 and 2; downtown. 415 Cedar St 83864. Fax: 208/263-3395. **Facility:** 70 units. 67 one-bedroom standard units, some with efficiencies. 3 one-bedroom suites ($169-$399), some with whirlpools. 2-3 stories, interior/exterior corridors. *Bath:* combo or shower only. **Parking:** on-site, winter plug-ins. **Terms:** small pets only (in designated units). **Amenities:** voice mail, irons, hair dryers. *Some:* dual phone lines. **Dining:** 6 am-10 pm, cocktails. **Pool(s):** small heated outdoor. **Leisure Activities:** whirlpool, exercise room. **Guest Services:** gift shop, valet laundry, area transportation-Amtrak station. **Business Services:** conference facilities. **Cards:** AX, DC, DS, MC, VI. **Special Amenities: free expanded continental breakfast and free local telephone calls.**

SOME UNITS

DATA PORT / VCR /

MONARCH MOUNTAIN LODGE **Phone:** (208)263-1222

Small-scale Hotel

6/2-10/1	1P: $49-$59	2P: $59-$89	XP: $6	F12
11/20-2/28	1P: $46-$59	2P: $56-$79	XP: $6	F12
3/1-6/1 & 10/2-11/19	1P: $39-$49	2P: $49-$69	XP: $6	F12

Location: 0.5 mi n on US 95 N from jct SR 200. Located next to a shopping mall. 363 Bonner Mall Way 83864 (PO Box 3025). Fax: 208/265-9472. **Facility:** 48 one-bedroom standard units, some with whirlpools. 2 stories (no elevator), interior corridors. **Parking:** on-site. **Terms:** cancellation fee imposed, [CP] meal plan available, pets ($5 extra charge, in designated units). **Amenities:** video library (fee). **Leisure Activities:** sauna, whirlpools, garden area with grills. **Guest Services:** coin laundry. **Cards:** AX, DS, MC, VI.

SOME UNITS

FEE / VCR FEE DATA PORT /

QUALITY INN SANDPOINT *Book at aaa.com* **Phone:** (208)263-2111

Small-scale Hotel

5/16-10/1	1P: $49-$89	2P: $49-$89	XP: $6	F18
3/1-5/15 & 10/2-2/28	1P: $44-$79	2P: $49-$79	XP: $6	F18

Location: US 2/95, just s of jct SR 200. 807 N 5th 83864 (PO Box 128). Fax: 208/263-3289. **Facility:** 62 units. 61 one-bedroom standard units. 1 one-bedroom suite. 2 stories (no elevator), interior corridors. *Bath:* combo or shower only. **Parking:** on-site, winter plug-ins. **Terms:** pets ($5 extra charge). **Amenities:** video library (fee), voice mail. **Pool(s):** small heated indoor. **Leisure Activities:** whirlpool. **Guest Services:** coin laundry. **Business Services:** meeting rooms. **Cards:** AX, CB, DC, DS, JC, MC, VI.

SOME UNITS

ASK FEE / VCR FEE DATA PORT /

SANDPOINT MOTEL 6 - 4163 **Phone:** 208/263-5383

Small-scale Hotel

All Year	1P: $34-$45	2P: $45-$55	XP: $6	F18

Location: 1.2 mi n on US 95 from jct SR 200. 477255 Hwy 95 N 83864. Fax: 208/263-0757. **Facility:** 70 one-bedroom standard units. 2 stories (no elevator), interior corridors. **Parking:** on-site, winter plug-ins. **Leisure Activities:** whirlpools. **Guest Services:** coin laundry. **Business Services:** meeting rooms. **Cards:** AX, DC, DS, MC, VI.

SOME UNITS

ASK DATA PORT / /

SELKIRK LODGE A RED LION HOTEL *Book at aaa.com* **Phone:** 208/265-0257

Small-scale Hotel

12/25-2/28	1P: $203-$223	2P: $223-$243	XP: $15	F17
3/1-4/11 & 11/20-12/24	1P: $133-$153	2P: $153-$173	XP: $15	F17
4/12-11/19	1P: $99-$149	2P: $119-$169	XP: $15	F17

Location: 2 mi n on US 95, then 10 mi w, follow signs. 10000 Schweitzer Mountain Rd 83864. Fax: 208/263-7961. **Facility:** Smoke free premises. 82 units. 81 one-bedroom standard units, some with whirlpools. 1 one-bedroom suite. 4 stories, interior corridors. *Bath:* combo or shower only. **Parking:** on-site. **Terms:** check-in 4 pm, 30 day cancellation notice. **Amenities:** video library, dual phone lines, voice mail, irons, hair dryers. **Pool(s):** heated outdoor. **Leisure Activities:** whirlpools, rental bicycles, hiking trails, jogging, playground, exercise room. *Fee:* downhill & cross country skiing, snowmobiling, horseback riding, massage. **Guest Services:** gift shop, coin laundry, area transportation (fee). **Business Services:** meeting rooms. **Cards:** AX, DC, MC, VI.

SOME UNITS

ASK FEE VCR DATA PORT / /

SUPER 8 MOTEL *Book at aaa.com* **Phone:** (208)263-2210

Small-scale Hotel

7/1-8/31	1P: $47	2P: $63	XP: $5	F17
9/1-2/28	1P: $42	2P: $53	XP: $5	F17
4/1-6/30	1P: $40	2P: $51	XP: $5	F17
3/1-3/31	1P: $33	2P: $46	XP: $5	F17

Location: 0.7 mi n on US 95 from jct SR 200. 476841 Hwy 95 N 83864. Fax: 208/263-2210. **Facility:** 61 one-bedroom standard units. 2 stories (no elevator), interior corridors. **Parking:** on-site. **Amenities:** safes (fee). **Leisure Activities:** whirlpool. **Cards:** AX, DC, JC, MC, VI.

SOME UNITS

WHITE PINE LODGE A RED LION HOTEL **Phone:** 208/265-0257

Small-scale Hotel

12/25-2/28	1P: $309	2P: $409-$499	XP: $15	F17
3/1-11/19	1P: $249	2P: $359-$429	XP: $15	F17
11/20-12/24	1P: $229	2P: $289-$339	XP: $15	F17

Location: 2 mi n on US 95, then 10 mi w, follow signs. Located at Schweitzer Mountain Resort. 145 Village Ln 83864 (10000 Schweitzer Mountain Rd). Fax: 208/263-7961. **Facility:** 50 units. 23 one-, 25 two- and 2 three-bedroom suites ($229-$799) with kitchens. 5 stories, interior corridors. **Parking:** on-site. **Terms:** check-in 4 pm, 21 day cancellation notice, in season-fee imposed, package plans - seasonal. **Amenities:** video library, dual phone lines, voice mail, irons, hair dryers. **Leisure Activities:** whirlpools, rental bicycles, hiking trails, jogging, playground, exercise room, horseshoes, shuffleboard, volleyball. *Fee:* downhill & cross country skiing, snowmobiling, tobogganing, horseback riding, massage. **Guest Services:** gift shop, complimentary laundry, area transportation (fee). **Business Services:** meeting rooms. *Fee:* administrative services, fax. **Cards:** AX, MC, VI.

SOME UNITS

FEE

WHERE TO DINE

CITY BEACH BISTRO **Dinner:** $16-$29 **Phone:** 208/255-1018

Nouvelle French

Location: Downtown. 204 N 1st Ave 83864. **Hours:** 5:30 pm-8:30 pm, Fri & Sat-9 pm; hours may vary. Closed: 11/25, 12/25; also Sun & Mon. **Reservations:** suggested. **Features:** The frequently changing menu boasts inventive, exciting "world food" and interesting daily specials and appetizers, such as foie gras, stuffed quail and USDA prime beef. Among hard-to-find items is wild Columbia River sturgeon. Casual dress; cocktails. **Parking:** street. **Cards:** AX, DS, MC, VI.

HYDRA **Lunch:** $6 **Dinner:** $7-$16 **Phone:** 208/263-7123

Steak & Seafood

Location: Just w of US 95 at 2nd and Lake sts; city center. 115 Lake St 83864. **Hours:** 11 am-3 & 5-10 pm, Fri & Sat-10:30 pm, Sun 10 am-9 pm. Closed: 11/25, 12/25. **Reservations:** accepted. **Features:** Dinners feature prime rib, steak and seafood specialties and creative pasta dishes served in a casual atmosphere. This comfortable, intimate eatery boasts a pleasant decor of stained glass, natural wood and greenery. Buffet lunch is offered Tuesday-Friday only. Casual dress; cocktails. **Parking:** on-site. **Cards:** AX, DC, DS, MC, VI.

IVANO'S RISTORANTE & CAFFE **Lunch:** $3-$5 **Dinner:** $7-$19 **Phone:** 208/263-0211

Regional Italian

Location: Downtown. 102 S 1st Ave 83864. **Hours:** 8 am-9 pm. Closed: 1/1, 11/25, 12/25; also Super Bowl Sun. **Reservations:** accepted. **Features:** Traditional Regional Italian cuisine is served in comfortable, casual surroundings enhanced by distinctive artwork and oak accents. Pasta, veal, chicken, beef and seafood all make a good showing, but it's the chocolate mousse that wins rave reviews. Seasonal outdoor seating is also an option at the busy downtown location. Casual dress; cocktails. **Parking:** on-site. **Cards:** AX, DC, DS, MC, VI.

JALAPENOS **Lunch:** $5-$8 **Dinner:** $6-$14 **Phone:** 208/263-2995

Mexican

Location: Downtown. 314 N Second Ave 83864. **Hours:** 11 am-10 pm; to 9 pm in winter. Closed major holidays. **Features:** Colorful, hand-painted murals and large, potted plants give the restaurant a tropical feel. Friendly service, good food and specialty drinks make it a favorite of tourists and locals alike. Casual dress; cocktails. **Parking:** street. **Cards:** AX, CB, DC, DS, JC, MC, VI.

SAND CREEK GRILL **Dinner:** $12-$26 **Phone:** 208/255-5736

International

Location: Downtown. 105 S First St 83864. **Hours:** 5 pm to closing, Sun 10 am-2 & 5 to closing. Closed: Mon & Tues. **Reservations:** accepted. **Features:** Guests can dine on creative international cuisine in the warm, lovingly decorated dining room or on the deck overlooking Sand Creek. A quiet atmosphere, subdued lighting and the occasional local musician round out the experience. Casual dress; beer & wine only. **Parking:** on-site. **Cards:** AX, MC, VI.

SODA SPRINGS pop. 3,381

WHERE TO STAY

J-R INN **Phone:** 208/547-3366

SAVE

Motel

All Year 1P: $35 2P: $47

Location: US 30. 179 W 2nd S 83276. Fax: 208/547-3003. **Facility:** 44 one-bedroom standard units. 1 story, exterior corridors. **Parking:** on-site, winter plug-ins. **Terms:** pets ($5 fee). **Leisure Activities:** basketball. **Business Services:** fax (fee). **Cards:** AX, CB, DC, DS, MC, VI. **Special Amenities: early check-in/late check-out and preferred room (subject to availability with advanced reservations).**

SOME UNITS

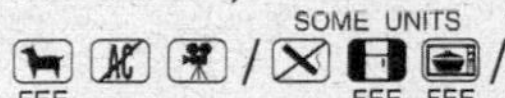
FEE FEE FEE

STANLEY pop. 100

WHERE TO STAY

MOUNTAIN VILLAGE LODGE — **Phone:** 208/774-3661

Small-scale Hotel

6/1-9/30	1P: $74-$121	2P: $74-$121	XP: $10	F10
12/26-2/28	1P: $64-$121	2P: $64-$121	XP: $10	F10
3/1-5/31 & 10/1-12/25	1P: $54-$121	2P: $54-$121	XP: $10	F10

Location: Jct US 75 and SR 21. Corner US 75 & SR 21 83278 (PO Box 150). Fax: 208/774-3761. **Facility:** 61 units. 58 one-bedroom standard units, some with efficiencies. 3 two-bedroom suites ($111-$121). 2 stories (no elevator), exterior corridors. **Parking:** on-site, winter plug-ins. **Terms:** 14 day cancellation notice, [AP] meal plan available, pets ($8 extra charge). **Dining:** restaurant, see separate listing. **Guest Services:** coin laundry. **Business Services:** meeting rooms. **Cards:** AX, DC, DS, MC, VI.

SOME UNITS

FEE

SALMON RIVER CABINS & MOTEL — **Phone:** 208/774-2290

SAVE

Cottage

6/1-9/12	1P: $85	2P: $95	XP: $10	F12
3/1-5/31	1P: $65-$75	2P: $75-$85	XP: $10	F12
9/13-10/31	1P: $75	2P: $85	XP: $10	F12
11/1-2/28	1P: $65	2P: $75	XP: $10	F12

Location: 1 mi n on US 75 from jct SR 21. (HC 67, Box 300). Fax: 208/774-3518. **Facility:** Designated smoking area. 24 units. 9 one-bedroom standard units, some with efficiencies. 1 one-bedroom suite with kitchen. 14 cabins ($60-$150). 2 stories (no elevator), exterior corridors. *Bath:* combo or shower only. **Parking:** on-site, winter plug-ins. **Terms:** cancellation fee imposed, pets ($10 extra charge). **Amenities:** video library (fee). **Business Services:** fax (fee). **Cards:** AX, DC, DS, MC, VI.

SOME UNITS

FEE

WHERE TO DINE

MOUNTAIN VILLAGE RESTAURANT — **Lunch:** $4-$8 **Dinner:** $5-$17 **Phone:** 208/774-3317

American

Location: Jct US 75 and SR 21; in Mountain Village Lodge. **Hours:** 7 am-10 pm; to 9 pm in winter. **Features:** Set in a high mountain valley with the rugged and impressive Sawtooth Mountains as a backdrop, the Mountain Village Restaurant serves up wholesome American food in a family friendly, Western-themed dining room. Catering to outdoor minded tourists who flock to the area for fly fishing, river rafting, hiking and appetite-stimulating, unpolluted mountain air. Casual dress; cocktails. **Parking:** on-site. **Cards:** AX, DS, MC, VI.

SUN VALLEY pop. 1,427

WHERE TO STAY

The following lodging was either not evaluated or did not meet AAA rating requirements but is listed for your information only.

SUN VALLEY LODGE & LODGE APARTMENTS — **Phone:** 208/622-4111

fyi

Not evaluated. **Location:** 1 mi n of Ketchum off SR 75. 1 Sun Valley Rd 83353 (Box 10). Facilities, services, and decor characterize an upscale property.

WHERE TO DINE

SUN VALLEY LODGE DINING ROOM — **Dinner:** $20-$32 **Phone:** 208/622-2150

Continental

Location: 1 mi n of Ketchum off SR 75; in Sun Valley Lodge & Lodge Apartments. 1 Sun Valley Rd 83353. **Hours:** 6:30 pm-9:30 pm; Sunday brunch 9 am-2 pm. Closed: Sun in season, Mon-Wed off season. **Reservations:** suggested. **Features:** A favorite choice for those seeking an elegant meal served with traditional flair in classic surroundings. The dining room is a study in rich brocades, gleaming brass and polished marble. The superb food is served, seemingly effortlessly, by tuxedo-clad waiters who go out of their way to ensure a memorable dining experience. Dressy casual; cocktails; entertainment. **Parking:** on-site and valet. **Cards:** AX, DC, DS, MC, VI.

The following restaurant has not been evaluated by AAA but is listed for your information only.

GRETCHEN'S — **Phone:** 208/622-4111

fyi

Not evaluated. **Location:** Sun Valley Rd. **Features:** On a menu of Continental food are game and pasta dishes and freshly baked desserts.

SWAN VALLEY pop. 213

WHERE TO STAY

The following lodging was either not evaluated or did not meet AAA rating requirements but is listed for your information only.

SOUTH FORK LODGE — **Phone:** 208/483-2112

fyi

Small-scale Hotel

Did not meet all AAA rating requirements for some guest rooms at time of last evaluation on 07/23/2002. **Location:** 4.9 mi n of jct US 26 and SR 31. 40 Conant Valley Loop 83449 (PO Box 22). Facilities, services, and decor characterize an upscale property.

WHERE TO DINE

SOUTH FORK — **Dinner:** $18-$24 — **Phone:** 208/483-2112

American

Location: 4.9 mi n of jct US 26 and SR 31; in South Fork Lodge. 40 Conant Valley Loop 83449. **Hours:** 7 am-10 & 4-9 pm. Closed: 3/18-5/24 & 10/27-12/13. **Reservations:** suggested. **Features:** Located in the South Fork Lodge this restaurant offers regional cuisine such as caribou, Canadian Walleye, Alaskan Halibut as well as other standbys like chicken and pasta. You can relax and enjoy the cuisine from the enclosed dining room or weather permitting, from the patio area. The restaurant offers a serene setting with spectacular views of the Snake River just a few yards away. Casual dress; cocktails. **Parking:** on-site. **Cards:** AX, CB, DC, DS, MC, VI.

TETON pop. 569

WHERE TO STAY

The following lodging was either not evaluated or did not meet AAA rating requirements but is listed for your information only.

TETON MOUNTAIN HIDEAWAYS — **Phone:** 208/787-3094

fyi

Not evaluated. **Location:** 219 Haighland Way 83455. Facilities, services, and decor characterize a mid-range property.

TETONIA pop. 247

WHERE TO STAY

TETON MOUNTAIN VIEW LODGE — **Phone:** (208)456-2741

AAA SAVE

Motel

6/1-11/30	2P: $65-$89	XP: $6	F18
3/1-5/31 & 12/1-2/28	2P: $38-$59	XP: $6	F18

Location: On SR 33. 510 Egbert Ave (Hwy 33) 83452 (PO Box 8). Fax: 208/456-2232. **Facility:** 24 units. 23 one- and 1 two-bedroom standard units. 2 stories (no elevator), exterior corridors. *Bath:* combo or shower only. **Parking:** on-site. **Terms:** [CP] meal plan available, package plans - seasonal, pets ($10 fee). **Leisure Activities:** whirlpool, outdoor grills, horseshoes. **Cards:** AX, DS, MC, VI. **Special Amenities: free continental breakfast and free local telephone calls.**

SOME UNITS

FEE

TWIN FALLS pop. 34,469

WHERE TO STAY

AMERITEL INN — ***Book at aaa.com*** — **Phone:** (208)736-8000

Small-scale Hotel

5/16-9/15 [ECP]	1P: $89-$119	2P: $89-$119	XP: $10	F18
3/1-5/15 & 9/16-2/28 [ECP]	1P: $69-$99	2P: $69-$99	XP: $10	F18

Location: I-84, exit 173, 3.9 mi s on US 93. 1377 Blue Lakes Blvd N 83301. Fax: 208/734-7777. **Facility:** 118 units. 117 one-bedroom standard units, some with efficiencies and/or whirlpools. 1 one-bedroom suite with efficiency. 3 stories, interior corridors. *Bath:* combo or shower only. **Parking:** on-site, winter plug-ins. **Amenities:** high-speed Internet, voice mail, irons, hair dryers. **Pool(s):** heated indoor. **Leisure Activities:** whirlpool, exercise room, sports court. **Guest Services:** valet and coin laundry. **Business Services:** meeting rooms. **Cards:** AX, CB, DC, DS, MC, VI. ***(See color ad p 186)***

SOME UNITS

ASK

DATA PORT

BEST WESTERN APOLLO MOTOR INN — ***Book at aaa.com*** — **Phone:** (208)733-2010

AAA SAVE

Motel

5/17-10/16 [ECP]	1P: $62-$76	2P: $66-$80	XP: $4	F17
3/1-5/16 & 10/17-2/28 [ECP]	1P: $54-$66	2P: $54-$66	XP: $4	F17

Location: I-84, exit 173, 5.7 mi s on US 93, 1.2 mi w. 296 Addison Ave W 83301. Fax: 208/734-0748. **Facility:** 50 units. 48 one-bedroom standard units. 2 one-bedroom suites. 1 story, exterior corridors. **Parking:** on-site. **Terms:** small pets only ($50 deposit, with prior approval). **Amenities:** irons, hair dryers. **Pool(s):** small heated outdoor. **Leisure Activities:** whirlpool. **Cards:** AX, CB, DC, DS, MC, VI. **Special Amenities: free expanded continental breakfast and free local telephone calls.**

SOME UNITS

DATA PORT

FEE

COMFORT INN *Book at aaa.com* **Phone:** 208/734-7494

Motel

All Year 1P: $79-$149 2P: $79-$149 XP: $10 F

Location: I-84, exit 173, 3.5 mi s on US 93. 1893 Canyon Springs Rd 83301. Fax: 208/735-9428. **Facility:** 52 one-bedroom standard units, some with whirlpools. 2 stories (no elevator), interior corridors. **Parking:** on-site, winter plug-ins. **Terms:** [ECP] meal plan available, pets ($10 extra charge, with prior approval). **Amenities:** safes (fee), irons, hair dryers. **Pool(s):** small heated indoor. **Leisure Activities:** whirlpool. **Guest Services:** valet laundry. **Cards:** AX, DC, DS, JC, MC, VI.

SOME UNITS

ASK / FEE

DAYS INN *Book at aaa.com* **Phone:** (208)324-6400

AAA SAVE

Motel

All Year 1P: $55-$65 2P: $55-$65 XP: $10 F18

Location: I-84, exit 173, just n on US 93. 1200 Centennial Spur 83338. Fax: 208/324-9207. **Facility:** 72 one-bedroom standard units. 3 stories, interior corridors. *Bath:* combo or shower only. **Parking:** on-site. **Terms:** cancellation fee imposed, weekly rates available, [CP] meal plan available, pets ($50 deposit, $10 extra charge). **Amenities:** video library (fee), hair dryers. *Some:* irons. **Leisure Activities:** whirlpool, exercise room. *Fee:* horse stables. **Guest Services:** coin laundry. **Business Services:** meeting rooms. **Cards:** AX, DC, DS, MC, VI. **Special Amenities: free continental breakfast and free local telephone calls.**

SOME UNITS

FEE / VCR

HOLIDAY INN EXPRESS HOTEL & SUITES *Book at aaa.com* **Phone:** 208/732-6001

Small-scale Hotel

All Year 1P: $89-$149 2P: $89-$149 XP: $10 F

Location: I-84, exit 173, 3.5 mi s. 1910 Fillmore St N 83301. Fax: 208/732-5974. **Facility:** 59 units. 57 one-bedroom standard units, some with whirlpools. 2 one-bedroom suites with whirlpools. 3 stories, interior corridors. *Bath:* combo or shower only. **Parking:** on-site, winter plug-ins. **Terms:** [ECP] meal plan available. **Amenities:** dual phone lines, voice mail, irons, hair dryers. **Pool(s):** small heated indoor. **Leisure Activities:** whirlpool, exercise room. **Guest Services:** valet and coin laundry. **Business Services:** meeting rooms. **Cards:** AX, CB, DC, DS, JC, MC, VI.

SOME UNITS

ASK

RED LION HOTEL CANYON SPRINGS *Book at aaa.com* **Phone:** (208)734-5000

AAA SAVE

Small-scale Hotel

5/1-9/30 1P: $70-$84 2P: $70-$84 XP: $10 F17

3/1-4/30 & 10/1-2/28 1P: $61-$84 2P: $61-$84 XP: $10 F17

Location: I-84, exit 173, 4 mi s on US 93. 1357 Blue Lakes Blvd N 83301. Fax: 208/733-3813. **Facility:** 112 one-bedroom standard units. 2 stories (no elevator), interior corridors. *Bath:* combo or shower only. **Parking:** on-site. **Terms:** cancellation fee imposed, package plans, small pets only (in designated units). **Amenities:** video games (fee), voice mail, irons, hair dryers. **Dining:** 2 restaurants, 6 am-9 pm, Sat & Sun from 7 am, cocktails. **Pool(s):** heated outdoor. **Leisure Activities:** sauna, whirlpool, exercise room. **Guest Services:** valet laundry. **Business Services:** conference facilities. **Cards:** AX, CB, DC, DS, MC, VI. **Special Amenities: free local telephone calls and free newspaper.** ***(See color ad p 226)***

SOME UNITS

TWIN FALLS SUPER 8 MOTEL *Book at aaa.com* **Phone:** (208)734-5801

Motel

6/1-8/31 [CP] 1P: $65-$80 2P: $79-$85 XP: $5 F13

9/1-2/28 [CP] 1P: $58-$70 2P: $65-$75 XP: $5 F13

3/1-5/31 [CP] 1P: $56-$75 2P: $61-$75 XP: $5 F13

Location: I-84, exit 173, 4.1 mi s on US 93. 1260 Blue Lakes Blvd N 83301. Fax: 208/734-7556. **Facility:** 94 one-bedroom standard units, some with whirlpools. 3 stories (no elevator), interior corridors. **Parking:** on-site, winter plug-ins. **Amenities:** hair dryers. **Leisure Activities:** exercise room. **Guest Services:** valet and coin laundry. **Cards:** AX, DC, DS, MC, VI.

SOME UNITS

ASK / VCR

WHERE TO DINE

IDAHO JOE'S **Lunch:** $4-$7 **Dinner:** $7-$12 **Phone:** 208/734-9403

AAA

American

Location: I-84, exit 173, 5 mi s. 598 Blue Lakes Blvd N 83301. **Hours:** 6 am-11 pm, Fri & Sat-midnight. Closed: 11/25, 12/25. **Features:** Try the house special: a Navajo taco made with homemade chili. The atmosphere is rustic here; the location convenient in Lynwood Shopping Center. Save room for dessert; there are more than 30 varieties of pie on the menu to choose from. Casual dress; beer & wine only. **Parking:** on-site. **Cards:** MC, VI.

LA CASITA **Lunch:** $3-$10 **Dinner:** $3-$10 **Phone:** 208/734-7974

Mexican

Location: I-84, exit 173, 6.5 mi s on US 93, then 1.3 mi sw on Shoshone St. 111 S Park Ave 83301. **Hours:** 11 am-9 pm, Fri & Sat-10 pm. Closed major holidays; also Sun. **Features:** Dine on classic Mexican cuisine featuring a variety of fresh-cooked shredded meat and chicken dishes — all hearty and tasty. This casual, contemporary local favorite offers quite a bang for your buck. Close to downtown. Casual dress; beer & wine only. **Parking:** on-site. **Cards:** AX, DS, MC, VI.

WALLACE pop. 960

WHERE TO STAY

BEST WESTERN WALLACE INN *Book at aaa.com* **Phone:** (208)752-1252

Small-scale Hotel

5/1-9/30	1P: $70-$76	2P: $84-$94	XP: $10	F12
10/1-2/28	1P: $66-$76	2P: $74-$86	XP: $10	F12
3/1-4/30	1P: $66-$76	2P: $72-$86	XP: $10	F12

Location: I-90, exit 61 (Business Rt 90), just se. 100 Front St 83873 (PO Box 867). Fax: 208/753-0981. **Facility:** 63 units. 61 one-bedroom standard units, some with whirlpools. 2 one-bedroom suites ($125-$250). 2 stories (no elevator), interior corridors. *Bath:* combo or shower only. **Parking:** on-site, winter plug-ins. **Terms:** check-in 4 pm, weekly rates available, package plans, pets ($10 deposit). **Amenities:** irons, hair dryers. **Dining:** JG's Restaurant, see separate listing. **Pool(s):** small heated indoor. **Leisure Activities:** sauna, whirlpool, steamroom, exercise room. **Guest Services:** gift shop, valet laundry. **Business Services:** conference facilities. **Cards:** AX, DC, MC, VI.

SOME UNITS

ASK FEE FEE DATA PORT / VCR FEE /

STARDUST MOTEL *Book at aaa.com* **Phone:** (208)752-1213

Motel

5/1-9/30	1P: $46-$56	2P: $56-$64	XP: $10	F12
10/1-2/28	1P: $42-$50	2P: $48-$58	XP: $10	F12
3/1-4/30	1P: $40-$48	2P: $46-$54	XP: $10	F12

Location: I-90, exit 61 (Business Rt 90), 0.7 mi e; downtown. Located in historic area. 410 Pine St 83873. Fax: 208/753-0981. **Facility:** 43 units. 42 one-bedroom standard units. 1 one-bedroom suite ($60-$78) with kitchen. 2 stories (no elevator), exterior corridors. **Parking:** on-site, winter plug-ins. **Terms:** office hours 7 am-10 pm, check-in 4 pm, weekly rates available, package plans, pets ($10 extra charge). **Amenities:** hair dryers. **Guest Services:** valet laundry. **Business Services:** meeting rooms. **Cards:** AX, DC, MC, VI.

SOME UNITS

ASK FEE FEE / /

WHERE TO DINE

HISTORIC JAMESON SALOON & RESTAURANT **Lunch:** $6-$9 **Dinner:** $8-$13 **Phone:** 208/556-6000

American

Location: Downtown. 304 6th St 83873. **Hours:** 11:30 am-8 pm. Closed: Sun & Mon. **Reservations:** accepted. **Features:** Patrons can step back in time for casual dining in the surroundings of a classic 19th-century saloon, complete with an ornate back bar and fixtures. The restaurant is in a historic mining town. Casual dress; cocktails. **Parking:** street. **Cards:** DS, MC, VI.

JG'S RESTAURANT **Lunch:** $5-$8 **Dinner:** $8-$13 **Phone:** 208/752-1252

American

Location: I-90, exit 61 (Business Rt 90), just se; in Best Western Wallace Inn. 100 Front St 83873. **Hours:** 7 am-8 pm, Fri & Sat-9 pm. **Reservations:** accepted. **Features:** Patrons can enjoy casual dining in bright and contemporary surroundings with friendly and attentive service. The menu's varied selection includes something for nearly every taste and member of the family. Casual dress; cocktails. **Parking:** on-site. **Cards:** DS, MC, VI.

WEISER pop. 5,343

WHERE TO STAY

INDIANHEAD MOTEL **Phone:** 208/549-0331

Motel

All Year	1P: $39-$60	2P: $50-$60

Location: 1 mi n at jct US 95 and Indianhead Rd. 747 Hillcrest Ave 83672. **Facility:** Smoke free premises. 8 units. 7 one- and 1 two-bedroom standard units. 1 story, exterior corridors. *Bath:* combo or shower only. **Parking:** on-site. **Terms:** 7 day cancellation notice-fee imposed. **Leisure Activities:** horseshoes. **Cards:** MC, VI.

WORLEY pop. 223

WHERE TO STAY

COEUR D'ALENE CASINO RESORT HOTEL **Phone:** (208)686-0248

AAA SAVE

Small-scale Hotel

5/16-9/1	1P: $80-$300	2P: $80-$300
3/1-5/15 & 9/2-2/28	1P: $65-$300	2P: $65-$300

Location: On US 95, 3 mi n. 27068 S Hwy 95 83876 (PO Box 236). Fax: 208/686-1842. **Facility:** 96 units. 93 one-bedroom standard units. 3 one-bedroom suites ($150-$300). 3 stories, interior corridors. *Bath:* combo or shower only. **Parking:** on-site, winter plug-ins. **Terms:** check-in 4 pm, [AP] meal plan available, package plans, pets ($25 deposit). **Amenities:** video games (fee), dual phone lines, voice mail, irons, hair dryers. **Dining:** 2 restaurants, 7 am-9 pm, cocktails, also, High Mountain Steakhouse, see separate listing. **Pool(s):** small heated indoor. **Leisure Activities:** whirlpool, exercise room, game room. *Fee:* golf-18 holes. **Guest Services:** gift shop, airport transportation (fee)-Spokane International Airport, area transportation-Cour d'Alene, Post Falls, Spokane. **Cards:** AX, DC, DS, MC, VI. **Special Amenities: free local telephone calls and free newspaper.**

SOME UNITS

FEE FEE 24 DATA PORT / FEE FEE /

WHERE TO DINE

HIGH MOUNTAIN STEAKHOUSE **Lunch:** $6-$10 **Dinner:** $6-$14 **Phone:** 208/686-0248

AAA

American

Location: On US 95, 3 mi n; in Coeur d'Alene Casino Resort Hotel. 27068 S Hwy 95 83876. **Hours:** 7 am-9 pm. **Reservations:** accepted. **Features:** This casual restaurant specializes in buffet service for the busy gambler, as well as cooked-to-order steak and seafood. Among elements of the Western-style setting are a large rock waterfall and a diorama depicting a canoe beached in the cattails of a lake. Casual dress; cocktails. **Parking:** on-site and valet. **Cards:** AX, CB, DC, DS, MC, VI.

Montana

Kintla Lake
Glacier National Park

ANACONDA pop. 9,417

WHERE TO STAY

The following lodging was either not evaluated or did not meet AAA rating requirements but is listed for your information only.

LODGE AT OLD WORKS

fyi

Small-scale Hotel

5/1-2/28 1P: $100-$150 2P: $100-$150 XP: $25 F18

Too new to rate, opening scheduled for May 2004. **Location:** I-90, exit 208, 7 mi on SR 1 to Cedar St. 1005 Pizzini Way 59711 (PO Box 1468). Fax: 406/563-7737. **Amenities:** 70 units, coffeemakers, microwaves, refrigerators. **Terms:** open 5/1-2/28, 2 night minimum stay, 3 day cancellation notice-fee imposed. **Cards:** AX, MC, VI.

WHERE TO DINE

BARCLAY II SUPPERCLUB & LOUNGE **Dinner:** $9-$26 **Phone:** 406/563-5541

Steak & Seafood

Location: I-90, exit Anaconda, just sw on SR 1, then 7.5 mi. 1300 E Commercial 59711. **Hours:** 5 pm-10 pm, Sun 4 pm-9:30 pm. Closed major holidays; also Mon. **Reservations:** suggested, weekends. **Features:** Patrons dine on large portions of steak and seafood specialties, including a notable tenderloin entree, in an informal setting just six miles from Fairmont Hot Springs. The crowd enjoys good food and pleasant service. Casual dress; cocktails. **Parking:** on-site. **Cards:** AX, DS, MC, VI.

BELGRADE pop. 5,728

WHERE TO STAY

GALLATIN RIVER LODGE *Book at aaa.com* **Phone:** (406)388-0148

Small-scale Hotel

6/1-9/30 [BP]	1P: $250	2P: $270	XP: $20	F8
3/1-5/31 & 10/1-2/28 [BP]	1P: $150	2P: $170	XP: $20	F8

Location: I-90, exit 298, 2.7 mi s on SR 85, 1 mi w on Valley Center Rd (gravel), then 0.5 mi s, follow sign. 9105 Thorpe Rd 59718. Fax: 406/388-6766. **Facility:** Smoke free premises. 6 one-bedroom standard units with whirlpools. 2 stories (no elevator), interior corridors. **Parking:** on-site, winter plug-ins. **Terms:** check-in 4 pm, 7 day cancellation notice-fee imposed, weekly rates available, [AP] meal plan available, package plans, pets ($20 deposit). **Amenities:** voice mail, hair dryers. **Leisure Activities:** fishing, hiking trails. *Fee:* horseback riding. **Business Services:** meeting rooms. **Cards:** MC, VI.

FEE

HOLIDAY INN EXPRESS *Book at aaa.com* **Phone:** (406)388-0800

Small-scale Hotel

All Year 1P: $90-$100

Location: I-90, exit 298, just s on SR 85. 6261 Jack Rabbit Ln 59714. Fax: 406/388-0804. **Facility:** Smoke free premises. 67 one-bedroom standard units. 3 stories, interior corridors. *Bath:* combo or shower only. **Parking:** on-site, winter plug-ins. **Terms:** cancellation fee imposed, [ECP] meal plan available. **Amenities:** voice mail, irons, hair dryers. **Leisure Activities:** exercise room. **Guest Services:** valet and coin laundry. **Business Services:** business center. **Cards:** AX, CB, DC, DS, JC, MC, VI.

SOME UNITS

LA QUINTA INN & SUITES *Book at aaa.com* **Phone:** (406)388-2222

AAA SAVE

Small-scale Hotel

6/15-8/31 [ECP]	1P: $89-$109	2P: $89-$109	XP: $10	F18
3/1-6/14 [ECP]	1P: $59-$99	2P: $59-$99	XP: $10	F18
9/1-10/31 [ECP]	1P: $69-$89	2P: $69-$89	XP: $10	F18
11/1-2/28 [ECP]	1P: $49-$69	2P: $49-$69	XP: $10	F18

Location: I-90, exit 298, just s on SR 85. 6445 Jackrabbit Ln 59714. Fax: 406/388-7501. **Facility:** 65 one-bedroom standard units, some with efficiencies and/or whirlpools. 3 stories, interior corridors. *Bath:* combo or shower only. **Parking:** on-site. **Amenities:** voice mail, irons, hair dryers. **Pool(s):** heated indoor. **Leisure Activities:** sauna, whirlpool, exercise room. **Guest Services:** coin laundry. **Business Services:** business center. **Cards:** AX, DC, DS, MC, VI. **Special Amenities: free expanded continental breakfast and free local telephone calls.**

SOME UNITS

BIGFORK pop. 1,421

WHERE TO STAY

BURGGRAF'S COUNTRY LANE BED N' BREAKFAST — **Phone:** (406)837-4608

Bed & Breakfast

5/15-9/15 [BP] 1P: $90 2P: $105-$140 XP: $25 F12

Location: Jct US 35, 3.3 mi e on SR 209 to fire station, 0.5 mi s on Ferndale Dr, 2 mi e on S Ferndale, then 2 mi s. 1 Rainbow Dr on Swan Lake 59911. Fax: 406/837-2468. **Facility:** A tree-shaded lakeshore is the setting for this log home decorated with artifacts and travel photos. Smoke free premises. 5 one-bedroom standard units, some with whirlpools. 2 stories (no elevator), interior corridors. *Bath:* combo or shower only. **Parking:** on-site. **Terms:** open 5/15-9/15, 14 day cancellation notice-fee imposed, weekly rates available. **Amenities:** video library. *Some:* hair dryers. **Leisure Activities:** rental boats, canoeing, rental paddleboats, boat dock, fishing, horseshoes.

SOME UNITS

ASK / VCR /

MOUNTAIN LAKE LODGE — **Phone:** (406)837-3800

AAA SAVE

Small-scale Hotel

6/24-9/6	1P: $165-$292	2P: $165-$292
9/7-10/6	1P: $99-$205	2P: $99-$205
3/1-6/23	1P: $85-$205	2P: $85-$205
10/7-2/28	1P: $85-$165	2P: $85-$165

Location: On US 35, 5 mi s. Located in a quiet area. 1950 Sylvan Dr 59911. Fax: 406/837-3861. **Facility:** Designated smoking area. 30 units. 21 one-bedroom standard units, some with whirlpools. 9 one-bedroom suites, some with kitchens. 1-3 stories (no elevator), exterior corridors. **Parking:** on-site, winter plug-ins. **Terms:** office hours 7:30 am-11:30 pm, check-in 4 pm, 7 day cancellation notice-fee imposed, small pets only ($15 extra charge). **Amenities:** irons, hair dryers. **Dining:** 2 restaurants, 11 am-9 pm; Fri& Sat from 6 pm, Sun 10 am-2 pm 10/1-5/15; closed Mon & Tues, cocktails. **Pool(s):** heated outdoor. **Leisure Activities:** whirlpool, putting green, exercise room. **Guest Services:** coin laundry. **Business Services:** meeting rooms. **Cards:** AX, DS, MC, VI.

DATA PORT

FEE

O'DUACHAIN COUNTRY INN — **Phone:** 406/837-6851

Bed & Breakfast

All Year [BP] 1P: $125-$195 2P: $125-$195 XP: $25 D6

Location: Jct US 35, 3.3 mi e on SR 209 to fire station, 1.5 mi ne. Located in a quiet area. 675 N Ferndale Dr 59911. Fax: 703/995-4300. **Facility:** Meadows, trees and a pond with flowering water lilies create a scenic backdrop to the inn's three-level log home with wraparound deck. Designated smoking area. 5 units. 4 one- and 1 two-bedroom standard units. 2 stories (no elevator), interior/exterior corridors. *Bath:* combo or shower only. **Parking:** on-site, winter plug-ins. **Terms:** 2 night minimum stay - 6/1-9/30, 30 day cancellation notice-fee imposed. **Leisure Activities:** whirlpool, hiking trails, jogging, basketball. **Cards:** AX, DS, MC, VI.

TIMBERS MOTEL — **Phone:** 406/837-6200

AAA SAVE

Motel

All Year [CP] 1P: $46-$88 2P: $46-$93 XP: $6

Location: Just n on US 35 from jct of SR 209. 8540 Hwy 35 59911 (PO Box 2214). Fax: 406/837-6203. **Facility:** 40 one-bedroom standard units. 2 stories (no elevator), exterior corridors. *Bath:* combo or shower only. **Parking:** on-site. **Terms:** 7 day cancellation notice, pets ($50 deposit, $5 extra charge). **Amenities:** voice mail. **Pool(s):** small heated outdoor. **Leisure Activities:** sauna, whirlpool. **Cards:** AX, DS, MC, VI. **Special Amenities: free continental breakfast and free local telephone calls.**

SOME UNITS

DATA PORT / /

FEE

The following lodgings were either not evaluated or did not meet AAA rating requirements but are listed for your information only.

ACCOMMODATIONS FLATHEAD LAKE — **Phone:** 406/837-5617

fyi

Not evaluated. **Location:** 520 Lake Ave 59911. Facilities, services, and decor characterize a mid-range property.

SWAN LAKE GUEST CABINS — **Phone:** 406/837-1137

fyi

Not evaluated. **Location:** SR Hwy 83, Milepost 78 59911 (PO Box 2559). Facilities, services, and decor characterize a mid-range property.

WHERE TO DINE

EL TOPO — **Dinner:** $5-$10 — **Phone:** 406/837-2114

Mexican

Location: On north end of town. 7987 SR 35 59911. **Hours:** 4:30 pm-9 pm. Closed: 1/1, 11/25, 12/25; also Sun in winter. **Features:** The wildly popular and lively gathering spot serves what many consider some of the area's best Mexican food. Fresh ingredients, careful preparation and friendly service are hallmarks. For a true taste treat, don't pass up the fish tacos. Casual dress; cocktails. **Parking:** on-site. **Cards:** AX, CB, DC, DS, JC, MC, VI.

LA PROVENCE RESTAURANT — **Lunch:** $4-$9 — **Dinner:** $15-$22 — **Phone:** 406/837-2923

AAA

French

Location: Downtown. 408 Bridge St 59911. **Hours:** 11 am-2 & 5:30-10 pm. Closed: 11/25, 12/25; also Sun & Mon in winter. **Reservations:** suggested. **Features:** La Provence is a small, bistro-style restaurant specializing in classic French Mediterranean cuisine as well as inventive and unique dishes utilizing local and seasonal produce. The French born chef/owner serves his tantalizing food from a main street location in this small, lakeside resort village which has become a favorite of tourists and locals alike. Casual dress; cocktails. **Parking:** street. **Cards:** AX, MC, VI.

SHOWTHYME — Dinner: $13-$22 — Phone: 406/837-0707

American

Location: Downtown. 548 Electric Ave 59911. **Hours:** 5 pm-10 pm; to 9 pm in winter. Closed: 1/1, 12/25. **Reservations:** suggested. **Features:** The top-notch staff treats every diner with special enthusiasm at this casual, fun eatery where imaginative fare is the norm. Seasonal menus feature creative entrees and dessert, such as truffle torte on creme Anglaise. Summer deck dining is available. Casual dress. **Parking:** street. **Cards:** AX, DS, MC, VI.

The following restaurants have not been evaluated by AAA but are listed for your information only.

BIGFORK INN — **Phone:** 406/837-6680

fyi

Not evaluated. **Location:** 604 Electric Ave 59911. **Features:** The Bigfork Inn is a long time dining tradition in this area and is very popular with locals and tourists alike.

COYOTE ROADHOUSE — **Phone:** 406/837-1233

fyi

Not evaluated. **Location:** 600 Three Eagle Ln 59911. **Features:** Set on the Flathead River in a rural location the Roadhouse affords beautiful views and casual country dining.

TUSCANY'S — **Phone:** 406/837-2505

fyi

Not evaluated. **Location:** 331 Bridge St 59911. **Features:** Casual dining in a small converted residential dwelling amid the pines of a popular resort town.

BIG SKY pop. 1,221

WHERE TO STAY

320 GUEST RANCH — **Phone:** (406)995-4283

AAA SAVE — Ranch

7/1-9/30 & 12/23-2/28 [CP]	1P: $132-$338	2P: $142-$338	XP: $15	F12
3/1-6/30	1P: $108-$283	2P: $124-$283	XP: $15	F12
10/1-12/22	1P: $87-$256	2P: $100-$256	XP: $15	F12

Location: 11.8 mi s on US 191. Located in the Gallatin National Forest. 205 Buffalo Horn Creek Rd 59730 (205 Buffalo Horn Creek Rd, GALLATIN GATEWAY). Fax: 406/995-4694. **Facility:** Luxury accommodations, including four rooms with fireplaces, are offered at this log ranch. 59 units. 38 one-bedroom standard units, some with efficiencies. 7 vacation homes and 14 cabins, some with whirlpools. 1-2 stories (no elevator), exterior corridors. **Parking:** on-site, winter plug-ins. **Terms:** 30 day cancellation notice-fee imposed, package plans - seasonal, pets ($10 extra charge). **Amenities:** hair dryers. *Some:* irons. **Dining:** 7 am-10 & 6-10 pm; 7 am-10 pm 6/15-10/1, cocktails. **Leisure Activities:** whirlpool, fishing, cross country skiing, snowmobiling, recreation programs, hiking trails, playground. *Fee:* sleigh rides, hayrides, horseback riding. **Guest Services:** gift shop, coin laundry. **Business Services:** meeting rooms. **Cards:** MC, VI. **Special Amenities: free continental breakfast and free local telephone calls.**

FEE — SOME UNITS

BEST WESTERN BUCK'S T-4 LODGE — *Book at aaa.com* — **Phone:** (406)995-4111

AAA SAVE — Small-scale Hotel

5/28-9/4 [BP]	1P: $89-$134	2P: $99-$144	XP: $10	F12
9/5-11/24 [BP]	1P: $79-$124	2P: $89-$134	XP: $10	F12
3/1-4/15 & 11/25-2/28 [BP]	1P: $99-$119	2P: $109-$129	XP: $10	F12

Location: US 191, 1 mi s of Big Sky entrance. 46625 Gallatin Rd 59716 (PO Box 160279). Fax: 406/995-2191. **Facility:** 74 units. 72 one- and 2 two-bedroom standard units, some with efficiencies and/or whirlpools. 2 stories (no elevator), interior/exterior corridors. *Bath:* combo or shower only. **Parking:** on-site, winter plug-ins. **Terms:** open 3/1-4/15 & 5/28-2/28, check-in 4 pm, 7 day cancellation notice, small pets only ($5 extra charge). **Amenities:** video library (fee), voice mail, irons, hair dryers. **Dining:** 3 restaurants, 5 pm-10 pm; from 4 pm in summer, cocktails. **Leisure Activities:** whirlpools, fishing, rafting, cross country skiing, snowmobiling, climbing wall, hiking trails, horseback riding. *Fee:* horseshoes, game room. **Business Services:** meeting rooms. **Cards:** AX, CB, DC, DS, JC, MC, VI. **Special Amenities: free full breakfast and free newspaper.** *(See color ad p 303)*

FEE — SOME UNITS — FEE

COMFORT INN AT BIG SKY — *Book at aaa.com* — **Phone:** (406)995-2333

Motel

6/1-9/4 [ECP]	1P: $89-$149	2P: $89-$149	XP: $10	F18
11/25-2/28 [ECP]	1P: $79-$149	2P: $79-$149	XP: $10	F18
3/1-5/31 & 9/5-11/24 [ECP]	1P: $69-$129	2P: $69-$129	XP: $10	F18

Location: US 191, 0.7 mi s of Big Sky entrance. 47214 Gallatin Rd 59716 (PO Box 161095). Fax: 406/995-2277. **Facility:** 62 units. 56 one- and 6 two-bedroom standard units, some with kitchens and/or whirlpools. 3 stories (no elevator), interior corridors. *Bath:* combo or shower only. **Parking:** on-site, winter plug-ins. **Terms:** cancellation fee imposed, package plans - seasonal, pets ($65 deposit, in smoking units). **Amenities:** voice mail, irons, hair dryers. **Pool(s):** heated indoor. **Leisure Activities:** whirlpool, waterslide, fishing, limited exercise equipment. **Guest Services:** coin laundry. **Business Services:** meeting rooms. **Cards:** AX, CB, DC, DS, JC, MC, VI.

ASK — FEE — SOME UNITS — FEE

MOUNTAIN INN — **Phone:** (406)995-7858

Small-scale Hotel

10/5-2/28 [ECP]	2P: $129-$197	XP: $25	F18
3/1-4/20 [ECP]	2P: $129-$149	XP: $25	F18
6/10-10/4 [ECP]	2P: $99-$134	XP: $25	F18

Location: From jct US 191 and SR 64, 9 mi w on SR 64. Located in Big Sky Mountain Village. 75 Sitting Bull Ln 59716. Fax: 406/995-7898. **Facility:** 90 one-bedroom standard units. 4 stories, interior corridors. *Bath:* combo or shower only. **Parking:** on-site. **Terms:** open 3/1-4/20 & 6/10-2/28, 30 day cancellation notice-fee imposed. **Amenities:** voice mail, irons, hair dryers. **Pool(s):** heated indoor. **Leisure Activities:** whirlpools, hiking trails, exercise room. **Guest Services:** sundries, coin laundry. **Business Services:** meeting rooms. **Cards:** AX, DC, DS, MC, VI.

ASK — SOME UNITS — FEE

RAINBOW RANCH LODGE *Book at aaa.com* **Phone:** (406)995-4132

AAA SAVE

6/16-10/16	1P: $245-$295	2P: $245-$295	XP: $30	F5
12/24-2/28	1P: $180-$215	2P: $180-$215	XP: $30	F5
3/1-6/15 & 10/17-12/23	1P: $145-$205	2P: $145-$205	XP: $30	F5

Motel

Location: 5 mi s on US 191. 42950 Gallatin Rd 59730 (PO Box 160336, 59716). Fax: 406/995-2861. **Facility:** Smoke free premises. 16 units. 14 one- and 2 two-bedroom standard units with whirlpools. 1 story, exterior corridors. **Parking:** on-site, winter plug-ins. **Terms:** 2-3 night minimum stay - seasonal, cancellation fee imposed, pets ($40 fee). **Amenities:** voice mail, irons, hair dryers. **Dining:** 5:30 pm-9 pm; 6 pm-9:30 pm in summer, cocktails. **Leisure Activities:** whirlpool, fishing, fly fishing outfitters, hiking trails. *Fee:* horseback riding, massage. **Guest Services:** area transportation. **Business Services:** meeting rooms, administrative services. **Cards:** AX, DS, MC, VI. **Special Amenities:** **free local telephone calls and free newspaper.**

FEE

The following lodgings were either not evaluated or did not meet AAA rating requirements but are listed for your information only.

ARROWHEAD **Phone:** 406/995-4800

fyi

Not evaluated. **Location:** Huntley Lodge Rd 59716. Facilities, services, and decor characterize a mid-range property.

BEAVERHEAD **Phone:** 406/995-4800

fyi

Not evaluated. **Location:** Sitting Bull Rd 59716. Facilities, services, and decor characterize a mid-range property.

BIG EZ LODGE **Phone:** 406/995-7000

fyi

Small-scale Hotel

Did not meet all AAA rating requirements for locking devices in some guest rooms at time of last evaluation on 07/24/2002. **Location:** From blinking light on US 191, 2.5 mi s, w on N Main Beaver Creek Rd (gravel), 1.2 mi to gate, then continue 4.8 mi s. 7000 Main Beaver Creek Rd 59730 (PO Box 160070, 59716). Facilities, services, and decor characterize an upscale property.

BIG HORN **Phone:** 406/995-4800

fyi

Not evaluated. **Location:** Bison Run Rd 59716. Facilities, services, and decor characterize a mid-range property.

BIG SKY HOUSE OF VIEWS **Phone:** 630/513-8535

fyi

Not evaluated. **Location:** 1470 Beaver Creek West Dr 59716. Facilities, services, and decor characterize a mid-range property.

BLUE GROUSE **Phone:** 406/995-4800

fyi

Not evaluated. **Location:** 3500 Ring Neck Rd 59716. Facilities, services, and decor characterize a mid-range property.

CRAIL CREEK CLUB **Phone:** 406/995-4800

fyi

Not evaluated. **Location:** 2000 Curley Bear Rd 59716. Facilities, services, and decor characterize a mid-range property.

EVANS BIG SKY HOME **Phone:** 941/489-2484

fyi

Not evaluated. **Location:** 2970 Looking Glass Rd 59716. Facilities, services, and decor characterize a mid-range property.

GLACIER CONDOMINIUMS **Phone:** 406/995-4800

fyi

Not evaluated. **Location:** 2575 Curley Bear Rd 59716. Facilities, services, and decor characterize a mid-range property.

HIDDEN VILLAGE **Phone:** 406/995-4800

fyi

Not evaluated. **Location:** Hidden Village Dr 59716. Facilities, services, and decor characterize a mid-range property.

PARK CONDOMINIUMS **Phone:** 406/995-4800

fyi

Not evaluated. **Location:** 1985 Yellowtail Rd 59716. Facilities, services, and decor characterize a mid-range property.

THE PINES **Phone:** 406/995-4800

fyi

Not evaluated. **Location:** 35 Blue Spruce Way 59716. Facilities, services, and decor characterize a mid-range property.

RESORT QUEST AT BIG SKY **Phone:** 406/995-4800

fyi

Not evaluated. **Location:** 3080 Pine Dr 59716. Facilities, services, and decor characterize a mid-range property.

RIVER ROCK LODGE-RESORTQUEST **Phone:** 406/995-4800

fyi

Small-scale Hotel

Did not meet all AAA rating requirements for locking devices in some guest rooms at time of last evaluation on 07/10/2003. **Location:** Jct US 191 and SR 64, 3 mi w on SR 4, then just s. 3080 Pine Dr 59716 (PO Box 160700). Facilities, services, and decor characterize a mid-range property.

SADDLE RIDGE **Phone:** 406/995-4800

fyi

Not evaluated. **Location:** Saddle Ridge Estates 59716. Facilities, services, and decor characterize a mid-range property.

SILVER BOW **Phone:** 406/995-4800

fyi

Not evaluated. **Location:** 2225 Black Otter Rd 59716. Facilities, services, and decor characterize a mid-range property.

SKY CREST **Phone:** 406/995-4800

fyi

Not evaluated. **Location:** 1700 Big Sky Rd 59716. Facilities, services, and decor characterize a mid-range property.

SOUTHFORK ANGLING AND SKI LODGE — **Phone:** 512/327-5896
fyi Not evaluated. **Location:** 1620 Big Sky Rd 59716. Facilities, services, and decor characterize a mid-range property.

STILLWATER — **Phone:** 406/995-4800
fyi Not evaluated. **Location:** Huntley Lodge Rd 59716. Facilities, services, and decor characterize a mid-range property.

YELLOWSTONE CONDOMINIUMS — **Phone:** 406/995-4800
fyi Not evaluated. **Location:** 2180 Yellowtail Rd 59716. Facilities, services, and decor characterize a mid-range property.

BIG TIMBER pop. 1,650

WHERE TO STAY

BIG TIMBER BUDGET HOST — **Phone:** (406)932-4943

Motel

6/2-9/30 [CP]	1P: $58-$68	2P: $68-$88	XP: $6	F12
3/1-6/1 & 10/1-2/28 [CP]	1P: $52-$58	2P: $58-$78	XP: $6	F12

Location: I-90, exit 367, just n, then 0.6 mi e. 600 W 2nd St 59011 (PO Box 1301). Fax: 406/932-6583. **Facility:** Smoke free premises. 22 one-bedroom standard units. 2 stories (no elevator), interior corridors. *Bath:* combo or shower only. **Parking:** on-site, winter plug-ins. **Terms:** small pets only ($20 deposit). **Cards:** AX, DS, MC, VI.

SOME UNITS
FEE / DATA PORT /

BIG TIMBER SUPER 8 MOTEL *Book at aaa.com* — **Phone:** (406)932-8888

Small-scale Hotel

5/1-9/30 [CP]	1P: $59-$89	2P: $64-$94	XP: $5	F12
10/1-2/28 [CP]	1P: $54-$84	2P: $59-$89	XP: $5	F12
3/1-4/30 [CP]	1P: $49-$79	2P: $54-$84	XP: $5	F12

Location: I-90, exit 367. 20A Big Timber Loop Rd 59011 (PO Box 1441). Fax: 406/932-4103. **Facility:** 41 one-bedroom standard units. 2 stories (no elevator), interior corridors. **Parking:** on-site, winter plug-ins. **Guest Services:** coin laundry. **Cards:** AX, CB, DC, DS, MC, VI.

SOME UNITS
ASK DATA PORT / /

BILLINGS pop. 89,847

WHERE TO STAY

BEST WESTERN BILLINGS *Book at aaa.com* — **Phone:** (406)248-9800

AAA SAVE

Small-scale Hotel

7/1-9/20 [ECP]	1P: $79-$109	2P: $79-$119	XP: $8	F16
5/1-6/30 [ECP]	1P: $69-$99	2P: $69-$99	XP: $8	F16
9/21-2/28 [ECP]	1P: $69-$89	2P: $69-$99	XP: $8	F16
3/1-4/30 [ECP]	1P: $65-$89	2P: $69-$99	XP: $8	F16

Location: I-90, exit 446, just s. 5610 S Frontage Rd 59101. Fax: 406/248-2500. **Facility:** 80 one-bedroom standard units, some with whirlpools. 3 stories, interior/exterior corridors. *Bath:* combo or shower only. **Parking:** on-site, winter plug-ins. **Terms:** small pets only. **Amenities:** video games (fee), voice mail, irons, hair dryers. *Some:* high-speed Internet, dual phone lines. **Pool(s):** small heated indoor. **Leisure Activities:** whirlpool, exercise room. **Guest Services:** valet and coin laundry. **Business Services:** meeting rooms. **Cards:** AX, CB, DC, DS, MC, VI. **Special Amenities: free expanded continental breakfast and free local telephone calls.**

SOME UNITS
DATA PORT / / FEE FEE

BEST WESTERN PONDEROSA INN *Book at aaa.com* — **Phone:** (406)259-5511

AAA SAVE

Small-scale Hotel

6/1-9/30 [CP]	1P: $60-$70	2P: $70-$80	XP: $10	F12
3/1-5/31 & 10/1-2/28 [CP]	1P: $55-$65	2P: $65-$75	XP: $10	F12

Location: On I-90 business loop; downtown. 2511 1st Ave N 59101 (PO Box 1791, 59103). Fax: 406/245-8004. **Facility:** 132 units. 131 one-bedroom standard units, some with whirlpools. 1 one-bedroom suite with whirlpool. 1-3 stories, interior/exterior corridors. *Bath:* combo or shower only. **Parking:** on-site, winter plug-ins. **Terms:** 3 day cancellation notice, small pets only. **Amenities:** voice mail, irons, hair dryers. **Dining:** 6 am-10 pm; to 9 pm in winter, wine/beer only. **Pool(s):** heated outdoor. **Leisure Activities:** sauna. **Guest Services:** valet and coin laundry, airport transportation-Billings Logan International Airport. **Business Services:** meeting rooms. **Cards:** AX, CB, DC, DS, JC, MC, VI. **Special Amenities: free local telephone calls and free room upgrade (subject to availability with advanced reservations).**

SOME UNITS
DATA PORT / /

BIG 5 MOTEL — **Phone:** 406/245-6646

Motel

All Year	1P: $33-$35	2P: $42-$48	XP: $6	F12

Location: I-90, exit 450, 1.6 mi n on 27th St, just e. 2601 4th Ave N 59101. Fax: 406/245-9358. **Facility:** 34 one-bedroom standard units. 2 stories (no elevator), exterior corridors. **Parking:** on-site, winter plug-ins. **Cards:** AX, CB, DC, DS, MC, VI.

SOME UNITS
/ DATA PORT /

BILLINGS HOTEL AND CONVENTION CENTER *Book at aaa.com* — **Phone:** (406)248-7151

Small-scale Hotel

All Year	1P: $59-$69	2P: $69-$79	XP: $10	F18

Location: I-90, exit 446, just s. 1223 Mullowney Ln 59101. Fax: 406/248-2054. **Facility:** 236 one-bedroom standard units, some with whirlpools. 2 stories (no elevator), interior corridors. **Parking:** on-site, winter plug-ins. **Terms:** cancellation fee imposed, small pets only ($50 deposit). **Amenities:** voice mail, irons, hair dryers. *Some:* CD players, fax. **Pool(s):** heated indoor. **Leisure Activities:** whirlpools, exercise room, volleyball. *Fee:* waterslide, massage, game room. **Guest Services:** gift shop, valet and coin laundry. **Business Services:** conference facilities. **Cards:** AX, DC, DS, MC, VI. ***(See color ad p 235)***

SOME UNITS
ASK FEE DATA PORT / /

THE BILLINGS INN *Book at aaa.com* **Phone:** (406)252-6800

AAA SAVE

Small-scale Hotel

All Year 1P: $58-$68 2P: $62-$72 XP: $5 F12

Location: I-90, exit 27th St, 2 mi n, just w on 9th Ave. Located across from the Deaconess Hospital. 880 N 29th St 59101. Fax: 406/252-6800. **Facility:** 60 one-bedroom standard units. 4 stories, interior corridors. **Parking:** on-site, winter plug-ins. **Terms:** [CP] meal plan available, pets ($5 extra charge). **Amenities:** irons, hair dryers. **Guest Services:** valet and coin laundry, airport transportation-Billings Logan International Airport. **Cards:** AX, DC, DS, MC, VI. **Special Amenities: free continental breakfast and free local telephone calls.**

(See color ad below)

SOME UNITS

DATA PORT / VCR /

FEE

BILLINGS SLEEP INN *Book at aaa.com* **Phone:** (406)254-0013

Small-scale Hotel

6/1-8/31 1P: $60-$70 2P: $68-$78 XP: $8 F18

3/1-5/31 & 9/1-2/28 1P: $53-$63 2P: $61-$71 XP: $6 F18

Location: I-90, exit 447, just w. Located opposite from the family fun park. 4904 Southgate Dr 59101. Fax: 406/254-9878. **Facility:** 75 one-bedroom standard units. 2 stories (no elevator), interior corridors. *Bath:* combo or shower only. **Parking:** on-site, winter plug-ins. **Amenities:** safes. *Some:* irons, hair dryers. **Cards:** AX, CB, DC, DS, JC, MC, VI.

SOME UNITS

ASK DATA PORT

BILLINGS
HOTEL
And Convention Center
The one with the waterslides!

Newly Remodeled
Complimentary Airport Limo
Special Group Rates
AAA Restaurant Discounts

- **Indoor Pool & Water Slides**
- **Restaurant**
- **Casino Lounge**
- **Jacuzzi Suites**

Toll Free
800/537-7286
Reservations
406/248-7151
1223 Mullowney Lane
Billings, MT 59101
I-90 Exit 446

Web
http://billingshotel.net
•
E-mail:
billingshotel@in-tch.com

"Quietly… one of the best."

Reservations:
1-800-231-7782

$49.99 Single/Double Subject to Availability

Located near Downtown, in the center of the Billings Medical Corridor.

By RIVERSTONE INNS

RIVERSTONE BILLINGS INN

- Free Continental Breakfast
- Business King Rooms
- Microwaves and Refrigerators
- Elevator
- In-Room Coffee
- Hair Dryers
- Pet Friendly
- Guest Laundry

880 North 29th Street, Billings, Montana 59101 • Visit our web site at: www.billingsinn.com

BILLINGS SUPER 8 MOTEL *Book at aaa.com* **Phone:** (406)248-8842

Small-scale Hotel

5/1-8/31	1P: $58-$78	2P: $58-$78	XP: $5	F12
3/1-4/30 & 9/1-2/28	1P: $48-$60	2P: $48-$60	XP: $5	F12

Location: I-90, exit 447, just n on S Billings Blvd, 0.8 mi w on King Ave, then just s on Parkway Ln. 5400 Southgate Dr 59102. Fax: 406/248-8842. **Facility:** 113 one-bedroom standard units. 3 stories, interior corridors. **Parking:** on-site, winter plug-ins. **Terms:** [CP] meal plan available, pets ($20 deposit). **Amenities:** *Fee:* video library, safes. **Guest Services:** coin laundry. **Cards:** AX, DC, DS, MC, VI.

SOME UNITS

BILLINGS TRAVEL WEST INN **Phone:** 406/245-6345

Motel

3/1-9/30 [CP]	1P: $49-$53	2P: $54-$60	XP: $5
10/1-2/28 [CP]	1P: $46-$50	2P: $50-$57	XP: $4

Location: Downtown. 3311 2nd Ave N 59101. Fax: 406/245-9882. **Facility:** 38 one-bedroom standard units. 2 stories (no elevator), interior/exterior corridors. *Bath:* combo or shower only. **Parking:** on-site, winter plug-ins. **Terms:** cancellation fee imposed. **Cards:** AX, DS, MC, VI.

SOME UNITS

BOOTHILL INN & SUITES *Book at aaa.com* **Phone:** 406/245-2000

AAA SAVE

Small-scale Hotel

All Year [ECP]	1P: $83	2P: $88

Location: I-90, exit 452, 1.8 mi n on US 87. 242 E Airport Rd 59105. Fax: 406/245-8591. **Facility:** 69 units. 66 one-bedroom standard units. 3 one-bedroom suites ($109). 4 stories, exterior corridors. *Bath:* combo or shower only. **Parking:** on-site. **Amenities:** high-speed Internet, dual phone lines, irons, hair dryers. **Pool(s):** heated indoor. **Leisure Activities:** whirlpools, exercise room. **Guest Services:** coin laundry, airport transportation-Billings Logan International Airport. **Business Services:** meeting rooms, PC. **Cards:** AX, DS, MC, VI. **Special Amenities: free expanded continental breakfast and free local telephone calls.**

SOME UNITS

CHERRY TREE INN **Phone:** 406/252-5603

AAA SAVE

Motel

All Year	1P: $45-$48	2P: $50-$55	XP: $5	F12

Location: I-90, exit 450, 2 mi n on 27th St, just w on 9th Ave. Located opposite the Deaconess Hospital. 823 N Broadway 59101. Fax: 406/254-0494. **Facility:** 65 units. 64 one-bedroom standard units. 1 one-bedroom suite ($50-$65). 2 stories, interior corridors. **Parking:** on-site, winter plug-ins. **Amenities:** irons, hair dryers. **Leisure Activities:** sauna, exercise room. **Guest Services:** coin laundry. **Cards:** AX, CB, DC, DS, MC, VI. **Special Amenities: free continental breakfast and free local telephone calls.** ***(See color ad below)***

SOME UNITS

C'MON INN **Phone:** 406/655-1100

Small-scale Hotel

4/1-9/30	1P: $65-$125	2P: $74-$140
3/1-3/31 & 10/1-2/28	1P: $60-$125,	2P: $64-$140

Location: I-90, exit 446, 0.5 mi n, then just s. 2020 Overland Ave 59102. Fax: 406/652-7672. **Facility:** 80 one-bedroom standard units, some with whirlpools. 2 stories, interior corridors. *Bath:* combo or shower only. **Parking:** on-site, winter plug-ins. **Terms:** 7 day cancellation notice, [ECP] meal plan available. **Amenities:** irons, hair dryers. *Some:* dual phone lines. **Pool(s):** heated indoor, wading. **Leisure Activities:** whirlpools, exercise room. *Fee:* game room. **Guest Services:** valet laundry. **Business Services:** meeting rooms. **Cards:** AX, DS, MC, VI. ***(See color ad p 237)***

SOME UNITS

COMFORT INN OF BILLINGS **Book at aaa.com** **Phone:** (406)652-5200

Small-scale Hotel

6/1-8/31 [ECP]	1P: $79-$99	2P: $79-$99	XP: $6	F
9/1-2/28 [ECP]	1P: $60-$75	2P: $60-$80	XP: $6	F
3/1-5/31 [ECP]	1P: $59-$75	2P: $59-$79	XP: $6	F

Location: I-90, exit 446, 0.5 mi n, then just s. 2030 Overland Ave 59102. Fax: 406/652-5200. **Facility:** 60 one-bedroom standard units. 2 stories (no elevator), interior corridors. **Parking:** on-site, winter plug-ins. **Terms:** small pets only ($15 extra charge). **Amenities:** irons, hair dryers. **Pool(s):** small heated indoor. **Leisure Activities:** whirlpool. **Guest Services:** valet laundry. **Cards:** AX, CB, DC, DS, MC, VI.

SOME UNITS

FEE

COUNTRY INN & SUITES BILLINGS @ METRA PARK **Book at aaa.com** **Phone:** (406)245-9995

Small-scale Hotel

All Year [ECP]	1P: $88	2P: $88	XP: $6	F17

Location: I-90, exit 452, 0.3 mi, follow Metra signs. 231 Main St 59105. Fax: 406/294-9999. **Facility:** 67 units. 55 one-bedroom standard units, some with whirlpools. 12 one-bedroom suites, some with whirlpools. 3 stories, interior corridors. *Bath:* combo or shower only. **Parking:** on-site. **Terms:** cancellation fee imposed. **Amenities:** high-speed Internet, voice mail, irons, hair dryers. **Pool(s):** heated indoor. **Leisure Activities:** whirlpool, exercise room. **Guest Services:** valet and coin laundry. **Business Services:** meeting rooms. **Cards:** AX, DC, DS, MC, VI.

(See color ad below)

SOME UNITS

DAYS INN **Book at aaa.com** **Phone:** (406)252-4007

Motel

6/1-8/31	1P: $65-$110	2P: $82-$130	XP: $5	F12
3/1-5/31 & 9/1-2/28	1P: $49-$99	2P: $55-$120	XP: $5	F12

Location: I-90, exit 447, just n on S Billings Blvd, 0.8 mi w on King Ave, then just s on Parkway Ln. 843 Parkway Ln 59101. Fax: 406/896-1147. **Facility:** 62 one-bedroom standard units. 2 stories (no elevator), interior corridors. *Bath:* combo or shower only. **Parking:** on-site, winter plug-ins. **Terms:** [ECP] meal plan available. **Amenities:** hair dryers. *Some:* irons. **Leisure Activities:** whirlpool. **Guest Services:** valet and coin laundry. **Cards:** AX, DC, DS, MC, VI.

SOME UNITS

FEE

DUDE RANCHER LODGE *Book at aaa.com* **Phone:** (406)259-5561

Motel

All Year	1P: $40-$75	2P: $45-$80	XP: $4	F16

Location: Just w of the 400 block of N 27th st; downtown. 415 N 29th St 59101. Fax: 406/259-0095. **Facility:** 56 one-bedroom standard units, some with efficiencies and/or whirlpools. 2 stories (no elevator), interior/exterior corridors. *Bath:* combo or shower only. **Parking:** on-site, winter plug-ins. **Terms:** pets ($5 extra charge). **Amenities:** hair dryers. **Guest Services:** valet laundry. **Cards:** AX, DC, DS, MC, VI. ***(See color ad below)***

ASK / FEE / SOME UNITS

FAIRFIELD INN BY MARRIOTT-BILLINGS *Book at aaa.com* **Phone:** (406)652-5330

Small-scale Hotel

6/1-8/31 [ECP]	1P: $69-$89	2P: $69-$89	XP: $6	F
3/1-5/31 & 9/1-2/28 [ECP]	1P: $59-$75	2P: $59-$79	XP: $6	F

Location: I-90, exit 446, 0.5 mi n, then just s. 2026 Overland Ave 59102. Fax: 406/652-5330. **Facility:** 63 one-bedroom standard units. 3 stories, interior corridors. **Parking:** on-site, winter plug-ins. **Amenities:** irons, hair dryers. **Pool(s):** small heated indoor. **Leisure Activities:** whirlpool. **Guest Services:** valet laundry. **Cards:** AX, CB, DC, DS, MC, VI.

DATA PORT / SOME UNITS

HAMPTON INN *Book at aaa.com* **Phone:** (406)248-4949

Small-scale Hotel

6/21-8/28 [ECP]	1P: $99-$104	2P: $99-$104
5/1-6/20 [ECP]	1P: $89-$94	2P: $89-$94
3/1-4/30 & 8/29-2/28 [ECP]	1P: $74-$79	2P: $74-$79

Location: I-90, exit 447, just n on Billings Blvd, just w on King Ave, then 0.4 mi sw. 5110 Southgate Dr 59101. Fax: 406/248-1011. **Facility:** 87 one-bedroom standard units. 4 stories, interior corridors. *Bath:* combo or shower only. **Parking:** on-site, winter plug-ins. **Terms:** pets ($10 extra charge). **Amenities:** high-speed Internet, voice mail, irons, hair dryers. **Pool(s):** heated indoor. **Leisure Activities:** whirlpool, exercise room. **Guest Services:** valet and coin laundry. **Business Services:** meeting rooms, business center. **Cards:** AX, DC, DS, MC, VI.

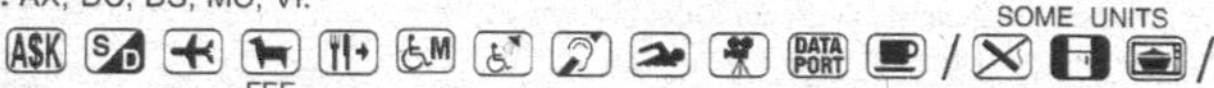

ASK / FEE / DATA PORT / SOME UNITS

HILLTOP INN ***Book at aaa.com*** **Phone:** (406)245-5000

SAVE

Small-scale Hotel

All Year 1P: $58-$68 2P: $62-$72 XP: $5 F12

Location: I-90, exit 450, 2 mi n, just w on 11th Ave, then just n. Located adjacent to St. Vincent Hospital. 1116 N 28th St 59101. Fax: 406/245-7851. **Facility:** 56 one-bedroom standard units. 3 stories, interior corridors. **Parking:** on-site, winter plug-ins. **Terms:** [ECP] meal plan available, pets ($5 extra charge). **Amenities:** irons, hair dryers. **Leisure Activities:** exercise room. **Guest Services:** valet and coin laundry, airport transportation-Billings Logan International Airport. **Cards:** AX, DC, DS, MC, VI. **Special Amenities: free continental breakfast and free local telephone calls.** *(See color ad p 238)*

SOME UNITS

FEE

THE HISTORIC NORTHERN HOTEL ***Book at aaa.com*** **Phone:** (406)245-5121

Large-scale Hotel

5/1-10/1 1P: $89 2P: $99 XP: $10 F17

3/1-4/30 & 10/2-2/28 1P: $79 2P: $89 XP: $10 F17

Location: Downtown. 19 N 28th St 59101. Fax: 406/259-9862. **Facility:** 160 units. 118 one-bedroom standard units. 42 one-bedroom suites ($99-$109). 10 stories, interior corridors. **Parking:** on-site, winter plug-ins. **Terms:** cancellation fee imposed. **Amenities:** video games, voice mail, irons, hair dryers. **Dining:** Golden Belle Restaurant, see separate listing. **Leisure Activities:** exercise room. **Guest Services:** gift shop, valet laundry. **Business Services:** conference facilities. **Cards:** AX, DC, DS, MC, VI.

SOME UNITS

HOLIDAY INN EXPRESS BILLINGS ***Book at aaa.com*** **Phone:** (406)259-8600

Small-scale Hotel

All Year 1P: $79-$109 2P: $79-$109 XP: $8 F

Location: I-90, exit 455, just s, then just e. 430 Cole St 59101. Fax: 406/259-8601. **Facility:** 66 one-bedroom standard units. 3 stories, interior corridors. *Bath:* combo or shower only. **Parking:** on-site, winter plug-ins. **Terms:** [ECP] meal plan available. **Amenities:** dual phone lines, voice mail, irons, hair dryers. **Pool(s):** small heated indoor. **Leisure Activities:** whirlpool, exercise room. **Business Services:** business center. **Cards:** AX, CB, DC, DS, JC, MC, VI.

SOME UNITS

HOLIDAY INN GRAND MONTANA BILLINGS ***Book at aaa.com*** **Phone:** (406)248-7701

SAVE

Large-scale Hotel

6/1-8/31 1P: $79-$109

3/1-5/31 & 9/1-2/28 1P: $69-$99

Location: I-90, exit 446. 5500 Midland Rd 59101. Fax: 406/248-8954. **Facility:** 317 units. 291 one-bedroom standard units. 26 one-bedroom suites, some with whirlpools. 7 stories, interior corridors. *Bath:* combo or shower only. **Parking:** on-site, winter plug-ins. **Terms:** check-in 4 pm, cancellation fee imposed, pets ($25 fee). **Amenities:** voice mail, irons, hair dryers. **Dining:** 2 restaurants, 6 am-2 & 5-10 pm, cocktails. **Pool(s):** heated indoor. **Leisure Activities:** sauna, whirlpool, exercise room, game room. **Guest Services:** gift shop, valet laundry, airport transportation-Billings Logan International Airport. **Business Services:** conference facilities. **Cards:** AX, DC, DS, MC, VI. **Special Amenities: free local telephone calls and free room upgrade (subject to availability with advanced reservations).** *(See color ad below & opposite title page)*

SOME UNITS

FEE

HOWARD JOHNSON EXPRESS INN ***Book at aaa.com*** **Phone:** (406)248-4656

Small-scale Hotel

6/1-2/28 [ECP] 1P: $75-$95 2P: $79-$99 XP: $4 F18

3/1-5/31 [ECP] 1P: $55-$85 2P: $59-$89 XP: $4 F18

Location: I-90, exit 450, just n on SR 3 (S 27th St). 1001 S 27th St 59101. Fax: 406/248-7268. **Facility:** 170 one-bedroom standard units. 3 stories, interior corridors. *Bath:* combo or shower only. **Parking:** on-site, winter plug-ins. **Terms:** 7 day cancellation notice, pets ($100 deposit). **Amenities:** video library (fee), voice mail, hair dryers. **Leisure Activities:** exercise room. **Guest Services:** valet and coin laundry, area transportation. **Business Services:** meeting rooms. **Cards:** AX, DC, DS, MC, VI.

SOME UNITS

FEE FEE FEE FEE

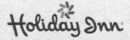

THE JOSEPHINE BED & BREAKFAST
Phone: (406)248-5898

Bed & Breakfast

All Year	1P: $75-$95	2P: $85-$105	XP: $10	F10

Location: Just w of 400 block of N 27th St; downtown. 514 N 29th St 59101. **Facility:** Smoke free premises. 5 units. 3 one-bedroom standard units. 2 one-bedroom suites ($105-$150), some with whirlpools. 2 stories (no elevator), interior corridors. *Bath:* combo or shower only. **Parking:** on-site, winter plug-ins. **Terms:** check-in 4 pm, age restrictions may apply, 30 day cancellation notice-fee imposed, [BP] meal plan available. **Amenities:** video library, irons, hair dryers. **Cards:** AX, DC, MC, VI.

SOME UNITS

KELLY INN *Book at aaa.com*
Phone: (406)252-2700

SAVE

Small-scale Hotel

6/1-9/20 [ECP]	1P: $59-$79	2P: $69-$89	XP: $5	F12
3/1-5/31 & 9/21-2/28 [ECP]	1P: $52-$68	2P: $62-$82	XP: $5	F12

Location: I-90, exit 446, just se. 5425 Midland Rd 59101. Fax: 406/252-1011. **Facility:** 88 units. 87 one-bedroom standard units. 1 one-bedroom suite ($79-$109) with kitchen. 2 stories, interior/exterior corridors. *Bath:* combo or shower only. **Parking:** on-site, winter plug-ins. **Terms:** small pets only. **Amenities:** video games, dual phone lines, irons, hair dryers. **Pool(s):** heated outdoor. **Leisure Activities:** sauna, whirlpool. **Guest Services:** valet and coin laundry, airport transportation-Billings Logan International Airport. **Cards:** AX, CB, DC, DS, MC, VI. **Special Amenities: free expanded continental breakfast and free local telephone calls.** *(See color ad below)*

SOME UNITS

QUALITY INN HOMESTEAD *Book at aaa.com*
Phone: (406)652-1320

Small-scale Hotel

6/1-8/31 [BP]	1P: $69-$89	2P: $69-$99	XP: $5	F17
9/1-2/28 [BP]	1P: $59-$89	2P: $59-$99	XP: $5	F17
3/1-5/31 [BP]	1P: $59-$79	2P: $59-$89	XP: $5	F17

Location: I-90, exit 446, n on King Ave W, just s, first stoplight. 2036 Overland Ave 59102. Fax: 406/652-1320. **Facility:** 119 units. 59 one-bedroom standard units. 60 one-bedroom suites ($69-$105). 2 stories (no elevator), interior corridors. **Parking:** on-site, winter plug-ins. **Terms:** pets ($5 extra charge). **Amenities:** video library (fee), voice mail, safes, irons, hair dryers. **Pool(s):** heated indoor. **Leisure Activities:** sauna, whirlpool. **Guest Services:** valet and coin laundry. **Business Services:** meeting rooms. **Cards:** AX, CB, DC, DS, JC, MC, VI. *(See color ad below)*

SOME UNITS
FEE FEE

RED ROOF INN - #269 *Book at aaa.com* **Phone:** (406)248-7551

Small-scale Hotel				
6/27-8/21	1P: $51-$62	2P: $56-$67	XP: $5	F18
5/23-6/26	1P: $47-$54	2P: $52-$59	XP: $5	F18
8/22-2/28	1P: $37-$47	2P: $42-$52	XP: $5	F18
3/1-5/22	1P: $36-$46	2P: $41-$51	XP: $5	F18

Location: I-90, exit 446, 0.5 mi se. 5353 Midland Rd 59102. Fax: 406/245-7032. **Facility:** 116 one-bedroom standard units. 2 stories (no elevator), interior corridors. *Bath:* combo or shower only. **Parking:** on-site, winter plug-ins. **Terms:** check-in 4 pm, small pets only. **Amenities:** video games (fee), voice mail. **Pool(s):** heated indoor. **Guest Services:** coin laundry. **Cards:** AX, CB, DC, DS, MC, VI.

SOME UNITS

DATA PORT / FEE FEE

RIMVIEW INN **Phone:** (406)248-2622

AAA SAVE

Motel

All Year	1P: $48-$57	2P: $55-$65	XP: $5

Location: I-90, exit 450, 2 mi n. 1025 N 27th St 59101. Fax: 406/248-2622. **Facility:** 54 units. 52 one-bedroom standard units, some with efficiencies. 2 one-bedroom suites ($60-$75). 3 stories (no elevator), interior/exterior corridors. *Bath:* combo or shower only. **Parking:** on-site, winter plug-ins. **Terms:** weekly rates available, [CP] meal plan available, pets ($5 extra charge). **Leisure Activities:** whirlpool. **Guest Services:** valet and coin laundry, airport transportation-Billings Logan International Airport. **Business Services:** meeting rooms. **Cards:** AX, CB, DC, DS, MC, VI. **Special Amenities: free continental breakfast and free local telephone calls.** *(See color ad below)*

SOME UNITS

FEE FEE / VCR FEE

SHERATON DOWNTOWN BILLINGS HOTEL *Book at aaa.com* Phone: (406)252-7400

Large-scale Hotel

All Year 1P: $109-$159 2P: $119-$169 XP: $10

Location: I-90 business loop and SR 3. 27 N 27th St 59101. Fax: 406/252-7020. **Facility:** 282 units. 281 one-bedroom standard units. 1 one-bedroom suite ($159-$300) with whirlpool. 23 stories, interior corridors. *Bath:* combo or shower only. **Parking:** on-site. **Terms:** [AP], [BP] & [CP] meal plans available, package plans. **Amenities:** high-speed Internet, voice mail, irons, hair dryers. *Some:* fax. **Pool(s):** small heated indoor, wading. **Leisure Activities:** saunas, whirlpool. *Fee:* game room. **Guest Services:** gift shop, valet laundry. **Business Services:** conference facilities. **Cards:** AX, DC, DS, JC, MC, VI.

SOME UNITS

WHERE TO DINE

C J'S RESTAURANT Lunch: $7-$14 Dinner: $7-$23 Phone: 406/656-1400

American

Location: I-90, exit 446, 1 mi w on King Ave, 1 mi n on 24th St, 0.3 mi w, s at light. 2456 Central Ave 59102. **Hours:** 11:30 am-3 & 5-9 pm, Fri & Sat 11:30 am-10 pm, Sun 11:30 am-9 pm. Closed major holidays; also Super Bowl Sun. **Reservations:** suggested. **Features:** Diners enjoy a great selection of ribs, steaks and seafood cooked over mesquite, oak and apple wood and served in a relaxed, contemporary atmosphere. The service is pleasant and prompt. Patio dining is available, weather permitting. Casual dress; cocktails. **Parking:** on-site. **Cards:** AX, DC, DS, MC, VI.

DOS MACHOS RESTAURANT Lunch: $7-$16 Dinner: $7-$16 Phone: 406/652-2020

Mexican

Location: I-90, exit 446, 1.3 mi nw on King Ave, then just s. 980 S 24th St W 59102. **Hours:** 11 am-10 pm, Sun 9 am-9 pm; to 9 pm in winter. Closed: 11/25, 12/25. **Features:** The popular restaurant is known for its large Mexican/American menu, which lists sizzling fajitas, San Lucas scampi and an eight-ounce top sirloin. A roaming, evening mariachi band and pleasant staff make for an enjoyable dining experience. Casual dress; cocktails. **Parking:** on-site. **Cards:** AX, DC, DS, MC, VI.

GOLDEN BELLE RESTAURANT Lunch: $6-$11 Dinner: $6-$26 Phone: 406/245-2232

Continental

Location: Downtown; in The Historic Northern Hotel. 19 N 28th St 59101. **Hours:** 6:30 am-2 & 5-9 pm, Fri & Sat-10 pm. **Reservations:** suggested. **Features:** The handsome dining room and upscale Western grill room provide perfect settings for intimate, business and casual dining. Prime rib, coconut shrimp and hand-cut Montana porterhouse are local favorites. Creative mixed-grill entrees and flaming dessert round out the menu. Service is pleasant and professional. Casual dress; cocktails. **Parking:** on-site. **Cards:** AX, DC, DS, JC, MC, VI.

JAKES OF BILLINGS Lunch: $6-$10 Dinner: $12-$29 Phone: 406/259-9375

American

Location: I-90 business loop and SR 3; downtown. 2701 1st Ave N 59101. **Hours:** 11:30 am-2 & 5-10:30 pm, Sat from 5:30 pm. Closed: 11/25, 12/25; also Sun. **Reservations:** suggested, weekends. **Features:** A 1930s, urban-Western ambience complements the varied menu at the informal, contemporary eatery. Locals and tourists flock here for steak, chicken and homemade desserts, along with made-to-order vegetarian dishes. Casual dress; cocktails. **Parking:** on-site (fee). **Cards:** AX, DS, MC, VI.

MACKENZIE RIVER PIZZA CO Lunch: $7-$18 Dinner: $7-$18 Phone: 406/254-0066

American

Location: I-90, exit 452, 1.3 mi w on I-90 business loop, 0.9 mi e on Main St; in Heights Target Complex. 405 Main St 59105. **Hours:** 11 am-midnight. Closed major holidays. **Features:** Known for its eclectic Western decor, the restaurant lets patrons choose from several microbrews to accompany a specialty pizza or large, innovative sandwich. Casual dress; beer & wine only. **Parking:** on-site. **Cards:** AX, DS, MC, VI.

MACKENZIE RIVER PIZZA CO Lunch: $7-$18 Dinner: $7-$18 Phone: 406/651-0068

American

Location: 4.5 mi w of city center. 3025 E Grand Ave 59102. **Hours:** 11 am-10 pm, Sun noon-9 pm; to 9 pm in winter. Closed major holidays. **Features:** Known for its eclectic Western decor, the restaurant lets patrons choose from several microbrews to accompany a specialty pizza or large, innovative sandwich. Casual dress; beer & wine only. **Parking:** on-site. **Cards:** AX, DS, MC, VI.

MCCORMICK CAFE Lunch: $6-$9 Phone: 406/255-9555

American

Location: Downtown. 2419 Montana Ave 59101. **Hours:** 7 am-4 pm, Sat 8 am-3 pm. Closed major holidays; also Sun. **Features:** Banana-stuffed French toast, grilled portobello sandwiches and moist, double-layer carrot cake are just a few of the excellent, made-from-scratch choices at the popular, sunny cafe. Mouthwatering aromas of roasted coffee beans and freshly squeezed fruit and vegetable juices fill the dining area. Breakfast is served until 10 am. Casual dress. **Parking:** on-site. **Cards:** AX, DS, MC, VI.

MONGOLIAN GRILL Lunch: $6-$8 Dinner: $7-$10 Phone: 406/651-2009

Mongolian

Location: 5 mi w of city center; located near west end shopping. 2202 Central Ave 59102. **Hours:** 11 am-9 pm, Fri & Sat-10 pm. **Reservations:** required. **Features:** After assembling a stir-fry from fresh vegetables, seafood, meats and a choice of 15 sauces, guests can watch their meals being cooked on the steel grill. Casual dress. **Parking:** on-site. **Cards:** AX, DS, MC, VI.

THE MUSTARD SEED Lunch: $5-$10 Dinner: $5-$10 Phone: 406/259-1400

Asian

Location: 3 mi w of city center; jct Grand Ave, near West Park Plaza. 1340 15th St W 59102. **Hours:** 11 am-9 pm, Fri & Sat-10 pm. Closed major holidays. **Features:** Fast food with a twist! The decor is fresh, bright and modern. You order at the cashier, take your seat and heaps of steaming, fragrant, visually appealing plates of food are brought to your table! Fresh ingredients are used and boy do the spices meld together! Casual dress; beer & wine only. **Parking:** on-site. **Cards:** AX, DS, MC, VI.

THE REX | **Lunch:** $8-$11 | **Dinner:** $15-$26 | **Phone:** 406/245-7477

American

Location: I-90, exit 450, 1.5 mi n on 27th St, just e. 2401 Montana Ave 59101. **Hours:** 11 am-10:30 pm. Closed: 11/25, 12/25. **Reservations:** accepted. **Features:** Among choices on the diverse menu are Montana-raised roasted buffalo, Tuscan pork loin, Cajun barbecued shrimp and the popular blackened prime rib. A patio bar and grill offers lighter fare and outside seating, weather permitting. Casual dress; cocktails. **Parking:** on-site. **Cards:** AX, DC, DS, MC, VI.

The following restaurants have not been evaluated by AAA but are listed for your information only.

DUTCH BROTHERS BAKERY GOODS | **Phone:** 406/252-1960

fyi

Not evaluated. **Location:** 1707 17th St W 59102. **Features:** Caramel cookie waffles, quiche and sausage rolls are among the eatery's dishes.

KING'S HAT | **Phone:** 406/259-4746

fyi

Not evaluated. **Location:** 105 S 37th St. **Features:** The drive-in serves specialty burgers, hot dogs, milkshakes and malts.

TERIYAKI BOWL EXPRESS | **Phone:** 406/652-6334

fyi

Not evaluated. **Location:** In Rimrock Mall Food Court. 2695 King Ave W 59102. **Features:** The quick-serve restaurant prepares traditional pot stickers, noodles and rice entrees.

BLACK EAGLE pop. 914

WHERE TO DINE

3D INTERNATIONAL Classic | **Lunch:** $9-$14 | **Dinner:** $9-$21 | **Phone:** 406/453-6561

International

Location: Jct 9th St and Smelter Ave, 0.5 mi e. 1825 Smelter Ave 59414. **Hours:** 11 am-2 & 5-10 pm, Fri-10:30 pm, Sat 4:30 pm-10:30 pm, Sun 4 pm-10 pm. Closed major holidays. **Reservations:** suggested. **Features:** 3D= Dine, Drink, Dance, and it has been an institution in Great Falls since 1946. While they used to promote big name acts and dancing, renovations took place in 1998. The neon lighting and original lounge seating was retained, creating an unique atmosphere in which to enjoy your Italian, Mongolian or Oriental cuisine. Casual dress; cocktails. **Parking:** on-site and street. **Cards:** AX, DS, MC, VI.

BORRIES | **Dinner:** $8-$26 | **Phone:** 406/761-0300

American

Location: Jct 9th St and Smelter Ave, 0.5 mi e. 1800 Smelter Ave 59414. **Hours:** 5 pm-10 pm, Fri-11 pm, Sun 4 pm-10 pm. Closed major holidays. **Reservations:** suggested, weekends. **Features:** In an older industrial neighborhood of a small mill town, the casual dining establishment prepares simple, hearty food and serves it in generous portions. In addition to steaks, the menu lists Southern Italian pasta dishes, including spaghetti and the signature ravioli. Many pictures and photographs evoke the history of the community when it was a center of the world's copper industry. Casual dress; cocktails. **Parking:** on-site. **Cards:** AX, DS, MC, VI.

BOZEMAN pop. 27,509

WHERE TO STAY

BEST VALUE INN *Book at aaa.com* | **Phone:** 406/585-7888

Small-scale Hotel

6/9-9/3	1P: $59-$79	2P: $64-$84	XP: $5	F15
9/4-11/15	1P: $54-$59	2P: $59-$64	XP: $5	F15
3/1-6/8	1P: $39-$49	2P: $44-$54	XP: $5	F15
11/16-2/28	1P: $39-$48	2P: $44-$54	XP: $5	F15

Location: I-90, exit 306, just n. 817 Wheat Dr 59718. Fax: 406/585-8842. **Facility:** 56 one-bedroom standard units. 2 stories (no elevator), interior corridors. *Bath:* combo or shower only. **Parking:** on-site, winter plug-ins. **Terms:** [CP] meal plan available. **Amenities:** *Some:* irons, hair dryers. **Pool(s):** small heated indoor. **Leisure Activities:** sauna, whirlpool. **Guest Services:** coin laundry. **Cards:** AX, DC, DS, MC, VI.

SOME UNITS

ASK / VCR /

BEST WESTERN GRANTREE INN *Book at aaa.com* | **Phone:** (406)587-5261

AAA SAVE

Small-scale Hotel

7/1-9/15	1P: $99-$119	2P: $99-$119
6/1-6/30	1P: $89-$109	2P: $89-$109
3/1-5/31 & 9/16-2/28	1P: $79-$99	2P: $79-$99

Location: I-90, exit 306, just s. 1325 N 7th Ave 59715. Fax: 406/587-9437. **Facility:** 119 units. 118 one-bedroom standard units, some with whirlpools. 1 one-bedroom suite ($99-$169) with whirlpool. 2 stories (no elevator), interior corridors. *Bath:* combo or shower only. **Parking:** on-site, winter plug-ins. **Terms:** check-in 4 pm, weekly rates available, [AP] meal plan available. **Amenities:** video games, dual phone lines, voice mail. *Some:* irons, hair dryers. **Dining:** 6 am-9 pm, Fri & Sat-10 pm, cocktails. **Pool(s):** heated indoor. **Leisure Activities:** whirlpool, exercise room. **Guest Services:** valet and coin laundry, airport transportation-Gallatin Field Airport. **Business Services:** conference facilities, business center. **Cards:** AX, CB, DC, DS, MC, VI. **Special Amenities: free newspaper and early check-in/late check-out.**

(See color ad p 244)

SOME UNITS

/ /

BOZEMAN DAYS INN *Book at aaa.com* | **Phone:** (406)587-5251

Small-scale Hotel

5/1-8/31	1P: $79-$99	2P: $79-$99	XP: $6	F17
9/1-12/31	1P: $59-$79	2P: $59-$79	XP: $6	F17
3/1-4/30 & 1/1-2/28	1P: $49-$69	2P: $49-$69	XP: $6	F17

Location: I-90, exit 306, just s. 1321 N 7th 59715. Fax: 406/587-5351. **Facility:** 79 one-bedroom standard units. 2 stories (no elevator), interior corridors. *Bath:* combo or shower only. **Parking:** on-site, winter plug-ins. **Terms:** [BP] & [ECP] meal plans available, pets ($10 deposit). **Amenities:** safes, irons, hair dryers. *Some:* dual phone lines. **Leisure Activities:** sauna, whirlpool, exercise room. **Guest Services:** coin laundry. **Business Services:** meeting rooms. **Cards:** AX, CB, DC, DS, JC, MC, VI.

SOME UNITS

ASK FEE / VCR FEE /

BOZEMAN INN

AAA SAVE — Motel — **Phone:** 406/587-3176

6/11-8/31 [CP]	1P: $55-$66	2P: $55-$79
3/1-6/10 & 9/1-10/15 [CP]	1P: $39-$49	2P: $39-$58
10/16-2/28 [CP]	1P: $39-$45	2P: $39-$55

Location: I-90, exit 306, just s. 1235 N 7th Ave 59715. Fax: 406/585-3591. **Facility:** 49 units. 48 one- and 1 two-bedroom standard units, some with whirlpools. 2 stories (no elevator), exterior corridors. *Bath:* combo or shower only. **Parking:** on-site, winter plug-ins. **Terms:** pets ($5 extra charge). **Pool(s):** heated outdoor. **Leisure Activities:** sauna, whirlpool. **Guest Services:** coin laundry. **Cards:** AX, DC, DS, MC, VI. **Special Amenities: free local telephone calls and early check-in/late check-out.**

SOME UNITS — FEE — FEE FEE

BOZEMAN SUPER 8

Small-scale Hotel — **Phone:** 406/586-1521

6/1-9/30	1P: $57-$69	2P: $62-$74	XP: $5	F15
3/1-5/31 & 10/1-2/28	1P: $45-$57	2P: $50-$62	XP: $5	F15

Location: I-90, exit 306, just n, then just w. 800 Wheat Dr 59715. Fax: 406/586-1521. **Facility:** 108 one-bedroom standard units. 3 stories (no elevator), interior corridors. **Parking:** on-site, winter plug-ins. **Terms:** [CP] meal plan available, pets ($5 extra charge). **Cards:** AX, CB, DC, DS, MC, VI.

SOME UNITS — ASK — FEE

BOZEMAN'S WESTERN HERITAGE INN

AAA SAVE — Small-scale Hotel — **Phone:** (406)586-8534

7/1-8/31	1P: $68-$88	2P: $68-$88	XP: $5	F15
6/1-6/30	1P: $58-$68	2P: $58-$78	XP: $5	F15
9/1-2/28	1P: $49-$58	2P: $49-$68	XP: $5	F15
3/1-5/31	1P: $44-$51	2P: $44-$56	XP: $5	F15

Location: I-90 business loop, exit 309, 0.5 mi w. 1200 E Main St 59715. Fax: 406/587-8729. **Facility:** 38 units. 37 one-bedroom standard units, some with whirlpools. 1 one-bedroom suite ($75-$145) with kitchen. 3 stories (no elevator), interior corridors. **Parking:** on-site, winter plug-ins. **Terms:** pets ($5 extra charge, small dogs only). **Amenities:** irons, hair dryers. **Leisure Activities:** whirlpool, steamroom, limited exercise equipment. **Guest Services:** valet and coin laundry. *Fee:* tanning facility. **Business Services:** meeting rooms. **Cards:** AX, DC, DS, MC, VI. ***(See color ad p 245)***

SOME UNITS — FEE — FEE FEE

COTTONWOOD INN BED & BREAKFAST — ***Book at aaa.com***

Bed & Breakfast — **Phone:** (406)763-5452

All Year [BP]	1P: $85-$129	2P: $85-$129	XP: $15	D16

Location: I-90, exit 305, 10.4 mi s on N 19th St (SR 412), 2.1 mi sw on Cottonwood Rd, then 0.9 mi s. 13515 Cottonwood Canyon Rd 59718. Fax: 406/763-5639. **Facility:** This upscale country bed and breakfast is nestled on the edge of the Gallatin Forest. Guest rooms and the wraparound porch offer excellent views. Smoke free premises. 5 one-bedroom standard units. 2 stories (no elevator), interior corridors. *Bath:* combo or shower only. **Parking:** on-site. **Terms:** check-in 4 pm, 14 day cancellation notice-fee imposed. **Amenities:** hair dryers. **Leisure Activities:** whirlpool, hiking trails. *Fee:* massage. **Cards:** AX, MC, VI.

SOME UNITS — ASK

FAIRFIELD INN BY MARRIOTT — ***Book at aaa.com***

Small-scale Hotel — **Phone:** (406)587-2222

6/1-8/31 [ECP]	1P: $79-$95	2P: $85-$99	XP: $6	F
9/1-2/28 [ECP]	1P: $59-$75	2P: $59-$79	XP: $6	F
3/1-5/31 [ECP]	1P: $55-$69	2P: $55-$75	XP: $6	F

Location: I-90, exit 306, just nw. 828 Wheat Dr 59715. Fax: 406/587-2222. **Facility:** 57 one-bedroom standard units. 3 stories, interior corridors. **Parking:** on-site, winter plug-ins. **Amenities:** high-speed Internet, irons, hair dryers. **Pool(s):** small heated indoor. **Leisure Activities:** whirlpool. **Guest Services:** valet laundry. **Cards:** AX, CB, DC, DS, MC, VI.

SOME UNITS

FOX HOLLOW BED AND BREAKFAST **Phone:** (406)582-8440

AAA SAVE

6/1-10/31 [BP]	1P: $109-$129	2P: $109-$129	XP: $20
3/1-5/31 & 11/1-2/28 [BP]	1P: $69-$109	2P: $69-$109	XP: $20

Bed & Breakfast **Location:** I-90, exit 305, just s on SR 412 (N 19th St), 3.1 mi w on SR 235 (Valley Center Rd), then 0.6 mi n. 545 Mary Rd 59718. Fax: 406/582-9752. **Facility:** This B&B offers gourmet breakfasts, a relaxed atmosphere and mountain and meadow views from guest rooms and the wraparound porch. Smoke free premises. 5 one-bedroom standard units, some with kitchens and/or whirlpools. 2 stories (no elevator), interior corridors. *Bath:* combo or shower only. **Parking:** on-site. **Terms:** check-in 4 pm, 14 day cancellation notice-fee imposed. **Amenities:** video library, hair dryers. **Leisure Activities:** whirlpool, yard games. **Cards:** AX, DS, MC, VI. **Special Amenities: free full breakfast and free local telephone calls.**

SOME UNITS

DATA PORT / TV VCR /

HAMPTON INN ***Book at aaa.com*** **Phone:** (406)522-8000

AAA SAVE

6/1-9/30 [ECP]	1P: $103-$109	2P: $107-$113
5/1-5/31 & 10/1-2/28 [ECP]	1P: $89-$93	2P: $93-$97
3/1-4/30 [ECP]	1P: $79-$83	2P: $83-$87

Small-scale Hotel **Location:** I-90, exit 306, just s on 7th Ave, just n. 75 Baxter Ln 59715. Fax: 406/522-7446. **Facility:** 70 one-bedroom standard units, some with whirlpools. 2 stories, interior corridors. *Bath:* combo or shower only. **Parking:** on-site, winter plug-ins. **Amenities:** voice mail, irons, hair dryers. **Pool(s):** small heated indoor. **Leisure Activities:** whirlpool, exercise room. **Guest Services:** valet and coin laundry, airport transportation-Gallatin Field Airport. **Business Services:** meeting rooms, business center. **Cards:** AX, DC, DS, MC, VI. **Special Amenities: free expanded continental breakfast and free local telephone calls.** *(See ad below)*

SOME UNITS

   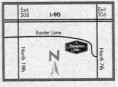 DATA PORT  /   /

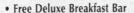

HOLIDAY INN BOZEMAN Book at aaa.com

Phone: (406)587-4561

SAVE

6/2-9/30	1P: $109-$159	2P: $109-$159
3/1-6/1 & 10/1-2/28	1P: $89-$129	2P: $89-$129

Small-scale Hotel

Location: I-90, exit 306, just s of jct I-90. 5 Baxter Ln 59715. Fax: 406/587-4413. **Facility:** 179 units. 178 one-bedroom standard units, some with whirlpools. 1 one-bedroom suite. 2 stories (no elevator), interior corridors. *Bath:* combo or shower only. **Parking:** on-site, winter plug-ins. **Terms:** check-in 4 pm, small pets only. **Amenities:** video games, high-speed Internet, voice mail, irons, hair dryers. **Dining:** 6 am-2 & 5-10 pm, cocktails. **Pool(s):** heated indoor. **Leisure Activities:** whirlpool, pool table, exercise room. *Fee:* massage. **Guest Services:** valet and coin laundry, airport transportation-Gallatin Field Airport. **Business Services:** meeting rooms. **Cards:** AX, DC, DS, MC, VI. **Special Amenities: free local telephone calls and early check-in/late check-out.** *(See color ad opposite title page)*

SOME UNITS

DATA PORT

HOWLERS INN BED & BREAKFAST

Phone: 406/586-0304

All Year	1P: $85-$275	2P: $85-$275

Bed & Breakfast

Location: I-90, exit 319 (Jackson Creek Rd), 3.1 mi n, then just e. 3185 Jackson Creek Rd 59715. **Facility:** A wolf sanctuary is on the grounds of this inn, which offers scenic views as well as proximity to downtown Bozeman, ski areas and a national forest. Smoke free premises. 8 units. 5 one-bedroom standard units. 1 one- and 2 two-bedroom suites ($170-$275), some with kitchens (utensils extra charge). 2-3 stories (no elevator), interior/exterior corridors. *Bath:* some shared or private, combo or shower only. **Parking:** on-site, winter plug-ins. **Terms:** check-in 4 pm, 10 day cancellation notice. **Amenities:** video library, hair dryers. *Some:* irons. **Leisure Activities:** sauna, whirlpool, exercise room. **Cards:** MC, VI.

SOME UNITS

VCR

LINDLEY HOUSE

Phone: (406)587-8403

4/16-2/28 [BP]	1P: $115-$350	2P: $115-$350	XP: $20	D
3/1-4/15 [BP]	1P: $100-$350	2P: $100-$350	XP: $20	D

Bed & Breakfast

Location: I-90, exit 306, 1.3 mi s on 7th Ave, 0.9 mi e on Main St, just s on Bozeman St, then just e on Olive St. 202 Lindley Pl 59715. Fax: 406/582-8112. **Facility:** Walking distance from Main Street, this B&B offers guest rooms with a mix of antiques, wicker and contemporary furnishings. Smoke free premises. 5 units. 4 one-bedroom standard units. 1 one-bedroom suite ($195-$350). 3 stories (no elevator), interior corridors. *Bath:* combo or shower only. **Parking:** on-site, winter plug-ins. **Terms:** 2 night minimum stay, 21 day cancellation notice-fee imposed, no pets allowed (owner's pet on premises). **Amenities:** high-speed Internet, irons, hair dryers. *Some:* CD players. **Leisure Activities:** whirlpool. **Cards:** DS, MC, VI.

SOME UNITS

VCR

MICROTEL INN & SUITES Book at aaa.com

Phone: (406)586-3797

All Year	1P: $49-$69	2P: $59-$89	XP: $5	F

Small-scale Hotel

Location: I-90, exit 306, just ne. 612 Nikles Dr 59715. Fax: 406/586-4247. **Facility:** 61 one-bedroom standard units, some with whirlpools. 3 stories, interior corridors. *Bath:* combo or shower only. **Parking:** on-site. **Terms:** weekly rates available, [CP] meal plan available, package plans - seasonal, pets ($10 fee). **Amenities:** high-speed Internet, voice mail. **Pool(s):** small heated indoor. **Leisure Activities:** whirlpool, hiking trails. **Business Services:** meeting rooms, business center. **Cards:** AX, DC, DS, MC, VI.

SOME UNITS

ASK DATA PORT

FEE

RAINBOW MOTEL **Phone:** (406)587-4201

Motel

5/1-9/30 [CP] 1P: $55 2P: $60-$75 XP: $5
3/1-4/30 & 10/1-2/28 [CP] 1P: $40-$50 2P: $45-$55 XP: $5

Location: I-90, exit 306, 0.8 mi s. 510 N 7th Ave 59715. Fax: 406/587-9737. **Facility:** 42 units. 39 one- and 3 two-bedroom standard units, some with efficiencies. 1-2 stories (no elevator), exterior corridors. *Bath:* combo or shower only. **Parking:** on-site, winter plug-ins. **Terms:** cancellation fee imposed, small pets only ($5 extra charge). **Pool(s):** heated outdoor. **Cards:** AX, DS, MC, VI.

SOME UNITS
FEE

RAMADA LIMITED *Book at aaa.com* **Phone:** (406)585-2626

Motel

All Year [CP] 1P: $39-$119 2P: $49-$149 XP: $10 F17

Location: I-90, exit 306, just n, then just w. 2020 Wheat Dr 59715. Fax: 406/585-2727. **Facility:** 50 units. 49 one-bedroom standard units. 1 one-bedroom suite ($79-$199) with kitchen. 2 stories (no elevator), interior corridors. **Parking:** on-site, winter plug-ins. **Amenities:** voice mail, irons, hair dryers. **Pool(s):** small heated indoor. **Leisure Activities:** whirlpool, waterslide. **Guest Services:** valet laundry. **Cards:** AX, DC, DS, MC, VI.

SOME UNITS

ROYAL "7" BUDGET INN **Phone:** 406/587-3103

Motel

6/1-9/30 [CP] 2P: $55-$66 XP: $4
3/1-5/31 & 10/1-2/28 [CP] 2P: $45-$49 XP: $4

Location: I-90, exit 306, 0.8 mi s on I-90 business loop. 310 N 7th Ave 59715. Fax: 406/587-3103. **Facility:** 47 units. 46 one- and 1 two-bedroom standard units. 1 story, exterior corridors. **Parking:** on-site, winter plug-ins. **Leisure Activities:** whirlpool, playground. **Cards:** AX, DS, MC. **Special Amenities: free continental breakfast and free local telephone calls.**

SOME UNITS

WINGATE INN OF BOZEMAN *Book at aaa.com* **Phone:** (406)582-4995

Small-scale Hotel

5/31-10/1 1P: $100-$115 2P: $100-$115 XP: $8 F18
10/2-2/28 1P: $85-$105 2P: $85-$105 XP: $8 F18
3/1-5/30 1P: $85-$100 2P: $85-$100 XP: $8 F18

Location: I-90, exit 305, just s on CR 41 (19th St), then just w on Valley Center Dr. 2305 Catron 59718. Fax: 406/582-7488. **Facility:** 86 units. 75 one-bedroom standard units. 11 one-bedroom suites ($115-$160), some with whirlpools. 3 stories, interior corridors. *Bath:* combo or shower only. **Parking:** on-site, winter plug-ins. **Terms:** check-in 4 pm, cancellation fee imposed, [ECP] meal plan available. **Amenities:** video games, high-speed Internet, dual phone lines, voice mail, safes, irons, hair dryers. **Pool(s):** heated indoor. **Leisure Activities:** whirlpool, exercise room. **Guest Services:** valet and coin laundry, airport transportation-Gallatin Field Airport. **Business Services:** meeting rooms, business center. **Cards:** AX, DC, DS, MC, VI. *(See color ad p 246)*

SOME UNITS

WHERE TO DINE

FRONTIER PIES RESTAURANT & BAKERY **Lunch:** $8-$15 **Dinner:** $9-$16 **Phone:** 406/586-5555

American

Location: I-90, exit 306, 1 mi s. 302 N 7th Ave 59715. **Hours:** 7 am-10 pm, Fri & Sat-11 pm. Closed: 12/25. **Features:** The dessert menu lists 26 varieties of homemade pie, great for savoring amid the rustic Old World decor peppered with antiques. The casual, cozy atmosphere makes for a nice family environment and complements the varied lunch and dinner selections. Casual dress. **Parking:** on-site. **Cards:** AX, DC, DS, MC, VI.

I-HO'S KOREAN GRILL **Lunch:** $4-$9 **Dinner:** $7-$13 **Phone:** 406/522-0949

Korean

Location: I-90, exit 306, 1 mi se, 0.5 mi w on W Main St, 1 mi se on 11th St, then just w; adjacent to Montana State University Campus. 1216 W Lincoln 59715. **Hours:** 11 am-9 pm, Sat from 5 pm. Closed: 11/25, 12/25. **Features:** You will love this authentic Korean food prepared in a traditional manner. The homey cafe is a big hit with the local college students and parents alike. If you're feeling bold, try the kim chee. Casual dress. **Parking:** on-site. **Cards:** MC, VI.

JOHN BOZEMAN'S BISTRO **Lunch:** $9-$13 **Dinner:** $14-$25 **Phone:** 406/587-4100

American

Location: Center. 125 W Main 59715. **Hours:** 11:30 am-2:30 & 5-9:30 pm. Closed: 1/1, 11/25, 12/25; also Sun & Mon. **Features:** The bistro provides eye-candy decor and a creative, international menu. Eclectic menu choices include inventive variations of sushi, buffalo, fish, tenderloin, poultry and vegetarian dishes. Seating in booths or on stools at the counter provides a casual feel, and the service is attentive, knowledgeable and friendly. Casual dress; beer & wine only. **Parking:** street. **Cards:** AX, DC, DS, MC, VI.

MACKENZIE RIVER PIZZA CO **Lunch:** $6-$17 **Dinner:** $6-$17 **Phone:** 406/587-0055

American

Location: City center. 232 E Main 59715. **Hours:** 11:30 am-9 pm, Fri & Sat-10 pm, Sun noon-9 pm; 11:30 am-10 pm, Sun from noon in summer. Closed major holidays; also 12/24. **Features:** Known for its eclectic Western decor, the restaurant lets patrons choose from several microbrews to accompany a specialty pizza or large, innovative sandwich. Casual dress; beer & wine only. **Parking:** street. **Cards:** AX, DS, MC, VI.

SANTA FE RED'S **Lunch:** $7-$14 **Dinner:** $7-$14 **Phone:** 406/587-5838

Mexican

Location: I-90, exit 306, just s. 1235 N 7th Ave 59715. **Hours:** 11 am-10 pm, Fri & Sat-11 pm, Sun-9 pm; 11 am-11 pm, Sun-10 pm in summer. Closed: 12/25. **Features:** The upbeat, bustling and popular Mexican restaurant serves such homemade Southwestern cuisine as fajitas, burritos and tacos. Guests can top off any meal with the signature dessert: fried ice cream. Casual dress; cocktails. **Parking:** on-site. **Cards:** AX, DS, MC, VI.

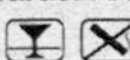

SAVORY OLIVE | **Lunch:** $6-$9 | **Dinner:** $16-$25 | **Phone:** 406/586-8320

American

Location: Downtown; in Baxter Hotel. 105 W Main St 59771. **Hours:** 11:30 am-2:30 & 5-10 pm, Sun 9 am-2 pm. Closed: 11/25, 12/25; also Mon. **Reservations:** suggested. **Features:** To say that this is just a Montana restaurant, just doesn't do it justice. The chef/owner utilizes the freshest of seasonal vegetables and spices to innovatively accentuate regionally available meats, poultry and seafood. To top it off, the desserts are made in house and all is presented with a creative flair. Located in the Historic Baxter Hotel, the decor is classic and intimate. Dressy casual; cocktails. **Parking:** street. **Cards:** AX, DS, MC, VI.

THE WOK | **Lunch:** $6-$9 | **Dinner:** $7-$16 | **Phone:** 406/585-1245

Chinese

Location: I-90, exit 306, 1 mi s. 319 N 7th Ave 59715. **Hours:** 11 am-10 pm. Closed: 11/25, 12/25. **Reservations:** accepted. **Features:** A very popular local favorite for family-style Oriental dining. Not only will you find the food tasty, the portions are hearty also. The staff is friendly and helpful. Good thing the dining room is large as this place can get quite busy at the dinner hour. Casual dress; beer & wine only. **Parking:** on-site. **Cards:** AX, DS, MC, VI.

The following restaurants have not been evaluated by AAA but are listed for your information only.

FAST LOOIES | **Phone:** 406/522-0800

fyi

Not evaluated. **Location:** 815 W College. **Features:** Across from the university campus, the restaurant welcomes patrons who want quick-serve variations of Indian, Asian and Italian dishes, as well as the ever-popular wraps.

THE PICKLE BARREL | **Phone:** 406/587-2411

fyi

Not evaluated. **Location:** 809 W College. **Features:** This eatery serves large, fresh deli sandwiches with dill pickles.

BROWNING pop. 1,065

WHERE TO STAY

WESTERN MOTEL | **Phone:** (406)338-7572

6/1-9/30	1P: $59-$95	2P: $59-$95	XP: $5
3/1-5/31 & 10/1-2/28	1P: $39-$80	2P: $45-$80	XP: $5

Motel

Location: On US 2; center of town. 121 Central Ave E 59417 (PO Box 788). Fax: 406/338-7572. **Facility:** 15 one-bedroom standard units. 1 story, exterior corridors. **Parking:** on-site, winter plug-ins. **Terms:** office hours 8 am-10 pm, cancellation fee imposed, small pets only. **Guest Services:** area transportation-train depot. **Cards:** AX, CB, DC, DS, MC, VI. **Special Amenities: free local telephone calls.**

SOME UNITS

BUTTE pop. 34,606

WHERE TO STAY

BEST WESTERN BUTTE PLAZA INN — *Book at aaa.com* — **Phone:** (406)494-3500

AAA SAVE

Small-scale Hotel

6/1-9/15	1P: $79-$99	2P: $89-$99	XP: $10	F12
3/1-5/31 & 9/16-2/28	1P: $72-$92	2P: $77-$97	XP: $10	F12

Location: I-90/15, exit 127 (Harrison Ave). 2900 Harrison Ave 59701. Fax: 406/494-7611. **Facility:** 134 units. 133 one-bedroom standard units. 1 one-bedroom suite ($100-$200) with whirlpool. 2 stories (no elevator), interior corridors. **Parking:** on-site, winter plug-ins. **Terms:** cancellation fee imposed, [ECP] meal plan available, pets ($50 deposit). **Amenities:** video games, voice mail, irons, hair dryers. **Dining:** 24 hours, cocktails. **Pool(s):** heated indoor. **Leisure Activities:** sauna, whirlpool, steamroom, exercise room. **Guest Services:** valet and coin laundry, airport transportation-Bert Mooney Airport, area transportation. **Business Services:** meeting rooms. **Cards:** AX, CB, DC, DS, JC, MC, VI. **Special Amenities: free continental breakfast and free newspaper.** ***(See color ad below)***

SOME UNITS

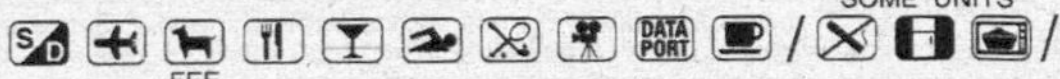

FEE

COMFORT INN OF BUTTE *Book at aaa.com* **Phone:** (406)494-8850

Motel

All Year	1P: $69-$99	2P: $75-$99	XP: $6	F18

Location: I-90/15, exit 127 (Harrison Ave), just s. 2777 Harrison Ave 59701. Fax: 406/494-2801. **Facility:** 145 units. 143 one-bedroom standard units, some with whirlpools. 2 one-bedroom suites, some with whirlpools. 3 stories, interior corridors. *Bath:* combo or shower only. **Parking:** on-site, winter plug-ins. **Terms:** pets ($5 extra charge). **Amenities:** video library (fee), hair dryers. *Some:* irons. **Pool(s):** heated indoor. **Leisure Activities:** sauna, whirlpools, exercise room. **Guest Services:** coin laundry, area transportation. **Business Services:** meeting rooms. **Cards:** AX, CB, DC, DS, MC, VI.

ASK FEE DATA PORT / SOME UNITS VCR FEE /

DAYS INN *Book at aaa.com* **Phone:** (406)494-7000

Small-scale Hotel

6/15-9/14 [CP]	1P: $79-$139	2P: $89-$139	XP: $8	F12
3/1-6/14 & 9/15-2/28 [CP]	1P: $60-$99	2P: $70-$99	XP: $8	F12

Location: I-90/15, exit 127 (Harrison Ave), just n. 2700 Harrison Ave 59701. Fax: 406/494-7000. **Facility:** 74 one-bedroom standard units, some with whirlpools. 3 stories, interior corridors. *Bath:* combo or shower only. **Parking:** on-site, winter plug-ins. **Amenities:** irons, hair dryers. *Some:* high-speed Internet. **Pool(s):** heated indoor. **Leisure Activities:** whirlpool, limited exercise equipment. **Guest Services:** valet and coin laundry. **Business Services:** meeting rooms. **Cards:** AX, CB, DC, DS, MC, VI.

ASK DATA PORT / SOME UNITS VCR FEE /

FINLEN HOTEL **Phone:** 406/723-5461

Small-scale Hotel

6/1-8/31	1P: $40-$52	2P: $44-$60
3/1-5/31 & 9/1-2/28	1P: $40-$48	2P: $40-$48

Location: I-90/15, exit 126, 1.4 mi n on Montana St, 0.3 mi e. 100 E Broadway 59701. Fax: 406/723-5461. **Facility:** 53 units. 48 one- and 5 two-bedroom standard units. 2-3 stories, interior/exterior corridors. *Bath:* combo or shower only. **Parking:** on-site. **Terms:** 5 day cancellation notice. **Cards:** AX, DC, DS, MC, VI.

ASK / SOME UNITS DATA PORT /

HAMPTON INN *Book at aaa.com* **Phone:** (406)494-2250

AAA SAVE

Small-scale Hotel

6/1-8/31	1P: $99-$119	2P: $99-$119
3/1-5/31 & 9/1-2/28	1P: $79-$99	2P: $79-$99

Location: I-90/15, exit 127 (Harrison Ave), 0.6 mi s. 3499 Harrison Ave 59701. Fax: 406/494-4404. **Facility:** 91 one-bedroom standard units. 3 stories, interior corridors. *Bath:* combo or shower only. **Parking:** on-site. **Terms:** [ECP] meal plan available. **Amenities:** video games, voice mail, irons, hair dryers. **Pool(s):** heated indoor. **Leisure Activities:** whirlpool, exercise room. **Guest Services:** valet and coin laundry, airport transportation-Bert Mooney Airport, area transportation-within 7 mi. **Business Services:** meeting rooms. **Cards:** AX, DC, DS, MC, VI. **Special Amenities: free expanded continental breakfast and free local telephone calls.** *(See color ad p 249)*

SOME UNITS

HOLIDAY INN EXPRESS PARKSIDE **Book at aaa.com** **Phone:** 406/494-6999

Small-scale Hotel

6/1-8/31 [ECP]	1P: $95	2P: $95
3/1-5/31 & 9/1-2/28 [ECP]	1P: $75-$79	2P: $75-$79

Location: I-90/15, exit 127 (Harrison Ave), just n to Cornell St, then just e, follow signs. Located across from a park and Greenway Walking Trail. 1 Holiday Park Dr 59701. Fax: 406/494-1300. **Facility:** 83 units. 66 one-bedroom standard units. 17 one-bedroom suites, some with whirlpools. 5 stories, interior corridors. *Bath:* combo or shower only. **Parking:** on-site, winter plug-ins. **Amenities:** dual phone lines, voice mail, irons, hair dryers. **Leisure Activities:** exercise room. **Guest Services:** valet and coin laundry. **Business Services:** meeting rooms, business center. **Cards:** AX, CB, DC, DS, JC, MC, VI.

ASK / SOME UNITS /

RAMADA INN COPPER KING **Book at aaa.com** **Phone:** (406)494-6666

AAA SAVE

Small-scale Hotel

6/1-8/31 [ECP]	1P: $65	2P: $65	XP: $5	F18
3/1-5/31 & 9/1-2/28 [ECP]	1P: $55	2P: $55	XP: $5	F18

Location: I-90/15, exit 127A, 2 mi s on SR 2 (Harrison Ave). 4655 Harrison Ave S 59701. Fax: 406/494-3274. **Facility:** 146 units. 144 one-bedroom standard units. 2 one-bedroom suites ($95) with whirlpools. 2 stories, interior corridors. **Parking:** on-site, winter plug-ins. **Terms:** package plans, pets ($10 extra charge). **Amenities:** video library, voice mail, safes (fee), irons, hair dryers. **Dining:** 2 restaurants, 6 am-2 & 5-9 pm, cocktails. **Pool(s):** heated indoor. **Leisure Activities:** sauna, whirlpool, 3 lighted indoor tennis courts, limited exercise equipment. **Guest Services:** valet and coin laundry, airport transportation-Bert Mooney Airport, area transportation. **Business Services:** conference facilities. **Cards:** AX, CB, DC, DS, MC, VI. **Special Amenities: free expanded continental breakfast and free local telephone calls.** *(See color ad p 250)*

FEE / SOME UNITS / FEE

RED LION HOTEL **Book at aaa.com** **Phone:** (406)494-7800

Small-scale Hotel

All Year [ECP]	1P: $59-$109	2P: $59-$119	XP: $10	F18

Location: I-90/15, exit 127B (Harrison Ave), just n, then just e. 2100 Cornell Ave 59701. Fax: 406/494-2875. **Facility:** 131 units. 125 one-bedroom standard units, some with whirlpools. 6 one-bedroom suites ($89-$169). 2 stories (no elevator), interior corridors. *Bath:* combo or shower only. **Parking:** on-site, winter plug-ins. **Terms:** [BP] meal plan available, package plans, pets ($25 deposit). **Amenities:** dual phone lines, voice mail, irons, hair dryers. **Pool(s):** heated indoor. **Leisure Activities:** sauna, whirlpool, exercise room. **Guest Services:** area transportation. **Business Services:** conference facilities, business center. **Cards:** AX, CB, DC, DS, MC, VI. *(See color ad p 250)*

ASK FEE / SOME UNITS /

ROCKER INN **Phone:** (406)723-5464

AAA SAVE

Motel

6/1-9/30	1P: $46-$48	2P: $50-$57	XP: $4	F12
3/1-5/31 & 10/1-2/28	1P: $38-$44	2P: $45-$53	XP: $4	F12

Location: I-90/15, exit 122 (Rocker). 122001 W Brown's Gulch Rd 59701. **Facility:** 49 one-bedroom standard units. 2 stories (no elevator), interior corridors. *Bath:* combo or shower only. **Parking:** on-site, winter plug-ins. **Terms:** pets ($5 extra charge). **Guest Services:** coin laundry, airport transportation-Bert Mooney Airport. **Cards:** AX, DS, MC, VI. **Special Amenities: early check-in/late check-out and preferred room (subject to availability with advanced reservations).**

FEE / SOME UNITS /

SUPER 8 MOTEL OF BUTTE **Book at aaa.com** **Phone:** 406/494-6000

Motel

6/1-9/30 [CP]	1P: $62-$72	2P: $67-$78	XP: $6	F12
4/1-5/31 [CP]	1P: $57-$66	2P: $61-$71	XP: $5	F12
3/1-3/31 & 10/1-2/28 [CP]	1P: $49-$57	2P: $53-$63	XP: $4	F12

Location: I-90/15, exit 127 (Harrison Ave), just s. Located opposite from a shopping mall. 2929 Harrison Ave 59701. Fax: 406/494-6000. **Facility:** 106 one-bedroom standard units. 3 stories (no elevator), interior corridors. **Parking:** on-site, winter plug-ins. **Terms:** pets ($5 fee, $50 deposit). **Amenities:** video library (fee). *Some:* irons. **Guest Services:** valet and coin laundry. **Business Services:** business center. **Cards:** AX, CB, DC, DS, JC, MC, VI.

ASK FEE / SOME UNITS FEE /

WHERE TO DINE

4 B'S RESTAURANT — American
Lunch: $6-$9 **Dinner:** $6-$9 **Phone:** 406/494-1199
Location: I-90/15, exit 127A, s on Harrison Ave, just w. 1905 Dewey Blvd 59701. **Hours:** 24 hours. Closed: 11/25, 12/25. **Features:** Sandwiches, soup, salad, chicken and a variety of additional entrees are served at this casual, family-style restaurant. Seating is open and unassuming; the service staff is prompt and friendly. A casino and lounge is housed next door. Casual dress. **Parking:** on-site. **Cards:** AX, DC, DS, MC, VI.

UPTOWN CAFE

Continental
Lunch: $4-$7 **Dinner:** $9-$22 **Phone:** 406/723-4735
Location: I-90/15, exit 126, 1.5 mi n on Montana St, just e. 47 E Broadway 59701. **Hours:** 11 am-2 & 5-10 pm, Sat from 5 pm, Sun from 4 pm. Closed major holidays. **Reservations:** suggested, for dinner. **Features:** An informal, modern decor and art gallery complement the house specials of fresh seafood, steak, poultry and pasta. Gourmet desserts include tortes and cakes, and the homemade bread is excellent. A convenient, upscale luncheon buffet is offered. Casual dress; cocktails. **Parking:** street. **Cards:** AX, DS, MC, VI.

CHINOOK pop. 1,386

WHERE TO STAY

CHINOOK MOTOR INN — Small-scale Hotel
Phone: (406)357-2248

3/1-10/31	1P: $55-$65	2P: $58-$68	XP: $5	F12
11/1-2/28	1P: $50-$55	2P: $55-$65	XP: $5	F12

Location: On US 2. 100 Indiana St 59523 (PO Box 1418). Fax: 406/357-2261. **Facility:** 38 one-bedroom standard units. 2 stories (no elevator), interior corridors. *Bath:* combo or shower only. **Parking:** on-site, winter plug-ins. **Terms:** pets ($5 extra charge). **Dining:** 6 am-10 pm; 7 am-9 pm in winter, cocktails. **Business Services:** meeting rooms. **Cards:** AX, DS, MC, VI.

SOME UNITS
FEE

CHOTEAU pop. 1,781

WHERE TO STAY

BIG SKY MOTEL — Motel
Phone: 406/466-5318
Property failed to provide current rates
Location: Just s of town center on US 89. 209 S Main Ave 59422 (PO Box 977). Fax: 406/466-5866. **Facility:** 12 units. 10 one-bedroom standard units, some with kitchens. 2 one-bedroom suites with kitchens. 1 story, exterior corridors. *Bath:* shower only. **Parking:** on-site, winter plug-ins. **Terms:** pets ($5 extra charge).

SOME UNITS
FEE

STAGE STOP INN — Small-scale Hotel
Phone: (406)466-5900

6/1-9/30 [CP]	1P: $67-$77	2P: $72-$82	XP: $5	F18
3/1-5/31 & 10/1-2/28 [CP]	1P: $58-$68	2P: $63-$73	XP: $5	F18

Location: N of town center on US 89. 1005 Main Ave N 59422 (PO Box 1238). Fax: 406/466-5907. **Facility:** 43 units. 39 one-bedroom standard units. 4 one-bedroom suites ($95-$110) with whirlpools. 2 stories (no elevator), interior corridors. *Bath:* combo or shower only. **Parking:** on-site, winter plug-ins. **Terms:** pets (at boarding kennel). **Pool(s):** heated indoor. **Leisure Activities:** whirlpool, exercise room. **Guest Services:** coin laundry. **Cards:** AX, CB, DC, DS, JC, MC, VI. **Special Amenities: free continental breakfast and free local telephone calls.**
(See color ad below)

SOME UNITS

WHERE TO DINE

JOHN HENRY'S

American
Lunch: $5-$8 **Dinner:** $7-$12 **Phone:** 406/466-5642
Location: On US 89; center. 215 N Main St 59422. **Hours:** 11 am-10 pm, Sun noon-8 pm. Closed: 12/24, 12/25. **Features:** You'll find affordable, tasty pizzas, burgers and family fare served in a casual, friendly atmosphere. Casual dress; beer & wine only. **Parking:** street. **Cards:** MC, VI.

CLINTON pop. 549

WHERE TO STAY

BLUE DAMSEL B&B ON ROCK CREEK — **Phone:** (406)825-3077

Bed & Breakfast

All Year	1P: $155-$200	2P: $155-$200	XP: $20

Location: I-90, exit 126 (Rock Creek Rd), 10.8 mi s. Located in a quiet, rural area. 1081 Rock Creek Rd 59825. Fax: 406/825-0085. **Facility:** A good trout-fishing stream serves as the backdrop for this well-constructed log home. Designated smoking area. 6 units. 3 one- and 1 two-bedroom standard units, some with whirlpools. 1 one-bedroom suite with kitchen. 1 cabin ($155-$200). 1-3 stories (no elevator), interior/exterior corridors. *Bath:* combo or shower only. **Parking:** on-site. **Terms:** 30 day cancellation notice-fee imposed, package plans. **Amenities:** CD players, hair dryers. **Leisure Activities:** fishing, cross country skiing, bicycles, hiking trails, jogging, horseshoes, volleyball. *Fee:* charter fishing. **Guest Services:** complimentary laundry. **Business Services:** PC, fax. **Cards:** AX, CB, DC, DS, MC, VI.

SOME UNITS

ASK VCR

WHERE TO DINE

EKSTROM'S STAGE STATION — **Lunch:** $7-$9 — **Dinner:** $7-$16 — **Phone:** 406/825-3183

American

Location: I-90, exit 126 (Rock Creek Rd), 0.5 mi s. 81 Rock Creek Rd 59825. **Hours:** Open 5/1-9/30; 8 am-10 pm. **Reservations:** accepted. **Features:** Dine in what was once the stable of a stagecoach station on recipes handed down from generation to generation in a family that has been in the hospitality business since 1883. Home-baked goods and trout are specialties and are served in a rustic decor. Casual dress; beer & wine only. **Parking:** on-site. **Cards:** MC, VI.

COLSTRIP pop. 2,346

WHERE TO STAY

LAKEVIEW BED & BREAKFAST — *Book at aaa.com* — **Phone:** (406)748-3653

Bed & Breakfast

All Year [BP]	1P: $75-$88	2P: $82-$95	XP: $10	D10

Location: 0.6 mi w from SR 39. 7437 Castle Rock Lake Dr 59323 (PO Box 483). Fax: 406/748-2275. **Facility:** This is a residential, lakefront home with charming, distinctive decor and a wide selection of books. Smoke free premises. 5 one-bedroom standard units. 3 stories (no elevator), interior/exterior corridors. *Bath:* some shared or private, combo or shower only. **Parking:** street. **Terms:** check-in 4 pm, 7 day cancellation notice-fee imposed. **Amenities:** video library, irons. *Some:* DVD players. **Leisure Activities:** boating, paddleboats, fishing. **Cards:** AX, DS, MC, VI.

SOME UNITS

ASK VCR DATA PORT

SUPER 8 MOTEL OF COLSTRIP LLC — **Phone:** 406/748-3400

Motel

4/1-9/30	1P: $62-$75	2P: $65-$85	XP: $5	F17
10/1-2/28	1P: $55-$70	2P: $58-$79	XP: $5	F17
3/1-3/31	1P: $53-$70	2P: $55-$79	XP: $5	F17

Location: SR 39. 6227 Main St 59323 (PO Box 1931). Fax: 406/748-3467. **Facility:** 39 one-bedroom standard units. 2 stories (no elevator), interior corridors. *Bath:* combo or shower only. **Parking:** on-site, winter plug-ins. **Terms:** pets ($5 deposit, in smoking units). **Amenities:** voice mail. *Some:* hair dryers. **Guest Services:** coin laundry. **Business Services:** meeting rooms. **Cards:** AX, DC, DS, MC, VI.

SOME UNITS

ASK DATA PORT FEE FEE FEE

COLUMBIA FALLS pop. 3,645—*See also GLACIER NATIONAL PARK.*

WHERE TO STAY

BAD ROCK COUNTRY BED & BREAKFAST — **Phone:** (406)892-2829

Bed & Breakfast

All Year [BP]	1P: $128-$168	2P: $128-$168	XP: $30

Location: Jct US 2 and SR 206, 2.4 mi s on SR 206, 0.9 mi w. Located in a quiet area. 480 Bad Rock Dr 59912. Fax: 406/892-2930. **Facility:** This B&B, which houses guests in two hand-hewn log buildings, is on 30 acres of manicured grounds offering sweeping mountain views. Smoke free premises. 7 one-bedroom standard units. 1-2 stories (no elevator), interior/exterior corridors. *Bath:* combo or shower only. **Parking:** on-site, winter plug-ins. **Terms:** office hours 7 am-10 pm, 2 night minimum stay, 30 day cancellation notice-fee imposed. **Amenities:** hair dryers. **Leisure Activities:** whirlpool. **Cards:** AX, CB, DC, DS, JC, MC, VI.

SOME UNITS

GLACIER PARK SUPER 8 *Book at aaa.com* **Phone:** 406/892-0888

AAA SAVE | 5/15-9/30 | 1P: $64-$79 | 2P: $69-$84 | XP: $5 | F12
3/1-5/14 & 10/1-2/28 | 1P: $40-$49 | 2P: $45-$53 | XP: $5 | F12

Small-scale Hotel

Location: Just ne on US 2 from jct SR 206. 7336 US 2 E 59912. Fax: 406/892-8808. **Facility:** 32 one-bedroom standard units, some with whirlpools. 2 stories (no elevator), interior/exterior corridors. **Parking:** on-site, winter plug-ins. **Leisure Activities:** whirlpool. **Business Services:** meeting rooms. **Cards:** AX, CB, DC, DS, JC, MC, VI. **Special Amenities: free local telephone calls.**

SOME UNITS

MEADOW LAKE RESORT **Phone:** (406)892-8700

AAA SAVE | 7/1-9/5 | 1P: $165-$565 | 2P: $165-$565
3/1-6/30 & 9/6-2/28 | 1P: $135-$480 | 2P: $135-$480

Condominium

Location: Jct US 2 and SR 40, 1.4 mi e on US 2, 1.1 mi n on Meadow Lake Blvd. 100 St Andrews Dr 59912. Fax: 406/892-8731. **Facility:** The complex features a golf course; accommodations include motel units, condos, townhouses and villas. 152 units. 24 one-bedroom standard units. 14 one- and 101 two-bedroom suites with kitchens, some with whirlpools. 13 vacation homes. 1-3 stories, interior/exterior corridors. **Parking:** on-site, winter plug-ins. **Terms:** office hours 6 am-midnight, check-in 4 pm, 2 night minimum stay - condos & vacation homes, 30 day cancellation notice. **Amenities:** voice mail. *Some:* irons. **Dining:** 7 am-10 pm; 5 pm-9 pm in winter, cocktails. **Pool(s):** heated outdoor, heated indoor. **Leisure Activities:** whirlpools, tennis court, cross country skiing, recreation programs, playground, exercise room, volleyball. *Fee:* golf-18 holes, massage. **Guest Services:** area transportation-ski area. **Business Services:** meeting rooms. **Cards:** AX, DC, MC, VI. **Special Amenities: free local telephone calls.** *(See color ad p 263)*

SOME UNITS

DATA PORT

WHERE TO DINE

THE BACK ROOM **Dinner:** $5-$14 **Phone:** 406/892-2191

American

Location: Just w of downtown. Hwy 2 E 59912. **Hours:** 4 pm-10 pm, Sun 2 pm-9 pm. **Features:** The casual eatery prepares excellent barbecue, steaks and seafood with few frills. Dedicated carnivores can sample any of three styles of ribs served with fry-bread. Casual dress; cocktails. **Parking:** on-site. **Cards:** AX, CB, DC, DS, JC, MC, VI.

COLUMBUS pop. 1,748

WHERE TO STAY

SUPER 8 OF COLUMBUS *Book at aaa.com* **Phone:** (406)322-4101

All Year | 1P: $59-$89 | 2P: $65-$99 | XP: $6 | F12

Small-scale Hotel

Location: I-90, exit 408, just s on SR 78. 602 8th Ave N 59019 (PO Box 88). Fax: 406/322-4636. **Facility:** 72 units. 71 one-bedroom standard units, some with kitchens. 1 one-bedroom suite with kitchen. 2 stories, interior corridors. *Bath:* combo or shower only. **Parking:** on-site, winter plug-ins. **Terms:** pets ($5 extra charge). **Leisure Activities:** sauna, whirlpool. **Guest Services:** coin laundry. **Business Services:** meeting rooms. **Cards:** AX, CB, DC, DS, MC, VI.

SOME UNITS

ASK FEE DATA PORT FEE FEE

CONRAD pop. 2,753

WHERE TO STAY

SUPER 8 MOTEL **Phone:** (406)278-7676

All Year | 1P: $59-$89 | 2P: $65-$99 | XP: $6 | F12

Small-scale Hotel

Location: I-15, exit 339, just w. 215 N Main 59425. Fax: 406/278-5370. **Facility:** 47 one-bedroom standard units. 2 stories (no elevator), interior corridors. **Parking:** on-site, winter plug-ins. **Terms:** pets ($5 extra charge). **Guest Services:** coin laundry. **Cards:** AX, CB, DC, DS, MC, VI.

SOME UNITS

ASK FEE DATA PORT

CORAM pop. 337—*See also GLACIER NATIONAL PARK.*

WHERE TO STAY

A WILD ROSE BED & BREAKFAST **Phone:** 406/387-4900

All Year [BP] | 1P: $100-$160 | 2P: $100-$160 | XP: $25

Bed & Breakfast

Location: Just n of town. Located in a quiet, rural area. 10280 US 2 E 59913 (PO Box 29, WEST GLACIER, 59936). **Facility:** A modern re-creation of a Victorian home, the B&B is nestled in the wooded hills of Montana, 6 miles from Glacier National Park. Smoke free premises. 4 one-bedroom standard units, some with whirlpools. 2 stories (no elevator), interior/exterior corridors. *Bath:* combo or shower only. **Parking:** on-site. **Terms:** office hours 8 am-9 pm, check-in 4 pm, 2 night minimum stay - seasonal, age restrictions may apply, 30 day cancellation notice-fee imposed. **Amenities:** hair dryers. **Leisure Activities:** whirlpool. **Cards:** DS, MC, VI.

SOME UNITS

CULBERTSON pop. 716

WHERE TO STAY

THE KINGS INN **Phone:** 406/787-6277

All Year | 1P: $40-$45 | 2P: $45-$55 | XP: $7 | F6

Motel

Location: Jct US 2 and SR 16, 0.3 mi e. 408 E 6th St 59218 (PO Box 665). Fax: 406/787-6177. **Facility:** 20 one-bedroom standard units. 1 story, interior corridors. **Parking:** on-site, winter plug-ins. **Cards:** AX, DC, DS, MC, VI.

SOME UNITS

CUT BANK pop. 3,105

WHERE TO STAY

CUT BANK SUPER 8 *Book at aaa.com* **Phone:** (406)873-5662

Motel

All Year | 1P: $49-$69 | 2P: $59-$69 | XP: $6 | F12

Location: On US 2, 0.3 mi w. 609 W Main St 59427. Fax: 406/873-3339. **Facility:** 61 one-bedroom standard units. 3 stories (no elevator), interior corridors. **Parking:** on-site, winter plug-ins. **Terms:** [CP] meal plan available. **Pool(s):** heated indoor. **Leisure Activities:** whirlpool, limited exercise equipment. **Cards:** AX, MC, VI. **Special Amenities: free continental breakfast and free local telephone calls.**

SOME UNITS

GLACIER GATEWAY INN **Phone:** 406/873-5544

Small-scale Hotel

All Year [ECP] | 1P: $46-$56 | 2P: $56-$74 | XP: $6 | F3

Location: US 2, just e from town center. 1121 E Railroad St 59427. Fax: 406/873-5546. **Facility:** 18 one-bedroom standard units. 1 story, interior corridors. **Parking:** on-site, winter plug-ins. **Terms:** cancellation fee imposed, small pets only ($3 extra charge). **Amenities:** video library (fee), hair dryers. **Leisure Activities:** whirlpool, exercise room. **Guest Services:** gift shop, airport transportation-Cut Bank Airport, area transportation-train depot. **Business Services:** fax (fee). **Cards:** AX, CB, DC, DS, MC, VI. **Special Amenities: free expanded continental breakfast and preferred room (subject to availability with advanced reservations).**

SOME UNITS

FEE FEE

GLACIER GATEWAY PLAZA **Phone:** 406/873-2566

Motel

All Year [ECP] | 1P: $59-$78 | 2P: $65-$84 | XP: $6 | D12

Location: Just e of town center on US 2. 1130 E Main St 59427 (1121 E Railroad St). Fax: 406/873-5546. **Facility:** 19 one-bedroom standard units. 1 story, interior corridors. **Parking:** on-site, winter plug-ins. **Terms:** cancellation fee imposed, small pets only ($3 extra charge, in smoking units). **Amenities:** video library (fee), voice mail, irons, hair dryers. **Pool(s):** heated indoor. **Leisure Activities:** whirlpool, exercise room. **Guest Services:** gift shop, coin laundry, airport transportation-Cut Bank Airport, area transportation-train depot & bus station. *Fee:* tanning facility. **Cards:** AX, CB, DC, DS, MC, VI. **Special Amenities: free expanded continental breakfast and free newspaper.**

SOME UNITS

FEE FEE

WHERE TO DINE

4 WINS SUPPER CLUB & CASINO **Lunch:** $2-$8 **Dinner:** $12-$23 **Phone:** 406/873-4401

Steak House

Location: US 2, east end of town. 918 E Main St 59427. **Hours:** 11 am-10 pm. Closed: 12/25. **Reservations:** accepted. **Features:** Casual dining and friendly service are hallmarks here. A large salad bar and good selection of steak and seafood keep the locals coming back to this popular eatery. Try the tender chicken strips, lightly breaded and accompanied by honey mustard sauce. Casual dress; cocktails. **Parking:** on-site. **Cards:** AX, DS, MC, VI.

DARBY pop. 710

WHERE TO STAY

RYE CREEK LODGE **Phone:** (406)821-3366

Cabin

4/1-10/31 | 1P: $225-$450 | 2P: $225-$450 | XP: $35 | F12

3/1-3/31 & 11/1-2/28 | 1P: $175 | 2P: $175 | XP: $35 | F12

Location: US 93, 4.5 mi s, 1.5 mi e. Located in a quiet, secluded setting. (PO Box 877). **Facility:** Nicely appointed log cabins. Smoke free premises. 6 units. 1 one- and 1 two-bedroom standard units with kitchens. 4 cabins, some with whirlpools. 1-2 stories (no elevator), exterior corridors. **Parking:** on-site, winter plug-ins. **Terms:** check-in 4 pm, 30 day cancellation notice-fee imposed, weekly rates available. **Amenities:** irons, hair dryers. *Some:* DVD players. **Leisure Activities:** fishing, badminton, croquet, horseshoes, volleyball. **Guest Services:** complimentary laundry. **Cards:** AX, DS, MC, VI. **Special Amenities: free local telephone calls and free room upgrade (subject to availability with advanced reservations).**

SOME UNITS

DEER LODGE pop. 3,421

WHERE TO STAY

SUPER 8 MOTEL *Book at aaa.com* **Phone:** (406)846-2370

Motel

5/16-9/30 [CP] | 1P: $60-$80 | 2P: $70-$80 | XP: $5 | F12

3/1-5/15 [CP] | 1P: $50-$74 | 2P: $63-$74 | XP: $5 | F12

10/1-2/28 [CP] | 1P: $56-$68 | 2P: $61-$68 | XP: $5 | F12

Location: I-90, exit 184, 0.3 mi s. 1150 N Main St 59722. Fax: 406/846-2373. **Facility:** 57 one-bedroom standard units. 2 stories (no elevator), interior corridors. *Bath:* combo or shower only. **Parking:** on-site, winter plug-ins. **Terms:** small pets only ($5 extra charge, in smoking units). **Amenities:** *Some:* hair dryers. **Cards:** AX, DC, DS, MC, VI. **Special Amenities: free continental breakfast and free local telephone calls.**

SOME UNITS

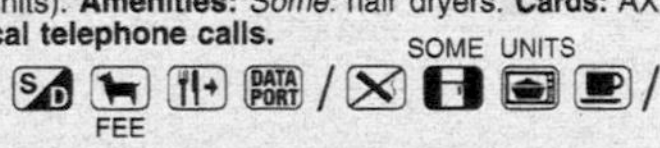

WHERE TO DINE

4 B'S RESTAURANT — Lunch: $6-$9 — Dinner: $6-$9 — Phone: 406/846-2620

American

Location: I-90, exit 184, 0.3 mi s. 130 Sam Beck Rd 59722. **Hours:** 5:30 am-midnight, Fri & Sat 24 hours. Closed: 11/25, 12/25. **Features:** Ample portions at reasonable prices are offered in an informal, family setting with comfortable booth and table seating. The menu features prime rib, hot sandwiches, burgers, salad, chicken and liver and onions, plus freshly baked pies. Casual dress. **Parking:** on-site. **Cards:** AX, DC, DS, MC, VI.

SCHARF'S FAMILY RESTAURANT — **Lunch:** $5-$11 — **Dinner:** $6-$11 — **Phone:** 406/846-3300

AAA — American

Location: On I-90 business loop; downtown; adjacent to Scharf's Motor Inn. 819 Main St 59722. **Hours:** 6:30 am-9 pm; 6 am-10 pm 4/1-10/1. Closed: 1/1, 11/25, 12/25. **Features:** This is a popular dining spot with the locals; the informal atmosphere and good food at this family-style restaurant are the reasons why. Daily soup bar and salad bar. The menu offers a varied selection of sandwiches, plus traditional dinner selections. Casual dress; beer & wine only. **Parking:** street. **Cards:** AX, MC, VI.

DILLON pop. 3,752

WHERE TO STAY

BEST WESTERN PARADISE INN — *Book at aaa.com* — **Phone:** (406)683-4214

AAA SAVE — Motel

3/1-10/15	1P: $55-$79	2P: $55-$79	XP: $6	F12
10/16-2/28	1P: $51-$68	2P: $51-$68	XP: $6	F12

Location: I-15, exit 63, 0.3 mi s on SR 41. 650 N Montana St 59725. Fax: 406/683-4216. **Facility:** 65 units. 62 one-bedroom standard units. 2 one- and 1 two-bedroom suites. 2 stories (no elevator), exterior corridors. **Parking:** on-site, winter plug-ins. **Terms:** small pets only. **Amenities:** irons, hair dryers. **Dining:** 6 am-10 pm; to 11 pm 5/16-10/31, cocktails. **Pool(s):** heated indoor. **Leisure Activities:** whirlpool. **Guest Services:** airport transportation-Dillon Airport. **Cards:** AX, CB, DC, DS, JC, MC, VI. **Special Amenities: free newspaper.**

SOME UNITS

DATA PORT

COMFORT INN OF DILLON — *Book at aaa.com* — **Phone:** (406)683-6831

Motel

All Year [ECP]	1P: $59-$89	2P: $65-$99	XP: $6	F18

Location: I-15, exit 63. 450 N Interchange 59725 (PO Box 666). Fax: 406/683-2021. **Facility:** 48 one-bedroom standard units. 2 stories (no elevator), interior corridors. **Parking:** on-site, winter plug-ins. **Terms:** pets ($5 extra charge). **Amenities:** *Some:* irons, hair dryers. **Pool(s):** small heated indoor. **Guest Services:** coin laundry. **Cards:** AX, CB, DC, DS, MC, VI.

SOME UNITS

ASK — FEE — DATA PORT

GUESTHOUSE INTERNATIONAL INNS & SUITES — *Book at aaa.com* — **Phone:** (406)683-3636

Small-scale Hotel

5/1-9/30	1P: $69-$79	2P: $79-$89	XP: $5	F17
3/1-4/30 & 10/1-2/28	1P: $59-$64	2P: $69-$79	XP: $5	F17

Location: I-15, exit 63. 580 Sinclair St 59725. Fax: 406/683-3637. **Facility:** 58 one-bedroom standard units, some with whirlpools. 2 stories (no elevator), interior corridors. *Bath:* combo or shower only. **Parking:** on-site. **Terms:** [BP] meal plan available, pets ($10 extra charge). **Amenities:** video library (fee), voice mail, irons, hair dryers. **Pool(s):** small heated indoor. **Leisure Activities:** whirlpool, exercise room. **Guest Services:** coin laundry. **Business Services:** meeting rooms, business center. **Cards:** AX, DC, DS, MC, VI.

SOME UNITS

ASK — FEE — VCR — DATA PORT

SUNDOWNER MOTEL — **Phone:** 406/683-2375

AAA SAVE — Motel

6/1-10/31	1P: $38-$40	2P: $41-$43	XP: $3
3/1-5/31 & 11/1-2/28	1P: $35-$37	2P: $38-$40	XP: $3

Location: I-15, exit 63, just s. Located in a commercial area. 500 N Montana St 59725. Fax: 406/683-6505. **Facility:** 32 one-bedroom standard units. 2 stories (no elevator), exterior corridors. **Parking:** on-site, winter plug-ins. **Terms:** pets (in designated units). **Leisure Activities:** playground. **Cards:** AX, DC, DS, MC, VI. **Special Amenities: free local telephone calls and preferred room (subject to availability with advanced reservations).**

SOME UNITS

FEE FEE

SUPER 8 MOTEL — *Book at aaa.com* — **Phone:** (406)683-4288

Motel

All Year [CP]	1P: $53-$60	2P: $56-$70	XP: $5	F13

Location: I-15, exit 63, just n on US 91. 550 N Montana St 59725. Fax: 406/683-4288. **Facility:** 47 one-bedroom standard units. 3 stories (no elevator), interior corridors. **Parking:** on-site, winter plug-ins. **Terms:** pets ($25 deposit). **Amenities:** safes. **Cards:** AX, CB, DC, DS, MC, VI.

SOME UNITS

ASK — FEE — DATA PORT

EAST GLACIER PARK pop. 396—*See also GLACIER NATIONAL PARK.*

WHERE TO STAY

DANCING BEARS INN LLC — **Phone:** (406)226-4402

AAA SAVE — Motel

6/1-9/30	1P: $59-$120	2P: $59-$120	XP: $5
3/1-5/31 & 10/1-2/28	1P: $39-$80	2P: $45-$80	XP: $5

Location: Just off US 2, follow signs; center. 40 Montana Ave 59434 (PO Box 149). Fax: 406/226-4402. **Facility:** 14 units. 12 one-bedroom standard units, some with efficiencies and/or whirlpools. 2 cabins ($80-$120). 1 story, interior/exterior corridors. *Bath:* combo or shower only. **Parking:** on-site, winter plug-ins. **Terms:** office hours 8:30 am-10 pm, cancellation fee imposed, small pets only. **Cards:** AX, CB, DC, DS, MC, VI.

SOME UNITS

JACOBSON'S SCENIC VIEW COTTAGES **Phone:** 406/226-4422

Cottage

6/15-9/14	1P: $49-$65	2P: $60-$75	XP: $6	F6
5/1-6/14 & 9/15-10/5	1P: $40-$50	2P: $49-$65	XP: $6	F6

Location: On SR 49, 0.8 mi n. 1204 Hwy 49 59434 (PO Box 454). **Facility:** 12 cottages. 1 story, exterior corridors. **Parking:** on-site. **Terms:** open 5/1-10/5. **Leisure Activities:** playground. **Cards:** AX, DS, MC, VI.

SOME UNITS

FEE FEE

MOUNTAIN PINE MOTEL **Phone:** 406/226-4403

Motel

6/15-9/14	1P: $53	2P: $58-$63	XP: $4
5/1-6/14 & 9/15-10/1	1P: $40	2P: $45-$49	XP: $4

Location: On SR 49, 0.5 mi n. Located adjacent to Glacier National Park. SR 49 N 59434 (PO Box 260). Fax: 406/226-9290. **Facility:** Smoke free premises. 27 units. 25 one-bedroom standard units. 1 vacation home and 1 cottage. 1 story, exterior corridors. *Bath:* combo or shower only. **Parking:** on-site. **Terms:** open 5/1-10/1. **Cards:** AX, DC, DS, MC, VI.

SOME UNITS

WHERE TO DINE

GLACIER VILLAGE RESTAURANT **Lunch:** $6-$9 **Dinner:** $9-$18 **Phone:** 406/226-4464

American

Location: US 2, at jct SR 49; opposite Glacier National Park gateway. 304-308 Hwy 2 E 59434. **Hours:** Open 6/1-9/29; 6:30 am-9:30 pm. **Reservations:** accepted. **Features:** The casual restaurant is a local favorite. The menu centers on traditional Native American and Montana foods, lots of sandwiches and burgers, roast turkey, buffalo, huckleberry pork chops and broiled steaks. Desserts are made in house. Guests can choose from many microbrew beers, imported teas and an espresso bar. Many historical photographs of Blackfeet Indians and Glacier National Park adorn the walls. Casual dress; beer & wine only. **Parking:** street. **Cards:** DS, MC, VI.

SERRANO'S **Dinner:** $9-$15 **Phone:** 406/226-9392

Mexican

Location: Center. 29 Dawson Ave 59434. **Hours:** Open 5/1-10/1; 5 pm-10 pm; to 9 pm 5/1-5/28 & 9/1-9/30. **Features:** Mexican/Southwest cuisine is served inside the historic former Dawson House where the atmosphere is intimate but bustling. (Expect a wait.) You can't go wrong with the sauteed red snapper, nor the strip steak. Patio seating is offered 7/1-8/31. Casual dress; cocktails. **Parking:** street. **Cards:** AX, DS, MC, VI.

EMIGRANT

WHERE TO STAY

MOUNTAIN SKY GUEST RANCH **Phone:** (406)333-4911

Ranch

5/5-10/15 [AP]	1P: $307	2P: $307

Location: US 89, 27 mi s of I-90, 6 mi s of Emigrant, then 4.5 mi w. Big Creek Rd 59027 (PO Box 1219). Fax: 406/333-4537. **Facility:** The ranch offers modern guest rooms and one- to three-bedroom rustic cabins. All are supplied with baskets of fruit, fine coffee and tea. 30 units. 10 one-bedroom standard units. 11 one- and 1 two-bedroom suites. 8 cabins. 1 story, exterior corridors. **Parking:** on-site. **Terms:** open 5/5-10/15, 7 night minimum stay - in summer, cancellation fee imposed, package plans. **Amenities:** *Some:* hair dryers. **Pool(s):** heated outdoor. **Leisure Activities:** sauna, whirlpool, fishing, fly fishing instruction, 2 tennis courts, recreation programs, ping pong, softball, hiking trails, horseback riding, horseshoes, volleyball. *Fee:* massage. **Guest Services:** gift shop, complimentary laundry, airport transportation (fee)-Gallatin Field Airport. **Business Services:** meeting rooms. **Cards:** MC, VI.

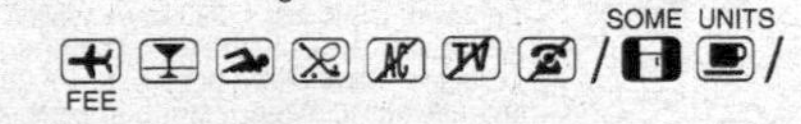

PARADISE GATEWAY BED & BREAKFAST & GUEST CABINS **Phone:** (406)333-4063

Bed & Breakfast

All Year [BP]	1P: $85-$115	2P: $85-$115	XP: $20

Location: US 89, 4.5 mi s of Emigrant, 0.3 mi e on gravel road, follow signs. PO Box 84 59027. Fax: 406/333-4626. **Facility:** The B&B's guest rooms are decorated with country touches such as dried-flower wreaths, lace doilies and quilted bedding; cabins include full kitchens. Smoke free premises. 6 units. 4 one-bedroom standard units. 2 cabins ($175-$220). 1-2 stories (no elevator), interior/exterior corridors. *Bath:* some shared or private, combo or shower only. **Parking:** on-site. **Terms:** check-in 4 pm, age restrictions may apply, 14 day cancellation notice-fee imposed, package plans - 12/1-4/1. **Amenities:** *Some:* CD players. **Leisure Activities:** fishing, hiking trails. **Guest Services:** TV in common area. **Cards:** MC, VI.

SOME UNITS

ENNIS pop. 840

WHERE TO STAY

EL WESTERN CABINS & LODGES **Phone:** 406/682-4217

Cabin

6/12-9/18	1P: $68-$115	2P: $68-$115	XP: $10	F8
4/23-6/11 & 9/19-10/18	1P: $62-$100	2P: $62-$100	XP: $10	F8

Location: 0.8 mi s. US Hwy 287 S 59729 (PO Box 487). Fax: 406/682-5207. **Facility:** On spacious grounds, these rustic log cabins are within walking distance of the river. 29 units. 1 vacation home ($205-$375) and 28 cabins ($68-$205), some with whirlpools. 1 story, exterior corridors. *Bath:* combo or shower only. **Parking:** on-site. **Terms:** open 4/23-10/18, 3 day cancellation notice-fee imposed, pets ($10 extra charge). **Amenities:** *Some:* irons. **Leisure Activities:** fishing, barbecue grills, croquet, horse corrals, volleyball. **Business Services:** meeting rooms. **Cards:** AX, DS, MC, VI.

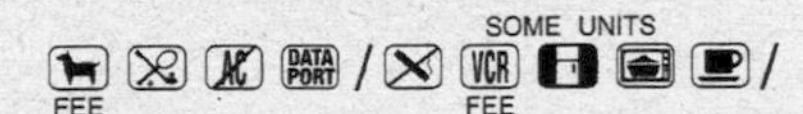

FAN MOUNTAIN INN **Phone:** 406/682-5200

AAA SAVE — Motel

All Year 1P: $40-$65 2P: $48-$70 XP: $5 F12

Location: US 287, just nw of city center. 204 N Main 59729 (PO Box 1350). Fax: 406/682-5266. **Facility:** 27 one-bedroom standard units. 2 stories (no elevator), exterior corridors. **Parking:** on-site, winter plug-ins. **Terms:** 10 day cancellation notice-fee imposed, pets ($5 extra charge). **Cards:** AX, DC, DS, MC, VI. **Special Amenities: free local telephone calls.**

SOME UNITS
FEE FEE FEE

RAINBOW VALLEY LODGE **Phone:** 406/682-4264

AAA SAVE — Motel

6/11-9/30 1P: $60-$70 2P: $75-$90
3/1-6/10 & 10/1-2/28 1P: $45-$55 2P: $55-$70

Location: On US 287, 1 mi s. S US 287 59729 (PO Box 26). Fax: 406/682-5012. **Facility:** 24 units. 16 one- and 8 two-bedroom standard units, some with efficiencies. 1 story, exterior corridors. **Parking:** on-site, winter plug-ins. **Terms:** 14 day cancellation notice-fee imposed, no pets allowed (owner's pet on premises). **Pool(s):** heated outdoor. **Leisure Activities:** spring creek fishing, RV spaces available. **Guest Services:** coin laundry. **Cards:** CB, DC, DS, MC, VI. **Special Amenities: free local telephone calls and free newspaper.** Affiliated with Best Value Inn Brand Membership.

SOME UNITS
DATA PORT

RIVERSIDE MOTEL & OUTFITTERS **Phone:** 406/682-4240

AAA SAVE — Motel

5/1-12/1 2P: $68-$108 XP: $10 F10

Location: US 287, e of town. 346 Main St 59729. Fax: 406/682-7727. **Facility:** 20 units. 14 one- and 6 two-bedroom standard units, some with efficiencies. 1 story, exterior corridors. *Bath:* combo or shower only. **Parking:** on-site, winter plug-ins. **Terms:** open 5/1-12/1, cancellation fee imposed, pets ($10 extra charge). **Amenities:** hair dryers. **Leisure Activities:** fishing, horse corrals, gas grills, horseshoes. **Cards:** AX, DC, JC. **Special Amenities: early check-in/late check-out and preferred room (subject to availability with advanced reservations).**

FEE DATA PORT

SPORTSMAN'S **Phone:** 406/682-4242

Cabin

6/1-9/20 1P: $50-$70 2P: $55-$80 XP: $6
3/1-5/31 & 9/21-2/28 1P: $40-$60 2P: $45-$70 XP: $4

Location: US 287, just nw of city center. 310 US Hwy 287 N 59729 (PO Box 305). Fax: 406/682-7565. **Facility:** 29 units. 11 one-bedroom standard units. 18 cabins. 1 story, exterior corridors. *Bath:* combo or shower only. **Parking:** on-site, winter plug-ins. **Terms:** 5 day cancellation notice-fee imposed, weekly rates available, pets ($5 extra charge). **Business Services:** meeting rooms. **Cards:** AX, DS, MC, VI.

SOME UNITS
FEE

WHERE TO DINE

AUNT JENNY'S DINER **Lunch:** $5-$9 **Phone:** 406/682-5555

American

Location: Center. 125 Main St 59729. **Hours:** 7 am-2 pm, Sun from 9 am. Closed major holidays. **Features:** More a restaurant than a diner, you'll be served innovative lunchtime sandwiches, salads and soups at this casual eatery. Casual dress; cocktails. **Parking:** street. **Cards:** AX, DS, MC, VI.

ESSEX —*See also GLACIER NATIONAL PARK.*

WHERE TO STAY

IZAAK WALTON INN ***Book at aaa.com*** **Phone:** (406)888-5700

Historic Country Inn

All Year 1P: $98-$118 2P: $98-$138 XP: $15

Location: US 2, just s. 290 Izaak Walton Inn Rd 59916. Fax: 406/888-5200. **Facility:** A lodge-style hotel, the inn was built in 1939 by the Great Northern Railway to house railroad workers; accommodations include caboose cottages. Smoke free premises. 37 units. 30 one- and 3 two-bedroom standard units. 4 cottages. 1-3 stories (no elevator), interior corridors. *Bath:* combo or shower only. **Parking:** on-site, winter plug-ins. **Terms:** office hours 7 am-10 pm, 45 day cancellation notice-fee imposed, [CP], [ECP] & [MAP] meal plans available, package plans. **Leisure Activities:** sauna, cross country skiing, ice skating, rental bicycles, hiking trails, volleyball. **Guest Services:** gift shop, coin laundry. **Business Services:** meeting rooms. **Cards:** MC, VI.

FORSYTH pop. 1,944

WHERE TO STAY

BEST WESTERN SUNDOWNER INN ***Book at aaa.com*** **Phone:** (406)346-2115

AAA SAVE — Motel

4/16-10/15 [CP] 1P: $67-$79 2P: $69-$79 XP: $5 F12
3/1-4/15 & 10/16-2/28 [CP] 1P: $67-$77 2P: $69-$79 XP: $5 F12

Location: I-94, exit 95, 0.5 mi nw on north frontage road. 1018 Front St 59327 (PO Box 1080). Fax: 406/346-2216. **Facility:** 40 one-bedroom standard units. 2 stories (no elevator), exterior corridors. **Parking:** on-site, winter plug-ins. **Terms:** small pets only ($5 extra charge). **Amenities:** voice mail, irons, hair dryers. **Guest Services:** coin laundry, airport transportation-Tillitt Field Airport. **Cards:** AX, CB, DC, DS, MC, VI. **Special Amenities: free continental breakfast and early check-in/late check-out.**

SOME UNITS
FEE DATA PORT

RAILS INN MOTEL **Phone:** (406)346-2242

AAA SAVE — Small-scale Hotel

All Year 1P: $57 2P: $62-$67 XP: $5 F12

Location: I-94, exit 93, just n, 0.5 mi e on frontage road. 3rd & Front sts 59327 (PO Box 1050). Fax: 406/346-7114. **Facility:** 50 one-bedroom standard units. 2 stories (no elevator), interior corridors. **Parking:** on-site. **Terms:** pets ($5 extra charge). **Dining:** 6 am-8 pm; to 9 pm in summer, cocktails. **Guest Services:** airport transportation-Tillitt Field Airport. **Business Services:** meeting rooms. **Cards:** AX, CB, DC, DS, MC, VI.

SOME UNITS
FEE DATA PORT

RESTWEL MOTEL *Book at aaa.com* **Phone:** (406)346-2771

AAA SAVE

Motel

5/1-10/31 [CP]	1P: $42-$53	2P: $47-$60	XP: $5	F10
3/1-4/30 & 11/1-2/28 [CP]	1P: $39-$50	2P: $45-$57	XP: $5	F10

Location: I-94, exit 95, 0.8 mi nw on north frontage road. 810 Front St 59327 (PO Box 287). Fax: 406/346-2645. **Facility:** 20 one-bedroom standard units, some with efficiencies and/or whirlpools. 1 story, exterior corridors. *Bath:* combo or shower only. **Parking:** on-site, winter plug-ins. **Terms:** weekly rates available, pets ($5 extra charge). **Cards:** AX, CB, DC, DS, MC, VI.

SOME UNITS

FEE

WESTWIND MOTOR INN **Phone:** (406)346-2038

AAA SAVE

Motel

All Year	1P: $55	2P: $60-$65

Location: I-94, exit 93, 0.3 mi n. 225 Westwind Ln 59327 (PO Box 5025). Fax: 406/346-2909. **Facility:** 33 units. 32 one- and 1 two-bedroom standard units. 2 stories (no elevator), interior corridors. **Parking:** on-site, winter plug-ins. **Terms:** pets ($5 extra charge). **Cards:** AX, CB, DC, MC, VI.

SOME UNITS

FEE

FORT BENTON pop. 1,594

WHERE TO STAY

GRAND UNION HOTEL *Book at aaa.com* **Phone:** (406)622-1882

AAA SAVE

Historic Small-scale Hotel

5/1-10/31 [ECP]	2P: $99-$119	XP: $12	F12
3/1-4/30 & 11/1-2/28 [ECP]	2P: $79-$99	XP: $12	F12

Location: City center. 1 Grand Union Sq 59442 (PO Box 119). Fax: 406/622-5985. **Facility:** This fully-restored 1882 hotel commands picturesque views of the Missouri River. All guest units are richly appointed. Seasonal outdoor riverside deck dining, a brewpub and a fine dining room round out the refinement of these luxurious accommodations. Smoke free premises. 26 one-bedroom standard units, some with whirlpools. 3 stories, interior corridors. **Parking:** street, winter plug-ins. **Terms:** check-in 4 pm, 7 day cancellation notice-fee imposed. **Amenities:** voice mail. *Some:* dual phone lines, irons, hair dryers. **Dining:** wine/beer only, also, Union Grille Restaurant, see separate listing. **Leisure Activities:** hiking trails, jogging. **Guest Services:** gift shop. **Business Services:** meeting rooms. **Cards:** AX, DS, MC, VI.

SOME UNITS

DATA PORT / VCR /

WHERE TO DINE

UNION GRILLE RESTAURANT Historic **Dinner:** $19-$29 **Phone:** 406/622-1882

AAA

Regional Continental

Location: City center; in Grand Union Hotel. 1 Grand Union Sq 59442. **Hours:** 5 pm-9 pm; closed Mon & Tues in winter. **Reservations:** suggested. **Features:** Traditional and innovative cuisine will give your taste buds something to sing about. Inside this historic hotel dining room, you'll find cozy wood accent decor which sets the stage for an intimate and impressive evening. The chef expertly chooses and prepares the freshest locally available ingredients into tasteful, exquisite productions. Dressy casual; cocktails. **Parking:** street. **Cards:** AX, DC, MC, VI.

GALLATIN GATEWAY

WHERE TO STAY

The following lodging was either not evaluated or did not meet AAA rating requirements but is listed for your information only.

GALLATIN GATEWAY INN **Phone:** 406/763-4672

fyi

Not evaluated. **Location:** Just n on US 191 (Gallatin Rd). 76405 Gallatin Rd Hwy 191 59715 (PO Box 376, 59730). Facilities, services, and decor characterize an upscale property.

WHERE TO DINE

GALLATIN GATEWAY INN RESTAURANT **Dinner:** $13-$25 **Phone:** 406/763-4672

Continental

Location: Just n on US 191 (Gallatin Rd); in Gallatin Gateway Inn. 76405 Gallatin Rd, Hwy 191 59730. **Hours:** 5:30 pm-9:30 pm. **Reservations:** suggested. **Features:** This restaurant is a place for more refined dining. Patrons should keep their eyes out for the sign, as the hotel is buffered from the highway with a wall of trees. The creative menu has a fine representation of various cuisines, all presented with artistic flair. Casual dress; cocktails. **Parking:** on-site. **Cards:** AX, DS, MC, VI.

THE GOURMET GAS STATION **Lunch:** $6-$11 **Dinner:** $9-$18 **Phone:** 406/763-4564

American

Location: Just n on US 191 (Gallatin Rd). 76250 Gallatin Rd (Hwy 191) 59730. **Hours:** 11 am-2 & 5-9 pm 9/15-5/15. Closed major holidays; also Mon 9/29-5/15. **Features:** Have you ever expected to find great tasting meals at a gas station eatery? Well, now you can, here at The Gourmet Gas Station. The chef creates everything from barbecue ribs to burritos, all delectable; although the real specialty at this cozy place is Mexican cuisine. Look for the rear end of a tanker truck poking out from the restaurant's overhang! Casual dress; cocktails. **Parking:** on-site. **Cards:** AX, MC, VI.

GARDINER pop. 851—*See also YELLOWSTONE NATIONAL PARK.*

WHERE TO STAY

BEEDE'S YELLOWSTONE RIVER COTTAGES

Phone: (406)848-9408

Cottage

All Year 1P: $125-$199 2P: $125-$199

Location: I-90, exit 333 (US 89S), 43 mi to Corwin Springs, cross bridge, then 3 mi s on Old Yellowstone Trail S (dirt road). 550 Old Yellowstone Tr S 59030. **Facility:** Smoke free premises. 11 cottages. 1 story, exterior corridors. *Bath:* combo or shower only. **Parking:** on-site, winter plug-ins. **Terms:** check-in 4 pm, 10 day cancellation notice, weekly rates available, [AP] & [BP] meal plans available. **Leisure Activities:** fishing. **Guest Services:** coin laundry. **Cards:** AX, DC, MC, VI.

ASK

BEST WESTERN BY MAMMOTH HOT SPRINGS

Book at aaa.com

Phone: (406)848-7311

AAA SAVE

Small-scale Hotel

6/8-10/7	1P: $95-$119	2P: $95-$119	XP: $5	F16
5/23-6/7	1P: $69-$85	2P: $69-$85	XP: $5	F16
3/1-5/22	1P: $49-$79	2P: $49-$79	XP: $5	F16
10/8-2/28	1P: $45-$79	2P: $45-$79	XP: $5	F16

Location: 0.5 mi n. S Hwy 89 59030 (PO Box 646). Fax: 406/848-7120. **Facility:** 85 units. 81 one- and 4 two-bedroom standard units, some with kitchens and/or whirlpools. 2 stories (no elevator), interior/exterior corridors. *Bath:* combo or shower only. **Parking:** on-site, winter plug-ins. **Terms:** check-in 4 pm, cancellation fee imposed, pets ($5 extra charge, in designated units). **Amenities:** irons, hair dryers. **Dining:** Yellowstone Mine Restaurant, see separate listing. **Pool(s):** heated indoor. **Leisure Activities:** saunas, whirlpool, fishing. **Guest Services:** coin laundry. **Business Services:** meeting rooms. **Cards:** AX, CB, DC, DS, JC, MC, VI. **Special Amenities: early check-in/late check-out and preferred room (subject to availability with advanced reservations).**

FEE / SOME UNITS /

COMFORT INN YELLOWSTONE NORTH

Book at aaa.com

Phone: (406)848-7536

Small-scale Hotel

6/16-9/30	1P: $89-$169	2P: $89-$169	XP: $10	F18
5/21-6/15	1P: $69-$99	2P: $69-$99	XP: $10	F18
3/1-5/20	1P: $49-$79	2P: $49-$79	XP: $10	F18
10/1-2/28	1P: $40-$79	2P: $40-$79	XP: $10	F18

Location: North entrance, just s on US 89. 107 Hellroaring Rd 59030 (PO Box 268). Fax: 406/848-7062. **Facility:** 78 units. 72 one- and 6 two-bedroom standard units, some with whirlpools. 3 stories, interior corridors. **Parking:** on-site. **Terms:** check-in 4 pm, 3 day cancellation notice, [CP] meal plan available. **Amenities:** *Some:* irons, hair dryers. **Dining:** The Antler Pub & Grill, see separate listing. **Leisure Activities:** whirlpools. **Guest Services:** coin laundry. *Fee:* tanning facility. **Business Services:** meeting rooms, fax (fee). **Cards:** AX, DS, MC, VI. ***(See color ad below)***

ASK / SOME UNITS /

HEADWATERS OF THE YELLOWSTONE BED & BREAKFAST & CABINS

Phone: 406/848-7073

Bed & Breakfast

All Year 2P: $85-$125

Location: 2.6 mi n on US 89. 9 Olson Ln 59030 (PO Box 25). Fax: 406/848-7420. **Facility:** Just minutes from Yellowstone's north entrance is one of the newest lodging offerings in this area. Having a river just feet away is enough to make any fisherman stay here, but families will be pleased with the kids play room. Rooms are done in modern furnishings with little extra adornments, but rather, offer a restful place to end the day. Smoke free premises. 7 units. 5 one-bedroom standard units. 2 cottages. 1-2 stories (no elevator), interior/exterior corridors. *Bath:* combo or shower only. **Parking:** on-site. **Terms:** check-in 4 pm, 14 day cancellation notice-fee imposed, [BP] meal plan available. **Leisure Activities:** fishing, playground, horseshoes. **Cards:** AX, MC, VI.

/ SOME UNITS /

NORTH YELLOWSTONE MOUNTAIN VIEW MOTEL — **Phone:** 406/848-7520

AAA SAVE — Motel

6/21-8/20	1P: $75-$85	2P: $75-$95	XP: $6	F17
5/21-6/20	1P: $59-$75	2P: $59-$75	XP: $6	F17
8/21-2/28	1P: $39-$75	2P: $39-$75	XP: $6	F17
3/1-5/20	1P: $39-$59	2P: $39-$59	XP: $6	F17

Location: North entrance, just s on US 89, 0.5 mi n of Yellowstone north gate. 109 Hellroaring St 59030 (PO Box 48). Fax: 406/848-7555. **Facility:** 40 one-bedroom standard units. 4 stories, exterior corridors. *Bath:* combo or shower only. **Parking:** on-site, winter plug-ins. **Terms:** 3 day cancellation notice. **Guest Services:** coin laundry. **Cards:** DS, MC, VI. **Special Amenities: free local telephone calls and early check-in/late check-out.**

SOME UNITS

DATA PORT

YELLOWSTONE BASIN INN — **Phone:** (406)848-7080

AAA SAVE — Motel

6/12-8/16 [CP]	1P: $88-$98	2P: $88-$220	XP: $8	F12
8/17-9/20 [CP]	1P: $71-$78	2P: $71-$168	XP: $8	F12
5/8-6/11 [CP]	1P: $50-$72	2P: $62-$160	XP: $8	F12
9/21-10/15 [CP]	1P: $62-$98	2P: $62-$128	XP: $8	F12

Location: 5 mi n on US 89 at MM 5. 4 Maiden Basin Dr 59030. Fax: 406/848-7083. **Facility:** Smoke free premises. 10 units. 8 one-bedroom standard units, some with kitchens and/or whirlpools. 1 one- and 1 two-bedroom suites ($108-$220) with kitchens. 2 stories (no elevator), exterior corridors. **Parking:** on-site. **Terms:** open 5/8-10/15, check-in 4 pm, weekly rates available. **Amenities:** hair dryers. *Some:* irons. **Leisure Activities:** whirlpool. **Cards:** AX, DS, MC, VI. **Special Amenities: free continental breakfast and free local telephone calls.** *(See color ad below)*

SOME UNITS

YELLOWSTONE RIVER MOTEL — **Phone:** (406)848-7303

AAA SAVE — Motel

6/15-9/14	1P: $63-$85	2P: $63-$85	XP: $5
5/1-6/14 & 9/15-10/31	1P: $45-$65	2P: $45-$65	XP: $5

Location: Just e of US 89. 14 E Park St 59030 (PO Box 223). Fax: 406/848-7304. **Facility:** 38 units. 35 one- and 3 two-bedroom standard units, some with kitchens. 1-2 stories (no elevator), exterior corridors. *Bath:* combo or shower only. **Parking:** on-site. **Terms:** open 5/1-10/31, pets ($5 fee). **Leisure Activities:** fishing. *Fee:* white-water rafting, horseback riding. **Cards:** AX, CB, DC, DS, MC, VI.

SOME UNITS

FEE

YELLOWSTONE SUPER 8-GARDINER — ***Book at aaa.com*** — **Phone:** (406)848-7401

Small-scale Hotel

6/1-9/30	1P: $89-$190	2P: $89-$190	XP: $5	F12
10/1-12/31	1P: $65-$150	2P: $65-$150	XP: $5	F12
3/1-5/31 & 1/1-2/28	1P: $50-$150	2P: $50-$150	XP: $5	F12

Location: On US 89. Hwy 89 S 59030 (PO Box 739). Fax: 406/848-9410. **Facility:** 66 units. 65 one-bedroom standard units. 1 two-bedroom suite ($69-$190) with kitchen. 2-3 stories (no elevator), interior corridors. **Parking:** on-site, winter plug-ins. **Terms:** check-in 4 pm, package plans - in winter, pets ($5 extra charge). **Pool(s):** heated indoor. **Guest Services:** coin laundry. **Cards:** AX, DS, MC, VI.

SOME UNITS

ASK DATA PORT

FEE FEE FEE

YELLOWSTONE VILLAGE INN — **Phone:** (406)848-7417

AAA SAVE — Small-scale Hotel

7/1-9/30	1P: $79-$99	2P: $89-$109	XP: $6	F12
5/14-6/30	1P: $39-$79	2P: $49-$89	XP: $6	F12
10/1-2/28	1P: $45-$69	2P: $45-$79	XP: $6	F12
3/1-5/13	1P: $39-$69	2P: $39-$79	XP: $6	F12

Location: 0.8 mi n on US 89. Yellowstone Park North Entrance 59030 (PO Box 93, YELLOWSTONE NATIONAL PARK, WY, 82190-0093). Fax: 406/848-7418. **Facility:** 43 units. 39 one-bedroom standard units. 2 one- and 2 two-bedroom suites ($95-$180), some with kitchens. 1-2 stories (no elevator), interior/exterior corridors. **Parking:** on-site, winter plug-ins. **Terms:** check-in 3:30 pm, [CP] meal plan available. **Pool(s):** heated indoor. **Leisure Activities:** sauna, weekend rodeos in summer, basketball. *Fee:* cross country skiing, snowmobiling, horseback riding. **Guest Services:** coin laundry. **Cards:** AX, DS, MC, VI. **Special Amenities: free continental breakfast and free local telephone calls.** *(See color ad p 177)*

SOME UNITS

VCR DATA PORT

FEE

WHERE TO DINE

THE ANTLER PUB & GRILL — **Dinner:** $8-$17 — **Phone:** 406/848-7536

American

Location: North entrance, just s on US 89; in Comfort Inn Yellowstone North. 107 Hellroaring St 59030. **Hours:** 5 pm-10 pm. **Reservations:** accepted. **Features:** A large dining room featuring wild game trophy mounts and rustic decor is the setting for this family style restaurant, which offers comfort food from a limited menu. Casual dress; beer & wine only. **Parking:** on-site. **Cards:** AX, DS, MC, VI.

YELLOWSTONE MINE RESTAURANT — **Dinner:** $8-$22 — **Phone:** 406/848-7336

Steak & Seafood

Location: 0.5 mi n; in Best Western by Mammoth Hot Springs. Hwy 89 S 59030. **Hours:** 6 am-11 & 5-9 pm; to 10 pm in summer. **Features:** Entering this eatery is like walking into an Old West mine, and it's not called The Mine for nothing. The dark restaurant is illuminated with soft lighting and table lamps. Chicken, steak and seafood are all good menu choices, and pasta primavera satisfies lighter eaters. Casual dress; cocktails. **Parking:** on-site. **Cards:** AX, DC, DS, MC, VI.

GLACIER NATIONAL PARK —*See also COLUMBIA FALLS*

WHERE TO STAY

APGAR VILLAGE LODGE — **Phone:** 406/888-5484

Cabin

5/5-10/4 — 1P: $71-$109 — 2P: $98-$126 — XP: $6 — F10

Location: 2 mi nw of West Glacier from jct US 2. Located in Apgar Village. 200 Going to the Sun Rd 59936 (PO Box 410, WEST GLACIER). Fax: 406/888-5273. **Facility:** 48 units. 20 one-bedroom standard units. 28 cabins ($109-$248). 1 story, exterior corridors. *Bath:* shower only. **Parking:** on-site. **Terms:** open 5/5-10/4, office hours 8 am-9 pm, check-in 4 pm, 3 day cancellation notice-fee imposed. **Leisure Activities:** rental boats, rental canoes, boat dock, fishing, hiking trails, jogging. **Guest Services:** area transportation (fee)-park shuttle. **Cards:** AX, DS, MC, VI.

SOME UNITS

The following lodgings were either not evaluated or did not meet AAA rating requirements but are listed for your information only.

GLACIER PARK LODGE **Phone:** 406/226-5600

fyi Not evaluated. **Location:** At southern entrance; on east side of Glacier National Park. SR 49 59434. Facilities, services, and decor characterize a mid-range property.

MANY GLACIER HOTEL **Phone:** 406/892-2525

fyi Not evaluated. **Location:** East side of Glacier National Park; 12 mi e of Babb Jct. (Swiftcurrent Lake, EAST GLACIER PARK, 59434). Facilities, services, and decor characterize a basic property.

WHERE TO DINE

EDDIE'S RESTAURANT **Lunch:** $5-$11 **Dinner:** $7-$16 **Phone:** 406/888-5361

American

Location: 2 mi nw of West Glacier from jct US 2; in Apgar Village. **Hours:** Open 6/1-9/22; 7 am-9 pm. **Features:** A friendly staff serves sandwiches, salad, soup and several dinner entrees such as pan fried trout and broasted chicken. Named for one of the earliest settlers, this is one of a handful of eateries inside the park and the only one privately owned. Casual dress; beer & wine only. **Parking:** on-site. **Cards:** DS, MC, VI.

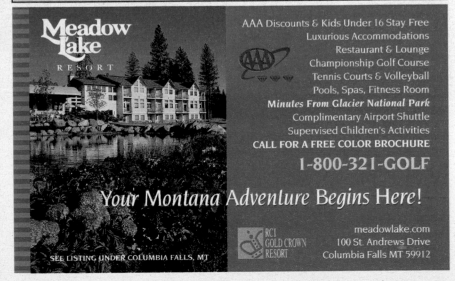

GLASGOW pop. 3,253

WHERE TO STAY

COTTONWOOD INN — Phone: (406)228-8213

Small-scale Hotel

All Year	1P: $53-$57	2P: $63-$73	XP: $5	F13

Location: 0.5 mi e of center on US 2. 45 1st Ave NE 59230 (PO Box 1240). Fax: 406/228-8248. **Facility:** 92 one-bedroom standard units. 2 stories (no elevator), interior corridors. *Bath:* combo or shower only. **Parking:** on-site, winter plug-ins. **Amenities:** irons, hair dryers. *Some:* high-speed Internet, fax. **Pool(s):** small heated indoor. **Leisure Activities:** sauna, whirlpool. **Guest Services:** valet and coin laundry. **Business Services:** meeting rooms. **Cards:** AX, DS, MC, VI.

SOME UNITS

ASK / VCR DATA PORT /

GLENDIVE pop. 4,729

WHERE TO STAY

BEST WESTERN JORDAN INN *Book at aaa.com* — Phone: (406)377-5555

AAA SAVE — Small-scale Hotel

5/16-9/30	1P: $75-$90	2P: $82-$106	XP: $7	F12
3/1-5/15 & 10/1-2/28	1P: $65-$75	2P: $72-$87	XP: $7	F12

Location: I-94, exit 215, on I-94 business loop; downtown. 223 N Merrill Ave 59330 (PO Box 741). Fax: 406/377-6233. **Facility:** 82 one-bedroom standard units. 2-3 stories, interior/exterior corridors. *Bath:* combo or shower only. **Parking:** on-site, winter plug-ins. **Terms:** 10 day cancellation notice, [BP] meal plan available, small pets only ($5 extra charge). **Amenities:** irons, hair dryers. **Dining:** 2 restaurants, 6 am-10 pm; to 9 pm in winter. **Pool(s):** small heated indoor. **Leisure Activities:** sauna. **Guest Services:** gift shop, valet and coin laundry, airport transportation-Dawson County Airport. **Business Services:** meeting rooms. **Cards:** AX, DC, DS, MC, VI. **Special Amenities: free full breakfast and free local telephone calls.**

SOME UNITS

FEE DATA PORT / /

SUPER 8 GLENDIVE *Book at aaa.com* — Phone: 406/365-5671

Motel

5/1-9/30	1P: $52-$60	2P: $62-$69	XP: $5	F12
10/1-2/28	1P: $49-$55	2P: $60-$67	XP: $5	F12
4/1-4/30	1P: $45-$50	2P: $55-$60	XP: $5	F12
3/1-3/31	1P: $43-$48	2P: $48-$55	XP: $5	F12

Location: I-94, exit 215, just n. 1904 Merrill Ave 59330. Fax: 406/365-5671. **Facility:** 52 one-bedroom standard units. 2 stories (no elevator), interior corridors. **Parking:** on-site, winter plug-ins. **Terms:** pets ($5 extra charge). **Amenities:** video library (fee). **Cards:** AX, CB, DC, DS, MC, VI.

SOME UNITS

FEE / VCR FEE /

GREAT FALLS pop. 56,690

WHERE TO STAY

BEST WESTERN HERITAGE INN *Book at aaa.com* — Phone: (406)761-1900

AAA SAVE — Small-scale Hotel

6/16-8/31	1P: $89-$109	2P: $89-$109
3/1-6/15 & 9/1-10/31	1P: $89-$99	2P: $89-$99
11/1-2/28	1P: $79-$99	2P: $79-$99

Location: I-15, exit 278, 0.8 mi e on 10th Ave S and US 87/89 and SR 3/200. 1700 Fox Farm Rd 59404. Fax: 406/761-0136. **Facility:** 235 units. 231 one-bedroom standard units. 4 one-bedroom suites ($99). 2 stories, interior corridors. **Parking:** on-site, winter plug-ins. **Terms:** [AP] meal plan available, small pets only. **Amenities:** video games, voice mail, irons, hair dryers. **Dining:** 6 am-10 pm, cocktails. **Pool(s):** small heated indoor. **Leisure Activities:** sauna, whirlpool, exercise room. **Guest Services:** gift shop, valet and coin laundry, airport transportation-Great Falls International Airport. **Business Services:** conference facilities, fax (fee). **Cards:** AX, CB, DC, DS, MC, VI. **Special Amenities: free newspaper and early check-in/late check-out.** *(See color ad p 266)*

SOME UNITS

DATA PORT / /

CENTRAL MOTEL — Phone: (406)453-0161

AAA SAVE — Motel

All Year [CP]	1P: $40-$50	2P: $45-$75	XP: $10	F18

Location: I-15, exit 280 (Central Ave), 0.7 mi e. 715 Central Ave W 59404. Fax: 406/453-7433. **Facility:** 29 units. 8 one-bedroom standard units. 17 one- and 4 two-bedroom suites ($75-$100), some with efficiencies or kitchens. 1 story, exterior corridors. **Parking:** on-site, winter plug-ins. **Terms:** 7 day cancellation notice-fee imposed, small pets only ($30 deposit). **Cards:** AX, DS, MC, VI. **Special Amenities: free continental breakfast and free local telephone calls.**

SOME UNITS

FEE DATA PORT / /

THE COLLINS MANSION BED & BREAKFAST — Phone: (406)452-6798

Historic Bed & Breakfast

5/1-8/31 [BP]	2P: $85-$95	XP: $15	D21
3/1-4/30 & 9/1-2/28 [BP]	2P: $75-$85		

Location: I-15, exit 280 (Central Ave), 1 mi e to 10th St NW, then just n. 1003 2nd Ave NW 59404. Fax: 406/452-6787. **Facility:** Built in 1891 and located in a residential area is this Queen Anne style mansion. Common areas are lavish with chandeliers, wainescoate walls and parquet floors. A large wraparound porch is ideal for relaxing and savoring the days adventures. All bedrooms are uniquely decorated with antiques and reproductions. Gregarious owner attends to guest needs. Smoke free premises. 5 one-bedroom standard units. 2 stories (no elevator), interior corridors. *Bath:* combo or shower only. **Parking:** on-site, winter plug-ins. **Terms:** check-in 5 pm. **Guest Services:** gift shop, complimentary laundry. **Cards:** AX, MC, VI.

ASK

COMFORT INN GREAT FALLS **Book at aaa.com** **Phone:** (406)454-2727

Small-scale Hotel

6/1-8/31 [ECP]	1P: $69-$89	2P: $75-$95	XP: $6	F
3/1-5/31 & 9/1-2/28 [ECP]	1P: $59-$79	2P: $65-$85	XP: $6	F

Location: I-15, exit 278, 3 mi e on 10th Ave S and US 87/89 and SR 3/200, then just s. Located next to a shopping mall. 1120 9th St S 59405. Fax: 406/454-2727. **Facility:** 64 one-bedroom standard units. 3 stories, interior corridors. **Parking:** on-site, winter plug-ins. **Terms:** pets ($10 extra charge). **Amenities:** irons, hair dryers. **Pool(s):** small heated indoor. **Leisure Activities:** whirlpool. **Cards:** AX, CB, DC, DS, MC, VI.

SOME UNITS

ASK / FEE / DATA PORT /

CRYSTAL INN **Book at aaa.com** **Phone:** (406)727-7788

Small-scale Hotel

All Year [ECP]	1P: $79-$99	2P: $79-$99	XP: $10	F18

Location: I-15, exit 277, just e. 3701 31st St SW 59404. Fax: 406/727-3935. **Facility:** 86 one-bedroom standard units, some with whirlpools. 3 stories, interior corridors. *Bath:* combo or shower only. **Parking:** on-site, winter plug-ins. **Amenities:** video library (fee), voice mail, irons, hair dryers. *Some:* high-speed Internet, dual phone lines. **Pool(s):** heated indoor. **Leisure Activities:** whirlpool, exercise room. **Guest Services:** valet and coin laundry, area transportation. **Business Services:** meeting rooms, PC. **Cards:** AX, DC, DS, MC, VI. ***(See color ad p 267)***

SOME UNITS

ASK VCR DATA PORT / /

DAYS INN OF GREAT FALLS **Book at aaa.com** **Phone:** (406)727-6565

Motel

5/28-9/6	1P: $71-$81	2P: $77-$87
3/1-5/27 & 9/7-2/28	1P: $57-$67	2P: $63-$73

Location: I-15, exit 280 (Central Ave), 1.3 mi e on Central Ave/Business 15, 0.8 mi n on 3rd St NW, then just w. Located next to a high school. 101 14th Ave NW 59404. Fax: 406/727-6308. **Facility:** 61 one-bedroom standard units. 2 stories (no elevator), interior corridors. **Parking:** on-site, winter plug-ins. **Terms:** [CP] meal plan available, pets ($5 extra charge, dogs only). **Amenities:** video library (fee), hair dryers. *Some:* irons. **Guest Services:** valet and coin laundry. **Cards:** AX, CB, DC, DS, MC, VI.

SOME UNITS

ASK FEE DATA PORT / VCR FEE /

FAIRFIELD INN BY MARRIOTT *Book at aaa.com* **Phone:** (406)454-3000

Small-scale Hotel

6/1-9/30 [ECP]	1P: $65-$79	2P: $65-$85	XP: $6	F
3/1-5/31 & 10/1-2/28 [ECP]	1P: $55-$69	2P: $55-$75	XP: $6	F

Location: I-15, exit 278, 3 mi e on 10th Ave S and US 87/89 and SR 3/200, then just n. Located across from a mall. 1000 9th Ave S 59405. Fax: 406/454-3000. **Facility:** 63 one-bedroom standard units. 3 stories, interior corridors. **Parking:** on-site. **Amenities:** irons, hair dryers. **Pool(s):** small heated indoor. **Leisure Activities:** whirlpool. **Guest Services:** valet laundry. **Cards:** AX, CB, DC, DS, MC, VI.

SOME UNITS

THE GREAT FALLS INN *Book at aaa.com* **Phone:** (406)453-6000

Small-scale Hotel

All Year	1P: $61-$66	2P: $66-$71	XP: $5	F12

Location: I-15, exit 278, 5.3 mi e on 10th Ave s, 0.3 mi s on 26th St S, then just e on 15th Ave S. Located next to a medical facility. 1400 28th St S 59405. Fax: 406/453-6078. **Facility:** 61 one-bedroom standard units. 4 stories, interior corridors. *Bath:* combo or shower only. **Parking:** on-site, winter plug-ins. **Terms:** [CP] meal plan available, pets ($5 extra charge). **Amenities:** irons, hair dryers. **Leisure Activities:** exercise room. **Guest Services:** valet and coin laundry. **Cards:** AX, DC, DS, MC, VI. **Special Amenities: free continental breakfast and free local telephone calls.** *(See color ad below)*

SOME UNITS

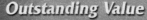

FEE

GREAT FALLS SUPER 8 MOTEL *Book at aaa.com* **Phone:** (406)727-7600

Small-scale Hotel

5/28-9/11	1P: $52-$74	2P: $57-$79	XP: $5	F13
3/1-5/27 & 9/12-2/28	1P: $46-$62	2P: $50-$66	XP: $5	F13

Location: I-15, exit 278, 2.7 mi e on 10th Ave S and US 87/89 and SR 3/200, then just s. Located next to a shopping mall. 1214 13th St S 59405. Fax: 406/727-7600. **Facility:** 114 one-bedroom standard units. 3 stories, interior corridors. **Parking:** on-site, winter plug-ins. **Terms:** weekly rates available, [CP] meal plan available, $2 service charge, small pets only. **Amenities:** safes (fee). *Some:* irons. **Cards:** AX, CB, DC, DS, MC, VI.

SOME UNITS

FEE FEE

HAMPTON INN *Book at aaa.com* **Phone:** 406/453-2675

SAVE

Small-scale Hotel

7/1-8/31	1P: $89-$99	2P: $89-$99
5/1-6/30	1P: $79-$99	2P: $79-$99
3/1-4/30 & 9/1-2/28	1P: $79-$89	2P: $79-$89

Location: I-15, exit 278, just sw. 2301 14th St SW 59404. Fax: 406/453-2676. **Facility:** 97 one-bedroom standard units, some with whirlpools. 4 stories, interior corridors. *Bath:* combo or shower only. **Parking:** on-site. **Terms:** check-in 4 pm, pets ($10 extra charge, no cats). **Amenities:** high-speed Internet, dual phone lines, voice mail, irons, hair dryers. **Pool(s):** heated indoor. **Leisure Activities:** whirlpool, exercise room. **Guest Services:** valet and coin laundry, airport transportation-Great Falls International Airport. **Business Services:** meeting rooms, business center. **Cards:** AX, DS, MC, VI. **Special Amenities: free continental breakfast and free local telephone calls.**

SOME UNITS

FEE

HOLIDAY INN *Book at aaa.com* **Phone:** (406)727-7200

Large-scale Hotel

6/1-9/30	1P: $99-$109	2P: $99-$109
3/1-5/31 & 10/1-2/28	1P: $89-$99	2P: $89-$99

Location: I-15, exit 278, 2 mi e on 10th Ave S, just s. Located in a commercial area. 400 10th Ave S 59405. Fax: 406/268-0472. **Facility:** 168 units. 164 one-bedroom standard units. 4 one-bedroom suites ($129-$199). 7 stories, interior corridors. *Bath:* combo or shower only. **Parking:** on-site. **Terms:** small pets only ($10 deposit). **Amenities:** video games (fee), voice mail, irons, hair dryers. *Some:* high-speed Internet. **Pool(s):** small heated outdoor. **Leisure Activities:** whirlpool, exercise room. **Guest Services:** valet and coin laundry. **Business Services:** meeting rooms, business center. **Cards:** AX, CB, DC, DS, MC, VI. ***(See color ad opposite title page)***

SOME UNITS

FEE

HOLIDAY INN EXPRESS HOTEL & SUITES *Book at aaa.com* **Phone:** (406)455-1000

Small-scale Hotel

7/1-10/31	1P: $89-$99	2P: $89-$99
3/1-6/30	1P: $69-$79	2P: $69-$79
11/1-2/28	1P: $59-$69	2P: $59-$69

Location: I-15, exit 278, just sw. 1801 Market Place Dr 59404. Fax: 406/455-6672. **Facility:** 95 units. 80 one-bedroom standard units. 15 one-bedroom suites ($99-$110). 4 stories, interior corridors. *Bath:* combo or shower only. **Parking:** on-site, winter plug-ins. **Terms:** [ECP] meal plan available. **Amenities:** high-speed Internet, dual phone lines, voice mail, irons, hair dryers. **Leisure Activities:** exercise room. **Guest Services:** valet and coin laundry, area transportation. **Business Services:** meeting rooms, business center. **Cards:** AX, DC, DS, MC, VI.

SOME UNITS

HOWARD JOHNSON PONDEROSA INN **Phone:** (406)761-3410

SAVE

Small-scale Hotel

5/1-9/30	1P: $60-$80	2P: $65-$90	XP: $5	F12
3/1-4/30 & 10/1-2/28	1P: $50-$70	2P: $55-$80	XP: $5	F12

Location: Downtown. 220 Central Ave 59401. Fax: 406/761-3411. **Facility:** 105 one-bedroom standard units. 4 stories, interior/exterior corridors. **Parking:** on-site, winter plug-ins. **Terms:** [ECP] meal plan available, small pets only ($5 extra charge). **Amenities:** video library (fee), voice mail, hair dryers. *Some:* high-speed Internet, irons. **Dining:** 11 am-10 pm, Sat from 4 pm; to 9 pm in winter; closed Sun, cocktails. **Pool(s):** heated outdoor. **Leisure Activities:** saunas. **Guest Services:** valet and coin laundry, airport transportation-Great Falls International Airport, area transportation-within city limits. **Business Services:** meeting rooms. **Cards:** AX, CB, DC, DS, MC, VI. **Special Amenities: free continental breakfast and free local telephone calls.**

SOME UNITS

FEE FEE

LA QUINTA INN & SUITES *Book at aaa.com* **Phone:** (406)761-2600

SAVE

Small-scale Hotel

6/1-8/31	1P: $89-$119
3/1-5/31 & 9/1-2/28	1P: $79-$109

Location: I-15, exit 278, 1.7 mi e on 10th Ave S, then 0.8 mi n. Located along the river. 600 River Dr S 59405. Fax: 406/761-2267. **Facility:** 71 units. 59 one-bedroom standard units, some with whirlpools. 12 one-bedroom suites ($109-$189) with kitchens. 3 stories, interior corridors. *Bath:* combo or shower only. **Parking:** on-site, winter plug-ins. **Terms:** [ECP] meal plan available, pets ($50 deposit). **Amenities:** video library (fee), dual phone lines, voice mail, irons, hair dryers. **Pool(s):** small heated indoor. **Leisure Activities:** sauna, whirlpool, exercise room. *Fee:* bicycles. **Guest Services:** valet and coin laundry. **Business Services:** meeting rooms, business center. **Cards:** AX, DC, DS, MC, VI. **Special Amenities: free expanded continental breakfast and free newspaper.**

SOME UNITS

FEE

MOTEL 6 #4238 *Book at aaa.com* **Phone:** 406/453-1602

SAVE

Motel

6/1-8/31	1P: $53	2P: $59	XP: $3	F
9/1-12/31	1P: $46	2P: $52	XP: $3	F
3/1-5/31	1P: $44	2P: $50	XP: $3	F
1/1-2/28	1P: $42	2P: $48	XP: $3	F

Location: I-15, exit 278, 0.8 mi e on 10th Ave S and US 87/89 and SR 3/200; next to Best Western. 2 Treasure State Dr 59404. Fax: 406/453-1602. **Facility:** 60 one-bedroom standard units. 2 stories (no elevator), interior corridors. **Parking:** on-site, winter plug-ins. **Terms:** small pets only. **Amenities:** voice mail, irons, hair dryers. **Guest Services:** airport transportation-Great Falls International Airport. **Cards:** AX, CB, DC, DS, VI.

SOME UNITS

O'HAIRE MOTOR INN **Phone:** (406)454-2141

AAA SAVE — Motel

All Year 1P: $49 2P: $55

Location: Center of downtown. 17 7th St S 59403 (PO Box 1667). Fax: 406/454-0211. **Facility:** 69 units. 66 one- and 3 two bedroom standard units. 3 stories, interior/exterior corridors. **Parking:** on-site, winter plug-ins. **Amenities:** *Some:* irons, hair dryers. **Dining:** 6 am-midnight, cocktails. **Pool(s):** heated indoor. **Guest Services:** valet laundry, airport transportation-Great Falls International Airport. **Business Services:** meeting rooms. **Cards:** AX, CB, DC, DS, MC, VI.

SOME UNITS

DATA PORT

PLAZA INN **Phone:** 406/452-9594

AAA SAVE — Motel

All Year 1P: $40-$50 2P: $50-$75 XP: $10

Location: I-15, exit 278, 2.4 mi e on 10th Ave S and US 87/89 and SR 3/200. 1224 10th Ave S 59405. Fax: 406/727-8450. **Facility:** 20 one-bedroom standard units. 1 story, exterior corridors. **Parking:** on-site, winter plug-ins. **Terms:** 7 day cancellation notice, [CP] meal plan available, small pets only ($10 fee). **Cards:** AX, DS, MC, VI. **Special Amenities: free continental breakfast and free local telephone calls.**

SOME UNITS

FEE

SKI'S WESTERN MOTEL **Phone:** (406)453-3281

AAA SAVE — Motel

All Year 1P: $40-$50 2P: $50-$75 XP: $10 F12

Location: I-15, exit 278, 5.2 mi e on 10th Ave S and US 87/89 and SR 3/200. Located in a busy, commercial area. 2420 10th Ave S 59405. Fax: 406/727-8450. **Facility:** 25 units. 22 one- and 3 two-bedroom standard units. 1 story, exterior corridors. *Bath:* combo or shower only. **Parking:** on-site, winter plug-ins. **Terms:** 7 day cancellation notice, pets ($10 extra charge). **Cards:** AX, DS, MC, VI. **Special Amenities: free continental breakfast and free local telephone calls.**

SOME UNITS

FEE

WHERE TO DINE

THE CATTLEMAN'S CUT SUPPER CLUB **Dinner:** $9-$22 **Phone:** 406/452-0702

Steak & Seafood

Location: I-15, exit 286, just w, then just n; next to Western Livestock Auction. 388 Vaughn Frontage Rd 59404. **Hours:** 5 pm-10 pm, Sun 4 pm-9 pm. Closed: 7/4, 11/25, 12/24, 12/25; also Mon. **Reservations:** suggested. **Features:** A really unlikely place to find quality prepared steaks, but here it is! Not only does the meat cut like butter, the taste is exquisite. The owner does it right—a bottomless salad bar, dessert and the entree...all for one affordable price! Casual dress; cocktails. **Parking:** on-site. **Cards:** AX, DS, MC, VI.

DANTE'S CREATIVE CUISINE **Lunch:** $5-$7 **Dinner:** $12-$21 **Phone:** 406/453-9599

Italian

Location: Jct 14th St and 8th Ave N. 1325 8th Ave N 59401. **Hours:** 11 am-10 pm, Sun from 2 pm. Closed: 7/4, 12/25. **Reservations:** accepted. **Features:** In an imposing red-brick structure that was built in 1908 as an ironworks, this casual dining restaurant offers good variety. The menu lists many traditional Italian dishes, as well as Mexican and Southwestern dishes, steaks, prime rib, and seafood. Signature dishes include the gorgonzola salad and sourdough bread served with olive oil and roasted garlic. The dining room has extensive oak woodwork and a pressed-tin ceiling. Casual dress; cocktails. **Parking:** on-site. **Cards:** AX, DS, MC, VI.

MACKENZIE RIVER PIZZA **Lunch:** $7-$14 **Dinner:** $10-$18 **Phone:** 406/761-0085

Pizza

Location: I-15, exit 278, 3 mi e on 10th Ave S and US 89/87 and SR 3/200. 1220 9th St S 59405. **Hours:** 11 am-9 pm, Fri & Sat-10 pm. Closed major holidays. **Features:** Specialty sandwiches, salads and gourmet pizzas are featured in the charmingly rustic restaurant. Of note is Athenian pizza, an eight-grain crust topped with chicken, jalapenos, red onions and black beans. Service is friendly and knowledgeable. Casual dress; cocktails. **Parking:** on-site. **Cards:** AX, DS, MC, VI.

PEKING GARDEN WEST **Lunch:** $5-$6 **Dinner:** $7-$10 **Phone:** 406/727-3913

Chinese

Location: 0.5 mi w of US 87 N and Smelter Ave. 801 Smelter Ave 59404-1912. **Hours:** 11:30 am-10 pm, Fri-11 pm, Sat noon-11 pm, Sun noon-10 pm. Closed: 11/25, 12/25; also for lunch major holidays. **Reservations:** accepted. **Features:** Authentic Chinese entrees, ranging from Mandarin and Szechuan to Peking and Shanghai, are served at this casual, family restaurant. Excellent menu choices are the chicken soup, fried shrimp and pork fried rice. American fare is also available. Casual dress; cocktails. **Parking:** on-site. **Cards:** AX, DS, MC, VI.

The following restaurant has not been evaluated by AAA but is listed for your information only.

PICKLE BARREL **Phone:** 406/452-2100

fyi

Not evaluated. **Location:** 20th and 10th Ave S. **Features:** This eatery serves large, fresh deli sandwiches with dill pickles.

HAMILTON pop. 3,705

WHERE TO STAY

BEST WESTERN HAMILTON INN *Book at aaa.com* **Phone:** (406)363-2142

AAA SAVE — Motel

5/11-9/30 1P: $65-$70 2P: $68-$70 XP: $5 F12

3/1-5/10 & 10/1-2/28 1P: $53-$61 2P: $57-$61 XP: $5 F12

Location: S of city center on US 93. 409 S 1st St (US 93) 59840. Fax: 406/363-2142. **Facility:** 36 one-bedroom standard units. 1-2 stories (no elevator), exterior corridors. **Parking:** on-site, winter plug-ins. **Terms:** office hours 6:30 am-10:30 pm, [CP] meal plan available. **Amenities:** voice mail, irons, hair dryers. **Leisure Activities:** whirlpool. **Business Services:** meeting rooms. **Cards:** AX, CB, DC, DS, MC, VI. **Special Amenities: free continental breakfast and free local telephone calls.**

SOME UNITS

DATA PORT

BITTERROOT RIVER INN HOLIDAY INN EXPRESS HAMILTON **Book at aaa.com** **Phone:** (406)375-2525

Small-scale Hotel

All Year 1P: $69-$99 2P: $69-$99

Location: US 93, 1 mi n, just w. Located next to city park, bird sanctuary and river. 139 Bitterroot Plaza Dr 59840. Fax: 406/363-9700. **Facility:** 65 units. 64 one-bedroom standard units, some with whirlpools. 1 one-bedroom suite ($109-$189). 3 stories, interior corridors. *Bath:* combo or shower only. **Parking:** on-site. **Terms:** cancellation fee imposed. **Amenities:** voice mail, irons, hair dryers. **Pool(s):** small heated indoor. **Leisure Activities:** sauna, whirlpool, hiking trails, jogging. **Guest Services:** coin laundry. **Business Services:** conference facilities. **Cards:** AX, DC, DS, MC, VI.

SOME UNITS

ASK FEE DATA PORT / VCR /

COMFORT INN OF HAMILTON **Book at aaa.com** **Phone:** (406)363-6600

Small-scale Hotel

All Year [ECP] 1P: $59-$89 2P: $65-$99 XP: $6 F18

Location: N of city center on US 93. 1113 N 1st St 59840. Fax: 406/363-5644. **Facility:** 64 one-bedroom standard units. 2 stories (no elevator), interior corridors. *Bath:* combo or shower only. **Parking:** on-site, winter plug-ins. **Terms:** pets ($4 extra charge). **Amenities:** video library (fee). *Some:* irons, hair dryers. **Leisure Activities:** sauna, whirlpool. **Guest Services:** coin laundry. **Cards:** AX, CB, DC, DS, MC, VI.

SOME UNITS

ASK FEE DATA PORT / VCR FEE /

HAMILTON SUPER 8 MOTEL **Book at aaa.com** **Phone:** (406)363-2940

AAA SAVE

Small-scale Hotel

All Year [CP] 1P: $47-$65 2P: $51-$69 XP: $6 F12

Location: US 93, north edge of town. 1325 N 1st St 59840. Fax: 406/363-2940. **Facility:** Smoke free premises. 40 one-bedroom standard units, some with whirlpools. 2 stories (no elevator), interior corridors. **Parking:** on-site, winter plug-ins. **Amenities:** hair dryers. **Guest Services:** coin laundry. **Cards:** AX, CB, DC, DS, MC, VI.

SOME UNITS

DATA PORT / VCR /

WHERE TO DINE

4 B'S RESTAURANT **Lunch:** $5-$7 **Dinner:** $5-$8 **Phone:** 406/363-4620

American

Location: US 93 S. 1105 N 1st St (US 93) 59840. **Hours:** 6 am-11 pm, Fri & Sat 24 hours. Closed: 11/25, 12/25. **Features:** The atmosphere is pleasant and informal at this family restaurant, located conveniently near area motels and shopping venues. The house specialties run the gamut of steak, chicken and seafood dishes. A notable variety of sandwiches also graces the menu. Casual dress. **Parking:** on-site. **Cards:** AX, DC, DS, MC, VI.

MANGY MOOSE GRILL **Lunch:** $5-$8 **Dinner:** $5-$16 **Phone:** 406/375-0102

American

Location: S of center. 310 S 1st St (US 93) 59840. **Hours:** 7 am-9 pm, Fri & Sat-10 pm; to 8 pm, Fri & Sat-9 pm in winter. Closed: 1/1, 11/25, 12/25. **Features:** The casual, friendly restaurant is a favorite of locals and tourists alike, and is located in a rustic looking log building, and the theme is carried through to the log tables and chairs. Casual dress; beer & wine only. **Parking:** on-site. **Cards:** AX, MC, VI.

The following restaurants have not been evaluated by AAA but are listed for your information only.

CHENG FAMILY INTERNATIONAL CUISINE **Phone:** 406/375-9139

fyi

Not evaluated. **Location:** 610 N 1st St, Suite 2 59840. **Features:** The family-owned restaurant specializes in Asian food of all types. Also on the menu are American dishes for those with less adventurous palates.

LULU FINE DINING **Phone:** 406/375-8330

fyi

Not evaluated. **Location:** 315 S 3rd St 59840. **Features:** The restaurant offers casual fine dining and friendly service in a Victorian house close to the downtown area.

HARDIN pop. 3,384

WHERE TO STAY

AMERICAN INN OF HARDIN — **Phone:** (406)665-1870

6/1-8/31	1P: $58-$68	2P: $69-$79	XP: $5	F12
5/1-5/31	1P: $55-$65	2P: $65-$75	XP: $5	F12
9/1-2/28	1P: $43-$65	2P: $46-$75	XP: $5	F12
3/1-4/30	1P: $43-$48	2P: $46-$49	XP: $5	F12

Small-scale Hotel **Location:** I-90, exit 495, just s on SR 47. 1324 N Crawford Ave 59034. Fax: 406/665-1492. **Facility:** 43 units. 42 one- and 1 two-bedroom standard units, some with kitchens. 2 stories, exterior corridors. **Parking:** on-site, winter plug-ins. **Terms:** cancellation fee imposed, pets ($5 extra charge). **Amenities:** hair dryers. **Dining:** 6 am-10 pm; 7:30 am-9 pm in winter. **Pool(s):** heated outdoor. **Leisure Activities:** whirlpool, waterslide, barbecue area. **Guest Services:** coin laundry. **Business Services:** meeting rooms, PC, fax. **Cards:** AX, DC, DS, MC, VI. **Special Amenities: free local telephone calls.**

(See color ad below)

SOME UNITS

FEE

WESTERN MOTEL — **Phone:** (406)665-2296

Motel

6/1-9/30	1P: $50-$65	2P: $55-$75	XP: $5	F12
3/1-5/31	1P: $35-$45	2P: $40-$65	XP: $5	F12
10/1-12/31	1P: $38-$55	2P: $43-$60	XP: $5	F12
1/1-2/28	1P: $28-$45	2P: $33-$50	XP: $5	F12

Location: I-90, exit 495 eastbound, 1.3 mi s on SR 47 and CR 313, just e; exit 497 westbound, 0.3 mi w on I-90 business loop, continue straight on 3rd St for 0.7 mi. 830 W 3rd St 59034. Fax: 406/665-2298. **Facility:** 28 units. 24 one- and 4 two-bedroom standard units. 2 stories, exterior corridors. **Parking:** on-site, winter plug-ins. **Terms:** pets ($2.50 extra charge). **Cards:** AX, DC, MC, VI.

SOME UNITS

FEE

HARLOWTON pop. 1,062

WHERE TO STAY

CORRAL MOTEL — **Phone:** 406/632-4331

Motel

All Year	1P: $40-$45	2P: $45-$50	XP: $10	F12

Location: 0.5 mi e at jct US 12 and 191. (PO Box 648, 59036). Fax: 406/632-4748. **Facility:** 18 units. 12 one- and 6 two-bedroom standard units, some with efficiencies (no utensils). 1 story, exterior corridors. *Bath:* combo or shower only. **Parking:** on-site, winter plug-ins. **Terms:** 3 day cancellation notice, $5 service charge. **Cards:** AX, DS, MC, VI.

SOME UNITS

COUNTRYSIDE INN — **Phone:** (406)632-4119

Motel

All Year	1P: $40-$42	2P: $51-$61	XP: $4

Location: US 12 E. 309 3rd St NE 59036 (PO Box 72). **Facility:** 15 one-bedroom standard units. 1 story, exterior corridors. *Bath:* combo or shower only. **Parking:** on-site, winter plug-ins. **Leisure Activities:** sauna, whirlpool, exercise room. **Cards:** AX, DS, MC, VI.

SOME UNITS

HAVRE pop. 9,621

WHERE TO STAY

BEST WESTERN GREAT NORTHERN INN *Book at aaa.com* — **Phone:** (406)265-4200

4/1-2/28 [ECP]	1P: $85-$99	2P: $89-$99	XP: $4	F18
3/1-3/31 [ECP]	1P: $81-$99	2P: $86-$99	XP: $5	F18

Small-scale Hotel **Location:** 0.7 mi e of town center on US 2. 1345 1st St 59501 (PO Box 1430). Fax: 406/265-3656. **Facility:** 64 units. 63 one-bedroom standard units, some with whirlpools. 1 one-bedroom suite ($129-$159). 3 stories, interior corridors. *Bath:* combo or shower only. **Parking:** on-site. **Amenities:** voice mail, irons, hair dryers. **Pool(s):** small heated indoor. **Leisure Activities:** whirlpool, steamroom, exercise room. **Guest Services:** valet laundry. **Business Services:** meeting rooms, PC. **Cards:** AX, DC, DS, MC, VI. **Special Amenities: free expanded continental breakfast and free local telephone calls.**

SOME UNITS

HELENA pop: 25,780

WHERE TO STAY

BARRISTER BED & BREAKFAST — **Phone:** (406)443-7330

Historic Bed & Breakfast

All Year [BP] 1P: $95-$110 2P: $95-$110 XP: $15 F6

Location: I-15, exit 192 (Prospect Ave), 1.5 mi sw via Prospect and Montana aves to 9th Ave, 0.8 mi w, then just s. Located across the street from St. Helena Cathedral. 416 N Ewing 59601. Fax: 406/442-7964. **Facility:** The bedrooms in this 1874 Victorian mansion have ornate fireplaces; common areas include a parlor, library, den and enclosed sun porch. Smoke free premises. 5 one-bedroom standard units. 3 stories (no elevator), interior corridors. *Bath:* combo or shower only. **Parking:** on-site, winter plug-ins. **Terms:** check-in 4 pm, 4 day cancellation notice, weekly rates available. **Amenities:** video library, hair dryers. *Some:* DVD players. **Business Services:** business center. **Cards:** AX, CB, DC, DS, MC, VI.

SOME UNITS

ASK / AC VCR DATA PORT /

BEST WESTERN HELENA GREAT NORTHERN HOTEL *Book at aaa.com* — **Phone:** (406)457-5500

Small-scale Hotel

5/15-10/15 1P: $110 2P: $155
3/1-5/14 & 10/16-2/28 1P: $95 2P: $135

Location: I-15, exit 193 (Cedar St), just e of jct Lyndale and Benton aves; downtown. 835 Great Northern Blvd 59601. Fax: 406/457-5501. **Facility:** Smoke free premises. 101 one-bedroom standard units. 4 stories, interior corridors. *Bath:* combo or shower only. **Parking:** on-site. **Terms:** [ECP] meal plan available, pets ($5 extra charge). **Amenities:** video games, high-speed Internet, voice mail, irons, hair dryers. **Pool(s):** heated indoor. **Leisure Activities:** whirlpool, exercise room. **Guest Services:** valet and coin laundry, area transportation. **Business Services:** conference facilities, business center. **Cards:** AX, CB, DC, DS, MC, VI.

SOME UNITS

ASK FEE DATA PORT / /

CAROLINA BED & BREAKFAST — **Phone:** 406/495-8095

AAA SAVE

Bed & Breakfast

All Year [BP] 1P: $95-$115 2P: $95-$115

Location: I-15, exit 192 (Prospect Ave), 1.5 mi sw via Prospect and Montana aves to 9th Ave, 0.8 mi w, then just s. 309 N Ewing St 59601. Fax: 406/495-0051. **Facility:** A beautiful and lovingly restored Victorian Arts & Crafts-style mansion. A newly renovated adjacent building is utilized as a conference facility. Smoke free premises. 6 units. 5 one-bedroom standard units. 1 two-bedroom suite with whirlpool. 3 stories (no elevator), interior corridors. *Bath:* combo or shower only. **Parking:** on-site. **Amenities:** voice mail, irons, hair dryers. **Guest Services:** complimentary evening beverages, airport transportation-Helena Regional Airport. **Business Services:** conference facilities. **Cards:** AX, MC, VI. **Special Amenities: free full breakfast and early check-in/late check-out.**

VCR DATA PORT

COMFORT INN OF HELENA *Book at aaa.com* — **Phone:** (406)443-1000

Small-scale Hotel

5/1-9/30 [ECP] 1P: $64-$84 2P: $69-$89 XP: $6 F
3/1-4/30 & 10/1-2/28 [ECP] 1P: $54-$69 2P: $54-$75 XP: $6 F

Location: I-15, exit 192 (Prospect Ave), just n. 750 N Fee St 59601. Fax: 406/443-1000. **Facility:** 56 one-bedroom standard units. 2 stories (no elevator), interior corridors. **Parking:** on-site, winter plug-ins. **Amenities:** irons, hair dryers. **Pool(s):** heated indoor. **Leisure Activities:** whirlpool. **Guest Services:** valet laundry. **Cards:** AX, CB, DC, DS, MC, VI.

SOME UNITS

ASK DATA PORT / /

DAYS INN HELENA *Book at aaa.com* — **Phone:** (406)442-3280

Small-scale Hotel

5/15-10/15 1P: $58-$85 2P: $68-$95 XP: $5 F17
3/1-5/14 & 10/16-2/28 1P: $53-$79 2P: $63-$89 XP: $5 F17

Location: I-15, exit 192 (Prospect Ave), just w. 2001 Prospect Ave 59601. Fax: 406/442-3108. **Facility:** 94 units. 93 one-bedroom standard units. 1 one-bedroom suite ($120) with kitchen. 2 stories (no elevator), interior corridors. *Bath:* combo or shower only. **Parking:** on-site, winter plug-ins. **Terms:** [BP] meal plan available, pets ($5 extra charge). **Amenities:** hair dryers. *Fee:* video library, safes. *Some:* irons. **Leisure Activities:** sauna, whirlpool, limited exercise equipment. **Guest Services:** valet and coin laundry. **Business Services:** meeting rooms. **Cards:** AX, DC, DS, MC, VI.

SOME UNITS

ASK FEE DATA PORT / VCR FEE /

ELKHORN MOUNTAIN INN *Book at aaa.com* — **Phone:** (406)442-6625

AAA SAVE

Small-scale Hotel

10/16-2/28 [ECP] 1P: $62-$69 2P: $69-$76 XP: $7 F12
5/16-10/15 [ECP] 1P: $65-$68 2P: $72-$75 XP: $7 F12
3/1-5/15 [ECP] 1P: $59-$62 2P: $66-$69 XP: $7 F12

Location: I-15, exit 187 (Montana City), just w. 1 Jackson Creek Rd 59634 (1 Jackson Creek Rd, MONTANA CITY). Fax: 406/449-8797. **Facility:** 22 one-bedroom standard units, some with whirlpools. 2 stories (no elevator), interior corridors. *Bath:* combo or shower only. **Parking:** on-site, winter plug-ins. **Terms:** check-in 4 pm, pets ($5 extra charge). **Amenities:** video library (fee). **Guest Services:** gift shop. **Business Services:** meeting rooms. **Cards:** AX, CB, DC, DS, MC, VI. **Special Amenities: free expanded continental breakfast and free newspaper.**

SOME UNITS

FEE VCR DATA PORT / /

FAIRFIELD INN HELENA *Book at aaa.com* — **Phone:** (406)449-9944

Small-scale Hotel

6/12-9/30 [ECP] 1P: $79-$95 2P: $85-$100 XP: $5 F18
3/1-6/11 & 10/1-2/28 [ECP] 1P: $72-$90 2P: $77-$95 XP: $5 F18

Location: I-15 S, exit 192B (Capital area); I-15 N exit west business district on US 12. 2150 11th Ave 59601. Fax: 406/449-9949. **Facility:** 60 one-bedroom standard units, some with whirlpools. 3 stories, interior corridors. *Bath:* combo or shower only. **Parking:** on-site, winter plug-ins. **Amenities:** video games, dual phone lines, voice mail, irons, hair dryers. *Some:* high-speed Internet. **Pool(s):** heated indoor. **Leisure Activities:** whirlpool, exercise room. **Guest Services:** valet and coin laundry. **Business Services:** meeting rooms. **Cards:** AX, CB, DC, DS, MC, VI. *(See color ad p 273)*

SOME UNITS

ASK DATA PORT / /

HAMPTON INN-HELENA *Book at aaa.com* **Phone:** 406/443-5800

Small-scale Hotel

5/1-12/31 [ECP]	1P: $79-$99	2P: $79-$99	XP: $10	F18
3/1-4/30 & 1/1-2/28 [ECP]	1P: $69-$89	2P: $69-$89	XP: $10	F18

Location: I-15, exit 192 eastbound; exit 192A westbound, just e on SR 12/287, then just n. 3000 Hwy 12 E 59601. Fax: 406/449-2592. **Facility:** 81 one-bedroom standard units. 3 stories, interior corridors. *Bath:* combo or shower only. **Parking:** on-site, winter plug-ins. **Terms:** cancellation fee imposed, pets ($20 fee). **Amenities:** dual phone lines, voice mail, irons, hair dryers. *Some:* high-speed Internet. **Pool(s):** heated indoor. **Leisure Activities:** whirlpool, exercise room. **Guest Services:** valet and coin laundry. **Business Services:** business center. **Cards:** AX, CB, DC, DS, MC, VI.
(See color ad below)

SOME UNITS
FEE

HELENA'S COUNTRY INN & SUITES **Phone:** (406)443-2300

SAVE

Motel

5/15-10/15	1P: $52-$99	2P: $57-$129	XP: $5	F11
3/1-5/14 & 10/16-2/28	1P: $42-$65	2P: $49-$89	XP: $5	F11

Location: I-15, exit 192 B (Capitol), just sw. 2101 E 11th Ave 59601. **Facility:** 72 one-bedroom standard units. 1 story, interior/exterior corridors. **Parking:** on-site, winter plug-ins. **Terms:** small pets only ($6 extra charge). **Amenities:** hair dryers. **Pool(s):** small heated indoor. **Leisure Activities:** whirlpool. **Guest Services:** valet and coin laundry, airport transportation-Helena Regional Airport. **Business Services:** meeting rooms. **Cards:** AX, DS, MC, VI. **Special Amenities: free continental breakfast and free room upgrade (subject to availability with advanced reservations).**

SOME UNITS
FEE

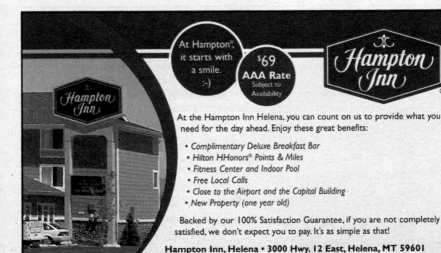

HOLIDAY INN EXPRESS HELENA **Book at aaa.com** **Phone:** (406)449-4000

AAA SAVE

7/1-9/30 [ECP]	1P: $89
4/1-6/30 [ECP]	1P: $85
3/1-3/31 & 10/1-2/28 [ECP]	1P: $69

Small-scale Hotel **Location:** I-15, exit 192 (Prospect Ave), just w on US 12; jct US 12 and I-15. 701 Washington St 59601. Fax: 406/449-4522. **Facility:** Smoke free premises. 75 one-bedroom standard units. 4 stories, interior corridors. *Bath:* combo or shower only. **Parking:** on-site, winter plug-ins. **Amenities:** high-speed Internet, dual phone lines, voice mail, irons, hair dryers. **Leisure Activities:** exercise room. **Guest Services:** valet and coin laundry, airport transportation-Helena Regional Airport. **Business Services:** meeting rooms, business center. **Cards:** AX, CB, DC, DS, MC, VI. **Special Amenities: free expanded continental breakfast and free local telephone calls.**

SOME UNITS

JORGENSON'S INN & SUITES **Book at aaa.com** **Phone:** (406)442-1770

AAA SAVE

All Year	1P: $59-$89	2P: $59-$89	XP: $5	F18

Small-scale Hotel **Location:** I-15, exit 192 (Prospect Ave), just w of I-15 and US 287/12. Located next to the shopping mall. 1714 11th Ave 59601 (PO Box 857, 59624). Fax: 406/449-0155. **Facility:** 111 one-bedroom standard units. 5 one-bedroom suites with whirlpools. 1-3 stories, interior/exterior corridors. *Bath:* combo or shower only. **Parking:** on-site, winter plug-ins. **Amenities:** *Some:* fax, irons, hair dryers. **Dining:** Jorgenson's Restaurant & Lounge, see separate listing. **Pool(s):** heated indoor. **Guest Services:** valet and coin laundry, airport transportation-Helena Regional Airport. **Business Services:** meeting rooms, business center. **Cards:** AX, CB, DC, DS, MC, VI. **Special Amenities: free local telephone calls and free newspaper.**

SOME UNITS

FEE

RED LION COLONIAL HOTEL *Book at aaa.com* **Phone:** (406)443-2100

Small-scale Hotel

6/1-10/15	1P: $82-$96	2P: $82-$96	XP: $10	F18
3/1-5/31 & 1/1-2/28	1P: $72-$86	2P: $72-$86	XP: $10	F18
10/16-12/31	1P: $65-$79	2P: $65-$79	XP: $10	F18

Location: I-15, exit 192 southbound; exit 192B northbound. 2301 Colonial Dr 59601. Fax: 406/442-0301. **Facility:** 149 one-bedroom standard units. 2 stories, interior corridors. **Parking:** on-site. **Terms:** pets ($5 extra charge, in smoking units). **Amenities:** video games (fee), voice mail, irons, hair dryers. **Pool(s):** heated outdoor, heated indoor. **Leisure Activities:** whirlpool, exercise room. **Guest Services:** gift shop, valet and coin laundry. **Business Services:** meeting rooms. **Cards:** AX, DC, DS, JC, MC, VI. ***(See color ad p 274)***

SOME UNITS

ASK / FEE / DATA PORT /

THE SANDERS-HELENA'S BED & BREAKFAST **Phone:** 406/442-3309

Bed & Breakfast

All Year [BP] 1P: $90-$110 2P: $105-$130 XP: $15

Location: 0.3 mi from Last Chance Gulch, 0.8 mi w of state capitol on 6th Ave, just n. 328 N Ewing St 59601. Fax: 406/443-2361. **Facility:** This restored 1875 mansion features period furnishings. Smoke free premises. 7 one-bedroom standard units. 3 stories (no elevator), interior corridors. *Bath:* combo or shower only. **Parking:** on-site, winter plug-ins. **Terms:** check-in 4 pm, 14 day cancellation notice-fee imposed. **Amenities:** hair dryers. **Business Services:** fax. **Cards:** AX, DC, DS, MC, VI.

SOME UNITS

CTV DATA PORT / VCR /

SUPER 8 MOTEL *Book at aaa.com* **Phone:** (406)443-2450

Small-scale Hotel

All Year 1P: $45-$55 2P: $50-$60 XP: $5 F12

Location: I-15, exit Capitol area southbound; exit west business district northbound on US 12. 2200 11th Ave 59601. Fax: 406/443-2450. **Facility:** 102 one-bedroom standard units. 3 stories, interior corridors. *Bath:* combo or shower only. **Parking:** on-site, winter plug-ins. **Terms:** weekly rates available, [CP] meal plan available. **Amenities:** video library (fee), safes. **Leisure Activities:** exercise room. **Guest Services:** valet and coin laundry. **Business Services:** meeting rooms. **Cards:** AX, DC, DS, MC, VI.

SOME UNITS

ASK DATA PORT / VCR FEE /

WINGATE INN *Book at aaa.com* **Phone:** (406)449-3000

Small-scale Hotel

All Year [ECP] 1P: $85-$105 2P: $90-$110 XP: $5 F16

Location: I-15, exit 193, just sw. 2007 Oakes 59601. Fax: 406/449-3001. **Facility:** 100 units. 92 one-bedroom standard units. 8 one-bedroom suites ($110-$225), some with whirlpools. 3 stories, interior corridors. *Bath:* combo or shower only. **Parking:** on-site, winter plug-ins. **Terms:** package plans - weekends. **Amenities:** video games, high-speed Internet, dual phone lines, voice mail, safes, irons, hair dryers. **Pool(s):** heated indoor. **Leisure Activities:** whirlpool, exercise room. **Guest Services:** valet and coin laundry. **Business Services:** meeting rooms, business center. **Cards:** AX, CB, DC, DS, MC, VI. ***(See color ad p 274)***

SOME UNITS

ASK DATA PORT / /

WHERE TO DINE

BENNY'S BISTRO **Lunch:** $6-$11 **Dinner:** $12-$21 **Phone:** 406/443-0105

American

Location: Center; in Historic downtown; across from the Chamber of Commerce. 108 E Sixth Ave 59601. **Hours:** 7:30 am-3 pm, Thurs & Fri also 5:30 pm-9 pm, Sat 11 am-3 & 5:30-9 pm. Closed major holidays. **Reservations:** accepted. **Features:** Whether you choose to dine here at lunch or at dinner, you'll always be served fresh, delicious, innovative cuisine. The foccacia bread is wonderful for any sandwich creation or as an accompaniment to an entree. Casual dress; beer & wine only. **Parking:** street. **Cards:** DS, MC, VI.

JADE GARDEN **Lunch:** $6-$10 **Dinner:** $8-$19 **Phone:** 406/443-8899

Chinese

Location: I-15, exit 192 (Prospect Ave), 0.9 mi w, then 1.8 mi n. 3128 N Montana Ave 59602. **Hours:** 11 am-9:30 pm, Fri & Sat-10:30 pm. Closed: 11/25, 12/25. **Features:** The traditional Chinese menu features Cantonese cooking and a wide selection of traditional favorites. The atmosphere is inviting and contemporary, and the service prompt and pleasant. A children's menu is available. Casual dress; beer & wine only. **Parking:** on-site. **Cards:** AX, DS, MC, VI.

JORGENSON'S RESTAURANT & LOUNGE **Lunch:** $5-$7 **Dinner:** $8-$18 **Phone:** 406/442-6380

AAA

American

Location: I-15, exit 192 (Prospect Ave), just w of I-15 and US 287/12; in Jorgenson's Inn & Suites. 1720 11th Ave 59601. **Hours:** 6:30 am-10 pm, Sun-9 pm. Closed major holidays. **Features:** This family restaurant serves up a variety of menu items, including seafood, beef and chicken entrees. Service is pleasant, casual and efficient. Casual dress; cocktails. **Parking:** on-site. **Cards:** AX, DC, DS, MC, VI.

MONTANA CITY GRILL AND SALOON **Lunch:** $6-$7 **Dinner:** $10-$23 **Phone:** 406/449-8890

American

Location: I-15, exit 187, just w. 4 Hwy 518 59634. **Hours:** 11 am-9 pm, Fri-10 pm, Sat 8 am-10 pm, Sun 8 am-9 pm. Closed: 12/25. **Features:** Specialties of the house include slow-roasted prime rib, fresh seafood, homemade soup, chicken, pasta, charbroiled steak and huckleberry barbecued pork ribs. The atmosphere is casual with some booth seating; the service is friendly and prompt. Good selection of microbrews and wines are offered. Casual dress; cocktails. **Parking:** on-site. **Cards:** DS, MC, VI.

ON BROADWAY **Dinner:** $11-$22 **Phone:** 406/443-1929

Italian

Location: Jct Cruse St; center; in Historic downtown. 106 Broadway 59601. **Hours:** 5:30 pm-9:30 pm. Closed major holidays; also Sun. **Features:** Yes, you may sit in the loft, overlooking the music stage or you may choose to be seated in the intimate dining room. Either way, expect friendly, knowledgeable service. The menu changes seasonally and the Chef's creative and well prepared offerings will delight you. Casual dress; beer & wine only. **Parking:** street. **Cards:** AX, DS, MC, VI.

OVERLAND EXPRESS **Lunch:** $6-$21 **Dinner:** $6-$22 **Phone:** 406/449-2635

Steak & Seafood

Location: I-15 S, exit Capital area; I-15 N, exit W business district on US 12. 2250 11th Ave 59601. **Hours:** 11 am-10 pm, Sat & Sun from 9 am. Closed: 7/4, 11/25, 12/25. **Reservations:** suggested. **Features:** Dine on traditional beef, fowl and seafood dishes, including a house favorite: prime rib, in a rustic wood atmosphere. The pastry chef prepares fresh desserts daily. There's also an extensive list of domestic, imported and microbrew beer. Patio seating is available in season. Casual dress; cocktails. **Parking:** on-site. **Cards:** AX, DC, DS, MC, VI.

RED FOX SUPPER CLUB **Lunch:** $4-$10 **Dinner:** $11-$26 **Phone:** 406/227-0099

American

Location: I-15, exit 192 (Prospect Ave), 3.1 mi e on US 12 to Wylie Rd, 3.8 mi n to York Rd, 2 mi e to Lake Helena Rd, just n, then just w; in Fox Ridge Golf Course Clubhouse. 4030 Fox Ridge Dr 59602. **Hours:** 11 am-9 pm, Fri & Sat-10 pm. Closed: 1/1, 12/24, 12/25. **Reservations:** suggested. **Features:** Steaks, prime rib, seafood and pasta make up the restaurant's menu. Casual dress; cocktails. **Parking:** on-site. **Cards:** AX, DS, MC, VI.

TOI'S THAI CUISINE **Dinner:** $8-$13 **Phone:** 406/443-6656

Thai

Location: Center; in Historic downtown. 423 N Last Chance Gulch 59601. **Hours:** 5 pm-8:30 pm. Closed major holidays; also Sun & Mon. **Reservations:** suggested. **Features:** What big flavors are created in this small kitchen! The spices are bold and the ingredients authentic. Be sure to make a reservation, as this place has very limited seating and is VERY popular. Casual dress. **Parking:** street. **Cards:** MC, VI.

WINDBAG SALOON **Lunch:** $5-$11 **Dinner:** $8-$22 **Phone:** 406/443-9669

American

Location: Jct Broadway; center; in Walking Mall. 19 S Last Chance Gulch 59601. **Hours:** 11 am-2 & 5:30-9 pm, Fri & Sat 11 am-2 & 5-9:30 pm. Closed major holidays; also Sun. **Features:** Bustling at lunch and dinner, you'll be served comfort foods in a causal atmosphere. The decor in this historic building is rustic and old-timey, the ambiance charming and the service friendly. Casual dress; cocktails. **Parking:** street. **Cards:** AX, DS, MC, VI.

HUNGRY HORSE pop. 934—*See also GLACIER NATIONAL PARK.*

WHERE TO STAY

GLACIER PARK INN B&B **Phone:** (406)387-5099

Bed & Breakfast

6/15-9/15 [BP]	1P: $90-$150	2P: $90-$150	XP: $10	F8
3/1-6/14 & 9/16-2/28 [BP]	1P: $75-$125	2P: $75-$125	XP: $10	F8

Location: On US 2, 0.5 mi e. 9128 Hwy 2 E 59919 (PO Box 190753). **Facility:** Smoke free premises. 4 one-bedroom standard units. 2 stories (no elevator), interior/exterior corridors. *Bath:* combo or shower only. **Parking:** on-site. **Terms:** 30 day cancellation notice-fee imposed, no pets allowed (owner's pet on premises). **Leisure Activities:** fishing, bicycles, hiking trails, jogging. **Business Services:** PC. **Cards:** DS, MC, VI.

SOME UNITS

HISTORIC 1907 TAMARACK LODGE **Phone:** (406)387-4420

SAVE

Motel

5/2-9/30 [CP]	1P: $75-$165	2P: $75-$165	XP: $10	F10
3/1-5/1 & 10/1-2/28	1P: $44-$99	2P: $44-$99	XP: $10	F10

Location: 1.6 mi n on US 2. 9549 US 2 E 59919 (PO Box 190236). Fax: 406/387-4450. **Facility:** 11 units. 8 one-bedroom standard units. 3 cabins ($125-$175). 1 story, exterior corridors. *Bath:* combo or shower only. **Parking:** on-site, winter plug-ins. **Terms:** 21 day cancellation notice-fee imposed. **Amenities:** *Some:* safes. **Leisure Activities:** fishing, cross country skiing, snowmobiling, hiking trails, jogging, horseshoes. **Business Services:** fax. **Cards:** CB, DC, DS, JC, MC, VI. **Special Amenities: free continental breakfast and free local telephone calls.**

SOME UNITS

MINI GOLDEN INNS MOTEL **Phone:** 406/387-4313

SAVE

Motel

5/1-10/31	1P: $72-$86	2P: $86-$96	XP: $10	F10
3/1-4/30 & 11/1-2/28	1P: $48-$56	2P: $56-$68	XP: $10	F10

Location: East end of town. 8955 US 2 E 59919. Fax: 406/387-4317. **Facility:** 38 units. 34 one- and 4 two-bedroom standard units, some with efficiencies. 1 story, exterior corridors. *Bath:* combo or shower only. **Parking:** on-site, winter plug-ins. **Terms:** office hours 7 am-10 pm, 45 day cancellation notice-fee imposed, [CP] meal plan available, small pets only. **Amenities:** hair dryers. **Guest Services:** coin laundry. **Cards:** AX, DC, DS, MC, VI. **Special Amenities: free continental breakfast and free local telephone calls.**

SOME UNITS

FEE

KALISPELL pop. 14,223—*See also GLACIER NATIONAL PARK.*

WHERE TO STAY

AERO INN **Phone:** (406)755-3798

SAVE

Motel

6/9-9/15 [CP]	1P: $72-$76	2P: $77-$81	XP: $5	F12
9/16-11/10 [CP]	1P: $48-$49	2P: $53-$54	XP: $5	F12
3/1-6/8 [CP]	1P: $37-$49	2P: $42-$54	XP: $5	F12
11/11-2/28 [CP]	1P: $37-$41	2P: $42-$46	XP: $5	F12

Location: 1.3 mi s on US 93 from jct of US 2. 1830 US 93 S 59901. Fax: 406/752-1304. **Facility:** 61 units. 60 one-bedroom standard units. 1 one-bedroom suite ($66-$120). 2 stories (no elevator), interior corridors. *Bath:* combo or shower only. **Parking:** on-site, winter plug-ins. **Terms:** pets ($10 deposit, in smoking units). **Amenities:** video library (fee). **Pool(s):** small heated indoor. **Leisure Activities:** sauna, whirlpool. **Cards:** AX, CB, DC, DS, MC, VI. **Special Amenities: free continental breakfast and free local telephone calls.**

SOME UNITS

FEE FEE

DAYS INN KALISPELL *Book at aaa.com* **Phone:** (406)756-3222

Small-scale Hotel

5/16-9/30	1P: $77-$95	2P: $83-$101	XP: $6	F12
3/1-5/15 & 10/1-2/28	1P: $51-$78	2P: $57-$84	XP: $6	F12

Location: 1.3 mi n on US 93 from jct of US 2. 1550 Hwy 93 N 59901. Fax: 406/756-3277. **Facility:** 53 one-bedroom standard units. 2 stories (no elevator), interior corridors. **Parking:** on-site, winter plug-ins. **Terms:** cancellation fee imposed, [CP] meal plan available, small pets only. **Amenities:** hair dryers. **Business Services:** meeting rooms. **Cards:** AX, CB, DC, DS, JC, MC, VI.

SOME UNITS

FOUR SEASONS MOTOR INN **Phone:** 406/755-6123

SAVE

Small-scale Hotel

6/16-9/15	1P: $69-$79	2P: $78-$98	XP: $6	F12
5/16-6/15	1P: $52-$62	2P: $60-$79	XP: $6	F12
9/16-2/28	1P: $43-$62	2P: $52-$79	XP: $6	F12
3/1-5/15	1P: $43-$53	2P: $52-$68	XP: $6	F12

Location: US 93, just n of jct US 2. 350 N Main St 59901. Fax: 406/755-1604. **Facility:** 101 one-bedroom standard units. 2 stories (no elevator), interior/exterior corridors. **Parking:** on-site, winter plug-ins. **Terms:** check-in 4 pm, cancellation fee imposed, [AP], [BP] & [CP] meal plans available, pets (in designated units). **Amenities:** *Some:* hair dryers. **Dining:** 6:30 am-4 pm, Thurs-Sat to 9 pm, Sun-2 pm. **Leisure Activities:** whirlpool. **Cards:** AX, CB, DC, DS, MC, VI. **Special Amenities: free continental breakfast.**

SOME UNITS

GLACIER GATEWAY MOTEL **Phone:** 406/755-3330

SAVE

Motel

6/1-9/30 [CP]	1P: $65-$73	2P: $74-$94	XP: $7
10/1-2/28 [CP]	1P: $48-$55	2P: $64-$72	XP: $7
3/1-5/31 [CP]	1P: $46-$62	2P: $59-$69	XP: $7

Location: Northwest corner of jct US 2 and 93. 264 N Main St 59901. Fax: 406/755-3366. **Facility:** 14 units. 5 one- and 9 two-bedroom standard units, some with efficiencies. 2 stories (no elevator), exterior corridors. **Parking:** on-site, winter plug-ins. **Terms:** office hours 6:30 am-11 pm, 3 day cancellation notice-fee imposed, weekly rates available, pets ($8 extra charge, limit 1 small dog with carrier, in designated units). **Amenities:** voice mail. **Business Services:** fax. **Cards:** AX, DS, MC, VI. **Special Amenities: free continental breakfast and free local telephone calls.**

SOME UNITS

FEE

HAMPTON INN-KALISPELL *Book at aaa.com* **Phone:** (406)755-7900

Small-scale Hotel

7/1-8/31 [ECP]	1P: $128	2P: $138
5/1-6/30 [ECP]	1P: $118	2P: $128
3/1-4/30 & 9/1-2/28 [ECP]	1P: $83	2P: $93

Location: 0.9 mi w on US 2 from jct of US 93. 1140 US 2 W 59901. Fax: 406/755-5056. **Facility:** 120 units. 116 one-bedroom standard units. 4 one-bedroom suites ($175-$225). 3 stories, interior corridors. *Bath:* combo or shower only. **Parking:** on-site, winter plug-ins. **Terms:** check-in 4 pm. **Amenities:** video games (fee), voice mail, irons, hair dryers. **Pool(s):** heated indoor. **Leisure Activities:** whirlpool, exercise room. **Guest Services:** gift shop, valet and coin laundry, area transportation. **Business Services:** meeting rooms, business center. **Cards:** AX, DC, DS, MC, VI. ***(See color ad below)***

SOME UNITS

KALISPELL/GLACIER INT'L AIRPORT AREA SUPER 8 MOTEL **Phone:** (406)755-1888

Small-scale Hotel

6/15-8/31 [ECP]	1P: $87-$106	2P: $94-$113	XP: $7	F12
4/1-6/14 [ECP]	1P: $73-$80	2P: $80-$87	XP: $7	F12
9/1-2/28 [ECP]	1P: $72-$79	2P: $79-$86	XP: $7	F12
3/1-3/31 [ECP]	1P: $48-$66	2P: $57-$73	XP: $7	F12

Location: 1.2 mi s on US 93 from jct of US 2. 1341 1st Ave E 59901. Fax: 406/755-1888. **Facility:** 74 one-bedroom standard units. 3 stories, interior corridors. **Parking:** on-site, winter plug-ins. **Terms:** pets ($10 extra charge). **Cards:** AX, DC, MC, VI.

SOME UNITS

FEE FEE FEE

KALISPELL GRAND HOTEL — **Phone:** (406)755-8100

Historic Small-scale Hotel

	1P	2P	XP	
6/1-9/30 [ECP]	1P: $76-$89	2P: $83-$96	XP: $7	F13
3/1-5/31 & 10/1-2/28 [ECP]	1P: $62-$76	2P: $69-$93	XP: $7	F13

Location: On US 93; downtown. 100 Main St 59901. Fax: 406/752-8012. **Facility:** Built in 1912, the hotel has been renovated and offers a variety of rooms. 40 one-bedroom standard units, some with whirlpools. 3 stories, interior corridors. *Bath:* combo or shower only. **Parking:** on-site. **Amenities:** hair dryers. *Some:* high-speed Internet. **Dining:** Painted Horse Grille, The Alley Connection, see separate listings. **Leisure Activities:** Fee: massage. **Guest Services:** gift shop, valet laundry. **Cards:** AX, DC, DS, MC, VI.

LA QUINTA INN & SUITES *Book at aaa.com* — **Phone:** (406)257-5255

AAA SAVE — Small-scale Hotel

	1P	2P	XP	
6/15-8/31 [ECP]	1P: $109-$159	2P: $109-$159	XP: $10	F18
3/1-6/14 & 9/1-2/28 [ECP]	1P: $59-$89	2P: $59-$89	XP: $10	F18

Location: Jct US 93 and 2, 1 mi e. 255 Montclair Dr 59901. Fax: 406/257-7361. **Facility:** 71 units. 59 one-bedroom standard units, some with efficiencies and/or whirlpools. 12 one-bedroom suites ($99-$199) with efficiencies. 2 stories, interior corridors. *Bath:* combo or shower only. **Parking:** on-site. **Terms:** package plans. **Amenities:** dual phone lines, voice mail, irons, hair dryers. **Pool(s):** heated indoor. **Leisure Activities:** sauna, whirlpool, exercise room. **Guest Services:** gift shop, valet and coin laundry. **Business Services:** meeting rooms, business center. **Cards:** AX, CB, DC, DS, MC, VI. **Special Amenities: free expanded continental breakfast and free local telephone calls.**

SOME UNITS

RED LION INN KALISPELL *Book at aaa.com* — **Phone:** (406)755-6700

AAA SAVE — Small-scale Hotel

	1P	2P	XP	
6/16-8/31 [CP]	1P: $99-$129	2P: $99-$129	XP: $10	F18
5/1-6/15 [CP]	1P: $79-$109	2P: $79-$109	XP: $10	F18
3/1-4/30 & 9/1-2/28 [CP]	1P: $69-$99	2P: $69-$99	XP: $10	F18

Location: 1 mi w on US 2 from jct of US 93. 1330 Hwy 2 W 59901. Fax: 406/755-6717. **Facility:** Some rooms with balconies or patios are offered at this inn. 64 units. 62 one-bedroom standard units. 2 one-bedroom suites. 2 stories (no elevator), interior corridors. **Parking:** on-site, winter plug-ins. **Terms:** pets ($10 extra charge). **Amenities:** voice mail, irons, hair dryers. **Dining:** 11 am-9 pm, Fri & Sat from 5 pm, cocktails. **Pool(s):** small heated outdoor. **Leisure Activities:** whirlpool, exercise room. **Guest Services:** valet and coin laundry. **Business Services:** fax. **Cards:** AX, DC, DS, MC, VI. **Special Amenities: free continental breakfast and free local telephone calls.** *(See color ad below)*

SOME UNITS

WESTCOAST KALISPELL CENTER *Book at aaa.com* **Phone:** (406)751-5050

7/1-9/15	1P: $117	2P: $127	XP: $10	F17
6/1-6/30	1P: $107	2P: $117	XP: $10	F17
3/1-5/31	1P: $80-$85	2P: $90-$95	XP: $10	F17
9/16-2/28	1P: $80	2P: $90	XP: $10	F17

Small-scale Hotel **Location:** Just s on US 93 from jct of US 2. Connected to Kalispell Center Mall, located adjacent to casino. 20 N Main St 59901. Fax: 406/751-5051. **Facility:** 132 one-bedroom standard units, some with efficiencies (no utensils) and/or whirlpools. 3 stories, interior corridors. **Parking:** on-site. **Terms:** check-in 4 pm, cancellation fee imposed, package plans. **Amenities:** video games (fee), voice mail, irons, hair dryers. **Dining:** 6:30 am-10 pm; to 9 pm 10/2-5/15, cocktails. **Pool(s):** small heated indoor. **Leisure Activities:** sauna, whirlpools, exercise room. **Guest Services:** valet laundry. **Business Services:** conference facilities. **Cards:** AX, DC, DS, MC, VI. **Special Amenities: free local telephone calls and free room upgrade (subject to availability with advanced reservations).** *(See color ad p 278)*

SOME UNITS

WESTCOAST OUTLAW HOTEL-KALISPELL **Phone:** (406)755-6100

7/1-9/15	1P: $107	2P: $117	XP: $10	F17
6/1-6/30	1P: $97	2P: $107	XP: $10	F17
3/1-5/31	1P: $70-$75	2P: $80-$95	XP: $10	F17
9/16-2/28	1P: $70	2P: $80	XP: $10	F17

Small-scale Hotel **Location:** 1.4 mi s on US 93 from jct US 2. 1701 Hwy 93 S 59901. Fax: 406/756-8994. **Facility:** 220 units. 196 one-bedroom standard units. 24 one-bedroom suites ($119-$149). 2-3 stories, interior corridors. **Parking:** on-site, winter plug-ins. **Terms:** check-in 4 pm, cancellation fee imposed, small pets only ($15 fee). **Amenities:** video games (fee), voice mail, irons, hair dryers. **Dining:** 6 am-10 pm; 6:30 am-2 & 5-9 pm 11/1-5/1, cocktails. **Pool(s):** 2 small heated indoor, wading. **Leisure Activities:** sauna, whirlpools, lighted tennis court, racquetball court, exercise room. **Guest Services:** valet laundry. **Business Services:** conference facilities. **Cards:** AX, DC, DS, MC, VI. **Special Amenities: free local telephone calls and free room upgrade (subject to availability with advanced reservations).** *(See color ad p 278)*

SOME UNITS

FEE

WHITE BIRCH MOTEL **Phone:** 406/752-4008

6/1-9/30	1P: $55-$75	2P: $58-$85	XP: $3	F10
3/1-5/31 & 10/1-2/28	1P: $36-$45	2P: $38-$50	XP: $2	F10

Motel **Location:** 0.4 mi e on SR 35 from jct US 2, just s. 17 Shady Ln 59901. Fax: 406/752-1106. **Facility:** 8 units. 7 one- and 1 two-bedroom standard units, some with efficiencies (utensil deposit required). 1 story, exterior corridors. **Parking:** on-site. **Terms:** 3 day cancellation notice. **Leisure Activities:** playground, basketball. **Guest Services:** coin laundry. **Cards:** AX, DS, MC, VI.

The following lodgings were either not evaluated or did not meet AAA rating requirements but are listed for your information only.

MONTANA VACATION RENTALS **Phone:** 406/752-4783

fyi Not evaluated. **Location:** 174 Lake Shore Dr 59901. Facilities, services, and decor characterize a mid-range property.

WHITE OAK OF MONTANA **Phone:** 406/857-2388

6/27-9/1	1P: $89-$99	2P: $99-$109	XP: $10	F12
3/1-6/26 & 12/1-2/28	1P: $79-$89	2P: $89-$99	XP: $10	F12
9/2-11/30	1P: $59	2P: $69	XP: $10	F12

fyi Small-scale Hotel. Too new to rate, opening scheduled for September 2003. **Location:** 7 mi s on US 2, jct SR 82. 4820 Hwy 93 S 59901. Fax: 406/857-2401. **Amenities:** 59 units, coffeemakers, microwaves, refrigerators, pool. **Terms:** cancellation fee imposed. **Cards:** AX, DS, MC, VI.

WHERE TO DINE

THE ALLEY CONNECTION **Lunch:** $3-$5 **Dinner:** $7-$13 **Phone:** 406/752-7077

Chinese. **Location:** On US 93; downtown; in Kalispell Grand Hotel. 22 1st St W 59901. **Hours:** 11 am-2:30 & 5-9 pm, Fri-9:30 pm, Sat noon-2:30 & 5-9:30 pm. Closed major holidays; also Sun. **Features:** Guests dine on a variety of Oriental dishes with foundations of steak, seafood and poultry. Asian beef—a lemongrass-marinated filet served with rice and stir-fried vegetables—proves to be a good choice. Servers are friendly and prompt. Casual dress; cocktails. **Parking:** on-site. **Cards:** AX, DS, MC, VI.

BOJANGLES DINER **Lunch:** $4-$10 **Dinner:** $4-$10 **Phone:** 406/755-3222

American. **Location:** 1.1 mi w from jct US 93. 1319 US 2 W 59901. **Hours:** 6 am-8 pm. Closed: 11/25, 12/25. **Features:** The 1950s are fondly remembered via memorabilia that covers nearly every available space. Home-style choices include all-day breakfast items and soups and pies prepared in house. Don't pass up huckleberry sour cream pie, which is made from berries collected in the nearby mountains. Casual dress. **Parking:** on-site. **Cards:** AX, DS, MC, VI.

THE BULLDOG PUB & STEAKHOUSE **Lunch:** $4-$6 **Dinner:** $8-$12 **Phone:** 406/752-7522

Steak & Seafood **Location:** Downtown. 208 1st Ave E 59901. **Hours:** 11 am-close. Closed major holidays; also Sun. **Reservations:** accepted, except Fri. **Features:** The longtime fixture and downtown favorite is where locals and visitors alike go for good food, good drink and good times. Traditional Irish pub decor is conducive to a convivial atmosphere. Casual dress; cocktails. **Parking:** on-site. **Cards:** AX, CB, DC, DS, JC, MC, VI.

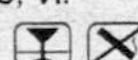

CAFE MAX — International — **Dinner:** $18-$26 — **Phone:** 406/755-7687

Location: Downtown. 121 Main St 59903. **Hours:** 5:30 pm-9 pm. Closed: 7/4, 11/25, 12/25; also Sun & Mon. **Reservations:** suggested. **Features:** The chef owns this inventive, upscale restaurant, which offers an eclectic and international menu centering on preparations of fresh meat and seafood and local, seasonal produce. On the town's main street, the unassuming storefront location gives no hint of the delights to be found within the walls. A favorite of locals and tourists alike, this place should be the destination of anyone seeking a satisfying dining experience in the Flathead Valley. Casual dress; beer & wine only. **Parking:** street. **Cards:** MC, VI.

CHINATOWN RESTAURANT — Chinese — **Lunch:** $5-$11 **Dinner:** $5-$11 — **Phone:** 406/755-2401

Location: 0.8 mi w from jct US 93. 1031 US 2 W 59901. **Hours:** 11 am-9:30 pm, Fri & Sat-10 pm. Closed: 11/25, 12/25. **Features:** Close to lodgings and shopping, the casual restaurant offers a buffet, as well as cooked-to-order menu items. Casual dress. **Parking:** on-site. **Cards:** AX, DS, MC, VI.

CISLO'S — American — **Lunch:** $5-$7 **Dinner:** $9-$12 — **Phone:** 406/756-7330

Location: Just n of jct US 2 and SR 82. 2046 US 2 E 59901. **Hours:** 6 am-8 pm, Sun 7 am-3 pm. **Features:** As it has for generations, the longtime family-owned favorite continues to serve no-nonsense home-style food to local families. The relaxed atmosphere evokes the feel of a home kitchen. Casual dress. **Parking:** on-site. **Cards:** AX, CB, DC, DS, JC, MC, VI.

FENDERS RESTAURANT — Steak & Seafood — **Dinner:** $10-$40 — **Phone:** 406/752-3000

Location: Jct US 2, 7.8 mi n on US 93. 4090 Hwy 93 N 59904. **Hours:** 4 pm-10 pm, Sun from 11 am. Closed: 12/25. **Reservations:** suggested. **Features:** The menu has something for everyone, with entrees based on a foundation of steak, seafood and pan-fried chicken. Try the hearty turkey soup — loaded with turkey and vegetables. The view of Flathead Valley is consistent with the pleasant country setting. Casual dress; cocktails. **Parking:** on-site. **Cards:** AX, DS, MC, VI.

FINISH LINE CASINO, RESTAURANT & LOUNGE — American — **Lunch:** $4-$12 **Dinner:** $4-$12 — **Phone:** 406/257-2441

Location: 0.7 mi w on US 2 from jct US 93, just s. 153 Meridian Rd 59901. **Hours:** 7 am-8 pm, Fri & Sat-10 pm. **Features:** Patrons can choose from a variety of foods at the casual, fun restaurant. Local blues society performances take place six nights a week. Casual dress; cocktails; entertainment. **Parking:** on-site. **Cards:** MC, VI.

GENKI — Asian — **Lunch:** $5-$8 **Dinner:** $5-$14 — **Phone:** 406/257-8889

Location: Downtown. 302 Main St 59901. **Hours:** 11 am-2:30 & 4-9:30 pm. Closed: 1/1, 11/25, 12/25; also Sun. **Reservations:** accepted. **Features:** The convenient downtown restaurant centers its menu on sushi and sashimi. Those who prefer their fish cooked also can choose from a full array of traditional Asian dishes. Casual dress; beer & wine only. **Parking:** on-site. **Cards:** AX, DC, MC, VI.

JULIE'S CENTER STREET CAFE — American — **Lunch:** $5-$8 — **Phone:** 406/755-7171

Location: Downtown. 200 E Center St 59901. **Hours:** 6:30 am-3 pm, Sun from 8 am. Closed: 11/25, 12/25; also Mon. **Features:** The cozy family restaurant serves breakfast all day, in addition to a variety of burgers, sandwiches, soups and salads. Made from a family recipe, the homemade sauerkraut, with or without a sandwich, is delicious. Casual dress. **Parking:** on-site. **Cards:** MC, VI.

THE KNEAD CAFE — International — **Lunch:** $4-$9 **Dinner:** $7-$15 — **Phone:** 406/755-7510

Location: Corner of 2nd Ave W and 1st St; downtown. 25 2nd Ave W 59901. **Hours:** 8 am-close, Sun 9 am-3 pm, Mon 8 am-3 pm. Closed: 1/1, 11/25, 12/25. **Reservations:** suggested. **Features:** Self-billed as "a spirited fusion of food, art and music," the cafe serves an eclectic mix of food from New Orleans gumbo to Mexican fajitas to Greek spanakopita. Breads baked in house are worth the visit themselves. Casual dress; beer & wine only. **Parking:** on-site. **Cards:** MC, VI.

MONTANA COFFEE TRADERS — Coffee/Espresso — **Lunch:** $4-$6 — **Phone:** 406/756-2326

Location: Downtown. 326 W Center St 59901. **Hours:** 7 am-5 pm, Sun 9 am-2 pm. Closed major holidays. **Features:** The eclectic, popular restaurant roasts its own coffee beans for sale and specializes in espresso drinks. Service is limited, but the soups, salads and sandwiches are generous and well-prepared. The in-house bakery produces some of the best dessert bars, muffins, scones and brownies in town. Casual dress. **Parking:** on-site. **Cards:** AX, MC, VI.

NICKEL CHARLIE'S CASINO & EATERY — American — **Lunch:** $4-$6 **Dinner:** $8-$14 — **Phone:** 406/257-7756

Location: 1.3 mi e of jct US 93. 1275 US 2 E 59901. **Hours:** 6 am-10 pm, Fri & Sat-11 pm. Closed: 12/25. **Features:** The restaurant, which serves good, attractively priced food in large portions, attracts locals and tourists alike. The staff provides service with a smile. Try a free pull on the antique slot machine for the chance to win prizes of food and discounts. Casual dress; beer & wine only. **Parking:** on-site. **Cards:** AX, DC, DS, MC, VI.

PAINTED HORSE GRILLE — American — **Lunch:** $6-$7 **Dinner:** $13-$20 — **Phone:** 406/257-7035

Location: On US 93; downtown; in Kalispell Grand Hotel. 110 Main St 59901. **Hours:** 11:30 am-2:30 & 5:30-9 pm, Sat from 5:30 pm. Closed major holidays; also Sun. **Reservations:** suggested. **Features:** The restaurant is a quietly elegant study in clean lines, neutral colors and soft lighting, which blend to create a quiet oasis equally perfect for a business lunch or special-occasion dinner. Whether it's large, hot or cold pasta dishes, sandwiches served on French baguettes or daily specials such as sauteed trout with lemon cream sauce, there is something here for everyone. Casual dress; cocktails. **Parking:** on-site (fee). **Cards:** AX, MC, VI.

ROCCO'S **Dinner:** $15-$20 **Phone:** 406/756-5834

Italian

Location: 8 mi ne from jct US 93. 3796 US 2 E 59901. **Hours:** 5 pm-close. Closed: 7/4, 11/25, 12/25; also Sun in winter & Mon. **Reservations:** suggested. **Features:** Although the menu of traditional fare focuses heavily on pasta selections, it also lists seafood and steak entrees. Everything, including the pasta, is made on the premises and cooked to order. Casual dress; beer & wine only. **Parking:** on-site. **Cards:** AX, DS, MC, VI.

SANDY'S MERIDIAN DELICATESSEN **Lunch:** $3-$7 **Phone:** 406/257-9525

Deli/Subs Sandwiches

Location: 0.7 mi w on US 2 from jct US 93, just n. 690 N Meridian Rd 59901. **Hours:** 10:30 am-4 pm, Sat 11 am-3 pm. Closed major holidays; also Sun. **Features:** In an office building, the bright, cheery restaurant prepares a variety of sandwiches with house-roasted meats and bread baked in house. Homemade soups are thick and rich, and the bakery produces wonderful desserts. Casual dress. **Parking:** on-site. **Cards:** AX, MC, VI.

SPENCER & CO **Dinner:** $11-$19 **Phone:** 406/756-8941

Steak House

Location: 7.3 mi n from jct US 2. 4010 US 93 N 59901. **Hours:** 5 pm-10 pm. Closed major holidays. **Features:** The classic steakhouse serves large, succulent cuts of beef on a sizzling platter. Although beef occupies the spotlight, chicken, seafood and pasta also have a place on the menu. Casual dress; cocktails. **Parking:** on-site. **Cards:** AX, MC, VI.

THING-A-MA-BOB'S **Lunch:** $4-$8 **Dinner:** $4-$13 **Phone:** 406/752-1447

American

Location: Jct of Center St; downtown. 7 1st Ave E 59901. **Hours:** 8 am-3 pm, Fri & Sat-8 pm; 8 am-8 pm 5/31-6/6. Closed: 4/11, 11/25, 12/25. **Features:** The casual, unpretentious restaurant specializes in breakfast and their signature sandwich, the Thing-a-Ma-Bob, which is a fresh chicken breast, broccoli, red onion and sweet red peppers grilled in a unique sauce, all served on a toasted baguette topped with a three-cheese blend. Casual dress. **Parking:** on-site. **Cards:** AX, CB, DC, DS, JC, MC, VI.

WHEAT MONTANA BAKERY & DELI **Lunch:** $4-$8 **Dinner:** $4-$8 **Phone:** 406/257-6530

Deli/Subs Sandwiches

Location: Downtown. 405 Main St 59901. **Hours:** 6:30 am-7 pm, Sun 8 am-4 pm. Closed major holidays. **Features:** The bright, comfortable restaurant specializes in fast takeout service or on-site dining on made-to-order sandwiches, soups, cinnamon rolls and muffins. Breads and bagels are made from chemical-free flour freshly ground from Montana wheat. Casual dress. **Parking:** on-site. **Cards:** MC, VI.

The following restaurants have not been evaluated by AAA but are listed for your information only.

BARLEY'S BREWHOUSE & GRILL **Phone:** 406/756-2222

fyi

Not evaluated. **Location:** 285 N Main St 59901. **Features:** The sleek, attractive restaurant features steaks, seafood and pasta, as well as a lunch menu with many sandwiches and salads.

ROMANO'S ITALIAN RISTORANTE **Phone:** 406/755-4441

fyi

Not evaluated. **Location:** 139 1st Ave W. **Features:** On the menu are fresh grilled seafood, pasta, filet mignon and oysters on the half shell.

THAI PALACE RESTAURANT **Phone:** 406/756-7956

fyi

Not evaluated. **Location:** 319 Main St 59901. **Features:** The casual storefront main street restaurant serves a variety of traditional Thai food as well as other Asian dishes.

LAKESIDE pop. 1,679

WHERE TO STAY

BAYSHORE RESORT MOTEL INC **Phone:** 406/844-3131

AAA SAVE

Motel

6/15-9/1	2P: $105-$165	XP: $7	F6
3/1-4/15	2P: $60-$105	XP: $7	F6
9/2-2/28	2P: $55-$105	XP: $7	F6
4/16-6/14	2P: $55-$95	XP: $7	F6

Location: On US 93; center. 616 Lakeside Blvd 59922 (PO Box 375). Fax: 406/844-2737. **Facility:** 16 units. 13 one- and 1 two-bedroom standard units with efficiencies. 2 one-bedroom suites ($95-$165) with kitchens. 2 stories, exterior corridors. **Parking:** on-site, winter plug-ins. **Terms:** office hours 8 am-11 pm, weekly rates available, package plans - off season. **Leisure Activities:** whirlpool, rental canoes, rental sailboats, boat dock, fishing. *Fee:* boat slips. **Business Services:** meeting rooms. **Cards:** MC, VI. **Special Amenities: free local telephone calls and preferred room (subject to availability with advanced reservations).**

SOME UNITS

FLATHEAD LAKE SUITES **Phone:** 406/844-2204

Condominium

6/16-9/15	1P: $115-$131	2P: $115-$131	XP: $35
3/1-6/15 & 9/16-2/28	1P: $90-$105	2P: $90-$105	XP: $35

Location: 1.7 mi s on US 93, 2 mi e, stay right on paved road. 829 Angel Point Rd 59922 (PO Box 768). **Facility:** A lakeside gazebo at this property features a grill and bench swings. Designated smoking area. 3 one-bedroom standard units with kitchens. 2 stories (no elevator), exterior corridors. **Parking:** on-site, winter plug-ins. **Terms:** 3 night minimum stay, 21 day cancellation notice-fee imposed. **Amenities:** *Some:* irons. **Leisure Activities:** boating, canoeing, boat dock, fishing, horseshoes.

SUNRISE VISTA INN
Phone: 406/844-0231

Motel

7/1-8/31	2P: $80-$125	XP: $5
5/24-6/30 & 9/1-9/30	2P: $72-$100	XP: $5

Location: North edge of town on US 93. 7005 US 93 59922 (PO Box 827). **Facility:** Designated smoking area. 9 units. 7 one-bedroom standard units. 2 one-bedroom suites. 1 story, exterior corridors. *Bath:* combo or shower only. **Parking:** on-site. **Terms:** open 5/24-9/30, office hours 8 am-11 pm, 10 day cancellation notice-fee imposed, small pets only ($10 fee). **Leisure Activities:** boat dock, fishing. **Cards:** DS, MC, VI.

SOME UNITS
ASK FEE / /

WHERE TO DINE

The following restaurant has not been evaluated by AAA but is listed for your information only.

BLUESTONE GRILL & TOP
Phone: 406/844-2583

fyi

Not evaluated. **Location:** 306 Stoner Loop Rd. **Features:** The warm and inviting restaurant evokes a western feel with the woodwork and stone decor and decorative lighting. Try the best of two worlds in the seafood Newburg pasta.

LAUREL pop. 6,255

WHERE TO STAY

LAUREL SUPER 8 *Book at aaa.com*
Phone: (406)628-6888

Small-scale Hotel

7/1-8/31 [ECP]	1P: $79-$94	2P: $84-$99
5/1-6/30 [ECP]	1P: $69-$84	2P: $74-$89
3/1-4/30 & 9/1-2/28 [ECP]	1P: $62-$79	2P: $67-$84

Location: I-90, exit 434, just n, just e. 205 SE 4th St 59044. Fax: 406/628-6888. **Facility:** 60 units. 51 one-bedroom standard units. 9 one-bedroom suites. 3 stories, interior corridors. *Bath:* combo or shower only. **Parking:** on-site, winter plug-ins. **Terms:** cancellation fee imposed, pets ($10 extra charge). **Amenities:** voice mail. *Some:* safes, hair dryers. **Pool(s):** heated indoor. **Leisure Activities:** whirlpool, exercise room. **Guest Services:** coin laundry. **Business Services:** meeting rooms. **Cards:** AX, DC, DS, MC, VI.

SOME UNITS
ASK FEE DATA PORT / /

LEWISTOWN pop. 5,813

WHERE TO STAY

B & B MOTEL
Phone: (406)538-5496

SAVE

Motel

5/15-11/15	1P: $41-$46	2P: $47-$60	XP: $4	F11
3/1-5/14 & 11/16-2/28	1P: $36-$45	2P: $40-$55	XP: $4	F11

Location: Downtown. 520 E Main St 59457. Fax: 406/538-4550. **Facility:** 36 units. 35 one- and 1 two-bedroom standard units, some with efficiencies. 2 stories (no elevator), exterior corridors. *Bath:* combo or shower only. **Parking:** on-site, winter plug-ins. **Terms:** pets ($3 extra charge). **Cards:** AX, DS, MC, VI. **Special Amenities: free local telephone calls and early check-in/late check-out.**

SOME UNITS
FEE / /

LIBBY pop. 2,626

WHERE TO STAY

SANDMAN MOTEL
Phone: (406)293-8831

Motel

5/1-10/31	1P: $39-$59	2P: $49-$62	XP: $8	F10
3/1-4/30	1P: $37-$47	2P: $39-$49	XP: $5	F10
11/1-2/28	1P: $35-$45	2P: $39-$49	XP: $5	F10

Location: Just w on US 2 from jct SR 37. Located in a quiet area. 688 US Hwy 2 W 59923. Fax: 406/293-3720. **Facility:** 16 one-bedroom standard units. 2 stories (no elevator), exterior corridors. **Parking:** on-site, winter plug-ins. **Terms:** office hours 7 am-10:30 pm, cancellation fee imposed, small pets only (in smoking units). **Cards:** AX, DS, MC, VI.

SOME UNITS
ASK / /

SUPER 8 MOTEL *Book at aaa.com*
Phone: 406/293-2771

SAVE

Small-scale Hotel

All Year	1P: $44-$60	2P: $50-$78	XP: $5

Location: Just w on US 2 from jct SR 37. 448 US 2 W 59923. Fax: 406/293-9871. **Facility:** 42 one-bedroom standard units. 2 stories (no elevator), interior corridors. **Parking:** on-site, winter plug-ins. **Terms:** pets ($5 extra charge). **Pool(s):** small heated indoor. **Business Services:** meeting rooms. **Cards:** AX, DC, DS, MC, VI. **Special Amenities: free local telephone calls and early check-in/late check-out.**

SOME UNITS
FEE DATA PORT / /

VENTURE MOTOR INN
Phone: (406)293-7711

SAVE

Small-scale Hotel

5/1-9/30	1P: $49-$69	2P: $59-$79	XP: $5	F5
3/1-4/30 & 10/1-2/28	1P: $47-$60	2P: $52-$69	XP: $5	F5

Location: Just w on US 2 from jct SR 37. 443 US 2 W 59923. Fax: 406/293-3326. **Facility:** 71 one-bedroom standard units. 3 stories, interior corridors. **Parking:** on-site, winter plug-ins. **Amenities:** *Some:* irons. **Dining:** 6 am-9 pm, Sat from 7 am, Sun 7 am-3 pm; 6 am-8 pm 10/1-5/1. **Pool(s):** heated indoor. **Leisure Activities:** whirlpool. **Guest Services:** valet laundry. **Business Services:** meeting rooms. **Cards:** AX, CB, DC, DS, MC, VI. **Special Amenities: free continental breakfast and free newspaper.**

SOME UNITS
DATA PORT / /

WHERE TO DINE

HENRY'S — American — **Lunch:** $4-$12 **Dinner:** $4-$12 **Phone:** 406/293-7911

Location: Just w on US 2 from jct SR 37. 405 W 9th St 59923. **Hours:** 6 am-9 pm. Closed: 11/25, 12/25. **Features:** Traditional homemade fare is served at this informal coffee shop and adjoining dining room that sports an antique-accented decor. The service staff's friendly demeanor adds a comfortably homey touch to your dining experience. The prices are good, too. Casual dress. **Parking:** on-site. **Cards:** MC, VI.

HIDDEN CHAPEL Historic — Continental — **Lunch:** $6-$7 **Dinner:** $10-$20 **Phone:** 406/293-2928

Location: Just e on US 2 from jct SR 37, just s. 1207 Utah Ave 59923. **Hours:** 11 am-2 & 5-10 pm. Closed: 1/1, 11/25, 12/25; also Sun. **Reservations:** suggested, holidays. **Features:** The Victorian decor complements this 1900s quaint neighborhood church. Lunch features sandwiches, soup and salad; dinner highlights beef, pasta, fresh seafood and chicken entrees. Seasonal patio dining is available. The food and water are chemical free. Casual dress; beer & wine only. **Parking:** street. **Cards:** MC, VI.

LINCOLN pop. 1,100

WHERE TO STAY

LEEPER'S PONDEROSA MOTEL — SAVE — Motel — **Phone:** 406/362-4333

All Year [CP] 1P: $40-$47 2P: $47-$52 XP: $5 F5

Location: Just w on SR 200. Hwy 200 & 1st Ave 59639 (PO Box 326). Fax: 406/362-4261. **Facility:** 15 one-bedroom standard units, some with efficiencies (no utensils). 1 story, exterior corridors. *Bath:* combo or shower only. **Parking:** on-site, winter plug-ins. **Terms:** 3 day cancellation notice-fee imposed, pets ($5 extra charge). **Leisure Activities:** sauna, whirlpool. **Cards:** AX, DS, MC, VI.

FEE / SOME UNITS

LIVINGSTON pop. 6,851

WHERE TO STAY

BEST WESTERN YELLOWSTONE INN & CONFERENCE CENTER — SAVE — Small-scale Hotel — *Book at aaa.com* — **Phone:** (406)222-6110

6/1-9/15 [ECP] 1P: $89-$129 2P: $89-$129 XP: $10 F17
3/1-5/31 & 9/16-2/28 [ECP] 1P: $49-$89 2P: $49-$89 XP: $10 F17

Location: I-90, exit 333, just n. 1515 W Park St 59047. Fax: 406/222-3357. **Facility:** 98 one-bedroom standard units. 3 stories, interior corridors. **Parking:** on-site, winter plug-ins. **Terms:** weekly rates available, small pets only ($10 extra charge). **Amenities:** irons, hair dryers. *Some:* high-speed Internet (fee). **Dining:** 6 am-2 & 4-9 pm, Fri & Sat-10 pm, cocktails. **Pool(s):** heated indoor. **Guest Services:** valet and coin laundry, airport transportation-Mission Field Airport. **Business Services:** meeting rooms, business center. **Cards:** AX, CB, DC, DS, JC, MC, VI. **Special Amenities: free expanded continental breakfast and free local telephone calls.**

FEE / SOME UNITS / DATA PORT

DEL MAR MOTEL INC — SAVE — Motel — **Phone:** 406/222-3120

6/9-8/28 1P: $48-$53 2P: $67-$74 XP: $5 F18
3/1-6/8 & 8/29-10/1 1P: $41-$46 2P: $55-$60 XP: $5 F18
10/2-2/28 1P: $34-$38 2P: $42-$47 XP: $5 F18

Location: I-90, exit 330, 1.9 mi e on I-90 business loop. Located in a quiet area. 1201 Hwy 10 W 59047. Fax: 406/222-5474. **Facility:** 32 one-bedroom standard units, some with kitchens. 1 story, exterior corridors. **Parking:** on-site, winter plug-ins. **Terms:** 3 day cancellation notice-fee imposed, pets ($5 extra charge). **Pool(s):** heated outdoor. **Leisure Activities:** barbecue grills, playground, basketball. **Cards:** AX, DS, MC, VI. **Special Amenities: free local telephone calls.**

FEE / SOME UNITS

ECONO LODGE — SAVE — Small-scale Hotel — *Book at aaa.com* — **Phone:** (406)222-0555

All Year [CP] 1P: $45-$99 2P: $45-$99 XP: $5 F18

Location: I-90, exit 333, just n on US 89, then just w. 111 Rogers Ln 59047 (PO Box 1379). Fax: 406/222-9588. **Facility:** 50 one-bedroom standard units. 2 stories (no elevator), interior corridors. *Bath:* combo or shower only. **Parking:** on-site, winter plug-ins. **Terms:** cancellation fee imposed, pets ($5 extra charge). **Pool(s):** heated indoor. **Leisure Activities:** whirlpool. **Guest Services:** coin laundry. **Business Services:** meeting rooms. **Cards:** AX, CB, DC, DS, MC, VI. **Special Amenities: free continental breakfast and free local telephone calls.**

FEE / SOME UNITS / DATA PORT

LIVINGSTON COMFORT INN — Small-scale Hotel — *Book at aaa.com* — **Phone:** 406/222-4400

All Year 1P: $50-$100 2P: $55-$105 XP: $5 F18

Location: I-90, exit 333, just s on US 89, then just w. 114 Loves Ln 59047. Fax: 406/222-7658. **Facility:** 49 units. 48 one-bedroom standard units. 1 one-bedroom suite with whirlpool. 2 stories (no elevator), interior/exterior corridors. **Parking:** on-site, winter plug-ins. **Terms:** [ECP] meal plan available. **Amenities:** safes (fee), irons, hair dryers. **Pool(s):** small heated indoor. **Leisure Activities:** whirlpool. **Guest Services:** coin laundry. **Business Services:** meeting rooms. **Cards:** AX, DC, DS, MC, VI.

ASK / SOME UNITS / DATA PORT

LIVINGSTON SUPER 8 MOTEL
Phone: 406/222-7711

Motel

6/10-8/25	1P: $63-$130	2P: $71-$130	
5/1-6/9	1P: $54-$110	2P: $59-$110	
8/26-2/28	1P: $58-$95	2P: $66-$95	
3/1-4/30	1P: $46-$95	2P: $61-$95	XP: $5 F12

Location: I-90, exit 333, just s on US 89. 105 Centennial Dr 59047 (PO Box 1385). Fax: 406/222-8654. **Facility:** 37 units. 36 one-bedroom standard units. 1 one-bedroom suite ($95-$130) with kitchen. 2 stories (no elevator), interior corridors. **Parking:** on-site, winter plug-ins. **Guest Services:** coin laundry. **Cards:** AX, DS, MC, VI.

SOME UNITS
ASK / /

TRAVELODGE LIVINGSTON *Book at aaa.com*
Phone: (406)222-6320

AAA SAVE
Motel

5/1-9/15	1P: $79-$89	2P: $89-$110	XP: $5
3/1-4/30 & 9/16-2/28	1P: $49-$59	2P: $59-$79	XP: $5

Location: I-90, exit 333, just n. 102 Rogers Ln 59047 (PO Box 1527). Fax: 406/222-2204. **Facility:** 43 one-bedroom standard units, some with whirlpools. 1 story, interior/exterior corridors. **Parking:** on-site, winter plug-ins. **Terms:** cancellation fee imposed, pets ($5 fee). **Amenities:** hair dryers. *Some:* DVD players. **Dining:** Clark's Crossing, Clark's Steak and Seafood, see separate listings. **Pool(s):** heated indoor. **Guest Services:** gift shop. **Business Services:** meeting rooms. **Cards:** AX, MC, VI. **Special Amenities: free full breakfast and free local telephone calls.**

SOME UNITS
FEE / /

WHERE TO DINE

BAGEL MANIA SISTER'S CAFE
Lunch: $3-$9 Phone: 406/222-8024

Deli/Subs Sandwiches

Location: I-90, exit 33, just n. 1178 Hwy 10 W 59047. **Hours:** 6 am-4 pm, Sat 8 am-2 pm, Sun 8 am-1 pm. Closed: 1/1, 12/25. **Features:** If you're looking for an alternative to the usual fast food, stop in and grab a bagel for the road! Sit and chat with the owners if you choose, but the seating is limited. Casual dress. **Parking:** on-site.

AC

CLARK'S CROSSING
Lunch: $5-$8 Dinner: $7-$18 Phone: 406/222-6320

American

Location: I-90, exit 333, just n; in Travelodge Livingston. 102 Rogers Ln 59047. **Hours:** 6 am-10 pm. Closed: 12/25. **Features:** This eatery offers tasty meals around the clock in an unpretentious atmosphere, and is located adjacent to the Travelodge Motel. Casual dress; cocktails. **Parking:** on-site. **Cards:** AX, DS, MC, VI.

CLARK'S STEAK AND SEAFOOD
Dinner: $11-$30 Phone: 406/222-6320

American

Location: I-90, exit 333, just n; in Travelodge Livingston. 102 Rogers Ln 59047. **Hours:** 5 pm-9 pm. Closed: 12/25. **Reservations:** accepted. **Features:** A bit more upscale than its sister eatery next door, the restaurant offers well-prepared steaks and seafoods in a casual, yet intimate setting. Casual dress; wine only. **Parking:** on-site. **Cards:** AX, DS, MC, VI.

MONTANA'S RIB & CHOP HOUSE
Lunch: $8-$18 Dinner: $8-$18 Phone: 406/222-9200

American

Location: Opposite train station; downtown. 119 W Park Rd 59047. **Hours:** 11:30 am-2 & 4-10 pm, Sat & Sun 4 pm-10 pm. Closed: 11/25, 12/25. **Features:** Restaurant specialties include 24-hour marinated baby back ribs and an 8-ounce Montana tenderloin, hand-cut, beef filet. Diners also can sink their teeth into a variety of chicken, seafood and other steak entrees. Casual dress; cocktails. **Parking:** street. **Cards:** AX, DS, MC, VI.

LOLO pop. 3,388

WHERE TO STAY

DAYS INN *Book at aaa.com*
Phone: 406/273-2121

Small-scale Hotel

5/1-12/31 [CP]	1P: $69-$99	2P: $69-$99	XP: $8
3/1-4/30 [CP]	1P: $59-$79	2P: $59-$79	XP: $8
1/1-2/28 [CP]	1P: $55-$75	2P: $55-$75	XP: $8

Location: North edge of town. 11225 US 93 S 59847. Fax: 406/273-0712. **Facility:** 40 units. 32 one-bedroom standard units. 8 one-bedroom suites ($65-$119) with efficiencies. 2 stories (no elevator), interior/exterior corridors. **Parking:** on-site. **Terms:** weekly rates available, pets ($10 extra charge). **Amenities:** hair dryers. **Cards:** AX, CB, DC, DS, MC, VI.

SOME UNITS
FEE / /

MALTA pop. 2,120

WHERE TO STAY

EDGEWATER INN & RV PARK
Phone: 406/654-1302

Motel

All Year	1P: $46-$56	2P: $51-$61	XP: $5

Location: Jct US 2 and US 191 N. 101 Hwy 2 W 59538 (PO Box 1630). Fax: 406/654-2104. **Facility:** 32 one-bedroom standard units. 1 story, exterior corridors. *Bath:* combo or shower only. **Parking:** on-site, winter plug-ins. **Amenities:** hair dryers. *Some:* irons. **Pool(s):** small heated indoor. **Leisure Activities:** sauna, whirlpool, exercise room. **Guest Services:** valet and coin laundry, area transportation. **Cards:** AX, DC, DS, MC, VI.

SOME UNITS
/ VCR /

MALTANA MOTEL Phone: 406/654-2610

SAVE

Motel

All Year 1P: $43-$50 2P: $48-$60 XP: $4 F6

Location: Just s of US 2 via US 191, just w; downtown. 138 S 1st Ave W 59538 (PO Box 1807). Fax: 406/654-1663. **Facility:** 19 one-bedroom standard units. 1 story, exterior corridors. **Parking:** on-site, winter plug-ins. **Guest Services:** airport transportation-Malta Municipie Airport. **Business Services:** fax (fee). **Cards.** AX, CB, DC, DS, MC, VI.

SOME UNITS

MANHATTAN pop. 1,396

WHERE TO DINE

The following restaurant has not been evaluated by AAA but is listed for your information only.

SIR SCOTT'S OASIS Phone: 406/284-6929

fyi

Not evaluated. **Location:** 204 W Railroad 59741. **Features:** A true Montana steakhouse. Known for serving large, quality cuts of Montana beef. Other choices include seafood and fried chicken. All meals come with vegetable tray, soup, salad and ice cream.

MARYSVILLE

WHERE TO DINE

THE MARYSVILLE HOUSE **Dinner:** $11-$35 **Phone:** 406/443-6677

Steak & Seafood

Location: SR 279, s at sign, 6 mi on gravel road, just n. 153 Main St 59640. **Hours:** 5 pm-10 pm. Closed: 1/1, 12/25; also Mon & Tues. **Features:** This very rustic, distinctive eatery in an old ghost town serves up T-bone steak, shrimp, oysters, grilled chicken, crab legs and lobster. Roast marshmallows over the campfire out back. A lively bar and down home service staff round out the experience. Casual dress; cocktails. **Parking:** street. **Cards:** MC, VI.

MILES CITY pop. 8,487

WHERE TO STAY

BEST WESTERN WAR BONNET INN *Book at aaa.com* **Phone:** (406)234-4560

SAVE

Motel

All Year [ECP] 1P: $65-$72 2P: $78 XP: $6 F17

Location: I-94, exit 138 (Broadus), 0.3 mi n. 1015 S Haynes Ave 59301 (PO Box 1055). Fax: 406/234-0363. **Facility:** 54 units. 51 one-bedroom standard units. 3 one-bedroom suites ($100-$120). 2 stories (no elevator), exterior corridors. **Parking:** on-site, winter plug-ins. **Terms:** pets ($5 extra charge). **Amenities:** irons, hair dryers. **Pool(s):** small heated indoor. **Leisure Activities:** sauna, whirlpool. **Business Services:** business center. **Cards:** AX, CB, DC, DS, MC, VI. **Special Amenities: free expanded continental breakfast and free local telephone calls.**

SOME UNITS

FEE

COMFORT INN MILES CITY **Phone:** 406/234-3141

Motel

5/16-9/16 [ECP]	1P: $75-$90	2P: $75-$90	XP: $5	F18
3/1-5/12 & 9/17-2/28 [ECP]	1P: $65-$80	2P: $70-$85	XP: $5	F18

Location: I-94, exit 138 (Broadus), just s. 1615 S Haynes Ave 59301. Fax: 406/234-2924. **Facility:** 49 one-bedroom standard units. 2 stories (no elevator), interior corridors. **Parking:** on-site, winter plug-ins. **Terms:** open 3/1-5/12 & 5/16-2/28. **Amenities:** *Some:* hair dryers. **Pool(s):** small heated indoor. **Leisure Activities:** whirlpool. **Guest Services:** valet and coin laundry, area transportation. **Business Services:** business center. **Cards:** AX, CB, DC, DS, JC, MC, VI.

SOME UNITS

ASK

GUESTHOUSE INTERNATIONAL INN & SUITES *Book at aaa.com* **Phone:** (406)232-3661

Small-scale Hotel

5/16-9/15	1P: $79-$139	2P: $79-$139	XP: $5	F17
9/16-11/30	1P: $72-$128	2P: $72-$128	XP: $5	F17
12/1-2/28	1P: $68-$125	2P: $68-$125	XP: $5	F17
3/1-5/15	1P: $65-$125	2P: $65-$125	XP: $5	F17

Location: I-94, exit 138 (Broadus), just s. 3111 Steel St 59301. Fax: 406/232-8943. **Facility:** 61 units. 56 one- and 2 two-bedroom standard units, some with whirlpools. 3 one-bedroom suites ($99-$150) with efficiencies. 2 stories (no elevator), interior corridors. *Bath:* combo or shower only. **Parking:** on-site. **Terms:** [BP] meal plan available, pets ($10 extra charge). **Amenities:** video library (fee), voice mail, irons, hair dryers. **Pool(s):** small heated indoor. **Leisure Activities:** whirlpool, exercise room. **Guest Services:** valet and coin laundry. **Business Services:** meeting rooms, business center. **Cards:** AX, CB, DC, DS, MC, VI.

SOME UNITS

ASK

FEE

HOLIDAY INN EXPRESS MILES CITY **Phone:** 406/234-1000

Small-scale Hotel

5/15-9/16 [ECP]	1P: $89-$115	2P: $89-$115	XP: $5	F18
3/1-5/14 & 9/17-2/28 [ECP]	1P: $75-$95	2P: $75-$95	XP: $5	F18

Location: I-94, exit 138 (Broadus), just s. 1720 S Haynes Ave 59301. Fax: 406/234-1365. **Facility:** 52 one-bedroom standard units, some with whirlpools. 2 stories (no elevator), interior corridors. *Bath:* combo or shower only. **Parking:** on-site, winter plug-ins. **Amenities:** irons, hair dryers. **Pool(s):** small heated indoor. **Leisure Activities:** whirlpool. **Guest Services:** valet and coin laundry. **Business Services:** meeting rooms. **Cards:** AX, CB, DC, DS, JC, MC, VI.

SOME UNITS

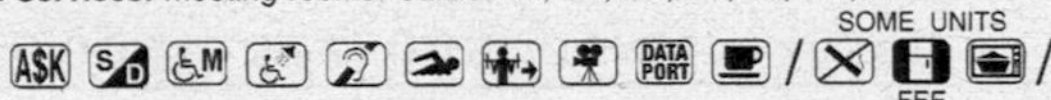

FEE

MISSOULA pop. 57,053

WHERE TO STAY

BEST INN & CONFERENCE CENTER-SOUTH *Book at aaa.com* **Phone:** (406)251-2665

Small-scale Hotel

5/1-9/30 [ECP]	1P: $84-$89	2P: $84-$89
10/1-2/28 [ECP]	1P: $65-$74	2P: $65-$74
3/1-4/30 [ECP]	1P: $65-$69	2P: $65-$69

Location: I-90, exit 101 (Reserve St), 5 mi s to Brooks (US 93), just w. 3803 Brooks St 59804. Fax: 406/251-5733. **Facility:** 91 one-bedroom standard units. 3 stories, interior corridors. *Bath:* combo or shower only. **Parking:** on-site, winter plug-ins. **Terms:** weekly rates available, package plans - 10/1-4/30. **Amenities:** irons, hair dryers. **Leisure Activities:** whirlpool. **Guest Services:** coin laundry, area transportation-community hospital. **Business Services:** meeting rooms. **Cards:** AX, CB, DC, DS, MC, VI. **Special Amenities: free expanded continental breakfast and free local telephone calls.** ***(See color ad below)***

SOME UNITS

BEST INN NORTH *Book at aaa.com* **Phone:** (406)542-7550

Small-scale Hotel

5/1-9/30 [ECP]	1P: $84-$89	2P: $84-$89
10/1-2/28 [ECP]	1P: $65-$74	2P: $65-$74
3/1-4/30 [ECP]	1P: $65-$69	2P: $65-$69

Location: I-90 W, exit 101 (Reserve St), just s. 4953 N Reserve St 59808. Fax: 406/721-5931. **Facility:** 67 one-bedroom standard units. 3 stories, interior corridors. *Bath:* combo or shower only. **Parking:** on-site, winter plug-ins. **Terms:** weekly rates available, package plans - 10/1-4/30, pets ($7 extra charge). **Amenities:** irons, hair dryers. **Leisure Activities:** whirlpool. **Guest Services:** coin laundry. **Cards:** AX, CB, DC, DS, MC, VI. ***(See color ad below)***

SOME UNITS

FEE FEE

BEST WESTERN GRANT CREEK INN *Book at aaa.com* **Phone:** (406)543-0700

Small-scale Hotel

6/1-9/30	1P: $119-$169	2P: $119-$169	XP: $10	F16
10/1-10/31	1P: $109-$159	2P: $109-$159	XP: $10	F16
11/1-2/28	1P: $89-$139	2P: $89-$139	XP: $10	F16
3/1-5/31	1P: $85-$135	2P: $85-$135	XP: $10	F16

Location: I-90, exit 101 (Reserve St), just n. 5280 Grant Creek Rd 59808. Fax: 406/543-0777. **Facility:** 126 units. 116 one-bedroom standard units. 10 one-bedroom suites ($135-$169). 4 stories, interior corridors. *Bath:* combo or shower only. **Parking:** on-site, winter plug-ins. **Terms:** [ECP] meal plan available, small pets only. **Amenities:** video games (fee), voice mail, irons, hair dryers. **Pool(s):** heated indoor. **Leisure Activities:** sauna, whirlpool, steamroom, exercise room. **Guest Services:** gift shop, valet and coin laundry, area transportation-mall & university. **Business Services:** meeting rooms. **Cards:** AX, CB, DC, DS, MC, VI. **Special Amenities: free expanded continental breakfast and free local telephone calls.**

SOME UNITS

FEE

BROOKS STREET MOTOR INN **Phone:** 406/549-5115

Motel

6/1-9/1 [CP]	1P: $54-$64	2P: $60-$70	XP: $6	F17
9/2-9/30 [CP]	1P: $50-$60	2P: $56-$66	XP: $6	F17
3/1-5/31 [CP]	1P: $40-$55	2P: $46-$61	XP: $6	F17
10/1-2/28 [CP]	1P: $40-$50	2P: $46-$56	XP: $6	F17

Location: I-90, exit 101 (Reserve St), 5 mi s, then just e. 3333 Brooks St 59801. **Facility:** 62 units. 58 one-bedroom standard units. 4 one-bedroom suites ($75-$125), some with whirlpools. 2 stories (no elevator), interior/exterior corridors. *Bath:* combo or shower only. **Parking:** on-site, winter plug-ins. **Terms:** cancellation fee imposed. **Guest Services:** coin laundry. **Cards:** AX, DS, MC, VI.

SOME UNITS

CAMPUS INN *Book at aaa.com* **Phone:** (406)549-5134

Motel

7/1-9/30 [ECP]	1P: $60-$120	2P: $60-$120
3/1-6/30 [ECP]	1P: $40-$100	2P: $40-$100
10/1-2/28 [ECP]	1P: $40-$80	2P: $40-$80

Location: I-90, exit 105 (Van Buren St), just s to Broadway, just w. 744 E Broadway 59802. **Facility:** 80 units. 73 one-bedroom standard units. 7 one-bedroom suites with kitchens (no utensils). 2 stories (no elevator), interior/exterior corridors. *Bath:* combo or shower only. **Parking:** on-site, winter plug-ins. **Terms:** pets ($6 extra charge). **Amenities:** video library (fee). **Pool(s):** small heated outdoor. **Leisure Activities:** whirlpool, limited exercise equipment. **Cards:** AX, CB, DC, DS, MC, VI.

SOME UNITS

FEE FEE

CITY CENTER MOTEL **Phone:** (406)543-3193

Motel

5/1-10/31	1P: $42-$48	2P: $45-$60	XP: $5	F12
3/1-4/30 & 11/1-2/28	1P: $35-$42	2P: $40-$45	XP: $5	F12

Location: I-90, exit 105 (Van Buren St), just s to Broadway, then just w. 338 E Broadway 59802. Fax: 407/728-3796. **Facility:** 16 units. 15 one- and 1 two-bedroom standard units. 2 stories (no elevator), interior/exterior corridors. *Bath:* combo or shower only. **Parking:** on-site, winter plug-ins. **Cards:** AX, DS, MC, VI. **Special Amenities: free local telephone calls and early check-in/late check-out.**

SOME UNITS

C'MON INN **Phone:** 406/543-4600

Small-scale Hotel

6/11-8/31	1P: $89-$109	2P: $89-$109	XP: $6	F13
4/30-6/10 & 9/1-2/28	1P: $79-$89	2P: $79-$89	XP: $6	F13
3/1-4/29	1P: $69-$79	2P: $69-$79	XP: $6	F13

Location: I-90, exit 101 (Reserve St), just n. 2775 Expo Pkwy 59808. Fax: 406/543-4664. **Facility:** 119 units. 105 one-bedroom standard units. 14 one-bedroom suites ($99-$179), some with kitchens. 3 stories, interior corridors. *Bath:* combo or shower only. **Parking:** on-site, winter plug-ins. **Terms:** [ECP] meal plan available. **Amenities:** irons, hair dryers. *Some:* high-speed Internet, dual phone lines. **Pool(s):** heated indoor, wading. **Leisure Activities:** whirlpools, exercise room. *Fee:* game room. **Guest Services:** valet laundry. **Business Services:** meeting rooms. **Cards:** AX, DS, MC, VI. ***(See color ad below)***

SOME UNITS

COMFORT INN *Book at aaa.com* **Phone:** (406)542-0888

Small-scale Hotel

4/30-9/30 [ECP]	1P: $90-$160	2P: $90-$160	XP: $10	F18
10/1-11/30 [ECP]	1P: $80-$150	2P: $80-$150	XP: $10	F18
3/1-4/29 & 12/1-2/28 [ECP]	1P: $70-$150	2P: $70-$150	XP: $10	F18

Location: I-90, exit 101 (Reserve St), 0.5 mi s. 4545 N Reserve St 59808. Fax: 406/543-6247. **Facility:** 52 one-bedroom standard units. 2 stories (no elevator), interior corridors. *Bath:* combo or shower only. **Parking:** on-site, winter plug-ins. **Terms:** 7 day cancellation notice, pets ($10 extra charge). **Amenities:** safes (fee), hair dryers. *Some:* irons. **Pool(s):** small heated indoor. **Leisure Activities:** whirlpool. **Guest Services:** valet and coin laundry. **Cards:** AX, CB, DC, DS, JC, MC, VI.

SOME UNITS

FEE FEE

DAYS INN/MISSOULA AIRPORT *Book at aaa.com* **Phone:** (406)721-9776

Small-scale Hotel

5/1-9/30 [CP]	1P: $79	2P: $84	XP: $5	F12
3/1-4/30 & 10/1-2/28 [CP]	1P: $56	2P: $61	XP: $5	F12

Location: I-90, exit 96, just n. Located next to truck parking. 8600 Truck Stop Rd 59808. Fax: 406/721-9781. **Facility:** 69 one-bedroom standard units. 2 stories (no elevator), interior corridors. **Parking:** on-site, winter plug-ins. **Terms:** pets ($5 extra charge). **Amenities:** hair dryers. **Leisure Activities:** whirlpool. **Guest Services:** valet and coin laundry. **Cards:** AX, DS, MC, VI. **Special Amenities: free continental breakfast and free local telephone calls.**

SOME UNITS

FEE

DOUBLETREE HOTEL MISSOULA/EDGEWATER *Book at aaa.com* **Phone:** (406)728-3100

Small-scale Hotel

5/13-10/15	1P: $129-$179	2P: $139-$189	XP: $10	F18
3/1-5/12 & 10/16-2/28	1P: $94-$139	2P: $104-$149	XP: $10	F18

Location: I-90, exit 105 (Van Buren St), just s, then w on Front St. 100 Madison 59802. Fax: 406/728-2530. **Facility:** 171 units. 170 one-bedroom standard units. 1 one-bedroom suite ($200-$275) with whirlpool. 2-3 stories, interior corridors. *Bath:* combo or shower only. **Parking:** on-site, winter plug-ins. **Terms:** [AP] meal plan available. **Amenities:** voice mail, irons. **Dining:** 6 am-10 pm, Fri & Sat-11 pm, cocktails. **Pool(s):** small heated outdoor. **Leisure Activities:** whirlpool, exercise room. **Guest Services:** gift shop, valet laundry. **Business Services:** meeting rooms. **Cards:** AX, CB, DC, DS, MC, VI. **Special Amenities: free newspaper.** ***(See color ad p 288)***

SOME UNITS

FEE

DOWNTOWN MOTEL — **Phone:** 406/549-5191

Motel

6/1-10/31	1P: $40-$43	2P: $45-$49	XP: $5	D7
3/1-5/31	1P: $38-$41	2P: $42-$45	XP: $5	D7
11/1-2/28	1P: $34-$36	2P: $40-$44	XP: $5	D7

Location: I-90, exit 105 (Van Buren St), just w. Located in a residential area. 502 E Broadway 59802. **Facility:** 22 one-bedroom standard units. 1 story, exterior corridors. *Bath:* combo or shower only. **Parking:** on-site, winter plug-ins. **Terms:** office hours 9 am-11 pm, cancellation fee imposed, pets ($6 extra charge). **Cards:** MC, VI. **Special Amenities: free local telephone calls and early check-in/late check-out.**

SOME UNITS

FEE

EXECUTIVE INN — **Phone:** (406)543-7221

Small-scale Hotel

7/1-8/31	1P: $69-$74	2P: $74-$79	XP: $8	F12
9/1-9/30	1P: $59-$64	2P: $64-$69	XP: $8	F12
3/1-6/30	1P: $54-$64	2P: $59-$69	XP: $8	F12
10/1-2/28	1P: $54-$59	2P: $59-$64	XP: $8	F12

Location: I-90, exit 104 (Orange St), 0.5 mi s to Broadway, 0.5 mi e to Washington, just s to Main St, just w. 201 E Main St 59802. **Facility:** 51 units. 50 one-bedroom standard units. 1 one-bedroom suite. 2 stories, exterior corridors. **Parking:** on-site, winter plug-ins. **Amenities:** irons, hair dryers. **Pool(s):** heated outdoor. **Cards:** AX, CB, DC, DS, MC, VI. **Special Amenities: free continental breakfast and free newspaper.**

SOME UNITS

FAMILY INN — **Phone:** (406)543-7371

Motel

6/16-9/5 [CP]	1P: $70-$74	2P: $74-$76	XP: $4
5/14-6/15 [CP]	1P: $58-$62	2P: $62-$66	XP: $4

Location: I-90, exit 105 (Van Buren St), just s, then just e. 1031 E Broadway 59802 (512 E Broadway). Fax: 406/549-9240. **Facility:** 30 one-bedroom standard units with efficiencies. 2 stories (no elevator), exterior corridors. *Bath:* shower only. **Parking:** on-site, winter plug-ins. **Terms:** open 5/14-9/5, office hours 6 am-11 pm, pets ($6 extra charge). **Pool(s):** small heated outdoor. **Guest Services:** coin laundry. **Cards:** AX, DS, MC, VI.

SOME UNITS

FEE

GOLDSMITH'S INN — **Phone:** (406)728-1585

Bed & Breakfast

5/15-10/1 [BP]	1P: $94-$134	2P: $104-$144	XP: $15	F10
10/2-2/28 [BP]	1P: $69-$109	2P: $79-$119	XP: $15	F10
3/1-5/14 [BP]	1P: $69-$95	2P: $79-$105	XP: $15	F10

Location: I-90, exit 105 (Van Buren St), just s, then just w. Located on the bank of the Clark Fork River. 809 E Front St 59802. Fax: 406/543-0045. **Facility:** A few blocks from the downtown business core, the inn is easily accessible to the university via a nearby pedestrian bridge. Smoke free premises. 8 one-bedroom standard units, some with whirlpools. 2 stories (no elevator), interior corridors. *Bath:* combo or shower only. **Parking:** on-site. **Terms:** 10 day cancellation notice-fee imposed. **Amenities:** irons, hair dryers. **Dining:** The Waterfront Pasta House, see separate listing. **Cards:** DS, MC, VI. **Special Amenities: free full breakfast.**

HAMPTON INN — *Book at aaa.com* — **Phone:** (406)549-1800

Small-scale Hotel

5/1-9/30	1P: $109-$119	2P: $109-$119
3/1-4/30 & 10/1-2/28	1P: $75-$85	2P: $75-$85

Location: I-90, exit 101 (Reserve St), just s. 4805 N Reserve St 59808. Fax: 406/549-1737. **Facility:** 61 one-bedroom standard units. 4 stories, interior corridors. *Bath:* combo or shower only. **Parking:** on-site. **Terms:** [ECP] meal plan available, package plans - in winter, pets ($10 fee). **Amenities:** voice mail, irons, hair dryers. **Pool(s):** heated indoor. **Leisure Activities:** whirlpool, exercise room. **Guest Services:** valet laundry. **Business Services:** business center. **Cards:** AX, DC, DS, MC, VI.

SOME UNITS

FEE

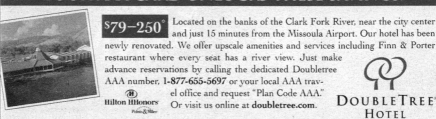

HOLIDAY INN EXPRESS-RIVERSIDE Book at aaa.com Phone: (406)549-7600

Small-scale Hotel

5/16-9/15 [CP] 1P: $89-$109
3/1-5/15 & 9/16-10/14 [CP] 1P: $70-$89
10/15-2/28 [CP] 1P: $69-$79

Location: I-90, exit 105 (Van Buren St), just s, then just e. 1021 E Broadway 59802. Fax: 406/543-2223. **Facility:** 95 units. 80 one-bedroom standard units. 15 one-bedroom suites ($140), some with whirlpools. 4 stories, interior corridors. *Bath:* combo or shower only. **Parking:** on-site, winter plug-ins. **Terms:** check-in 4 pm. **Amenities:** high-speed Internet, dual phone lines, voice mail, irons, hair dryers. **Leisure Activities:** exercise room. **Guest Services:** valet and coin laundry. **Business Services:** meeting rooms, business center. **Cards:** AX, CB, DC, DS, MC, VI.

SOME UNITS

HOLIDAY INN MISSOULA-PARKSIDE Book at aaa.com Phone: (406)721-8550

Small-scale Hotel

All Year 1P: $69-$119 2P: $69-$119

Location: I-90, exit 104 (Orange St), 0.5 mi s to Broadway, just e to Pattee St, then just s. 200 S Pattee St 59802. Fax: 406/721-7427. **Facility:** 200 one-bedroom standard units. 3 stories, interior corridors. **Parking:** on-site. **Terms:** check-in 4 pm, 3 day cancellation notice, small pets only (in selected units). **Amenities:** high-speed Internet (fee), voice mail, irons, hair dryers. **Pool(s):** small heated indoor. **Leisure Activities:** sauna, whirlpool, exercise room. **Guest Services:** gift shop, valet laundry. **Business Services:** meeting rooms. **Cards:** AX, CB, DC, DS, JC, MC, VI.
(See color ad below & opposite title page)

SOME UNITS

HUBBARD'S PONDEROSA LODGE Phone: 406/543-3102

Motel

5/1-10/31 1P: $55 2P: $60-$65 XP: $5
3/1-4/30 & 11/1-2/28 1P: $45 2P: $50-$55 XP: $5

Location: I-90, exit 105 (Van Buren St), just s to Broadway, then w. 800 E Broadway 59802. **Facility:** 37 one-bedroom standard units. 2 stories (no elevator), interior/exterior corridors. **Parking:** on-site, winter plug-ins. **Cards:** AX, DC, DS, MC, VI. **Special Amenities: free local telephone calls and preferred room (subject to availability with advanced reservations).** Affiliated with Best Value Inn Brand Membership.

SOME UNITS

INN ON BROADWAY Book at aaa.com Phone: (406)543-7231

Small-scale Hotel

6/1-9/30 [ECP] 1P: $87-$97 2P: $94-$104 XP: $7 F18
3/1-5/31 & 10/1-11/30 [ECP] 1P: $67-$77 2P: $74-$84 XP: $7 F18
12/1-2/28 [ECP] 1P: $67-$74 2P: $74-$81 XP: $7 F18

Location: I-90, exit 104 (Orange St), 0.5 mi s, 1 mi w. 1609 W Broadway 59808. Fax: 406/728-1930. **Facility:** 79 one-bedroom standard units. 2 stories (no elevator), interior corridors. **Parking:** on-site. **Amenities:** voice mail, hair dryers. *Some:* dual phone lines. **Dining:** 2 restaurants, 11 am-10 pm, cocktails. **Pool(s):** small heated outdoor. **Leisure Activities:** whirlpool, exercise room. **Guest Services:** coin laundry. **Business Services:** meeting rooms. **Cards:** AX, DC, DS, MC, VI. **Special Amenities: free expanded continental breakfast and free local telephone calls.** ***(See color ad p 290)***

SOME UNITS

MICROTEL INN & SUITES Book at aaa.com Phone: (406)543-0959

Small-scale Hotel

5/1-10/14 [BP] 1P: $60-$80 2P: $70-$90 XP: $10 F16
3/1-4/30 & 10/15-2/28 [BP] 1P: $40-$60 2P: $50-$70 XP: $10 F16

Location: I-90, exit 101 (Reserve St), just s. 5059 N Reserve St 59808 (PO Box 16085). Fax: 406/543-0960. **Facility:** 81 one-bedroom standard units, some with whirlpools. 3 stories, interior corridors. *Bath:* combo or shower only. **Parking:** on-site. **Terms:** small pets only ($10 fee). **Amenities:** voice mail. *Some:* irons. **Business Services:** meeting rooms, business center. **Cards:** AX, DS, MC, VI.

SOME UNITS

FEE

MOUNTAIN VALLEY INN Phone: (406)728-4500

Small-scale Hotel

All Year [BP] 1P: $59-$149 2P: $69-$159 XP: $10 D15

Location: I-90, exit 104 (Orange St), 0.5 mi s, then just w. 420 W Broadway 59802. Fax: 406/728-9565. **Facility:** 60 one-bedroom standard units. 3 stories, interior/exterior corridors. *Bath:* combo or shower only. **Parking:** on-site, winter plug-ins. **Terms:** package plans. **Amenities:** hair dryers. **Guest Services:** coin laundry. **Cards:** AX, DS, MC, VI. **Special Amenities: free full breakfast and free local telephone calls.**
(See color ad p 290)

SOME UNITS

RAMADA LIMITED *Book at aaa.com* **Phone:** (406)721-3610

Small-scale Hotel

All Year	1P: $85	2P: $85	XP: $10	F18

Location: I-90, exit 104 (Orange St), just s. 801 N Orange St 59802. Fax: 406/721-8875. **Facility:** 81 one-bedroom standard units. 3 stories, interior corridors. **Parking:** on-site, winter plug-ins. **Terms:** [ECP] meal plan available, pets ($5 extra charge, in limited units). **Amenities:** video library (fee), hair dryers. **Leisure Activities:** exercise room. **Business Services:** meeting rooms. **Cards:** AX, CB, DC, DS, MC, VI. **Special Amenities: free expanded continental breakfast and free local telephone calls.**

SOME UNITS

FEE FEE

RED LION INN *Book at aaa.com* **Phone:** (406)728-3300

Small-scale Hotel

6/1-9/30	1P: $109-$119	2P: $119-$129	XP: $10	F17
10/1-10/31	1P: $89-$99	2P: $99-$109	XP: $10	F17
3/1-5/31	1P: $79-$89	2P: $89-$99	XP: $10	F17
11/1-2/28	1P: $69-$79	2P: $79-$89	XP: $10	F17

Location: I-90, exit 104 (Orange St), just s, then just w. 700 W Broadway 59802. Fax: 406/728-4441. **Facility:** 76 one-bedroom standard units. 2 stories (no elevator), exterior corridors. *Bath:* combo or shower only. **Parking:** on-site, winter plug-ins. **Terms:** cancellation fee imposed, [CP] meal plan available, pets ($5 extra charge). **Amenities:** voice mail, irons, hair dryers. **Pool(s):** heated outdoor. **Leisure Activities:** whirlpool, exercise room. **Guest Services:** sundries, valet and coin laundry. **Business Services:** meeting rooms, business center. **Cards:** AX, CB, DC, DS, MC, VI. ***(See ad below)***

SOME UNITS

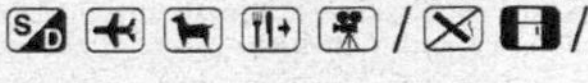

FEE FEE FEE FEE

REDWOOD LODGE **Phone:** (406)721-2110

Motel

All Year	1P: $55-$65	2P: $65-$75	XP: $5

Location: I-90, exit 96, just s. Located adjacent to truck parking. 8060 Hwy 93 N 59808. Fax: 406/721-2110. **Facility:** 41 units. 40 one-bedroom standard units. 1 two-bedroom suite with kitchen. 2 stories (no elevator), exterior corridors. *Bath:* combo or shower only. **Parking:** on-site. **Amenities:** hair dryers. **Guest Services:** coin laundry. **Cards:** AX, CB, DC, DS, MC, VI. **Special Amenities: free full breakfast and free local telephone calls.**

SOME UNITS

ROYAL MOTEL **Phone:** 406/542-2184

Motel

5/1-9/29	1P: $40-$44	2P: $44-$48	XP: $5
3/1-4/30 & 9/30-11/30	1P: $36-$40	2P: $40-$44	XP: $5
12/1-2/28	1P: $32-$36	2P: $36-$40	XP: $5

Location: I-90, exit 105 (Van Buren St), just s, then 0.5 mi w on Broadway. 338 Washington St 59802. **Facility:** 12 units. 8 one- and 4 two-bedroom standard units. 1 story, exterior corridors. **Parking:** on-site, winter plug-ins. **Terms:** weekly rates available, pets ($4 extra charge). **Cards:** AX, DS, MC, VI. **Special Amenities: free local telephone calls and early check-in/late check-out.**

SOME UNITS

FEE

RUBY'S INN & CONVENTION CENTER **Phone:** (406)721-0990

6/15-9/30 [BP]	1P: $85-$105	2P: $90-$120
5/1-6/14 [BP]	1P: $75-$95	2P: $80-$110
10/1-2/28 [BP]	1P: $69-$89	2P: $75-$105
3/1-4/30 [BP]	1P: $65-$85	2P: $70-$105

Small-scale Hotel **Location:** I-90, exit 101 (Reserve St), just s. 4825 N Reserve St 59808. Fax: 406/721-0990. **Facility:** 126 one-bedroom standard units, some with kitchens. 2 stories, interior/exterior corridors. *Bath:* combo or shower only. **Parking:** on-site, winter plug-ins. **Terms:** pets ($10 extra charge). **Amenities:** voice mail, irons, hair dryers. *Some:* high-speed Internet. **Pool(s):** heated outdoor. **Leisure Activities:** sauna, whirlpool, horseshoes. **Guest Services:** valet and coin laundry. **Business Services:** conference facilities, business center. **Cards:** AX, CB, DC, DS, MC, VI. **Special Amenities: free full breakfast and free local telephone calls.** ***(See color ad p 291)***

SOME UNITS

FEE / FEE FEE

SLEEP INN ***Book at aaa.com*** **Phone:** (406)543-5883

6/1-8/31 [ECP]	1P: $64-$79	2P: $64-$85	XP: $6 F
3/1-5/31 & 9/1-2/28 [ECP]	1P: $49-$69	2P: $55-$75	XP: $6 F

Small-scale Hotel **Location:** I-90, exit 101 (Reserve St), 5 mi s, then just e on Brooks St. 3425 Dore Ln 59801. Fax: 406/543-5883. **Facility:** 59 one-bedroom standard units. 3 stories, interior corridors. *Bath:* combo or shower only. **Parking:** on-site, winter plug-ins. **Terms:** small pets only (in smoking units). **Amenities:** irons. *Some:* hair dryers. **Pool(s):** small heated indoor. **Leisure Activities:** whirlpool. **Guest Services:** valet laundry. **Cards:** AX, CB, DC, DS, MC, VI.

SOME UNITS

SOUTHGATE INN — Phone: (406)251-2250

Small-scale Hotel

4/30-9/25 [ECP]	1P: $55-$85	2P: $55-$85
9/26-2/28 [ECP]	1P: $45-$72	2P: $45-$72
3/1-4/29 [ECP]	1P: $45-$62	2P: $45-$62

Location: I-90, exit 101 (Reserve St), 5 mi s to Brooks St, just e. 3530 Brooks St 59801. Fax: 406/251-2006. **Facility:** 81 one-bedroom standard units, some with whirlpools. 2 stories (no elevator), exterior corridors. *Bath:* combo or shower only. **Parking:** on-site, winter plug-ins. **Terms:** check-in 4 pm, weekly rates available, package plans, pets ($5-$8 extra charge). **Pool(s):** small heated outdoor. **Leisure Activities:** sauna, whirlpool, exercise room. **Guest Services:** valet and coin laundry. **Business Services:** meeting rooms. **Cards:** AX, DC, DS, MC, VI. **Special Amenities: free expanded continental breakfast and free local telephone calls.**

SOME UNITS FEE

SUPER 8-BROOKS ST *Book at aaa.com* — Phone: (406)251-2255

Small-scale Hotel

5/1-9/30 [ECP]	1P: $62-$75	2P: $66-$75	XP: $3	F12
10/1-2/28 [ECP]	1P: $50-$58	2P: $53-$58	XP: $3	F12
3/1-4/30 [ECP]	1P: $49-$57	2P: $52-$57	XP: $3	F12

Location: I-90, exit 101 (Reserve St), 5 mi s, just w. 3901 Brooks St 59804. Fax: 406/251-2989. **Facility:** 103 one-bedroom standard units. 3 stories (no elevator), interior corridors. **Parking:** on-site, winter plug-ins. **Terms:** pets ($3.50 extra charge, dogs only). **Guest Services:** coin laundry. **Cards:** AX, DC, DS, MC, VI.

SOME UNITS FEE FEE FEE

SUPER 8 MOTEL-RESERVE ST — Phone: 406/549-1199

Small-scale Hotel

5/1-9/30	1P: $65-$75	2P: $69-$79	XP: $3	F12
4/1-4/30	1P: $57-$67	2P: $60-$70	XP: $3	F12
10/1-2/28	1P: $50-$60	2P: $53-$63	XP: $3	F12
3/1-3/31	1P: $49-$59	2P: $52-$62	XP: $3	F12

Location: I-90, exit 101 (Reserve St), 0.4 mi s. 4703 N Reserve St 59808. Fax: 406/549-0677. **Facility:** 58 one-bedroom standard units. 3 stories, interior corridors. *Bath:* combo or shower only. **Parking:** on-site, winter plug-ins. **Terms:** cancellation fee imposed, weekly rates available, [CP] meal plan available. **Leisure Activities:** whirlpool. **Guest Services:** coin laundry. **Cards:** AX, DC, DS, MC, VI.

SOME UNITS

THUNDERBIRD MOTEL — Phone: (406)543-7251

Motel

5/1-9/30	1P: $75	2P: $75-$85	XP: $5
3/1-4/30 & 10/1-2/28	1P: $60	2P: $60-$70	XP: $5

Location: I-90, exit 105 (Van Buren St), just s to Broadway, then just e. 1009 E Broadway 59802. Fax: 406/543-7251. **Facility:** 30 units. 26 one- and 4 two-bedroom standard units, some with whirlpools. 2 stories (no elevator), interior/exterior corridors. **Parking:** on-site, winter plug-ins. **Amenities:** hair dryers. **Pool(s):** small heated indoor. **Leisure Activities:** whirlpool, exercise room. **Guest Services:** coin laundry. **Business Services:** meeting rooms. **Cards:** AX, DC, DS, MC, VI. ***(See color ad p 292)***

SOME UNITS

TRAVELERS INN MOTEL — Phone: (406)728-8330

Motel

5/16-9/30 [CP]	1P: $59-$69	2P: $59-$69	XP: $5	F12
3/1-5/15 & 10/1-2/28 [CP]	1P: $45-$59	2P: $49-$59	XP: $3	F12

Location: I-90, exit 101 (Reserve St), just s. 4850 N Reserve St 59808 (5453 Prospect Dr). Fax: 406/728-4435. **Facility:** 29 one-bedroom standard units. 1 story, exterior corridors. *Bath:* combo or shower only. **Parking:** on-site, winter plug-ins. **Terms:** small pets only. **Cards:** AX, CB, DC, DS, MC, VI. **Special Amenities: free continental breakfast and free local telephone calls.**

SOME UNITS

VAL-U-INN **Book at aaa.com**

Small-scale Hotel

6/1-8/31 [ECP]	1P: $55-$60	2P: $68-$72	XP: $6	F12
3/1-5/31 & 9/1-2/28 [ECP]	1P: $56-$60	2P: $66-$70	XP: $6	F12

Phone: 406/721-9600

Location: I-90, exit 101 (Reserve St), 5 mi s to US 93, 0.7 mi e. Located adjacent to a shopping mall. 3001 Brooks St 59801. Fax: 406/721-7208. **Facility:** 84 one-bedroom standard units. 3 stories, interior corridors. *Bath:* combo or shower only. **Parking:** on-site, winter plug-ins. **Amenities:** video library (fee), voice mail, hair dryers. *Some:* irons. **Leisure Activities:** sauna, whirlpool. **Guest Services:** valet and coin laundry. **Business Services:** meeting rooms. **Cards:** AX, CB, DC, DS, MC, VI.

SOME UNITS DATA PORT / VCR FEE /

WINGATE INN MISSOULA **Book at aaa.com**

SAVE

Small-scale Hotel

All Year [ECP]	1P: $94-$210	2P: $94-$210	XP: $10	F17

Phone: (406)541-8000

Location: I-90, exit 99 (Airway Blvd), just s to E Harrier. 5252 Airway Blvd 59808. Fax: 406/541-8008. **Facility:** 100 units. 96 one-bedroom standard units. 4 one-bedroom suites, some with whirlpools. 3 stories, interior corridors. *Bath:* combo or shower only. **Parking:** on-site. **Amenities:** video games (fee), high-speed Internet, dual phone lines, voice mail, safes, irons, hair dryers. **Pool(s):** heated indoor, wading. **Leisure Activities:** whirlpool, waterslide, indoor water park. **Guest Services:** coin laundry, area transportation. **Business Services:** meeting rooms, business center. **Cards:** AX, CB, DC, DS, JC, MC, VI. **Special Amenities: free expanded continental breakfast and free local telephone calls.** *(See color ad p 292)*

SOME UNITS DATA PORT / /

WHERE TO DINE

THE DEPOT Historic — **Dinner:** $11-$20 — **Phone:** 406/728-7007

American

Location: I-90, exit 104 (Orange St), just s, e on Spruce, then n on Ryman. 201 W Railroad St 59802. **Hours:** 5:30 pm-10:30 pm. Closed: 11/25, 12/25; also Super Bowl Sun. **Reservations:** suggested. **Features:** This historic railroad hotel offers casual dining either in the pub or the dining room and features fresh seafood, hand cut steak, pasta and choice prime rib. The atmosphere is bustling and busy; the service prompt. Patio seating is available in season. Casual dress; cocktails. **Parking:** on-site. **Cards:** AX, DC, DS, MC, VI.

THE MUSTARD SEED ASIAN CAFE — **Lunch:** $6-$9 — **Dinner:** $9-$12 — **Phone:** 406/542-7333

International

Location: I-90, exit 101 (Reserve St), 5 mi s to US 93, 0.7 mi e, just n; in Southgate Mall. 2901 Brooks St 59801. **Hours:** 11 am-9 pm, Fri & Sat-10 pm. Closed major holidays. **Features:** Located in Southgate Mall with convenient private entrance, the restaurant serves a blend of Pacific Rim cuisines geared to American tastes. Casual dress; cocktails. **Parking:** on-site. **Cards:** AX, CB, DC, DS, JC, MC, VI.

PERUGIA — **Dinner:** $17-$27 — **Phone:** 406/543-3757

American

Location: I-90, exit 104 (Orange St), s to Broadway, then just w. 1106 W Broadway 59802. **Hours:** 5 pm-9 pm, Fri & Sat-10 pm. Closed: Sun. **Reservations:** suggested. **Features:** Original ceramic and fabric art accents the family-owned eatery, which specializes in Old World hospitality and comparable cuisine. The menu—Mediterranean, European and Japanese—is nearly as eclectic as the decor. The service staff is knowledgeable and will offer guests an extensive menu of clever martinis and one of the best single-malt scotch lists in town. Casual dress; cocktails. **Parking:** on-site. **Cards:** AX, DS, MC, VI.

RED BIRD — **Dinner:** $15-$29 — **Phone:** 406/549-2906

Specialty

Location: I-90, exit 104 (Orange St), s to Broadway, e to Higgins Ave, s to Front St, then just w; main entrance in alley between Front St and Main. 120 W Front St 59802. **Hours:** 5 pm-9:30 pm. Closed: 7/4; also Sun, Mon & 12/24-12/28. **Reservations:** suggested. **Features:** This chef-owned, intimate hideaway is known for inventive seasonal cuisine served in quiet, architecturally dramatic surroundings. The menu consists of beef, chicken and seafood, along with appetizers such as won tons stuffed with brie and candied pecans. Casual dress; beer & wine only. **Parking:** street. **Cards:** AX, DS, MC, VI.

THE SHACK CAFE 222 — **Lunch:** $5-$9 — **Dinner:** $7-$16 — **Phone:** 406/549-9903

American

Location: Downtown. 222 W Main St 59801. **Hours:** 7 am-3 & 5-9:30 pm, Sat & Sun 7 am-9:30 pm, Mon & Tues 7 am-3 pm. Closed: 12/25. **Features:** Innovative freshly prepared foods, a multitude of vegetarian dishes and exceptional breakfast items are a hallmark here. Try the light Greek fettuccine, resplendent with olives, feta cheese and fresh spinach leaves. Patio seating is available in summer. Casual dress; beer & wine only. **Parking:** street. **Cards:** AX, MC, VI.

SHADOWS KEEP — **Dinner:** $16-$24 — **Phone:** 406/728-5132

Steak & Seafood

Location: I-90, exit 101 (Reserve St), 5.4 mi s to 39th St, 1.2 mi e to High Park Way, 0.6 mi s to Whitaker Dr, 0.5 mi w to Ben Hogan Dr, then just s. 102 Ben Hogan Dr 59803. **Hours:** 5 pm-10 pm. Closed: 12/25. **Reservations:** suggested. **Features:** In a quiet residential area high on a hill overlooking the city, the restaurant resides in an impressive building—a turreted faux castle structure with heavy stone/masonry construction and attractively landscaped grounds. A favorite with the locals, this landmark is often busy, making reservations a near necessity. Whether in the dining room or on the seasonal patio, diners enjoy steak, seafood and vegetarian dishes and friendly service. Dressy casual; cocktails. **Parking:** on-site. **Cards:** AX, DS, MC, VI.

TWO SISTERS — **Lunch:** $6-$13 — **Dinner:** $9-$22 — **Phone:** 406/327-8438

American

Location: Just w of Higgins Ave; downtown. 127 W Alder 59801. **Hours:** 8 am-10 pm, Mon & Tues-5 pm. Closed: 7/4, 11/25, 12/25. **Reservations:** accepted. **Features:** Having trained in New Orleans and worked in New York, the chef-owner here is nationally known. The eclectic menu is difficult to classify, running the gamut between classic French cuisine and comfort food such as fried chicken with mashed potatoes and cream gravy. However, guests can rest assured that, as much as possible, the food is freshly prepared in house. A homemade dessert is the perfect finish to any meal. Casual dress; beer & wine only. **Parking:** street. **Cards:** MC, VI.

THE WATERFRONT PASTA HOUSE **Dinner:** $7-$12 **Phone:** 406/549-8826

Italian

Location: I-90, exit 105 (Van Buren St), just s, then just w; in Goldsmith's Inn. 809 E Front St 59802. **Hours:** 5 pm-9 pm, Fri & Sat-10 pm. Closed major holidays. **Features:** The casual, family-friendly restaurant features Italian cuisine and deliciously rich ice cream made on the premises. During the summer, diners vie for tables on the patio, which overlooks the Clark Fork River. Children can color their own menus with provided crayons. Casual dress; beer & wine only. **Parking:** on-site. **Cards:** DS, MC, VI.

The following restaurants have not been evaluated by AAA but are listed for your information only.

CHINA BOWL RESTAURANT **Phone:** 406/721-9888

fyi

Not evaluated. **Location:** 3445 American Way 59801. **Features:** Near shopping and theaters, the comfortable family restaurant prepares traditional and inventive Asian dishes.

CURLEY'S BROILER **Phone:** 406/721-4133

fyi

Not evaluated. **Location:** 2915 Brooks St. **Features:** Jazz music plays in the dining room, where beef specialties and other dishes are served.

HOB NOB CAFE **Phone:** 406/542-3188

fyi

Not evaluated. **Location:** 208 E Main. **Features:** This restaurant serves food as eclectic as its kitschy "living room" decor, but it is always interesting and satisfying. The location in the rear of the Union Club bar makes it a choice mostly for adults.

STEELHEAD GRILL **Phone:** 406/541-3755

fyi

Not evaluated. **Location:** 140 W Pine. **Features:** The large, casual restaurant presents a menu of eclectic fare. A dance floor and live music are in a separate room.

NOXON pop. 230

WHERE TO STAY

BIGHORN LODGE BED & BREAKFAST **Phone:** 406/847-4676

Bed & Breakfast

All Year [BP]	1P: $75	2P: $125	XP: $25

Location: 6.7 mi w on US 200 to SR 56, 7.3 mi n. 2 Bighorn Ln 59853. Fax: 406/847-0069. **Facility:** This blend of Southern plantation and contemporary Western lodge overlooks a river which runs between two mountain ranges. Designated smoking area. 6 units. 5 one-bedroom standard units. 1 cottage. 2 stories (no elevator), interior/exterior corridors. *Bath:* combo or shower only. **Parking:** on-site. **Terms:** office hours 9 am-9 pm, 14 day cancellation notice-fee imposed, package plans. **Amenities:** *Some:* irons. **Leisure Activities:** whirlpool, boating, canoeing, fishing, cross country skiing, snowmobiling, bicycles, hiking trails, jogging, horseshoes, volleyball. *Fee:* charter fishing, horseback riding. **Guest Services:** TV in common area, complimentary evening beverages. **Cards:** MC, VI.

ASK / SOME UNITS

OVANDO pop. 71

WHERE TO STAY

LAKE UPSATA GUEST RANCH **Phone:** (406)793-5890

Ranch

6/16-9/7 [AP]	1P: $275	2P: $440
5/16-6/15 [AP]	1P: $215	2P: $340
3/1-5/15 & 9/8-2/28 [AP]	1P: $115	2P: $180

Location: 7.5 mi w on SR 200 to MM 38, 3.4 mi n on Woodworth Rd, then 1 mi e. Located in a quiet, rural area. 201 Lower Lakeside Ln 59854 (PO Box 6). Fax: 406/793-5894. **Facility:** On a lake near a picturesque wilderness area, the ranch is well suited for cookouts and campfires. Designated smoking area. 9 units. 1 one-bedroom standard unit. 8 cabins. 1 story, exterior corridors. *Bath:* shower only. **Parking:** on-site. **Terms:** 4 night minimum stay - in summer, 30 day cancellation notice, package plans. **Leisure Activities:** whirlpool, boating, canoeing, paddleboats, boat dock, fishing, recreation programs, bicycles, hiking trails, jogging, horseback riding, horseshoes. **Cards:** MC, VI.

FEE

POLSON pop. 4,041

WHERE TO STAY

BAYVIEW INN **Phone:** (406)883-3120

Motel

7/1-8/31 [CP]	1P: $60-$70	2P: $70-$80	XP: $5	F16
5/15-6/30 [CP]	1P: $55-$65	2P: $60-$70	XP: $5	F16
3/1-5/14 & 9/1-2/28 [CP]	1P: $35-$55	2P: $40-$60	XP: $5	F16

Location: Just s; downtown. 914 Hwy 93 59860. Fax: 406/883-2325. **Facility:** 25 one-bedroom standard units. 2 stories (no elevator), exterior corridors. **Parking:** on-site, winter plug-ins. **Terms:** weekly rates available, pets ($5 extra charge). **Cards:** AX, DS, MC, VI.

ASK FEE DATA PORT / SOME UNITS VCR FEE

BEST VALUE PORT POLSON INN *Book at aaa.com* **Phone:** (406)883-5385

SAVE

Small-scale Hotel

6/1-9/15 [CP]	1P: $79-$89	2P: $89-$99	XP: $10	F12
3/18-5/31 [CP]	1P: $60-$70	2P: $66-$76	XP: $10	F12
9/16-2/28 [CP]	1P: $46-$70	2P: $50-$76	XP: $10	F12
3/1-3/17 [CP]	1P: $46	2P: $50-$60	XP: $10	F12

Location: Just s; downtown. 502 Hwy 93 59860 (PO Box 1411). Fax: 406/883-3998. **Facility:** 43 units. 41 one-bedroom standard units, some with efficiencies. 2 one-bedroom suites ($75-$200) with kitchens. 2 stories (no elevator), interior/exterior corridors. **Parking:** on-site, winter plug-ins. **Terms:** office hours 7 am-10 pm. **Amenities:** *Some:* irons, hair dryers. **Leisure Activities:** sauna, whirlpools, exercise room. **Guest Services:** coin laundry. **Cards:** AX, DC, DS, MC, VI. **Special Amenities: free continental breakfast and free local telephone calls.** *(See color ad p 296)*

SOME UNITS

BEST WESTERN KWATAQNUK RESORT *Book at aaa.com* **Phone:** (406)883-3636

AAA SAVE

6/1-9/15	1P: $104-$124	2P: $114-$134	XP: $10	F12
3/1-5/31 & 9/16-2/28	1P: $62-$82	2P: $72-$92	XP: $10	F12

Small-scale Hotel **Location:** Just s of downtown on US 93. 303 US Hwy 93 E 59860. Fax: 406/883-5392. **Facility:** 112 units. 111 one-bedroom standard units. 1 one-bedroom suite with whirlpool. 2-3 stories, interior corridors. **Parking:** on-site, winter plug-ins. **Terms:** 3 day cancellation notice-fee imposed, package plans. **Amenities:** voice mail, irons, hair dryers. *Some:* dual phone lines. **Dining:** 7 am-2 & 5-9 pm; to 10 pm in summer, cocktails. **Pool(s):** small heated outdoor, small heated indoor. **Leisure Activities:** whirlpool, rental boats, rental canoes. *Fee:* marina, waterskiing, charter fishing, jet skis, lake cruises. **Business Services:** conference facilities. **Cards:** AX, DC, DS, MC, VI. **Special Amenities: free local telephone calls and free newspaper.** ***(See color ad below)***

SOME UNITS

FEE FEE

WHERE TO DINE

THE PEMMICAN RESTAURANT **Lunch:** $5-$8 **Dinner:** $12-$20 **Phone:** 406/883-3636

American

Location: Just s of downtown on US 93. 303 US Hwy 93 E 59860. **Hours:** 7 am-2 & 5-9 pm; to 10 pm in summer. Closed: 12/25. **Reservations:** accepted. **Features:** Try a buffalo burger or steak at this family restaurant located in the largest hotel on the shores of Flathead Lake. The lake and mountain views from the dining room are stunning and are a perfect complement to a relaxing dining experience. Casual dress; cocktails. **Parking:** on-site. **Cards:** AX, CB, DC, DS, MC, VI.

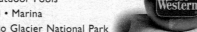

PRAY

WHERE TO STAY

The following lodging was either not evaluated or did not meet AAA rating requirements but is listed for your information only.

CHICO HOT SPRINGS LODGE **Phone:** 406/333-4933
fyi Not evaluated. **Location:** (PO Drawer D). Facilities, services, and decor characterize a basic property.

WHERE TO DINE

The following restaurant has not been evaluated by AAA but is listed for your information only.

CHICO HOT SPRINGS RESTAURANT **Phone:** 406/333-4933
fyi Not evaluated. **Location:** In Chico Hot Springs Lodge. PO Drawer D 59065. **Features:** Menu items include rack of lamb, prime rib, Grand Marnier duckling and halibut.

RED LODGE pop. 2,177—*See also YELLOWSTONE NATIONAL PARK.*

WHERE TO STAY

BEST WESTERN LU PINE INN *Book at aaa.com* **Phone:** (406)446-1321

Small-scale Hotel

5/28-9/25	1P: $79-$99	2P: $79-$99
12/18-2/28	1P: $69-$99	2P: $69-$99
3/1-5/27 & 9/26-12/17	1P: $69-$79	2P: $69-$79

Location: 0.4 mi s, just w of US 212. 702 S Hauser 59068 (PO Box 30). Fax: 406/446-1465. **Facility:** 46 one-bedroom standard units, some with efficiencies (utensils extra charge). 2 stories (no elevator), interior corridors. *Bath:* combo or shower only. **Parking:** on-site, winter plug-ins. **Terms:** [CP] meal plan available. **Amenities:** irons, hair dryers. **Pool(s):** heated indoor. **Leisure Activities:** sauna, whirlpool, exercise room. **Guest Services:** coin laundry. **Business Services:** meeting rooms. **Cards:** AX, CB, DC, DS, MC, VI.

SOME UNITS

ASK / / FEE

COMFORT INN OF RED LODGE *Book at aaa.com* **Phone:** (406)446-4469

Small-scale Hotel

6/16-9/15 [ECP]	1P: $79-$99	2P: $79-$99	XP: $10	F18
12/21-2/28 [ECP]	1P: $60-$90	2P: $60-$90	XP: $10	F18
9/16-12/20 [ECP]	1P: $60-$80	2P: $60-$80	XP: $10	F18
3/1-6/15 [ECP]	1P: $50-$80	2P: $50-$80	XP: $10	F18

Location: Jct US 212 and SR 78, north entrance. 612 N Broadway 59068 (PO Box 1970). Fax: 406/446-4669. **Facility:** 53 one-bedroom standard units, some with whirlpools. 2 stories (no elevator), interior corridors. *Bath:* combo or shower only. **Parking:** on-site, winter plug-ins. **Terms:** pets ($25 deposit). **Amenities:** video library, dual phone lines. *Some:* irons, hair dryers. **Pool(s):** small heated outdoor. **Leisure Activities:** whirlpool. **Guest Services:** coin laundry. **Business Services:** meeting rooms. **Cards:** AX, CB, DC, DS, MC, VI.

SOME UNITS

ASK FEE / VCR FEE /

ROCK CREEK RESORT **Phone:** 406/446-1111

AAA SAVE

Resort Small-scale Hotel

All Year	1P: $95-$120	2P: $95-$120	XP: $20	F10

Location: 5.8 mi s. Located bordering a wilderness area. US 212 S 59068 (HC 49, Box 3500). Fax: 406/237-9851. **Facility:** The resort offers townhouse, condominium and standard lodgings. Elevator is in the main building only. 87 units. 84 one-bedroom standard units, some with efficiencies, kitchens and/or whirlpools. 2 three-bedroom suites with kitchens. 1 cabin ($275) with whirlpool. 1-3 stories, interior/exterior corridors. **Parking:** on-site. **Terms:** 15 day cancellation notice-fee imposed. **Amenities:** voice mail. **Dining:** 7:30 am-2 pm; hours vary in winter, cocktails, also, Old Piney Dell, see separate listing. **Pool(s):** heated indoor. **Leisure Activities:** sauna, whirlpool, fishing, 4 tennis courts, cross country skiing, snow shoe rental, cross country ski rental, soccer field, rental bicycles, playground, exercise room, volleyball. *Fee:* adventure challenge course. **Guest Services:** gift shop, coin laundry. **Business Services:** meeting rooms. **Cards:** AX, DC, DS, MC, VI. ***(See ad below)***

SOME UNITS

DATA PORT / VCR /

SUPER 8 OF RED LODGE — **Phone:** 406/446-2288

Motel

	1P	2P	XP
All Year	1P: $50-$100	2P: $50-$100	XP: $9

Location: Just s on US 212. 1223 S Broadway Ave 59068 (HC 49, Box 3375). Fax: 406/446-3162. **Facility:** 50 one-bedroom standard units, some with kitchens and/or whirlpools. 2 stories, interior/exterior corridors. **Parking:** on-site, winter plug-ins. **Terms:** 30 day cancellation notice-fee imposed, [CP] meal plan available, pets ($5 extra charge). **Pool(s):** heated indoor. **Leisure Activities:** whirlpools. *Fee:* game room. **Guest Services:** coin laundry. **Business Services:** meeting rooms. **Cards:** AX, CB, DC, DS, MC, VI. **Special Amenities: free continental breakfast and free local telephone calls.**

SOME UNITS / FEE

YODELER MOTEL — **Phone:** (406)446-1435

Motel

	1P	2P	XP	
6/11-9/10	1P: $59-$79	2P: $59-$79	XP: $5	D16
12/24-2/28	1P: $55-$79	2P: $55-$79	XP: $5	D16
3/1-6/10	1P: $49-$75	2P: $49-$75	XP: $5	D16
9/11-12/23	1P: $49-$69	2P: $49-$69	XP: $5	D16

Location: Just s on US 212. 601 S Broadway 59068 (PO Box 1336). Fax: 406/446-1436. **Facility:** 23 units. 18 one- and 5 two-bedroom standard units, some with kitchens and/or whirlpools. 2 stories (no elevator), exterior corridors. **Parking:** on-site, winter plug-ins. **Terms:** cancellation fee imposed, pets (in designated units). **Amenities:** voice mail. **Leisure Activities:** whirlpool, ski wax room. **Cards:** AX, CB, DC, DS, MC, VI. **Special Amenities: free local telephone calls and preferred room (subject to availability with advanced reservations).**

SOME UNITS

WHERE TO DINE

BOGART'S — **Lunch:** $6-$17 — **Dinner:** $6-$17 — **Phone:** 406/446-1784

American

Location: City center. 11 S Broadway Ave 59068. **Hours:** 11 am-9 pm, Sun-8:30 pm; to 10 pm in summer. Closed: 11/25, 12/25. **Features:** The local-favorite restaurant offers specialty pizzas, Mexican dishes and standard American cuisine amid Humphrey Bogart memorabilia, wild animal busts and varied antiques. Large portions of homemade sour cream chicken enchiladas, charbroiled burgers, pasta and surf and turf are served. Casual dress; cocktails. **Parking:** street. **Cards:** MC, VI.

OLD PINEY DELL — **Dinner:** $17-$24 — **Phone:** 406/446-1196

American

Location: 5.8 mi s; in Rock Creek Resort. 6380 US 212 59068. **Hours:** 5:30 pm-9 pm, Fri & Sat-10 pm, 6/1-9/30; hours may vary in winter. Closed: Mon & Tues in winter. **Reservations:** suggested. **Features:** Steak, seafood, veal and pasta entrees head up the list of eclectic selections served in this rustic, 1920s log cabin, adjacent to Rock Creek. Casual dress; cocktails. **Parking:** on-site. **Cards:** AX, DC, DS, MC, VI. *(See ad p 297)*

The following restaurant has not been evaluated by AAA but is listed for your information only.

RED BOX CAR DRIVE-IN — **Phone:** 406/446-2152

fyi

Not evaluated. **Location:** S on US 212. 1300 S Broadway 59068. **Features:** Popular with the locals, the summer drive-in is known for its burgers, hot dogs and shakes. Guests can relax on the patio next to Rock Creek.

RONAN pop. 1,812

WHERE TO STAY

STARLITE MOTEL **Phone:** 406/676-7000

Motel

6/1-9/15	1P: $52-$57	2P: $67-$71	XP: $5	F11
9/16-2/28	1P: $49-$58	2P: $58-$68	XP: $5	F11
3/1-5/31	1P: $49-$58	2P: $60-$67	XP: $5	F11

Location: Just w of jct US 93 and Main St. 18 Main St SW 59864. Fax: 406/676-7000. **Facility:** 15 one-bedroom standard units. 2 stories (no elevator), exterior corridors. **Parking:** on-site, winter plug-ins. **Terms:** office hours 7 am-10 pm, cancellation fee imposed, weekly rates available, pets ($10 fee, in limited units). **Amenities:** voice mail. **Cards:** AX, DC, DS, MC, VI.

SOME UNITS

ASK FEE DATA PORT

TWIN CREEKS BED & BREAKFAST **Phone:** 406/676-8800

Bed & Breakfast

All Year [BP]	1P: $60-$135	2P: $60-$135

Location: Jct US 93 and Terrace Lake Rd, 1.3 mi e to N Foothills Rd, 2.5 mi n to Twin Creeks Rd, then 0.7 mi e. 2295 Twin Creeks Way 59864. Fax: 406/676-2662. **Facility:** Designated smoking area. 4 one-bedroom standard units, some with whirlpools. 2 stories (no elevator), interior corridors. **Parking:** on-site, winter plug-ins. **Terms:** check-in 5 pm, 10 day cancellation notice, package plans - 10/13-2/28, no pets allowed (owner's dog on premises). **Leisure Activities:** sauna, whirlpool. *Fee:* massage. **Guest Services:** gift shop. **Cards:** AX, MC, VI.

SOME UNITS

DATA PORT

ROUNDUP pop. 1,931

WHERE TO DINE

BUSY BEE RESTAURANT & GIFT SHOP **Lunch:** $4-$16 **Dinner:** $4-$16 **Phone:** 406/323-2204

AAA

American

Location: South edge of city on US 12 and 87. 317 1st Ave W 59072. **Hours:** 6 am-9 pm, Fri & Sat-10 pm; 6 am-8 pm, Fri & Sat-9 pm in winter. Closed: 1/1, 12/24, 12/25. **Reservations:** suggested, major holidays. **Features:** Both the Honeycomb and Fireside dining rooms are well suited to family dining. Selections include crisp chicken, tender beer-battered shrimp, creations from the fresh salad bar and homemade pie. Prime rib is offered weekend evenings. Casual dress; beer & wine only. **Parking:** on-site. **Cards:** AX, DS, MC, VI.

ST. IGNATIUS pop. 788

WHERE TO STAY

SUNSET MOTEL **Phone:** 406/745-3900

Motel

5/1-9/30	1P: $52-$62	2P: $62-$72
3/1-4/30 & 10/1-2/28	1P: $39	2P: $49

Location: Just s of downtown, exit on US 93. 32670 Hwy 93 59865 (PO Box 566). Fax: 406/745-3110. **Facility:** 10 one-bedroom standard units, some with kitchens (no utensils). 2 stories (no elevator), exterior corridors. **Parking:** on-site. **Terms:** weekly rates available, pets ($5 extra charge, dogs only). **Cards:** DC, MC, VI.

FEE

ST. MARY —*See also GLACIER NATIONAL PARK.*

WHERE TO DINE

TWO SISTERS CAFE **Lunch:** $5-$11 **Dinner:** $7-$20 **Phone:** 406/732-5535

AAA

American

Location: On US 89, 4.5 mi n. US 89 59411. **Hours:** Open 5/31-9/9; 8 am-10 pm. **Features:** Driving down the road from Glacier National Park, you can't miss the bright, multi-colored cafe. As innovative as their sister restaurant in Missoula, this eatery, with their funky decor serves up tasty twists on tradtional favorites in a casual, family friendly setting. Casual dress; cocktails. **Parking:** on-site. **Cards:** MC, VI.

ST. REGIS pop. 315

WHERE TO STAY

LITTLE RIVER MOTEL **Phone:** (406)649-2713

AAA SAVE

Motel

6/26-8/25	1P: $50-$65	2P: $50-$65	XP: $5	F12
3/1-6/25 & 8/26-10/15	1P: $40-$55	2P: $40-$55	XP: $5	F12
10/16-2/28	1P: $35-$55	2P: $35-$55	XP: $5	F12

Location: I-90, exit 33, just n to flashing light, just w, then just sw. 50 Old US Hwy 10 W 59866. **Facility:** 11 units. 7 one-bedroom standard units. 4 cottages. 1 story, exterior corridors. *Bath:* combo or shower only. **Parking:** on-site, winter plug-ins. **Terms:** weekly rates available, small pets only ($5 fee). **Leisure Activities:** hiking trails, jogging. **Cards:** DS, MC, VI.

SOME UNITS

FEE

SEELEY LAKE pop. 1,436

WHERE TO STAY

THE EMILY A BED & BREAKFAST — Phone: 406/677-3474

Bed & Breakfast

5/1-10/15 [BP] 1P: $120-$150 2P: $120-$150 XP: $15 F6

Location: 5 mi n on SR 83, just n of MM 20. Located in a quiet, secluded area. Hwy 83 N (MM 20) 59868 (PO Box 350). Fax: 406/677-3474. **Facility:** Birds and other wildlife are often sighted from this elegant log home tucked amid mountains, a river and a lake. Smoke free premises. 6 units. 5 one-bedroom standard units. 1 two-bedroom suite ($150) with kitchen. 2 stories (no elevator), interior corridors. *Bath:* some shared or private. **Parking:** on-site, winter plug-ins. **Terms:** open 5/1-10/15, office hours 9 am-7 pm, 7 day cancellation notice, weekly rates available. **Leisure Activities:** canoeing, fishing, hiking trails, volleyball. **Guest Services:** coin laundry. **Business Services:** meeting rooms. **Cards:** MC, VI.

ASK

WILDERNESS GATEWAY INN — Phone: 406/677-2095

SAVE

Motel

5/15-10/15 1P: $49-$55 2P: $52-$61 XP: $3 F10

3/1-5/14 & 10/16-2/28 1P: $40-$45 2P: $43-$51 XP: $3 F10

Location: South end of town on SR 83. Located in a quiet, secluded area. 2996 Hwy 83 N 59868 (PO Box 661). Fax: 406/677-2095. **Facility:** 19 one-bedroom standard units. 2 stories (no elevator), exterior corridors. **Parking:** on-site, winter plug-ins. **Terms:** pets ($5 extra charge). **Leisure Activities:** horseshoes. **Cards:** AX, DS, MC, VI. **Special Amenities: free local telephone calls and early check-in/late check-out.**

SOME UNITS

DATA PORT

FEE

WHERE TO DINE

LINDEY'S PRIME STEAK HOUSE — **Dinner:** $15-$21 — Phone: 406/677-9229

Steak House

Location: Just s. SR 83 59868. **Hours:** 5 pm-10 pm; to 9 pm in winter. Closed: 11/25, 12/25; also Tues-Wed 10/1-4/15. **Features:** Bring your appetite for beef because the menu features only flavorful aged prime sirloin and beef. "Dinner sharing" is available. Overlooking Seeley Lake, casual outdoor summer dining fare showcases thick "bayburgers.". Casual dress; cocktails. **Parking:** on-site. **Cards:** MC, VI.

SHELBY pop. 3,216

WHERE TO STAY

COMFORT INN OF SHELBY — *Book at aaa.com* — Phone: (406)434-2212

Small-scale Hotel

All Year [ECP] 1P: $59-$89 2P: $65-$99 XP: $6 F18

Location: I-15, exit 363, just e, then just s on McKinley Ave. 50 Frontage Rd 59474. Fax: 406/434-2493. **Facility:** 72 units. 71 one-bedroom standard units, some with efficiencies and/or whirlpools. 1 one-bedroom suite with whirlpool. 3 stories, interior corridors. *Bath:* some combo or shower only. **Parking:** on-site, winter plug-ins. **Terms:** pets ($5 extra charge). **Amenities:** *Some:* irons, hair dryers. **Leisure Activities:** sauna, whirlpool, exercise room. **Guest Services:** coin laundry. **Business Services:** meeting rooms. **Cards:** AX, CB, DC, DS, MC, VI.

SOME UNITS

ASK DATA PORT

FEE

CROSSROADS INN — Phone: (406)434-5134

SAVE

Motel

5/20-9/30 [CP] 1P: $52 2P: $60 XP: $8 F12

3/1-5/19 & 10/1-2/28 [CP] 1P: $46 2P: $52 XP: $6 F12

Location: Just w of town center on US 2. 1200 Roosevelt Hwy 59474 (PO Box 926). Fax: 406/434-2937. **Facility:** 52 units. 50 one-bedroom standard units. 2 one-bedroom suites. 2 stories (no elevator), interior corridors. **Parking:** on-site, winter plug-ins. **Terms:** 7 day cancellation notice, small pets only ($10 extra charge, in smoking units). **Pool(s):** heated indoor. **Leisure Activities:** whirlpool. **Guest Services:** coin laundry. **Business Services:** meeting rooms, fax (fee). **Cards:** AX, CB, DC, DS, MC, VI.

SOME UNITS

DATA PORT

FEE

O'HAIRE MANOR MOTEL — Phone: (406)434-5555

SAVE

Motel

All Year 1P: $35-$50 2P: $50-$65 XP: $5

Location: Just s of Main St via Maple St. 204 2nd St S 59474. Fax: 406/434-2702. **Facility:** 36 one-bedroom standard units. 2 stories (no elevator), interior/exterior corridors. *Bath:* combo or shower only. **Parking:** on-site, winter plug-ins. **Terms:** weekly rates available, small pets only ($5 extra charge). **Amenities:** *Some:* irons. **Leisure Activities:** whirlpool, limited exercise equipment. **Guest Services:** coin laundry, airport transportation-Toole County Airport, area transportation-train depot & bus station. **Cards:** AX, CB, DC, DS, MC, VI. **Special Amenities: free local telephone calls and preferred room (subject to availability with advanced reservations).**

SOME UNITS

FEE

SHERIDAN pop. 659

WHERE TO STAY

MORIAH MOTEL — Phone: 406/842-5491

Motel

All Year 1P: $40-$45 2P: $48-$56 XP: $5 F10

Location: SR 287 S. 220 S Main St 59749. Fax: 406/842-5488. **Facility:** 12 one-bedroom standard units. 1 story, exterior corridors. *Bath:* combo or shower only. **Parking:** on-site, winter plug-ins. **Terms:** pets ($7 extra charge). **Amenities:** voice mail. **Cards:** AX, DC, MC, VI.

SOME UNITS

FEE

SIDNEY pop. 4,774

WHERE TO STAY

RICHLAND MOTOR INN — **Phone:** (406)433-6400

Motel

All Year [ECP] 1P: $65-$75 2P: $70-$80 XP: $6 F16

Location: 1.5 mi n of jct SR 200 and 16. 1200 S Central Ave 59270. Fax: 406/433-4743. **Facility:** 61 one-bedroom standard units. 2 stories (no elevator), interior corridors. *Bath:* combo or shower only. **Parking:** on-site, winter plug-ins. **Terms:** pets (in smoking units). **Amenities:** hair dryers. *Some:* irons. **Leisure Activities:** whirlpools, exercise room. *Fee:* massage. **Business Services:** meeting rooms, business center. **Cards:** AX, CB, DC, DS, MC, VI.

SOME UNITS

SOMERS pop. 556

WHERE TO STAY

SOMERS BAY LOG CABIN LODGING — **Phone:** 406/857-3881

Cabin

All Year 2P: $69-$109 XP: $10

Location: Just s. 5496 US 93 S 59932 (PO Box 447). Fax: 406/857-3871. **Facility:** The cozy log cabins are nestled in the trees just across the road from Flathead Lake and are close to restaurants and adjacent to a lake cruise boat. 7 cabins. 1-2 stories (no elevator), exterior corridors. **Parking:** on-site, winter plug-ins. **Terms:** office hours 8 am-10 pm, cancellation fee imposed. **Leisure Activities:** whirlpool, playground, horseshoes. **Cards:** AX, DS, MC, VI.

STEVENSVILLE pop. 1,553

WHERE TO STAY

BIG CREEK PINE'S BED & BREAKFAST — **Phone:** 406/642-6475

Bed & Breakfast

All Year [BP] 1P: $80 2P: $90 XP: $20

Location: 4.7 mi s on US 93; between MM 62 and 63. Located in a quiet area. 2986 US 93 N 59870. **Facility:** Each room is accessorized differently at this B&B, which is in the Bitterroot Valley countryside and adjacent to a creek. Designated smoking area. 4 one-bedroom standard units. 2 stories (no elevator), interior corridors. **Parking:** on-site. **Terms:** 14 day cancellation notice-fee imposed. **Guest Services:** TV in common area, complimentary evening beverages. **Business Services:** meeting rooms. **Cards:** MC, VI.

ASK

SUPERIOR pop. 893

WHERE TO STAY

BUDGET HOST BIG SKY MOTEL — **Phone:** (406)822-4831

Motel

6/1-2/28	1P: $48-$54	2P: $54-$60	XP: $6	F12
3/1-5/31	1P: $44-$48	2P: $48-$52	XP: $4	F12

Location: I-90, exit 47, just n. 103 4th Ave E 59872 (PO Box 458). Fax: 406/822-4371. **Facility:** 24 one-bedroom standard units. 2 stories (no elevator), exterior corridors. **Parking:** on-site, winter plug-ins. **Terms:** office hours 7 am-11 pm, small pets only (in designated units). **Cards:** AX, DS, MC, VI.

SOME UNITS

THOMPSON FALLS pop. 1,321

WHERE TO STAY

THE RIVERFRONT — **Phone:** 406/827-3460

Motel

All Year 1P: $56-$79 2P: $69-$107

Location: 1 mi w of city center. 4907 Scenic SR 200 W 59873 (PO Box 22). **Facility:** Designated smoking area. 14 units. 13 one-bedroom standard units, some with efficiencies. 1 cottage ($89-$229) with whirlpool. 1-2 stories (no elevator), exterior corridors. *Bath:* combo or shower only. **Parking:** on-site. **Terms:** office hours 8 am-9:30 pm, cancellation fee imposed, pets ($7 extra charge). **Leisure Activities:** fishing, hiking trails, horseshoes. **Guest Services:** gift shop. **Cards:** AX, DS, MC, VI.

FEE

THREE FORKS pop. 1,728

WHERE TO STAY

BROKEN SPUR MOTEL — **Phone:** (406)285-3237

Motel

All Year 1P: $38-$50 2P: $48-$66 XP: $6 F12

Location: I-90, exit 278 westbound, 1.3 mi sw on SR 2; exit 274 eastbound, 1 mi s on SR 287 to jct SR 2, 3 mi se on SR 2. 124 W Elm (Hwy 2) 59752 (PO Box 1009). Fax: 406/285-3237. **Facility:** 24 units. 23 one-bedroom standard units, some with efficiencies. 1 cabin ($50-$75). 2 stories (no elevator), exterior corridors. *Bath:* combo or shower only. **Parking:** on-site, winter plug-ins. **Terms:** weekly rates available, [CP] meal plan available, pets ($5 extra charge). **Cards:** AX, DS, MC, VI. **Special Amenities: free continental breakfast and free local telephone calls.**

SOME UNITS

FEE FEE FEE

FORT THREE FORKS MOTEL & RV PARK — Phone: 406/285-3233

Motel

5/1-8/31 [CP]	1P: $55	2P: $70-$85	XP: $5	F11
3/1-4/30 & 9/1-2/28 [CP]	1P: $49	2P: $66-$85	XP: $5	F11

Location: I-90, exit 274. 10776 Hwy 287 59752 (PO Box 1074). Fax: 406/285-4362. **Facility:** 24 one-bedroom standard units. 2 stories (no elevator), exterior corridors. *Bath:* combo or shower only. **Parking:** on-site, winter plug-ins. **Terms:** pets ($10 extra charge). **Leisure Activities:** playground. **Guest Services:** coin laundry. **Cards:** AX, MC, VI.

SOME UNITS

FEE

WHERE TO DINE

HISTORIC HEADWATERS RESTAURANT — Historic — **Lunch:** $6-$10 — **Dinner:** $9-$22 — **Phone:** 406/285-4511

Regional American

Location: I-90, exit 278, 1 mi s. 105 S Main St 59752. **Hours:** 11 am-10 pm, Sun 11 am-3 & 5-10 pm; 11 am-8 pm, Sun-3 pm 10/1-4/30. Closed: 1/1, 12/25; also Mon & Tues, Wed 10/1-4/30. **Reservations:** accepted. **Features:** You wouldn't expect to find a gourmet experience in such a small town, but here it is. Nightly specials may vary, but this Kansas City chef's culinary talent holds steadfast in whichever dish you choose. A short drive out of your way to dine in this historic building is well worthwhile. The Sunday buffet is renowned around these parts. Dressy casual; beer & wine only. **Parking:** street. **Cards:** AX, DS, MC, VI.

VICTOR pop. 859

WHERE TO STAY

WILDLIFE ADVENTURES — **Phone:** (406)642-3262

Ranch

All Year [BP]	1P: $90-$150	2P: $105-$170	XP: $15	F6

Location: Jct US 93 and Fifth St, 0.9 mi w, 3.2 mi s. 1765 Pleasant View DR 59875. Fax: 406/642-3462. **Facility:** Smoke free premises. 6 one-bedroom standard units. 2 stories (no elevator), interior corridors. **Parking:** on-site. **Terms:** 30 day cancellation notice-fee imposed, weekly rates available, [AP], [CP] & [MAP] meal plans available, package plans, $10 service charge. **Leisure Activities:** whirlpool, hiking trails, jogging. *Fee:* horseback riding. **Business Services:** meeting rooms. **Cards:** AX, CB, DC, DS, JC, MC, VI.

ASK

WEST GLACIER —*See also GLACIER NATIONAL PARK.*

WHERE TO STAY

GLACIER RAFT COMPANY CABINS — ***Book at aaa.com*** — **Phone:** (406)888-5454

AAA SAVE

Cabin

All Year	1P: $195-$295	2P: $195-$295

Location: On US 2, 0.5 mi w. 11957 US Hwy 2 E 59936 (PO Box 210). Fax: 406/888-5541. **Facility:** Individual log cabins are available throughout the property, from which you can enjoy the river rafting or explore Glacier National Park. Smoke free premises. 9 cabins. 1-2 stories (no elevator), exterior corridors. **Parking:** on-site. **Terms:** office hours 7:30 am-9 pm, check-in 4 pm, 14 day cancellation notice-fee imposed, package plans. **Leisure Activities:** fishing, fly-fishing instruction, outdoor equipment, fishing supplies, cross country skiing, rental bicycles, hiking trails, horseshoes, volleyball. *Fee:* charter fishing. **Guest Services:** gift shop. **Cards:** AX, DS, MC, VI. **Special Amenities: early check-in/late check-out.**

GREAT NORTHERN WHITEWATER RESORT — **Phone:** (406)387-5340

AAA SAVE

Cabin

7/1-9/10	1P: $197-$280	2P: $197-$280
3/1-6/30	1P: $116-$263	2P: $116-$263
9/11-9/30	1P: $163-$216	2P: $163-$216
10/1-2/28	1P: $116-$179	2P: $116-$179

Location: On US 2, 1 mi w. 12127 US 2 59936 (PO Box 270). Fax: 406/387-9007. **Facility:** These log chalets surround a pond and offer mountain views. 5 cabins. 2 stories (no elevator), exterior corridors. *Bath:* combo or shower only. **Parking:** on-site. **Terms:** office hours 8:30 am-7 pm, 3 night minimum stay - 6/16-9/15, 45 day cancellation notice-fee imposed. **Amenities:** *Some:* DVD players. **Leisure Activities:** swim spa, river rafting, volleyball. **Guest Services:** area transportation-West Glacier Train Depot. **Cards:** AX, DC, DS, MC, VI. ***(See color ad p 98)***

SOME UNITS

SILVERWOLF CHALETS — **Phone:** (406)387-4448

AAA SAVE

Cabin

7/1-8/31 [ECP]	1P: $145-$158	2P: $145-$158
5/15-6/30 & 9/1-10/17 [ECP]	1P: $105-$136	2P: $105-$136

Location: 6 mi w on US 2. Located in a quiet, rural area. 160 Gladys Glen Rd 59936 (PO Box 115). **Facility:** In a forest setting, these log cabins feature fireplaces, lodgepole furniture and handmade quilts. Smoke free premises. 10 cabins. 1 story, exterior corridors. *Bath:* shower only. **Parking:** on-site. **Terms:** open 5/15-10/17, office hours 8 am-7 pm, age restrictions may apply, 31 day cancellation notice-fee imposed. **Leisure Activities:** barbecue area with grills & picnic tables. **Cards:** DC, MC, VI. **Special Amenities: free local telephone calls.**

The following lodging was either not evaluated or did not meet AAA rating requirements but is listed for your information only.

BELTON CHALET — **Phone:** 406/888-5000

fyi

Not evaluated. **Location:** US 2E, at west entrance to Glacier National Park. 12575 US 2 E 59936 (PO Box 206). Facilities, services, and decor characterize a mid-range property.

WEST YELLOWSTONE pop. 1,177—*See also YELLOWSTONE NATIONAL PARK.*

WHERE TO STAY

ALPINE MOTEL **Phone:** (406)646-7544

AAA SAVE — Motel

6/11-9/20	1P: $44-$58	2P: $53-$69	XP: $4
5/10-6/10 & 9/21-11/1	1P: $35-$45	2P: $39-$49	XP: $4

Location: Just w from park entrance. 120 Madison 59758 (PO Box 1497). Fax: 406/646-0158. **Facility:** Smoke free premises. 15 units. 13 one-bedroom standard units. 2 one-bedroom suites ($60-$110), some with kitchens. 1-2 stories (no elevator), exterior corridors. *Bath:* combo or shower only. **Parking:** on-site. **Terms:** open 5/10-11/1, 3 day cancellation notice-fee imposed. **Amenities:** hair dryers. **Cards:** AX, DS, MC, VI. **Special Amenities: early check-in/late check-out and preferred room (subject to availability with advanced reservations).**

SOME UNITS / FEE

AL'S WESTWARD HO MOTEL **Phone:** 406/646-7331

AAA SAVE — Motel

6/11-9/20	2P: $48-$66	XP: $4	D16
5/1-6/10 & 9/21-11/1	2P: $38-$56	XP: $4	D16

Location: Just n of park entrance. Located in a quiet, secluded area. 16 Boundary St 59758 (PO Box 49). **Facility:** Smoke free premises. 33 units. 30 one-bedroom standard units, some with kitchens. 1 one- and 2 two-bedroom suites, some with kitchens. 1-2 stories (no elevator), interior/exterior corridors. *Bath:* combo or shower only. **Parking:** on-site. **Terms:** open 5/1-11/1, 5 day cancellation notice. **Guest Services:** airport transportation-West Yellowstone Airport. **Cards:** DS, MC, VI.

SOME UNITS

BEST WESTERN CROSS WINDS MOTOR INN *Book at aaa.com* **Phone:** (406)646-9557

AAA SAVE — Small-scale Hotel

6/12-9/21 [CP]	1P: $79-$109	2P: $89-$124
1/28-2/28 [CP]	1P: $49-$79	2P: $49-$89
3/1-6/11 [CP]	1P: $39-$79	2P: $49-$89
9/22-1/27 [CP]	1P: $39-$69	2P: $42-$79

Location: Just w of US 191 and 287, on US 20 at Dunraven St and Firehole Ave. Located next to city park. 201 Firehole Ave 59758 (PO Box 340). Fax: 406/646-9592. **Facility:** 70 one-bedroom standard units. 2 stories (no elevator), exterior corridors. **Parking:** on-site, winter plug-ins. **Terms:** 3 day cancellation notice. **Amenities:** irons, hair dryers. **Pool(s):** heated indoor. **Leisure Activities:** whirlpool. **Guest Services:** airport transportation-West Yellowstone Airport. **Cards:** AX, CB, DC, DS, MC, VI. **Special Amenities: free continental breakfast.**

SOME UNITS / DATA PORT

BEST WESTERN DESERT INN *Book at aaa.com* **Phone:** (406)646-7376

AAA SAVE — Motel

6/12-9/21 [CP]	1P: $89-$139	2P: $89-$139
1/28-2/28 [CP]	1P: $49-$109	2P: $49-$109
3/1-6/11 & 9/22-1/27 [CP]	1P: $49-$99	2P: $49-$99

Location: US 191 at jct US 20, corner of Canyon and Firehole aves. 133 Canyon Ave 59758 (PO Box 340). Fax: 406/646-7759. **Facility:** 76 one-bedroom standard units, some with kitchens. 3 stories, interior corridors. *Bath:* combo or shower only. **Parking:** on-site, winter plug-ins. **Terms:** 3 day cancellation notice. **Amenities:** irons, hair dryers. **Pool(s):** heated indoor. **Leisure Activities:** whirlpool. **Guest Services:** valet and coin laundry, airport transportation-West Yellowstone Airport. **Business Services:** meeting rooms. **Cards:** AX, CB, DC, DS, MC, VI. **Special Amenities: free continental breakfast.**

SOME UNITS / DATA PORT

BRANDIN' IRON INN Book at aaa.com **Phone:** (406)646-9411

AAA SAVE — Small-scale Hotel

6/11-9/20 [ECP]	1P: $71-$94	2P: $71-$104
12/18-2/28 [ECP]	1P: $57-$63	2P: $57-$74
9/21-12/17 [ECP]	1P: $48-$60	2P: $48-$71
3/1-6/10 [ECP]	1P: $48-$63	2P: $48-$63

Location: Just w and n of park entrance. 201 Canyon Ave 59758 (PO Box 978). Fax: 406/646-9436. **Facility:** 79 one-bedroom standard units. 2 stories (no elevator), exterior corridors. *Bath:* combo or shower only. **Parking:** on-site, winter plug-ins. **Terms:** 20 day cancellation notice, in winter, 3 day in summer-fee imposed, package plans - in winter. **Amenities:** hair dryers. **Leisure Activities:** whirlpools. *Fee:* snowmobiling, guided snowmobile tours, summer park tours, guided fly fishing. **Guest Services:** valet and coin laundry, airport transportation-West Yellowstone Airport. **Business Services:** meeting rooms. **Cards:** AX, DC, DS, MC, VI. **Special Amenities: free expanded continental breakfast and free local telephone calls.** *(See color ad below)*

SOME UNITS

CITY CENTER MOTEL **Phone:** (406)646-7337

AAA SAVE — Motel

6/11-9/20	1P: $59-$69	2P: $59-$89
12/18-2/28	1P: $49-$55	2P: $49-$59
3/1-6/10	1P: $39-$49	2P: $39-$59
9/21-12/17	1P: $39	2P: $39-$49

Location: W off US 191 at Madison Ave and Dunraven St; just nw of park entrance. 214 Madison Ave 59758 (PO Box 580). Fax: 406/646-7337. **Facility:** 25 units. 21 one- and 4 two-bedroom standard units. 1-2 stories (no elevator), exterior corridors. *Bath:* combo or shower only. **Parking:** on-site. **Terms:** 20 day cancellation notice-fee imposed. **Leisure Activities:** whirlpool. *Fee:* snowmobiling. **Business Services:** meeting rooms. **Cards:** AX, DS, MC, VI. *(See color ad below)*

SOME UNITS

COMFORT INN Book at aaa.com **Phone:** (406)646-4212

AAA SAVE — Small-scale Hotel

6/16-9/30 [ECP]	1P: $79-$149	2P: $79-$149	XP: $8	F18
12/21-2/28 [ECP]	1P: $79-$129	2P: $79-$129	XP: $8	F18
3/1-6/15 [ECP]	1P: $49-$129	2P: $49-$129	XP: $8	F18
10/1-12/20 [ECP]	1P: $49-$99	2P: $49-$99	XP: $8	F18

Location: US 191, 0.6 mi w; e from US 20, 0.4 mi s on Iris St. 638 Madison Ave 59758 (PO Box 1050). Fax: 406/646-4212. **Facility:** 78 one-bedroom standard units. 3 stories, interior corridors. **Parking:** on-site, winter plug-ins. **Terms:** 3 day cancellation notice-fee imposed, package plans. **Amenities:** irons, hair dryers. **Pool(s):** heated indoor. **Leisure Activities:** whirlpool, limited exercise equipment. **Guest Services:** coin laundry, airport transportation-West Yellowstone Airport. **Business Services:** meeting rooms. **Cards:** AX, CB, DC, DS, JC, MC, VI. **Special Amenities: free expanded continental breakfast and free local telephone calls.** *(See color ad p 305)*

SOME UNITS

DAYS INN WEST YELLOWSTONE *Book at aaa.com* **Phone:** (406)646-7656

AAA SAVE

Small-scale Hotel

1/1-2/28	1P: $69-$135	2P: $79-$165	XP: $10	F12
6/1-9/30	1P: $104-$125	2P: $125-$155	XP: $10	F12
3/1-5/01 & 10/1 12/31	1P: $59-$125	2P: $69-$155	XP: $10	F12

Location: W off US 191; just nw of park entrance. 301 Madison Ave 59758. Fax: 406/646-7965. **Facility.** 110 one bedroom standard units, some with whirlpools. 3 stories, interior/exterior corridors. *Bath:* combo or shower only. **Parking:** on-site, winter plug-ins. **Terms:** 14 day cancellation notice-fee imposed, small pets only ($9 extra charge). **Amenities:** voice mail, hair dryers. *Some:* safes, irons. **Dining:** 7 am-1 & 5-9 pm; hours may vary in spring & fall. **Pool(s):** heated indoor. **Leisure Activities:** whirlpools, waterslide. *Fee:* snowmobiling. **Guest Services:** coin laundry. **Business Services:** meeting rooms. **Cards:** AX, DS, MC, VI. **Special Amenities: free local telephone calls and free newspaper.**

SOME UNITS

FEE

EVERGREEN MOTEL **Phone:** 406/646-7655

AAA SAVE

Motel

All Year	1P: $39-$69	2P: $39-$79	XP: $5

Location: Just w of Canyon Ave; on US 20 and 191. 229 Firehole Ave 59758 (PO Box 631). Fax: 406/646-4103. **Facility:** 16 units. 15 one-bedroom standard units, some with kitchens. 1 one-bedroom suite. 1 story, exterior corridors. *Bath:* combo or shower only. **Parking:** on-site. **Terms:** 7 day cancellation notice-fee imposed. **Guest Services:** coin laundry. **Cards:** AX, DS, MC, VI. **Special Amenities: free local telephone calls.**

SOME UNITS

FAIRFIELD INN BY MARRIOTT *Book at aaa.com* **Phone:** (406)646-4892

SAVE — Small-scale Hotel

6/1-9/30 [ECP]	1P: $79-$149	2P: $79-$149	XP: $10	F16
12/23-2/28 [ECP]	1P: $69-$109	2P: $69-$109	XP: $10	F16
4/24-5/31 [ECP]	1P: $59-$99	2P: $59-$99	XP: $10	F16
10/1-10/28 [ECP]	1P: $59-$79	2P: $59-$79	XP: $10	F16

Location: Just sw of jct US 191, 187 and 20, just w of park entrance. 105 S Electric St 59758 (PO Box 1745). Fax: 406/646-4893. **Facility:** 77 one-bedroom standard units, some with whirlpools. 3 stories, interior corridors. **Parking:** on-site, winter plug-ins. **Terms:** open 4/24-10/28 & 12/23-2/28, package plans - in winter. **Amenities:** video games, irons, hair dryers. **Pool(s):** heated indoor. **Leisure Activities:** whirlpool, exercise room. **Guest Services:** coin laundry, airport transportation-West Yellowstone Airport. **Business Services:** meeting rooms. **Cards:** AX, CB, DC, DS, MC, VI. **Special Amenities: free expanded continental breakfast and free local telephone calls.** *(See color ad p 305)*

SOME UNITS — FEE FEE

GRAY WOLF INN & SUITES *Book at aaa.com* **Phone:** (406)646-0000

SAVE — Motel

6/1-9/15	1P: $79-$139	2P: $79-$139	XP: $5	F18
9/16-2/28	1P: $59-$129	2P: $59-$129	XP: $5	F18
3/1-5/31	1P: $59-$99	2P: $59-$99	XP: $5	F18

Location: Just w of Yellowstone National Park entrance. 250 S Canyon Ave 59758 (PO Box 1449). Fax: 406/646-4232. **Facility:** 103 units. 85 one-bedroom standard units. 16 one- and 2 two-bedroom suites ($159-$299) with kitchens. 3 stories, interior corridors. *Bath:* combo or shower only. **Parking:** on-site, winter plug-ins. **Terms:** package plans - weekends, pets ($5 extra charge). **Amenities:** video games, voice mail, hair dryers. *Some:* irons. **Pool(s):** small heated indoor. **Leisure Activities:** sauna, whirlpool. **Guest Services:** coin laundry, airport transportation-West Yellowstone Airport. **Cards:** AX, DS, MC, VI. **Special Amenities: free expanded continental breakfast and free local telephone calls.** *(See color ad p 307)*

SOME UNITS — FEE

HEBGEN LAKE MOUNTAIN INN **Phone:** 406/646-5100

SAVE — Small-scale Hotel

3/1-9/15	2P: $140	XP: $10	F12
9/16-2/28	2P: $95	XP: $10	F12

Location: 8 mi n on US 191, w at jct US 191/287, then 7 mi w on US 287. Located across the highway from lake. 15475 Hebgen Lake Rd 59758. Fax: 406/646-0530. **Facility:** 16 one-bedroom suites with kitchens. 2 stories (no elevator), exterior corridors. **Parking:** on-site. **Terms:** 10 day cancellation notice-fee imposed, pets ($50 deposit). **Amenities:** honor bars. **Dining:** 11 am-11 pm, Sun from 9:30 am; hours may vary in winter. **Leisure Activities:** whirlpool, boat dock, fishing, hunting. *Fee:* boats. **Guest Services:** airport transportation-West Yellowstone Airport, area transportation-witin 25 mi. **Cards:** AX, DS, MC, VI. **Special Amenities: free local telephone calls and early check-in/late check-out.**

SOME UNITS — FEE

HOLIDAY INN SUNSPREE RESORT WEST YELLOWSTONE CONFERENCE HOTEL *Book at aaa.com* **Phone:** (406)646-7365

SAVE — Small-scale Hotel

6/1-9/30	1P: $99-$139	2P: $99-$139	XP: $8	F18
12/17-2/28	1P: $109-$119	2P: $109-$119	XP: $8	F18
3/1-5/31	1P: $79-$119	2P: $79-$119	XP: $8	F18
10/1-12/16	1P: $79-$99	2P: $79-$99	XP: $8	F18

Location: Just w of park entrance. 315 Yellowstone Ave 59758 (PO Box 470). Fax: 406/646-4433. **Facility:** 123 units. 110 one- and 13 two-bedroom standard units, some with whirlpools. 3 stories, interior corridors. *Bath:* combo or shower only. **Parking:** on-site, winter plug-ins. **Terms:** check-in 4 pm, cancellation fee imposed. **Amenities:** video games, dual phone lines, voice mail, irons, hair dryers. **Dining:** 6:30 am-11 & 5:30-10 pm; hours may vary in spring & fall. **Pool(s):** small heated indoor. **Leisure Activities:** sauna, whirlpool, exercise room. **Guest Services:** gift shop, valet and coin laundry, airport transportation-West Yellowstone Airport, area transportation. **Business Services:** conference facilities. **Cards:** AX, CB, DC, DS, JC, MC, VI. *(See color ad p 308 & opposite title page)*

SOME UNITS

KELLY INN *Book at aaa.com* **Phone:** (406)646-4544

AAA SAVE

Small-scale Hotel

6/1-9/30 [ECP]	1P: $79-$149	2P: $79-$149
12/24-2/28 [ECP]	1P: $69-$109	2P: $69-$109
3/1-5/31 [ECP]	1P: $59-$99	2P: $59-$99
10/1-12/23 [ECP]	1P: $59-$79	2P: $59-$79

Location: S of jct US 191, 287 and 20, just w of park entrance. 104 S Canyon Ave 59758 (PO Box 1482). Fax: 406/646-9838. **Facility:** 78 one-bedroom standard units, some with whirlpools. 3 stories, interior/exterior corridors. *Bath:* combo or shower only. **Parking:** on-site, winter plug-ins. **Terms:** check-in 4 pm, package plans - in winter, pets ($20 deposit). **Amenities:** video games, irons, hair dryers. **Pool(s):** heated indoor. **Leisure Activities:** sauna, whirlpool. **Guest Services:** coin laundry, airport transportation-West Yellowstone Airport. **Business Services:** meeting rooms. **Cards:** AX, CB, DC, DS, MC, VI. **Special Amenities: free expanded continental breakfast and free local telephone calls.**
(See color ad p 306)

SOME UNITS

FEE

LAZY G MOTEL **Phone:** 406/646-7586

AAA SAVE

Motel

3/1-3/31 & 5/1-2/28	1P: $32-$66	2P: $32-$66	XP: $7

Location: 0.6 mi w of park entrance on Yellowstone Ave, n on Hayden St, e via US 20, then just s. 123 Hayden St 59758 (PO Box 218). Fax: 406/646-4342. **Facility:** 15 units. 13 one- and 2 two-bedroom standard units, some with efficiencies. 1-2 stories (no elevator), exterior corridors. *Bath:* combo or shower only. **Parking:** on-site, winter plug-ins. **Terms:** open 3/1-3/31 & 5/1-2/28, 2 night minimum stay, 5 day cancellation notice, 30 day in winter-fee imposed. **Amenities:** hair dryers. **Leisure Activities:** fish cleaning & freezing facilities. *Fee:* snowmobiling. **Guest Services:** airport transportation-West Yellowstone Airport. **Cards:** DS, MC, VI. **Special Amenities: free local telephone calls.**

SOME UNITS

ONE HORSE MOTEL **Phone:** 406/646-7677

AAA SAVE

Motel

All Year	1P: $49-$69	2P: $49-$79	XP: $5

Location: Just w of US 191 and 287, on US 20 at Dunraven St and Firehole Ave. Located next to a city park. 216 Dunraven St 59758 (PO Box 878). Fax: 406/646-4103. **Facility:** Smoke free premises. 19 one-bedroom standard units. 1 story, exterior corridors. **Parking:** on-site, winter plug-ins. **Terms:** 7 day cancellation notice-fee imposed. **Guest Services:** coin laundry. **Business Services:** fax (fee). **Cards:** AX, DS, MC, VI. **Special Amenities: free local telephone calls and early check-in/late check-out.**

SOME UNITS

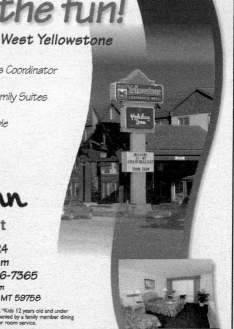

ROUNDUP MOTEL & DUDE MOTOR INN — **Phone:** (406)646-7301

AAA SAVE — Motel

5/21-10/1	1P: $69-$119	2P: $69-$119
5/10-5/20	1P: $45-$89	2P: $45-$89
12/15-2/28	1P: $60-$70	2P: $60-$70

Location: Just n of park entrance. 3 Madison Ave 59758 (PO Box 709). Fax: 406/646-7919. **Facility:** 58 units. 57 one-bedroom standard units, some with kitchens (no utensils). 1 cabin. 1-2 stories (no elevator), exterior corridors. **Parking:** on-site, winter plug-ins. **Terms:** open 5/10-10/1 & 12/15-2/28, 3 day cancellation notice, [CP] meal plan available, pets ($5 extra charge). **Pool(s):** heated outdoor. **Leisure Activities:** whirlpool. **Guest Services:** airport transportation-West Yellowstone Airport. **Cards:** AX, MC, VI.

SOME UNITS — FEE

STAGE COACH INN *Book at aaa.com* — **Phone:** (406)646-7381

AAA SAVE — Small-scale Hotel

6/16-9/30 & 12/16-2/28	1P: $89-$139	2P: $89-$139	XP: $10	F
3/1-6/15 & 10/1-12/15	1P: $49-$119	2P: $49-$119	XP: $10	F

Location: Corner of Dunraven St and Madison Ave, just w of park entrance. 209 Madison Ave 59758 (PO Box 169). Fax: 406/646-9575. **Facility:** 83 one-bedroom standard units. 2 stories, interior/exterior corridors. *Bath:* combo or shower only. **Parking:** on-site, winter plug-ins. **Terms:** cancellation fee imposed, package plans - in winter, pets ($50 deposit, in smoking units). **Amenities:** hair dryers. **Dining:** 7 am-11 & 5-10 pm; hours vary in spring & fall. **Leisure Activities:** sauna, whirlpools. *Fee:* snowmobiling. **Guest Services:** gift shop, coin laundry, airport transportation-West Yellowstone Airport. **Business Services:** meeting rooms. **Cards:** AX, CB, DC, DS, MC, VI. **Special Amenities: free local telephone calls.** *(See color ad p 307)*

SOME UNITS — FEE

SUPER 8 WEST YELLOWSTONE LIONSHEAD RESORT *Book at aaa.com* — **Phone:** (406)646-9584

AAA SAVE — Motel

5/28-9/30	1P: $79-$99	2P: $79-$102	XP: $5	F12
3/1-5/27 & 10/1-2/28	1P: $47-$74	2P: $49-$77	XP: $5	F12

Location: 8 mi w of west park entrance, on US 20. 1545 Targhee Pass Hwy 59758. Fax: 406/646-7404. **Facility:** 44 one-bedroom standard units. 2 stories (no elevator), interior corridors. **Parking:** on-site, winter plug-ins. **Terms:** check-in 4 pm. **Dining:** 7 am-10 & 5-9 pm, cocktails. **Leisure Activities:** sauna, whirlpool, square dancing, playground. *Fee:* fishing. **Guest Services:** coin laundry. **Cards:** AX, DS, MC, VI. **Special Amenities: free local telephone calls.**

SOME UNITS

THREE BEAR MOTOR LODGE — **Phone:** 406/646-7353

AAA SAVE — Motel

6/1-9/30 [CP]	1P: $70-$90	2P: $70-$99	XP: $10	F12
12/15-2/28 [CP]	1P: $70-$90	2P: $70-$90	XP: $10	F12
4/26-5/31 & 10/1-11/15	1P: $50-$60	2P: $50-$60	XP: $5	F12

Location: Just w of park entrance. 217 Yellowstone Ave 59758 (PO Box 1590). Fax: 406/646-4567. **Facility:** 73 units. 61 one- and 12 two-bedroom standard units, some with whirlpools. 1-2 stories (no elevator), interior/exterior corridors. **Parking:** on-site, winter plug-ins. **Terms:** open 4/26-11/15 & 12/15-2/28, cancellation fee imposed, small pets only ($5 extra charge). **Amenities:** irons, hair dryers. **Dining:** restaurant, see separate listing. **Pool(s):** small heated outdoor. **Leisure Activities:** whirlpools, limited exercise equipment. *Fee:* snowmobiling. **Guest Services:** airport transportation-West Yellowstone Airport. **Business Services:** meeting rooms. **Cards:** AX, DS, MC, VI. **Special Amenities: free continental breakfast and free local telephone calls.** *(See color ad p 309)*

SOME UNITS — DATA PORT — FEE

TRAVELERS LODGE — **Phone:** 406/646-9561

AAA SAVE — Motel

5/15-10/30 [CP]	1P: $69-$79	2P: $79-$95	XP: $5	F12
12/15-2/28 [CP]	1P: $70-$80	2P: $85	XP: $5	F12

Location: Just w of park entrance. 225 Yellowstone Ave 59758 (PO Box 930). Fax: 406/646-4478. **Facility:** 44 one-bedroom standard units. 2 stories (no elevator), exterior corridors. *Bath:* some combo or shower only. **Parking:** on-site. **Terms:** open 5/15-10/30 & 12/15-2/28, 14 day cancellation notice, in winter-fee imposed, small pets only ($50 deposit, $6 extra charge). **Amenities:** *Some:* safes. **Pool(s):** small heated outdoor. **Leisure Activities:** sauna, whirlpool. **Guest Services:** coin laundry, airport transportation-West Yellowstone Airport. **Cards:** AX, DS, MC, VI. **Special Amenities: free continental breakfast and free local telephone calls.**

SOME UNITS — FEE

YELLOWSTONE COUNTRY INN — **Phone:** (406)646-7622

AAA SAVE — Small-scale Hotel

6/16-9/30 [CP]	1P: $49-$129	2P: $49-$129	XP: $8
12/20-2/28 [CP]	1P: $49-$119	2P: $49-$119	XP: $8
3/1-6/15 & 10/1-12/19 [CP]	1P: $39-$109	2P: $39-$109	XP: $8

Location: On US 20 and 191, just w of Canyon Ave, corner of Firehole Ave and Electric St. 234 Firehole Ave 59758 (PO Box 67). Fax: 406/646-9443. **Facility:** 45 units. 38 one- and 7 two-bedroom standard units, some with efficiencies. 2 stories (no elevator), interior/exterior corridors. **Parking:** on-site, winter plug-ins. **Terms:** 30 day cancellation notice-fee imposed, pets ($5 extra charge). **Amenities:** voice mail. *Some:* DVD players. **Dining:** Rustler's Roost, see separate listing. **Pool(s):** small heated outdoor. **Leisure Activities:** sauna, whirlpool. *Fee:* heated snowcoach, dog sleds. **Guest Services:** valet and coin laundry. **Business Services:** meeting rooms. **Cards:** AX, CB, DC, DS, MC, VI. **Special Amenities: free local telephone calls.** *(See color ad below)*

SOME UNITS — DATA PORT — VCR — FEE

YELLOWSTONE LODGE — Book at aaa.com — **Phone:** (406)646-0020

AAA SAVE — Small-scale Hotel

6/16-9/15	1P: $89-$129	2P: $89-$129	XP: $10	F17
12/16-2/28	1P: $59-$119	2P: $59-$119	XP: $10	F17
3/1-6/15 & 9/16-12/15	1P: $49-$79	2P: $49-$79	XP: $10	F17

Location: Just w of park entrance. 251 S Electric St 59758 (PO Box 607). Fax: 406/646-0110. **Facility:** 77 units. 75 one- and 2 two-bedroom standard units. 3 stories, interior corridors. *Bath:* combo or shower only. **Parking:** on-site, winter plug-ins. **Terms:** cancellation fee imposed, [CP] meal plan available, package plans - seasonal, pets ($50 deposit). **Amenities:** voice mail, hair dryers. **Pool(s):** small heated indoor. **Leisure Activities:** whirlpool. **Guest Services:** valet and coin laundry. **Business Services:** meeting rooms. **Cards:** AX, CB, DC, DS, MC, VI. **Special Amenities: free expanded continental breakfast and free local telephone calls.** *(See color ad p 307)*

SOME UNITS — DATA PORT — FEE

WHERE TO DINE

ALICE'S RESTAURANT **Lunch:** $6-$14 **Dinner:** $6-$14 **Phone:** 406/646-7296

AAA

American

Location: 8 mi w of west park entrance on US 20. 1545 Targhee Pass Hwy 59758. **Hours:** 7 am-10 & 5-9 pm; 7 am-9 pm in winter. **Reservations:** suggested. **Features:** Set away from the tourist bustle of West Yellowstone, the eatery is surrounded by forested hills and wide, open spaces. Patrons can count on good home-style cooking with selections of chicken, steaks, fish, salads and sandwiches. Homemade desserts and strawberry butter for the bread are house specialties. Casual dress; cocktails. **Parking:** on-site. **Cards:** AX, DC, DS, MC, VI.

BULLWINKLE'S SALOON & EATERY **Lunch:** $6-$10 **Dinner:** $9-$22 **Phone:** 406/646-7974

American

Location: Just w and n of park entrance. 19 Madison Ave 59758. **Hours:** 11 am-10:30 pm. Closed: 11/25. **Features:** Even though the dining room is a large one, during the summer months, you may find a wait for a table at this extremely popular place. The decor is rustic Montana, with lots of wood accents and the overall feel is family friendly. Casual dress; cocktails. **Parking:** street. **Cards:** AX, DS, MC, VI.

CHINATOWN RESTAURANT **Lunch:** $5-$7 **Dinner:** $6-$12 **Phone:** 406/646-7088

Chinese

Location: Just w of park entrance. 100 Madison St 59758. **Hours:** 11 am-10 pm. Closed: 4/1-4/30 & 11/1-11/30. **Features:** The popular restaurant serves traditional Chinese cuisine with little variation from the standards. This is one of the few places in the area that is open for a late lunch. Casual dress. **Parking:** street. **Cards:** MC, VI.

THE GUSHER PIZZA AND SANDWICH SHOPPE **Lunch:** $6-$14 **Dinner:** $6-$14 **Phone:** 406/646-9050

American

Location: Corner of Madison & Dunraven sts. 40 Dunraven St 59758. **Hours:** 11:30 am-9:30 pm; Fri, Sat & 5/1-10/20 to 10:30 pm. Closed: 12/25; also 10/21-12/1 & 3/25-4/30. **Features:** The popular restaurant features pizza, sandwiches, burgers and steaks. Take-out and delivery are available. Casual dress; beer & wine only. **Parking:** on-site. **Cards:** AX, DS, MC, VI.

KIMMI'S ALASKAN GRILL **Dinner:** $12-$22 **Phone:** 406/646-1162

American

Location: W of park entrance; in Travelodge. 236 Dunraven 59758. **Hours:** Open 3/1-10/31 & 12/15-2/28; 6 am-11 & 5-10 pm; hours may vary in winter. **Features:** You're in a casual eatery in Montana, but when you close your eyes, you'll imagine being in Alaska dining on all the fresh bounty Alaskan waters offer. Depending on the time of year, Salmon species will vary, but all are guaranteed to please a seafood lovers palate. Casual dress. **Parking:** street. **Cards:** AX, DS, MC, VI.

RUNNING BEAR PANCAKE HOUSE **Lunch:** $4-$8 **Phone:** 406/646-7703

American

Location: 0.6 mi w of park entrance on Yellowstone Ave, just n on Hayden St. 538 Madison Ave 59758. **Hours:** 7 am-2 pm; hours may vary in season. Closed: 12/25; also 4/1-4/30 & 11/1-11/30. **Features:** These pancakes aren't the ones you usually make at home. One recent meal consisted of two huge pancakes loaded with walnuts and served with hot maple syrup. There are also several specialties like the veggie omelet, taco salad and homemade cinnamon rolls. Large salad bar is available at lunchtime. Casual dress. **Parking:** on-site. **Cards:** DS, MC, VI.

RUSTLER'S ROOST **Lunch:** $7-$17 **Dinner:** $13-$24 **Phone:** 406/646-7622

American

Location: On US 20 and 191, just w of Canyon Ave, corner of Firehole Ave and Electric St; in Yellowstone Country Inn. 234 Firehole Ave 59758. **Hours:** 6:30 am-10 pm; 5 pm-10 pm 3/19-5/17 & 11/3-12/17. **Features:** This pleasant eatery with great views of the sunset specializes in prime rib, seafood, elk, buffalo and fresh home-baked goods. The restaurant itself is situated in a volcano caldera. Meals are served in the lounge during the off season. Casual dress; cocktails. **Parking:** street. **Cards:** AX, DC, DS, MC, VI.
(See color ad p 310)

THREE BEAR RESTAURANT **Dinner:** $8-$25 **Phone:** 406/646-7811

American

Location: Just w of park entrance; in Three Bear Motor Lodge. 205 Yellowstone Ave 59758. **Hours:** Open 5/15-10/15 & 12/1-2/28; 6:30 am-11 & 5-10 pm; 6:30 am-10:30 & 5-9:30 pm in winter. **Features:** Varied dishes—ranging from selections of beef and fish to sandwiches, soups and salads—are likely to please just about anyone at this family restaurant. Home-baked pastries are mouthwatering treats. The rustic decor is reminiscent of historic days of Yellowstone and its residents. Casual dress; cocktails. **Parking:** street. **Cards:** DS, MC, VI. *(See color ad p 309)*

UNCLE LAURIE'S RIVERSIDE CAFE **Lunch:** $5-$8 **Phone:** 406/464-7040

American

Location: Just w of Canyon Ave, corner of Firehole Ave and Electric St, on US 20 and 191. 237 Hwy 20 59758. **Hours:** 7 am-3 pm. Closed major holidays; also Sun. **Features:** Don't be afraid to ask Laurie why she's called "Uncle". The story is a cute one and will bring you closer to the family feel conveyed by Laurie and her staff. The casual eatery is only open for breakfast and lunch, so beat the crowds clammering for the fresh and delicious foods by arriving early. Casual dress. **Parking:** on-site.

The following restaurant has not been evaluated by AAA but is listed for your information only.

ERNIE'S BIGHORN DELI **Phone:** 406/646-9467

fyi

Not evaluated. **Location:** 406 Hwy Ave 59758. **Features:** The bakery/deli specializes in made-from-scratch soups, deli sandwiches and desserts.

WHITEFISH pop. 5,032—*See also GLACIER NATIONAL PARK.*

WHERE TO STAY

ALPINGLOW INN **Phone:** (406)862-6966

SAVE

Small-scale Hotel

3/1-4/10	1P: $105-$135	2P: $105-$135	XP: $15	F12
6/11-2/28	1P: $85-$135	2P: $85-$135	XP: $15	F12

Location: Jct US 93 and SR 487, 2.4 mi n on SR 487, 5.2 mi n at flashing light. 3900 Big Mountain Rd 59937 (PO Box 1770). Fax: 406/862-0076. **Facility:** 54 one-bedroom standard units. 3 stories (no elevator), interior corridors. *Bath:* combo or shower only. **Parking:** on-site. **Terms:** open 3/1-4/10 & 6/11-2/28, check-in 4 pm, 30 day cancellation notice-fee imposed, [CP] meal plan available, package plans - in winter. **Dining:** 7:30-11 am, 11:30-2 & 5:30-9:30 pm; closed in summer, wine/beer only. **Leisure Activities:** saunas, whirlpools, 4 lighted tennis courts, rental bicycles, hiking trails, jogging. *Fee:* downhill & cross country skiing, snowmobiling, horseback riding, massage. **Guest Services:** gift shop, coin laundry. **Cards:** AX, DC, MC, VI. **Special Amenities: free continental breakfast and free local telephone calls.**

SOME UNITS

BAY POINT ON THE LAKE **Phone:** (406)862-2331

SAVE

Condominium

7/1-8/31	1P: $145-$165	2P: $145-$165	XP: $10	F13
3/1-6/30 & 9/1-2/28	1P: $89-$129	2P: $89-$129	XP: $10	F13

Location: Jct US 93 and SR 487, 0.6 mi n on SR 487 to Skyles Pl, 0.3 mi w to Dakota Ave, 0.3 mi n, then just w. 300 Bay Point Dr 59937 (PO Box 35). Fax: 406/862-5556. **Facility:** 50 units. 40 one-, 8 two- and 2 three-bedroom suites with kitchens. 2 stories (no elevator), exterior corridors. *Bath:* combo or shower only. **Parking:** on-site, winter plug-ins. **Terms:** office hours 8:30 am-5 pm, check-in 4 pm, 2 night minimum stay, 30 day cancellation notice-fee imposed, pets (in designated units). **Amenities:** voice mail, irons. *Some:* hair dryers. **Pool(s):** heated indoor. **Leisure Activities:** sauna, whirlpools, rental canoes, boat dock, waterskiing, fishing, playground, volleyball. *Fee:* game room. **Guest Services:** coin laundry. **Business Services:** meeting rooms. **Cards:** AX, MC, VI. **Special Amenities: free local telephone calls.** *(See color ad p 313)*

SOME UNITS

BEST WESTERN ROCKY MOUNTAIN LODGE *Book at aaa.com* **Phone:** (406)862-2569

SAVE

Small-scale Hotel

6/1-9/30	1P: $98-$116	2P: $98-$116	XP: $10	F12
12/26-2/28	1P: $71-$98	2P: $71-$98	XP: $10	F12
3/1-5/31 & 10/1-12/25	1P: $71	2P: $71	XP: $10	F12

Location: 1.3 mi s on US 93 from jct of SR 487. 6510 Hwy 93 S 59937. Fax: 406/862-1154. **Facility:** 79 one-bedroom standard units. 2-3 stories, interior/exterior corridors. *Bath:* combo or shower only. **Parking:** on-site, winter plug-ins. **Terms:** [ECP] meal plan available, package plans - in winter, small pets only ($10 fee, in designated units). **Amenities:** irons, hair dryers. **Pool(s):** small heated outdoor. **Leisure Activities:** whirlpool, exercise room. **Guest Services:** valet and coin laundry, area transportation-Amtrak station. **Business Services:** meeting rooms. **Cards:** AX, CB, DC, DS, MC, VI. **Special Amenities: free continental breakfast.**

SOME UNITS

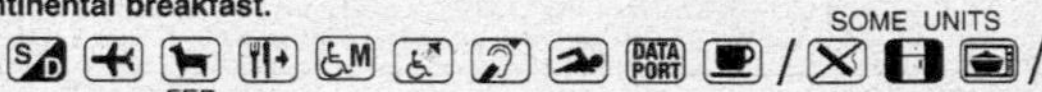

BIG MOUNTAIN RESORT **Phone:** (406)862-1960

AAA SAVE

Condominium

3/1-4/11 & 12/17-2/28	1P: $145-$350	2P: $145-$350	XP: $20	F12
11/25-12/16	1P: $120-$300	2P: $120-$300	XP: $20	F12
4/12-11/24	1P: $100-$215	2P: $100-$215	XP: $20	F12

Location: Jct of US 93 and SR 487, 2.4 mi n on SR 487, 5.2 mi n at flashing light. Big Mountain Rd 59937 (PO Box 1400). Fax: 406/862-1969. **Facility:** 30 units. 1 one-bedroom standard unit with kitchen. 11 one-, 10 two- and 8 three-bedroom suites with kitchens. 2-4 stories (no elevator), interior corridors. *Bath:* combo or shower only. **Parking:** on-site, winter plug-ins. **Terms:** off-site registration, check-in 4 pm, 30 day cancellation notice-fee imposed, weekly rates available, package plans. **Amenities:** video library (fee), voice mail, irons. **Pool(s):** heated indoor. **Leisure Activities:** whirlpool, recreation programs, archery, rental bicycles, hiking trails, jogging. *Fee:* 4 lighted tennis courts, downhill & cross country skiing, snowmobiling, horseback riding. **Guest Services:** coin laundry. *Fee:* airport transportation-in winter, area transportation-train depot in winter. **Cards:** AX, DC, MC, VI. **Special Amenities: free local telephone calls.**
(See color ad p 264)

SOME UNITS

FEE

CHALET MOTEL **Phone:** (406)862-5581

AAA SAVE

Motel

6/16-9/15	1P: $70-$80	2P: $80-$90	XP: $5	F11
5/21-6/15	1P: $55-$65	2P: $65-$80	XP: $5	F11
3/1-5/20 & 9/16-2/28	1P: $45-$55	2P: $50-$65	XP: $5	F11

Location: 1 mi n on US 93 from jct SR 40. 6430 US 93 S 59937. Fax: 406/862-3103. **Facility:** 33 one-bedroom standard units. 2 stories (no elevator), exterior corridors. *Bath:* combo or shower only. **Parking:** on-site, winter plug-ins. **Terms:** office hours 7 am-11 pm. **Pool(s):** small heated indoor. **Leisure Activities:** whirlpool. **Cards:** AX, DC, MC, VI. **Special Amenities: free local telephone calls and free newspaper.**

SOME UNITS

CHEAP SLEEP MOTEL **Phone:** (406)862-5515

Small-scale Hotel

7/1-9/12	1P: $60-$70	2P: $60-$70	XP: $5	F15
3/1-6/30 & 9/13-2/28	1P: $40-$50	2P: $40-$50	XP: $5	F15

Location: US 93, 1 mi s. 6400 Hwy 93 S 59937. Fax: 406/862-5510. **Facility:** 48 one-bedroom standard units. 2 stories (no elevator), interior corridors. **Parking:** on-site, winter plug-ins. **Terms:** office hours 7 am-11 pm, pets ($5 extra charge). **Pool(s):** small heated outdoor. **Leisure Activities:** whirlpool. **Guest Services:** coin laundry. **Cards:** AX, CB, DC, DS, MC, VI.

SOME UNITS

FEE

DUCK INN LODGE **Phone:** 406/862-3825

Bed & Breakfast

3/1-10/31 & 2/1-2/28	1P: $69-$109	2P: $69-$109	XP: $5

Location: On US 93, 1.5 mi n of jct SR 40, just e at Columbia Ave (Conoco Station). 1305 Columbia Ave 59937. **Facility:** Though not far from town, the Duck Inn is on the tree-shaded banks of a river where wildlife is often sighted. Designated smoking area. 10 one-bedroom standard units. 2 stories (no elevator), interior corridors. **Parking:** on-site. **Terms:** open 3/1-10/31 & 2/1-2/28, office hours 8 am-6 pm, 7 day cancellation notice. **Leisure Activities:** whirlpool. **Guest Services:** area transportation. **Cards:** AX, CB, DC, DS, MC, VI. ***(See ad p 314)***

EDELWEISS CONDOMINIUMS — Phone: (406)862-1960

Condominium

	1P	2P	XP	
4/12-11/24	1P: $105-$250	2P: $105-$250	XP: $20	F12
3/1-4/11 & 12/17-2/28	1P: $155-$225	2P: $155-$225	XP: $20	F12
11/25-12/16	1P: $130-$200	2P: $130-$200	XP: $20	F12

Location: US 93 and SR 487, 2.4 mi n on SR 487, 5.2 mi n. Big Mountain Rd 59937 (PO Box 1400). Fax: 406/862-1969. **Facility:** 47 units. 4 one-bedroom standard units with kitchens. 26 one- and 17 two-bedroom suites with kitchens. 3 stories (no elevator), interior/exterior corridors. **Parking:** on-site. **Terms:** office hours 8 am-5 pm, off-site registration, check-in 4 pm, 30 day cancellation notice-fee imposed, weekly rates available, package plans. **Amenities:** video library (fee), irons. **Pool(s):** heated indoor. **Leisure Activities:** sauna, whirlpool, 2 lighted tennis courts, rental bicycles, hiking trails, jogging. *Fee:* downhill & cross country skiing, snowmobiling, horseback riding. **Guest Services:** coin laundry. **Cards:** AX, DC, MC, VI.

SOME UNITS

GASTHAUS WENDLINGEN — Phone: (406)862-4886

Bed & Breakfast

6/15-9/15 [BP]	2P: $90-$135	XP: $25
9/16-1/4 [BP]	2P: $60-$110	XP: $25
3/1-6/14 & 1/5-2/28 [BP]	2P: $60-$80	XP: $25

Location: 0.5 mi n on US 93 from jct of SR 40, 1.7 mi e on JP and Monegan rds. Located in a quiet area. 700 Monegan Rd 59937. Fax: 406/862-4886. **Facility:** This log-and-cedar house on eight acres features a covered front porch and a river-rock fireplace. Designated smoking area. 4 one-bedroom standard units. 2 stories (no elevator), interior corridors. *Bath:* some shared or private, combo or shower only. **Parking:** on-site, winter plug-ins. **Terms:** office hours 6 am-10 pm, check-in 4 pm, 14 day cancellation notice-fee imposed. **Leisure Activities:** steamroom, cross country skiing. **Cards:** MC, VI.

SOME UNITS

GOOD MEDICINE LODGE — Phone: (406)862-5488

AAA SAVE — **Bed & Breakfast**

	1P	2P	XP	
6/15-9/30	1P: $95-$180	2P: $95-$180	XP: $20	F12
12/22-2/28	1P: $95-$155	2P: $95-$155	XP: $20	F12
10/1-12/21	1P: $75-$145	2P: $95-$145	XP: $20	F12
3/1-6/14	1P: $75-$145	2P: $85-$145	XP: $20	F12

Location: Jct US 93 and SR 487, 0.5 mi n on SR 487. 537 Wisconsin Ave 59937. Fax: 406/862-5489. **Facility:** Custom lodgepole furniture and locally inspired fabrics decorate this cedar lodge. Designated smoking area. 9 units. 8 one-bedroom standard units. 1 one-bedroom suite with whirlpool. 2 stories (no elevator), interior corridors. *Bath:* combo or shower only. **Parking:** on-site. **Terms:** 14 day cancellation notice. **Amenities:** hair dryers. **Leisure Activities:** whirlpool, ski room with boot & glove dryer. **Guest Services:** coin laundry, area transportation-train & ski area. **Business Services:** meeting rooms. **Cards:** AX, DS, MC, VI. **Special Amenities: free full breakfast and early check-in/late check-out.**

GROUSE MOUNTAIN LODGE — ***Book at aaa.com*** — Phone: 406/862-3000

AAA SAVE — **Small-scale Hotel**

	1P	2P	XP	
6/1-10/16	1P: $175-$255	2P: $175-$255	XP: $10	F12
12/25-2/28	1P: $119-$239	2P: $119-$239	XP: $10	F12
3/1-5/31	1P: $125-$175	2P: $125-$175	XP: $10	F12
10/17-12/24	1P: $115-$165	2P: $115-$165	XP: $10	F12

Location: 1 mi w on US 93 from jct of SR 487. 2 Fairway Dr 59937. Fax: 406/862-0326. **Facility:** 145 units. 133 one-bedroom standard units. 12 one-bedroom suites ($159-$255), some with efficiencies and/or whirlpools. 3 stories, interior corridors. **Parking:** on-site, winter plug-ins. **Terms:** check-in 4 pm, 15 day cancellation notice-fee imposed. **Amenities:** hair dryers. *Some:* irons. **Dining:** The Grill & Wine Room, see separate listing. **Pool(s):** heated indoor. **Leisure Activities:** sauna, whirlpools, exercise room. *Fee:* game room. **Guest Services:** gift shop, valet and coin laundry, area transportation-train depot, downtown. **Business Services:** conference facilities, business center. **Cards:** AX, MC, VI.

(See ad p 263)

SOME UNITS

HIDDEN MOOSE LODGE — Phone: (406)862-6516

Bed & Breakfast

	1P	2P	XP	
6/11-10/2	1P: $139-$199	2P: $139-$199	XP: $10	F6
10/3-2/28	1P: $105-$179	2P: $105-$179	XP: $10	F6
3/1-6/10	1P: $99-$159	2P: $99-$159	XP: $10	F6

Location: Jct US 93 and SR 487, 1.5 mi n on SR 487. 1735 E Lakeshore Dr 59937. Fax: 406/862-6514. **Facility:** Each guest room at this upscale yet rustic lodge, which is close to a mountain stream, has a private balcony or patio with a flower box. Designated smoking area. 13 units. 12 one-bedroom standard units, some with whirlpools. 1 one-bedroom suite with whirlpool. 2 stories (no elevator), interior/exterior corridors. **Parking:** on-site, winter plug-ins. **Terms:** office hours 7:30 am-11 pm, check-in 4 pm, 30 day cancellation notice-fee imposed. **Amenities:** DVD players, irons, hair dryers. **Leisure Activities:** whirlpool, canoeing, bicycles, hiking trails, playground. **Guest Services:** complimentary evening beverages, complimentary laundry, area transportation. **Cards:** AX, DS, MC, VI.

KANDAHAR LODGE **Phone:** (406)862-6098

AAA SAVE

Small-scale Hotel

1/3-2/28	1P: $149-$339	2P: $149-$339	XP: $10	F12
6/1-10/1	1P: $99-$299	2P: $99-$299	XP: $10	F12
11/25-1/2	1P: $99-$289	2P: $99-$289	XP: $10	F12

Location: Jct of US 93 and SR 487, 2.4 mi n on SR 487, 5.2 mi n at flashing light. 3824 Big Mountain Rd 59937 (PO Box 278). Fax: 406/862-6095. **Facility:** Smoke free premises. 50 units. 49 one-bedroom standard units, some with efficiencies. 1 three-bedroom suite ($450-$699) with kitchen. 4 stories (no elevator), interior corridors. *Bath:* combo or shower only. **Parking:** on-site. **Terms:** open 6/1-10/1 & 11/25-2/28, check-in 4 pm, 30 day cancellation notice-fee imposed. **Amenities:** hair dryers. **Dining:** 7:30 am-10:30 & 5:30-9:30 pm; closed 4/19-5/20 & 10/10-11/20, cocktails. **Leisure Activities:** sauna, whirlpool, steamrooms, outdoor garden tub/soaking pool, ski in & out, "walk in the tree tops", rental bicycles, hiking trails, exercise room. *Fee:* downhill & cross country skiing. **Guest Services:** coin laundry, area transportation-ski area in winter. **Business Services:** meeting rooms, business center. **Cards:** AX, DS, MC, VI. **Special Amenities: free expanded continental breakfast and early check-in/late check-out.** ***(See color ad below)***

SOME UNITS

DATA PORT

KINTLA LODGE **Phone:** (406)862-1960

Condominium

3/1-4/11 & 12/17-2/28	1P: $175-$500	2P: $175-$500	XP: $20	F12
11/25-12/16	1P: $125-$400	2P: $125-$400	XP: $20	F12
4/12-11/24	1P: $120-$375	2P: $120-$375	XP: $20	F12

Location: Jct of US 93 and SR 487, 2.4 mi n on SR 487, 5.2 mi n at flashing light. 3840 Big Mountain Rd 59937 (PO Box 1400). Fax: 406/862-1969. **Facility:** Ski-in/ski-out access is featured at this lodge. Smoke free premises. 20 units. 11 one- and 9 two-bedroom suites with kitchens. 4 stories, interior corridors. **Parking:** on-site. **Terms:** office hours 8 am-5 pm, off-site registration, check-in 4 pm, 30 day cancellation notice-fee imposed, weekly rates available, package plans. **Amenities:** video library (fee), voice mail, irons, hair dryers. **Leisure Activities:** sauna, whirlpool, 2 lighted tennis courts, recreation programs, rental bicycles, hiking trails, jogging. *Fee:* downhill & cross country skiing, snowmobiling, horseback riding. **Guest Services:** gift shop, complimentary laundry, area transportation (fee). **Business Services:** meeting rooms. **Cards:** AX, DC, MC, VI.

ASK FEE VCR

KRISTIANNA MOUNTAIN HOMES ***Book at aaa.com*** **Phone:** (406)862-2860

AAA SAVE

Condominium

3/1-4/11 & 11/25-2/28	1P: $138-$220	2P: $220-$308	XP: $20	F12
4/12-11/24	1P: $100-$220	2P: $138-$230	XP: $10	F12

Location: Jct US 93 and SR 487, 2.4 mi n on SR 487, at flashing light go 5.2 mi on Big Mountain Rd, just n on Gelande, then just w on Kristanna Close. Located in a quiet, secluded area. 3842 Winter Ln 59937 (PO Box 1545). Fax: 406/862-0782. **Facility:** 9 units. 6 two- and 3 three-bedroom suites with kitchens. 4 stories (no elevator), interior/exterior corridors. **Parking:** on-site, winter plug-ins. **Terms:** cancellation fee imposed, pets (in designated units). **Amenities:** video games, CD players, voice mail, irons, hair dryers. **Leisure Activities:** sauna, whirlpool, catch & release fishing in Jumping Rainbow Pond, 4 lighted tennis courts, adjacent to chair 3 with ski in/ski out access, mountain biking trails, rental bicycles, hiking trails, jogging. *Fee:* downhill & cross country skiing, snowmobiling, horseback riding, massage. **Guest Services:** coin laundry, area transportation (fee)-train depot. **Cards:** AX, DC, MC, VI.

FEE

MORNING EAGLE — Phone: (406)862-1960

Condominium

12/18-2/28	1P: $250-$625	2P: $250-$625	XP: $20	F12
3/1-4/11	1P: $200-$525	2P: $200-$525	XP: $20	F12
11/25-12/17	1P: $150-$425	2P: $150-$425	XP: $20	F12
4/12-11/24	1P: $125-$375	2P: $125-$375	XP: $20	F12

Location: Jct US 93 and SR 487, 2.4 mi n on SR 487, then 5.2 mi n at flashing light. Big Mountain Rd 59937 (PO Box 1400). Fax: 406/862-1969. **Facility:** The newest addition to the lodging scene on Big Mountain offers spacious, fully contained condominiums which are beautifully appointed and decorated. 49 units. 4 one-bedroom standard units with kitchens. 15 one-, 18 two- and 12 three-bedroom suites with kitchens. 4 stories, interior corridors. **Parking:** on-site. **Terms:** check-in 4 pm, 30 day cancellation notice-fee imposed, package plans - in winter. **Amenities:** DVD players, CD players, voice mail, irons, hair dryers. **Pool(s):** heated indoor. **Leisure Activities:** whirlpool, recreation programs, rental bicycles, hiking trails, jogging. *Fee:* 4 lighted tennis courts, downhill & cross country skiing, snowmobiling, horseback riding. **Guest Services:** complimentary laundry, area transportation (fee). **Cards:** AX, DS, MC, VI.

ASK DATA PORT
FEE

NORTH FORTY RESORT — Phone: (406)862-7740

Cabin

6/15-9/15 & 12/21-2/28	2P: $90-$215	XP: $10	F13
3/1-6/14 & 9/16-12/20	2P: $69-$159	XP: $10	F13

Location: 2.5 mi e on SR 40 from jct of US 93. Located in a quiet, secluded area. 3765 Hwy 40 W 59912 (PO Box 4250, 59937). Fax: 406/862-7741. **Facility:** On 40 wooded acres, these cabins each feature paved parking, fireplaces and two televisions. Designated smoking area. 22 cabins. 1 story, exterior corridors. **Parking:** on-site, winter plug-ins. **Terms:** office hours 7 am-10 pm, check-in 4 pm, 14 day cancellation notice, in season-fee imposed, pets ($10 extra charge, in designated units). **Leisure Activities:** sauna, whirlpools, hiking trails. **Cards:** AX, DS, MC, VI.

FEE

PINE LODGE — Phone: (406)862-7600

AAA SAVE

Small-scale Hotel

6/25-9/5 [CP]	1P: $110-$125	2P: $120-$130
9/6-1/1 [CP]	1P: $80-$110	2P: $90-$120
1/2-2/28 [CP]	1P: $70-$90	2P: $75-$95
3/1-6/24 [CP]	1P: $70-$80	2P: $75-$85

Location: 1 mi s on US 93. 920 Spokane Ave 59937. Fax: 406/862-7616. **Facility:** 76 units. 66 one-bedroom standard units. 10 one-bedroom suites ($95-$190), some with kitchens. 3 stories, interior corridors. *Bath:* combo or shower only. **Parking:** on-site, winter plug-ins. **Terms:** check-in 4 pm, cancellation fee imposed. **Amenities:** hair dryers. *Some:* irons. **Pool(s):** small heated indoor/outdoor. **Leisure Activities:** whirlpool, exercise room. **Guest Services:** valet and coin laundry. **Business Services:** meeting rooms. **Cards:** AX, CB, DC, DS, MC, VI. **Special Amenities: free continental breakfast and free local telephone calls.**

SOME UNITS
DATA PORT / /

SUPER 8 MOTEL — Phone: 406/862-8255

6/26-8/21	1P: $84	2P: $89	XP: $5	F12
3/1-6/25	1P: $44-$60	2P: $49-$65	XP: $5	F12
8/22-9/12	1P: $60	2P: $65	XP: $5	F12
9/13-2/28	1P: $44	2P: $49	XP: $5	F12

Small-scale Hotel **Location:** 1 mi s on US 93 from jct of SR 487. 800 Spokane Ave 59937. Fax: 406/862-8255. **Facility:** 40 one-bedroom standard units. 2 stories (no elevator), interior corridors. **Parking:** on-site, winter plug-ins. **Terms:** pets ($5 extra charge). **Leisure Activities:** whirlpool. **Guest Services:** coin laundry. **Cards:** AX, CB, DC, DS, MC, VI. **Special Amenities: free continental breakfast and free local telephone calls.**

SOME UNITS
FEE

WHITEFISH LAKE LODGE & MARINA — Phone: (406)862-2929

6/27-9/2 & 12/19-2/28	1P: $99-$490	2P: $99-$490
3/1-6/26 & 9/3-12/18	1P: $80-$390	2P: $80-$390

Condominium **Location:** Jct US 93 and SR 487, 1.5 mi n on SR 487. 1400 Wisconsin Ave 59937 (PO Box 2040). Fax: 406/862-3550. **Facility:** These contemporary condos, most with a fireplace and private balcony, overlook a lake. 32 units. 7 one-, 15 two- and 10 three-bedroom suites ($430-$490) with kitchens. 3 stories, exterior corridors. **Parking:** on-site, winter plug-ins. **Terms:** office hours 9 am-5 pm, check-in 4 pm, 3 night minimum stay - seasonal, 45 day cancellation notice-fee imposed, package plans. **Pool(s):** heated outdoor. **Leisure Activities:** whirlpools, rental boats, rental canoes, rental paddleboats, boat dock, fishing. *Fee:* waterskiing, pontoons, waverunners, waterski equipment. **Guest Services:** coin laundry. **Cards:** AX, MC, VI.

SOME UNITS
VCR

WHERE TO DINE

THE GRILL & WINE ROOM — **Lunch:** $7-$10 — **Dinner:** $12-$21 — **Phone:** 406/862-3000

American — **Location:** 1 mi w on US 93 from jct of SR 487; in Grouse Mountain Lodge. 2 Fairway Dr 59937. **Hours:** 7 am-2 & 5:30-9:30 pm. **Reservations:** suggested. **Features:** You'll discover fine dining in a mountain resort atmosphere and a menu to support an array of taste temptations. Limited lunch fare includes inventive burgers and sandwiches, all well prepared and made to order. Side dishes are varied and similarly tasty. Casual dress; cocktails. **Parking:** on-site. **Cards:** AX, DC, DS, MC, VI.

MAMBO ITALIANO — **Dinner:** $5-$14 — **Phone:** 406/863-9600

Italian — **Location:** Downtown. 234 2nd St E 59937. **Hours:** 5 pm-10 pm. Closed: 12/25. **Reservations:** accepted. **Features:** The family-owned restaurant serves traditional and inventive dishes in casual and comfortable surroundings. Casual dress; beer & wine only. **Parking:** street. **Cards:** AX, CB, DC, DS, JC, MC, VI.

ORIENT EXPRESS RESTAURANT — **Lunch:** $4-$7 — **Dinner:** $7-$14 — **Phone:** 406/862-7818

Chinese — **Location:** Just n of jct SR 40. 6155 US 93 S 59937. **Hours:** 11 am-3:30 & 4:30-9:30 pm. Closed major holidays; also Mon. **Reservations:** accepted. **Features:** The casual family restaurant overlooks a par-three executive golf course. Friendly servers aim to please. Casual dress; cocktails. **Parking:** on-site. **Cards:** CB, DC, DS, JC, MC, VI.

POLLO GRILL — **Dinner:** $11-$23 — **Phone:** 406/863-9400

American — **Location:** 2 mi n on Wisconsin Ave, follow signs to Big Mountain Rd. 1705 Wisconsin Ave 59937. **Hours:** 5 pm-10 pm; to 9 pm weekdays in winter. **Reservations:** suggested. **Features:** This popular eatery features a variety of entrees, many of which are prepared on a rotisserie grill. Portions are ample and side dishes of garlic mashed potatoes and home-style vegetables tasty. The setting is casual with a rural, dark wood decor. Casual dress; beer & wine only. **Parking:** on-site. **Cards:** AX, DS, MC, VI.

TRUBY'S WOOD-FIRED PIZZA — **Lunch:** $5-$9 — **Dinner:** $7-$15 — **Phone:** 406/862-4979

Pizza — **Location:** Downtown. 115 Central Ave 59937. **Hours:** 11 am-10 pm, Sun from 4 pm. Closed: 4/11, 11/25, 12/25. **Features:** Wood-fired ovens at the casual, family-friendly restaurant produce pizzas that are widely popular with locals and the ski crowd from nearby Big Mountain. Also good are the steaks, ribs and pasta dishes. Smoking is not permitted here. Casual dress; cocktails. **Parking:** street. **Cards:** AX, DS, MC, VI.

TUPELO GRILLE AND WINE BAR — **Dinner:** $13-$21 — **Phone:** 406/862-6136

Continental — **Location:** Downtown. 17 Central Ave 59937. **Hours:** 5:30 pm-close. Closed: 4/11, 11/25, 12/25. **Features:** In keeping with the experience of the owners, who hail from the South, the menu's Continental dishes show hints of Southern Creole and Cajun influences. Casual dress; beer & wine only. **Parking:** street. **Cards:** AX, MC, VI.

WASABI SUSHI BAR & THE GINGER GRILL — **Dinner:** $15-$20 — **Phone:** 406/863-9283

Asian — **Location:** Downtown. 419 E Second St 59937. **Hours:** 5 pm-close. Closed: 11/25, 12/25; also Mon & Super Bowl Sun. **Reservations:** accepted. **Features:** The menu centers on sushi and Asian-influenced dishes grilled with a contemporary flair. The lively, colorful dining room displays original artwork in oils, acrylics and fiber. Casual dress; beer & wine only. **Parking:** street. **Cards:** MC, VI.

WHITEFISH LAKE GOLF CLUB RESTAURANT **Lunch:** $4-$8 **Dinner:** $11-$25 **Phone:** 406/862-5285

Steak & Seafood

Location: 1 mi w. Hwy 93 N 59937. **Hours:** 11 am-9:30 pm; from 5:30 pm 10/15-4/15. Closed: 11/25; also Thurs 5/1-8/31. **Reservations:** suggested. **Features:** Located on one of the areas finest golf courses, the restaurant is housed in a structure made of logs from the surrounding forests. Guest dine on steak and seafood as well as inventive specials created nightly. Casual dress; cocktails. **Parking:** on-site. **Cards:** AX, DS, MC, VI.

WHITE SULPHUR SPRINGS pop. 984

— WHERE TO STAY —

ALL SEASONS SUPER 8 MOTEL *Book at aaa.com* **Phone:** (406)547-8888

Motel

5/1-11/30 [CP]	1P: $45-$50	2P: $53-$58	XP: $6	F13
3/1-4/30 & 12/1-2/28 [CP]	1P: $41-$45	2P: $48-$53	XP: $6	F13

Location: On US 89, south end of town. 808 3rd Ave SW 59645 (PO Box 626). Fax: 406/547-2573. **Facility:** 32 one-bedroom standard units. 2 stories (no elevator), interior corridors. **Parking:** on-site, winter plug-ins. **Terms:** cancellation fee imposed, pets ($20 deposit). **Amenities:** hair dryers. **Leisure Activities:** whirlpool. **Guest Services:** coin laundry. **Cards:** AX, DS, MC, VI.

SOME UNITS

ASK / / FEE

FOXWOOD INN **Phone:** 406/547-2106

Historic Bed & Breakfast

All Year [BP]	1P: $46	2P: $56-$60	XP: $10	F5

Location: US 12 and 89, 0.3 mi w on SR 360, just s on SW 10th Ave, 0.5 mi w on gravel road. Located in a quiet, rural area. 52 Miller Rd 59645 (PO Box 368). Fax: 406/547-3380. **Facility:** Quaint home built in 1890 situated in a valley. Guest units offer varying styles of furnishings. Smoke free premises. 11 units. 9 one- and 2 two-bedroom standard units. 2 stories (no elevator), interior corridors. *Bath:* shared. **Parking:** on-site. **Terms:** cancellation fee imposed. **Amenities:** video library. **Guest Services:** TV in common area.

Wyoming

Devil's Tower National Monument / © Henryk T. Kaiser / Camerique Inc., Int'l/Robertstock

AFTON pop. 1,818

WHERE TO STAY

THE CORRAL

Phone: 307/885-5424

Cabin

5/1-11/1 | 1P: $45-$50 | 2P: $50-$55 | XP: $5

Location: On US 89; center. 161 Washington St (US Hwy 89) 83110 (PO Box 442). Fax: 307/885-5464. **Facility:** Smoke free premises. 15 cabins. 1 story, exterior corridors. *Bath:* combo or shower only. **Parking:** on-site. **Terms:** open 5/1-11/1, small pets only (with prior approval). **Leisure Activities:** playground, volleyball. **Cards:** AX, CB, DC, DS, MC, VI.

SOME UNITS

HI COUNTRY INN

Phone: (307)885-3856

Motel

All Year | 1P: $75-$85 | 2P: $95-$100 | XP: $10 | F12

Location: On US 89, 0.8 mi s. 689 S Washington St (US Hwy 89) 83110-0907 (PO Box 0907). Fax: 307/885-9318. **Facility:** 30 one-bedroom standard units. 1 story, exterior corridors. **Parking:** on-site, winter plug-ins. **Terms:** 5 day cancellation notice, small pets only. **Pool(s):** heated outdoor. **Leisure Activities:** whirlpool, cross country skiing, snowmobiling, volleyball. **Business Services:** fax (fee). **Cards:** AX, CB, DC, DS, MC, VI.

SOME UNITS

LAZY B MOTEL

Phone: 307/885-3187

Motel

All Year | 1P: $50-$60 | 2P: $65-$75 | XP: $7

Location: On US 89; center. 219 Washington St (US Hwy 89) 83110 (PO Box 430). Fax: 307/885-3035. **Facility:** 25 one-bedroom standard units. 1 story, exterior corridors. *Bath:* combo or shower only. **Parking:** on-site, winter plug-ins. **Pool(s):** heated outdoor. **Leisure Activities:** playground. *Fee:* horse corral. **Guest Services:** coin laundry, airport transportation-Afton Municipal Airport. **Business Services:** fax (fee). **Cards:** AX, CB, DC, DS, MC, VI. **Special Amenities: free local telephone calls and preferred room (subject to availability with advanced reservations).**

SOME UNITS

FEE

MOUNTAIN INN

Phone: 307/885-3156

Motel

All Year | 1P: $50-$80 | 2P: $65-$85 | XP: $5 | D10

Location: On US 89, 1.5 mi s. 83542 Hwy 89 83110. Fax: 307/885-3645. **Facility:** 20 one-bedroom standard units. 1 story, exterior corridors. *Bath:* combo or shower only. **Parking:** on-site, winter plug-ins. **Terms:** pets ($5 extra charge). **Pool(s):** heated outdoor. **Leisure Activities:** sauna, whirlpool, cross country skiing, snowmobiling. **Cards:** MC, VI.

SOME UNITS

ASK

FEE

ALPINE pop. 550

WHERE TO STAY

BEST WESTERN FLYING SADDLE LODGE Book at aaa.com **Phone:** 307/654-7561

AAA SAVE

Motel

5/1-10/31 1P: $116-$180

Location: 0.5 mi e of jct US 26 and 89. 118878 Jct US 26 & 89 83128 (PO Box 3227). Fax: 307/654-7563. **Facility:** 26 units. 20 one-bedroom standard units, some with whirlpools. 6 cabins ($171-$180). 1 story, exterior corridors. **Parking:** on-site. **Terms:** open 5/1-10/31, [BP] & [MAP] meal plans available, package plans, pets ($50 deposit, with prior approval). **Amenities:** voice mail, irons, hair dryers. **Dining:** The Canyon Restaurant, see separate listing. **Pool(s):** small heated outdoor. **Leisure Activities:** whirlpools, fishing, tennis court, hiking trails, jogging. *Fee:* charter fishing. **Cards:** AX, DS, MC, VI. **Special Amenities: free continental breakfast and early check-in/late check-out.**

SOME UNITS

FEE FEE

WHERE TO DINE

THE CANYON RESTAURANT **Dinner:** $8-$27 **Phone:** 307/654-7561

AAA

American

Location: 0.5 mi e of jct US 26 and 89; in Best Western Flying Saddle Lodge. Jct US 26 & 89 83128. **Hours:** Open 3/1-11/1 & 12/20-2/28; 7 am-11 & 6-10 pm. **Reservations:** suggested. **Features:** This small, intimate dining room is attractively furnished and has a large tropical fish tank. The Flying Saddle selections always include elk, buffalo, pork loin, a few pasta as well as chicken dishes, fresh fish, prawns and homemade bread and dessert. The formally attired staff offers warm, Western professionalism and enjoy live piano music some evenings. Casual dress; cocktails. **Parking:** on-site. **Cards:** AX, DS, MC, VI.

GUNNAR'S PIZZA **Lunch:** $7-$18 **Dinner:** $7-$18 **Phone:** 307/654-7778

American

Location: Center. US 89 83128. **Hours:** 11 am-9 pm, Fri & Sat-10 pm. Closed: 11/25, 12/25. **Features:** Wonderful bread, salad, soup and subs abound here, with the substantial fare and restaurant location attracting plenty of river rafters and those in search of great mountain views. The tasty, fresh salad selections are varied and quite plentiful, too. Casual dress; beer only. **Parking:** on-site. **Cards:** MC, VI.

ALTA pop. 400

WHERE TO STAY

GRAND TARGHEE RESORT Book at aaa.com **Phone:** (307)353-2300

AAA SAVE

Resort Small-scale Hotel

11/19-2/28	1P: $81-$519	2P: $81-$519	XP: $12	F14
6/5-9/5	1P: $73-$284	2P: $73-$284	XP: $12	F14

Location: 12 mi e on Little Ave, follow signs. (PO Box SKI). Fax: 307/353-8619. **Facility:** At the base of a ski area in a picturesque, European-style village, the resort has rustic guest rooms, some with adobe-style stoves and bunk beds. Smoke free premises. 96 units. 88 one- and 8 two-bedroom standard units, some with efficiencies. 2-4 stories (no elevator), interior/exterior corridors. *Bath:* combo or shower only. **Parking:** on-site. **Terms:** open 6/5-9/5 & 11/19-2/28, check-in 4 pm, 30 day cancellation notice-fee imposed, package plans - seasonal. **Amenities:** video library (fee). **Dining:** 2 restaurants, 7 am-10 pm, cocktails. **Pool(s):** heated outdoor. **Leisure Activities:** sauna, whirlpools, 2 tennis courts, cross country skiing, ice skating, recreation programs, climbing wall, ropes course, scenic chairlift rides, summer frisbee golf, yoga instruction, rental bicycles, hiking trails, exercise room, sports court, horseshoes. *Fee:* tubing, downhill skiing, dog sledding, sleigh ride, snowboarding, horseback riding, massage, game room. **Guest Services:** gift shop, coin laundry. *Fee:* airport transportation-Jackson Hole Airport, area transportation-Idaho Falls. **Business Services:** meeting rooms, PC. **Cards:** AX, DS, MC, VI. **Special Amenities: free local telephone calls.**

SOME UNITS

FEE FEE

BIG HORN pop. 198

WHERE TO STAY

SPAHN'S BIG HORN MOUNTAIN BED & BREAKFAST LLC **Phone:** 307/674-8150

Bed & Breakfast

All Year [BP]	1P: $110-$150	2P: $110-$150	XP: $25

Location: 6 mi w of Big Horn, last 1.4 mi on gravel road; in Big Horn Mountains (call for directions). Located in a quiet, secluded area. 70 Upper Hideaway Ln 82833 (PO Box 579). **Facility:** This log home and two cabins are nestled in the Big Horn Mountains, amid a pine forest and 100-mile views; binoculars are handed out with breakfast. Smoke free premises. 5 units. 3 one-bedroom standard units. 2 cabins. 1-4 stories (no elevator), interior/exterior corridors. *Bath:* shower only. **Parking:** on-site. **Terms:** check-in 4 pm, 21 day cancellation notice-fee imposed. **Leisure Activities:** hiking trails.

SOME UNITS

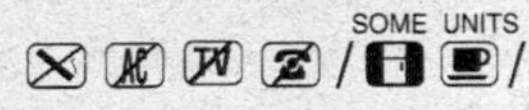

BUFFALO pop. 3,900

WHERE TO STAY

ARROWHEAD MOTEL **Phone:** 307/684 9453

Motel

5/15-8/15	1P: $32-$42	2P: $42-$60	XP: $5
8/16-10/31	1P: $35-$40	2P: $40-$50	XP: $5
11/1-2/28	1P: $32-$36	2P: $36-$50	XP: $3
3/1-5/14	1P: $28-$32	2P: $35-$45	XP: $3

Location: Jct US 16, 87 and Business Loop I-25, 0.6 mi w. 749 Fort St 82834. **Facility:** 13 one-bedroom standard units, some with efficiencies. 1 story, exterior corridors. *Bath:* combo or shower only. **Parking:** on-site, winter plug-ins. **Terms:** pets ($5 extra charge). **Cards:** MC, VI.

SOME UNITS

FEE

BIG HORN MOTEL — AAA SAVE — Motel — **Phone:** 307/684-7822

6/1-2/28	1P: $45-$55	2P: $55-$65	XP: $5	D10
3/1-5/31	1P: $37-$47	2P: $47-$57	XP: $5	D10

Location: On US 16; downtown. 209 N Main St 82834. **Facility:** 20 units. 15 one- and 5 two-bedroom standard units. 1 story, exterior corridors. *Bath:* combo or shower only. **Parking:** on-site. **Terms:** 3 day cancellation notice-fee imposed, weekly rates available, [CP] meal plan available. **Cards:** AX, DC, DS, MC, VI. **Special Amenities: free continental breakfast and free local telephone calls.**

SOME UNITS

CANYON MOTEL — Motel — **Phone:** (307)684-2957

5/15-10/31	1P: $40-$46	2P: $50-$60	XP: $3
3/1-5/14 & 11/1-2/28	1P: $32-$36	2P: $34-$48	XP: $3

Location: Jct US 16/87/Business Loop I-25, 0.9 mi w on US 16. 997 Fort St 82834 (PO Box 56). **Facility:** 18 one-bedroom standard units, some with efficiencies or kitchens. 1 story, exterior corridors. *Bath:* combo or shower only. **Parking:** on-site, winter plug-ins. **Terms:** weekly rates available, pets ($3 extra charge). **Cards:** AX, DC, DS, MC, VI.

SOME UNITS

FEE

CLEAR CREEK BED & BREAKFAST — Bed & Breakfast — **Phone:** 307/684-2317

All Year [BP]	1P: $65-$85	2P: $65-$85	XP: $10	D16

Location: I-25, exit 298, 0.7 mi nw on Business Loop I-25/US 87. 330 S Main St 82834. **Facility:** 4 units. 3 one-bedroom standard units. 1 one-bedroom suite. 2 stories (no elevator), interior corridors. *Bath:* some shared or private, combo or shower only. **Parking:** street. **Terms:** check-in 4 pm, 3 day cancellation notice, weekly rates available. **Amenities:** *Some:* hair dryers. **Cards:** MC, VI.

SOME UNITS

COMFORT INN ***Book at aaa.com*** — Small-scale Hotel — **Phone:** (307)684-9564

7/31-9/4	1P: $70-$120	2P: $70-$120	XP: $5	F18
5/16-7/30	1P: $60-$99	2P: $60-$99	XP: $5	F18
9/5-2/28	1P: $45-$90	2P: $45-$90		
3/1-5/15	1P: $45-$70	2P: $45-$70	XP: $5	F18

Location: I-25, exit 299 (US 16), just e; I-90, exit 58, 1.3 mi w. 65 Hwy 16 E 82834. Fax: 307/684-9564. **Facility:** 41 one-bedroom standard units. 2 stories (no elevator), interior/exterior corridors. **Parking:** on-site, winter plug-ins. **Terms:** [ECP] meal plan available, pets ($5 extra charge, in limited units). **Amenities:** irons, hair dryers. **Leisure Activities:** whirlpool. **Cards:** AX, DC, DS, MC, VI. ***(See color ad below)***

SOME UNITS

FEE

HISTORIC MANSION HOUSE INN AND MOTEL — AAA SAVE — Motel — **Phone:** (307)684-2218

6/15-8/31 [CP]	1P: $50-$60	2P: $70-$75	XP: $5	F5
3/1-6/14 & 9/1-10/31 [CP]	1P: $45-$50	2P: $58-$65	XP: $5	F5
11/1-2/28 [CP]	1P: $40-$45	2P: $48-$58	XP: $5	F5

Location: US 16; downtown. 313 N Main St 82834. **Facility:** 17 one-bedroom standard units. 1-2 stories (no elevator), interior/exterior corridors. *Bath:* combo or shower only. **Parking:** on-site, winter plug-ins. **Terms:** check-in 4 pm, 3 day cancellation notice. **Leisure Activities:** whirlpool. **Cards:** DS, MC, VI. **Special Amenities: free continental breakfast and free local telephone calls.** ***(See color ad p 323)***

SOME UNITS

MOUNTAIN VIEW MOTEL & CAMPGROUND **Phone:** 307/684-2881

Cabin

5/1-10/31	1P: $49-$99
3/1-4/30 & 11/1-2/28	1P: $35-$75

Location: Jct US 16/87 and Business Loop I-25, 0.4 mi w on US 16. 585 Fort St 82834. Fax: 307/684-9465. **Facility:** 13 cabins ($35-$99). 1 story, exterior corridors. *Bath:* combo or shower only. **Parking:** on-site. **Terms:** 7 day cancellation notice-fee imposed, pets (in smoking units). **Guest Services:** coin laundry. **Cards:** MC, VI.

SOME UNITS

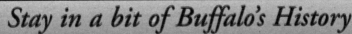

SUPER 8 MOTEL OF BUFFALO ***Book at aaa.com*** **Phone:** (307)684-2531

Small-scale Hotel

5/21-9/1 [CP]	1P: $74-$99	2P: $84-$120	XP: $5	F12
9/2-10/31 [CP]	1P: $55-$74	2P: $65-$84	XP: $5	F12
3/1-5/20 [CP]	1P: $44-$70	2P: $55-$80	XP: $5	F12
11/1-2/28 [CP]	1P: $44-$55	2P: $55-$65	XP: $5	F12

Location: I-25, exit 299 (US 16), just w; I-90, exit 58, 1.3 mi w. 655 E Hart St 82834. Fax: 307/684-7954. **Facility:** 48 one-bedroom standard units. 2 stories (no elevator), interior corridors. **Parking:** on-site, winter plug-ins. **Terms:** 3 day cancellation notice-fee imposed, pets ($5.25 extra charge). **Amenities:** safes (fee). *Some:* hair dryers. **Leisure Activities:** hiking trails. *Fee:* miniature golf, ferris wheel, carousel, outdoor museum. **Guest Services:** gift shop. **Cards:** AX, CB, DC, DS, MC, VI. **Special Amenities: free continental breakfast and free local telephone calls.** *(See color ad below)*

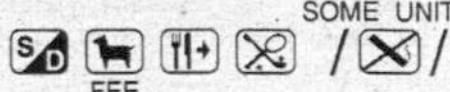

WYOMING MOTEL *Book at aaa.com* **Phone:** (307)684-5505

AAA SAVE ♦♦ **Motel**

6/7-8/20 [CP]	1P: $69-$74	2P: $69-$97	XP: $8	F
8/21-9/30 [CP]	1P: $40-$65	2P: $40-$87	XP: $8	F
3/1-6/6 [CP]	1P: $35-$60	2P: $35-$64	XP: $8	F
10/1-2/28 [CP]	1P: $27-$46	2P: $27-$51	XP: $8	F

Location: I-25, exit 299 (US 16), just w; I-90, exit 58, 1.3 mi w. 610 E Hart St 82834. Fax: 307/684-5442. **Facility:** 27 one-bedroom standard units, some with efficiencies and/or whirlpools. 1 story, exterior corridors. **Parking:** on-site, winter plug-ins. **Terms:** cancellation fee imposed, pets (in designated units, with prior approval). **Pool(s):** small heated outdoor. **Leisure Activities:** whirlpool, playground. **Guest Services:** airport transportation-Johnson County Airport. **Cards:** AX, CB, DC, DS, MC, VI. **Special Amenities: free continental breakfast and free local telephone calls.** *(See color ad below)*

SOME UNITS

Z-BAR MOTEL **Phone:** 307/684-5535

AAA SAVE ♦♦ **Cabin**

6/11-9/30	1P: $48-$62	2P: $53-$67	XP: $4	D12
3/1-6/10 & 10/1-2/28	1P: $34-$49	2P: $40-$54	XP: $4	D12

Location: Jct US 16, 87 and Business Loop I-25, 0.5 mi w on US 16. 626 Fort St 82834. Fax: 307/684-5538. **Facility:** 26 units. 4 one-bedroom standard units. 22 cabins. 1 story, exterior corridors. *Bath:* combo or shower only. **Parking:** on-site, winter plug-ins. **Terms:** 30 day cancellation notice, pets ($4 extra charge). **Leisure Activities:** playground. **Cards:** AX, DC, DS, MC, VI. **Special Amenities: free local telephone calls and early check-in/late check-out.** *(See color ad below)*

SOME UNITS

FEE

WHERE TO DINE

BOZEMAN'S TRAIL STEAKHOUSE **Lunch:** $5-$8 **Dinner:** $8-$22 **Phone:** 307/684-5555

AAA ♦ **American**

Location: I-25, exit 299 (US 16), just w. 675 E Hart St 82834. **Hours:** 11 am-10 pm; to 9 pm in winter. Closed: 4/11, 11/25, 12/25. **Features:** Colonel Bozeman's offers a varied menu that includes a few Mexican items, burgers, buffalo steak, shrimp dinners and the house specialty, baby back ribs. The decor creates a Western and Plains Indian ambience. Casual dress; cocktails. **Parking:** on-site. **Cards:** AX, CB, DS, MC, VI. *(See color ad p 323)*

CHINA GARDEN **Lunch:** $6-$8 **Dinner:** $8-$13 **Phone:** 307/684-2186

♦ Chinese

Location: US 16; downtown. 386 N Main St 82834. **Hours:** 11 am-9:30 pm. Closed major holidays. **Reservations:** accepted. **Features:** A surprise find of extremely tasty, well prepared authentic cuisine in this small town. The atmosphere is casual. Casual dress; beer & wine only. **Parking:** on-site. **Cards:** MC, VI.

WINCHESTER STEAK HOUSE **Dinner:** $10-$24 **Phone:** 307/684-8636

Steak House

Location: I-25, exit 299 (US 16), 0.5 mi e; I-90, exit 58, just e. 117 US Hwy 16 E 82834. **Hours:** 5 pm-9 pm. Closed: 11/25, 12/25; also Sun; Mon in winter. **Features:** Voted best steak and seafood in Buffalo, this family run restaurant attracts folks from miles around to enjoy a casual dinner at a location convenient to both interstates as well as downtown. Casual dress; cocktails. **Parking:** on-site. **Cards:** AX, DS, MC, VI.

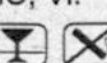

CASPER pop. 49,644

WHERE TO STAY

DAYS INN CASPER *Book at aaa.com* **Phone:** (307)234-1159

Small-scale Hotel

5/16-9/15 [ECP]	1P: $76-$86
9/16-2/28 [ECP]	1P: $74-$81
3/1-5/15 [ECP]	1P: $72-$79

Location: I-25, exit 188A, just w. 301 E 'E' St 82601. Fax: 307/265-0829. **Facility:** 121 units. 120 one-bedroom standard units. 1 one-bedroom suite with kitchen (no utensils). 2 stories (no elevator), interior corridors. **Parking:** on-site, winter plug-ins. **Terms:** cancellation fee imposed, small pets only. **Amenities:** DVD players (fee), video games, hair dryers. *Some:* irons. **Pool(s):** heated outdoor. **Leisure Activities:** exercise room. **Guest Services:** valet and coin laundry. **Business Services:** meeting rooms. **Cards:** AX, CB, DC, DS, JC, MC, VI.

SOME UNITS

ASK / FEE FEE

HAMPTON INN *Book at aaa.com* **Phone:** (307)235-6668

6/1-8/31 [ECP]	1P: $96-$106	2P: $101-$111
3/1-5/31 [ECP]	1P: $91-$101	2P: $96-$106
9/1-2/28 [ECP]	1P: $86-$96	2P: $91-$101

Small-scale Hotel

Location: I-25, exit 188A, just e. 400 W 'F' St 82601. Fax: 307/235-2027. **Facility:** 121 one-bedroom standard units. 2 stories (no elevator), interior corridors. **Parking:** on-site, winter plug-ins. **Terms:** 3 day cancellation notice-fee imposed. **Amenities:** voice mail, irons, hair dryers. **Pool(s):** heated outdoor. **Leisure Activities:** exercise room. **Guest Services:** valet laundry, airport transportation-Netrona County International Airport. **Business Services:** meeting rooms. **Cards:** AX, DC, DS, MC, VI. **Special Amenities: free expanded continental breakfast and free local telephone calls.** *(See color ad p 325)*

SOME UNITS

HEARTHSIDE **Phone:** (307)232-5100

10/1-2/28	1P: $74-$108	2P: $74-$108	XP: $6	F
7/1-9/30	1P: $71-$104	2P: $71-$104	XP: $6	F
3/1-6/30	1P: $68-$97	2P: $68-$97	XP: $6	F

Small-scale Hotel

Location: I-25, exit 186, 0.5 mi s to 1st St, then 0.4 mi w. 111 S Wilson St 82601. Fax: 307/232-5197. **Facility:** 66 units. 59 one-bedroom standard units with efficiencies. 4 one- and 3 two-bedroom suites ($74-$114) with efficiencies. 3 stories, interior corridors. *Bath:* combo or shower only. **Parking:** on-site, winter plug-ins. **Terms:** pets ($50 fee). **Amenities:** dual phone lines, voice mail, hair dryers. **Leisure Activities:** exercise room. **Guest Services:** coin laundry. **Business Services:** meeting rooms, PC. **Cards:** AX, DC, DS, MC, VI. **Special Amenities: free local telephone calls and early check-in/late check-out.**

FEE

HOLIDAY INN *Book at aaa.com* **Phone:** (307)235-2531

6/1-9/1	1P: $109	2P: $109
3/1-5/31 & 9/2-2/28	1P: $99	2P: $99

Small-scale Hotel

Location: I-25, exit 188A, just e. 300 W 'F' St 82601. Fax: 307/473-3100. **Facility:** 200 units. 192 one-bedroom standard units. 8 one-bedroom suites ($149-$199), some with kitchens. 2 stories (no elevator), interior corridors. *Bath:* combo or shower only. **Parking:** on-site, winter plug-ins. **Terms:** 3 day cancellation notice, pets ($50 deposit). **Amenities:** dual phone lines, voice mail, irons, hair dryers. **Dining:** 6 am-2 & 5-10 pm, cocktails. **Pool(s):** small heated indoor. **Leisure Activities:** whirlpool, exercise room. *Fee:* game room. **Guest Services:** complimentary evening beverages: Tues, valet and coin laundry, airport transportation-Natrona County International Airport, area transportation. **Business Services:** conference facilities. **Cards:** AX, CB, DC, DS, JC, MC, VI. **Special Amenities: free local telephone calls.** *(See color ad below & opposite title page)*

SOME UNITS

FEE FEE FEE FEE

PARKWAY PLAZA HOTEL & CONVENTION CENTRE **Phone:** (307)235-1777

6/1-9/30	1P: $85-$90	2P: $90-$95	XP: $5	F18
10/1-2/28	1P: $80	2P: $95	XP: $5	F18
3/1-5/31	1P: $75	2P: $80	XP: $5	F18

Small-scale Hotel

Location: I-25, exit 188A, just w. 123 W 'E' St 82601. Fax: 307/235-8068. **Facility:** 285 units. 260 one-bedroom standard units. 25 one-bedroom suites ($125-$325), some with kitchens and/or whirlpools. 2-4 stories, interior/exterior corridors. *Bath:* combo or shower only. **Parking:** on-site, winter plug-ins. **Terms:** [BP] meal plan available, pets ($25 deposit). **Amenities:** irons. *Some:* DVD players, CD players, dual phone lines. **Dining:** 2 restaurants, 6 am-10 pm, cocktails. **Pool(s):** heated indoor, wading. **Leisure Activities:** sauna, whirlpool, miniature golf, exercise room. **Guest Services:** gift shop, valet and coin laundry, airport transportation-Natrona County Airport. **Business Services:** conference facilities, PC. **Cards:** AX, CB, DC, DS, JC, MC, VI. **Special Amenities: free local telephone calls and free newspaper.** *(See color ad p 327)*

SOME UNITS

FEE

QUALITY INN & SUITES *Book at aaa.com* **Phone:** (307)266-2400

AAA SAVE

Small-scale Hotel

6/1-9/30 [ECP]	1P: $75-$85	2P: $85-$95	XP: $5	F18
1/1-2/28 [ECP]	1P: $70-$80	2P: $75-$85	XP: $5	F18
3/1-5/31 & 10/1-12/31 [ECP]	1P: $65-$75	2P: $70-$80	XP: $5	F18

Location: I-25, exit 188B, just e. 821 N Poplar St 82601. Fax: 307/266-1146. **Facility:** 92 units. 82 one-bedroom standard units. 10 one-bedroom suites ($95-$145), some with whirlpools. 2 stories (no elevator), interior corridors. *Bath:* combo or shower only. **Parking:** on-site, winter plug-ins. **Terms:** pets ($5 extra charge, with prior approval). **Amenities:** video games (fee), voice mail, irons, hair dryers. **Guest Services:** valet and coin laundry. **Business Services:** meeting rooms. **Cards:** AX, CB, DC, DS, JC, MC, VI. **Special Amenities: free expanded continental breakfast and free local telephone calls.** *(See color ad below)*

SOME UNITS

FEE FEE

PARKWAY PLAZA
HOTEL & CONVENTION CENTRE

Toll Free Reservations in Casper 1-800-270-7829

- 300 Guest Rooms & Suites
- Indoor Pool/Sauna & Spa
- Gift Shop & 2 Hair Salons
- 2 Restaurants & Lounge
- Family Fun Park
- River Walk Location
- Downtown Casper

...& more, of course!

- Free deluxe continental breakfast
- Free high-speed internet
- 27" color TV's, cable, pay per view movies, free HBO
- Hairdryers, irons, coffee makers
- Private 2 room and whirlpool suites
- King/Queen Serta beds
- Guest laundry, voicemail
- Fitness Center, Pet Friendly
- 1000 square foot meeting room
- Business center
- 10% discount at adjacent restaurant

Quality Inn & Suites
821 North Poplar
Casper, WY 82601
Phone: 307.266.2400
Fax: 307.266.1146
Toll Free: 800.4.CHOICE

800.228.1AAA
choicehotels.com

We'll see you there.℠

BY CHOICE HOTELS

RADISSON HOTEL CASPER *Book at aaa.com* **Phone:** (307)266-6000

Large-scale Hotel

All Year 1P: $84-$99 2P: $89-$105 XP: $5 F18

Location: I-25, exit 188B, just e. 800 N Poplar St 82601. Fax: 307/473-1010. **Facility:** 228 one-bedroom standard units, some with whirlpools. 5 one-bedroom suites ($119-$204). 6 stories, interior corridors. *Bath:* combo or shower only. **Parking:** on-site, winter plug-ins. **Terms:** [AP] meal plan available, small pets only ($35 deposit). **Pool(s):** heated indoor. **Leisure Activities:** whirlpool, exercise room. *Fee:* game room. **Guest Services:** gift shop, valet laundry. **Business Services:** conference facilities. **Cards:** AX, CB, DC, DS, JC, MC, VI. ***(See color ad below)***

FEE SOME UNITS FEE

SUPER 8 MOTEL *Book at aaa.com* **Phone:** (307)266-3480

Small-scale Hotel

All Year 1P: $50-$55 2P: $57-$62

Location: I-25, exit 188B, 1.7 mi w on S Poplar St (SR 220), 1.8 mi n. 3838 CY Ave 82604. Fax: 307/266-3480. **Facility:** 66 one-bedroom standard units. 3 stories (no elevator), interior corridors. **Parking:** on-site, winter plug-ins. **Terms:** [ECP] meal plan available, pets ($3 extra charge). **Amenities:** video library (fee), hair dryers. *Some:* irons. **Guest Services:** coin laundry. **Cards:** AX, CB, DC, DS, MC, VI.

FEE SOME UNITS FEE

WHERE TO DINE

ARMOR SILVER FOX RESTAURANT & LOUNGE **Lunch:** $6-$8 **Dinner:** $9-$24 **Phone:** 307/235-3000

American

Location: I-25, exit 188B, 4.2 mi sw on SR 220. 3422 S Energy Ln 82604. **Hours:** 11 am-2 & 5-9:30 pm, Fri & Sat 5 pm-10 pm. Closed major holidays; also Sun. **Features:** Well-prepared dishes of prime rib are served in an attractive, relaxing setting that affords a nice mountain view. A most recent dining experience included a cup of tasty, hearty and spicy chicken and sausage gumbo and a delicious Caesar salad. Casual dress; cocktails. **Parking:** on-site. **Cards:** AX, CB, DC, DS, MC, VI.

BOSCO'S ITALIAN RESTAURANT **Lunch:** $4-$8 **Dinner:** $9-$20 **Phone:** 307/265-9658

Italian

Location: I-25, exit 187, 0.3 mi w on McKinley St, just sw. 847 East A St 82601. **Hours:** 11 am-2 & 5-10 pm, Sat from 5 pm. Closed major holidays; also Sun & Mon. **Reservations:** suggested, for dinner. **Features:** Although difficult to find, the casual, child-friendly restaurant is worth the effort. Entree choices include create-your-own Alfredo dishes and traditional veal, chicken, shrimp and gnocchi preparations. Casual dress; cocktails. **Parking:** street. **Cards:** AX, CB, DC, DS, MC, VI.

SOUTH SEA CHINESE RESTAURANT **Lunch:** $5-$14 **Dinner:** $5-$14 **Phone:** 307/237-4777

Chinese

Location: I-25, exit 185, 0.4 mi s on Wyoming, then 0.6 mi w. 3400 E 2nd St 82609. **Hours:** 11 am-9 pm. Closed: 12/25; also Sun. **Features:** The diverse menu lists 102 budget-friendly choices of traditional Oriental food. The locally popular combination seafood sizzling platter is entertaining and tasty. Servers are friendly. Casual dress; beer & wine only. **Parking:** on-site. **Cards:** AX, DS, MC, VI.

CHEYENNE pop. 53,011

WHERE TO STAY

BEST WESTERN HITCHING POST INN RESORT & CONFERENCE CENTER *Book at aaa.com* **Phone:** (307)638-3301

Small-scale Hotel

All Year 1P: $79-$149 2P: $89-$159 XP: $10 F17

Location: I-25, exit 9, 0.8 mi e on I-80 business loop/US 30. 1700 W Lincolnway 82001 (PO Box 1769). Fax: 307/778-7194. **Facility:** 166 one-bedroom standard units. 2 stories (no elevator), interior/exterior corridors. *Bath:* combo or shower only. **Parking:** on-site, winter plug-ins. **Amenities:** video games (fee), high-speed Internet, voice mail, irons, hair dryers. **Dining:** 6 am-10 pm, also, Cheyenne Cattle Company, The Cheyenne Cattle Company, see separate listings, entertainment. **Pool(s):** heated indoor. **Leisure Activities:** saunas, whirlpool, exercise room. *Fee:* massage, game room. **Guest Services:** gift shop, valet and coin laundry, airport transportation-Cheyenne Airport. **Business Services:** conference facilities, business center. **Cards:** AX, CB, DC, DS, JC, MC, VI. **Special Amenities: free newspaper and early check-in/late check-out.** ***(See color ad below)***

SOME UNITS

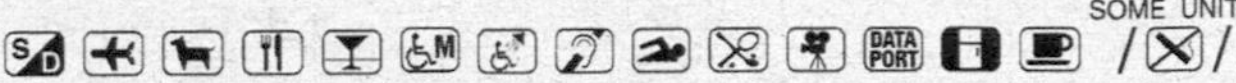

CHEYENNE SUPER 8 MOTEL *Book at aaa.com* **Phone:** (307)635-8741

Motel

All Year [ECP] 1P: $46-$150 2P: $51-$150 XP: $5 F18

Location: I-25, exit 9, 0.7 mi e. 1900 W Lincolnway 82001. Fax: 307/635-8741. **Facility:** 61 one-bedroom standard units. 3 stories (no elevator), interior corridors. *Bath:* combo or shower only. **Parking:** on-site, winter plug-ins. **Terms:** 14 day cancellation notice. **Amenities:** *Fee:* video library, safes. *Some:* irons. **Cards:** AX, CB, DC, DS, MC, VI.

SOME UNITS

FEE

COMFORT INN OF CHEYENNE *Book at aaa.com* **Phone:** (307)638-7202

Small-scale Hotel

All Year [ECP]	1P: $79-$109	2P: $79-$109	XP: $10	F17

Location: I-25, exit 7, just w. 2245 Etchepare Dr 82007. Fax: 307/635-8560. **Facility:** 77 one-bedroom standard units. 2 stories, interior corridors. **Parking:** on-site, winter plug-ins. **Terms:** pets ($20 deposit). **Amenities:** video library (fee), irons, hair dryers. **Pool(s):** heated outdoor. **Leisure Activities:** exercise room. **Guest Services:** valet and coin laundry, area transportation. **Cards:** AX, DC, DS, MC, VI. *(See color ad below)*

SOME UNITS

FEE

DAYS INN CHEYENNE *Book at aaa.com* **Phone:** (307)778-8877

Small-scale Hotel

4/16-9/30 [ECP]	1P: $69-$84	2P: $74-$89	XP: $5	F17
10/1-12/31 [ECP]	1P: $64-$79	2P: $69-$84	XP: $5	F17
3/1-4/15 & 1/1-2/28 [ECP]	1P: $59-$74	2P: $64-$79	XP: $5	F17

Location: I-25, exit 9, just e on US 30/I-80 business loop. 2360 W Lincolnway 82001 (PO Box 1286, 82003). Fax: 307/778-8697. **Facility:** 72 one-bedroom standard units. 2 stories (no elevator), interior corridors. *Bath:* combo or shower only. **Parking:** on-site, winter plug-ins. **Terms:** pets ($25 deposit, in designated units). **Amenities:** safes (fee), hair dryers. *Some:* irons. **Leisure Activities:** sauna, whirlpool. **Cards:** AX, CB, DC, DS, JC, MC, VI.

SOME UNITS

FEE

EXPRESS INN **Phone:** (307)632-7556

AAA SAVE

Small-scale Hotel

7/1-9/30 [CP]	1P: $50-$140	2P: $50-$140	XP: $6	F16
3/1-6/30 [CP]	1P: $60-$70	2P: $60-$70	XP: $6	F16
1/1-2/28 [CP]	1P: $40-$45	2P: $44-$58	XP: $6	F16

Location: I-25, exit 9, just e. 2512 W Lincolnway 82001. Fax: 307/635-9141. **Facility:** 60 one-bedroom standard units. 2 stories (no elevator), interior corridors. **Parking:** on-site, winter plug-ins. **Terms:** 7 day cancellation notice, weekly rates available, small pets only ($5 extra charge). **Pool(s):** heated indoor. **Leisure Activities:** whirlpool. **Guest Services:** coin laundry. **Cards:** AX, DS, MC, VI. **Special Amenities: free continental breakfast and free local telephone calls.** *(See color ad below)*

SOME UNITS

FEE

FAIRFIELD INN BY MARRIOTT-CHEYENNE *Book at aaa.com* **Phone:** (307)637-4070

Small-scale Hotel

5/1-9/30 [ECP]	1P: $69-$89	2P: $69-$95	XP: $6	F
10/1-2/28 [ECP]	1P: $59-$79	2P: $64-$84	XP: $6	F
3/1-4/30 [ECP]	1P: $59-$74	2P: $59-$79	XP: $6	F

Location: 1.2 mi e of jct Dell Range Blvd and Yellowstone Rd. Located on the north side of the airport. 1415 Stillwater Ave 82001. Fax: 307/637-4070. **Facility:** 62 one-bedroom standard units. 3 stories, interior corridors. *Bath:* combo or shower only. **Parking:** on-site, winter plug-ins. **Amenities:** irons, hair dryers. **Pool(s):** heated indoor. **Leisure Activities:** whirlpool, jogging. **Guest Services:** valet laundry. **Cards:** AX, CB, DC, DS, MC, VI.

SOME UNITS

FLEETWOOD MOTEL — **Phone:** (307)638-8908

Motel

6/2-9/7	1P: $46-$52	2P: $55-$59	XP: $5	F10
3/1-6/1 & 9/8-2/28	1P: $39-$42	2P: $47-$52	XP: $5	F10

Location: I-80, exit 364, 1.2 mi n on N College Dr (SR 212), just w on I-80/US 30 business loop. Located in a quiet area. 3800 E Lincolnway 82001. Fax: 307/773-8537. **Facility:** 22 one-bedroom standard units, some with efficiencies. 2 stories (no elevator), exterior corridors. **Parking:** on-site, winter plug-ins. **Terms:** 7 day cancellation notice, small pets only ($5 extra charge). **Pool(s):** heated outdoor. **Cards:** AX, CB, DC, DS, MC, VI.

ASK — FEE — SOME UNITS

HAMPTON INN OF CHEYENNE — *Book at aaa.com* — **Phone:** (307)632-2747

AAA SAVE — Small-scale Hotel

7/23-8/1	1P: $119-$179	2P: $129-$189	XP: $10	F12
8/2-9/1	1P: $109-$155	2P: $119-$165	XP: $10	F12
9/2-2/28	1P: $79-$125	2P: $89-$135	XP: $10	F12
3/1-7/22	1P: $99-$119	2P: $109-$129	XP: $10	F12

Location: I-25, exit 9, just e on I-80 business loop/US 30, just n. 1781 Fleischli Pkwy 82001. Fax: 307/632-2745. **Facility:** 64 units. 62 one-bedroom standard units, some with whirlpools. 2 one-bedroom suites ($119-$179). 3 stories, interior corridors. *Bath:* combo or shower only. **Parking:** on-site. **Terms:** [ECP] meal plan available. **Amenities:** video games (fee), high-speed Internet, voice mail, irons, hair dryers. **Pool(s):** heated indoor. **Leisure Activities:** whirlpool, sun deck, exercise room. **Guest Services:** valet and coin laundry. **Business Services:** meeting rooms, business center. **Cards:** AX, CB, DC, DS, MC, VI. **Special Amenities: free continental breakfast and free local telephone calls.**

SOME UNITS

HOLIDAY INN CHEYENNE DREAM IN THE WEST — *Book at aaa.com* — **Phone:** 307/638-4466

AAA SAVE — Small-scale Hotel

7/1-8/17	1P: $99-$189	2P: $99-$189
6/1-6/30	1P: $89-$129	2P: $89-$129
8/18-2/28	1P: $69-$129	2P: $69-$129
3/1-5/31	1P: $69-$109	2P: $69-$109

Location: I-80, exit 362, just s. 204 W Fox Farm Rd 82007. Fax: 307/638-3677. **Facility:** 244 units. 235 one-bedroom standard units. 9 one-bedroom suites. 6 stories, interior corridors. *Bath:* combo or shower only. **Parking:** on-site, winter plug-ins. **Terms:** package plans - seasonal, pets ($25 fee). **Amenities:** voice mail, irons, hair dryers. **Dining:** 6 am-2 & 5-10 pm, cocktails. **Pool(s):** heated indoor. **Leisure Activities:** whirlpool, sun deck, exercise room. *Fee:* game room. **Guest Services:** gift shop, valet and coin laundry. **Business Services:** conference facilities, PC. **Cards:** AX, CB, DC, DS, JC, MC, VI. **Special Amenities: early check-in/late check-out and free room upgrade (subject to availability with advanced reservations).** *(See color ad below & opposite title page)*

FEE — SOME UNITS — FEE FEE

LA QUINTA INN CHEYENNE — *Book at aaa.com* — **Phone:** 307/632-7117

AAA SAVE — Small-scale Hotel

All Year	1P: $70-$90	2P: $70-$90

Location: I-25, exit 9, just e. 2410 W Lincolnway 82009. Fax: 307/638-7807. **Facility:** 105 units. 102 one-bedroom standard units. 3 one-bedroom suites. 3 stories, interior corridors. **Parking:** on-site, winter plug-ins. **Terms:** [ECP] meal plan available, small pets only. **Amenities:** video games, voice mail, irons, hair dryers. **Pool(s):** heated outdoor. **Guest Services:** valet and coin laundry. **Cards:** AX, CB, DC, DS, MC, VI. **Special Amenities: free expanded continental breakfast and free local telephone calls.**

SOME UNITS

LITTLE AMERICA HOTEL — Phone: (307)775-8400

Small-scale Hotel

6/15-9/30	1P: $86-$119	2P: $96-$129	XP: $10	F12
3/1-6/14 & 10/1-2/28	1P: $76-$109	2P: $86-$119	XP: $10	F12

Location: I-25, exit 9, just w on US 30. Located in a quiet, secluded area. 2800 W Lincolnway 82009 (PO Box 1529, 82003). Fax: 307/775-8425. **Facility:** 188 one-bedroom standard units. 1-3 stories (no elevator), interior/exterior corridors. **Parking:** on-site. **Terms:** package plans - weekends. **Amenities:** dual phone lines, voice mail, irons, hair dryers. *Some:* honor bars. **Dining:** 2 restaurants, 5 am-1 am, also, Western Gold Dining Room, see separate listing. **Pool(s):** heated outdoor. **Leisure Activities:** croquet, badminton, jogging, exercise room, volleyball. *Fee:* golf-9 holes. **Guest Services:** gift shop, valet and coin laundry, airport transportation (fee)-Denver International & Cheyenne airports. **Business Services:** meeting rooms. **Cards:** AX, CB, DC, DS, MC, VI. ***(See color ad below)***

SOME UNITS

FEE

NAGLE WARREN MANSION B & B — *Book at aaa.com* — Phone: (307)637-3333

Historic Bed & Breakfast

7/1-9/30	1P: $138	2P: $138		
10/1-2/28	1P: $128	2P: $128		
5/1-6/30	1P: $128	2P: $128	XP: $20	D6
3/1-4/30	1P: $118	2P: $118	XP: $20	D6

Location: I-80, exit 362, 1.2 mi n on I-25 business loop/US 85/87 business route, just e; downtown. 222 E 17th St 82001. Fax: 307/638-6879. **Facility:** Handmade tiles adorn the fireplaces in most guest rooms at this Romanesque-style 1888 building; furnishings include a variety of period antiques. 12 units. 11 one-bedroom standard units. 1 one-bedroom suite ($148-$168). 3 stories (no elevator), interior corridors. *Bath:* combo or tub only. **Parking:** street. **Terms:** age restrictions may apply, 3 day cancellation notice, [BP] meal plan available, pets ($20 extra charge, in Carriage House only). **Amenities:** CD players, high-speed Internet, voice mail, irons, hair dryers. **Leisure Activities:** whirlpool, bicycles, exercise room. *Fee:* massage. **Guest Services:** complimentary evening beverages, valet laundry, airport transportation-Cheyenne Airport, area transportation. **Business Services:** meeting rooms. **Cards:** AX, DC, MC, VI. **Special Amenities: free local telephone calls and early check-in/late check-out.**

SOME UNITS

FEE

OAK TREE INN — *Book at aaa.com* — Phone: (307)778-6620

Small-scale Hotel

5/1-8/31 [BP]	1P: $59-$100	2P: $65-$100	XP: $5	F12
3/1-4/30 & 9/1-2/28 [BP]	1P: $55-$65	2P: $65-$100	XP: $5	F12

Location: 1.2 mi e of jct Dell Range Blvd and Yellowstone Rd, 0.4 mi s. Located on the north side of the airport. 1625 Stillwater 82009. Fax: 307/778-8085. **Facility:** Smoke free premises. 60 one-bedroom standard units. 2 stories (no elevator), interior/exterior corridors. *Bath:* combo or shower only. **Parking:** on-site. **Terms:** weekly rates available, [AP] meal plan available, pets ($10 fee). **Amenities:** *Some:* irons, hair dryers. **Dining:** 24 hours. **Leisure Activities:** whirlpool, exercise room. **Guest Services:** coin laundry. **Business Services:** meeting rooms, business center. **Cards:** AX, CB, DC, DS, JC, MC, VI. **Special Amenities: free full breakfast and free local telephone calls.**

SOME UNITS

FEE

THE PLAINS HOTEL ***Book at aaa.com*** **Phone:** (307)638-3311

Historic Small-scale Hotel

3/1-9/30	1P: $79-$199	2P: $89-$209	XP: $10	F18
10/1-2/28	1P: $69-$199	2P: $79-$199	XP: $10	F18

Location: I-80, exit 362, 1 mi n on I-180/I-25 business loop/US 85/87 business route, just w on I-80 business loop/US 30; downtown. 1600 Central Ave 82001. Fax: 307/635-2022. **Facility:** This 1911 hotel has been fully restored to its original grandeur, with public areas reflecting the Western elegance of the early 1900s. 131 units. 122 one-bedroom standard units. 9 one-bedroom suites, some with whirlpools. 5 stories, interior corridors. *Bath:* combo or shower only. **Parking:** street. **Terms:** [AP] meal plan available, package plans, pets ($35 deposit). **Amenities:** voice mail, irons, hair dryers. *Some:* high-speed Internet. **Leisure Activities:** exercise room. **Guest Services:** gift shop, valet laundry, area transportation. **Business Services:** meeting rooms. **Cards:** AX, DS, MC, VI. ***(See color ad below)***

SOME UNITS

FEE FEE FEE

PORCH SWING BED & BREAKFAST **Phone:** 307/778-7182

Historic Bed & Breakfast

All Year [BP]	1P: $65-$75	2P: $85	XP: $20	D

Location: I-80, exit 362, 1.8 mi n on I-25 business loop/US 85/87 business route, just e; downtown. 502 E 24th St 82001. Fax: 307/778-7182. **Facility:** Built in 1917, this Prairie-style bungalow features a library as well as a back-yard herb garden. Smoke free premises. 2 one-bedroom standard units, some with whirlpools. 1 story, interior corridors. *Bath:* shared. **Parking:** street. **Terms:** check-in 4 pm, 30 day cancellation notice, weekly rates available, pets (with prior approval). **Amenities:** video library, irons, hair dryers. *Some:* CD players. **Leisure Activities:** bicycles. **Guest Services:** complimentary evening beverages, area transportation. **Cards:** MC, VI.

SOME UNITS

WINDY HILLS GUEST HOUSE **Phone:** 307/632-6423

AAA SAVE

Bed & Breakfast

All Year	1P: $96-$200	2P: $98-$200	XP: $20	F7

Location: I-25, exit 10B, 22 mi w on SR 210 (Happy Jack Rd), 1 mi s on private gravel road. Located in a quiet, rural area. 393 Happy Jack Rd 82007. Fax: 307/632-8906. **Facility:** This property on 60 acres offers accommodations in a log building as well as in a hillside building featuring good views of a lake and park. Smoke free premises. 9 units. 8 one- and 1 two-bedroom standard units, some with efficiencies, kitchens and/or whirlpools. 1-3 stories (no elevator), exterior corridors. *Bath:* combo or shower only. **Parking:** on-site. **Terms:** check-in 4 pm, 3 day cancellation notice-fee imposed, [BP] meal plan available, 3% service charge, pets ($10 fee, in kennel). **Amenities:** video library, DVD players, hair dryers. *Some:* irons. **Leisure Activities:** steamroom, canoeing, paddleboats, boat dock, fishing, cross country skiing, sledding hill, exercise room, horseshoes, volleyball. *Fee:* sauna, whirlpool, bicycles, massage. **Guest Services:** coin laundry, airport transportation-Cheyenne Airport, area transportation-within 25 mi. **Business Services:** meeting rooms. **Cards:** MC, VI. **Special Amenities: free local telephone calls and early check-in/late check-out.**

SOME UNITS

FEE

WHERE TO DINE

CHEYENNE CATTLE COMPANY **Dinner:** $15-$24 **Phone:** 307/638-3301

American

Location: I-25, exit 9, 0.8 mi e on I-80 business loop/US 30; in Best Western Hitching Post Inn Resort & Conference Center. 1700 W Lincolnway 82001. **Hours:** 6 pm-10 pm. Closed major holidays. **Reservations:** suggested. **Features:** Enjoy intimate dining in casual elegance, complete with ample portions and tableside prep by a friendly, capable wait staff. Specials include filet mignon, veal Oscar and rack of lamb. A martini/cigar patio is open, along with seasonal outdoor dining. Casual dress; cocktails. **Parking:** on-site. **Cards:** AX, CB, DC, DS, JC, MC, VI.

THE CHEYENNE CATTLE COMPANY **Lunch:** $9 **Dinner:** $11-$27 **Phone:** 307/638-3301

Steak House

Location: I-25, exit 9, 0.8 mi e on I-80 business loop/US 30; in Best Western Hitching Post Inn Resort & Conference Center. 1700 W Lincolnway 82001. **Hours:** 11 am-1:30 & 5:30-10 pm, Sat & Sun from 5:30 pm. **Reservations:** accepted. **Features:** The nicely presented luncheon buffet is notable at this locally popular restaurant. Menu portions are ample and flavorful. A special thumbs-up goes to the great soups and eye-appealing desserts, such as death by chocolate cake. Casual dress; cocktails. **Parking:** on-site. **Cards:** AX, CB, DC, DS, JC, MC, VI.

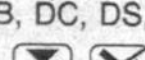

LOS AMIGOS RESTAURANT **Lunch:** $5-$11 **Dinner:** $5-$11 **Phone:** 307/638-8591

Mexican

Location: I-80, exit 362, 0.3 mi n on frontage road. 620 Central Ave 82007. **Hours:** 11 am-8:30 pm, Fri & Sat-9 pm. Closed major holidays; also Sun. **Features:** Fast, friendly service in a festive, bustling atmosphere is what you'll find here. Great homemade tortilla chips and zesty salsa accompany your Mexican meal, along with a good selection of beer and margaritas. Be sure to take note of the ceiling mural. Casual dress; cocktails. **Parking:** on-site. **Cards:** AX, DC, DS, MC, VI.

POOR RICHARDS **Lunch:** $8-$15 **Dinner:** $8-$15 **Phone:** 307/635-5114

American

Location: I-80, exit 364, just n on N College Dr (SR 212); 1.5 mi w on I-80 business loop/US 30. 2233 E Lincolnway 82001. **Hours:** 11 am-2:30 & 5-10 pm, Fri & Sat-11 pm, Sun 5 pm-10 pm. Closed: 11/25, 12/25; also Super Bowl Sun. **Features:** Well-prepared dishes include such items as slow-smoked baby back ribs, Cajun snapper, veal, pasta and roast duck. Thirst quenchers range from Italian soda and microbrews to cappuccino and espresso. Saturday brunch and "home cookin' Sunday dinner" are offered. Seasonal patio dining is available. Casual dress; cocktails. **Parking:** on-site. **Cards:** AX, CB, DC, DS, MC, VI.

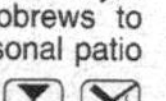

SANFORD'S GRUB & PUB **Lunch:** $6-$20 **Dinner:** $6-$20 **Phone:** 307/634-3381

American

Location: I-80, exit 362, 1.2 mi n on I-25 business loop/US 85/87 business route, just w. 115 E 17th St 82001. **Hours:** 11 am-10 pm. Closed major holidays. **Features:** This very casual, busily decorated restaurant features a varied menu which includes Cajun chicken, catfish and finger foods as well as bottled beers. On Wednesday nights, guests can feast on all-you-can-eat ribs. Casual dress; cocktails. **Parking:** street. **Cards:** AX, DS, MC, VI.

SENATOR'S RESTAURANT & BRASS BUFFALO SALOON **Lunch:** $6-$8 **Dinner:** $6-$23 **Phone:** 307/634-4171

Steak House

Location: I-25, exit 2, 2.6 mi se on Terry Ranch Rd; in Terry Bison Ranch RV Park & Resort. 51 I-25 Service Rd E 82007. **Hours:** Open 4/1-10/31; 7 am-9 pm. Closed: 1/1, 12/25. **Reservations:** accepted, weekends. **Features:** The rustic pine dining room at this working ranch is the perfect setting for dining on the house specialty: barbecued and grilled bison. Casual dress; cocktails; entertainment. **Parking:** on-site. **Cards:** DS, MC, VI. *(See color ad p 141)*

WESTERN GOLD DINING ROOM **Lunch:** $7-$9 **Dinner:** $14-$23 **Phone:** 307/775-8404

Continental

Location: I-25, exit 9, just w on US 30; in Little America Hotel. 2800 W Lincoln Way 82009. **Hours:** 11 am-2 & 5-10 pm. **Reservations:** accepted. **Features:** Traditional elegance and style set the popular restaurant apart. Favorites include T-bone, New York and filet mignon steaks, as well as pan-fried trout, seafood and pasta. The signature dish is Grecian-style lamb chops. Tableside preparations of bananas Foster or snowy range flambe create an exciting end to a special-occasion meal. Casual dress; cocktails; entertainment. **Parking:** on-site. **Cards:** AX, CB, DC, DS, MC, VI.

CHUGWATER pop. 244

WHERE TO STAY

SUPER 8 MOTEL-CHUGWATER **Phone:** 307/422-3248

Small-scale Hotel

5/26-9/30	1P: $50-$60	2P: $60-$80	XP: $7	F12
10/1-2/28	1P: $36-$52	2P: $55-$70	XP: $7	F12
3/1-5/25	1P: $39-$55	2P: $52-$70	XP: $7	F12

Location: I-25, exit 54, just ne. 100 Buffalo Dr 82210. Fax: 307/422-3219. **Facility:** 24 one-bedroom standard units. 2 stories (no elevator), interior corridors. *Bath:* combo or shower only. **Parking:** on-site, winter plug-ins. **Terms:** pets ($9.50 extra charge, in designated units). **Dining:** Miss Kitty's Grill, see separate listing. **Pool(s):** small heated outdoor. **Guest Services:** gift shop. **Business Services:** meeting rooms. **Cards:** AX, DC, MC, VI.

SOME UNITS

ASK / FEE

WHERE TO DINE

MISS KITTY'S GRILL **Lunch:** $5-$8 **Dinner:** $5-$11 **Phone:** 307/422-3463

American

Location: I-25, exit 54, just ne; in Super 8 Motel-Chugwater. 98 Buffalo Dr 82210. **Hours:** 6 am-8 pm, Sun-3 pm. **Features:** Burgers prepared with fresh buffalo meat are the specialty at the small, basic restaurant. Casual dress. **Parking:** on-site. **Cards:** AX, DS, MC, VI.

CODY pop. 8,835—*See also YELLOWSTONE NATIONAL PARK.*

WHERE TO STAY

AMERICINN LODGE & SUITES *Book at aaa.com* **Phone:** (307)587-7716

SAVE

Small-scale Hotel

6/1-7/31 [ECP]	1P: $89-$209	2P: $89-$209	XP: $6	F12
8/1-9/30 [ECP]	1P: $129-$199	2P: $129-$199	XP: $6	F12
3/1-5/31 [ECP]	1P: $69-$169	2P: $69-$169	XP: $6	F12
10/1-2/28 [ECP]	1P: $89-$119	2P: $89-$119	XP: $6	F12

Location: On US 14/16/20, 1.9 mi w. 508 Yellowstone Ave 82414. Fax: 307/587-7716. **Facility:** 46 units. 43 one-bedroom standard units, some with whirlpools. 3 one-bedroom suites with whirlpools. 2 stories, interior corridors. *Bath:* combo or shower only. **Parking:** on-site, winter plug-ins. **Terms:** cancellation fee imposed. **Amenities:** hair dryers. *Some:* irons. **Pool(s):** heated indoor. **Leisure Activities:** sauna, whirlpool. **Guest Services:** coin laundry, airport transportation-Yellowstone Regional Airport. **Business Services:** meeting rooms. **Cards:** AX, DC, DS, MC, VI. **Special Amenities: free local telephone calls and free newspaper.** *(See color ad p 336)*

SOME UNITS

DATA PORT

BEARTOOTH INN *Book at aaa.com* **Phone:** (307)527-5505

Motel

6/11-9/15 [CP]	1P: $102-$110	2P: $121-$131	XP: $5	F12
9/16-2/28 [CP]	1P: $76-$86	2P: $89-$99	XP: $5	F12
5/16-6/10 [CP]	1P: $69-$79	2P: $79-$89	XP: $5	F12
3/1-5/15 [CP]	1P: $55-$69	2P: $69-$79	XP: $5	F12

Location: 1.5 mi e on US 14/16/20. Located in a quiet area. 2513 Greybull Hwy 82414. Fax: 307/527-5001. **Facility:** 50 one-bedroom standard units, some with whirlpools. 2 stories (no elevator), interior/exterior corridors. **Parking:** on-site, winter plug-ins. **Terms:** cancellation fee imposed. **Amenities:** irons, hair dryers. **Leisure Activities:** sauna, whirlpool. **Guest Services:** coin laundry, airport transportation-Yellowstone Regional Airport. **Cards:** AX, DS, MC, VI. **Special Amenities: free continental breakfast and free newspaper.** *(See color ad below)*

SOME UNITS

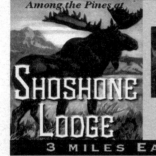

BEST VALUE INN CODY *Book at aaa.com* **Phone:** (307)587-4258

AAA SAVE — Motel

6/12-8/27 [CP]	1P: $69-$94	2P: $72-$98	XP: $4
5/10-6/11 & 8/28-11/15 [CP]	1P: $52-$64	2P: $55-$65	XP: $4
3/1-5/9 [CP]	1P: $42-$48	2P: $42-$48	XP: $4

Location: 0.4 mi e. Located in a quiet area. 1807 Sheridan Ave 82414. Fax: 307/527-6990. **Facility:** 24 units. 23 one-bedroom standard units. 1 one-bedroom suite. 1 story, exterior corridors. *Bath:* combo or shower only. **Parking:** on-site, winter plug-ins. **Terms:** open 3/1-11/15. **Guest Services:** coin laundry, airport transportation-Yellowstone Regional Airport. **Cards:** AX, DS, MC, VI. **Special Amenities: free continental breakfast and free local telephone calls.** ***(See color ad below)***

SOME UNITS

DATA PORT

BEST VALUE INN WEST **Phone:** (307)587-4208

Motel

6/12-8/27 [CP]	1P: $69-$94	2P: $72-$98	XP: $4
5/10-6/11 & 8/28-11/15 [CP]	1P: $52-$64	2P: $55-$65	XP: $4
3/1-5/9 [CP]	1P: $42-$48	2P: $42-$48	XP: $4

Location: 1.4 mi w on US 14/16/20. 720 Yellowstone Ave 82414 (PO Box 1446). Fax: 307/587-0217. **Facility:** 40 one-bedroom standard units. 1 story, exterior corridors. **Parking:** on-site. **Terms:** open 3/1-11/15, small pets only. **Pool(s):** heated outdoor. **Guest Services:** coin laundry. **Cards:** AX, DS, MC, VI. ***(See color ad below & p 343)***

SOME UNITS

ASK

BEST WESTERN SUNSET MOTOR INN *Book at aaa.com* **Phone:** (307)587-4265

AAA SAVE — Small-scale Hotel

5/24-9/25	1P: $99-$115	2P: $99-$139	XP: $10	F18
3/1-5/23	1P: $55-$89	2P: $55-$99	XP: $10	F18
9/26-2/28	1P: $55-$79	2P: $55-$89	XP: $10	F18

Location: 0.8 mi w on US 14/16/20. 1601 8th St 82414 (PO Box 1720). Fax: 307/587-9029. **Facility:** 120 units. 118 one-bedroom standard units. 2 one-bedroom suites ($95-$185). 1-2 stories (no elevator), exterior corridors. *Bath:* combo or shower only. **Parking:** on-site, winter plug-ins. **Terms:** small pets only. **Amenities:** voice mail, irons, hair dryers. **Dining:** 6 am-9 pm; from 8 am in winter, cocktails. **Pool(s):** heated outdoor, heated indoor. **Leisure Activities:** whirlpool, playground, exercise room. **Guest Services:** coin laundry. **Business Services:** meeting rooms. **Cards:** AX, CB, DC, DS, MC, VI. ***(See color ad p 338)***

SOME UNITS

DATA PORT

BIG BEAR MOTEL **Phone:** 307/587-3117

AAA SAVE — Motel

6/13-8/19	1P: $65	2P: $70	XP: $5
5/25-6/12 & 8/20-10/31	1P: $40	2P: $49	XP: $5
5/1-5/24	1P: $34	2P: $39	XP: $5

Location: 2 mi w on US 14/16/20, from city center. 139 W Yellowstone Hwy 82414. **Facility:** 42 one-bedroom standard units. 1 story, exterior corridors. **Parking:** on-site. **Terms:** open 5/1-10/31. **Pool(s):** heated outdoor. **Cards:** AX, DS, MC, VI. ***(See color ad p 338)***

SOME UNITS

BUFFALO BILL VILLAGE RESORT — **Phone:** (307)587-5544

AAA SAVE

Historic Cabin

6/1-9/30	1P: $89-$139	2P: $89-$139	XP: $10	F
5/1-5/31	1P: $49-$99	2P: $49-$99		

Location: US 14/16/20 and SR 120, just e n of jct SR 120. 1701 Sheridan Ave 82414. Fax: 307/527-7757. **Facility:** This complex of closely spaced log cabins was built between 1920 and 1923. 83 cabins. 1 story, exterior corridors. **Parking:** on-site. **Terms:** open 5/1-9/30, 3 day cancellation notice-fee imposed. **Amenities:** high-speed Internet, voice mail, irons, hair dryers. **Dining:** 6 am-2 & 5-10 pm; to 8 pm 10/1-4/30, cocktails. **Leisure Activities:** pool privileges, exercise room. *Fee:* rafting. **Guest Services:** gift shop, coin laundry, airport transportation-Yellowstone Regional Airport. **Business Services:** meeting rooms. **Cards:** AX, DC, DS, MC, VI. **Special Amenities: free local telephone calls and free room upgrade (subject to availability with advanced reservations).** *(See color ad p 339)*

SOME UNITS

DATA PORT

BURL INN — **Phone:** (307)587-2084

AAA SAVE

Small-scale Hotel

6/19-8/21	1P: $85	2P: $90	XP: $5	F6
3/1-6/18 & 8/22-10/31	1P: $65	2P: $70	XP: $5	F6
2/1-2/28	1P: $45	2P: $50	XP: $5	F6

Location: Just e of jct US 14/16/20. 1213 17th St 82414. Fax: 307/587-3031. **Facility:** 40 one-bedroom standard units, some with whirlpools. 2 stories (no elevator), interior corridors. *Bath:* combo or tub only. **Parking:** on-site. **Terms:** open 3/1-10/31 & 2/1-2/28. **Guest Services:** airport transportation-Yellowstone Regional Airport. **Cards:** AX, DS, MC, VI. **Special Amenities: free local telephone calls and early check-in/late check-out.**

SOME UNITS

CARRIAGE HOUSE **Phone:** 307/587-2572

Cottage

6/13-8/19	1P: $60-$70	2P: $60-$70	XP: $5
5/25-6/12 & 8/20-10/15	1P: $40-$50	2P: $40-$50	XP: $5
5/1-5/24	1P: $34-$40	2P: $34-$40	XP: $5

Location: Just w of Buffalo Bill Historical Center on US 14/20. 1816 8th St 82414. Fax: 307/587-2572. **Facility:** Smoke free premises. 27 units. 20 one- and 4 two-bedroom standard units. 3 vacation homes ($135-$150). 1 story, exterior corridors. *Bath:* combo or shower only. **Parking:** on-site. **Terms:** open 5/1-10/15. **Amenities:** *Some:* irons, hair dryers. **Leisure Activities:** playground. **Guest Services:** airport transportation-Yellowstone Regional Airport. ***(See color ad p 340)***

SOME UNITS

CODY MOTOR LODGE **Phone:** (307)527-6291

AAA SAVE ♦♦ Motel

6/1-8/31 [CP]	1P: $99-$110	2P: $105-$120	XP: $10	D13
9/1-11/30 [CP]	1P: $65-$75	2P: $75-$85	XP: $10	D13
3/1-5/31 [CP]	1P: $65-$69	2P: $69-$75	XP: $5	D13
12/1-2/28 [CP]	1P: $45-$55	2P: $55-$59	XP: $5	D13

Location: Just w on US 14/16/20 and SR 120. 1455 Sheridan Ave 82414. Fax: 307/527-6291. **Facility:** 31 units. 30 one-bedroom standard units. 1 two-bedroom suite ($165-$185). 2 stories, interior corridors. *Bath:* combo or shower only. **Parking:** on-site, winter plug-ins. **Terms:** weekly rates available. **Guest Services:** coin laundry, airport transportation-Yellowstone Regional Airport. **Cards:** AX, DS, MC, VI. ***(See color ad below)***

SOME UNITS

CODY SUPER 8 MOTEL ***Book at aaa.com*** **Phone:** 307/527-6214

♦♦ Motel

6/1-9/30	1P: $131-$169	2P: $131-$169	XP: $5	F12
3/1-5/31	1P: $58-$78	2P: $68-$88	XP: $5	F12
10/1-2/28	1P: $58-$68	2P: $68-$78	XP: $5	F12

Location: On US 14/16, 1 mi w of city center. 730 Yellowstone Rd 82414 (PO Box 1123). Fax: 307/527-6214. **Facility:** 64 one-bedroom standard units. 2 stories, interior corridors. **Parking:** on-site, winter plug-ins. **Amenities:** *Some:* fax. **Cards:** AX, CB, DC, DS, JC, MC, VI.

SOME UNITS

COMFORT INN AT BUFFALO BILL VILLAGE RESORT ***Book at aaa.com*** **Phone:** (307)587-5556

AAA SAVE ♦♦♦ Small-scale Hotel

6/16-10/15 [ECP]	1P: $89-$179	2P: $89-$179	XP: $10	F19
5/16-6/15 [ECP]	1P: $59-$139	2P: $59-$139	XP: $10	F19
10/16-2/28 [ECP]	1P: $49-$99	2P: $49-$99		
3/1-5/15 [ECP]	1P: $49-$89	2P: $49-$89		

Location: US 14/16/20 and SR 120. 1601 Sheridan Ave 82414 (PO Box 30). Fax: 307/587-8727. **Facility:** 75 units. 74 one-bedroom standard units. 1 one-bedroom suite ($129-$279). 2 stories (no elevator), interior corridors. **Parking:** on-site, winter plug-ins. **Terms:** 3 day cancellation notice-fee imposed. **Amenities:** irons, hair dryers. **Leisure Activities:** pool privileges. **Guest Services:** coin laundry, airport transportation-Yellowstone Regional Airport. **Cards:** AX, DC, DS, MC, VI. ***(See color ad p 339)***

SOME UNITS

DAYS INN ***Book at aaa.com*** **Phone:** (307)527-6604

SAVE	6/11-10/15	1P: $105-$155	2P: $115-$155	XP: $10	F10
	4/1-6/10	1P: $50-$140	2P: $55-$140	XP: $10	F10
	10/16-2/28	1P: $39-$140	2P: $45-$140	XP: $10	F10
	3/1-3/31	1P: $39-$110	2P: $45-$110	XP: $10	F10

Small-scale Hotel **Location:** Jct US 14/16/20 and SR 120, 1.8 mi w. 524 Yellowstone Rd 82414. Fax: 307/527-7341. **Facility:** 52 units. 50 one-bedroom standard units. 2 one-bedroom suites ($100-$200) with whirlpools. 2 stories (no elevator), interior corridors. *Bath:* combo or shower only. **Parking:** on-site, winter plug-ins. **Terms:** [CP] meal plan available. **Amenities:** hair dryers. **Pool(s):** heated indoor. **Leisure Activities:** whirlpool. **Guest Services:** coin laundry. **Cards:** AX, CB, DC, DS, MC, VI. **Special Amenities: free continental breakfast and free local telephone calls.**

SOME UNITS

ECONO LODGE MOOSE CREEK ***Book at aaa.com*** **Phone:** (307)587-2221

	6/7-8/16 [CP]	1P: $84-$146	2P: $94-$156		
	8/17-9/30 [CP]	1P: $68-$122	2P: $78-$132		
Motel	10/1-11/30 [CP]	1P: $42-$72	2P: $52-$82		
	4/1-6/6 [CP]	1P: $42-$72	2P: $52-$82	XP: $8	F18

Location: On US 14/16/20; downtown. 1015 Sheridan Ave 82414 (PO Box 772). Fax: 307/587-2222. **Facility:** 53 one-bedroom standard units. 1-2 stories (no elevator), interior/exterior corridors. *Bath:* combo or shower only. **Parking:** on-site. **Terms:** open 4/1-11/30, 3 day cancellation notice-fee imposed. **Pool(s):** small heated indoor. **Guest Services:** coin laundry. **Cards:** AX, CB, DC, DS, JC, MC, VI. ***(See color ad below)***

SOME UNITS

GREEN GABLES INN

Phone: (307)587-6886

Motel

6/21-8/15 [CP]	1P: $99	2P: $99
6/7-6/20 [CP]	1P: $69-$79	2P: $69-$79
8/16-10/15 [CP]	1P: $59-$69	2P: $59-$69
5/15-6/6 [CP]	1P: $49-$59	2P: $49-$59

Location: Just e on US 14/16/20 and SR 120. 1636 Central Ave 82414. **Facility:** 15 one-bedroom standard units, some with whirlpools. 2 stories (no elevator), exterior corridors. **Parking:** on-site. **Terms:** open 5/15-10/15, small pets only. **Amenities:** irons, hair dryers. **Guest Services:** coin laundry. **Cards:** AX, DS, MC, VI. ***(See color ad p 343)***

SOME UNITS

HOLIDAY INN AT BUFFALO BILL VILLAGE RESORT

Phone: (307)587-5555

AAA SAVE

Small-scale Hotel

6/16-10/15	1P: $89-$179	2P: $89-$179	XP: $10	F19
5/16-6/15	1P: $59-$139	2P: $59-$139	XP: $10	F19
10/16-2/28	1P: $49-$99	2P: $49-$99		
3/1-5/15	1P: $49-$89	2P: $49-$89		

Location: US 14/16/20 and SR 120. 1701 Sheridan Ave 82414. Fax: 307/527-7757. **Facility:** 189 units. 188 one-bedroom standard units. 1 one-bedroom suite ($129-$279). 2 stories (no elevator), interior corridors. *Bath:* combo or shower only. **Parking:** on-site, winter plug-ins. **Terms:** 3 day cancellation notice-fee imposed. **Amenities:** high-speed Internet, voice mail, irons, hair dryers. *Some:* dual phone lines. **Dining:** 6 am-2 & 5-10 pm, Sat 6 am-11 & 5-10 pm; to 8 pm 10/1-4/30, cocktails. **Pool(s):** heated outdoor. **Leisure Activities:** exercise room. *Fee:* rafting. **Guest Services:** valet laundry, airport transportation-Yellowstone Regional Airport. **Business Services:** conference facilities. **Cards:** AX, DC, DS, MC, VI. **Special Amenities: free local telephone calls.** ***(See color ad p 339 & opposite title page)***

SOME UNITS

THE LOCKHART BED & BREAKFAST INN AKA GRANDMA'S HOUSE

Phone: (307)587-6074

AAA SAVE

Bed & Breakfast

6/13-8/15 [BP]	1P: $95-$135	2P: $95-$135	XP: $15	D5
8/16-10/31 [BP]	1P: $85-$115	2P: $85-$115	XP: $15	D5
3/1-6/12 [BP]	1P: $65-$90	2P: $65-$90	XP: $15	D5
11/1-2/28 [BP]	1P: $65-$85	2P: $65-$85	XP: $15	D5

Location: W on US 14/16/20, 2.3 mi from city center. 109 W Yellowstone Ave 82414. Fax: 307/587-8644. **Facility:** Smoke free premises. 6 one-bedroom standard units. 2 stories (no elevator), interior corridors. *Bath:* combo or tub only. **Parking:** on-site, winter plug-ins. **Terms:** check-in 4 pm, 30 day cancellation notice-fee imposed, weekly rates available. **Leisure Activities:** croquet, swing set. **Cards:** DS, MC, VI. **Special Amenities: free full breakfast and free local telephone calls.**

THE MAYOR'S BED & BREAKFAST INN

Phone: (307)587-0887

Historic Country Inn

5/15-10/15 [BP]	1P: $95-$205	2P: $95-$205	XP: $15
10/16-2/28 [BP]	1P: $70-$150	2P: $85-$150	XP: $15
3/1-5/14 [BP]	1P: $70-$150	2P: $70-$150	XP: $15

Location: Just n off Sheridan Ave at 14th St. 1413 Rumsey Ave 82414-3714. Fax: 307/587-0890. **Facility:** This turn-of-the-century mansion was built to house Cody's first mayor. Many antiques and collectibles adorn this lovely home. Smoke free premises. 4 units. 3 one-bedroom standard units, some with whirlpools. 1 cottage. 1-2 stories (no elevator), interior/exterior corridors. *Bath:* combo or shower only. **Parking:** street. **Terms:** 30 day cancellation notice-fee imposed. **Amenities:** CD players, hair dryers. **Cards:** AX, MC, VI.

SOME UNITS

PARSON'S PILLOW BED & BREAKFAST **Book at aaa.com** **Phone:** (307)587-2382

Bed & Breakfast

5/16-9/15 [BP]	1P: $80-$90	2P: $85-$95	XP: $15	F6
9/16-2/28 [BP]	1P: $70	2P: $75		
3/1-5/15 [BP]	1P: $70	2P: $75	XP: $15	F6

Location: Just s of US 14/16/20. 1202 14th St 82414. Fax: 307/587-2382. **Facility:** Smoke free premises. 5 one-bedroom standard units. 2 stories (no elevator), interior corridors. *Bath:* combo or tub only. **Parking:** street, winter plug-ins. **Terms:** age restrictions may apply, 14 day cancellation notice. **Guest Services:** TV in common area. **Cards:** AX, DC, DS, MC, VI.

ASK

RAINBOW PARK MOTEL **Book at aaa.com** **Phone:** 307/587-6251

SAVE

Motel

6/16-8/21	1P: $54-$64	2P: $57-$75	XP: $3
8/22-9/30	1P: $35-$45	2P: $38-$55	XP: $3
3/1-6/15 & 10/1-2/28	1P: $32-$45	2P: $36-$50	XP: $3

Location: Just e on US 14/16/20 and SR 120. 1136 17th St 82414. Fax: 307/527-5531. **Facility:** 39 one-bedroom standard units, some with kitchens (no utensils). 1 story, exterior corridors. *Bath:* combo or shower only. **Parking:** on-site, winter plug-ins. **Terms:** cancellation fee imposed. **Leisure Activities:** playground. **Guest Services:** coin laundry. **Cards:** AX, DC, DS, MC, VI. **Special Amenities: free local telephone calls and early check-in/late check-out.** *(See color ad p 342)*

SOME UNITS

SKYLINE MOTOR INN — **Phone:** 307/587-4201

Motel

6/16-8/24	1P: $48-$64	2P: $60-$74	XP: $4
3/1-6/15 & 10/1-2/28	1P: $28-$42	2P: $40-$52	XP: $4
8/25-9/30	1P: $35-$44	2P: $38-$48	XP: $4

Location: 0.8 mi e on US 14/16/20 and SR 120. 1919 17th St 82414. **Facility:** 46 one-bedroom standard units. 1-2 stories (no elevator), exterior corridors. **Parking:** on-site, winter plug-ins. **Pool(s):** small heated outdoor. **Leisure Activities:** playground. **Guest Services:** valet laundry. **Cards:** AX, MC, VI. ***(See color ad p 335)***

SOME UNITS

SUNRISE MOTOR INN — **Phone:** (307)587-5566

Motel

6/7-8/14 [CP]	1P: $89	2P: $89-$110
8/15-9/19 [CP]	1P: $67	2P: $67-$83
5/1-6/6 [CP]	1P: $44-$67	2P: $49-$79
9/20-10/25 [CP]	1P: $45	2P: $45-$49

Location: 0.8 mi w on US 14/16/20. Located next to Buffalo Bill Historical Center. 1407 8th St 82414 (PO Box 1446). Fax: 307/587-0217. **Facility:** 40 one-bedroom standard units. 1 story, exterior corridors. **Parking:** on-site. **Terms:** open 5/1-10/25, small pets only. **Amenities:** irons, hair dryers. **Pool(s):** heated outdoor. **Guest Services:** coin laundry. **Cards:** AX, CB, DC, DS, MC, VI. ***(See color ad p 343)***

SOME UNITS

WHERE TO DINE

ADRIANO'S ITALIAN RESTAURANT — **Lunch:** $5-$8 **Dinner:** $9-$18 **Phone:** 307/527-7320

Italian

Location: On US 14/16/20; downtown. 1244 Sheridan Ave 82414. **Hours:** 11 am-9 pm; hours may vary in summer. Closed major holidays; also Mon. **Features:** The smells of authentic Italian pizza are what hit your nose as you enter Adriano's. Partake of the pizza or enjoy some of their other Italian entrees at this family style restaurant. Casual dress; cocktails. **Parking:** street. **Cards:** AX, DS, MC, VI.

BUBBA'S BAR-B-QUE RESTAURANT — **Lunch:** $6-$14 **Dinner:** $6-$14 **Phone:** 307/587-7427

Barbecue

Location: US 14/16/20, 1.9 mi w. 512 Yellowstone Ave 82414. **Hours:** 7 am-9 pm; to 10 pm in summer. Closed: 11/25, 12/25. **Features:** Texas meats are slow-smoked over a hickory fire. Although spare ribs are the house specialty, guests also can try catfish with hush puppies, charbroiled steak or the popular sloppy Bubba sandwich. Casual dress. **Parking:** on-site. **Cards:** AX, MC, VI.

LA COMIDA — **Lunch:** $5-$14 **Dinner:** $5-$14 **Phone:** 307/587-9556

Mexican

Location: On US 14/16/20. 1385 Sheridan Ave 82414. **Hours:** 11 am-8:30 pm, Fri & Sat-9 pm, Sun noon-9 pm; 11 am-10 pm, Sun from noon in summer. Closed: 4/11, 11/25, 12/25. **Reservations:** suggested, wkends & summer. **Features:** Family owned, very popular restaurant. Patio dining in summer. Relaxed, attractive setting. Daily homemade soup, American dishes and traditional as well as inventive Mexican fare. Good sized, attractively presented courses. Pleasant, expedient service. Tasty margaritas. Casual dress; cocktails. **Parking:** street. **Cards:** AX, DS, MC, VI.

STEFAN'S RESTAURANT — **Lunch:** $7-$13 **Dinner:** $9-$24 **Phone:** 307/587-8511

American

Location: On US 14/16/20; downtown. 1367 Sheridan Ave 82414. **Hours:** 11 am-2 & 5-8 pm, Fri & Sat-9 pm. Closed major holidays. **Reservations:** suggested. **Features:** This intimate restaurant, in a converted downtown storefront is a wonderful respite from the hustle and bustle of Cody. Relax and enjoy well prepared pasta or seafood. Casual dress; cocktails. **Parking:** street. **Cards:** AX, DS, MC, VI.

DIAMONDVILLE pop. 716

WHERE TO STAY

ENERGY INN — **Phone:** 307/877-6901

Motel

All Year	1P: $50-$55	2P: $63-$68	XP: $5	F10

Location: Jct US 30 and 189. (PO Box 494). Fax: 307/877-6901. **Facility:** 41 one-bedroom standard units, some with kitchens. 1-2 stories (no elevator), interior/exterior corridors. **Parking:** on-site, winter plug-ins. **Guest Services:** valet laundry. **Cards:** AX, DC, DS, MC, VI.

SOME UNITS

DOUGLAS pop. 5,288

WHERE TO STAY

BEST WESTERN DOUGLAS INN & CONFERENCE CENTER — ***Book at aaa.com*** — **Phone:** (307)358-9790

Small-scale Hotel

6/1-9/30	1P: $75-$85	2P: $85-$95	XP: $10	F18
3/1-5/31 & 10/1-2/28	1P: $65-$75	2P: $75-$85	XP: $10	F18

Location: I-25, exit 140, 0.8 mi e. 1450 Riverbend Dr 82633. Fax: 307/358-6251. **Facility:** 117 one-bedroom standard units, some with whirlpools. 2 stories (no elevator), interior corridors. **Parking:** on-site, winter plug-ins. **Terms:** [AP] meal plan available, pets ($25 deposit). **Amenities:** irons, hair dryers. *Some:* dual phone lines. **Dining:** Chutes Eatery & Saloon, see separate listing. **Pool(s):** heated indoor. **Leisure Activities:** saunas, whirlpool, dart boards, pool tables, exercise room. *Fee:* game room. **Guest Services:** valet and coin laundry. **Business Services:** meeting rooms. **Cards:** AX, CB, DC, DS, JC, MC, VI. **Special Amenities: free local telephone calls and free room upgrade (subject to availability with advanced reservations).**

SOME UNITS

FEE

WHERE TO DINE

CHUTES EATERY & SALOON **Lunch:** $6-$8 **Dinner:** $10-$24 **Phone:** 307/358-9790
American
Location: I-25, exit 140, 0.8 mi e; in Best Western Douglas Inn & Conference Center. 1450 Riverbend Dr 82633. **Hours:** 6 am-2 & 5-10 pm. Closed: 12/25. **Features:** The contemporary, Western atmosphere evident at the relaxed restaurant complements the array of menu selections. House specials include buffalo rib-eye and whiskey peppercorn filet. Casual dress; cocktails. **Parking:** on-site. **Cards:** AX, CB, DC, DS, MC, VI.

DUBOIS pop. 962

WHERE TO STAY

BALD MOUNTAIN INN *Book at aaa.com* **Phone:** 307/455-2844
Motel
5/15-2/28 1P: $42-$105 2P: $45-$125 XP: $10
Location: 1.6 mi w on US 26 and 287. 1349 W Ramshorn St 82513 (PO Box 847). Fax: 307/455-3167. **Facility:** 16 one-bedroom standard units, some with kitchens and/or whirlpools. 2 stories (no elevator), exterior corridors. **Parking:** on-site, winter plug-ins. **Terms:** open 5/15-2/28, 3 day cancellation notice, pets ($10-$15 extra charge). **Leisure Activities:** whirlpool, fishing, horseshoes. **Guest Services:** gift shop, area transportation. **Cards:** MC, VI.
SOME UNITS
FEE FEE

BLACK BEAR COUNTRY INN **Phone:** (307)455-2344
SAVE
Motel

7/1-9/5	1P: $50-$60	2P: $55-$65	XP: $3	F12
5/25-6/30 & 9/6-10/31	1P: $40-$50	2P: $45-$55	XP: $3	F12

Location: 0.5 mi w on US 26 and 287. 505 N Ramshorn St 82513 (PO Box 595). Fax: 307/455-2626. **Facility:** 15 units. 14 one-bedroom standard units. 1 two-bedroom suite with kitchen (no utensils). 1 story, exterior corridors. *Bath:* combo or shower only. **Parking:** on-site, winter plug-ins. **Terms:** open 5/25-10/31, small pets only (with prior approval). **Leisure Activities:** fishing, picnic tables & grills. **Guest Services:** gift shop. **Cards:** AX, CB, DC, DS, JC, MC, VI. **Special Amenities: free local telephone calls and early check-in/late check-out.**
SOME UNITS

BRANDING IRON INN **Phone:** (307)455-2893
SAVE
Cottage

6/1-10/3	1P: $40-$90	2P: $40-$90	XP: $5	F12
3/1-5/31 & 10/4-2/28	1P: $45-$65	2P: $45-$65	XP: $5	F12

Location: 0.3 mi w on US 26 and 287. 401 W Ramshorn St 82513 (PO Box 705). Fax: 307/455-2446. **Facility:** 23 cabins. 1 story, exterior corridors. *Bath:* combo or shower only. **Parking:** on-site, winter plug-ins. **Terms:** cancellation fee imposed, weekly rates available, pets ($5 extra charge). **Leisure Activities:** picnic tables, horse corals. **Cards:** AX, MC, VI.
SOME UNITS
FEE

CHINOOK WINDS MT. LODGE **Phone:** (307)455-2987
Motel
5/15-10/15 [CP] 1P: $35-$70 2P: $45-$70 XP: $5 F12
Location: 0.8 mi e on US 26 and 287. 640 S First St 82513 (PO Box 1497). Fax: 307/455-2634. **Facility:** Smoke free premises. 18 one-bedroom standard units. 1-2 stories (no elevator), exterior corridors. *Bath:* combo or shower only. **Parking:** on-site, winter plug-ins. **Terms:** open 5/15-10/15, weekly rates available, pets ($5 extra charge). **Leisure Activities:** whirlpool, fishing, basketball. **Cards:** AX, DS, MC, VI.
SOME UNITS
ASK FEE DATA PORT

PINNACLE BUTTES LODGE & CAMPGROUND **Phone:** 307/455-2506
Motel

3/1-4/14 & 12/15-2/28	2P: $95
5/25-12/14	2P: $50
4/15-5/24	2P: $40

Location: 20 mi w on US 26 and 287. Located in Shoshone National Forest. 3577 US Hwy 26 W 82513. Fax: 307/455-3874. **Facility:** 10 one-bedroom standard units. 1-2 stories, exterior corridors. **Parking:** on-site. **Terms:** 14 day cancellation notice, pets ($50 deposit). **Amenities:** video library. **Pool(s):** small outdoor. **Leisure Activities:** whirlpool, fishing, cross country skiing. *Fee:* snowmobiling. **Guest Services:** gift shop. **Cards:** DS, MC, VI.
SOME UNITS
FEE VCR

RIVERSIDE INN & CAMPGROUND — **Phone:** 307/455-2337

Motel

5/1-11/30 1P: $30-$35 2P: $40-$50 XP: $4

Location: 3 mi e of town center on US 26 and 287. 5810 US Hwy 26 82513 (PO Box 642). Fax: 307/455-2866. **Facility:** 14 units. 13 one- and 1 two-bedroom standard units, some with kitchens. 1 story, exterior corridors. *Bath:* combo or shower only. **Parking:** on-site. **Terms:** open 5/1-11/30, pets ($5 fee, dogs only). **Leisure Activities:** fishing, hiking trails, playground. *Fee:* horseback riding. **Guest Services:** coin laundry. **Cards:** DS, MC, VI.

SOME UNITS

FEE

STAGECOACH MOTOR INN — **Phone:** (307)455-2303

SAVE

Small-scale Hotel

5/1-9/30 1P: $40-$56 2P: $50-$74 XP: $5 F5
3/1-4/30 & 10/1-2/28 1P: $40-$50 2P: $44-$64 XP: $5 F5

Location: On US 26 and 287; center. Located in a quiet area. 103 Ramshorn St 82513 (PO Box 216). Fax: 307/455-3903. **Facility:** 48 units. 46 one- and 2 two-bedroom standard units, some with kitchens. 1-2 stories (no elevator), exterior corridors. *Bath:* combo or shower only. **Parking:** on-site, winter plug-ins. **Terms:** weekly rates available, pets ($5 extra charge). **Pool(s):** heated outdoor. **Leisure Activities:** whirlpool, fishing, playground, horseshoes. **Guest Services:** coin laundry, area transportation. **Cards:** AX, DS, MC, VI. **Special Amenities: early check-in/late check-out and preferred room (subject to availability with advanced reservations).** *(See color ad p 345)*

SOME UNITS

VCR

FEE

TWIN PINES LODGE & CABINS Book at aaa.com — **Phone:** (307)455-2600

SAVE

Historic Cabin

6/1-9/30 1P: $50-$70 2P: $60-$80 XP: $5 F8
3/1-5/31 & 10/1-2/28 1P: $40-$60 2P: $50-$70 XP: $5 F8

Location: Center. 218 Ramshorn St 82513 (PO Box 1150). Fax: 307/455-2608. **Facility:** Some lodge rooms contain original furnishings. Some new cabins. Lodge open by reservation in winter. Smoke free premises. 15 units. 4 one- and 1 two-bedroom standard units. 10 cabins. 1-2 stories (no elevator), interior/exterior corridors. *Bath:* combo or shower only. **Parking:** on-site. **Amenities:** video library. **Leisure Activities:** picnic area with grill, horseshoes. **Cards:** AX, DS, MC, VI. **Special Amenities: free expanded continental breakfast and early check-in/late check-out.** *(See color ad below)*

SOME UNITS

VCR

EVANSTON pop. 11,507

WHERE TO STAY

BEST WESTERN DUNMAR INN Book at aaa.com — **Phone:** (307)789-3770

SAVE

Small-scale Hotel

5/28-9/5 & 1/1-2/28 1P: $69-$89 2P: $79-$99 XP: $6 F
3/1-5/27 & 9/6-12/31 1P: $59-$79 2P: $69-$89 XP: $6 F

Location: I-80, exit 3 (Harrison Dr). 1601 Harrison Dr 82930 (PO Box 0768, 82931). Fax: 307/789-3758. **Facility:** 165 one-bedroom standard units, some with kitchens (no utensils) and/or whirlpools. 1 story, exterior corridors. **Parking:** on-site, winter plug-ins. **Amenities:** dual phone lines, voice mail, irons, hair dryers. *Some:* honor bars. **Dining:** Dunmar's Legal Tender Dining & Lounge, see separate listing. **Pool(s):** small heated outdoor. **Leisure Activities:** sauna, whirlpool, exercise room. **Guest Services:** gift shop, valet laundry, area transportation-within 5 mi. **Business Services:** conference facilities. **Cards:** AX, CB, DC, DS, MC, VI. **Special Amenities: free local telephone calls and free newspaper.** *(See color ad p 347)*

SOME UNITS

DATA PORT

COMFORT INN *Book at aaa.com* **Phone:** (307)789-7799

Small-scale Hotel

All Year 1P: $65-$99 2P: $65-$99 XP: $5 F18

Location: I-80, exit 3 (Harrison Dr). 1931 Harrison Dr 82930. Fax: 307/789-7733. **Facility:** 56 one-bedroom standard units, some with whirlpools. 2 stories (no elevator), interior corridors. *Bath:* combo or shower only. **Parking:** on-site, winter plug-ins. **Terms:** [CP] meal plan available, pets ($10 fee). **Amenities:** voice mail, irons, hair dryers. **Pool(s):** small heated indoor. **Leisure Activities:** whirlpool, exercise room. **Guest Services:** coin laundry. **Cards:** AX, CB, DC, DS, JC, MC, VI.

SOME UNITS

ASK FEE

PRAIRIE INN **Phone:** (307)789-2920

AAA SAVE

Motel

All Year 1P: $40-$50 2P: $50-$65 XP: $7 F12

Location: I-80, exit 6, 0.3 mi n. 264 Bear River Dr 82930. Fax: 307/789-2475. **Facility:** 31 one-bedroom standard units. 1 story, interior/exterior corridors. **Parking:** on-site, winter plug-ins. **Terms:** [CP] meal plan available, pets ($5 extra charge). **Cards:** AX, DS, MC, VI.

SOME UNITS

FEE

RENDEZVOUS LODGE **Phone:** (307)789-2220

Small-scale Hotel

5/2-2/28	1P: $75-$150	2P: $75-$150	XP: $10	F12
3/1-5/1	1P: $55-$120	2P: $65-$130	XP: $10	F12

Location: I-80, exit 3 (Harrison Dr), just n to Wasatch Rd. 339 Wasatch Rd 82930. Fax: 307/789-4122. **Facility:** 113 one-bedroom standard units, some with kitchens and/or whirlpools. 3 stories (no elevator), interior corridors. **Parking:** on-site, winter plug-ins. **Terms:** weekly rates available, pets ($10 fee). **Amenities:** *Some:* hair dryers. **Leisure Activities:** sauna, whirlpool. **Guest Services:** coin laundry. **Business Services:** meeting rooms. **Cards:** AX, DC, DS, MC, VI.

SOME UNITS

ASK FEE

WHERE TO DINE

DUNMAR'S LEGAL TENDER DINING & LOUNGE **Lunch:** $5-$10 **Dinner:** $10-$30 **Phone:** 307/789-3770

AAA

American

Location: I-80, exit 3 (Harrison Dr); in Best Western Dunmar Inn. 1601 Harrison Dr 82930. **Hours:** 5:30 am-9:30 pm. Closed: 12/25. **Reservations:** accepted. **Features:** The fresh salad beckons many locals as well as being a favorite with guests. Friendly, efficient service of American fare in a casual, relaxed atmosphere. Casual dress; cocktails; entertainment. **Parking:** on-site. **Cards:** AX, CB, DC, DS, MC, VI.

(See color ad below)

EVANSVILLE pop. 2,255

WHERE TO STAY

COMFORT INN-CASPER *Book at aaa.com* **Phone:** (307)235-3038

Small-scale Hotel

6/1-8/31 [ECP]	1P: $75-$89	2P: $75-$95	XP: $6	F
3/1-5/31 & 9/1-2/28 [ECP]	1P: $65-$79	2P: $65-$85	XP: $6	F

Location: I-25, exit 185, just e. 480 Lathrop Rd 82636. Fax: 307/235-3038. **Facility:** 56 one-bedroom standard units. 2 stories (no elevator), interior corridors. *Bath:* combo or shower only. **Parking:** on-site, winter plug-ins. **Terms:** pets (in smoking units). **Amenities:** irons, hair dryers. **Pool(s):** small heated indoor. **Leisure Activities:** whirlpool. **Cards:** AX, CB, DC, DS, MC, VI.

ASK DATA PORT / SOME UNITS /

GILLETTE pop. 19,646

WHERE TO STAY

BEST WESTERN TOWER WEST LODGE *Book at aaa.com* **Phone:** (307)686-2210

AAA SAVE

Small-scale Hotel

8/2-8/20	1P: $79-$149	2P: $89-$159	XP: $8	F18
6/2-8/1	1P: $54-$109	2P: $59-$129	XP: $8	F18
3/1-6/1	1P: $49-$99	2P: $54-$109	XP: $6	F18
8/21-2/28	1P: $44-$99	2P: $49-$109		

Location: I-90, exit 124, just n. 109 N US Hwy 14-16 82716. Fax: 307/682-5105. **Facility:** 189 units. 183 one-bedroom standard units. 6 one-bedroom suites, some with whirlpools. 2 stories (no elevator), interior corridors. *Bath:* combo or shower only. **Parking:** on-site, winter plug-ins. **Terms:** [AP] meal plan available. **Amenities:** video games (fee), high-speed Internet, dual phone lines, voice mail, irons, hair dryers. **Dining:** 6 am-2 & 5-10 pm, Sun-9 pm, cocktails. **Pool(s):** heated indoor. **Leisure Activities:** whirlpool, exercise room. *Fee:* game room. **Guest Services:** valet and coin laundry, airport transportation-Campbell County Airport. **Business Services:** meeting rooms, business center. **Cards:** AX, CB, DC, DS, JC, MC, VI. **Special Amenities: free newspaper and early check-in/late check-out.** *(See color ad below)*

DATA PORT / SOME UNITS VCR /

CLARION WESTERN PLAZA *Book at aaa.com* **Phone:** (307)686-3000

Small-scale Hotel

6/1-8/31	1P: $80-$90	2P: $80-$90
9/1-10/31	1P: $60-$70	2P: $60-$70
3/1-5/31 & 11/1-2/28	1P: $55-$65	2P: $55-$65

Location: I-90, exit 126, just se. 2009 S Douglas Hwy 59 82718. Fax: 307/686-4018. **Facility:** 159 units. 147 one-bedroom standard units. 12 one-bedroom suites ($120-$160), some with efficiencies, kitchens (no utensils) and/or whirlpools. 3 stories, interior/exterior corridors. **Parking:** on-site, winter plug-ins. **Terms:** [AP] & [BP] meal plans available. **Amenities:** dual phone lines, voice mail, irons, hair dryers. **Pool(s):** heated indoor, wading. **Leisure Activities:** sauna, whirlpool, playground, exercise room. *Fee:* game room. **Guest Services:** gift shop, valet and coin laundry. **Business Services:** conference facilities, business center. **Cards:** AX, CB, DC, DS, MC, VI.

ASK DATA PORT / SOME UNITS VCR FEE /

COMFORT INN & SUITES ***Book at aaa.com*** **Phone:** 307/685-2223

Small-scale Hotel

6/16-8/20 [ECP]	1P: $59-$149	2P: $64-$159	XP: $6
3/1-6/15 [ECP]	1P: $49-$109	2P: $54-$119	XP: $6
8/21-10/15 [ECP]	1P: $49-$109	2P: $54-$109	XP: $6
10/16-2/28 [ECP]	1P: $48-$88	2P: $52-$92	XP: $6

Location: I-90, exit 124, just ne. 1607 W 2nd Ave 82716. Fax: 307/685-5615. **Facility:** 60 one-bedroom standard units, some with whirlpools. 3 stories, interior corridors. **Parking:** on-site. **Terms:** cancellation fee imposed. **Amenities:** high-speed Internet, dual phone lines, voice mail, irons, hair dryers. **Pool(s):** heated indoor. **Leisure Activities:** whirlpool, exercise room. **Guest Services:** coin laundry. **Business Services:** meeting rooms, business center. **Cards:** AX, CB, DC, DS, JC, MC, VI.

(See color ad below)

SOME UNITS

GILLETTE WINGATE INN *Book at aaa.com* **Phone:** (307)685-2700

Small-scale Hotel

7/15-8/15 [ECP]	1P: $119-$159	2P: $119-$159	XP: $10	F18
6/1-7/14 [ECP]	1P: $99-$109	2P: $99-$109	XP: $10	F18
3/1-5/31 & 8/16-2/28 [ECP]	1P: $89-$99	2P: $89-$99	XP: $10	F18

Location: I-90, exit 126, just s to Boxelder Rd, then just e. 1801 Cliff Davis Dr 82718. Fax: 307/685-6635. **Facility:** 84 one-bedroom standard units, some with whirlpools. 3 stories, interior corridors. *Bath:* combo or shower only. **Parking:** on-site. **Terms:** check-in 4 pm. **Amenities:** video games, high-speed Internet, dual phone lines, voice mail, safes, irons, hair dryers. **Pool(s):** heated indoor. **Leisure Activities:** whirlpool, exercise room. **Guest Services:** valet and coin laundry. **Business Services:** meeting rooms, business center. **Cards:** AX, CB, DC, DS, MC, VI. **Special Amenities: free expanded continental breakfast and free newspaper.** *(See color ad p 349)*

SOME UNITS

HAMPTON INN *Book at aaa.com* **Phone:** (307)686-2000

Small-scale Hotel

All Year [ECP]	1P: $59-$199	2P: $59-$199

Location: I-90, exit 124, just n. 211 Decker Ct 82716. Fax: 307/686-1201. **Facility:** 57 one-bedroom standard units, some with whirlpools. 3 stories, interior corridors. *Bath:* combo or shower only. **Parking:** on-site. **Amenities:** voice mail, irons, hair dryers. **Pool(s):** heated indoor. **Leisure Activities:** whirlpool, exercise room. **Guest Services:** valet and coin laundry. **Business Services:** meeting rooms, fax (fee). **Cards:** AX, DC, DS, MC, VI.

SOME UNITS

HOLIDAY INN EXPRESS HOTEL & SUITES *Book at aaa.com* **Phone:** (307)686-9576

Small-scale Hotel

7/17-8/15	1P: $93-$159	2P: $93-$159
6/1-7/16	1P: $93-$139	2P: $93-$139
8/16-2/28	1P: $83-$139	2P: $83-$139
3/1-5/31	1P: $83-$119	2P: $83-$119

Location: I-90, exit 126. 1908 Cliff Davis Dr 82718. Fax: 307/686-9573. **Facility:** 83 one-bedroom standard units, some with whirlpools. 3 stories, interior corridors. *Bath:* combo or shower only. **Parking:** on-site, winter plug-ins. **Terms:** [ECP] meal plan available, pets (in designated units). **Amenities:** video games, high-speed Internet, voice mail, irons, hair dryers. **Pool(s):** heated indoor. **Leisure Activities:** whirlpool, exercise room. **Guest Services:** valet and coin laundry. **Business Services:** meeting rooms, business center. **Cards:** AX, DC, DS, MC, VI.

SOME UNITS

QUALITY INN *Book at aaa.com* **Phone:** (307)682-2616

Motel

All Year	1P: $59-$79	2P: $59-$79	XP: $10	F17

Location: I-90, exit 128, 1 mi w. 1004 E Hwy 14-16 82716. Fax: 307/687-7002. **Facility:** 74 one-bedroom standard units. 2 stories (no elevator), interior/exterior corridors. **Parking:** on-site, winter plug-ins. **Amenities:** irons, hair dryers. **Guest Services:** valet laundry. **Cards:** AX, DC, DS, MC, VI.

SOME UNITS

FEE FEE FEE

WHERE TO DINE

BAILEY'S BAR & GRILL **Lunch:** $4-$8 **Dinner:** $7-$16 **Phone:** 307/686-7678

American

Location: Center. 301 S Gillette Ave 82716. **Hours:** 9 am-3 & 5-9 pm, Sat 11 am-3 pm. Closed major holidays; also Sun. **Reservations:** accepted. **Features:** This restored 1935 post office boasts a casual dining experience with emphasis on light meals and homemade fruit and cream pie. House specials run the gamut from sandwiches to steak and are served a relaxing and comfortable family atmosphere. Casual dress; cocktails. **Parking:** street. **Cards:** AX, DS, MC, VI.

CASA DEL REY **Lunch:** $6-$9 **Dinner:** $8-$12 **Phone:** 307/682-4738

Mexican

Location: I-90, exit 128, 2 mi w on US 14/16. 409 W Second St 82716. **Hours:** 11 am-11 pm, Sun-10 pm; 11 am-10 pm in winter. Closed: 11/25, 12/25. **Features:** All-you-can-eat Mexican food and fresh-fruit margaritas are restaurant hallmarks. Casual dress; cocktails. **Parking:** on-site. **Cards:** AX, DS, MC, VI.

THE CHOPHOUSE RESTAURANT **Lunch:** $6-$10 **Dinner:** $11-$33 **Phone:** 307/682-6805

Steak & Seafood

Location: I-90, exit 124, just n, 1.5 mi e on 2nd St, then just n. 113 S Gillette Ave 82716. **Hours:** 11 am-10 pm. Closed major holidays; also Sun, except Mother's Day. **Reservations:** suggested. **Features:** Prime beef cuts are cooked to your liking in this upscale restaurant. A warm and inviting dining room with a menu laden with fish and shellfish specialties prepared as you wish or with an interesting interpretation of classic dishes. Dressy casual; cocktails. **Parking:** on-site. **Cards:** AX, DS, MC, VI.

HONG KONG RESTAURANT **Lunch:** $5-$6 **Dinner:** $6-$14 **Phone:** 307/682-5829

Chinese

Location: I-90, exit 124, just n to US 14/16, then just e. 1612 W Second St 82716. **Hours:** 11 am-9:30 pm. Closed: 12/25. **Reservations:** accepted. **Features:** The restaurant presents traditional Chinese cuisine, including daily specials. Casual dress; cocktails. **Parking:** on-site. **Cards:** AX, DS, MC, VI.

GLENROCK pop. 2,231

WHERE TO STAY

ALL AMERICAN INN **Phone:** 307/436-2772

Motel

All Year	1P: $35-$40	2P: $50-$60	XP: $10	F12

Location: I-25, exit 165, 2.2 mi n. 500 W Aspen 82637. Fax: 307/436-2532. **Facility:** 21 one-bedroom standard units. 1-2 stories (no elevator), exterior corridors. **Parking:** on-site. **Terms:** weekly rates available, pets ($25 deposit). **Cards:** AX, DC, MC, VI. *(See color ad p 325)*

SOME UNITS

FEE

Everything you need to travel. Including this handy bookmark.

Book in advance and as a AAA/CAA member you'll always save at Choice hotels.* Plus, it's easy to earn nights or flights with our reward programs at any of our over 3,000 locations across the U.S. Just visit your local AAA/CAA office or call 800.228.1AAA to book your next stay.

CHOICE HOTELS INTERNATIONAL®

choicehotels.com
800.228.1AAA

*Advance reservations required. Offer cannot be combined with any other discount. Visit choicehotels.com for complete reward program details.

The Power of Being There. GO®

CHOICE HOTELS INTERNATIONAL

Call us at 800.228.1AAA or visit us on the Web at choicehotels.com for more information and reservations.

TourBookMark

Lodging Listing Symbols

Member Values

(see pg. 14)

- Official Appointment
- Offers minimum 10% discount
- SYC&S chain partners
- May offer discount
- Offers senior discount
- Informational listing only

Member Services

- Airport transportation
- Pets allowed
- Restaurant on premises
- Restaurant off premises (walking distance)
- 24-hour room service
- Cocktail lounge
- Child care

Accessibility Features

(see pg. 18)

- Accessibility features
- Roll-in showers
- Hearing impaired

Leisure Activities

- Full Service Casino
- Pool
- Health Club on premises
- Health Club off premises
- Recreational activities

In-Room Amenities

- Non-smoking rooms
- No air conditioning
- No TV
- No Cable TV
- VCR
- Movies
- Data port/modem line
- No telephones
- Refrigerator
- Microwave
- Coffee maker

Call property for detailed information about fees & restrictions relating to the lodging listing symbols.

CHOICE HOTELS INTERNATIONAL®

GRAND TETON NATIONAL PARK —*See also DRIGGS*

WHERE TO STAY

FLAGG RANCH RESORT **Phone:** (307)543-2001

AAA SAVE

Resort
Large-scale Hotel

5/21-9/26 1P: $150-$165 2P: $150-$165 XP: $15 F17

Location: US 89 and 191; 2 mi s of Yellowstone National Park south entrance; 5 mi n of Grand Teton National park north entrance. (PO Box 187, MORAN, 83013). Fax: 307/543-2356. **Facility:** Large log cabin exterior with modern decor. Some rooms with view of Tetons. 92 one-bedroom standard units. 1 story, exterior corridors. **Parking:** on-site. **Terms:** open 5/21-9/26, check-in 4 pm, 7 day cancellation notice-fee imposed, pets ($5 extra charge). **Amenities:** voice mail. **Dining:** 7 am-10 pm, cocktails. **Leisure Activities:** fishing, cross country skiing, snowshoeing, recreation programs, ranger talks, hiking trails, jogging. *Fee:* snowmobiling, horseback riding. **Guest Services:** gift shop, coin laundry. *Fee:* airport transportation-Jackson Hole Airport, area transportation-Jackson. **Business Services:** meeting rooms. **Cards:** AX, DS, MC, VI. ***(See color ad p 394)***

SOME UNITS

FEE FEE

JACKSON LAKE LODGE **Phone:** 307/543-2811

Resort
Large-scale Hotel

5/21-10/6 1P: $137-$240 2P: $137-$240 XP: $10 F11

Location: 5 mi nw of Moran at jct US 89 and 287. (PO Box 240, MORAN, 83013). Fax: 307/543-3143. **Facility:** Lake and mountain views enhance this lodge on spacious, landscaped grounds. 385 one-bedroom standard units, some with whirlpools. 1-3 stories, interior/exterior corridors. **Parking:** on-site. **Terms:** open 5/21-10/6, check-in 4 pm, 7 day cancellation notice-fee imposed, pets (in limited units). **Amenities:** dual phone lines, voice mail. **Dining:** The Mural Room, see separate listing. **Pool(s):** heated outdoor. **Leisure Activities:** fishing, recreation programs, hiking trails, playground. *Fee:* horseback riding. **Guest Services:** gift shop, valet laundry, area transportation (fee). **Business Services:** meeting rooms. **Cards:** AX, MC, VI. ***(See color ad p 361)***

SOME UNITS

FEE

JENNY LAKE LODGE **Phone:** 307/733-4647

Historic Resort
Cabin

5/28-10/8 [MAP] 1P: $378 2P: $465

Location: 3 mi off Interpark Rd at jct N Jenny Lake. Located in a quiet area. (PO Box 240, MORAN, 83013). Fax: 307/543-3358. **Facility:** This property, set in a pine shaded location at the foot of the majestic Grand Tetons, offers hardwood floors, high beamed ceilings, willow and pine furnishings and upscale appointments. Smoke free premises. 37 units. 6 one-bedroom suites ($600-$650), some with whirlpools. 31 cabins ($378-$465). 1 story, exterior corridors. **Parking:** on-site. **Terms:** open 5/28-10/8, check-in 4 pm, 28 day cancellation notice-fee imposed. **Amenities:** irons, hair dryers. **Leisure Activities:** fishing, recreation programs, bicycles, hiking trails, horseback riding. **Guest Services:** gift shop, complimentary evening beverages: Mon, valet laundry. **Business Services:** fax (fee). **Cards:** AX, MC, VI. ***(See color ad p 361)***

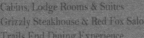

LUTON'S TETON CABINS — Phone: 307/543-2489

Cabin

6/16-8/31	2P: $175	XP: $15
9/1-11/30	2P: $160	XP: $15
5/1-6/15	2P: $150	XP: $15

Location: 5 mi e of Moran at jct US 26 and 287, south side of road. (PO Box 48, MORAN, 83013). **Facility:** These duplex log cabins are in an open meadow and offer sweeping views of the mountains. Smoke free premises. 11 cabins ($150-$295). 1 story, exterior corridors. **Parking:** on-site, winter plug-ins. **Terms:** open 5/1-11/30, 30 day cancellation notice-fee imposed, weekly rates available, no pets allowed (owner's pet on premises). **Leisure Activities:** picnic tables & grills, horse corrals, hiking trails, horseshoes, volleyball. **Guest Services:** coin laundry. **Business Services:** meeting rooms. **Cards:** DS, MC, VI.

SIGNAL MOUNTAIN LODGE — **Phone:** (307)543-2831

Small-scale Hotel

5/8-10/16	1P: $98-$250	2P: $98-$250	XP: $12

Location: Teton Park Rd, 2 mi s of US 89, 191 and 287. (PO Box 50, MORAN, 83013). Fax: 307/543-2569. **Facility:** Smoke free premises. 79 units. 32 one- and 20 two-bedroom standard units. 27 cabins ($98-$250). 2 stories (no elevator), exterior corridors. **Parking:** on-site. **Terms:** open 5/8-10/16, 4 day cancellation notice-fee imposed, pets ($5 extra charge). **Amenities:** voice mail. *Some:* hair dryers. **Dining:** The Peaks, see separate listing. **Leisure Activities:** rental boats, rental canoes, marina, fishing, hiking trails. **Guest Services:** gift shop, coin laundry. **Business Services:** meeting rooms. **Cards:** AX, DS, MC, VI.

SOME UNITS

FEE

TOGWOTEE MOUNTAIN LODGE — **Phone:** (307)543-2847

Cabin

5/21-9/15 [ECP]	1P: $99-$159	2P: $109-$169	XP: $10	F12
12/1-2/28 [ECP]	1P: $199-$249			

Location: 16.5 mi e of Moran at jct US 26 and 287. (PO Box 91, MORAN, 83013). Fax: 307/543-2391. **Facility:** 82 units. 28 one-bedroom standard units. 54 cabins ($199-$249). 1-3 stories (no elevator), interior/exterior corridors. **Parking:** on-site. **Terms:** open 5/21-9/15 & 12/1-2/28, check-in 4 pm, 30 day cancellation notice-fee imposed, package plans - seasonal, 5% service charge. **Dining:** The Grizzly Steakhouse, see separate listing. **Leisure Activities:** whirlpools, fishing, cross country skiing, recreation programs, playground. *Fee:* snowmobiling, dog sledding, horseback riding, massage. **Guest Services:** gift shop, complimentary evening beverages: in winter, coin laundry, airport transportation (fee)-Jackson Hole Airport. **Business Services:** meeting rooms. **Cards:** AX, DS, MC, VI. **Special Amenities: free expanded continental breakfast and free local telephone calls.** *(See color ad p 351)*

SOME UNITS

DATA PORT

FEE

The following lodging was either not evaluated or did not meet AAA rating requirements but is listed for your information only.

COLTER BAY VILLAGE & CABINS — **Phone:** 307/543-2811

fyi

Not evaluated. **Location:** 10 mi nw of Moran at jct US 89 and 287. (PO Box 240, MORAN, 83013). Facilities, services, and decor characterize a basic property. ***(See color ad p 361)***

WHERE TO DINE

THE GRIZZLY STEAKHOUSE — **Lunch:** $5-$7 **Dinner:** $7-$21 **Phone:** 307/543-2847

American

Location: 16.5 mi e of Moran at jct US 26 and 287; in Togwotee Mountain Lodge. **Hours:** 7 am-2:30 & 5:30-9 pm. Closed: 4/16-5/31 & 10/21-12/10. **Features:** Enjoy family dining in a mountain lodge, where a varied menu takes center stage. This eatery, located in a national forest, is known for its plentiful plates at breakfast and notable French toast. The service staff is attentive and pleasant. Casual dress; cocktails. **Parking:** on-site. **Cards:** AX, DS, MC, VI.

THE MURAL ROOM — **Lunch:** $5-$13 **Dinner:** $15-$30 **Phone:** 307/543-2811

American

Location: 5 mi nw of Moran at jct US 89 and 287; in Jackson Lake Lodge. US Hwy 89 N 83013. **Hours:** Open 5/17-10/14; 7 am-9:30, 11:30-1:30 & 5:30-9 pm. **Reservations:** suggested. **Features:** A wonderful view of the Tetons outside and murals depicting the history of Jackson Hole inside set the stage for your dining experience. The extensive menu features some game dishes, and the wine list is extensive. An outdoor barbecue is served nightly. Casual dress; cocktails. **Parking:** on-site. **Cards:** AX, DC, MC, VI.

THE PEAKS — **Dinner:** $17-$26 **Phone:** 307/543-2831

American

Location: Teton Park Rd, 2 mi s of US 89, 191 and 287; in Signal Mountain Lodge. **Hours:** Open 5/10-10/19; 5:30 pm-10 pm. **Features:** Situated on Jackson Lake with a great view of the Grand Tetons, this popular, contemporary rustic eatery, features a varied menu to include roasted garlic soup, pan seared trout, Mediterranean pasta, Thai chicken, walnut crusted salmon and elk medallions. Expect a wait at peak times. Casual dress; cocktails. **Parking:** on-site. **Cards:** AX, DS, MC, VI.

GREEN RIVER pop. 11,808

WHERE TO STAY

COACHMAN INN MOTEL — **Phone:** (307)875-3681

Motel

5/15-10/15	1P: $36-$40	2P: $42-$49	XP: $5	D8
3/1-5/14 & 10/16-2/28	1P: $34-$38	2P: $40-$47	XP: $5	D8

Location: I-80, exit 89, just e on I-80 business loop. 470 E Flaming Gorge Way 82935 (PO Box 352, LYMAN, 82937). **Facility:** 18 one-bedroom standard units. 1 story, exterior corridors. **Parking:** on-site, winter plug-ins. **Terms:** pets ($7-$10 fee). **Amenities:** voice mail. **Cards:** AX, DC, DS, MC, VI. **Special Amenities: free local telephone calls and early check-in/late check-out.**

SOME UNITS

DATA PORT

FEE

OAK TREE INN *Book at aaa.com* **Phone:** (307)875-3500

SAVE

Small-scale Hotel

5/1-9/30 [BP]	1P: $64-$74	2P: $69-$79	XP: $5	F12
3/1-4/30 & 10/1-2/28 [BP]	1P: $59-$69	2P: $64-$74	XP: $5	F12

Location: I-80, exit 89, just s. 1170 W Flaming Gorge Way 82935. Fax: 307/875-4889. **Facility:** Smoke free premises. 191 one-bedroom standard units. 2 stories (no elevator), interior/exterior corridors. *Bath:* combo or shower only. **Parking:** on-site. **Terms:** pets ($5 extra charge). **Amenities:** *Some:* irons, hair dryers. **Dining:** 24 hours. **Leisure Activities:** whirlpool, exercise room. **Guest Services:** coin laundry. **Business Services:** meeting rooms. **Cards:** AX, DC, DS, JC, MC, VI. **Special Amenities: free full breakfast and free local telephone calls.**

SOME UNITS

FEE

GREYBULL pop. 1,815

WHERE TO STAY

ANTLER MOTEL **Phone:** (307)765-4404

SAVE

Motel

5/1-11/30	1P: $45	2P: $50-$60	XP: $5	D15
3/1-4/30 & 12/1-2/28	1P: $35	2P: $40-$50	XP: $5	D15

Location: 0.8 mi w on US 14/16/20. 1116 N 6th St 82426. Fax: 307/765-4719. **Facility:** 12 units. 11 one- and 1 two-bedroom standard units. 1 story, exterior corridors. *Bath:* combo or shower only. **Parking:** on-site. **Terms:** pets ($10 extra charge). **Leisure Activities:** playground. *Fee:* miniature golf. **Guest Services:** gift shop, coin laundry. **Cards:** AX, DS, MC, VI. **Special Amenities: free local telephone calls and preferred room (subject to availability with advanced reservations).**

SOME UNITS

FEE

BUDGET HOST WHEELS MOTEL **Phone:** (307)765-2105

SAVE

Motel

6/1-9/6	1P: $52-$62	2P: $62-$72	XP: $7	F5
3/1-5/31 & 9/7-2/28	1P: $45-$52	2P: $52-$65	XP: $7	F5

Location: On US 14/16/20, north end of town. 1324 N 6th St 82426. Fax: 307/765-4735. **Facility:** 29 one-bedroom standard units. 1 story, exterior corridors. **Parking:** on-site, winter plug-ins. **Terms:** cancellation fee imposed. **Leisure Activities:** exercise room. **Guest Services:** coin laundry. **Cards:** AX, DS, MC, VI. **Special Amenities: free local telephone calls and preferred room (subject to availability with advanced reservations).**

SOME UNITS

YELLOWSTONE MOTEL **Phone:** 307/765-4456

SAVE

Motel

6/1-8/31	1P: $55-$67	2P: $72-$79	XP: $6	F12
3/1-5/31 & 11/1-2/28	1P: $45-$52	2P: $52-$65	XP: $6	F12
9/1-10/31	1P: $50-$55	2P: $55-$60	XP: $6	F12

Location: 0.4 mi e on US 14. 247 Greybull Ave 82426. Fax: 307/765-2108. **Facility:** 35 units. 32 one- and 2 two-bedroom standard units, some with kitchens. 1 cottage. 1 story, exterior corridors. *Bath:* combo or shower only. **Parking:** on-site, winter plug-ins. **Terms:** 3 day cancellation notice-fee imposed, small pets only ($5 extra charge). **Pool(s):** small heated outdoor. **Leisure Activities:** putting green. **Cards:** AX, CB, DC, DS, MC, VI. **Special Amenities: free local telephone calls and preferred room (subject to availability with advanced reservations).**

SOME UNITS

FEE

WHERE TO DINE

BEIJING GARDEN **Lunch:** $5-$8 **Dinner:** $7-$12 **Phone:** 307/765-9826

Chinese

Location: 0.4 mi e on US 14. 510 Greybull Ave 82426. **Hours:** 11 am-9:30 pm. Closed major holidays. **Features:** In a converted storefront building downtown, this restaurant offers a relaxed, casual dining experience. Oriental dishes are well prepared and the service is friendly. Casual dress. **Parking:** street. **Cards:** AX, DC, DS, MC, VI.

LISA'S **Lunch:** $6-$8 **Dinner:** $6-$18 **Phone:** 307/765-4765

American

Location: 0.4 mi e on US 14. 200 Greybull Ave 82426. **Hours:** 7 am-10 pm; 11 am-9 pm in winter. Closed major holidays; also Sun in winter. **Features:** Lisa's offers up a mixture of Western and Southwestern courses as well as a number of micro-brewed beers. Locally raised beef is featured on the varied steak menu. Farmers pasta, fajitas, chicken fried steak, shrimp and hot sandwiches are also available. Relax and unwind amidst stucco walls and an adobe fireplace. Casual dress; cocktails. **Parking:** on-site. **Cards:** DS, MC, VI.

GUERNSEY pop. 1,147

WHERE TO STAY

THE BUNKHOUSE MOTEL **Phone:** 307/836-2356

Motel

All Year	1P: $44	2P: $51

Location: On US 26; center. 350 W Whalen 82214 (PO Box 40). Fax: 307/836-2328. **Facility:** 31 one-bedroom standard units. 1 story, exterior corridors. **Parking:** on-site. **Terms:** pets ($3 extra charge). **Amenities:** voice mail. **Cards:** AX, DC, MC, VI.

SOME UNITS

FEE

HULETT pop. 408

WHERE TO STAY

HULETT MOTEL **Phone:** 307/467-5220

Motel

4/15-12/1 1P: $65-$85 2P: $65-$85

Location: SR 24 at north end of town. 202 Main St 82720 (PO Box 489). **Facility:** 15 units. 7 one- and 4 two-bedroom standard units. 4 cabins. 1 story, exterior corridors. *Bath:* combo or shower only. **Parking:** on-site. **Terms:** open 4/15-12/1, pets ($10 extra charge). **Leisure Activities:** gazebo, sun deck. **Guest Services:** gift shop. **Cards:** DS, MC, VI. **Special Amenities: free local telephone calls.**

SOME UNITS

FEE

JACKSON pop. 8,647—*See also GRAND TETON NATIONAL PARK & YELLOWSTONE NATIONAL PARK.*

WHERE TO STAY

49'ER INN AND SUITES (QUALITY INN AND SUITES) *Book at aaa.com* **Phone:** (307)733-7550

Small-scale Hotel

5/21-9/30 [ECP]	1P: $89-$199	2P: $95-$199	XP: $10	F12
12/21-2/28 [ECP]	1P: $74-$169	2P: $78-$179	XP: $10	F12
3/1-5/20 [ECP]	1P: $64-$106	2P: $68-$110	XP: $10	F12
10/1-12/20 [ECP]	1P: $56-$104	2P: $60-$108	XP: $10	F12

Location: Just w and just s of town square. 330 W Pearl St 83001 (PO Box 1948). Fax: 307/733-2002. **Facility:** 142 units. 137 one- and 5 two-bedroom standard units, some with kitchens and/or whirlpools. 3 stories, interior/exterior corridors. **Parking:** on-site, winter plug-ins. **Terms:** 14 day cancellation notice, in winter-fee imposed. **Amenities:** voice mail, irons, hair dryers. **Leisure Activities:** sauna, whirlpool, large indoor Roman bath, exercise room. **Guest Services:** valet and coin laundry, area transportation-ski shuttle. **Business Services:** meeting rooms. **Cards:** AX, CB, DC, DS, JC, MC, VI. **Special Amenities: free expanded continental breakfast and free newspaper.** *(See color ad p 355)*

SOME UNITS

4 WINDS MOTEL **Phone:** 307/733-2474

Small-scale Hotel

6/11-9/5	2P: $88-$110	XP: $10	F12
9/6-9/25	2P: $75-$95	XP: $10	F12
9/26-10/15	2P: $65-$95	XP: $10	F12
5/1-6/10	2P: $55-$95	XP: $10	F12

Location: Just n of US 26/89/187/191. Located across from city park. 150 N Millward St 83001 (PO Box 66). **Facility:** Smoke free premises. 21 one-bedroom standard units. 2 stories, exterior corridors. **Parking:** on-site, winter plug-ins. **Terms:** open 5/1-10/15, check-in 4 pm, 3 day cancellation notice-fee imposed. **Cards:** AX, DS, MC, VI. *(See color ad below)*

THE ALPINE HOUSE

Phone: (307)739-1570

Bed & Breakfast

6/1-10/31 [BP]	1P: $165-$225	2P: $165-$225	XP: $25
12/1-2/28 [BP]	1P: $125-$200	2P: $125-$200	XP: $25
3/1-4/30 [BP]	1P: $115-$190	2P: $115-$190	XP: $25
5/1-5/31 [BP]	1P: $100-$150	2P: $100-$150	XP: $25

Location: 0.3 mi n, turn n on Glenwood or w on Mercil Ave from US 26/89/191. 285 N Glenwood 83001 (PO Box 1126). Fax: 307/734-2850. **Facility:** The house, reminiscent of a Norwegian inn, features a mural, wood furniture and an airy dining space; 14 units have balconies and fireplaces. Smoke free premises. 21 units. 20 one-bedroom standard units, some with whirlpools. 1 one-bedroom suite ($180-$265) with whirlpool. 3 stories (no elevator), interior corridors. **Parking:** on-site, winter plug-ins. **Terms:** open 3/1-10/31 & 12/1-2/28, check-in 4 pm, 30 day cancellation notice-fee imposed, package plans. **Amenities:** voice mail, hair dryers. **Leisure Activities:** sauna, whirlpool. *Fee:* massage. **Business Services:** meeting rooms. **Cards:** AX, MC, VI.

SOME UNITS

DATA PORT

ANGLER'S INN

Phone: (307)733-3682

SAVE

Small-scale Hotel

6/1-9/30	1P: $105-$155	2P: $105-$165	XP: $5	F12
3/1-5/31 & 10/1-2/28	1P: $65-$85	2P: $65-$85	XP: $5	F12

Location: Just nw of town square, n on Millward St or w on Mercil Ave from US 26/89/191. 265 N Millward 83001 (PO Box 1247). Fax: 307/733-8662. **Facility:** Smoke free premises. 28 one-bedroom standard units. 2 stories, exterior corridors. **Parking:** on-site, winter plug-ins. **Terms:** 3 day cancellation notice, package plans - in winter. **Amenities:** irons, hair dryers. **Cards:** AX, DS, MC, VI. **Special Amenities: free local telephone calls and free newspaper.** *(See color ad below)*

ANTLER INN

Phone: (307)733-2535

SAVE

Small-scale Hotel

5/21-10/15	1P: $92-$105	2P: $97-$110	XP: $5	F8
3/1-5/20 & 10/16-2/28	1P: $70-$80	2P: $75-$85	XP: $5	F8

Location: Just s of town square. 43 W Pearl St 83001 (PO Box 575). Fax: 307/733-4158. **Facility:** 100 units. 97 one- and 3 two-bedroom standard units. 2 stories, interior/exterior corridors. **Parking:** on-site, winter plug-ins. **Terms:** 14 day cancellation notice, pets (must be attended). **Amenities:** voice mail, irons, hair dryers. **Leisure Activities:** whirlpool, exercise room. **Guest Services:** valet and coin laundry. **Business Services:** meeting rooms. **Cards:** AX, CB, DC, DS, MC, VI. *(See color ad p 355)*

SOME UNITS

DATA PORT

BUCKRAIL LODGE

Phone: 307/733-2079

SAVE

Motel

6/7-9/1	1P: $83-$121	2P: $83-$121	XP: $7	D12
9/2-9/30	1P: $83-$99	2P: $83-$99	XP: $7	D12
5/1-6/6 & 10/1-10/20	1P: $55-$83	2P: $55-$83	XP: $7	D12

Location: Just s and e of US 26/89/187/189, 0.3 mi s of town square via King St; at jct of Karns Ave and King St. Located in a quiet, residential area. 110 E Karns Ave 83001 (PO Box 23). Fax: 307/734-1663. **Facility:** Smoke free premises. 12 one-bedroom standard units. 1 story, exterior corridors. *Bath:* combo or shower only. **Parking:** on-site. **Terms:** open 5/1-10/20, 7 day cancellation notice-fee imposed. **Amenities:** hair dryers. **Leisure Activities:** whirlpool. **Business Services:** fax. **Cards:** AX, DS, MC, VI. *(See color ad p 358)*

SOME UNITS

COWBOY VILLAGE RESORT — **Phone:** (307)733-3121

AAA SAVE — Cabin

6/1-9/20	1P: $139-$179	2P: $139-$179	XP: $5	F12
3/1-5/31 & 9/21-12/20	1P: $89-$149	2P: $89-$149	XP: $5	F12
12/21-2/28 [CP]	1P: $99-$135	2P: $99-$135	XP: $5	F12

Location: 0.3 mi w on Broadway to Flat Creek Dr, just s; downtown. 120 S Flat Creek Dr 83002 (PO Box 8040). Fax: 307/739-1955. **Facility:** A small village of various sized log cabins near ski lift, each with picnic table and barbecue grill. 82 cabins. 1 story, exterior corridors. **Parking:** on-site, winter plug-ins. **Terms:** package plans - seasonal. **Amenities:** voice mail, hair dryers. **Leisure Activities:** whirlpools. **Guest Services:** coin laundry, area transportation-Jackson Hole Ski Resort. **Business Services:** meeting rooms, fax. **Cards:** AX, CB, DC, DS, MC, VI. **Special Amenities: free local telephone calls and free newspaper.** *(See color ad p 359)*

SOME UNITS

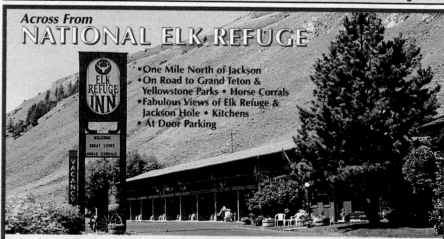

DAYS INN OF JACKSON HOLE *Book at aaa.com* **Phone:** (307)733-0033

6/1-9/15 [ECP]	1P: $159	2P: $159	XP: $10	F17
1/1-2/28 [ECP]	1P: $99-$139	2P: $99-$139	XP: $10	F17
9/16-12/31 [ECP]	1P: $79-$119	2P: $79-$119	XP: $10	F17
3/1-5/31 [ECP]	1P: $79	2P: $79	XP: $10	F17

Small-scale Hotel **Location:** 1.5 mi s on US 26/89/191. 350 S Hwy 89 83001 (PO Box 2986). Fax: 307/733-0044. **Facility:** 90 one-bedroom standard units, some with whirlpools. 3 stories, interior corridors. *Bath:* combo or shower only. **Parking:** on-site, winter plug-ins. **Terms:** 7 day cancellation notice. **Amenities:** hair dryers. *Some:* irons. **Leisure Activities:** sauna, whirlpool, ski racks. **Guest Services:** valet laundry. **Business Services:** fax. **Cards:** AX, CB, DC, DS, MC, VI. **Special Amenities: free expanded continental breakfast and free local telephone calls.**

SOME UNITS

ELK COUNTRY INN **Phone:** 307/733-2364

3/1-5/20	1P: $56-$122	2P: $60-$126	XP: $6	F10
5/21-9/30	1P: $70-$136		XP: $6	F10
12/21-2/28	1P: $54-$108		XP: $6	F10
10/1-12/20	1P: $52-$82		XP: $6	F10

Small-scale Hotel **Location:** Just w, then just s of town square. 480 W Pearl St 83001 (PO Box 1255). Fax: 307/733-4465. **Facility:** 88 units. 71 one-bedroom standard units, some with kitchens. 1 one-bedroom suite ($88-$184) with kitchen. 16 cabins ($76-$158). 1-2 stories, interior/exterior corridors. *Bath:* combo or shower only. **Parking:** on-site, winter plug-ins. **Terms:** 14 day cancellation notice, in winter, pets (except in cabins). **Amenities:** voice mail, hair dryers. *Some:* irons. **Leisure Activities:** whirlpool, pet park, picnic and lawn area with barbecue grills, playground. **Guest Services:** valet and coin laundry. **Cards:** AX, CB, DC, DS, MC, VI. **Special Amenities: free local telephone calls.** ***(See color ad p 355)***

SOME UNITS

ELK REFUGE INN **Phone:** (307)733-3582

6/15-9/15 [CP]	1P: $98-$110	2P: $98-$120	XP: $10	F12
5/23-6/14	1P: $75-$80	2P: $75-$90	XP: $10	F12
9/16-2/28	1P: $50-$75	2P: $55-$90	XP: $10	F12
3/1-5/22	1P: $50-$60	2P: $55-$85	XP: $10	F12

Motel **Location:** 1.5 mi n on US 26/89/191. 1755 N Hwy 89 83001 (PO Box 2834). Fax: 307/734-1580. **Facility:** Smoke free premises. 22 one-bedroom standard units, some with kitchens. 2 stories (no elevator), exterior corridors. **Parking:** on-site, winter plug-ins. **Terms:** check-in 4 pm, 3 day cancellation notice-fee imposed, package plans - in winter. **Leisure Activities:** horse corrals, trailer parking, picnic areas, barbecue grills. **Cards:** AX, DS, MC, VI. ***(See color ad p 358)***

SOME UNITS

THE GOLDEN EAGLE INN — **Phone:** 307/733-2042

AAA SAVE — Motel

6/11-9/11	2P: $99-$125	XP: $10	F12
9/12-9/30	2P: $75-$105	XP: $10	F12
10/1-2/28	2P: $65-$97	XP: $10	F12
3/1-6/10	2P: $55-$95	XP: $10	F12

Location: Just c. Located in a quiet, residential area. 325 E Broadway 83001 (PO Box 1107). **Facility:** Smoke free premises. 23 one-bedroom standard units. 2 stories (no elevator), exterior corridors. **Parking:** on-site, winter plug-ins. **Terms:** 3 day cancellation notice-fee imposed. **Amenities:** voice mail. **Pool(s):** heated outdoor. **Cards:** AX, DS, MC, VI. ***(See color ad p 354)***

DATA PORT

THE GRAND VICTORIAN LODGE — **Phone:** (307)739-2294

Small-scale Hotel

All Year	1P: $89-$279	2P: $89-$279

Location: Just n and w from town square. 85 Perry Ave 83001 (PO Box 20147). Fax: 307/733-9704. **Facility:** Smoke free premises. 11 one-bedroom standard units, some with whirlpools. 3 stories (no elevator), interior corridors. **Parking:** on-site. **Terms:** 30 day cancellation notice-fee imposed, package plans - seasonal, weekends. **Amenities:** irons, hair dryers. **Leisure Activities:** whirlpool. **Guest Services:** complimentary evening beverages, valet laundry. **Cards:** AX, MC, VI.

ASK DATA PORT

JACKSON HOLE LODGE <u>*Book at aaa.com*</u> — **Phone:** (307)733-2992

AAA SAVE — **Small-scale Hotel**

6/1-10/1	1P: $109	2P: $124
3/1-5/31	1P: $79-$94	2P: $104-$119
12/10-2/28	1P: $94	2P: $119
10/2-12/9	1P: $79	2P: $104

Location: 0.3 mi w on US 26/89/191. 420 W Broadway 83001 (PO Box 1805). Fax: 307/739-2144. **Facility:** 59 units. 30 one-bedroom standard units. 15 one- and 14 two-bedroom suites ($159-$299) with kitchens and whirlpools. 3 stories (no elevator), exterior corridors. **Parking:** on-site, winter plug-ins. **Terms:** check-in 4 pm, 14 day cancellation notice-fee imposed, small pets only ($50 deposit). **Amenities:** voice mail, irons. *Some:* hair dryers. **Pool(s):** heated indoor, wading. **Leisure Activities:** sauna, whirlpools, sun deck, ski lockers. *Fee:* game room. **Business Services:** meeting rooms, fax. **Cards:** AX, DC, DS, MC, VI. **Special Amenities: free newspaper.** ***(See color ad p 362)***

FEE DATA PORT / SOME UNITS VCR /

PAINTED BUFFALO INN Book at aaa.com

Phone: (307)733-4340

Small-scale Hotel

6/16-9/18	1P: $89-$149	2P: $99-$159	XP: $15	F16
12/25-2/28	1P: $70-$120	2P: $75-$130	XP: $15	F16
3/1-6/15 & 9/19-12/24	1P: $60-$90	2P: $70-$99	XP: $15	F16

Location: Just w of town square. 400 W Broadway 83001 (PO Box 2547). Fax: 307/733-7953. **Facility:** 136 units. 135 one- and 1 two-bedroom standard units. 2 stories, exterior corridors. **Parking:** on-site, winter plug-ins. **Terms:** check-in 4 pm, small pets only ($10 fee). **Pool(s):** heated indoor. **Leisure Activities:** sauna. *Fee:* massage. **Guest Services:** valet laundry. **Cards:** AX, DC, MC, VI. **Special Amenities: free local telephone calls and early check-in/late check-out.** *(See color ad p 363)*

SOME UNITS

FEE FEE FEE

PARKWAY INN Book at aaa.com

Phone: (307)733-3143

Small-scale Hotel

6/5-9/19 [ECP]	1P: $159-$199	2P: $159-$199	XP: $15
3/1-6/4 & 12/1-2/28 [ECP]	1P: $99-$149	2P: $99-$149	XP: $15
9/20-10/31 [ECP]	1P: $99-$139	2P: $99-$139	XP: $15

Location: Just n of jct Broadway and Jackson aves; 0.3 mi w of town square. 125 N Jackson St 83001 (PO Box 494). Fax: 307/733-0955. **Facility:** Smoke free premises. 49 units. 37 one-bedroom standard units. 12 one-bedroom suites ($125-$235). 2 stories, interior/exterior corridors. **Parking:** on-site. **Terms:** open 3/1-10/31 & 12/1-2/28, 30 day cancellation notice, in winter, 7 day in summer-fee imposed, monthly rates available, package plans - in winter. **Amenities:** hair dryers. *Some:* CD players, irons. **Leisure Activities:** saunas, whirlpools, exercise room. **Guest Services:** valet laundry. **Cards:** AX, CB, DC, DS, MC, VI. **Special Amenities: free expanded continental breakfast and free local telephone calls.** *(See color ad p 366 & p 364)*

SOME UNITS

RAWHIDE MOTEL Book at aaa.com

Phone: (307)733-1216

Motel

6/10-9/25	1P: $85-$120	2P: $109-$129	XP: $10	F15
9/26-10/20	1P: $65-$85	2P: $99-$109	XP: $10	F15
5/1-6/9	1P: $65-$75	2P: $75-$95	XP: $10	F15

Location: Just s of US 26/89/191. 75 S Millward St 83001 (PO Box 4800). Fax: 307/734-1335. **Facility:** 23 one-bedroom standard units. 2 stories, exterior corridors. **Parking:** on-site. **Terms:** open 5/1-10/20. **Amenities:** voice mail. **Cards:** AX, DS, MC, VI. **Special Amenities: free local telephone calls and free newspaper.**

SOME UNITS

RED LION WYOMING INN OF JACKSON Book at aaa.com

Phone: (307)734-0035

Small-scale Hotel

7/4-9/30 [ECP]	1P: $259-$329	2P: $259-$329	XP: $10	F17
10/1-2/28 [ECP]	1P: $229-$299	2P: $229-$299	XP: $10	F17
5/16-7/3 [ECP]	1P: $209-$289	2P: $209-$289	XP: $10	F17
3/1-5/15 [ECP]	1P: $109-$199	2P: $109-$199	XP: $10	F17

Location: 0.5 mi s on US 26/89/191. 930 W Broadway 83001 (PO Box 8820, 83002). Fax: 307/734-0037. **Facility:** Smoke free premises. 73 one-bedroom standard units, some with kitchens. 1-3 stories, interior corridors. **Parking:** on-site. **Terms:** check-in 4 pm, 3 day cancellation notice-fee imposed, package plans - in winter. **Amenities:** irons, hair dryers. *Some:* DVD players. **Leisure Activities:** Fee: massage. **Guest Services:** airport transportation-Jackson Hole Airport. **Business Services:** PC. **Cards:** AX, DC, MC, VI. **Special Amenities: free expanded continental breakfast and early check-in/late check-out.** *(See color ad p 365)*

SOME UNITS

RUSTY PARROT LODGE & SPA — **Phone:** (307)733-2000

AAA SAVE — Country Inn

9/29-2/28 [BP]	1P: $199-$395	2P: $199-$395	XP: $30
5/24-9/28 [BP]	1P: $284-$355	2P: $284-$355	XP: $30
3/1-3/27 [BP]	1P: $245-$325	2P: $245-$325	XP: $30
3/28-5/23 [BP]	1P: $164-$219	2P: $164-$219	XP: $30

Location: Just nw from town square. 175 N Jackson St 83001 (PO Box 1657). Fax: 307/733-5566. **Facility:** Featured at the modern lodge are pine-log beds, Southwestern-style decor and cooked-to-order breakfasts; spa treatments are available. Smoke free premises. 31 units. 30 one-bedroom standard units, some with whirlpools. 1 one-bedroom suite with whirlpool. 3 stories (no elevator), interior corridors. **Parking:** on-site and valet, winter plug-ins. **Terms:** check-in 4 pm, 3 night minimum stay - seasonal, 21 day cancellation notice-fee imposed. **Amenities:** dual phone lines, voice mail, irons, hair dryers. **Dining:** 6 pm-10 pm, cocktails. **Leisure Activities:** whirlpool, sun deck, spa. **Guest Services:** valet laundry, airport transportation (fee)-Jackson Hole Airport. **Business Services:** PC. **Cards:** AX, DS, MC, VI. **Special Amenities: free full breakfast and free newspaper.** *(See color ad p 366)*

SOME UNITS

FEE DATA PORT / VCR /

SNOW KING RESORT Book at aaa.com

Phone: (307)733-5200

Large-scale Hotel

6/12-8/21	1P: $220-$720	2P: $230-$720	XP: $10	F13
8/22-10/9	1P: $170-$400	2P: $180-$400	XP: $10	F13
3/1-6/11 & 10/10-2/28	1P: $130-$400	2P: $140-$400	XP: $10	F13

Location: Just se of town square. 400 E Snow King Ave 83001 (PO Box SKI). Fax: 307/733-4086. **Facility:** 269 units. 204 one-bedroom standard units. 45 one- and 20 three-bedroom suites ($160-$450) with kitchens, some with whirlpools. 2-7 stories, interior corridors. *Bath:* combo or shower only. **Parking:** on-site, winter plug-ins. **Terms:** check-in 4 pm, cancellation fee imposed, small pets only ($50 fee, $50 deposit). **Amenities:** voice mail, hair dryers. *Some:* DVD players, CD players, safes, irons. **Dining:** 6:30 am-9:30 pm, cocktails. **Pool(s):** heated outdoor. **Leisure Activities:** sauna, whirlpools, cross country skiing, hiking trails, exercise room. *Fee:* miniature golf, downhill skiing, ice skating, ski equipment, snow tubing park, snowboarding park, alpine slide, horseback riding, massage. **Guest Services:** gift shop, complimentary evening beverages: Wed 12/1-3/31, valet and coin laundry, airport transportation-Jackson Hole Airport, area transportation-within ski area. **Business Services:** conference facilities, administrative services, PC. **Cards:** AX, CB, DC, DS, MC, VI. *(See color ad p 367 & p 158)*

FEE / SOME UNITS DATA PORT / VCR /

SPRING CREEK RANCH Book at aaa.com

Phone: (307)733-8833

Resort
Small-scale Hotel

6/1-10/15	1P: $250-$2000	2P: $250-$2000
10/16-2/28	1P: $150-$2000	2P: $150-$2000
3/1-3/31	1P: $195-$1600	2P: $195-$1600
4/1-5/31	1P: $150-$1600	2P: $150-$1600

Location: 2 mi w on US 89/189/191, 0.5 mi w on SR 22, then 1 mi n on Spring Gulch Rd, follow signs. Located in a rural area. 1800 Spirit Dance Rd 83001 (PO Box 4780). Fax: 307/733-1524. **Facility:** This activity-oriented ranch offers sweeping views of the mountains. 124 units. 90 one- and 8 two-bedroom standard units. 10 one- and 8 three-bedroom suites, some with kitchens and/or whirlpools. 8 vacation homes ($1600-$2000) with whirlpools. 2-3 stories (no elevator), exterior corridors. **Parking:** on-site, winter plug-ins. **Terms:** check-in 4 pm, 15 day cancellation notice-fee imposed. **Amenities:** voice mail, hair dryers. *Some:* irons. **Dining:** Granary, see separate listing. **Pool(s):** heated outdoor. **Leisure Activities:** whirlpools, 2 tennis courts, cross country skiing, hiking trails, jogging, exercise room, spa. *Fee:* horseback riding. **Guest Services:** gift shop, valet laundry, area transportation. **Business Services:** meeting rooms. **Cards:** AX, MC, VI.

SOME UNITS DATA PORT / VCR /

SUPER 8 MOTEL Book at aaa.com

Phone: (307)733-6833

Small-scale Hotel

6/16-9/30	1P: $119	2P: $125
5/1-6/15	1P: $69	2P: $89
3/1-4/30 & 10/1-2/28	1P: $45	2P: $49

Location: Jct US 26/89/189, 0.5 mi s. 750 S US Hwy 89 83001 (PO Box 1382). Fax: 307/739-1828. **Facility:** 97 one-bedroom standard units. 3 stories (no elevator), interior corridors. **Parking:** on-site, winter plug-ins. **Terms:** check-in 4 pm, 10 day cancellation notice. **Amenities:** safes. **Guest Services:** coin laundry. **Cards:** AX, DS, MC, VI.

SOME UNITS ASK DATA PORT / /

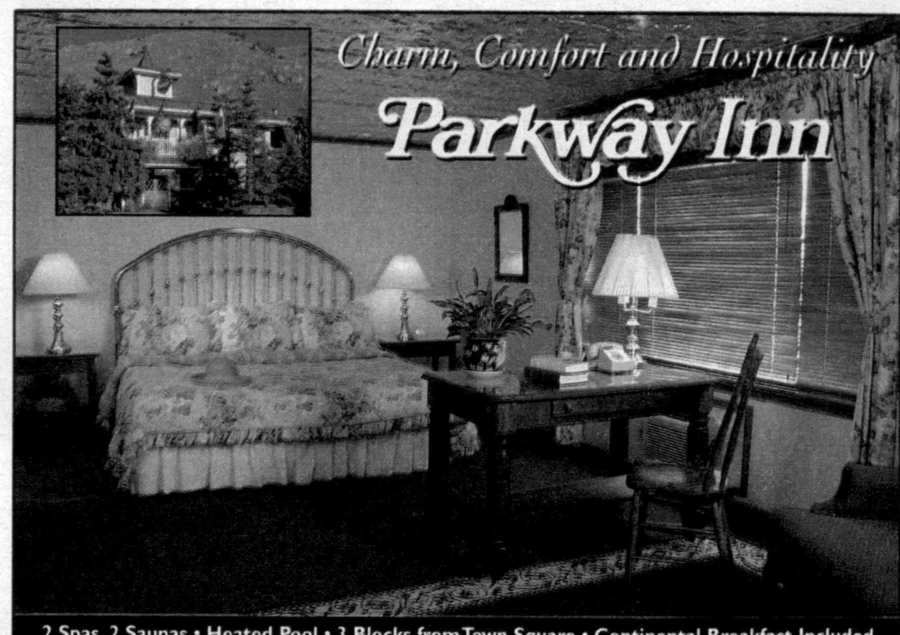

TRAPPER INN *Book at aaa.com* **Phone:** (307)733-2648

6/11-9/30	1P: $107-$180	2P: $107-$180	XP: $10	F12
5/21-6/10	1P: $83-$125	2P: $83-$125	XP: $10	F12
3/1-5/20 & 10/1-2/28	1P: $58-$90	2P: $58-$90	XP: $10	F12

Small-scale Hotel **Location:** Just n on US 26/89/191; downtown. 235 N Cache Dr 83001-1712 (PO Box 1712, 83001). Fax: 307/739-9351. **Facility:** Smoke free premises. 54 one-bedroom standard units, some with whirlpools. 1-2 stories, exterior corridors. **Parking:** on-site, winter plug-ins. **Terms:** 14 day cancellation notice, package plans. **Amenities:** voice mail. *Some:* hair dryers. **Leisure Activities:** whirlpools, ski lockers. **Guest Services:** coin laundry. **Business Services:** meeting rooms, fax. **Cards:** AX, CB, DC, MC, VI. **Special Amenities: free local telephone calls and early check-in/late check-out.** *(See color ad p 368)*

SOME UNITS

VIRGINIAN LODGE — **Phone:** (307)733-2792

AAA SAVE

Small-scale Hotel

5/23-9/30	1P: $95-$165	2P: $95-$165	XP: $7	F11
3/1-5/22	1P: $52-$165	2P: $52-$165	XP: $7	F11
10/1-2/28	1P: $52-$125	2P: $52-$125	XP: $7	F11

Location: Just w. 750 W Broadway 83001 (PO Box 1052). Fax: 307/733-4063. **Facility:** 170 units. 149 one-bedroom standard units. 18 one- and 3 two-bedroom suites with efficiencies, some with whirlpools. 1-2 stories, interior/exterior corridors. **Parking:** on-site, winter plug-ins. **Terms:** check-in 4 pm, cancellation fee imposed. **Amenities:** *Some:* irons, hair dryers. **Dining:** 7 am-11 & 5-10 pm, cocktails. **Pool(s):** heated outdoor. **Leisure Activities:** whirlpool. **Guest Services:** coin laundry, airport transportation (fee)-Jackson Hole Airport. **Business Services:** conference facilities, fax (fee). **Cards:** AX, CB, DC, DS, MC, VI. ***(See color ad below)***

SOME UNITS

FEE

WAGON WHEEL VILLAGE | **Phone:** (307)733-2357

AAA SAVE — Three Diamond — Motel

5/16-9/15	1P: $90-$100	2P: $99-$110
3/1-5/15 & 9/16-2/28	1P: $45-$85	2P: $50-$95

Location: 0.5 mi n on US 26/89/189/191. 435 N Cache Dr 83001 (PO Box 525). Fax: 307/733-0568. **Facility:** Smoke free premises. 97 units. 84 one-bedroom standard units, some with efficiencies and/or whirlpools. 7 one-bedroom suites ($135-$175), some with efficiencies, kitchens and/or whirlpools. 6 cabins. 2 stories, exterior corridors. *Bath:* combo or shower only. **Parking:** on-site. **Terms:** cancellation fee imposed. **Amenities:** voice mail. *Some:* hair dryers. **Dining:** 6 am-10 pm, cocktails. **Leisure Activities:** whirlpools. **Guest Services:** gift shop, valet and coin laundry, airport transportation-Jackson Hole Airport. **Business Services:** meeting rooms. **Cards:** AX, DS, MC, VI.
(See color ad below)

SOME UNITS

WORT HOTEL | ***Book at aaa.com*** | **Phone:** (307)733-2190

AAA SAVE — Three Diamond — Historic Small-scale Hotel

	1P	2P	XP	
All Year [BP]	1P: $160-$275	2P: $160-$275	XP: $25	F14

Location: Center of downtown. 50 N Glenwood 83001 (PO Box 69). Fax: 307/733-2067. **Facility:** Established hotel with colorful history. 60 units. 59 one-bedroom standard units. 1 one-bedroom suite ($325-$550) with whirlpool. 2 stories, interior corridors. *Bath:* combo or shower only. **Parking:** valet. **Terms:** check-in 4 pm, 14 day cancellation notice, 4/7-9/30-fee imposed. **Amenities:** voice mail, irons, hair dryers. **Dining:** Silver Dollar Grill, see separate listing. **Leisure Activities:** whirlpools, exercise room. **Guest Services:** gift shop, valet laundry, area transportation-ski shuttle. **Business Services:** meeting rooms, fax (fee). **Cards:** AX, DS, MC, VI. **Special Amenities: free local telephone calls and free newspaper.** ***(See color ad p 366)***

SOME UNITS

FEE

WHERE TO DINE

BLUE LION **Dinner:** $13-$30 **Phone:** 307/733-3912

American

Location: US 26/89/189/191, just n; opposite Miller Park. 160 N Millward St 83001. **Hours:** 6 pm-10 pm; from 5:30 pm 6/1-9/30. Closed: 11/25. **Reservations:** suggested. **Features:** This casual, art-filled restaurant offers an intimate atmosphere in a refurbished older home with outdoor seating. Menu selections include game, fresh fish, pasta, fowl, creative vegetarian dishes and the house specialty, rack of lamb. Homemade desserts. Casual dress; cocktails. **Parking:** street. **Cards:** AX, DS, MC, VI.

BUBBA'S BAR-B-QUE RESTAURANT **Lunch:** $6-$8 **Dinner:** $9-$15 **Phone:** 307/733-2288

Barbecue

Location: 0.5 mi w on US 26/89/191. 515 W Broadway 83001. **Hours:** 7 am-10 pm; to 9 pm in winter. Closed major holidays. **Features:** This very popular local favorite offers pit barbecue fare accented with homemade sauce. A good choice is the sloppy Bubba sandwich — barbecued turkey, pork and beef with a side of curly fries. Expect to sign-in and wait during busy periods. Casual dress. **Parking:** on-site. **Cards:** AX, DS, MC, VI.

THE BUNNERY, BAKERY & RESTAURANT **Lunch:** $6-$10 **Dinner:** $7-$18 **Phone:** 307/733-5474

American

Location: Just n of downtown center. 130 N Cache St 83001. **Hours:** 7 am-3 & 5-9 pm; to 2 pm in winter. Closed: 12/25. **Features:** Locals love the light meals, sandwiches and fresh all-natural bakery items, served in generous portions. The quaint interior boasts pine walls, large windows and artworks depicting local wildlife. Deck seating is available in summer. Casual dress; beer & wine only. **Parking:** street. **Cards:** MC, VI.

CADILLAC GRILLE **Lunch:** $6-$12 **Dinner:** $15-$28 **Phone:** 307/733-3279

AAA

Regional American

Location: US 26/89/189. 55 N Cache St 83001. **Hours:** Open 3/1-11/1 & 12/1-2/28; 11:30 am-10 pm. **Reservations:** suggested. **Features:** Featured are fresh seafood, game and homemade pasta in a casual, contemporary atmosphere. House specials, such as elk T-bone & Black Angus tenderloin, center on the wood-fired oven. Casual dress; cocktails. **Parking:** street. **Cards:** AX, MC, VI.

GRANARY **Lunch:** $8-$14 **Dinner:** $22-$34 **Phone:** 307/733-8833

Continental

Location: 2 mi w on US 89/189/191, 0.5 mi w on SR 22, then 1 mi n on Spring Gulch Rd, follow signs; in Spring Creek Ranch. 1800 Spirit Dance Rd 83001. **Hours:** 7:30 am-10, noon-2 & 6-10 pm. **Reservations:** suggested. **Features:** In search of fine, upscale dining with a world-class view? You've found the right place. A favorite dish is the elk short loin. An extensive wine list featuring the finest California vintages, including Chalk Hill, is offered. Casual dress; cocktails. **Parking:** on-site. **Cards:** AX, DC, DS, MC, VI.

HARVEST BAKERY AND CAFE **Lunch:** $4-$8 **Phone:** 307/733-5418

Natural/Organic

Location: Just nw of town center. 130 W Broadway 83001. **Hours:** 8 am-6 pm; 7 am-8 pm in summer; 10 am-6 pm 11/1-11/30 & 4/1-4/30. Closed: 1/1, 12/25. **Features:** Reminiscent of European cafes, Harvest offers healthy, creative and energizing dishes such as chickpea lentil dal and veggie sandwiches.You can also sample the fine tea, coffee, smoothies and espressos while browsing in the bookstore. Casual dress. **Parking:** on-site. **Cards:** DS, MC, VI.

THE MERRY PIGLETS MEXICAN GRILL AND CARRY-OUT **Lunch:** $5-$12 **Dinner:** $5-$12 **Phone:** 307/733-2966

Mexican

Location: Just n of town square; next to Ripley's. 160 N Cache St 83001. **Hours:** 11:30 am-9:30 pm. Closed: 4/11, 12/25. **Features:** Since 1969, this eatery has served fresh Mexican fare in a fun and lively setting. Regulars like to meet for a snack of nachos or quesadillas as well as dine on fire roasted mesquite grilled fajitas. Thumbs up to the conqueso and ranchero Tex Mex sauces. Casual dress; cocktails. **Parking:** street. **Cards:** MC, VI.

MOUNTAIN HIGH PIZZA PIE **Lunch:** $4-$12 **Dinner:** $6-$18 **Phone:** 307/733-3646

Italian

Location: Just w of town square; downtown. 120 W Broadway 83001. **Hours:** 11-midnight; to 10 pm in winter. Closed: 11/25, 12/25. **Features:** A large selection of salad, subs and sandwiches as well as creative pizza is available at this friendly neighborhood pizza parlor with indoor/outdoor dining. This is a great place to sit outside and watch the crowd while enjoying a meal or quick snack. Casual dress; beer & wine only. **Parking:** on-site. **Cards:** DS, MC, VI.

OFF BROADWAY GRILL **Dinner:** $14-$28 **Phone:** 307/733-9777

AAA

Continental

Location: Just nw of town square. 30 S King St 83001. **Hours:** 5:30 pm-10 pm. Closed: 11/25, 12/25. **Reservations:** suggested. **Features:** You will find this attractive, minimalist style dining room with low lighting, muted colors and soft jazz. Try the house favorite, Chilean sea bass, or choose from fresh seafood, pasta, wild game and homemade dessert. Patio dining is available in summer. Casual dress; cocktails. **Parking:** street. **Cards:** AX, MC, VI.

OLD YELLOWSTONE GARAGE **Dinner:** $18-$32 **Phone:** 307/734-6161

Italian

Location: Downtown. 175 Center St 83001. **Hours:** 6 pm-10 pm. Closed major holidays; also Mon. **Reservations:** suggested. **Features:** You will encounter an authentic northern Italian dining experience at the Old Yellowstone Garage. An extensive wine list, featuring many wines from small Italian vineyards, complements the meals very nicely here. Casual dress; cocktails. **Parking:** street. **Cards:** AX, DS, MC, VI.

SILVER DOLLAR GRILL **Lunch:** $6-$12 **Dinner:** $7-$33 **Phone:** 307/733-2190

American

Location: Center of downtown; in Wort Hotel. 50 N Glenwood 83001. **Hours:** 7 am-10 pm. **Reservations:** suggested. **Features:** This restaurant specializes in American-style chop-house cuisine. You can choose from Black Angus beef, seafood specialties and local wild game dishes. Breakfast and lunch are also served. Casual dress; cocktails. **Parking:** street. **Cards:** AX, MC, VI.

SNAKE RIVER BREWING CO RESTAURANT & BREWERY **Lunch:** $6-$12 **Dinner:** $6-$12 **Phone:** 307/739-2337

American

Location: Just s of Broadway. 265 S Millward St 83001. **Hours:** 11:30 am-midnight, Fri & Sat-1 am. Closed: 11/25, 12/25. **Features:** Wood-fired oven pizza, calzone, bread, sandwiches, pasta and daily homemade soup fill the menu. Beer lovers will like the selection of ales and lagers. Patio seating is available outside this bustling eatery. Casual dress; beer & wine only. **Parking:** on-site. **Cards:** AX, MC, VI.

SWEETWATER RESTAURANT Historic **Lunch:** $6-$12 **Dinner:** $17-$24 **Phone:** 307/733-3553

Continental

Location: Just se of town square, corner of King and Pearl sts. 85 King St 83001. **Hours:** 11:30 am-3 & 6-10 pm; 11:30 am-2:30 & 6-9:30 pm in winter. Closed: 11/25, 12/25; also 4/1-4/15. **Reservations:** suggested. **Features:** Housed in a restored log cabin, the attentive and well trained staff deliver unique daily specials including fresh fish and steak, phyllo creations, vegetarian specials. Indoor-outdoor dining is available. Casual dress; cocktails. **Parking:** street. **Cards:** AX, DS, MC, VI.

LANDER pop. 6,867

WHERE TO STAY

BALDWIN CREEK BED & BREAKFAST **Phone:** 307/332-7608

Cabin

5/1-9/30 [BP]	1P: $80-$85	2P: $90-$95	XP: $10	F3
3/1-4/30 & 10/1-2/28 [BP]	1P: $60-$65	2P: $65-$75	XP: $10	F3

Location: 4.8 mi w on Baldwin Creek Rd from jct US 287. Located in a quiet area. 2343 Baldwin Creek Rd 82520. Fax: 307/332-7608. **Facility:** These four cabins, which are decorated in a Western theme, are nestled on a mountaintop overlooking a canyon. Smoke free premises. 6 units. 2 one-bedroom standard units. 4 cabins. 2 stories (no elevator), interior/exterior corridors. *Bath:* combo or shower only. **Parking:** on-site. **Terms:** 14 day cancellation notice-fee imposed, weekly rates available, pets ($5 extra charge, with prior approval). **Leisure Activities:** hiking trails. **Business Services:** meeting rooms, fax (fee). **Cards:** MC, VI.

SOME UNITS

FEE

BLUE SPRUCE INN **Phone:** 307/332-8253

Historic Bed & Breakfast

5/1-10/31 [BP]	1P: $70	2P: $85	XP: $10
3/1-4/30 & 11/1-2/28 [BP]	1P: $65	2P: $80	XP: $10

Location: 0.4 mi w of jct US 287. 677 S 3rd St 82520. Fax: 307/332-1386. **Facility:** Theme rooms such as Civil War and Native American are offered at this 1920 property; a recreation room features a wet bar, darts and a pool table. Smoke free premises. 4 one-bedroom standard units. 3 stories (no elevator), interior corridors. *Bath:* combo or shower only. **Parking:** on-site. **Terms:** check-in 4 pm, age restrictions may apply, 7 day cancellation notice-fee imposed. **Amenities:** hair dryers. *Some:* irons. **Leisure Activities:** bicycles. **Guest Services:** complimentary laundry. **Business Services:** meeting rooms, fax. **Cards:** AX, DS, MC, VI.

SOME UNITS

DATA PORT

FEE

BUDGET HOST PRONGHORN LODGE *Book at aaa.com* **Phone:** 307/332-3940

SAVE | 5/1-10/15 | 1P: $56 | 2P: $61-$90 | XP: $5 | F11
3/1-4/30 & 10/16-2/28 | 1P: $42 | 2P: $46-$55 | XP: $5 | F11

Small-scale Hotel

Location: Just n of jct US 287 and SR 789. 150 E Main St 82520. Fax: 307/332-2651. **Facility:** 56 units. 51 one-bedroom standard units, some with efficiencies (no utensils). 5 one-bedroom suites ($84-$90), some with efficiencies (no utensils) and/or whirlpools. 1-2 stories (no elevator), exterior corridors. *Bath:* combo or shower only. **Parking:** on-site, winter plug-ins. **Terms:** package plans - seasonal, pets ($10 extra charge, with approval). **Amenities:** irons, hair dryers. **Dining:** The Oxbow Restaurant, see separate listing. **Leisure Activities:** whirlpool, exercise room. **Guest Services:** coin laundry. **Business Services:** meeting rooms. **Cards:** AX, CB, DC, DS, JC, MC, VI. **Special Amenities: free continental breakfast and free local telephone calls.** *(See color ad p 371)*

SOME UNITS
FEE

HOLIDAY LODGE **Phone:** 307/332-2511

SAVE | All Year [CP] | 1P: $44-$54 | 2P: $48-$54 | XP: $5 | F3

Motel

Location: Just e of jct US 287 and SR 789. 210 McFarlane Dr 82520. Fax: 307/332-2256. **Facility:** 40 one-bedroom standard units, some with efficiencies. 2 stories (no elevator), exterior corridors. **Parking:** on-site, winter plug-ins. **Terms:** cancellation fee imposed, pets ($10 extra charge). **Leisure Activities:** whirlpool. **Guest Services:** coin laundry. **Cards:** AX, CB, DC, DS, MC, VI. **Special Amenities: free continental breakfast and preferred room (subject to availability with advanced reservations).**

SOME UNITS
FEE

SILVER SPUR MOTEL **Phone:** (307)332-5189

SAVE | 5/1-10/31 | 1P: $45 | 2P: $50-$55 | XP: $5
4/1-4/30 | 1P: $30 | 2P: $35-$40 | XP: $5

Motel

Location: 1.5 mi n on US 287. 1240 W Main St 82520. **Facility:** 25 units. 22 one- and 3 two-bedroom standard units, some with efficiencies. 2 stories (no elevator), exterior corridors. *Bath:* combo or shower only. **Parking:** on-site, winter plug-ins. **Terms:** open 4/1-10/31, pets ($5 extra charge). **Pool(s):** heated outdoor. **Cards:** AX, DS, MC, VI. **Special Amenities: free local telephone calls and preferred room (subject to availability with advanced reservations).**

SOME UNITS
FEE

WHERE TO DINE

HITCHING RACK **Dinner:** $8-$22 **Phone:** 307/332-4322

American

Location: 0.5 mi s on US 287. 785 E Main St 82520. **Hours:** 5:30 pm-9:30 pm, Fri & Sat-10 pm. Closed major holidays; also Sun. **Reservations:** accepted. **Features:** Dine on steak, seafood, chicken, pasta or prime rib, but leave room for one of the homemade desserts. Attentive service from a well-trained staff rounds out the experience. Plenty of microbrew beer is offered. **Parking:** on-site. **Cards:** DS, MC, VI.

THE OXBOW RESTAURANT **Lunch:** $6-$9 **Dinner:** $8-$15 **Phone:** 307/332-0233

American

Location: Just n of jct US 287 and SR 789; in Budget Host Pronghorn Lodge. 170 E Main St 82520. **Hours:** 6 am-9 pm; to 10 pm in summer. Closed: 11/25, 12/25. **Features:** Classic American dining with casual, fast service with a smile. Daily specials include steak, pasta, chicken, seafood and ribs, but always features the ample soup and salad bar. Casual dress; cocktails. **Parking:** on-site. **Cards:** AX, CB, DC, DS, MC, VI.

LARAMIE pop. 27,204

WHERE TO STAY

1ST INN GOLD — **Phone:** (307)742-3721

SAVE — Small-scale Hotel

5/1-10/31 [ECP]	1P: $79-$89	2P: $89-$99	XP: $8	F16
3/1-4/30 & 11/1-2/28 [ECP]	1P: $49-$59	2P: $57-$67	XP: $8	F16

Location: I-80, exit 313, just n on US 287. 421 Boswell 82070. Fax: 307/742-5473. **Facility:** 79 one-bedroom standard units. 2 stories (no elevator), interior/exterior corridors. **Parking:** on-site, winter plug-ins. **Terms:** 15 day cancellation notice, pets ($8 fee). **Dining:** 11 am-10 pm, Fri & Sat-11 pm, Sun-8:30 pm, cocktails. **Pool(s):** heated outdoor. **Leisure Activities:** whirlpool. **Guest Services:** valet and coin laundry, airport transportation-Laramie Regional Airport, area transportation-Ivanson Memorial Hospital. **Business Services:** meeting rooms. **Cards:** AX, DC, DS, MC, VI. **Special Amenities: free expanded continental breakfast and free local telephone calls.**

SOME UNITS — FEE — DATA PORT

BEST VALUE INN *Book at aaa.com* — **Phone:** (307)721-8860

SAVE — Motel

5/14-9/30	1P: $55-$69	2P: $59-$75	XP: $6	F16
3/1-5/13 & 10/1-2/28	1P: $42-$50	2P: $45-$52	XP: $6	F16

Location: I-80, exit 311, just s. 523 S Adams St 82070. Fax: 307/721-6290. **Facility:** 33 one-bedroom standard units. 2 stories (no elevator), interior/exterior corridors. **Parking:** on-site. **Amenities:** voice mail. **Guest Services:** coin laundry. **Cards:** AX, CB, DC, DS, MC, VI. **Special Amenities: free local telephone calls and preferred room (subject to availability with advanced reservations).**

SOME UNITS — DATA PORT

BEST WESTERN CENTER HOTEL — **Phone:** (307)742-6611

Small-scale Hotel

7/23-8/1	1P: $129-$139	2P: $149-$199
8/2-9/1	1P: $89-$119	2P: $99-$129
3/1-7/22	1P: $79-$99	2P: $89-$109
9/2-2/28	1P: $79-$89	2P: $89-$109

Location: I-80, exit 313, just s on US 287. 2313 Soldier Springs Rd 82070. Fax: 307/745-8371. **Facility:** 100 one-bedroom standard units. 2 stories (no elevator), interior/exterior corridors. **Parking:** on-site. **Terms:** 14 day cancellation notice, [AP] meal plan available, pets ($10 extra charge). **Amenities:** high-speed Internet, voice mail, irons, hair dryers. **Pool(s):** heated indoor. **Leisure Activities:** whirlpool, exercise room. **Guest Services:** gift shop, valet and coin laundry, area transportation. **Business Services:** meeting rooms. **Cards:** AX, CB, DC, DS, JC, MC, VI.

SOME UNITS — ASK — FEE — DATA PORT

DAYS INN *Book at aaa.com* — **Phone:** (307)745-5678

Small-scale Hotel

6/16-9/15	1P: $75-$95	2P: $95-$105	XP: $7	F12
5/16-6/15	1P: $65-$85	2P: $75-$95	XP: $7	F12
3/1-5/15 & 9/16-2/28	1P: $55-$65	2P: $65-$85	XP: $7	F12

Location: I-80, exit 310, just e. 1368 McCue St 82072 (PO Box 988). Fax: 307/742-8934. **Facility:** 53 one-bedroom standard units, some with kitchens and/or whirlpools. 2 stories (no elevator), interior corridors. *Bath:* combo or shower only. **Parking:** on-site, winter plug-ins. **Terms:** [ECP] meal plan available, pets ($15 extra charge). **Amenities:** voice mail, irons, hair dryers. *Some:* dual phone lines. **Pool(s):** small heated indoor. **Leisure Activities:** whirlpool, exercise room. **Guest Services:** coin laundry. **Cards:** AX, CB, DC, DS, MC, VI.

SOME UNITS — ASK — FEE — DATA PORT — VCR

GAS LITE INN MOTEL — **Phone:** (307)742-6616

SAVE — Motel

3/1-9/30	1P: $56-$61	2P: $61-$66
10/1-2/28	1P: $36-$46	2P: $46-$56

Location: I-80, exit 313, 1.6 mi n on US 287; downtown. 960 N 3rd St 82072. Fax: 307/742-6616. **Facility:** 30 one-bedroom standard units. 2 stories (no elevator), exterior corridors. **Parking:** on-site, winter plug-ins. **Terms:** weekly rates available, [CP] meal plan available, pets ($5 extra charge). **Amenities:** hair dryers. *Some:* DVD players. **Pool(s):** heated indoor. **Guest Services:** coin laundry. **Cards:** AX, CB, DC, MC, VI. **Special Amenities: free continental breakfast and free local telephone calls.**

SOME UNITS — FEE — DATA PORT

HOWARD JOHNSON INN *Book at aaa.com* — **Phone:** (307)742-8371

SAVE — Small-scale Hotel

5/14-9/1 [BP]	1P: $69-$120	2P: $77-$128	XP: $8	F17
9/2-2/28 [BP]	1P: $59-$93	2P: $67-$100	XP: $8	F17
3/1-5/13 [BP]	1P: $49-$79	2P: $57-$87	XP: $8	F17

Location: I-80, exit 311, just s. 1555 Snowy Range Rd 82072 (PO Box 580, 82070). Fax: 307/742-0884. **Facility:** 112 one-bedroom standard units. 2 stories (no elevator), exterior corridors. **Parking:** on-site, winter plug-ins. **Terms:** [AP] meal plan available, pets ($10 extra charge). **Amenities:** voice mail, irons, hair dryers. **Dining:** 6 am-10 pm, cocktails. **Pool(s):** heated indoor. **Leisure Activities:** whirlpool. **Guest Services:** gift shop, airport transportation-Laramie Regional Airport. **Business Services:** meeting rooms. **Cards:** AX, CB, DC, DS, JC, MC, VI. **Special Amenities: free full breakfast and free room upgrade (subject to availability with advanced reservations).**

SOME UNITS — FEE — DATA PORT

SUNSET INN — **Phone:** (307)742-3741

SAVE — Motel

5/1-9/30	1P: $60-$65	2P: $65-$75	XP: $8	F16
3/1-4/30 & 10/1-2/28	1P: $45-$50	2P: $52-$58	XP: $8	F16

Location: I-80, exit 313, just n on US 287. 1104 S 3rd St 82070. Fax: 307/745-9305. **Facility:** 51 one-bedroom standard units. 2 stories (no elevator), exterior corridors. **Parking:** on-site, winter plug-ins. **Terms:** cancellation fee imposed, small pets only. **Amenities:** *Some:* irons. **Pool(s):** heated outdoor. **Leisure Activities:** whirlpool. **Cards:** AX, DC, DS, MC, VI. **Special Amenities: free local telephone calls.**

SOME UNITS

TRAVEL INN — **Phone:** (307)745-4853

SAVE — Motel

5/1-9/2	1P: $45-$65	2P: $55-$85	XP: $5	F10
3/1-4/30	1P: $40-$45	2P: $45-$50	XP: $5	F10
9/3-2/28	1P: $35-$45	2P: $45-$50	XP: $5	F10

Location: I-80, exit 313, 1.1 mi n on US 287 loop; downtown. 262 N 3rd St 82072. Fax: 307/721-4943. **Facility:** 29 one-bedroom standard units. 2 stories (no elevator), exterior corridors. *Bath:* combo or shower only. **Parking:** on-site, winter plug-ins. **Terms:** cancellation fee imposed, weekly rates available, [CP] meal plan available. **Amenities:** voice mail. *Some:* irons, hair dryers. **Pool(s):** heated outdoor. **Cards:** AX, DC, DS, MC, VI. **Special Amenities: free continental breakfast and early check-in/late check-out.**

SOME UNITS

TRAVELODGE DOWNTOWN — **Phone:** (307)742-6671

SAVE — Motel

7/1-9/30	1P: $55-$60	2P: $60-$65	XP: $5	F17
4/1-6/30 & 10/1-2/28	1P: $45-$50	2P: $50-$55	XP: $5	F17
3/1-3/31	1P: $40-$45	2P: $45-$50	XP: $5	F17

Location: I-80, exit 313, 1 mi n on US 287; downtown. 165 N 3rd St 82072. Fax: 307/742-6671. **Facility:** 30 units. 29 one- and 1 two-bedroom standard units. 2 stories (no elevator), exterior corridors. **Parking:** on-site, winter plug-ins. **Terms:** check-in 4 pm, cancellation fee imposed, [CP] meal plan available, pets ($50 deposit). **Amenities:** hair dryers. *Some:* high-speed Internet (fee), irons. **Cards:** AX, DS, MC, VI. **Special Amenities: free continental breakfast and free local telephone calls.**

FEE SOME UNITS

WHERE TO DINE

THE CAVALRYMAN SUPPER CLUB — **Lunch:** $15-$30 **Dinner:** $15-$30 **Phone:** 307/745-5551

American

Location: I-80, exit 313, 1.8 mi s on US 287. 4452 S 3rd St 82073. **Hours:** 4:30 pm-10 pm; from noon on holidays. Closed: 12/24, 12/25. **Reservations:** accepted. **Features:** Built on the location of Fort Sanders, this locally popular restaurant serves up their specialty of tender, aged prime rib and New York sirloin. A trip to the overflowing salad and soup bar is a must! Casual dining amongst moose, deer and antelope trophies. Complimentary appetizers and desserts gives hospitality a thumbs up. Casual dress; cocktails. **Parking:** on-site. **Cards:** AX, CB, DC, DS, MC, VI.

OVERLAND RESTAURANT — **Lunch:** $4-$7 **Dinner:** $8-$19 **Phone:** 307/721-2800

International

Location: Center. 100 Ivinson St 82070. **Hours:** 7 am-8 pm, Mon-Wed from 11 am. Closed major holidays. **Features:** Diners can unwind in casual surroundings, inside or out, at this cozy corner restaurant. The bistro-style cuisine features homemade soups, savory sandwiches and vegetarian specialties. International options broaden at dinner time, when such dishes as pork medallions, Cajun shrimp, manicotti, broiled salmon, quesadillas and Greek pasta share center stage on the menu with several heart-healthy items. The pastry chef offers a wide variety of hand-crafted gourmet desserts along with daily specials. Casual dress; cocktails. **Parking:** street. **Cards:** AX, DS, MC, VI.

LITTLE AMERICA pop. 56

WHERE TO STAY

LITTLE AMERICA HOTEL & TRAVEL CENTER *Book at aaa.com* **Phone:** (307)875-2400

SAVE

Small-scale Hotel

5/1-9/30	1P: $66-$92	2P: $72-$98	XP: $6	F12
10/1-2/28	1P: $62-$76	2P: $68-$82	XP: $6	F12
3/1-4/30	1P: $59-$73	2P: $65-$79	XP: $6	F12

Location: I-80, exit 68. (PO Box 1). Fax: 307/872-2666. **Facility:** 140 units. 128 one-bedroom standard units. 12 one-bedroom suites ($96). 1-2 stories (no elevator), interior/exterior corridors. *Bath:* combo or shower only. **Parking:** on-site. **Amenities:** *Some:* hair dryers. **Dining:** 4 restaurants, 24 hours, cocktails. **Pool(s):** heated outdoor. **Leisure Activities:** deck, exercise room. **Guest Services:** gift shop, coin laundry. **Business Services:** meeting rooms. **Cards:** AX, CB, DC, DS, MC, VI. *(See color ad below)*

SOME UNITS

LUSK pop. 1,447

WHERE TO STAY

BEST VALUE COVERED WAGON MOTEL *Book at aaa.com* **Phone:** (307)334-2836

SAVE

Motel

All Year [CP]	1P: $47-$71	2P: $61-$90	XP: $10	F12

Location: Just n of jct US 20/85. 730 S Main St 82225 (PO Box 236). Fax: 307/334-2977. **Facility:** 51 one-bedroom standard units. 1-2 stories (no elevator), interior/exterior corridors. **Parking:** on-site, winter plug-ins. **Terms:** package plans. **Amenities:** hair dryers. **Pool(s):** heated indoor. **Leisure Activities:** sauna, whirlpool, patio, barbecue grill, playground, limited exercise equipment, basketball, shuffleboard. **Guest Services:** coin laundry. **Business Services:** meeting rooms. **Cards:** AX, CB, DC, DS, MC, VI. **Special Amenities: free continental breakfast and free local telephone calls.**

SOME UNITS

FEE FEE

BEST WESTERN PIONEER *Book at aaa.com* **Phone:** 307/334-2640

SAVE

Motel

All Year [CP]	1P: $49-$120	2P: $49-$120	XP: $10	F12

Location: Just n of jct US 20/85. 731 S Main St 82225 (PO Box 87). Fax: 307/334-2660. **Facility:** 30 one-bedroom standard units. 1 story, exterior corridors. **Parking:** on-site, winter plug-ins. **Terms:** cancellation fee imposed. **Amenities:** irons, hair dryers. **Pool(s):** small heated outdoor. **Guest Services:** coin laundry. **Cards:** AX, DC, DS, MC, VI. **Special Amenities: free continental breakfast and free local telephone calls.**

SOME UNITS

TOWN HOUSE MOTEL Phone: 307/334-2376

Motel

6/1-8/6	1P: $38-$50	2P: $42-$68	XP: $5	F12
3/1-5/31 & 8/7-2/28	1P: $35-$45	2P: $40-$60	XP: $5	F12

Location: On US 20/85, just n. 525 S Main St 82225 (PO Box 33). Fax: 307/334-4033. **Facility:** 20 one-bedroom standard units. 1 story, exterior corridors. *Bath:* combo or shower only. **Parking:** on-site, winter plug-ins. **Terms:** weekly rates available, [CP] meal plan available, pets ($5 extra charge, in designated units). **Cards:** AX, DC, DS, MC, VI.

SOME UNITS

ASK / FEE

TRAIL MOTEL Phone: (307)334-2530

SAVE

Motel

All Year [CP]	1P: $25-$75	2P: $30-$80	XP: $5	F12

Location: Just sw on US 20/18. 305 W 8th St 82225 (PO Box 1087). Fax: 307/334-3136. **Facility:** 22 one-bedroom standard units. 1 story, exterior corridors. *Bath:* combo or shower only. **Parking:** on-site. **Terms:** 3 day cancellation notice-fee imposed, weekly rates available, small pets only ($10 extra charge). **Pool(s):** heated outdoor. **Leisure Activities:** playground. **Guest Services:** airport transportation-Lusk Airport. **Cards:** AX, CB, DC, DS, MC, VI. **Special Amenities: free continental breakfast and free local telephone calls.**

SOME UNITS

FEE FEE

MEETEETSE pop. 351

WHERE TO DINE

OUTLAW STEAK AND RIB HOUSE **Lunch:** $5-$20 **Dinner:** $5-$20 **Phone:** 307/868-2585

American

Location: Center. 1936 State St 82433. **Hours:** 11 am-10 pm. **Features:** Known for its Captain Morgan's molasses and rum ribs and Jack Daniel's honey and whiskey ribs, the hometown cafe serves a variety of well-prepared, homemade dishes. On the menu are buffalo steaks, hand-tossed pizzas, thick sourdough sandwiches and fresh, from-scratch pies. Next door is the Cowboy Bar and Saloon, established in 1893. Casual dress; cocktails. **Parking:** street. **Cards:** MC, VI.

MOOSE —*See also GRAND TETON NATIONAL PARK.*

WHERE TO STAY

The following lodging was either not evaluated or did not meet AAA rating requirements but is listed for your information only.

THE LOST CREEK RANCH **Phone:** 307/733-3435

fyi

Not evaluated. **Location:** 8 mi n. 1 Old Ranch Rd 83012 (PO Box 95). Facilities, services, and decor characterize an upscale property.

MORAN —*See GRAND TETON NATIONAL PARK.*

NEWCASTLE pop. 3,065

WHERE TO STAY

AUTO INN MOTEL *Book at aaa.com* **Phone:** 307/746-2734

SAVE

Motel

5/15-10/31	1P: $40-$48	2P: $59-$69	XP: $6	F11
3/1-5/14 & 11/1-2/28	1P: $32-$38	2P: $42-$52	XP: $6	F11

Location: West end of town on US 16. 2503 W Main St 82701. Fax: 307/746-4067. **Facility:** 21 one-bedroom standard units. 1 story, exterior corridors. **Parking:** on-site, winter plug-ins. **Terms:** cancellation fee imposed, pets ($6 extra charge). **Guest Services:** coin laundry. **Cards:** AX, CB, DC, DS, MC, VI. ***(See color ad below)***

SOME UNITS

FEE

PINES MOTEL — **Phone:** (307)746-4334

AAA SAVE — Motel

5/16-10/31	1P: $45-$50	2P: $50-$75	XP: $5	F10
3/1-5/15 & 11/1-2/28	1P: $34-$40	2P: $42-$55	XP: $5	F10

Location: Just e from jct US Business Rt 16; downtown. Located in a residential area. 248 E Wentworth St 82701. Fax: 307/746-3409. **Facility:** Smoke free premises. 12 units. 11 one-bedroom standard units, some with efficiencies or kitchens. 1 two-bedroom suite with kitchen. 1 story, exterior corridors. *Bath:* combo or shower only. **Parking:** on-site, winter plug-ins. **Terms:** [CP] meal plan available, small pets only. **Leisure Activities:** whirlpool, barbecue grill, picnic area. **Cards:** AX, CB, DC, DS, MC, VI.

SOME UNITS

SAGE MOTEL — **Phone:** (307)746-2724

AAA SAVE — Motel

5/1-10/31	1P: $44-$48	2P: $52-$60	XP: $5	F12
3/1-4/30	1P: $40-$44	2P: $44-$50	XP: $5	F12
11/1-2/28	1P: $36-$40	2P: $42-$50	XP: $5	F12

Location: 0.3 mi s of jct US 16 on US 85, just w. 1227 S Summit Ave 82701. Fax: 307/746-3496. **Facility:** 12 one-bedroom standard units. 1 story, exterior corridors. **Parking:** on-site, winter plug-ins. **Terms:** 3 day cancellation notice-fee imposed, small pets only ($5 extra charge). **Leisure Activities:** barbecue grills, picnic tables. **Cards:** AX, DS, MC, VI.

FEE

SOME UNITS

PAINTER

WHERE TO STAY

HUNTER PEAK RANCH — **Phone:** 307/587-3711

Ranch

All Year	1P: $115-$150	2P: $115-$150	XP: $22

Location: SR 296, 5 mi s of US 212; 40 mi n of SR 120. 4027 Crandall Rd 82414 (Box 1731, Painter Rt, CODY). **Facility:** Smoke free premises. 8 units. 6 one-bedroom standard units. 2 cabins. 1-2 stories (no elevator), exterior corridors. *Bath:* combo or shower only. **Parking:** on-site, winter plug-ins. **Terms:** check-out 9 am, 90 day cancellation notice-fee imposed, weekly rates available, [AP] meal plan available, pets ($10 extra charge). **Leisure Activities:** fishing, recreation programs, hiking trails, jogging, horseshoes, volleyball. *Fee:* horseback riding. **Cards:** MC, VI.

FEE

PINEDALE pop. 1,412

WHERE TO STAY

BEST WESTERN PINEDALE INN *Book at aaa.com* — **Phone:** (307)367-6869

AAA SAVE — Small-scale Hotel

All Year [CP]	1P: $69-$129	2P: $69-$129

Location: 0.5 mi n on US 191. 850 W Pine St 82941 (P O Box 849). Fax: 307/367-6897. **Facility:** 58 units. 57 one-bedroom standard units. 1 one-bedroom suite with kitchen. 2 stories (no elevator), interior corridors. **Parking:** on-site, winter plug-ins. **Terms:** 30 day cancellation notice-fee imposed. **Amenities:** irons, hair dryers. **Pool(s):** heated indoor. **Leisure Activities:** whirlpool. **Guest Services:** coin laundry. **Business Services:** meeting rooms. **Cards:** AX, CB, DC, DS, MC, VI. **Special Amenities: free continental breakfast and free local telephone calls.**

SOME UNITS

THE LODGE AT PINEDALE — **Phone:** 307/367-8800

AAA SAVE — Small-scale Hotel

5/1-8/31	1P: $98	2P: $108
9/1-11/15	1P: $81	2P: $88
11/16-2/28	1P: $70	2P: $76
3/1-4/30	1P: $70	2P: $75

Location: 0.7 mi n on US 191. 1054 W Pine St 82941 (PO Box 8). Fax: 307/367-8812. **Facility:** Smoke free premises. 43 units. 41 one-bedroom standard units. 2 one-bedroom suites ($98-$135). 3 stories, interior corridors. **Parking:** on-site, winter plug-ins. **Terms:** pets ($10 extra charge). **Amenities:** hair dryers. **Pool(s):** small heated indoor. **Leisure Activities:** whirlpool. **Guest Services:** coin laundry. **Cards:** AX, DC, DS, MC, VI. **Special Amenities: free continental breakfast and free local telephone calls.**

FEE

SUN DANCE MOTEL — **Phone:** 307/367-4336

AAA SAVE — Motel

7/1-9/30	1P: $65-$80	2P: $80-$105	XP: $5	F16
5/1-6/30	1P: $50-$85	2P: $56-$90	XP: $5	F16
3/1-4/30	1P: $40-$55	2P: $50-$70	XP: $5	F16
10/1-2/28	1P: $35-$55	2P: $45-$60	XP: $5	F16

Location: US 191; city center. 148 E Pine St 82941 (PO Box 622). **Facility:** 19 units. 16 one- and 3 two-bedroom standard units, some with efficiencies. 1 story, exterior corridors. *Bath:* combo or shower only. **Parking:** on-site, winter plug-ins. **Guest Services:** gift shop. **Cards:** AX, DC, MC, VI. **Special Amenities: free local telephone calls and early check-in/late check-out.**

SOME UNITS

WAGON WHEEL MOTEL — **Phone:** 307/367-2871

AAA SAVE — Motel

All Year	1P: $40-$85	2P: $45-$115	XP: $5

Location: Just s of town center. 407 S Pine St 82941 (PO Box 407). Fax: 307/367-2872. **Facility:** 15 one-bedroom standard units. 1 story, exterior corridors. **Parking:** on-site, winter plug-ins. **Terms:** cancellation fee imposed. **Guest Services:** airport transportation-Pinedale Airport. **Cards:** AX, CB, DC, DS, MC, VI. **Special Amenities: free local telephone calls and free room upgrade (subject to availability with advanced reservations).**

SOME UNITS

WHERE TO DINE

MCGREGORS PUB **Lunch:** $5-$7 **Dinner:** $9-$30 **Phone:** 307/367-4443

American

Location: Just w, then n; back of Cowboy Shop. 21 N Franklin Ave 82941. **Hours:** 11:30 am-2 & 5:30-10 pm. Closed: 11/25, 12/25. **Reservations:** suggested. **Features:** Contemporary menu items can be found in the Old West! Dine in the comfortable dining room after a cocktail or dine on the patio in the summer. Specializing in hand-cut steak grilled to perfection, oven roasted prime rib or pork, pasta, and a wide selection of seafood. Casual dress; cocktails. **Parking:** on-site. **Cards:** AX, CB, DC, DS, MC, VI.

STOCKMENS RESTAURANT **Lunch:** $4-$10 **Dinner:** $9-$17 **Phone:** 307/367-4563

American

Location: Center. 117 W Pine St 82941. **Hours:** 6 am-10:30 pm; to 10 pm in winter. Closed: 12/25. **Reservations:** accepted. **Features:** Succulent prime rib, large juicy prawns or Australian Lamb are a few of the local favorites to be enjoyed in an Old West atmosphere. Southern hospitality is served with a smile. Casual dress; cocktails; entertainment. **Parking:** on-site. **Cards:** AX, DC, DS, MC, VI.

POWELL pop. 5,373

WHERE TO STAY

KINGS INN **Phone:** (307)754-5117

Small-scale Hotel

6/10-8/20	1P: $69-$79	2P: $77-$87
3/1-6/9 & 8/21-2/28	1P: $54-$60	2P: $58-$64

Location: 0.3 mi e on US 14A. 777 E 2nd St 82435 (PO Box 933). Fax: 307/754-2198. **Facility:** 49 one-bedroom standard units. 2 stories, exterior corridors. **Parking:** on-site, winter plug-ins. **Terms:** small pets only. **Amenities:** *Some:* dual phone lines, hair dryers. **Pool(s):** heated outdoor. **Business Services:** meeting rooms. **Cards:** AX, DC, DS, MC, VI.

SOME UNITS

ASK / /

PARK MOTEL **Phone:** (307)754-2233

Motel

6/10-8/20	1P: $55-$59	2P: $65-$69	XP: $3	F3
3/1-6/9 & 8/21-9/30	1P: $39-$45	2P: $45-$49	XP: $3	F3
10/1-2/28	1P: $37-$39	2P: $39-$48	XP: $3	F3

Location: 0.4 mi e on US 14A. 737 E 2nd St 82435. Fax: 307/754-2233. **Facility:** 18 units. 17 one-bedroom standard units, some with efficiencies and/or whirlpools. 1 one-bedroom suite. 1 story, exterior corridors. *Bath:* combo or shower only. **Parking:** on-site, winter plug-ins. **Terms:** no pets allowed (owner's pet on premises). **Cards:** AX, DS, MC, VI.

SOME UNITS

DATA PORT / /

RAWLINS pop. 8,538

WHERE TO STAY

BEST WESTERN COTTONTREE INN

Book at aaa.com — **Phone:** (307)324-2737

AAA SAVE — Small-scale Hotel

6/1-10/31	1P: $84-$99	2P: $89-$119	XP: $5	F17
3/1-5/31 & 11/1-2/28	1P: $79-$89	2P: $84-$99	XP: $5	F17

Location: I-80, exit 211, just n. 2221 W Spruce St 82301 (PO Box 387). Fax: 307/324-5011. **Facility:** 122 one-bedroom standard units. 2 stories (no elevator), interior/exterior corridors. **Parking:** on-site, winter plug-ins. **Terms:** 14 day cancellation notice, [AP] meal plan available, pets ($10 fee). **Amenities:** high-speed Internet, irons, hair dryers. **Dining:** The Hungry Miner, see separate listing. **Pool(s):** heated indoor. **Leisure Activities:** sauna, whirlpool. **Guest Services:** valet laundry. **Business Services:** meeting rooms. **Cards:** AX, CB, DC, DS, MC, VI. **Special Amenities: free newspaper.**

FEE / SOME UNITS FEE

THE LODGE AT RAWLINS

Phone: (307)324-2783

AAA SAVE — Small-scale Hotel

6/1-9/30	1P: $65-$75	2P: $70-$80	XP: $5	F18
10/1-2/28	1P: $50-$55	2P: $55-$60	XP: $5	F18
3/1-5/31	1P: $45-$55	2P: $50-$60	XP: $5	F18

Location: I-80, exit 215, just w of jct US 287. 1801 E Cedar 82301. Fax: 307/328-1011. **Facility:** 130 one-bedroom standard units. 2 stories (no elevator), interior corridors. **Parking:** on-site, winter plug-ins. **Terms:** pets ($50 deposit). **Amenities:** irons, hair dryers. **Dining:** 6 am-9 pm, cocktails. **Pool(s):** small heated outdoor. **Leisure Activities:** Fee: game room. **Guest Services:** gift shop, valet laundry. **Business Services:** meeting rooms. **Cards:** AX, CB, DC, DS, MC, VI. **Special Amenities: free local telephone calls and early check-in/late check-out.** *(See color ad below)*

FEE / SOME UNITS

WHERE TO DINE

ASPEN HOUSE RESTAURANT

Lunch: $6-$12 **Dinner:** $12-$26 **Phone:** 307/324-4787

American

Location: Just s of jct US 30/SR 78/I-80 business loop; center. 318 5th St 82301. **Hours:** 11 am-2 & 5-9 pm, Sat from 5 pm. Closed major holidays; also Sun. **Reservations:** suggested. **Features:** Unique dining choices with Eastern and Western influences. Oriental with Szechuan, blackened and Cajun dishes, grilled steaks, stir-frys and seafoods are all made fresh and brought to you by a friendly, willing staff. Casual dress; cocktails. **Parking:** street. **Cards:** AX, MC, VI.

THE HUNGRY MINER

Lunch: $5-$10 **Dinner:** $7-$16 **Phone:** 307/328-2181

American

Location: I-80, exit 211, just n; in Best Western CottonTree Inn. 2221 W Spruce St 82301. **Hours:** 6 am-10 pm; to 9 pm in winter. Closed: 1/1, 11/25, 12/25. **Features:** Casual dining in a rustic, all-wood frontier atmosphere of the Old West with mining memorabilia and antiques. A hearty selection of favorite sandwiches can be accompanied by a visit to the well-stocked soup and salad bar. Mexican fare is another popular calling as well as steak, seafood and pot roast. All diners are served with their signature cornbread. Casual dress; cocktails. **Parking:** on-site. **Cards:** AX, MC, VI.

THE PANTRY

Lunch: $4-$7 **Dinner:** $9-$19 **Phone:** 307/324-7860

AAA — **American**

Location: I-80 business loop; city center. 221 W Cedar 82301. **Hours:** 11 am-9 pm. Closed: 1/1, 12/25; also Sun. **Features:** Fresh baked bread, homemade soup, and pie are the specialities of the house. A wide variety of tastes can be satisfied with the house favorite of prime rib. Also grilled steak, variety of chicken, Italian favorites and juicy sandwiches made with their fresh bread are enjoyed in casual and historic surroundings. Casual dress. **Parking:** on-site. **Cards:** AX, DC, DS, MC, VI.

RIVERTON pop. 9,310

WHERE TO STAY

DAYS INN *Book at aaa.com* **Phone:** (307)856-9677

Small-scale Hotel

5/1-9/30	1P: $50-$80	2P: $55-$90	XP: $5	F12
3/1-4/30 & 10/1-2/28	1P: $40-$60	2P: $50-$70	XP: $5	F12

Location: 0.5 mi nw on US 26. 909 W Main St 82501. Fax: 307/856-9677. **Facility:** 33 one-bedroom standard units. 2 stories (no elevator), exterior corridors. *Bath:* combo or shower only. **Parking:** on-site, winter plug-ins. **Terms:** [ECP] meal plan available, pets ($5 extra charge). **Amenities:** hair dryers. **Cards:** AX, DC, DS, MC, VI.

SOME UNITS

FEE

HOLIDAY INN CONVENTION CENTER *Book at aaa.com* **Phone:** (307)856-8100

SAVE

Small-scale Hotel

6/1-9/20	1P: $89-$119	2P: $89-$109	XP: $8	F12
3/1-5/31 & 9/21-2/28	1P: $79-$99	2P: $79-$99	XP: $8	F12

Location: 0.8 mi ne on US 26/SR 789. 900 E Sunset Dr 82501. Fax: 307/856-0266. **Facility:** 122 one-bedroom standard units. 2 stories (no elevator), interior corridors. **Parking:** on-site, winter plug-ins. **Terms:** pets ($20 fee). **Amenities:** dual phone lines, voice mail, irons, hair dryers. **Dining:** 6 am-2 & 5-10 pm, cocktails. **Pool(s):** heated indoor. **Leisure Activities:** exercise room. **Guest Services:** valet and coin laundry, airport transportation-Riverton Regional Airport. **Business Services:** meeting rooms, fax (fee). **Cards:** AX, CB, DC, DS, MC, VI. **Special Amenities: free local telephone calls and early check-in/late check-out.**
(See ad below & color ad opposite title page)

SOME UNITS

FEE FEE FEE

PAINTBRUSH MOTEL **Phone:** 307/856-9238

Motel

All Year	1P: $36-$39	2P: $46-$49

Location: 1.3 mi ne on US 26/SR 789. 1550 N Federal Blvd 82501. Fax: 307/856-5594. **Facility:** 23 one-bedroom standard units. 1 story, exterior corridors. **Parking:** on-site, winter plug-ins. **Cards:** AX, DS, MC, VI.

SOME UNITS

SUPER 8 MOTEL *Book at aaa.com* **Phone:** (307)857-2400

Small-scale Hotel

7/1-8/31	1P: $50-$55	2P: $60-$70	XP: $5	F12
3/1-6/30	1P: $35-$50	2P: $45-$65	XP: $5	F12
9/1-9/30	1P: $45-$50	2P: $50-$60	XP: $5	F12
10/1-2/28	1P: $35-$40	2P: $45-$50	XP: $5	F12

Location: 1 mi ne on US 26/SR 789. 1040 N Federal Blvd 82501. Fax: 307/857-2400. **Facility:** 32 one-bedroom standard units. 2 stories (no elevator), interior corridors. **Parking:** on-site, winter plug-ins. **Terms:** 7 day cancellation notice, weekly rates available, [CP] meal plan available, small pets only ($5 extra charge). **Amenities:** hair dryers. *Some:* irons. **Business Services:** fax (fee). **Cards:** AX, DS, MC, VI.

SOME UNITS

FEE

THUNDERBIRD MOTEL **Phone:** 307/856-9201

SAVE

Motel

3/1-6/30	1P: $38-$46	2P: $38-$52	XP: $4	F
7/1-9/30	1P: $38-$51	2P: $38-$51	XP: $4	F
10/1-2/28	1P: $35-$46	2P: $36-$46	XP: $4	F

Location: Just n of US 26; downtown. 302 E Fremont 82501. Fax: 307/856-5486. **Facility:** 45 one-bedroom standard units. 2 stories (no elevator), exterior corridors. *Bath:* combo or shower only. **Parking:** on-site, winter plug-ins. **Terms:** pets ($4 extra charge, in designated units, with prior approval). **Guest Services:** valet and coin laundry. **Cards:** AX, DC, DS, MC, VI. **Special Amenities: free local telephone calls.**

SOME UNITS

FEE

TOMAHAWK MOTOR LODGE — Phone: (307)856-9205

Motel

6/1-9/30 [CP]	1P: $55	2P: $65	XP: $10	F
4/1-5/31 [CP]	1P: $50	2P: $60	XP: $10	F
3/1-3/31 & 10/1-2/28 [CP]	1P: $42	2P: $57	XP: $10	F

Location: On US 26; downtown. 208 E Main St 82501. Fax: 307/856-2879. **Facility:** 32 units. 30 one- and 2 two-bedroom standard units. 2 stories (no elevator), interior/exterior corridors. **Parking:** on-site, winter plug-ins. **Terms:** cancellation fee imposed, weekly rates available, pets ($10 deposit, with prior approval). **Guest Services:** valet laundry. **Cards:** AX, CB, DC, DS, JC, MC, VI.

SOME UNITS

ASK / DATA PORT / FEE

WHERE TO DINE

THE BROKER RESTAURANT — **Lunch:** $6-$14 **Dinner:** $7-$19 **Phone:** 307/856-0555

American

Location: On US 26; downtown. 203 E Main St 82501. **Hours:** 11 am-2 & 5-9:30 pm. Closed major holidays. **Reservations:** accepted. **Features:** Prime rib, seafood and a full line of traditional Mexican fare are served in a historic setting, appointed with antiques and old books and lending to a quiet, intimate ambience. The lunch menu emphasizes burgers, sandwiches, soups and salads. Casual dress; cocktails. **Parking:** street. **Cards:** AX, MC, VI.

ROCK SPRINGS pop. 18,708

WHERE TO STAY

BEST WESTERN OUTLAW INN — *Book at aaa.com* — **Phone:** (307)362-6623

AAA SAVE — Small-scale Hotel

5/16-9/15	1P: $84-$94	2P: $94-$104		
9/16-2/28	1P: $64-$74	2P: $70-$80		
3/1-5/15	1P: $64-$74	2P: $70-$80	XP: $7	F18

Location: I-80, exit 104 (Elk St), just n. 1630 Elk St 82901 (PO Box 1570). Fax: 307/362-2633. **Facility:** 101 one-bedroom standard units. 1-2 stories (no elevator), interior/exterior corridors. **Parking:** on-site, winter plug-ins. **Amenities:** high-speed Internet, irons, hair dryers. **Dining:** Outlaw Inn Restaurant, see separate listing. **Pool(s):** heated indoor. **Guest Services:** valet laundry, airport transportation-Rock Springs Sweetwater Airport. **Business Services:** meeting rooms. **Cards:** AX, DC, DS, MC, VI. **Special Amenities: free local telephone calls and free room upgrade (subject to availability with advanced reservations).** *(See color ad p 382)*

SOME UNITS

DATA PORT / VCR

BUDGET HOST INN — **Phone:** (307)362-6673

AAA SAVE — Motel

6/1-9/30 [CP]	1P: $44-$54	2P: $54-$70	XP: $5
3/1-5/31 [CP]	1P: $36-$45	2P: $49-$59	XP: $5
10/1-2/28 [CP]	1P: $36-$45	2P: $45-$55	XP: $5

Location: I-80, exit 102 (Dewar Dr), 1.3 mi se. 1004 Dewar Dr 82901. Fax: 307/362-6673. **Facility:** 32 one-bedroom standard units. 1-2 stories (no elevator), exterior corridors. **Parking:** on-site, winter plug-ins. **Terms:** pets ($5 extra charge, in designated units). **Cards:** AX, DC, DS, MC, VI. **Special Amenities: free continental breakfast and free local telephone calls.**

SOME UNITS

FEE

COMFORT INN — *Book at aaa.com* — **Phone:** (307)382-9490

Small-scale Hotel

5/16-9/15	1P: $76	2P: $82	XP: $6	F18
3/1-5/15 & 9/16-2/28	1P: $64	2P: $70	XP: $6	F18

Location: I-80, exit 102 (Dewar Dr), 0.3 mi s, then just w. 1670 Sunset Dr 82901. Fax: 307/382-7333. **Facility:** 103 units. 102 one-bedroom standard units. 1 one-bedroom suite. 1 story, exterior corridors. *Bath:* combo or shower only. **Parking:** on-site, winter plug-ins. **Terms:** [ECP] meal plan available, small pets only ($10 extra charge). **Amenities:** dual phone lines, voice mail, safes (fee), irons, hair dryers. **Pool(s):** small heated outdoor. **Leisure Activities:** whirlpool, playground, exercise room. **Guest Services:** complimentary evening beverages, coin laundry. **Business Services:** meeting rooms. **Cards:** AX, CB, DC, DS, JC, MC, VI.

SOME UNITS

ASK / DATA PORT / FEE

ECONO LODGE — *Book at aaa.com* — **Phone:** (307)382-4217

Small-scale Hotel

5/1-10/31 [ECP]	1P: $55-$65	2P: $60-$75	XP: $6	F16
3/1-4/30 & 11/1-2/28 [ECP]	1P: $50-$60	2P: $55-$65	XP: $6	F16

Location: I-80, exit 104 (Elk St), just n. 1635 Elk St 82901. Fax: 307/362-4150. **Facility:** 95 one-bedroom standard units. 2 stories (no elevator), exterior corridors. **Parking:** on-site, winter plug-ins. **Terms:** 7 day cancellation notice, pets ($5 fee). **Amenities:** irons, hair dryers. **Pool(s):** small heated outdoor. **Leisure Activities:** whirlpool. **Guest Services:** coin laundry. **Cards:** AX, CB, DC, DS, MC, VI.

SOME UNITS

ASK / FEE

HOLIDAY INN — *Book at aaa.com* — **Phone:** (307)382-9200

Small-scale Hotel

All Year	1P: $75-$110	2P: $75-$110

Location: I-80, exit 102 (Dewar Dr), 0.3 mi sw. 1675 Sunset Dr 82901. Fax: 307/362-1064. **Facility:** 170 one-bedroom standard units, some with whirlpools. 4 stories, interior/exterior corridors. *Bath:* combo or shower only. **Parking:** on-site, winter plug-ins. **Terms:** pets ($10 fee). **Amenities:** high-speed Internet, voice mail, irons, hair dryers. **Pool(s):** heated indoor, wading. **Leisure Activities:** whirlpool, exercise room. *Fee:* game room. **Guest Services:** valet and coin laundry. **Business Services:** conference facilities. **Cards:** AX, CB, DC, DS, JC, MC, VI.

SOME UNITS

ASK / DATA PORT / FEE

MOTEL 6 - 395 **Book at aaa.com**

Motel

Phone: 307/362-1850

5/27-9/5	1P: $43-$53	2P: $49-$59	XP: $3	F17
9/6-10/2	1P: $41-$51	2P: $47-$57	XP: $3	F17
10/3-2/28	1P: $36-$46	2P: $42-$52	XP: $3	F17
3/1-5/26	1P: $29-$39	2P: $35-$45	XP: $3	F17

Location: I-80, exit 102 (Dewar Dr), n to Foothills Blvd, just e. 2615 Commercial Way 82901. Fax: 307/362-5998. **Facility:** 99 one-bedroom standard units. 2 stories (no elevator), exterior corridors. *Bath:* shower only. **Parking:** on-site. **Terms:** small pets only. **Pool(s):** small heated outdoor. **Guest Services:** coin laundry. **Cards:** AX, CB, DC, DS, MC, VI.

SOME UNITS

RAMADA LIMITED **Book at aaa.com**

Small-scale Hotel

Phone: (307)362-1770

5/1-9/30	1P: $75-$85	2P: $85-$95	XP: $6	F17
10/1-2/28	1P: $70-$80	2P: $80-$90	XP: $6	F17
3/1-4/30	1P: $60-$70	2P: $70-$80	XP: $6	F17

Location: I-80, exit 102 (Dewar Dr), just n. 2717 Dewar Dr 82901. Fax: 307/362-2830. **Facility:** 129 one-bedroom standard units. 2 stories (no elevator), interior corridors. **Parking:** on-site, winter plug-ins. **Terms:** [ECP] meal plan available, small pets only ($5 extra charge, in designated units). **Amenities:** video games, irons, hair dryers. **Pool(s):** small heated outdoor. **Leisure Activities:** exercise room. **Guest Services:** valet and coin laundry. **Business Services:** meeting rooms. **Cards:** AX, CB, DC, DS, MC, VI.

SOME UNITS

SPRINGS MOTEL **Phone:** 307/362-6683

SAVE

Motel

5/1-9/30	1P: $45-$52	2P: $56-$64	XP: $6
10/1-12/31	1P: $40-$45	2P: $48-$50	XP: $6
3/1-4/30	1P: $38-$45	2P: $40-$48	XP: $6
1/1-2/28	1P: $38-$40	2P: $40-$48	XP: $6

Location: I-80, exit 107, 0.3 mi w. 1525 9th St 82901. **Facility:** 23 one-bedroom standard units. 1 story, exterior corridors. **Parking:** on-site, winter plug-ins. **Terms:** small pets only. **Cards:** AX, DS, MC.

SOME UNITS

WHERE TO DINE

THE LOG INN **Dinner:** $13-$59 **Phone:** 307/362-7166

American

Location: I-80, exit 99; in back of Conoco Truck Stop. 12 Purple Sage Rd 82901. **Hours:** 5:30 pm-10 pm. Closed major holidays; also Sun. **Reservations:** accepted. **Features:** Comfortable Western style dining in an original log cabin. Intimate booth seating available with friendly attentive staff. Favorites include deep-fried lobster tail, steak, chicken, pasta and selected desserts. Casual dress; cocktails. **Parking:** on-site. **Cards:** AX, CB, DC, DS, MC, VI.

OUTLAW INN RESTAURANT **Lunch:** $5-$9 **Dinner:** $7-$20 **Phone:** 307/362-6623

American

Location: I-80, exit 104 (Elk St), just n; in Best Western Outlaw Inn. 1630 Elk St 82901. **Hours:** 6 am-10 pm. Closed: 12/25. **Features:** A favorite local dining spot where friendly home town service to all is provided by an attentive staff. House dinner specialties include Black Angus prime rib cooked to order. Daily specials include a variety of cooking styles. Casual dress; cocktails. **Parking:** on-site. **Cards:** AX, CB, DC, DS, MC, VI.

SARATOGA pop. 1,726

WHERE TO STAY

FAR OUT WEST BED & BREAKFAST **Phone:** 307/326-5869

Bed & Breakfast

All Year [BP]	1P: $85-$115	2P: $100-$130	XP: $15

Location: Just n; center. Located in a residential area. 304 N 2nd St 82331-1230 (PO Box 1230, 82331). Fax: 307/326-9864. **Facility:** Modern amenities and Western-style decor are featured in guest rooms at this B&B. Smoke free premises. 6 units. 5 one-bedroom standard units. 1 cottage. 1-2 stories (no elevator), interior/exterior corridors. **Parking:** on-site. **Terms:** 10 day cancellation notice. **Amenities:** *Some:* irons. **Business Services:** fax. **Cards:** AX, DS, MC, VI.

SOME UNITS

DATA PORT / VCR /

HACIENDA MOTEL — **Phone:** (307)326-5751

Motel

5/1-10/31	1P: $56-$66	2P: $66-$76	XP: $5	F11
3/1-4/30 & 11/1-2/28	1P: $46-$56	2P: $56-$66	XP: $5	F11

Location: 0.5 mi s on SR 130. Located adjacent to airport. 1500 S First St 82331 (PO Box 960). Fax: 307/326-5751. **Facility:** 32 one-bedroom standard units, some with efficiencies (no utensils). 2 stories (no elevator), interior corridors. *Bath:* combo or shower only. **Parking:** on-site, winter plug-ins. **Terms:** pets ($5 extra charge). **Amenities:** *Some:* irons. **Cards:** AX, CB, DC, DS, MC, VI.

SOME UNITS

FEE FEE

SHERIDAN pop. 15,804

WHERE TO STAY

BEST WESTERN SHERIDAN CENTER *Book at aaa.com* — **Phone:** (307)674-7421

SAVE

Small-scale Hotel

6/1-9/15	1P: $119-$149	2P: $119-$149
9/16-10/31	1P: $89-$119	2P: $89-$119
3/1-5/31	1P: $79-$109	2P: $79-$109
11/1-2/28	1P: $59-$99	2P: $59-$99

Location: I-90, exit 20, 1.7 mi s. 612 N Main St 82801. Fax: 307/672-3018. **Facility:** 138 one-bedroom standard units. 2 stories (no elevator), interior/exterior corridors. **Parking:** on-site, winter plug-ins. **Terms:** pets ($15 extra charge). **Amenities:** high-speed Internet (fee), voice mail, irons, hair dryers. **Dining:** 6 am-9 pm, cocktails. **Pool(s):** small heated outdoor, heated indoor. **Leisure Activities:** whirlpool. *Fee:* game room. **Guest Services:** coin laundry, airport transportation-Sheridan Airport. **Business Services:** conference facilities, business center. **Cards:** AX, CB, DC, DS, JC, MC, VI. **Special Amenities: free local telephone calls.** *(See color ad below)*

SOME UNITS

FEE

BUDGET HOST INN — **Phone:** 307/674-7496

SAVE

Motel

6/1-9/15 [CP]	1P: $50-$55	2P: $65-$70	XP: $5	F10
3/1-5/31 & 9/16-10/15	1P: $40-$45	2P: $55-$60	XP: $5	F10
10/16-2/28	1P: $35-$40	2P: $50-$55	XP: $5	F10

Location: I-90, exit 20, 0.7 mi s; on I-90 business loop. 2007 N Main St 82801. Fax: 307/674-7687. **Facility:** 44 one-bedroom standard units. 1 story, exterior corridors. **Parking:** on-site, winter plug-ins. **Terms:** 10 day cancellation notice, pets ($5 extra charge). **Guest Services:** coin laundry. **Business Services:** fax (fee). **Cards:** AX, DC, DS, JC, MC, VI. *(See color ad p 385)*

SOME UNITS

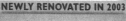

FEE

HOLIDAY INN ATRIUM & CONVENTION CENTER *Book at aaa.com* **Phone:** (307)672-8931

AAA SAVE

Small-scale Hotel

6/1-9/30	1P: $119	2P: $119
3/1-5/31 & 10/1-2/28	1P: $79	2P: $79

Location: I-90, exit 25, 0.3 mi nw. 1809 Sugarland Dr 82801. Fax: 307/672-6388. **Facility:** 212 units. 205 one-bedroom standard units. 7 one-bedroom suites. 5 stories, interior corridors. *Bath:* combo or shower only. **Parking:** on-site, winter plug-ins. **Terms:** pets ($50 deposit). **Amenities:** video games, voice mail, irons, hair dryers. **Dining:** 6 am-2 & 5-10 pm, cocktails. **Pool(s):** heated indoor. **Leisure Activities:** saunas, whirlpool, putting green, racquetball court, exercise room, basketball. *Fee:* game room. **Guest Services:** gift shop, valet and coin laundry, airport transportation-Sheridan County Airport, area transportation-within town. **Business Services:** conference facilities, business center. **Cards:** AX, DC, DS, MC, VI. **Special Amenities: free local telephone calls.**
(See color ad opposite title page & below)

SOME UNITS

FEE

MILL INN **Phone:** 307/672-6401

AAA SAVE

Historic Motel

6/1-9/15 [ECP]	1P: $89-$110	2P: $94-$120	XP: $5
3/1-5/31 & 9/16-2/28 [ECP]	1P: $50-$80	2P: $55-$85	XP: $5

Location: I-90, exit 25, 0.3 mi w. 2161 Coffeen Ave 82801. Fax: 307/672-6401. **Facility:** A converted flour mill houses this inn offering some rooms with mountain views. 45 units. 42 one- and 1 two-bedroom standard units, some with whirlpools. 2 two-bedroom suites ($125-$175), some with kitchens. 2 stories, interior/exterior corridors. **Parking:** on-site, winter plug-ins. **Amenities:** voice mail, irons, hair dryers. **Leisure Activities:** exercise room. **Business Services:** fax (fee). **Cards:** AX, DS, MC, VI. **Special Amenities: free expanded continental breakfast and free local telephone calls.** *(See color ad below)*

SOME UNITS

S/D DATA PORT / VCR /

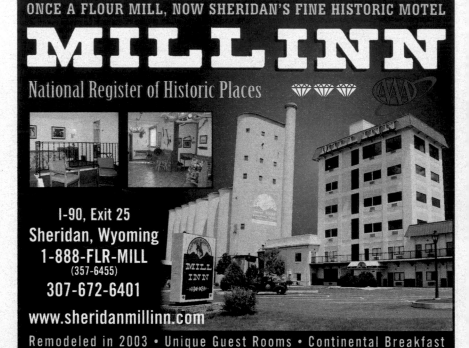

WHERE TO DINE

GOLDEN STEER **Lunch:** $6-$7 **Dinner:** $9-$19 **Phone:** 307/674-9334

American

Location: I-90, exit 20, 0.8 mi s; on I-90 business loop. 2071 N Main St 82801. **Hours:** 11 am-2 & 4-9 pm, Fri & Sat-10 pm, Sun 4 pm-9 pm; 11 am-2 & 4-10 pm, Sun 4 pm-9 pm in summer. Closed major holidays. **Features:** Steak, seafood and family fare are served in a large, comfortable, contemporary dining room whose decor is Western. The smothered burrito with lean beef, green chili, olives and onions is ample and flavorful. Sunday brunch is offered 10/1-5/14. Casual dress; cocktails. **Parking:** on-site. **Cards:** AX, DC, DS, MC, VI.

OLIVER'S BAR & GRILL **Lunch:** $7-$15 **Dinner:** $10-$25 **Phone:** 307/672-2838

American

Location: Corner of Main and Brundage sts; downtown. 55 N Main St 82801. **Hours:** 11 am-2 & 6-11 pm. Closed: 7/4, 11/25, 12/25; also Sun. **Reservations:** accepted. **Features:** The casually upscale bistro in downtown Sheridan offers continental cuisine and Italian specialties. Casual dress; cocktails. **Parking:** street. **Cards:** AX, DS, MC, VI.

STORY pop. 887

WHERE TO DINE

WAGON BOX RESTAURANT Historic **Lunch:** $5-$10 **Dinner:** $10-$26 **Phone:** 307/683-2444

American

Location: I-90, exit 44, 7.2 mi nw. 108 N Piney 82842. **Hours:** 11:30 am-9 pm, Fri & Sat-10 pm, Sun noon-8 pm; hours may vary in winter. Closed: 12/25. **Reservations:** accepted. **Features:** Worth the short drive off I-90, the restaurant was built in 1907 and has the feel of an old supper club decorated in a Western theme. Locals favor the steak and seafood along with the nightly special, and hot bread that melts in your mouth. Casual dress; cocktails. **Parking:** on-site. **Cards:** AX, CB, DC, DS, MC, VI.

WALDORF A' STORY AT PINEY CREEK GROCERY **Lunch:** $3-$8 **Dinner:** $6-$9 **Phone:** 307/683-2400

American

Location: I-90, exit 37 eastbound; exit 44 westbound, 5 mi w, follow signs to Story, then just n. 19 N Piney Rd 82842. **Hours:** 7:30 am-7:30 pm; Fri & Sat-9:30 pm 5/15-9/15. **Features:** Rustic and small town charm are all rolled into one in this eatery. Some of the daily specials have been created by the waitstaff. All ingredients are fresh and gathered locally when available. While the connecting grocery store carries staples for the pantry, you'll also be able to find gourmet & unique gift items. Casual dress; beer & wine only. **Parking:** on-site. **Cards:** MC, VI.

SUNDANCE pop. 1,161

WHERE TO STAY

BEST WESTERN INN AT SUNDANCE ***Book at aaa.com*** **Phone:** (307)283-2800

SAVE

6/1-8/31 [ECP]	1P: $74-$109	2P: $79-$114	XP: $5	F17
9/1-9/30 [ECP]	1P: $66-$79	2P: $74-$89	XP: $5	F17
3/1-5/31 & 10/1-2/28 [ECP]	1P: $52-$69	2P: $57-$74	XP: $5	F17

Small-scale Hotel

Location: I-90, exit 189, just n, then just w on I-90 business loop. 2719 E Cleveland 82729 (PO Box 927). Fax: 307/283-2727. **Facility:** 44 one-bedroom standard units. 2 stories (no elevator), interior corridors. **Parking:** on-site, winter plug-ins. **Terms:** pets ($5 extra charge). **Amenities:** irons, hair dryers. **Pool(s):** small heated indoor. **Leisure Activities:** whirlpool. **Guest Services:** coin laundry. **Business Services:** meeting rooms. **Cards:** AX, DC, DS, MC, VI. **Special Amenities: free expanded continental breakfast and free local telephone calls.**

SOME UNITS

DATA PORT / /

FEE

BUDGET HOST ARROWHEAD MOTEL **Phone:** 307/283-3307

SAVE

5/15-9/20	1P: $49-$59	2P: $59-$69	XP: $5	D16
9/21-12/1	1P: $40-$45	2P: $45-$55	XP: $5	D16
3/1-5/14	1P: $36-$45	2P: $39-$50	XP: $4	D16
12/2-2/28	1P: $36-$45	2P: $39-$49	XP: $4	D16

Motel

Location: I-90 business loop and US 14. 214 Cleveland 82729 (PO Box 366). **Facility:** 12 one-bedroom standard units. 1 story, exterior corridors. **Parking:** on-site, winter plug-ins. **Terms:** pets ($5 extra charge). **Cards:** AX, CB, DC, DS, MC, VI. **Special Amenities: free local telephone calls and early check-in/late check-out.**

SOME UNITS

/ /

FEE

SUNDANCE MOUNTAIN INN **Phone:** (307)283-3737

SAVE

7/1-7/31 [CP]	1P: $83-$97	2P: $83-$97	XP: $5	F17
8/1-8/31 [CP]	1P: $80-$93	2P: $80-$93	XP: $5	F17
5/24-6/30 [CP]	1P: $58-$89	2P: $58-$89	XP: $5	F17
9/1-10/15 [CP]	1P: $58-$75	2P: $58-$75	XP: $5	F17

Motel

Location: I-90, exit 187, 0.4 mi n. 26 SR 585 82729 (PO Box 947). Fax: 307/283-3738. **Facility:** 42 units. 41 one- and 1 two-bedroom standard units. 1-2 stories (no elevator), exterior corridors. **Parking:** on-site, winter plug-ins. **Terms:** open 5/24-10/15, 14 day cancellation notice, small pets only ($25 deposit). **Pool(s):** small heated indoor. **Leisure Activities:** whirlpool. **Guest Services:** coin laundry. **Cards:** AX, DC, DS, MC, VI. **Special Amenities: free continental breakfast.**

SOME UNITS

/ / /

FEE

WHERE TO DINE

ARO FAMILY RESTAURANT **Lunch:** $4-$12 **Dinner:** $4-$15 **Phone:** 307/283-2000

American

Location: I-90 business loop and US 14. 205 Cleveland Ave 82729. **Hours:** 7 am-9 pm; to 10 pm in summer. Closed: 12/25. **Reservations:** accepted. **Features:** Get your taste buds ready for true home-style cooking in an unpretentious setting. House specialties include smothered burritos, rib eye steak, prime rib and a decadent devil's tower dessert of brownies, ice cream, chocolate syrup with a dollop of whipped cream. Casual dress; cocktails. **Parking:** on-site. **Cards:** AX, DS, MC, VI.

TETON VILLAGE pop. 175—*See also GRAND TETON NATIONAL PARK.*

WHERE TO STAY

THE ALPENHOF LODGE *Book at aaa.com* **Phone:** (307)733-3242

Small-scale Hotel

3/1-4/6	1P: $188-$498	2P: $188-$498	XP: $30	F12
9/23-2/28	1P: $128-$498	2P: $128-$498	XP: $30	F12
6/6-9/22	1P: $128-$440	2P: $128-$440	XP: $30	F12
5/2-6/5	1P: $108-$425	2P: $108-$425	XP: $30	F12

Location: Center. 3255 W Village Dr 83025 (PO Box 288). Fax: 307/739-1516. **Facility:** 42 units. 41 one-bedroom standard units, some with whirlpools. 1 two-bedroom suite ($318-$538) with whirlpool. 4 stories, interior corridors. **Parking:** on-site. **Terms:** open 3/1-4/6 & 5/2-2/28, 10 day cancellation notice-fee imposed, 2% service charge. **Amenities:** video library (fee), hair dryers. **Dining:** 2 restaurants, 7 am-10:30 pm, cocktails, also, Alpenrose, see separate listing. **Pool(s):** heated outdoor. **Leisure Activities:** sauna, whirlpool, hiking trails. *Fee:* massage. **Guest Services:** valet laundry. **Business Services:** meeting rooms. **Cards:** AX, DC, DS, MC, VI. ***(See color ad p 357)***

SOME UNITS

FEE

BEST WESTERN INN AT JACKSON HOLE *Book at aaa.com* **Phone:** 307/733-2311

Small-scale Hotel

10/12-2/28	1P: $89-$279	2P: $89-$279	XP: $10	F14
5/30-8/23	1P: $129-$259	2P: $129-$259	XP: $10	F14
3/1-5/29	1P: $89-$249	2P: $89-$249	XP: $10	F14
8/24-10/11	1P: $139-$199	2P: $139-$199	XP: $10	F14

Location: Center. 3345 W Village Dr 83025 (PO Box 328). Fax: 307/733-0844. **Facility:** Smoke free premises. 83 units. 82 one-bedroom standard units, some with efficiencies. 1 one-bedroom suite with kitchen. 3-4 stories, exterior corridors. **Parking:** on-site. **Terms:** check-in 4 pm, 30 day cancellation notice. **Amenities:** video games (fee), voice mail, irons, hair dryers. **Dining:** 7 am-9:30 & 5:30-10 pm, cocktails, also, Masa Sushi, see separate listing. **Pool(s):** heated outdoor. **Leisure Activities:** sauna, whirlpools, ski lockers, hiking trails. *Fee:* horseback riding, massage. **Guest Services:** valet and coin laundry. **Business Services:** meeting rooms. **Cards:** AX, DC, DS, MC, VI. ***(See color ad p 357)***

SOME UNITS

SNAKE RIVER LODGE & SPA, A ROCK RESORT *Book at aaa.com* **Phone:** (307)732-6000

Small-scale Hotel

6/1-9/25	1P: $299-$4500	2P: $299-$4500	XP: $20	F14
3/1-4/3 & 9/26-2/28	1P: $279-$4500	2P: $279-$4500	XP: $20	F14
4/4-5/31	1P: $139-$4500	2P: $139-$4500	XP: $20	F14

Location: Center. 7710 Granite Loop Rd 83025 (PO Box 348). Fax: 307/732-6004. **Facility:** Many luxuries are offered at this contemporary four-season resort set alongside the slopes for easy ski-in access. Smoke free premises. 130 units. 114 one-bedroom standard units, some with whirlpools. 16 two-bedroom suites with kitchens. 5 stories, interior corridors. **Parking:** on-site (fee) and valet. **Terms:** check-in 4 pm, 30 day cancellation notice-fee imposed, package plans - seasonal. **Amenities:** video games (fee), dual phone lines, voice mail, safes, honor bars, irons, hair dryers. *Some:* CD players. **Dining:** 7 am-10, noon-2 & 6-9 pm, cocktails. **Pool(s):** heated indoor/outdoor. **Leisure Activities:** saunas, whirlpools, steamrooms, exercise room, spa. *Fee:* downhill & cross country skiing, horseback riding. **Guest Services:** gift shop, valet laundry. **Business Services:** meeting rooms. **Cards:** AX, DC, DS, MC, VI. **Special Amenities: free newspaper.** ***(See color ad p 367)***

FEE

TETON MOUNTAIN LODGE *Book at aaa.com* **Phone:** (307)734-7111

Small-scale Hotel

3/1-4/4 & 12/8-2/28	1P: $149-$1200	2P: $149-$1200
4/5-12/7	1P: $129-$1100	2P: $129-$1100

Location: Center. 3385 W Village Dr 83025 (PO Box 564). Fax: 307/734-7999. **Facility:** Smoke free premises. 129 units. 112 one-bedroom standard units. 17 one-bedroom suites ($250-$1200). 5 stories, interior corridors. *Bath:* combo or shower only. **Parking:** valet and street. **Terms:** check-in 4 pm, 31 day cancellation notice-fee imposed, [BP] meal plan available, 4% service charge. **Amenities:** video games (fee), voice mail, irons, hair dryers. *Some:* DVD players. **Pool(s):** small outdoor, heated indoor. **Leisure Activities:** whirlpools, spa. **Guest Services:** valet and coin laundry. **Business Services:** meeting rooms. **Cards:** AX, DC, DS, MC, VI.

VILLAGE CENTER INN **Phone:** (307)733-3990

Condominium

4/6-2/28	1P: $75-$300
3/1-3/21	1P: $140-$155
3/22-4/5	1P: $115-$145

Location: Center. Located next to a ski lift. 3275 W Village Dr 83025 (PO Box 510). Fax: 307/733-0244. **Facility:** Smoke free premises. 16 one-bedroom standard units with efficiencies. 3 stories (no elevator), exterior corridors. **Parking:** on-site. **Terms:** check-in 4 pm, 31 day cancellation notice-fee imposed. **Amenities:** voice mail, irons. **Leisure Activities:** cross country skiing, hiking trails. *Fee:* downhill skiing, snowmobiling, horseback riding, massage. **Guest Services:** coin laundry. **Cards:** AX, MC, VI.

The following lodging was either not evaluated or did not meet AAA rating requirements but is listed for your information only.

FOUR SEASONS RESORT JACKSON HOLE **Phone:** 307/734-5040

fyi

Small-scale Hotel

All Year	1P: $275-$3000	2P: $275-$3000	XP: $50	F18

Too new to rate, opening scheduled for December 2003. **Location:** Located at the base of Jackson Hole Mountain Resort. 7680 Granite Loop 83025 (PO Box 544). Fax: 307/734-1182. **Amenities:** 124 units, pets, restaurant, coffeemakers, refrigerators, pool, winter sports. **Terms:** 30 day cancellation notice-fee imposed. **Cards:** AX, DC, MC, VI. ***(See color ad p 360)***

WHERE TO DINE

ALPENROSE — AAA — Two Diamonds — Nouvelle French
Dinner: $21-$32 **Phone:** 307/733-3462
Location: Center; in The Alpenhof Lodge. 3255 W Village Dr 83025. **Hours:** Open 3/1-10/14 & 12/2-2/28; 7 am-11 & 5:30-9 pm; 7 am-10 & 6-9:30 pm 12/1-4/6. Closed: 4/7-5/15 & for dinner Mon. **Reservations:** suggested. **Features:** A professional staff assists diners with the extensive wine list that features finer California and European varieties as well as a nice selection of after-dinner drinks. The atmosphere is European and offers a strong menu variety, including game dishes. Casual dress; cocktails. **Parking:** on-site. **Cards:** AX, CB, DC, DS, MC, VI.

MANGY MOOSE RESTAURANT AND SALOON — Two Diamonds — Regional American
Lunch: $4-$9 **Dinner:** $15-$30 **Phone:** 307/733-4913
Location: Center of village. 1 McCollister Dr 83025. **Hours:** 7 am-10 pm. **Features:** Diners can watch village activity while eating prime rib, trout or beef stroganoff. The buffalo prime rib is a favorite but often goes quickly. This two-level dining room is covered with nostalgic items. Casual dress; cocktails. **Parking:** on-site. **Cards:** AX, MC, VI.

MASA SUSHI — Two Diamonds — Japanese
Dinner: $8-$25 **Phone:** 307/732-2962
Location: Center; in Best Western Inn at Jackson Hole. 3345 W Village Dr 83025. **Hours:** 5:30 pm-9:30 pm. Closed: Mon. **Reservations:** suggested. **Features:** Chef Masa Kitami delights guests with traditional sushi and sashimi as well as his own inventive creations like the tasty Jackson Hole steak roll. The atmosphere is relaxing and scenic with great views of the surrounding mountains, skiers and tram. Casual dress; cocktails. **Parking:** on-site. **Cards:** MC, VI.

VISTA GRANDE — Two Diamonds — Mexican
Dinner: $10-$16 **Phone:** 307/733-6964
Location: From Jackson, 5 mi w on SR 22 to SR 390, then 1.3 mi n. 2550 Moose Wilson Rd 83014. **Hours:** 5:30 pm-9 pm; 5 pm-10 pm 5/31-9/6. Closed: 12/25; also Sun. **Features:** Vista Grande serves up both standard and creative Mexican fare such as seafood enchiladas, a variety of chimichangas and carne asada. The open dining room is decorated with colorful Mexican artwork. Outdoor dining is also available. Casual dress; cocktails. **Parking:** on-site. **Cards:** MC, VI.

THERMOPOLIS pop. 3,172

WHERE TO STAY

BEST WESTERN (THE PLAZA HOTEL) — Three Diamonds — Small-scale Hotel **Phone:** 307/864-2939

5/1-9/15 [ECP]	1P: $65-$149	2P: $65-$149	XP: $5	F18
3/1-4/30 & 9/16-2/28 [ECP]	1P: $55-$129	2P: $55-$129	XP: $5	F18

Location: In Hot Springs State Park. 116 E Park St 82433 (PO Box 866). Fax: 307/864-2927. **Facility:** 36 units. 18 one-bedroom standard units. 18 one-bedroom suites. 2 stories (no elevator), interior corridors. **Parking:** on-site. **Amenities:** irons, hair dryers. **Pool(s):** heated outdoor. **Guest Services:** gift shop. **Business Services:** meeting rooms. **Cards:** AX, CB, DC, DS, JC, MC, VI.

ASK / SOME UNITS

HOLIDAY INN OF THE WATERS — *Book at aaa.com* — Two Diamonds — Small-scale Hotel **Phone:** (307)864-3131

5/28-9/6	1P: $89-$129	2P: $99-$139	XP: $10	F19
3/1-5/27	1P: $79-$99	2P: $89-$109	XP: $10	F19
9/7-2/28	1P: $79-$99	2P: $89-$99	XP: $10	F19

Location: In Hot Springs State Park. 115 E Park St 82443 (PO Box 1323). Fax: 307/864-3131. **Facility:** 80 one-bedroom standard units. 2 stories (no elevator), interior/exterior corridors. *Bath:* combo or shower only. **Parking:** on-site, winter plug-ins. **Terms:** [BP] meal plan available, package plans. **Amenities:** voice mail, irons, hair dryers. *Some:* dual phone lines. **Dining:** The Safari Club, see separate listing. **Pool(s):** heated outdoor. **Leisure Activities:** sauna, whirlpool, jogging, exercise room. *Fee:* racquetball courts, massage. **Guest Services:** coin laundry. *Fee:* tanning facility. **Business Services:** meeting rooms. **Cards:** AX, CB, DC, DS, MC, VI. ***(See color ad below & opposite title page)***

ASK / SOME UNITS / VCR FEE

HOT SPRINGS SUPER 8 **Phone:** 307/864-5515

Small-scale Hotel

All Year 1P: $59-$129 2P: $59-$129 XP: $5 F10

Location: On US 20, just se. Lane 5, Hwy 20 S 82443 (PO Box 569). Fax: 307/864-5447. **Facility:** Smoke free premises. 52 units. 51 one-bedroom standard units. 1 one-bedroom suite ($189-$209) with whirlpool. 2 stories (no elevator), interior corridors. *Bath:* combo or shower only. **Parking:** on-site. **Terms:** [CP] meal plan available, package plans - seasonal. **Amenities:** video library, safes (fee), hair dryers. *Some:* video games (fee), high-speed Internet. **Pool(s):** heated indoor. **Leisure Activities:** whirlpool. **Guest Services:** coin laundry. **Business Services:** meeting rooms. **Cards:** AX, CB, DC, MC, VI.

SOME UNITS

WHERE TO DINE

THE SAFARI CLUB **Lunch:** $5-$9 **Dinner:** $7-$21 **Phone:** 307/864-3131

American

Location: In Hot Springs State Park; in Holiday Inn of the Waters. 115 E Park St 82443. **Hours:** 5 am-10 pm; 6 am-2 & 5-9 pm, Fri & Sat-10 pm, Sun 6 am-9 pm in winter. **Features:** Hundreds of different types of mounted fish, birds and animals decorate the restaurant and lounge where house specials like prime rib and pork chops are served in a fun and lively atmosphere. Sunday breakfast and buffet is available 7 am-2 pm. Casual dress; cocktails. **Parking:** on-site. **Cards:** AX, DC, DS, JC, MC, VI.

TORRINGTON pop. 5,776

WHERE TO STAY

KINGS INN **Phone:** 307/532-4011

Small-scale Hotel

3/1-9/30 1P: $42-$53 2P: $50-$60 XP: $7 F12
10/1-2/28 1P: $39-$53 2P: $46-$56 XP: $7 F12

Location: Just s of jct US 26 and 85. 1555 Main St 82240. Fax: 307/532-7202. **Facility:** 52 one-bedroom standard units. 2 stories (no elevator), interior corridors. **Parking:** on-site, winter plug-ins. **Terms:** cancellation fee imposed, [BP] meal plan available, pets ($5 extra charge, in designated units). **Amenities:** *Some:* hair dryers. **Dining:** 5 pm-10 pm, cocktails. **Pool(s):** heated indoor. **Leisure Activities:** whirlpool, limited exercise equipment. **Guest Services:** coin laundry. **Business Services:** meeting rooms. **Cards:** AX, CB, DC, DS, JC, MC, VI. **Special Amenities: free local telephone calls.**

SOME UNITS

FEE

MAVERICK MOTEL **Phone:** (307)532-4064

Motel

All Year 1P: $38-$40 2P: $42-$46 XP: $5 D10

Location: 1.7 mi w on US 26/85. US 26 W 82240 (Rt 1, Box 354). Fax: 307/532-2577. **Facility:** 13 one-bedroom standard units, some with efficiencies (no utensils). 1 story, exterior corridors. **Parking:** on-site, winter plug-ins. **Terms:** pets ($5 fee). **Cards:** AX, DC, DS, MC, VI. **Special Amenities: free local telephone calls.**

SOME UNITS

FEE

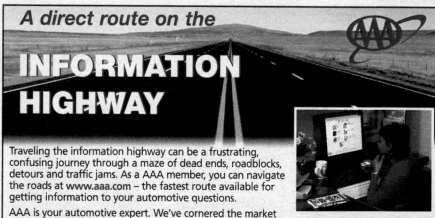

SUPER 8 MOTEL — **Phone:** 307/532-7118

Motel

6/1-9/30	1P: $55-$65	2P: $63-$75	XP: $10	F12
3/1-5/31 & 10/1-2/28	1P: $47-$55	2P: $55-$65	XP: $10	F12

Location: Just s of jct US 26 and 85. 1548 S Main 82240. Fax: 307/532-2876. **Facility:** 57 one-bedroom standard units. 2 stories (no elevator), interior corridors. **Parking:** on-site, winter plug-ins. **Terms:** 14 day cancellation notice, [ECP] meal plan available. **Pool(s):** heated indoor. **Leisure Activities:** whirlpool. **Guest Services:** coin laundry. **Business Services:** meeting rooms. **Cards:** AX, DC, DS, MC, VI.

SOME UNITS

ASK / DATA PORT

UCROSS

WHERE TO STAY

THE RANCH AT UCROSS — **Phone:** (307)737-2281

AAA SAVE — Ranch

6/1-9/30 [AP]	1P: $239-$299	2P: $239-$299	XP: $20	F19
5/1-5/31 [AP]	1P: $199-$239	2P: $199-$239	XP: $10	F19

Location: Jct US 14/16, 0.5 mi w on US 14. Located in a rural area. 2673 US Hwy 14 E 82835. Fax: 307/737-2211. **Facility:** Mountain scenery and a manicured lawn dotted with cottonwood trees create an appealing setting at this ranch offering annex rooms and four cabins. 31 units. 23 one-bedroom standard units. 8 cabins. 1-2 stories (no elevator), interior/exterior corridors. **Parking:** on-site. **Terms:** open 5/1-9/30, 3 day cancellation notice-fee imposed, pets ($100 deposit). **Dining:** 7 am-8:30 & 7-9 pm, cocktails. **Pool(s):** small heated outdoor. **Leisure Activities:** fishing, 2 tennis courts, croquet, hiking trails, horseshoes, game room. *Fee:* horseback riding. **Guest Services:** gift shop. **Business Services:** meeting rooms. **Cards:** AX, DC, DS, MC, VI. **Special Amenities: free full breakfast.** ***(See ad p 386)***

SOME UNITS

DATA PORT FEE

WAPITI —*See also YELLOWSTONE NATIONAL PARK.*

WHERE TO STAY

BILL CODY RANCH — **Phone:** (307)587-2097

AAA SAVE — Ranch

6/8-9/8	1P: $115-$260	2P: $115-$260	XP: $15
5/15-6/7 & 9/9-9/30	1P: $78-$175	2P: $78-$175	XP: $10

Location: 6 mi w on US 14/16/20. Located in the Shoshone National Forest. 2604 Yellowstone Hwy 82414 (2604-A Yellowstone Hwy). Fax: 307/587-6272. **Facility:** These log cabins in the woods offer Western decor and mountain views. Designated smoking area. 14 cabins. 1-2 stories (no elevator), interior/exterior corridors. **Parking:** on-site. **Terms:** open 5/15-9/30, check-in 3:30 pm, 30 day cancellation notice-fee imposed, weekly rates available, [AP], [BP] & [MAP] meal plans available, no pets allowed (owner's pet on premises). **Dining:** 7:30 am-9 & 6-8 pm, cocktails. **Leisure Activities:** fishing, recreation programs, hiking trails, playground, basketball, horseshoes. *Fee:* horseback riding, game room. **Cards:** DS, MC, VI. **Special Amenities: free local telephone calls and early check-in/late check-out.** ***(See color ad p 393)***

GREEN CREEK INN — **Phone:** (307)587-5004

AAA SAVE — Motel

6/7-8/31	1P: $50-$57	2P: $57-$70	XP: $5	F13
5/1-6/6 & 9/1-11/15	1P: $35-$40	2P: $40-$45	XP: $5	F13

Location: 2.8 mi w on US 14/16/20. Located in a quiet, rural area. 2908 Yellowstone Hwy 82450. **Facility:** 17 units. 15 one-bedroom standard units. 2 two-bedroom suites ($60-$80). 1 story, exterior corridors. **Parking:** on-site. **Terms:** open 5/1-11/15, cancellation fee imposed, package plans, pets ($5 extra charge). **Leisure Activities:** playground, horseshoes. **Cards:** AX, DS, MC, VI. **Special Amenities: free local telephone calls and early check-in/late check-out.** ***(See color ad p 341)***

SOME UNITS

CTV FEE

SHOSHONE LODGE — **Phone:** (307)587-4044

AAA SAVE — Cabin

6/1-8/31	1P: $80-$90	2P: $90-$120	XP: $20
9/1-9/30	1P: $50-$80	2P: $50-$90	XP: $20
4/30-5/31 & 10/1-11/8	1P: $50-$70	2P: $50-$80	XP: $20

Location: 28 mi w on US 14/16/20. Located in a quiet, secluded area. 349 Yellowstone Hwy 82414. Fax: 307/587-2681. **Facility:** Smoke free premises. 16 cabins ($100-$180). 1 story, exterior corridors. *Bath:* combo or shower only. **Parking:** on-site. **Terms:** open 4/30-11/8, 45 day cancellation notice-fee imposed, weekly rates available, [BP] & [MAP] meal plans available, package plans. **Dining:** 7 am-9 & 6-8 pm. **Leisure Activities:** fishing, hiking trails, playground. *Fee:* horseback riding. **Cards:** AX, DS, MC, VI. ***(See color ad p 395 & p 336)***

SOME UNITS

WHEATLAND pop. 3,548

WHERE TO STAY

BEST WESTERN TORCHLITE MOTOR INN *Book at aaa.com* — **Phone:** 307/322-4070

AAA SAVE — Small-scale Hotel

All Year	1P: $43-$75	2P: $48-$80	XP: $5	F12

Location: I-25, exit 78, just e; 1.5 mi n on US 87/I-25 business loop (16th St). 1809 N 16th St 82201 (PO Box 637). Fax: 307/322-4072. **Facility:** 50 one-bedroom standard units. 2 stories (no elevator), exterior corridors. **Parking:** on-site, winter plug-ins. **Terms:** pets ($25 deposit). **Amenities:** irons, hair dryers. **Pool(s):** heated outdoor. **Leisure Activities:** whirlpool, barbecue grill, picnic area. **Guest Services:** airport transportation-Phifer Airport. **Business Services:** meeting rooms. **Cards:** AX, CB, DC, DS, MC, VI. **Special Amenities: free local telephone calls and early check-in/late check-out.**

SOME UNITS

DATA PORT FEE

MOTEL WEST WINDS

Phone: 307/322-2705

Motel

All Year	1P: $38-$48	2P: $43-$53	XP: $5	F16

Location: I-25, exit 78, just e; 0.4 mi n on US 87/I-25 business loop (16th St). 1756 South Rd 82201. Fax: 307/322-9169. **Facility:** 30 one-bedroom standard units. 2 stories (no elevator), exterior corridors. *Bath:* combo or shower only. **Parking:** on-site, winter plug-ins. **Terms:** cancellation fee imposed, weekly rates available. **Cards:** AX, CB, DC, DS, MC, VI.

SOME UNITS

ASK / DATA PORT /

VIMBO'S MOTEL

Phone: (307)322-3842

AAA SAVE

Motel

7/19-8/1	1P: $69	2P: $74-$77	XP: $5	F12
6/1-7/18	1P: $59	2P: $64-$67	XP: $5	F12
3/1-5/31 & 8/2-2/28	1P: $39	2P: $44-$47	XP: $5	F12

Location: I-25, exit 78, just e; just n on US 87/I-25 business loop (16th St). 203 16th St 82201. Fax: 307/322-2677. **Facility:** 41 units. 38 one-bedroom standard units. 3 one-bedroom suites ($60-$90) with kitchens. 2 stories (no elevator), interior/exterior corridors. **Parking:** on-site, winter plug-ins. **Terms:** weekly rates available, small pets only. **Amenities:** *Some:* irons, hair dryers. **Dining:** restaurant, see separate listing. **Guest Services:** gift shop, airport transportation-Phifer Airport. **Business Services:** meeting rooms. **Cards:** AX, DC, MC, VI.

SOME UNITS

DATA PORT / /

WHERE TO DINE

CASEY'S TIMBERHAUS FAMILY RESTAURANT AND LOUNGE **Lunch:** $5-$10 **Dinner:** $5-$10 **Phone:** 307/322-4932

American

Location: I-25, exit 78, just e, 1.5 mi n on US 87/I-25 business loop (16th St). 1803 N 16th St 82201. **Hours:** 6 am-9 pm, Fri & Sat-9:30 pm; 7 am-8 pm, Fri & Sat-9 pm 11/1-3/31. Closed: 1/1, 11/25, 12/25. **Features:** The creative use of woodwork, and regional wildlife displays give Casey's more than just good food. Rustic and homey, you'll appreciate the timber atmosphere. Cocktails. **Parking:** on-site. **Cards:** AX, DC, DS, MC, VI.

VIMBO'S "DUSTY BOOTS" RESTAURANT **Lunch:** $5-$9 **Dinner:** $7-$15 **Phone:** 307/322-3725

AAA

American

Location: I-25, exit 78, just e; just n on US 87/I-25 business loop (16th St); beside Vimbo's Motel. 203 16th St 82201. **Hours:** 6 am-9 pm, Fri & Sat-10 pm. Closed: 11/25, 12/25. **Features:** Casual, family dining offers an impressive lunch buffet with salad, soup, broasted chicken, real mashed potatoes and gravy, plus much more. Friday night seafood buffet and nightly steak specials are highly popular with locals. Freshly baked bread and dessert complement your great meal. Casual dress; cocktails. **Parking:** on-site. **Cards:** AX, DS, MC, VI.

WILSON pop. 1,294—*See also GRAND TETON NATIONAL PARK.*

WHERE TO STAY

SASSY MOOSE INN OF JACKSON HOLE

Phone: (307)733-1277

Bed & Breakfast

12/6-2/28	1P: $139-$189	2P: $139-$189		
5/11-10/31	1P: $129-$189	2P: $129-$189	XP: $15	F12
3/1-5/10	1P: $79-$139	2P: $79-$189	XP: $15	F12
11/1-12/5	1P: $79-$129	2P: $79-$129		

Location: 2 mi n on SR 390 from jct SR 22; 5 mi s from Teton Village; 6 mi nw from Jackson. Located in a quiet area. 3859 Miles Rd 83014. Fax: 307/739-0793. **Facility:** Smoke free premises. 5 one-bedroom standard units. 2 stories, interior corridors. *Bath:* combo or shower only. **Parking:** on-site. **Terms:** check-in 4 pm, 30 day cancellation notice-fee imposed, [BP] meal plan available, 2% service charge, pets ($10 fee). **Amenities:** video library. **Leisure Activities:** whirlpool. **Guest Services:** complimentary evening beverages. **Business Services:** fax. **Cards:** AX, MC, VI.

VCR

FEE

WORLAND pop. 5,250

WHERE TO STAY

COMFORT INN OF WORLAND *Book at aaa.com*

Phone: (307)347-9898

Small-scale Hotel

6/1-8/31	1P: $80-$105	2P: $85-$110
9/1-10/31	1P: $60-$85	2P: $65-$90
3/1-5/31 & 11/1-2/28	1P: $55-$85	2P: $60-$90

Location: On US 16, 1.4 mi e. 100 N Road 11 82401. Fax: 307/347-6734. **Facility:** 50 units. 48 one-bedroom standard units, some with whirlpools. 2 one-bedroom suites ($109-$150) with whirlpools. 2 stories (no elevator), interior corridors. *Bath:* combo or shower only. **Parking:** on-site, winter plug-ins. **Terms:** cancellation fee imposed, [ECP] meal plan available, small pets only ($6 extra charge). **Amenities:** hair dryers. *Some:* irons. **Pool(s):** small heated indoor. **Leisure Activities:** whirlpool, limited exercise equipment. **Guest Services:** coin laundry. **Cards:** AX, CB, DC, DS, JC, MC, VI.

SOME UNITS

ASK DATA PORT / /

FEE

DAYS INN *Book at aaa.com*

Phone: (307)347-4251

Motel

6/1-10/31	1P: $65-$85	2P: $70-$90
3/1-5/31 & 11/1-2/28	1P: $50-$70	2P: $55-$75

Location: 0.5 mi n on US 20. 500 N 10th St 82401. Fax: 307/347-6500. **Facility:** 42 one-bedroom standard units. 1 story, exterior corridors. *Bath:* combo or shower only. **Parking:** on-site, winter plug-ins. **Terms:** cancellation fee imposed, [CP] meal plan available, small pets only ($5 extra charge). **Amenities:** voice mail, hair dryers. **Guest Services:** coin laundry. **Cards:** AX, CB, DC, DS, JC, MC, VI.

SOME UNITS

ASK DATA PORT / /

FEE

WHERE TO DINE

RAM'S HORN CAFE — **Lunch:** $5-$17 — **Dinner:** $7-$17 — **Phone:** 307/347-6351

American

Location: On US 16; city center. 629 Big Horn Ave 82401. **Hours:** 6 am-9 pm, Sun to 8:30 pm. Closed: 12/25. **Reservations:** accepted. **Features:** There's a coffee shop on one side and dining room and lounge on the other, where chicken fried steak, salmon and pies reign as the specialties of the house. The atmosphere is casual and friendly throughout and attracts locals and tourists alike. Casual dress; cocktails. **Parking:** street. **Cards:** AX, MC, VI.

YELLOWSTONE NATIONAL PARK —*See also CODY*

WHERE TO STAY

ABSAROKA MOUNTAIN LODGE — **Phone:** (307)587-3963

Cabin

5/1-9/30 — 1P: $76-$175 — 2P: $76-$175

Location: 11 mi e of east entrance. Located in the Shoshone National Forest. 1231 E Yellowstone Hwy 82450 (1231 E Yellowstone Hwy, CODY, 82414). **Facility:** Smoke free premises. 16 cabins ($76-$175). 1 story, exterior corridors. *Bath:* combo or shower only. **Parking:** on-site. **Terms:** open 5/1-9/30, 2 night minimum stay, 30 day cancellation notice-fee imposed, [AP] meal plan available, package plans, 9% service charge. **Leisure Activities:** fishing, recreation programs, hiking trails, playground, basketball, horseshoes. *Fee:* horseback riding. **Guest Services:** gift shop. **Cards:** DS, MC, VI. ***(See color ad p 175)***

SOME UNITS

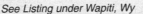

FEE

ELEPHANT HEAD LODGE — Cabin — **Phone:** (307)587-3980

6/10-8/19	1P: $95-$110	2P: $110-$125	XP: $10
5/20-6/9 & 8/20-9/30	1P: $84-$97	2P: $99-$112	XP: $10

Location: 7 mi e of east entrance. 1170 Yellowstone Hwy 82450 (1170 Yellowstone Hwy, CODY, 82414). Fax: 307/527-6850. **Facility:** Cozy wilderness cabins, including three with lofts, are featured at this lodge. Smoke free premises. 14 cabins ($110-$225). 1 story, exterior corridors. *Bath:* combo or shower only. **Parking:** on-site. **Terms:** open 5/20-9/30, 30 day cancellation notice-fee imposed, [AP] meal plan available, package plans. **Dining:** 7:30 am-9:30 & 6:30-8:30 pm, cocktails. **Leisure Activities:** fishing, recreation programs, hiking trails, playground, horseshoes. *Fee:* portable TV/VCRs, horseback riding. **Cards:** AX, DS, MC, VI. *(See color ad p 174 & p 393)*

SOME UNITS

The following lodgings were either not evaluated or did not meet AAA rating requirements but are listed for your information only.

CANYON LODGE **Phone:** 307/344-7311

fyi Not evaluated. **Location:** Canyon Jct 82190. Facilities, services, and decor characterize a basic property.

LAKE LODGE & CABINS **Phone:** 307/344-7311

fyi Not evaluated. **Location:** 1.5 mi s of Lake Jct. Lake Station, Box 3307 82190. Facilities, services, and decor characterize a basic property.

LAKE YELLOWSTONE HOTEL & CABINS **Phone:** 307/344-7311

fyi Not evaluated. **Location:** 1 mi s of Lake Jct. Lake Station, Box 3307 82190. Facilities, services, and decor characterize a basic property.

MAMMOTH HOT SPRINGS HOTEL & CABINS **Phone:** 307/344-7311

fyi Not evaluated. **Location:** Mammoth Hot Springs. Mammoth Hot Springs 82190. Facilities, services, and decor characterize a basic property.

OLD FAITHFUL INN **Phone:** 307/344-7311

fyi Not evaluated. **Location:** Opposite Old Faithful Geyser between West Thumb and Madison jcts. West Thumb & Madison 82190 (#1 Old Faithful Inn). Facilities, services, and decor characterize a basic property.

AAA SAFETY POSTER PROGRAM

AAA SAFETY POSTER PROGRAM

Promotes safety on the road and off

Each year, hundreds of posters from around the United States and Canada flood to AAA to be judged and recognized for their distinguished achievement in executing a traffic safety message.

Through art education, the AAA Traffic Safety Poster Program encourages students to think about traffic safety practices, learn, and have fun by doing.

Prizes totaling more than $30,000 in U.S. savings bonds and scholarships are awarded each year.

Contact the **Traffic Safety Department** of the main office of your local AAA club for more information.

National Poster Program Headquarters: (407) 444-7073

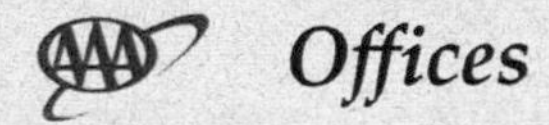

Offices

Cities with main offices are listed in **BOLD TYPE** and toll-free member service numbers in *ITALIC TYPE*.
All are closed Saturdays, Sundays and holidays unless otherwise indicated.

The type of service provided is designated below the name of the city where the office is located:

- ✚ Auto travel services, including books/maps, marked maps and on-demand Triptik maps
- ● Auto travel services, including books/maps, marked maps, but no on-demand Triptik maps
- ■ Provides books/maps only. No marked maps or on-demand Triptik maps available
- ▲ Travel agency services

NATIONAL OFFICE: 1000 AAA DRIVE, HEATHROW, FLORIDA 32746-5063, (407) 444-7000

IDAHO

BOISE—AAA OREGON/IDAHO, 7155 W DENTON ST, 83704. MON-FRI 8-5:30. (208) 342-9391, *(800) 999-9391*.✚▲

COEUR D'ALENE—AAA WASHINGTON/INLAND, 296 W SUNSET AVE #26, 83815. MON-FRI 8-5. (208) 664-5868.✚▲

LEWISTON—AAA WASHINGTON/INLAND, 2116 12TH AVE, 83501. MON-FRI 8-5. (208) 746-0407, *(800) 356-2228*.✚▲

POCATELLO—AAA OREGON/IDAHO, 1135 YELLOWSTONE AVE #A, 83201. MON-FRI 8:30-5:30. (208) 237-2225.✚▲

TWIN FALLS—AAA OREGON/IDAHO, 1445 FILLMORE ST #1100, 83301. MON-FRI 8:30-5:30. (208) 734-6441, *(800) 999-6441*.✚▲

MONTANA

BILLINGS—AAA MOUNTAINWEST, 3220 4TH AVE N, 59101. MON-FRI 8:30-5:30. (406) 248-7738, *(800) 391-4222*.✚▲

BOZEMAN—AAA MOUNTAINWEST, 711 W MAIN, 59715. MON-FRI 8:30-5:30. (406) 586-6156, *(800) 391-4222*.✚▲

GREAT FALLS—AAA MOUNTAINWEST, 505 10TH AVE S, 59405. MON-FRI 8:30-5:30. (406) 727-2900, *(800) 391-4222*.✚▲

HELENA—AAA MOUNTAINWEST, 2100 11TH AVE, 59601. MON-FRI 8:30-5:30, SAT 9-1. (406) 447-8100, *(800) 332-6119*.✚▲

KALISPELL—AAA MOUNTAINWEST, 440 W IDAHO, 59901. MON-FRI 8:30-5:30. (406) 758-6980, *(800) 391-4222*.✚▲

MISSOULA—AAA MOUNTAINWEST, 1200 S RESERVE SUITE B, 59801. MON-FRI 8:30-5:30. (406) 829-5500, *(800) 391-4222*.✚▲

WYOMING

CHEYENNE—AAA MOUNTAINWEST, 1450 STILLWATER AVE, 82009. MON-FRI 8:30-5:30. (307) 634-8861, *(800) 391-4222*.✚▲

SHERIDAN—AAA MOUNTAINWEST, 941 SUGARLAND DR, 82801. MON-FRI 8:30-5:30. (307) 672-3447, *(800) 391-4222*.■▲

Do you know the facts?

AAA publishes the Digest of Motor Laws to assist traveling motorists. Filled with facts and information, this one-of-a-kind compilation includes a comprehensive description of the laws that govern motor vehicle registration and operation in the United States and Canada. This guide has a new, easy-to-read format with graphics, state-by-state tax summary tables and detailed information on occupant protection laws, driver licensing laws, automated enforcement laws and motor vehicle fees and taxes.

You can easily locate various licensing and motor laws governing the states in which you are traveling. In addition to vehicle registration and operation laws, the Digest contains information and facts about alcohol laws, traffic safety laws and more.

Call your local club or 1-877-AAA-BOOK to obtain a copy of the Digest.

The book retails for $13.95.

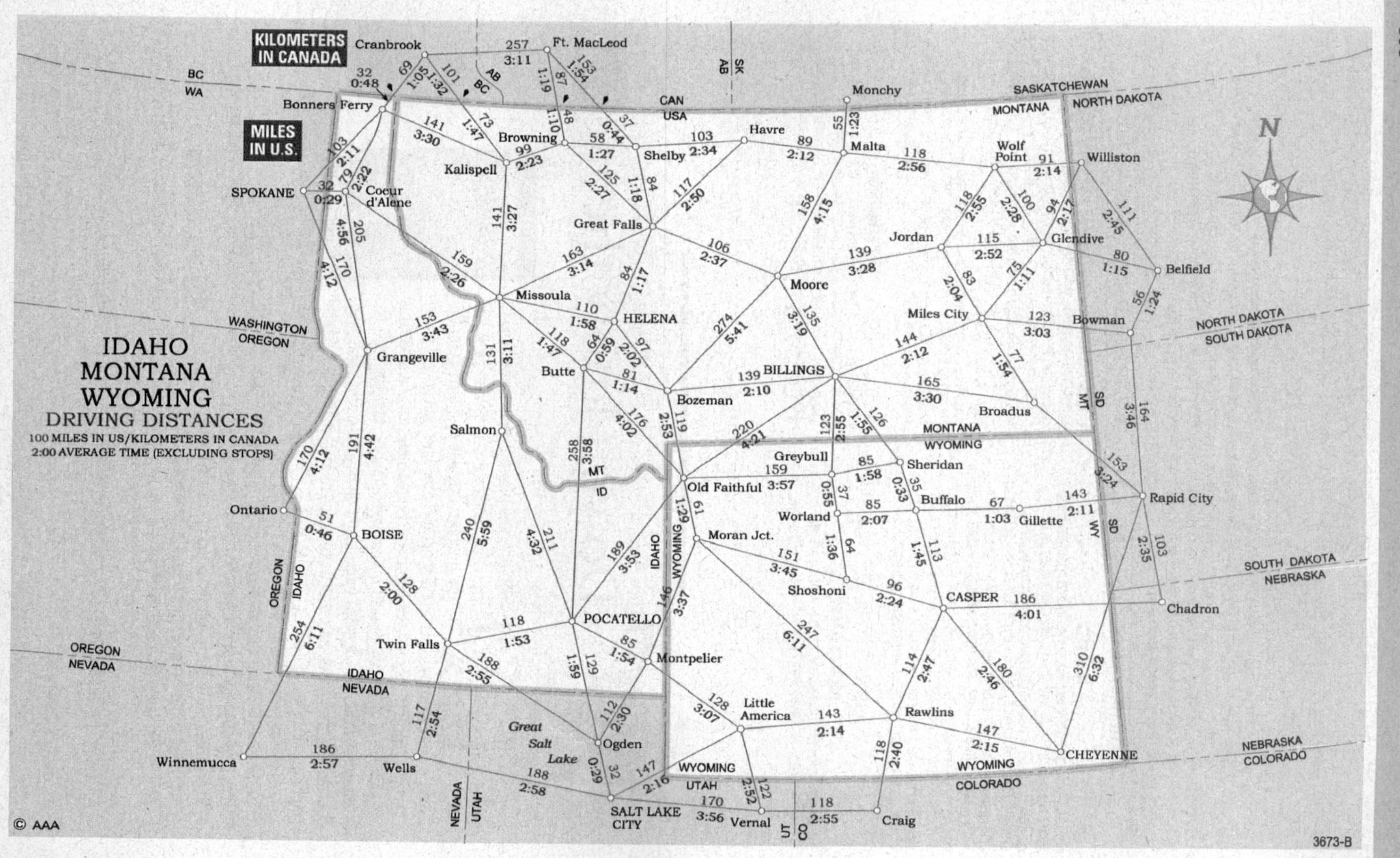
IDAHO
MONTANA
WYOMING
DRIVING DISTANCES
100 MILES IN US/KILOMETERS IN CANADA
2:00 AVERAGE TIME (EXCLUDING STOPS)
KILOMETERS IN CANADA
MILES IN U.S.
N
Cranbrook
Ft. MacLeod
Bonners Ferry
Monchy
SPOKANE
Coeur d'Alene
Kalispell
Browning
Shelby
Havre
Malta
Wolf Point
Williston
Glendive
Belfield
Jordan
Great Falls
Moore
Miles City
Bowman
Missoula
HELENA
Grangeville
Butte
BILLINGS
Bozeman
Broadus
Salmon
Old Faithful
Greybull
Sheridan
Buffalo
Gillette
Rapid City
Worland
Moran Jct.
Shoshoni
CASPER
Chadron
Ontario
BOISE
POCATELLO
Twin Falls
Montpelier
Little America
Rawlins
CHEYENNE
Ogden
Great Salt Lake
Winnemucca
Wells
SALT LAKE CITY
Vernal
Craig
BC
WA
AB
SK
CAN
USA
SASKATCHEWAN
NORTH DAKOTA
MONTANA
WASHINGTON
OREGON
NORTH DAKOTA
SOUTH DAKOTA
MT
SD
MONTANA
WYOMING
ID
IDAHO
WYOMING
WY
SOUTH DAKOTA
NEBRASKA
OREGON
IDAHO
OREGON
NEVADA
IDAHO
NEVADA
NEVADA
UTAH
WYOMING
UTAH
UT
CO
WYOMING
COLORADO
NEBRASKA
COLORADO
© AAA
3673-B

GOLDEN PASSPORTS

Golden Passports, available in three types, offer benefits and significant savings to individuals who plan to visit federal recreation sites.

The Golden Eagle Passport, available for a **$65** annual fee, is valid for entrance only to all federal recreation areas that have an entrance fee. Sites include those operated by the National Forest Service, National Park Service, Bureau of Land Management and the U.S. Fish and Wildlife Service. The passport admits all occupants of a private vehicle at locations where entrance is on a per vehicle basis. At locations where a per person fee is charged, the pass covers the pass holder, spouse, parents and children.

Citizens or permanent residents of the United States who are 62 and older can obtain *Golden Age Passports* for a one-time **$10** fee. Proof of age is required.

Golden Access Passports are free to citizens or permanent residents of the United States (regardless of age) who are medically blind or permanently disabled.

Both *Golden Age* and *Golden Access passports* cover entrance fees for the holder and accompanying private party to all national parks and sites managed by the U.S. Fish and Wildlife Service, the U.S. Forest Service and the Bureau of Land Management, plus half off camping and other fees. When a per person fee is imposed, the pass covers the pass holder, spouse and children. Apply in person at a federally operated area where an entrance fee is charged.

NATIONAL PARKS PASS

The *National Parks Pass*, valid for 1 year from its first use in a park, allows unlimited admissions to all U.S. national parks. The **$50** pass covers all occupants of a private vehicle at parks where the entrance fee is per vehicle. At parks with individual entry fees, the pass covers the pass holder, spouse, parents and children.

As a result of a partnership with the National Park Foundation, AAA members may purchase the pass for **$48**, either through AAA's internet site (www.aaa.com) or by visiting a participating AAA office. Members may also phone the National Park Foundation at **(888) 467-2757** or purchase the pass online at www.nationalparks.org. Non-members may purchase the pass through participating AAA offices for the full **$50** price or online at www.nationalparks.org.

For an upgrade fee of **$15**, a Golden Eagle hologram sticker can be added to a *National Parks Pass*. The hologram covers entrance fees not just at national parks, but at any federal recreation area that has an admission fee. Valid for the duration of the *National Parks Pass* to which it is affixed, the Golden Eagle hologram is available at National Park Service, Fish and Wildlife Service and Bureau of Land Management fee stations.

Border Information

FOR CANADIAN RESIDENTS ENTERING THE UNITED STATES

PASSPORTS to enter the United States or return to Canada are not required for native-born citizens of either country. However, **a Canadian passport remains the best internationally accepted evidence of Canadian citizenship and its use is strongly suggested.** Proof of citizenship must be carried; a certified birth certificate, accompanied by a photo ID will usually suffice. Proof of residence also may be required. Unmarried parents who share custody of children should carry copies of the legal custody documents.

UNITED STATES CUSTOMS permits you to bring, free of duty, for personal use and not intended for sale: clothing, personal effects and equipment appropriate to the trip. Personal effects may include 200 cigarettes ***or*** 50 cigars ***or*** 4.4 pounds (2 kgs) of smoking tobacco ***or*** proportionate amounts of each, and 1 litre of alcoholic beverage. **Cuban cigars are denied entry.**

If you are planning to be in the United States **at least 72 hours,** you may bring gifts up to a fair retail value of $100 (U.S.), provided you have not claimed this exemption within the preceding 6 months. Family members may not combine their gift exemptions. Perfume containing alcohol and valued at more than $5 retail, tobacco products (except for 100 cigars) and alcoholic beverages are excluded from the gift provision.

RADIO COMMUNICATION EQUIPMENT: You may use your Family Radio Service (FRS) radio and cellular phone in the United States without any restrictions.

RETURNING TO CANADA

CANADIAN CUSTOMS allows you to bring, free of duty and taxes, goods valued up to $200 (Canadian) any number of times per year, provided you have been in the United States **48 hours or more.** All goods must accompany you; a written declaration may be required.

You may claim a $50 (Canadian) exemption on goods, excluding alcoholic beverages and tobacco products, if you are returning after an absence of **24 hours or more** and are not using any other exemption. If more than $50 worth of goods are brought back, the regular rate of duty and taxes will be levied on the entire value. This exemption may apply any number of times in a year.

If you are returning after **7 days or more** in the United States (not counting the day of departure from Canada), you may claim an exemption on goods valued up to $750 (Canadian). Goods, other than alcohol and tobacco products, are not required to accompany you; a written declaration may be required.

Permitted within the $200 and $750 exemptions are up to 50 cigars, 200 cigarettes, 200 tobacco sticks and 7 ounces (200 gm) of tobacco and up to 40 ounces (1.14 L) of liquor ***or*** 1.6 quarts (1.5 L) of wine ***or*** 9 quarts (8.5 L) of beer and/or ale (or its equivalent of 24 twelve-ounce bottles or cans). You must meet the minimum age requirement of the province entered to claim alcohol or tobacco products. Northwest Territories and Nunavut do not allow you to bring in more than the duty-free allowance of alcohol.

There is nothing to prevent you from importing any quantity of goods, even if you do not qualify for any kind of personal exemption, provided the goods you are importing are not restricted and you pay the full rate of duty and taxes

Special Tariff: When you exceed your $200 or $750 exemptions, a special rate of 7 percent combined duty and taxes is levied on the next $300 value in goods (except tobacco and alcohol) in excess of maximum exemptible amounts, provided the goods are of U.S. origin. Regular duties apply on any amount over that. For detailed information concerning specific duty rates, consult Canadian Customs before leaving on your trip.

All exemptions are individual and may not be combined with those of another person. You may be asked to verify the length of your visit; dated receipts normally constitute proof.

GIFTS to the value of $60 (Canadian) may be sent from abroad, free of duty or taxes. These may not include alcoholic beverages, tobacco products or advertising matter. Gifts valued at over $60 (Canadian) are subject to duty and taxes on the amount in excess of $60. Gifts sent from abroad do not count against your personal exemption, but gifts brought back must be included as part of your exemption.

Bed & Breakfast Lodgings Index

Some bed and breakfasts listed below might have historical significance. Those properties are also referenced in the Historical index. The indication that continental [CP] or full breakfast [BP] is included in the room rate reflects whether a property is a Bed-and-Breakfast facility.

IDAHO

ACCOMMODATIONS

MONTANA

ACCOMMODATIONS

WYOMING

ACCOMMODATIONS

Country Inns Index

Some of the following country inns can also be considered as bed-and-breakfast operations. The indication that continental [CP] or full breakfast [BP] is included in the room rate reflects whether a property is a Bed-and-Breakfast facility.

IDAHO

ACCOMMODATION

MONTANA

ACCOMMODATION

WYOMING

ACCOMMODATIONS

Historical Lodgings & Restaurants Index

Some of the following historical lodgings can also be considered as bed-and-breakfast operations. The indication that continental [CP] or full breakfast [BP] is included in the room rate reflects whether a property is a Bed-and-Breakfast facility.

Resorts Index

Many establishments are located in resort areas; however, the following places have extensive on-premises recreational facilities:

Points of Interest Index

Index Legend

NB.................................national battlefield
NBP..........................national battlefield park
NC..................................national cemetery
NF.....................................national forest
NHM....................national historic(al) monument
NHP..........................national historic(al) park
NHS...........................national historic(al) site
NL...................................national lakeshore
NME.................................national memorial
NMO...............................national monument
NMP..............................national military park
NP.......................................national park
NRA.........................national recreation area
NR..national river
NS...................................national seashore
NWR...........................national wildlife refuge
PHP.........................provincial historic(al) park
PHS..........................provincial historic(al) site
PP..provincial park
SF..state forest
SHM.......................state historic(al) monument
SHP..............................state historic(al) park
SHS...............................state historic(al) site
SME.....................................state memorial
SP...state park
SRA..............................state recreation area

GEM: Points of Interest Offering a *Great Experience for Members*®

EXHIBITS & COLLECTIONS-ANIMALS & BIRDS

EXHIBITS & COLLECTIONS-AVIATION

EXHIBITS & COLLECTIONS-CIVIL WAR HISTORY

EXHIBITS & COLLECTIONS-COINS

EXHIBITS & COLLECTIONS-DOLLS & TOYS

EXHIBITS & COLLECTIONS-HISTORICAL

EXHIBITS & COLLECTIONS-INDIAN

FORTS & MILITARY INSTALLATIONS

FOSSILS

GAPS & PASSES

GARDENS

GENEALOGICAL INFORMATION

GEOLOGICAL FORMATIONS

GHOST TOWNS

GRAVES & TOMBS

HALLS OF FAME

HISTORIC BUILDINGS & HOUSES

HISTORIC DOCUMENTS, MANUSCRIPTS & RARE BOOKS

HISTORIC SITES

INDIAN MOUNDS, REMAINS & RUINS

INDIAN PICTOGRAPHS & PETROGLYPHS

INDIAN RESERVATIONS & VILLAGES

INDUSTRIAL TOURS

JAILS

LAKES, PONDS & RESERVOIRS

MUSIC HALLS & OPERA HOUSES

NATURAL BRIDGES

NATURAL PHENOMENA

NATURE CENTERS

NATURE TRAILS

OBSERVATORIES

PAINTINGS

PARKS, CITY; STATE; PROVINCIAL

PARKS, NATIONAL

PLANETARIUMS

RACETRACKS-AUTO

RACETRACKS-HORSE

RAILROADS

RAILROADS-LOCOMOTIVES & CARS

RAILROADS & SKI LIFTS, CABLE; COG; INCLINE; NARROW GAUGE

RANCHES

RECREATION-SUMMER ACTIVITIES

RECREATION-WINTER ACTIVITIES

RESEARCH ORGANIZATIONS

RESTORED VILLAGES & SETTLEMENTS

RIVERS

ROCKS

SCENIC DRIVES

SCHOOL BUILDINGS

SCHOOLS

SCHOOLS-COLLEGES & UNIVERSITIES

SCHOOLS-INSTITUTES

SELF-GUIDING TOURS

SHIPS & BOATS

SHOPS, FIRMS & STORES

SIGHTSEEING-AIRCRAFT RIDES & TOURS

SIGHTSEEING TOURS

SIGHTSEEING TOURS-BOATS

SIGHTSEEING TOURS-RAFTING & CANOEING

SPORTS ARENAS

SPRINGS

STATUES

STREETS, PLAZAS, SQUARES, CITY AREAS

THEATERS-BUILDINGS

THEATERS-PLAYS, DRAMAS & MUSICALS

TREES

VIEWS

VISITOR CENTERS

VISITOR INFORMATION

WALKING TOURS

WATERFALLS

WATER PARKS

WILDERNESS AREAS

WILDLIFE SANCTUARIES

WINERIES

ZOOLOGICAL PARKS & EXHIBITS

ZOOLOGICAL PARKS & EXHIBITS-CHILDREN'S ZOOS

SAVE *Attraction Admission Discount Index*

IDAHO

MONTANA

WYOMING

Comprehensive City Index

Here is an alphabetical list of all cities appearing in this TourBook® guide. Cities are presented by state/province. Page numbers under the POI column indicate where points of interest text begins. Page numbers under the L&R column indicate where lodging and restaurant listings begin.

COMPREHENSIVE CITY INDEX (CONT'D)

Which place is best for each vehicle to travel?

Help the car, the airplane and the cruise ship find a path to the right spot.

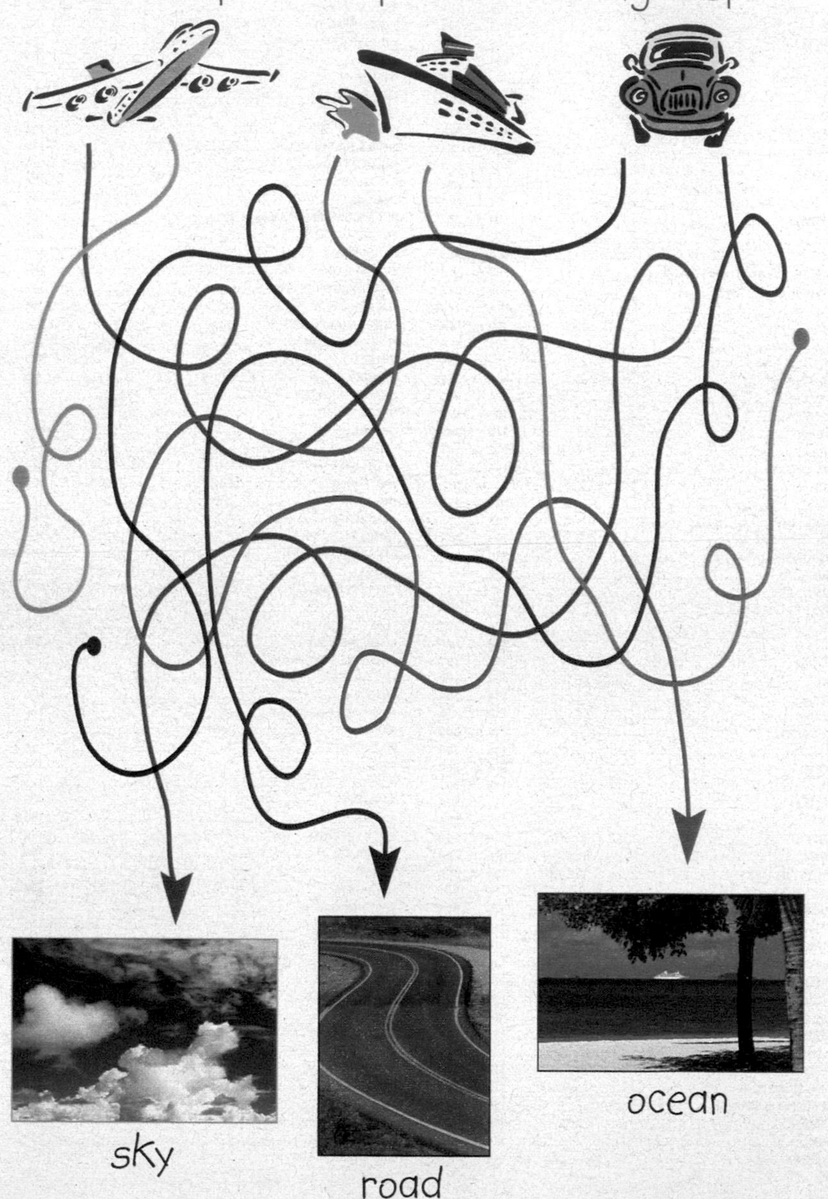

Word Search

A H T R E S T A U R A N T F D T A H M F C V N S Q H F H
G J H E R S P O O D A R D G V R J M A P N S T L C C V B
A S D S A P O E I H A K L D V A A K D F G H A A I W E U
T Y A E G H A H O T E L E Y P V O R T G T H E E J K W F
T H J R R B L N N W O G F P Y E F G H W A B U S S R E A
E I W V D T K E A O O E C V N L A P E D S E E N M S T I
K L E A H H S T P N P A D S A R S G M A D A N V D T Y R
C D A T E A B G U Y L O J D C A A W E Y T J S E I L N P
I E B I A L N G D Y A W H G I H F A P G J F U N V N M O
T E T O J I C X Z A N F T H I E E M A N E U I Z P W M R
F T M N M P Q A G J E R D S N Y T B R E W S T I J B S T
K F A M G H I U A A R E F P I B Y O K A B T C A R V J V
D L I F S A E G M T Y D I K A A C N O G D A A D Y T S A
R W C B B N F S A S O P L S R E F V B Z Q R S E E A N T
S A R H S B M E N O Z E M I T D R M C P F H E C I T Y S

Suitcase	Plane	Train	Swimming Pool
Travel	Time Zone	Reservation	Restaurant
Ticket	Hotel	Bus	City
Car	Beach	Theme Park	Highway
Map	Fun	Safety	Airport